Learning ActionScript 2.0 for Macromedia® FLASH® 8

Jen deHaan, Peter deHaan

macromedia®
PRESS

Learning ActionScript 2.0 for Macromedia Flash 8

Jen deHaan, Peter deHaan

Macromedia Press books are published by:

Peachpit
1249 Eighth Street
Berkeley, CA 94710
510/524-2178 510/524-2221 (fax)
Find us on the World Wide Web at:
www.peachpit.com   www.macromedia.com

To report errors, please send a note to errata@peachpit.com

Copyright © 2004–2006 Macromedia, Inc.

ISBN 0-321-39415-1

9 8 7 6 5 4 3 2 1

Printed and bound in the United States of America

Credits

Macromedia

Project Management: Sheila McGinn

Writing: Jen deHaan; Peter deHaan, Joey Lott

Managing Editor: Rosana Francescato

Lead Editor: Lisa Stanziano

Editing: Linda Adler, Geta Carlson, Evelyn Eldridge, John Hammett, Mary Kraemer, Noreen Maher, Jessie Wood, Anne Szabla

Production Management: Patrice O'Neill, Kristin Conradi, Yuko Yagi

Media Design and Production: Adam Barnett, Aaron Begley, Paul Benkman. John Francis, Geeta Karmarkar, Masayo Noda, Paul Rangel, Arena Reed, Mario Reynoso

Special thanks to Jody Bleyle, Mary Burger, Lisa Friendly, Stephanie Gowin, Bonnie Loo, Mary Ann Walsh, Erick Vera, the beta testers, and the entire Flash and Flash Player engineering and QA teams.

Macromedia Press

Macromedia Press Editor: Angela C. Kozlowski

Production Editor: Pat Christenson

Product Marketing Manager: Zigi Lowenberg

Cover Design: Charlene Charles Will

Dedication

The Studio 8 Documentation Team recognizes and honors Patrice O'Neill, who inspires all of us with her dedication and commitment.

Contents

Introduction

Macromedia Flash Basic 8 and Macromedia Flash Professional 8 are the professional standard authoring tools for producing high-impact web experiences. ActionScript is the language you use to add interactivity to Flash applications, whether your applications are simple animated SWF files or more complex rich Internet applications. You don't have to use ActionScript to use Flash, but if you want to provide basic or complex user interactivity, work with objects other than those built into Flash (such as buttons and movie clips), or otherwise turn a SWF file into a more robust user experience, you'll probably want to use ActionScript.

For more information, see the following topics:

Intended audience

This manual assumes that you have already installed Flash Basic 8 or Flash Professional 8 and know how to use the user interface. You should know how to place objects on the Stage and manipulate them in the Flash authoring environment. If you have used a scripting language before, ActionScript will seem familiar. But if you're new to programming, ActionScript basics are easy to learn. You can start with simple commands and build more complexity as you progress. You can add a lot of interactivity to your files without having to learn (or write) a lot of code.

System requirements

ActionScript 2.0 does not have any system requirements in addition to Flash 8.

This manual assumes that you are using the default publishing settings for your Flash files: Flash Player 8 and ActionScript 2.0. If you change either of these settings, explanations and code samples in the documentation might not work correctly. If you develop applications for earlier versions of Flash Player, see Appendix D, "Writing Scripts for Earlier Versions of Flash Player," on page 803.

Updating Flash XML files

It is important that you always have the latest Flash XML files installed. Macromedia sometimes introduces features in dot releases (minor releases) of Flash Player. When such a release is available, you should update your version of Flash to get the latest XML files. Otherwise, the Flash 8 compiler might generate errors if you use new properties or methods that were unavailable in the version of Flash Player that came with your Flash installation.

For example, Flash Player 7 (7.0.19.0) contained a new method for the System object, `System.security.loadPolicyFile`. To access this method, you must use the Player Updater installer to update all the Flash players that are installed with Flash. Otherwise, the Flash compiler displays errors.

Remember that you can install a Player Updater that is one or more major versions ahead of your version of Flash. By doing this, you will get the XML files that you need but shouldn't have any compiler errors when you publish to older versions of Flash Player. Sometimes new methods or properties are available to older versions, and having the latest XML files minimizes the compiler errors you get when you try to access older methods or properties.

About the documentation

This manual provides an overview of ActionScript syntax and information on how to use ActionScript when working with different types of objects. For details on the syntax and usage of every language element, see the *ActionScript 2.0 Language Reference* in Flash Help.

For more information, see the following topics:

- "Learning ActionScript 2.0 book overview" on page 11
- "About the sample files" on page 15
- "Terms used in this document" on page 13
- "Copy and paste code" on page 13

Learning ActionScript 2.0 book overview

The following list summarizes the contents of this manual:

- Chapter 1, "What's New in Flash 8 ActionScript," describes features that are new in ActionScript, changes to the compiler and debugger, and the new programming model for the ActionScript 2.0 language.

- Chapter 2, "Writing and Editing ActionScript 2.0," describes features of the ActionScript editor within Flash that make it easier to write code.

- Chapter 3, "About ActionScript," outlines what the ActionScript language is and details how to choose between which version of ActionScript to use.

- Chapter 4, "Data and Data Types," describes the terminology and basic concepts about data, data types, and variables. You use these concepts throughout the manual.

- Chapter 5, "Syntax and Language Fundamentals," describes the terminology and basic concepts of the ActionScript language. You use these concepts throughout the manual.

- Chapter 6, "Functions and Methods," describes how to write different kinds of functions and methods and how to use them in your application.

- Chapter 7, "Classes," describes how to create custom classes and objects in ActionScript. This chapter also lists the built-in classes in ActionScript and provides a brief overview of how you use them to access powerful features in ActionScript.

- Chapter 8, "Inheritance," describes inheritance in the ActionScript language and describes how to extend built-in or custom classes.

- Chapter 9, "Interfaces," describes how to create and work with interfaces in ActionScript.

- Chapter 10, "Handling Events," describes a few different ways to handle events: event handler methods, event listeners, and button and movie clip event handlers.

- Chapter 11, "Working with Movie Clips," describes movie clips and the ActionScript you can use to control them.

- Chapter 12, "Working with Text and Strings," describes the different ways you can control text and strings in Flash and includes information on text formatting and FlashType (advanced text rendering, such as anti-alias text).

- Chapter 13, "Animation, Filters, and Drawings," describes how to create code-based animation and images, add filters to objects, and draw using ActionScript.

- Chapter 14, "Creating Interaction with ActionScript," describes some simple ways in which you can create more interactive applications, including controlling when SWF files play, creating custom pointers, and creating sound controls.

- Chapter 15, "Working with Images, Sound, and Video," describes how to import external media files, such as bitmap images, MP3 files, Flash Video (FLV) files, and other SWF files, in your Flash applications. This chapter also provides an overview of how to work with video in your applications, and how to create progress bar loading animations.

- Chapter 16, "Working with External Data," describes how to process data from external sources using server- or client-side scripts in your applications. This chapter describes how to integrate data with your applications.

- Chapter 17, "Understanding Security," explains security in Flash Player, as it pertains to working with SWF files locally on your hard disk. This chapter also explains cross-domain security issues, and how to load data from servers, or across domains.

- Chapter 18, "Debugging Applications," describes the ActionScript debugger within Flash that makes it easier to write applications.

- Chapter 19, "Best Practices and Coding Conventions for ActionScript 2.0," explains the best practices for using Flash and writing ActionScript. This chapter also lists standardized coding conventions, such as naming variables, and other conventions.

- Appendix A, "Error Messages," lists the error messages that the Flash compiler can generate.

- Appendix B, "Deprecated Flash 4 operators," lists all the deprecated Flash 4 operators and their associativity.

- Appendix C, "Keyboard Keys and Key Code Values," lists all the keys on a standard keyboard and the corresponding ASCII key code values that are used to identify the keys in ActionScript.

- Appendix D, "Writing Scripts for Earlier Versions of Flash Player," provides guidelines to help you write scripts that are syntactically correct for the player version you are targeting.

- Appendix E, "Object-Oriented Programming with ActionScript 1.0," provides information on using the ActionScript 1.0 object model to write scripts.

- Appendix F, "Terminology," lists commonly used terminology when working with the ActionScript language and provides descriptions for the terms.

This manual explains how to use the ActionScript language. For information on the language elements themselves, see the *ActionScript 2.0 Language Reference* in Flash Help.

Typographical conventions

This manual uses the following typographical conventions:

- `Code font` indicates ActionScript code.
- `Bold code font`, typically within a procedure, indicates code that you need to modify or add to code you have already added to your FLA file. In some case, it might be used to highlight code to look at.
- **Boldface text** indicates data you need to type into the user interface, such as a filename or instance name.
- *Italic text* indicates a new term defined in the text that follows. In a file path, it might indicate a value that should be replaced (for example, with a directory name on your own hard disk).

Terms used in this document

The following terms are used in this manual:

- *You* refers to the developer who is writing a script or application.
- *The user* refers to the person who is running your scripts and applications.
- *Compile time* is the time at which you publish, export, test, or debug your document.
- *Runtime* is the time at which your script is running in Flash Player.

ActionScript terms such as *method* and *object* are defined in Appendix F, "Terminology," on page 821.

Copy and paste code

When you paste ActionScript from the Help panel into your FLA or ActionScript file, you have to be careful about special characters. Special characters include special quotation marks (also called curly quotation marks or smart quotation marks). These characters are not interpreted by the ActionScript editor, so your code throws an error if you try to compile it in Flash.

You can determine that your quotation mark characters are special characters if they do not color-code correctly. That is, if all your strings do not change in color in the code editor, you need to replace the special characters with regular straight quotation mark characters. If you type a single or double quotation mark character directly into the ActionScript editor, you always type a straight quotation mark character. The compiler (when you test or publish a SWF file) throws an error and lets you know if there are the wrong kind (special quotation marks or curly quotation marks) of characters in your code.

> **NOTE** You might also encounter special quotation marks if you paste ActionScript from other locations, such as a web page or a Microsoft Word document.

Be cautious of proper line breaks when you copy and paste code. If you paste your code from some locations, the line of code might break in an improper location. Make sure that the color coding of your syntax is correct in the ActionScript editor if you think line breaks might be a problem. You might want to compare your code in the Actions panel to that in the Help panel to see if it matches. Try turning on Word Wrap in the ActionScript editor to help solve surplus line breaks in your code (select View > Word Wrap in the Script window, or Word Wrap from the Actions panel pop-up menu.)

Additional resources

In addition to this manual about ActionScript, there are manuals on other Flash topics, such as components and Macromedia Flash Lite. You can access each manual in the Help panel (Help > Flash Help), by viewing the default Table of Contents. Click the Clear button to see each manual that's available; for more information, see "Where to find documentation on other subjects" on page 17.

For more information about other available resources, see the following topics:

- "About the sample files" on page 15
- "Where to find PDF files or printed documentation" on page 15
- "About LiveDocs" on page 16
- "Additional online resources" on page 17
- "Where to find documentation on other subjects" on page 17

About the sample files

There are numerous ActionScript-based sample files available that install with Flash. These sample files show you how code works in a FLA file; this is often a useful learning tool. The chapters in this manual often reference these files, but we recommend that you also check out the sample files folder on your hard disk.

The sample files include application FLA files that use common Flash functionality installed with Flash. These applications were designed to introduce new Flash developers to the capabilities of Flash applications, as well as show advanced developers how Flash features work in context.

You can find the ActionScript-focused sample source files in the Samples folder on your hard disk.

- In Windows, browse to *boot drive*\Program Files\Macromedia\Flash 8\Samples and Tutorials\Samples\ActionScript\.

- On the Macintosh, browse to *Macintosh HD*/Applications/Macromedia Flash 8/Samples and Tutorials/Samples/ActionScript/.

You might find the following components-focused sample files useful, because they contain a lot of ActionScript code. They're also in the Samples folder on your hard disk:

- In Windows, browse to *boot drive*\Program Files\Macromedia\Flash 8\Samples and Tutorials\Samples\Components\.

- On the Macintosh, browse to *Macintosh HD*/Applications/Macromedia Flash 8/Samples and Tutorials/Samples/Components/.

You can also find additional sample files for download on the Internet. The following web page contains links and descriptions of additional sample files: www.macromedia.com/go/flash_samples/.

Where to find PDF files or printed documentation

If you prefer to read documentation in printed format, the PDF versions of each Help manual are available for downloading. Go to www.macromedia.com/support/documentation/ and select the product you're interested in. You can view or download the PDF or link to the LiveDocs version of the manual.

Often, you can also purchase printed documentation. For updated information, go to the Documentation support site and select Flash Basic 8 or Flash Professional 8.

About LiveDocs

You can access documentation at the LiveDocs website, in addition to accessing it from the Help panel. The LiveDocs website contains all of the Flash Help pages and might contain comments that clarify, update, or correct parts of the documentation. Click View Comments on LiveDocs at the bottom of a page in the Help panel to display the equivalent page on the LiveDocs website. Go to http://livedocs.macromedia.com to see a list of all of the available documentation in the LiveDocs format.

Technical writers monitor the LiveDocs website. One of the advantages of LiveDocs is seeing comments that clarify the documentation or correct any errata or issues that arise after a software release. LiveDocs is not the place to make help requests, such as asking questions about your code that doesn't work, comment on problems with software or installation, or ask how to create something with Flash. It is the correct place to provide feedback about the documentation (for example, you notice a sentence or paragraph that could be clarified).

When you click the button to add a comment on LiveDocs, there are several points about the kinds of comments that are acceptable on the system. Please read these guidelines closely, or your comment might be removed from the website.

If you have a question about Flash, please ask it on the Macromedia web forums: www.macromedia.com/support/forums/. The web forums are the best place to ask questions, because there are many Macromedia employees, Team Macromedia volunteers, Macromedia user group managers and members, and even technical writers who monitor these forums.

Engineers do not monitor the LiveDocs system but do monitor the Flash wish list. If you think you have found a bug in the software, or you would like to request an enhancement to Flash, please fill out the wishform at www.macromedia.com/go/wish. If you report your bug or enhancement request on LiveDocs, it will not be officially added to the bug database. You must use the wishform instead, if you want an engineer to see your bug or request.

Remember to be careful about special characters and line breaks when you paste from the web, including LiveDocs. Macromedia has made every effort to remove all special characters from code samples, but if you have problems pasting code, see "Copy and paste code" on page 13.

Additional online resources

There are several resources online that offer a wealth of instruction, help, and guidance to help you learn Macromedia Flash 8. Check the following websites often for updates:

The Macromedia Developer Center website (www.macromedia.com/devnet) is updated regularly with the latest information on Flash, plus advice from expert users, advanced topics, examples, tips, tutorials (including multipart tutorials), and other updates. Check the website often for the latest news on Flash and how to get the most out of the program.

The Macromedia Flash Support Center (www.macromedia.com/support/flash) provides TechNotes, documentation updates, and links to additional resources in the Flash community.

The Macromedia Weblogs website (http://weblogs.macromedia.com) provides a list of both Macromedia employee and community weblogs (also known as *blogs*).

The Macromedia web forums (http://webforums.macromedia.com) provides numerous forums for asking specific questions about Flash, your applications, or the ActionScript language. The forums are monitored by Team Macromedia volunteers and often visited by Macromedia employees as well. If you're not sure where to go, or how to solve a problem, a Flash forum is a good place to start.

The Macromedia Community website (www.macromedia.com/community) regularly hosts Macrochats, a series of live presentations on a variety of topics by Macromedia employees or community members. Check the website often for updates and to register for Macrochats.

Where to find documentation on other subjects

The following manuals offer additional information on subjects commonly associated with ActionScript 2.0:

- For information about the elements that compose the ActionScript language, see the *ActionScript 2.0 Language Reference* in Flash Help.
- For information about working in the Flash authoring environment, see *How to Use Help*.
- For information about working with components, see *Using Components* in Flash Help.

CHAPTER 1

What's New in Flash 8 ActionScript

Macromedia Flash Basic 8 and Macromedia Flash Professional 8 provide several enhancements that make it easy for you to write robust scripts using the ActionScript (AS) language. The new features, which are discussed in this chapter, include new language elements (see "Additions to the ActionScript language" on page 22), improved editing tools (see "ActionScript editing changes" on page 27), changes to the security model, and other ActionScript-related improvements to the authoring tool.

For more information, see the following topics:

New in ActionScript 2.0 and Flash 8

The ActionScript language has grown and developed since its introduction several years ago. With each new release of Flash, additional keywords, objects, methods, and other language elements were added to ActionScript. There are also ActionScript-related improvements to the Flash 8 authoring environments. Flash Basic 8 and Flash Professional 8 introduce several new language elements for expressive features, such as filters and blending modes, and application development, such as JavaScript integration (ExternalInterface) and file input and output (FileReference and FileReferenceList).

This section provides an overview of the ActionScript language elements and classes that are new or changed in Flash 8 and ActionScript-related improvements to the authoring tool. For a list of specific additions to ActionScript 2.0, see "Additions to the ActionScript language" on page 22. To use any of the new language elements in your scripts, you must target Flash Player 8 (the default) when you publish your documents.

The following features were added to both Flash Basic 8 and Flash Professional 8 (unless noted otherwise):

- ActionScript editor enhancements let you show hidden characters in your scripts. For more information, see "Showing hidden characters" on page 55.

- Debug options are now available in the Script window, as well as the Actions panel, for ActionScript files.

- The Configuration directory that includes XML files and Class files is reorganized. See "Configuration files that install with Flash 8" on page 66 for details.

- You can set a preference to reload modified script files when working on an application, which helps you avoid working with older versions of script files, and overwriting newer script files. For more information, see "About ActionScript preferences" on page 44.

- The Script window feature is available in Flash Basic 8 and Flash Professional 8. That means you can now create an ActionScript file in either program.

- Script Assist (similar to Normal Mode in earlier editions of Flash) helps you code without needing to understand syntax. For more information on Script Assist, see "About Script Assist" on page 60.

- You can load new kinds of image files at runtime, which include progressive JPEG images, and non-animated GIF and PNG files. If you load an animated file, the first frame of the animation appears.

- You can assign linkage identifiers to bitmap and sound files stored in the Library, which means that you can attach images to the Stage or work with these assets in shared libraries.

- Bitmap caching lets you improve the performance of your applications at runtime by caching a bitmap representation of your instances. You can use ActionScript code to access this property. For more information, see "About bitmap caching, scrolling, and performance" on page 490.

- 9-slice scaling lets you scale movie clip instances without widening the strokes that outline the movie clip. You can use ActionScript code to access this feature in Flash Basic 8 and Flash Professional 8, or in the Flash 8 authoring tool. For more information, see "Working with 9-slice scaling in ActionScript" on page 571. For information about accessing 9-slice scaling in the authoring tool, see "About 9-slice scaling and movie clip symbols" on page 79 in Flash Help.

- You can now add metadata information to your FLA files in the Publish Settings dialog box. You can add a name and description to your FLA file using the dialog box to help increase online search visibility.

- The Strings panel is improved to include multiline support in the String field and a language XML file. For more information, see "About the Strings panel" on page 461.

- A new garbage collector is built into Flash Player, which uses an incremental collector to improve performance.

- The workflow for creating accessible applications is improved. Flash Player 8 no longer requires developers to add all objects to the tab index for content to be read correctly by a screen reader. For more information on tab index, see `tabIndex (Button.tabIndex property)`, `tabIndex (MovieClip.tabIndex property)`, and `tabIndex (TextField.tabIndex property)` in the *ActionScript 2.0 Language Reference* in Flash Help.

- Flash Player has improved local file security, for additional safety when running SWF files on your hard disk. For information on local file security, see "About local file security and Flash Player" on page 693.

- Using ActionScript code, you can use the Drawing API to control the line style of strokes that you draw. For information on new line styles, see "Using line styles" on page 560.

- Using ActionScript code, you can use the Drawing API to create more complex gradients that you fill shapes with. For information on gradient fills, see "Using complex gradient fills" on page 559.

- You can use ActionScript code to apply many filters to objects on the Stage (such as movie clip instances). For information on filters and ActionScript, see "Working with filters using ActionScript" on page 515.

- You can use the FileReference and FileReferenceList API to upload files to a server. For more information, see "About file uploading and downloading" on page 657.

- You can use ActionScript code to access new and advanced ways of applying and manipulating colors. For more information, see "Setting color values" on page 586 and `ColorTransform (flash.geom.ColorTransform)` in the *ActionScript 2.0 Language Reference* in Flash Help.

- Numerous improvements are made to text handling, including new options, properties, and parameters in the TextField and TextFormat classes. For more information, see `TextField` and `TextFormat` in the *ActionScript 2.0 Language Reference* in Flash Help.

- You can use ActionScript code to access advanced anti-aliasing features (FlashType). For more information, see "About font rendering and anti-alias text" on page 415.

- You can delete ASO files when you test your application. Select Control > Delete ASO files or Control > Delete ASO files and Test Movie in the authoring tool. For information, see "Using ASO files" on page 288.

For a list of specific classes, language elements, methods, and properties added to ActionScript 2.0 in Flash 8, see "Additions to the ActionScript language" on page 22.

Additions to the ActionScript language

This section lists additions to ActionScript language elements and classes that are new or changed in Flash 8. The following classes and language elements are new additions or newly supported in Flash Player 8.

The following classes were added to ActionScript 2.0 in Flash 8:

- The BevelFilter class (in flash.filters package) lets you add bevel effects to objects.
- The BitmapData class (in flash.display package) lets you create and manipulate arbitrarily sized transparent or opaque bitmap images.
- The BitmapFilter class (in flash.display package) is a base class for filter effects.
- The BlurFilter class lets you apply blurs to objects in Flash.
- The ColorMatrixFilter class (in flash.filters package) lets you apply transformations to ARGB colors and alpha values.
- The ColorTransform class (in the flash.geom package) lets you adjust color values in movie clips. The Color class is deprecated in favor of this class.
- The ConvolutionFilter class (in the flash.filters package) lets you apply matrix convolution filter effects.
- The DisplacementMapFilter class (in the flash.filters package) lets you use pixel values from a BitmapData object to perform displacement on an object.
- The DropShadowFilter class (in the flash.filters package) lets you add drop shadows to objects.
- The ExternalInterface class (in the flash.external package) lets you communicate by using ActionScript with the Flash Player container (the system holding the Flash application, such as a browser with JavaScript, or the desktop application).
- The FileReference class (in the flash.net package) lets you upload and download files between the user's computer and a server.
- The FileReferenceList class (in the flash.net package) lets you select one or more files to upload.
- The GlowFilter class (in the flash.filters package) lets you add glow effects to objects.
- The GradientBevelFilter class (in the flash.filters package) lets you add gradient bevels to objects.
- TheGradientGlowFilter class (in the flash.filters package) lets you add gradient glow effects to objects.
- The IME class (in the System class) lets you manipulate the operating system's input method editor (IME) within Flash Player.

- The Locale class (in the mx.lang package) lets you control how multilanguage text appears in a SWF file.

- The Matrix class (in the flash.geom package) represents a transformation matrix that determines how to map points from one coordinate space to another.

- The Point class (in the flash.geom package) represents a location in a two-dimensional coordinate system (x represents the horizontal axis, and y represents the vertical axis).

- The Rectangle class (in the flash.geom package) lets you create and modify Rectangle objects.

- The TextRenderer class (in the flash.text package) provides functionality for anti-aliasing embedded fonts.

- The Transform class (in the flash.geom package) collects data about color transformations and coordinates manipulations that you apply to a MovieClip instance.

> **NOTE** Official support is added for the AsBroadcaster class in Flash 8.

New language elements, methods, and functions added to existing classes in ActionScript include:

- The showRedrawRegions global function provides the ability for the debugger player to outline the regions of the screen that are being redrawn (that is, dirty regions that are being updated). The function has the player show what was redrawn, but does not let you control redraw regions.

- The blendMode property in the Button class, which sets the blending mode for the button instance.

- The cacheAsBitmap property in the Button class, which lets you cache the object as an internal bitmap representation of the instance.

- The filters property in the Button class, which is an indexed array that contains each filter object associated with the button.

- The scale9Grid property in the Button class, which is the rectangular region that defines nine scaling regions for the instance.

- The hasIME property in the System.capabilities class, which indicates if the system has an IME installed.

- The getUTCYear property in the Date class, which returns the year of this date, according to universal time.

- The isAccessible() method in the Key class returns a Boolean value that indicates whether the last key pressed may be accessed by other SWF files, depending on security restrictions.

- The `onHTTPStatus` event handler of the LoadVars class returns the status code that's returned from the server (for example, the value 404 for page not found). For more information, see `onHTTPStatus (LoadVars.onHTTPStatus handler)` in the *ActionScript 2.0 Language Reference* in Flash Help.

- The `attachBitmap()` method of the MovieClip class, which attaches a bitmap image to a movie clip. For information, see the `BitmapData (flash.display.BitmapData)` in the *ActionScript 2.0 Language Reference* in Flash Help.

- The `beginBitmapFill()` method of the MovieClip class, which fills a movie clip with a bitmap image.

- The `spreadMethod`, `interpolationMethod`, and `focalPointRatio` parameters of the `beginGradientFill()` method in the MovieClip class. This method fills a drawing area with a bitmap image, and the bitmap can be repeated or tiled to fill the area.

- The `blendMode` property of the MovieClip class, which lets you set the blending mode for the instance.

- The `cacheAsBitmap` property of the MovieClip class, which lets you cache the object as an internal bitmap representation of the instance.

- The `filters` property of the MovieClip class, which is an indexed array that contains each filter object that's currently associated with the instance.

- The `getRect()` method of the MovieClip class, which returns properties that are the minimum and maximum coordinate values of the specified instance.

- The `lineGradientStyle()` method of the MovieClip class, which specifies a gradient line style that Flash uses when drawing a path.

- The `pixelHinting`, `noScale`, `capsStyle`, `jointStyle`, and `miterLimit` parameters of the `lineStyle()` method in the MovieClip class. These parameters specify kinds of line styles you can use when drawing lines.

- The `opaqueBackground` property of the MovieClip class, which sets the color of the movie clip's opaque (not transparent) background to the color that the RGB hexadecimal value specifies.

- The `scale9Grid` property of the MovieClip class, which is the rectangular region that defines nine scaling regions for the instance.

- The `scrollRect` property of the MovieClip class, which lets you quickly scroll movie clip content and have a window viewing larger content.

- The `transform` property of the MovieClip class, which lets you make settings regarding a movie clip's matrix, color transform, and pixel bounds. For more information, see `Transform (flash.geom.Transform)` in the *ActionScript 2.0 Language Reference* in Flash Help.

- The `status` parameter of the `MovieClipLoader.onLoadComplete` event handler returns the status code that's returned from the server (for example, the value 404 for page not found). For more information, see `onLoadComplete` (`MovieClipLoader.onLoadComplete event listener`) in the *ActionScript 2.0 Language Reference* in Flash Help.

- The `onLoadError` event handler of the MovieClipLoader class is invoked when a file loaded with `MovieClipLoader.loadClip()` fails to load.

- The `secure` parameter of the `SharedObject.getLocal()` method determines whether access to this shared object is restricted to SWF files delivered over an HTTPS connection. For more information, see `getLocal` (`SharedObject.getLocal method`) in the *ActionScript 2.0 Language Reference* in Flash Help.

- The sandboxType property of the System.security class indicates the type of security sandbox in which the calling SWF file is operating. For more information, see `sandboxType` (`security.sandboxType property`) in the *ActionScript 2.0 Language Reference* in Flash Help.

- The `antiAliasType` property in the TextField class, which sets the type of anti-aliasing that you use for the TextField instance.

- The `filters` property in the TextField class, which is an indexed array that contains each filter object that's currently associated with the TextField instance.

- The `gridFitType` property in the TextField class, which sets the type of grid fitting that you use for the instance. For information on grid fitting and TextField.gridFitType, see `gridFitType` (`TextField.gridFitType property`) in the *ActionScript 2.0 Language Reference* in Flash Help.

- The `sharpness` property in the TextField class, which sets the sharpness of the glyph edges for the TextField instance. You must set the `antiAliasType()` method to advanced if you use this property.

- The `thickness` property in the TextField class, which sets the thickness of the glyph edges in the TextField instance. You must set the `antiAliasType()` method to advanced if you use this property.

- The `justify` value for the `align` property of the TextFormat class, which lets you justify a specified paragraph.

- The `indent` property of the TextFormat class, which lets you use negative values.

- The `kerning` property in the TextFormat class, which lets you turn kerning on or off for the TextFormat object.

- The `leading` property of the TextFormat class, which lets you use negative leading, so the space between lines is less than the text height. This lets you put lines of text close together in your applications.

- The `letterSpacing` property in the TextFormat class, which lets you specify the amount of space that is uniformly distributed between characters.

- The `_alpha` property in the Video class, which is the specified amount of transparency for the video object.

- The `_height` property in the Video class, which indicates the height of the video instance.

- The `_name` property in the Video class, which indicates the instance name of the video.

- The `_parent` property in the Video class, which indicates the movie clip instance or object that contains the video instance.

- The `_rotation` property in the Video class, which lets you set the amount of rotation of the video instance in degrees.

- The `_visible` property in the Video class, which lets you set the visibility of a video instance.

- The `_width` property in the Video class, which lets you set the width of the video instance.

- The `_x` property in the Video class, which lets you set the *x* coordinate of the video instance.

- The `_xmouse` property in the Video class, which lets you set the *x* coordinate of the mouse pointer position.

- The `_xscale` property in the Video class, which lets you set the horizontal scale percentage of the video instance.

- The `_y` property in the Video class, which lets you set the *y* coordinate of the video instance.

- The `_ymouse` property in the Video class, which lets you set the *y* coordinate of the mouse pointer position.

- The `_yscale` property in the Video class, which lets you set the vertical scale percentage of the video instance.

- The `onHTTPStatus` event handler in the XML class returns the status code that's returned from the server (for example, the value 404 for page not found). For more information, see `onHTTPStatus` (`XML.onHTTPStatus handler`) in the *ActionScript 2.0 Language Reference* in Flash Help.

- The `localName` property of the XMLNode class, which returns the full name of the XML node object (including both the prefix and the local name).

- The `namespaceURI` property of the XMLNode class, which reads the URI of the namespace to which the XML node's prefix resolves. For more information, see `namespaceURI` (`XMLNode.namespaceURI property`) in the *ActionScript 2.0 Language Reference* in Flash Help.

- The `prefix` property of the XMLNode class, which reads the prefix of the node name.
- The `getNamespaceForPrefix()` method of the XMLNode class, which returns the namespace URI associated with the specified prefix for the node.
- The `getPrefixForNamespace` method of the XMLNode class, which returns the prefix associated with a specified namespace URI for the node.

About deprecated language elements

Some language elements are deprecated in Flash Player 8. For a list of deprecated language elements, and alternatives to use in Flash Player 8, see the following sections in the *ActionScript 2.0 Language Reference* in Flash Help:

- Deprecated Class summary
- Deprecated Function summary
- Deprecated Property summary
- Deprecated Operator summary

ActionScript editing changes

The ActionScript editor in the Actions panel and Script window has been updated in several ways to make it more robust and easier to use than earlier versions of the tool. The changes are summarized in this section.

View hidden characters   You can now use the Options pop-up menu in the Script pane, Debugger panel, and Output panel to view or hide hidden characters when you're writing script files in the Actions panel or Script window. For information on this feature, see "Showing hidden characters" on page 55.

Script assist added to Actions panel   In previous versions of Flash, you could work in the Actions panel either in *normal mode*, in which you filled in options and parameters to create code, or in *expert mode*, in which you added commands directly into the Script pane. These options were not available in Flash MX 2004 or Flash MX Professional 2004. However, in Flash Basic 8 and Flash Professional 8, you can work in *Script Assist mode*, which is similar to (and more robust than) normal mode. For information on Script Assist, see "Writing ActionScript with Script Assist" in Flash Help. For a tutorial on Script Assist, see "Creating a startDrag/stopDrag event using Script Assist" in Flash Help.

Reload modified files   You can reload modified script files when working on an application. A warning message appears, prompting you to reload the modified script files associated with the application you're working on. This feature is particularly beneficial to teams working on applications at the same time, in that it helps you avoid working with outdated scripts, or overwriting newer versions of a script. If a script file was moved or deleted, a warning message appears and prompts you to save the files as necessary. For more information, see "About ActionScript preferences" on page 44.

Changes to security model for locally installed SWF files

Flash Player 8 has a new, improved security model in which Flash applications and SWF files on a local computer can communicate with the Internet and the local file system, rather than run from a remote web server. When you develop a Flash application, you must indicate whether a SWF file is allowed to communicate with a network or with a local file system.

> **NOTE**
> In this description, a *local SWF file* is a SWF file that is locally installed on a user's computer, not served from a website, and does not include projector (EXE) files.

In previous versions of Flash Player, local SWF files could interact with other SWF files and load data from any remote or local computer without configuring security settings. In Flash Player 8, a SWF file cannot make connections to the local file system and the network (such as the Internet) in the same application without making a security setting. This is for your safety, so a SWF file cannot read files on your hard disk and then send the contents of those files across the Internet.

This security restriction affects all locally deployed content, whether it's legacy content (a FLA file created in an earlier version of Flash) or created in Flash 8. Using the Flash MX 2004 or earlier authoring tool, you could test a Flash application that runs locally and also accesses the Internet. In Flash Player 8, this application now prompts the user for permission to communicate with the Internet.

When you test a file on your hard disk, there are several steps to determine whether the file is a local trusted (safe) document or a potentially untrusted (unsafe) document. If you create the file in the Flash authoring environment (for example, when you select Control > Test Movie), your file is trusted because it is in the test environment.

In Flash Player 7 and earlier, local SWF files had permissions to access both the local file system and the network. In Flash Player 8, local SWF files can have three levels of permission:

- Access the local file system only (the default level). The local SWF file can read from the local file system and universal naming convention (UNC) network paths and cannot communicate with the Internet.

- Access the network only. The local SWF file can access the network only (such as the Internet) and not the local file system where the SWF file is installed.

- Access to both the local file system and the network. The local SWF file can read from the local file system where the file is installed, read from and write to any server that grants it permission, and can cross-script other SWF files on either the network or the local file system that grant it permission.

For more details about each level of permission, see "About local file security and Flash Player" on page 693.

There are also minor changes to System.security.allowDomain and improvements to System.security.allowInsecureDomain. For more information on local file security, see Chapter 17, "Understanding Security."

CHAPTER 2

Writing and Editing ActionScript 2.0

2

When you write ActionScript code in Macromedia Flash Basic 8 or Macromedia Flash Professional 8, you use the Actions panel or Script window. The Actions panel and Script window contain a full-featured code editor (called the *ActionScript editor*) that includes code hinting and coloring, code formatting, syntax highlighting, syntax checking, debugging, line numbers, word wrapping, and support for Unicode in two different views. For more information about the ActionScript editor, see "Using the Actions panel and Script window" on page 36.

You can use one of two methods to write ActionScript code in Flash. You can write scripts that are part of your Flash document (that is, scripts that are embedded in the FLA file), or you can write external scripts (scripts or classes that are stored in external files). You cannot use the Actions panel to write external scripts.

When you write scripts inside a FLA file, you use the ActionScript editor in the Actions panel. The Actions panel contains the ActionScript editor in a Script pane and supporting tools to make writing scripts easier. These tools include the Actions toolbox, which gives you quick access to the core ActionScript language elements; the Script navigator, which helps you navigate between all of the scripts in your document; and Script Assist mode, in which you are prompted for the elements needed to create scripts. For more information about the Actions panel, see "About the Actions panel" on page 37. For more information about Script Assist, see "About Script Assist" on page 60.

When you need to create an external script, you use the ActionScript editor in the Script window to create a new ActionScript file. (You can also use your favorite text editor to create an external AS file.) In the Script window, the ActionScript editor includes code-assistance features like code hinting and coloring, syntax checking, and so on just like the Actions panel. For more information about the Script window, see "About the Script window" on page 38.

Flash offers further scripting assistance through behaviors. Behaviors are predefined ActionScript functions that you can attach to objects in your Flash document without having to create the ActionScript code yourself. For more information about behaviors, see "About behaviors" on page 63.

For more information on handling events, see the following sections:

About ActionScript and events

In Macromedia Flash Basic 8 and Macromedia Flash Professional 8, ActionScript code is executed when an event occurs: for example, when a movie clip is loaded, when a keyframe on the timeline is entered, or when the user clicks a button. Events can be triggered either by the user or by the system. Users click mouse buttons and press keys; the system triggers events when specific conditions are met or processes completed (the SWF file loads, the timeline reaches a certain frame, a graphic finishes downloading, and so on).

When an event occurs, you write an *event handler* to respond to the event with an action. Understanding when and where events occur will help you to determine how and where you will respond to the event with an action, and which ActionScript tools to use in each case. For more information, see "About writing scripts to handle events" on page 35.

Events can be grouped into a number of categories: mouse and keyboard events, which occur when a user interacts with your Flash application through the mouse and keyboard; clip events, which occur within movie clips; and frame events, which occur within frames on the timeline.

For information about the kinds of scripts you can write to handle events, see "About writing scripts to handle events" on page 35.

Mouse and keyboard events

A user interacting with your SWF file or application triggers mouse and keyboard events. For example, when the user rolls over a button, the `Button.onRollOver` or `on(rollOver)` event occurs; when the user clicks a button, the `Button.onRelease` event occurs; if a key on the keyboard is pressed, the `on(keyPress)` event occurs. You can write code on a frame or attach scripts to an instance to handle these events and add all the interactivity you desire.

Clip events

Within a movie clip, you may react to a number of clip events that are triggered when the user enters or exits the scene or interacts with the scene by using the mouse or keyboard. You might, for example, load an external SWF file or JPG image into the movie clip when the user enters the scene, or allow the user's mouse movements to reposition elements in the scene.

Frame events

On a main or movie clip timeline, a system event occurs when the playhead enters a keyframe—this is known as a *frame event*. Frame events are useful for triggering actions based on the passage of time (moving through the timeline) or for interacting with elements that are currently visible on the Stage. When you add a script to a keyframe, it is executed when the keyframe is reached during playback. A script attached to a frame is called a *frame script*.

One of the most common uses of frame scripts is to stop the playback when a certain keyframe is reached. This is done with the `stop()` function. You select a keyframe and then add the `stop()` function as a script element in the Actions panel.

```
1  stop();
2  //do something
```

When you've stopped the SWF file at a certain keyframe, you need to take some action. You could, for example, use a frame script to dynamically update the value of a label, to manage the interaction of elements on the Stage, and so on.

Organizing ActionScript code

You may attach scripts to keyframes and to object instances (movie clips, buttons, and other symbols). However, if your ActionScript code is scattered over many keyframes and object instances, debugging your application will be much more difficult. It will also be difficult to share your code between different Flash applications. Therefore, it's important to follow best practices for coding when you create ActionScript in Flash.

Rather than attaching your scripts to elements like keyframes, movie clips, and buttons, you should respond to events by calling functions that reside in a central location. One method is to attach embedded ActionScript to the first or second frame of a timeline whenever possible so you don't have to search through the FLA file to find all your code. A common practice is to create a layer called *actions* and place your ActionScript code there.

When you attach all your scripts to individual elements, you're embedding all your code in the FLA file. If sharing your code between other Flash applications is important to you, use the Script window or your favorite text editor to create an external ActionScript (AS) file.

By creating an external file, you make your code more modular and well organized. As your project grows, this convenience becomes much more useful than you might imagine. An external file aids debugging and also source control management if you're working on a project with other developers.

To use the ActionScript code contained in an external AS file, you create a script within the FLA file and then use the #include statement to access the code you've stored externally, as shown in the following example:

```
#include "../core/Functions.as"
```

You can also use ActionScript 2.0 to create custom classes. You must store custom classes in external AS files and use `import` statements in a script to get the classes exported into the SWF file, instead of using `#include` statements. For more information on writing class files, see "Writing custom class files" on page 241 and "About importing class files" on page 245 about importing class files. You can also use components (prebuilt movie clips) to share code and functionality, such as UI elements and scripts.

When you write ActionScript in Flash 8, you use the Actions panel, the Script window, or both. When you use the Actions panel or Script window is dictated by how you respond to events, how you organize your code, and, most importantly, coding best practices.

For more information about coding best practices and conventions, see "ActionScript coding conventions" on page 759.

When you use behaviors, which are predefined ActionScript functions (see "About behaviors" on page 63), other workflow and code organization issues must be considered.

About writing scripts to handle events

Writing code for events can be categorized into two major groups: events that occur on the timeline (in keyframes) and those that occur on object instances (move clips, buttons, and components). The interactivity of your SWF file or application can be scattered over the many elements in your project, and you may be tempted to add scripts directly to these elements. However, Macromedia recommends that you do not add scripts directly to these elements (keyframes and objects). Instead, you should respond to events by calling functions that reside in a central location, as described in "Organizing ActionScript code" on page 34.

Using the Actions panel and Script window

To create scripts within a FLA file, you enter ActionScript directly into the Actions panel. To create external scripts that you include or import into your application, you can use the Script window (File > New and then select ActionScript File) or your preferred text editor.

When you use the Actions panel or Script window, you are using features of the ActionScript editor to write, format, and edit your code. Both the Actions panel and Script window have the Script pane (which is where you type your code) and the Actions toolbox. The Actions panel offers a few more code-assistance features than the Script window. Flash offers these features in the Actions panel because they are especially useful in the context of editing ActionScript within a FLA file.

To display the Actions panel, do one of the following:

- Select Window > Actions.
- Press F9.

To display the Script window, do one of the following:

- To begin writing a new script, select File > New and then select ActionScript File.
- To open an existing script, select File > Open, and then open an existing AS file.
- To edit a script that is already open, click the document tab that shows the script's name.

For more information, see the following topics:

- "About the Actions panel" on page 37
- "About the Script window" on page 38

About the Actions panel

You use the Actions panel to create ActionScript in a Flash document (a FLA file). The Actions panel consists of three panes, each of which supports you in creating and managing scripts.

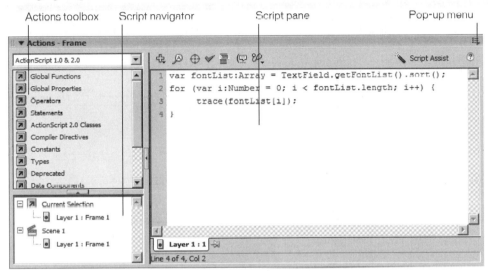

Actions toolbox   Use the Actions toolbox to browse a categorical list of ActionScript language elements (functions, classes, types, and so on) and then insert them into the Script pane. You can insert a script element into the Script pane either by double-clicking or dragging it directly into the Script pane. You can also add language elements to your scripts by using the Add (+) button on the Actions panel toolbar. For more information, see "About the Actions panel and Script window toolbars" on page 40.

Script navigator   The Script navigator displays a hierarchical list of Flash elements (movie clips, frames, and buttons) that contain scripts. Use the Script navigator to move quickly between all the scripts in your Flash document.

If you click an item in the Script navigator, the script associated with that item appears in the Script pane and the playhead moves to that position on the timeline. If you double-click an item in the Script navigator, the script gets *pinned* (locked in place). For more information, see "Pinning scripts in the Actions panel" on page 60.

Script pane   The Script pane is where you type your code. The Script pane provides you with tools to create scripts in a full-featured editor (called the *ActionScript editor*) that includes code syntax formatting and checking, code hinting, code coloring, debugging, and other features that simplify creating scripts. For more information, see "Using the Actions panel and Script window" on page 36.

For information on each of the buttons in the Actions panel toolbar, see "About coding in the Actions panel and Script window" on page 39. For more information on features in the Actions panel, see the following topics:

About the Script window

You can write and edit ActionScript in the Script window when you create a new ActionScript, Flash Communication, or Flash JavaScript file. You use the Script window to write and edit external script files. Syntax coloring, code hinting, and other editor options are supported in the Script window.

You can create external ActionScript, ActionScript communication, and Flash JavaScript files in the Script window. Depending upon the type of external script file you create, the Actions toolbox provides you with a complete list of the language elements available for each.

When you use the Script window, you'll notice that some of the other code-assistance features like Script navigator, Script Assist mode, and behaviors are unavailable. This is because these features are only useful in the context of creating a Flash document, not for creating an external script file.

You will also notice that many of the options available in the Actions panel are unavailable in the Script window. The Script window supports the following editor options: the Actions toolbox, find and replace, syntax checking, automatic formatting, code hinting, and debug options (ActionScript files only). Additionally, the Script window supports displaying line numbers, hidden characters, and word wrap.

To display the Script window:

1. Select File > New.

2. Select the type of external file you want to create (ActionScript file, Flash Communication file, or Flash JavaScript file).

You can have multiple external files open at the same time; filenames are displayed on tabs across the top of the Script window. For more information on features in the Script window, see the following topics:

- "About the Actions panel and Script window toolbars" on page 40
- "About ActionScript editing options" on page 42
- "About code hinting in Flash" on page 46
- "Formatting code" on page 52
- "Using syntax highlighting" on page 53
- "Using line numbers and word wrap" on page 54
- "Using Escape shortcut keys" on page 54
- "Showing hidden characters" on page 55
- "Using the Find tool" on page 56
- "Checking syntax and punctuation" on page 57
- "Importing and exporting scripts" on page 57

About coding in the Actions panel and Script window

The Script pane, where you edit code, is the primary element of both the Actions panel and the Script window. The Actions panel and Script window offer basic script editing and code-assistance features like code hinting, coloring, automatic formatting, and so on.

Features that help you edit code are accessible from the toolbar in the Actions panel or Script window, through the menu system, and in the Script pane itself.

The following topics present the many features of the ActionScript editor (Actions panel and Script window):

- "About the Actions panel and Script window toolbars" on page 40
- "About ActionScript editing options" on page 42
- "About ActionScript preferences" on page 44
- "About code hinting in Flash" on page 46
- "Formatting code" on page 52
- "Using syntax highlighting" on page 53
- "Using line numbers and word wrap" on page 54
- "Using Escape shortcut keys" on page 54
- "Showing hidden characters" on page 55
- "Using the Find tool" on page 56
- "Checking syntax and punctuation" on page 57
- "Importing and exporting scripts" on page 57

For features specific only to the Actions panel, such as script pinning and the Script navigator, see "About Actions panel features" on page 59.

About the Actions panel and Script window toolbars

The Actions panel and Script window toolbars contain links to the code-assistance features that help simplify and streamline coding in ActionScript. The toolbars are different depending on whether you are using the ActionScript editor in the Actions panel or the Script pane. The following image displays features found in the Actions panel toolbar. The marked options are only available in the Actions panel.

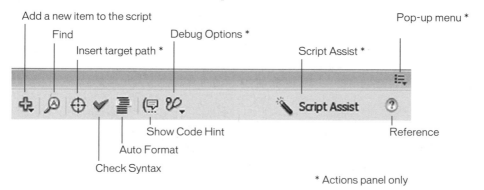

The features you find in the toolbar are discussed in detail in "Using the Actions panel and Script window" on page 36. A quick summary of the buttons you find on the toolbars of both the Actions panel and the Script window follows.

> **NOTE** Some of the following options are found in the Actions panel only. These features are marked *Actions panel only.*

Add a new item to the script   Display all of the language elements that are also in the ActionScript toolbox. Selecting an item from the categorized list of language elements adds it to the script.

Find   Find and replace text in your ActionScript code. For more information, see "Using the Find tool" on page 56.

Insert target path   *Actions panel only.* Assists you in setting an absolute or relative target path for an action in the script. For more information, see "Inserting target paths" on page 62.

Check Syntax   Check for syntax errors in the current script. Syntax errors are listed in the Output panel. For more information, see "Checking syntax and punctuation" on page 57.

Auto Format   Format your script for proper coding syntax and improved readability. You can set autoformatting preferences in the Preferences dialog box, which is available from the Edit menu or from the Actions panel pop-up menu. For more information, see "Formatting code" on page 52.

Show Code Hint   If you've turned off automatic code hinting, you can use Show Code Hint to manually display a code hint for the line of code you're working on. For more information, see "About Script Assist" on page 60.

Debug Options   Set and remove breakpoints in your script so that when you debug your Flash document, you can stop and then proceed line by line through your script. Debug options are now available in the Script window as well as the Actions panel, but only for ActionScript files. This option is disabled for ActionScript Communication and Flash JavaScript files. For more information about debugging your Flash documents, see "Debugging your scripts" on page 725. For information about setting and removing breakpoints, see "Setting and removing breakpoints" on page 734.

Script Assist   *Actions panel only.* In Script Assist mode, you are prompted to enter the elements needed to create scripts. For more information, see "About Script Assist" on page 60.

Reference   Display a reference Help topic for the ActionScript language element that is selected in the Script pane. For example, if you click an `import` statement and then click Reference, the Help topic for `import` appears in the Help panel.

Pop-up menu   *Actions panel only.* Contains the many commands and preferences that apply to the Actions panel or Script window. For example, you can set line numbers and word wrapping in the ActionScript editor, access the ActionScript preferences, and import or export scripts. For more information, see "About ActionScript editing options" on page 42.

About ActionScript editing options

The Script window and Actions panel provide you with many code-assistance features—tools that make writing and maintaining your scripts much easier. These tool options are available from the Actions panel or Script window toolbar and the Actions panel pop-up menu. When you edit ActionScript in the Script window, these options are available in the toolbar and the Flash menu system.

The Actions panel provides more options than are available in the Script window. This is because these additional options are useful in the context of creating ActionScript embedded into a Flash document, but not when writing external ActionScript files. For information about which of these options are available in the Script window, see "About the Script window" on page 38.

The options that are available in the Script window and Actions panel are discussed in "About the Actions panel and Script window toolbars" on page 40.

The following options are available from the Actions panel pop-up menu, and from a variety of menus in the Script window.

 NOTE Some of the following options are found in the Actions panel only. These features are marked *Actions panel only.*

Reload code hints   *Actions panel only.* If you customize the Script assist mode by writing custom methods, you can reload code hints without restarting Flash 8.

Pin script   *Actions panel only.* Pins (locks in place) the script currently displayed in the Script pane. For more information, see "Pinning scripts in the Actions panel" on page 60.

Close script   *Actions panel only.* Closes the currently open script.

Close all scripts   *Actions panel only.* Closes all currently open scripts.

Go to line   Locates and highlights the specified line in the Script pane.

Find and replace   Finds and replaces text within your scripts in the Script pane. For more information, see "Using the Find tool" on page 56.

Find again   Repeats the find action for the last search string that you entered in the Find tool. For more information, see "Using the Find tool" on page 56.

Import script   Allows you to import a script file (ActionScript) into the Script pane. For more information, see "Import and export preferences" on page 58.

Export script   Exports the current script to an external ActionScript (AS) file. For more information, see "Import and export preferences" on page 58.

Esc shortcut keys   Quickly enter common language elements and syntax structures into your scripts. For example, when you press Esc+g+p in the Script pane, the `gotoAndPlay()` function is inserted into the script. When you select the Esc Shortcut Keys option from the Actions panel pop-up menu, all of the available Escape shortcut keys appear in the Actions toolbox. For more information, see "Using Escape shortcut keys" on page 54.

Hidden characters   View hidden characters in your script. Hidden characters are spaces, tabs, and line breaks. For more information, see "Showing hidden characters" on page 55.

Line numbers   Displays line numbers in the Script pane. For more information, see "Using line numbers and word wrap" on page 54.

Preferences   *Actions panel only.* Displays the ActionScript preferences dialog box. For more information, see "About ActionScript preferences" on page 44.

Word wrap   To wrap the lines of your script that exceed the current size of the Script window, select Word Wrap from the Actions panel pop-up menu. When you are using the Script window, select Word Wrap from the View menu. For more information, see "Using line numbers and word wrap" on page 54.

Group Actions with   *Actions panel only.* Allows you to group the Actions panel (which includes the Actions toolbox and the Script navigator) with other panels within the Flash authoring environment.

In addition, the Actions panel pop-up menu includes the Print, Help, and panel resizing commands.

About ActionScript preferences

Whether you edit code in the Actions panel or the Script window, you can set and modify a single set of preferences. You can, for example, control automatic indentation, code hinting and coloring, and a number of other basic code editing features.

To access ActionScript preferences:

1. To access ActionScript preferences in a FLA file with the Actions panel, select Preferences from the pop-up menu, or Edit > Preferences (Windows) or Flash > Preferences (Macintosh), and click ActionScript in the Category list.

2. To access ActionScript preferences in the Script window, select Edit > Preferences and then click ActionScript (Windows) or Flash > Preferences and then click ActionScript (Macintosh).

The following image shows the ActionScript settings you can change in Flash 8.

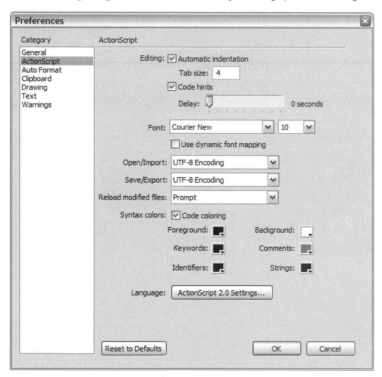

You can set the following preferences:

Automatic indentation   When automatic indentation is turned on, the text you type after an opening parenthesis [(] or opening curly brace ({) is automatically indented according to the Tab Size setting in ActionScript preferences. For more information, see "Formatting code" on page 52.

Tab size   Specifies the number of characters a new line is offset by when automatic indentation is turned on.

Code hints   Enables code hinting in the Script pane. For more information about using code hinting, see "About code hinting in Flash" on page 46.

Delay   Specifies the delay (in seconds) before code hints are displayed.

Font   Specifies the font used in the Script pane.

Use dynamic font mapping   Checks to ensure that the selected font family has the necessary glyphs to render each character. If not, Flash substitutes a font family that contains the necessary characters. For more information, see "Formatting code" on page 52.

Encoding   Specifies the character encoding used when opening, saving, importing, and exporting ActionScript files. For more information, see "Importing and exporting scripts" on page 57.

Reload modified files   Lets you select when to see warnings about whether a script file is modified, moved, or deleted. Select between Always, Never, or Prompt.

- **Always**   No warning is displayed when a change is detected, and the file is automatically reloaded.

- **Never**   No warning is displayed when a change is detected, and the file remains in the current state.

- **Prompt**   (Default) Warning is displayed when a change is detected, and you can choose whether or not to reload the file.

When building applications that involve external script files, this feature helps you avoid overwriting a script that a team member has modified since you opened the application, or publishing the application with older versions of scripts. The warnings let you automatically close a script, and reopen the newer, modified version.

Syntax colors   Specifies the colors for code coloring in your scripts. With code coloring enabled, you can select the colors to be displayed in the Script pane.

Language   Opens the ActionScript Settings dialog box. For more information, see "Modifying the classpath" on page 65.

About code hinting in Flash

When you use the Actions panel or the Script window, you can use several features to help you write syntactically correct code. Code hints help you write code quickly and accurately. Code hinting includes tooltips that contain correct syntax, and menus that let you select method and property names. The following sections show you how to write code that uses these features.

- "About triggering code hints" on page 46
- "Using code hints" on page 46
- "About typing objects to trigger code hints" on page 49
- "About using suffixes to trigger code hints" on page 50
- "About using comments to trigger code hints" on page 51

About triggering code hints

When you work in the Actions panel or Script window, Flash can detect what action you are entering and display a *code hint*. The two different styles of code hint are a tooltip that contains the complete syntax for that action, and a pop-up menu that lists possible method or property names (sometimes referred to as a form of *code completion*). A pop-up menu appears for parameters, properties, and events when you use strict typing or naming for your objects, as discussed in the rest of this section.

Code hints sometimes appear if you double-click an item in the Actions toolbox or click Add (+) in the Actions panel or Script window toolbar to add actions to the Script pane. For information on using code hints when they appear, see "Using code hints" on page 46.

 NOTE Code hinting is enabled automatically for native classes that don't require you to create and name an instance of the class, such as Math, Key, Mouse, and so on.

To ensure that code hints are enabled, the Code Hints options must be selected in the ActionScript Preferences dialog box. For more information, see "About the Actions panel" on page 37.

Using code hints

Code hints are enabled by default. By setting preferences, you can disable code hints or determine how quickly they appear. When code hints are disabled in preferences, you can still display a code hint for a specific command.

To specify settings for automatic code hints, do one of the following:

■ In the Actions panel or Script window, select Edit > Preferences (Windows) or Flash > Preferences (Macintosh), click ActionScript in the Category list, and then enable or disable Code Hints.

■ In the Actions panel, select Preferences from the pop-up menu (at the upper-right of the Actions panel) and enable or disable Code Hints in the ActionScript preferences.

If you enable code hints, you can also specify a delay in seconds before the code hints should appear. For example, if you are new to ActionScript, you might prefer no delay, so that code hints always appear immediately. However, if you usually know what you want to type and need hints only when you use unfamiliar language elements, you can specify a delay so that code hints don't appear when you don't plan to use them.

To specify a delay for code hints:

1. In the Actions panel or Script window, select Edit > Preferences (Windows) or Flash > Preferences (Macintosh) from the main menu.

2. Click ActionScript in the Category list.

3. Use the slider to select an amount of delay.

   The amount of delay is in seconds.

To work with tooltip-style code hints:

1. Display the code hint by typing an opening parenthesis [(] after an element that requires parentheses (for example, after a method name, a command such as if or do..while, and so on).

   The code hint appears.

> **NOTE**
> If a code hint doesn't appear, make sure you didn't disable Code Hints in the ActionScript preferences (Edit > Preferences (Windows) or Flash > Preferences (Macintosh) and then click ActionScript in the Category list). To display code hints for a variable or object you created, make sure that you named your variable or object correctly (see "About using suffixes to trigger code hints" on page 50) or that you use strict typing for your variable or object (see "About typing objects to trigger code hints" on page 49).

2. Enter a value for the parameter.

If more than one parameter is present, separate the values with commas. For functions or statements, such as the `for` loop, separate the parameters with semicolons.

Overloaded commands (functions or methods that can be invoked with different sets of parameters) such as `gotoAndPlay()` or `for` display an indicator that lets you select the parameter you want to set. Click the small arrow buttons or press Control+Left Arrow and Control+Right Arrow to select the parameter.

3. To dismiss the code hint, do one of the following:

- Type a closing parens [)].
- Click outside the statement.
- Press Escape.

To work with menu-style code hints:

1. Display the code hint by typing a period after the variable or object name.

The code hint menu appears.

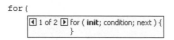

 NOTE If a code hint doesn't appear, make sure you didn't disable code hints in the ActionScript preferences (Edit > Preferences (Windows) or Flash > Preferences (Macintosh) and then click ActionScript in the Category list). To display code hints for a variable or object you created, make sure that you named your variable or object correctly (see "About using suffixes to trigger code hints" on page 50) or that you used strict typing for your variable or object (see "About typing objects to trigger code hints" on page 49).

2. To navigate through the code hints, use the Up and Down Arrow keys.

3. To select an item in the menu, press Enter or Tab, or double-click the item.

4. To dismiss the code hint, do one of the following:

- Select one of the menu items.
- Click above or below the menu window.
- Type a closing parens [)] if you've already typed an opening parens [(].
- Press Escape.

To manually display a code hint:

1. Click in a code location where code hints can appear, such as in the following locations:

- After the dot (.) following a statement or command, where a property or method must be entered
- Between parentheses [()] in a method name

2. Do one of the following:

- Click Show Code Hint in the Actions panel or Script window toolbar.
- Press Control+Spacebar (Windows) or Command+Spacebar (Macintosh).
- If you are working in the Actions panel, select Show Code Hint from the pop-up menu.

About typing objects to trigger code hints

When you use ActionScript 2.0, you can use strict typing for a variable that is based on a built-in class, such as Button, Array, and so on. If you do so, the Script pane displays code hints for the variable. For example, suppose you type the following code:

```
var names:Array = new Array();
names.
```

As soon as you type the period (.), Flash displays a list of methods and properties available for Array objects in a pop-up menu, because you have typed the variable as an array. For more information on data typing, see "About assigning data types and strict data typing" on page 83. For information on using code hints when they appear, see "Using code hints" on page 46.

About using suffixes to trigger code hints

If you use ActionScript 1 or you want to display code hints for objects you create without strictly typing them (see "About typing objects to trigger code hints" on page 49), you must add a special suffix to the name of each object when you create it. For example, the suffixes that trigger code hinting for the Array class and the Camera class are _array and _cam, respectively. For example, if you type the following code

```
var my_array = new Array();
var my_cam = Camera.get();
```

you can type either of the following (the variable name followed by a period):

```
my_array.
my_cam.
```

Code hints for the Array and Camera objects will appear.

For objects that appear on the Stage, use the suffix in the Instance Name text box in the Property inspector. For example, to display code hints for MovieClip objects, use the Property inspector to assign instance names with the _mc suffix to all MovieClip objects. Then, whenever you type the instance name followed by a period, code hints appear.

Although suffixes are not required for triggering code hints when you use strict typing for an object, using suffixes consistently helps make your code understandable.

The following table lists the suffixes required for support of automatic code hinting:

Object type	Variable suffix
Array	_array
Button	_btn
Camera	_cam
Color	_color
ContextMenu	_cm
ContextMenuItem	_cmi
Date	_date
Error	_err
LoadVars	_lv
LocalConnection	_lc
Microphone	_mic
MovieClip	_mc
MovieClipLoader	_mcl

Object type	Variable suffix
PrintJob	_pj
NetConnection	_nc
NetStream	_ns
SharedObject	_so
Sound	_sound
String	_str
TextField	_txt
TextFormat	_fmt
Video	_video
XML	_xml
XMLNode	_xmlnode
XMLSocket	_xmlsocket

For information on using code hints when they appear, see "Using code hints" on page 46.

About using comments to trigger code hints

You can also use ActionScript comments to specify an object's class for code hints. The following example tells ActionScript that the class of the `theObject` instance is Object, and so on. If you were to enter `mc` followed by a period after these comments, code hints that display the list of MovieClip methods and properties would appear. If you were to enter `theArray` followed by a period, a menu that displays a list of Array methods and properties would appear, and so on.

```
// Object theObject;
// Array theArray;
// MovieClip theMc;
```

However, Macromedia recommends that instead of this technique, you use strict data typing (see "About typing objects to trigger code hints" on page 49) or suffixes (see "About using suffixes to trigger code hints" on page 50) because these techniques enable code hints automatically and make your code more understandable. For more information on using code hints, see "Using code hints" on page 46.

Formatting code

You can specify settings to determine if your code is formatted and indented automatically or manually. In addition, you can select whether to use dynamic font mapping, which ensures that the correct fonts are used when working with multilingual text.

To set format options:

1. In the Actions panel, select Preferences from the pop-up menu (at the upper right of the Actions panel). In the Preferences dialog box, select Auto Format.

Alternatively, in the Script window, select Edit > Preferences (Windows) or Flash > Preferences (Macintosh). In the Preferences dialog box, select Auto Format.

2. Select any of the Auto Format options.

To see the effect of each selection, look in the Preview pane.

After you set Auto Format options, your settings are applied automatically to code you write, but not to existing code; you must apply your settings to existing code manually. You must manually format code that was formatted using different settings, code that you imported from another editor, and so on.

To format code according to Auto Format settings, do one of the following:

- Click the Auto Format button in the Actions panel or Script window toolbar.
- In the Actions panel, select Auto Format from the pop-up menu.
- Press Control+Shift+F (Windows) or Command+Shift+F (Macintosh).
- In the Script window, select Tools > Auto Format.

To use dynamic font mapping:

- To turn dynamic font mapping on or off, select or deselect Use dynamic font mapping in the Preferences dialog box.

Dynamic font mapping is turned off by default because it increases performance time when you are scripting. If you are working with multilingual text, turn on dynamic font mapping because it helps to ensure that the correct fonts are used.

To use automatic indentation:

- To turn automatic indentation on or off, select or deselect Automatic indentation in the Preferences dialog box.

  When automatic indentation is turned on, the text you type after an opening parenthesis [(] or opening curly brace ({) is automatically indented according to the Tab size setting in ActionScript preferences.

  In your scripts, you can indent a line by selecting the line and pressing Tab. To remove the indent, select the line and press Shift+Tab.

Using syntax highlighting

In ActionScript, as in any language, *syntax* is the way elements are put together to create meaning. If you use incorrect ActionScript syntax, your scripts cannot work.

When you write scripts in Flash Basic 8 and Flash Professional 8, commands that are not supported by the version of the player you are targeting appear in yellow in the Actions toolbox. For example, if the Flash Player SWF file version is set to Flash 7, ActionScript that is supported only by Flash Player 8 appears in yellow in the Actions toolbox. (For information on setting the Flash Player SWF file version, see "Setting publish options for the Flash SWF file format" in Flash Help.

You can also set a preference to have Flash color-code parts of your scripts as you write them, which brings attention to typing errors. For example, suppose you set the Syntax coloring preference to make keywords appear in deep blue. While you type code, if you type var, the word var appears in blue. However, if you mistakenly type vae, the word vae remains black, which shows that you made a typing error. For information on keywords, see "About keywords" on page 142.

To set preferences for syntax coloring as you type, do one of the following:

- Select Edit > Preferences (Windows) or Flash > Preferences (Macintosh), click ActionScript in the Category list, and specify Syntax coloring settings.
- In the Actions panel, select Preferences from the pop-up menu (at the upper right of the Actions panel) and specify Syntax coloring settings in ActionScript preferences.
- With the mouse pointer focused in the Script pane, press Control-U (Windows) or Command-U (Macintosh).

You can change the color settings for keywords, comments, identifiers, and strings. For information on identifiers and strings, see "Terminology" on page 821 and "String data type" on page 82. For information on commenting, see "About comments" on page 135.

Using line numbers and word wrap

You can select whether to view line numbers and whether to wrap long lines of code. Typically, you should enable line numbers and word wrap to make editing code much easier. Line numbers make code easier to scroll and parse when you're editing or modifying the code. Word wrap helps you avoid horizontally scrolling long lines of code (especially when you work in the authoring environment, or at low screen resolutions).

To enable or disable line numbers, do one of the following:

- In the Actions panel, select Line Numbers from the pop-up menu.
- In the Script window, select Tools > Line Numbers.
- Press Control+Shift+L (Windows) or Command+Shift+L (Macintosh).

To enable or disable line word wrap, do one of the following:

- In the Actions panel, select Word Wrap from the pop-up menu.
- In the Script window, select Tools > Word Wrap.
- Press Control+Shift+W (Windows) or Command+Shift+W (Macintosh).

Using Escape shortcut keys

You can add many elements to a script by using Escape shortcut keys (pressing the Escape key, and then two other keys).

> **NOTE** These shortcuts are different from the keyboard shortcuts that initiate certain menu commands.

For example, if you are working in the Script pane and press Escape+d+o, the following code is placed in your script:

```
do {
} while ();
```

The insertion point is placed immediately following the word `while`, so you can begin typing your condition. Similarly, if you press Escape+c+h, the following code is placed in your script, and the insertion point is placed between the parentheses [()], so you can begin typing your condition:

```
catch () {
}
```

If you want to learn (or be reminded) about which commands have Escape shortcut keys, you can show them next to elements in the ActionScript toolbox.

To show or hide Escape shortcut keys:

 ■ From the Actions panel pop-up menu, select or deselect Esc Shortcut Keys.

Escape shortcut keys appear next to elements in the ActionScript toolbox.

Showing hidden characters

As you write and format ActionScript code, you will enter spaces, tabs, and line breaks into your script. These of course are good and necessary to the visual organization of your code. However, the Flash compiler generates errors if it encounters double-byte spaces that are not part of a string value. Showing hidden characters in the Script pane allows you to see and then remove double-byte spaces.

The following symbols are used to display each hidden character:

single-byte space	.
double-byte space	‖
tab	≫
line break	¶

To show hidden characters, do one of the following:

■ Select Hidden Characters from the pop-up menu.

■ Press Control+Shift+8 (Windows) or Command+Shift+8 (Macintosh).

With hidden characters shown, the Script pane looks like this:

```
43 ····private·function·calculate():Void¶
44 »    {¶
45 ········var·percent:Number·=·Number(radioGroup.selection.data)
46 ····»    var·tip:Number·=·Number(subtotal.text)·*·percent;¶
47 ········if·(isNaN(tip))·{»    »    »    »    »    ·¶
48 ············gratuity.text·=·"";¶
49 ········}·else·{¶
50 ············gratuity.text·=·formatCurrency(tip);¶
51 ········}¶
52 »    }¶
53 ¶
54 ····//·Event·handler·for·"change"¶
55 ····//·If·user·changes·subtotal,·recalculate·gratuity¶
56 ····public·function·change(event:Object):Void¶
57 »    {¶
```

Script Assist

Layer 1 : 1

Line 3 of 77, Col 37

Using the Find tool

The Find tool allows you to find and optionally replace text string in your scripts. You may replace the first or all occurrences of the text in your script. You may also match the case of the text.

To find text in a script:

1. From the Actions panel or Script window toolbar, select the Find tool or press Control+F (Windows) or Command+F (Macintosh).

2. Enter the search string that you want to locate in the script.

3. Click Find Next.

   If the text or characters are present in the script, the words or characters will be highlighted in the Script pane.

To find and replace text in a script:

1. From the Actions panel or Script window toolbar, click the Find tool or press Control+F (Windows) or Command+F (Macintosh).

2. Enter the search string that you want to locate and replace in the script.

3. In the Replace text box, enter the new string.

4. Click Find Next.

   If the string is present in the script, it is highlighted.

5. Click Replace to replace the string, or click Replace All to replace all occurrences of the string.

After you've entered a search string in the Find tool, you can repeat the search by selecting Find Again from the pop-up menu.

Checking syntax and punctuation

To determine whether the code you wrote performs as planned, you need to publish or test the file. However, you can do a quick check of your ActionScript code without leaving the FLA file. Syntax errors are listed in the Output panel. You can also check to see if a set of parentheses, curly braces, or brackets around a block of code is balanced.

When you check syntax, the current script is checked. If the current script calls ActionScript 2.0 classes, those classes are compiled and their syntax is also checked. Other scripts that might be in the FLA file are not checked.

To check syntax, do one of the following:

- Click Check Syntax in the Actions panel or Script window toolbar.
- In the Actions panel, select Check Syntax from the pop-up menu.
- Select the Script pane (so it has focus), and then press Control+T (Windows) or Command+T (Macintosh).

> **NOTE**
> If you click Check Syntax in an external ActionScript 2.0 class file in the Script window, the global class path affects this process. Sometimes you will generate errors—even if the global class path is set correctly—because the compiler is not aware that this class is being compiled. For more information on compiling classes, see "Compiling and exporting classes" on page 286.

To check for punctuation balance, do one of the following:

- Click between braces ({}), brackets ([]), or parentheses [()] in your script.
- For Windows, press Control+' (single quote), or for Macintosh, press Command+' (single quote) to highlight the text between braces, brackets, or parentheses.

  The highlighting helps you check that opening punctuation has corresponding closing punctuation.

Importing and exporting scripts

You may both import a script into the Actions panel or Script window and export your scripts to external ActionScript files. Both can be useful for sharing code between different Flash applications and development teams.

To import an external AS file:

- To import an external script into a script that you're working on in the Script pane, place the insertion point where you want the first line of the external script to be located and then do either of the following:
  - In the Actions panel, select Import Script from the pop-up menu or press Control+Shift+I (Windows) or Command+Shift+I (Macintosh).
  - In the Script window, select Import Script from the File menu or press Control+Shift+I (Windows) or Command+Shift+I (Macintosh).

You can export a script from the Actions panel. When you use the Script window, exporting is unnecessary because you can instead save the AS file.

To export a script from the Actions panel:

1. Select the script to export and then select Export Script from the pop-up menu or press Control+Shift+X (Windows) or Command+Shift+X (Macintosh).

   The Save As dialog box appears.

2. Save the ActionScript (AS) file.

Flash supports a number of different character encoding formats (including Unicode) and you may specify which format to use when importing and exporting scripts. For more information, see "Importing and exporting scripts" on page 57 and "Import and export preferences" on page 58.

Unicode support for ActionScript

Flash 8 supports Unicode text encoding for ActionScript. This means that you can include text in different languages in an ActionScript file. For example, you can include text in English, Japanese, and French in the same file.

> **CAUTION**
>
> When you use a non-English application on an English system, the Test Movie command (see "Debugging your scripts" on page 725) fails if any part of the SWF file path has characters that cannot be represented by using the Multibyte Character Sets (MBCS) encoding scheme. For example, Japanese paths, which work on a Japanese system, won't work on an English system. All areas of the application that use the external player are subject to this limitation.

Import and export preferences

You can set ActionScript preferences to specify the type of encoding to use when importing or exporting ActionScript files. You can select UTF-8 encoding or Default Encoding. UTF-8 is 8-bit Unicode format; Default Encoding is the encoding form supported by the language your system is currently using, also called the *traditional code page*.

In general, if you are importing or exporting ActionScript files in UTF-8 format, use the UTF-8 preference. If you are importing or exporting files in the traditional code page in use on your system, use the Default Encoding preference.

If text in your scripts doesn't look as expected when you open or import a file, change the import encoding preference. If you receive a warning message when you export ActionScript files, you can change the export encoding preference or turn this warning off in ActionScript preferences.

To select text encoding options for importing or exporting ActionScript files:

1. In the Preferences dialog box (Edit > Preferences (Windows) or Flash > Preferences (Macintosh)), click ActionScript in the Category list.

2. Under Editing Options, do one or both of the following:

   - For Open/Import, select UTF-8 Encoding to open or import using Unicode encoding, or select Default Encoding to open or import using the encoding form of the language currently used by your system.

   - For Save/Export, select UTF-8 Encoding to save or export using Unicode encoding, or select Default Encoding to save or export using the encoding form of the language currently used by your system.

To turn the export encoding warning off or on:

1. In the Flash system menu, select Edit > Preferences (Windows) or Flash > Preferences (Macintosh), and click Warnings from the Category list.

2. Select or deselect Warn on encoding conflicts when exporting ActionScript files.

About Actions panel features

The following features are only available in the Actions panel. These features are not available in the Script window. Even though the Actions panel has all the features of the Script window, the Script window is used for a different functionality. The Actions panel has to support some FLA file-related functionality, which you'll read about in the following sections. For features that are available in both the Script window and the Actions panel, see the sections in "About coding in the Actions panel and Script window" on page 39.

For features only available in the Actions panel, see these sections:

- "About Script Assist" on page 60
- "Pinning scripts in the Actions panel" on page 60
- "Inserting target paths" on page 62

About Script Assist

Script Assist prompts you to enter the elements of a script, helping you to more easily add simple interactivity to your Flash SWF file or application. Script Assist mode is ideal for users who either aren't comfortable writing their own scripts or who just appreciate the convenience the tool provides.

Used in conjunction with the Actions panel, Script Assist prompts you to select options and enter parameters. For example, instead of writing a new script, you can select a language element from the Actions toolbox (or the Add (+) command on the toolbar), drag it into the Script pane, and then use Script Assist to help you complete the script.

In the example below, the `gotoAndPlay` function was added to the Script pane. Script Assist displays all of the prompts needed to use this ActionScript function—in this case, the scene name, the type, and the frame number.

Pinning scripts in the Actions panel

If you don't centralize your code within a FLA file in one location (discussed in "Organizing ActionScript code" on page 34) or if you're using behaviors (see "About behaviors" on page 63), you can *pin* multiple scripts in the Actions panel to make it easier to move among them. To pin a script means that you can keep the location of the code open in the Actions panel, and easily click between each open script.

In the following figure, the script associated with the current location on the timeline is on Frame 1 of the layer named Cleanup. (The tab at the far left always follows your location along the timeline.) That script is also pinned (it is shown as the right-most tab). Two other scripts are pinned: one on Frame 1 and the other on Frame 15 of the layer named Intro. You can move among the pinned scripts by clicking on the tabs or by using keyboard shortcuts, such as Control+Shift+. (period). Moving among pinned scripts does not change your current position on the timeline. As you can see in the following figure, multiple scripts are open in the Actions panel, and you can click each tab to move between the scripts.

> **TIP** If the content in the Script pane doesn't change to reflect the location that you select on the timeline, the Script pane is probably showing a pinned script. Click the left tab at the lower left of the Script pane to show the ActionScript associated with your location along the timeline.

To pin a script:

1. Position your mouse pointer on the Timeline so the script appears in a tab at the lower left of the Script pane in the Actions panel.

2. Do one of the following:

   - Click the pushpin icon to the right of the tab.
   - Right-click (Windows) or Control-click (Macintosh) on the tab, and select Pin Script.

   - Select Pin Script from the pop-up menu (at the upper right of the Actions panel).
   - With the mouse pointer focused in the Script pane, press Control+= (equal sign) in Windows or Command+= on the Macintosh.

To unpin one or more scripts, do one of the following:

- If a pinned script appears in a tab at the lower left of the Script pane in the Actions panel, click the pushpin icon on the right of the tab.
- Right-click (Windows) or Control-click (Macintosh) on a tab, and select Close Script or Close All Scripts.
- Select Close Script or Close All Scripts from the pop-up menu (at the upper right of the Actions panel).
- With the mouse pointer focused in the Script pane, press Control+-(minus sign) in Windows or Command+- on Macintosh.

To use keyboard shortcuts with pinned scripts:

■ You can use the following keyboard shortcuts to work with pinned scripts:

Action	Windows shortcut key	Macintosh shortcut key
Pin script	Control+= (equal sign)	Command+=
Unpin script	Control+- (minus sign)	Command+-
Move focus to tab on the right	Control+Shift+. (period)	Command+Shift+.
Move focus to tab on the left	Control+Shift+, (comma)	Command+Shift+,
Unpin all scripts	Control+Shift+- (minus)	Command+Shift+-

Inserting target paths

Many of the actions that you create in your script will affect movie clips, buttons, and other symbol instances. To apply actions to instances on a timeline, you set a *target path*—the address of the instance you want to target. You can set either an absolute or relative target path.

The Target Path tool, which is available in the Actions panel, prompts you to enter the target path for the selected action in your script.

To insert a target path:

1. Select and position the pointer in an action in your script.
2. Click Target Path on the Actions panel toolbar.

   The Insert Target Path dialog box appears.
3. Do one of the following:
   - Manually enter the path to the target instance.
   - Select the target from the list of available targets.
4. Select either the Absolute or Relative path option.
5. Click OK.

   The path is appended to the action.

About behaviors

Behaviors are predefined ActionScript functions that you can attach to objects in your Flash document without having to create the ActionScript code yourself. Behaviors provide you with prewritten ActionScript functionality, such as frame navigation, loading of external SWF files and JPEGs, controlling the stacking order of movie clips, and movie clip dragging.

You can use behaviors as a convenience when building your Flash application—as a way to avoid having to write ActionScript, or conversely as a way to learn how ActionScript works in certain situations.

Behaviors are available to you only when you are working in a Flash document, not in an external script file. Typically, you select a triggering object in your document, a movie clip or a button, select Add on the Behaviors panel to display the available behaviors, and then select the behavior you want, as shown in the following example:

The behavior is added to the object and is displayed in the Actions panel.

```
1
2      //load Graphic Behavior
3      this.loadMovie("1.jpg");
4      //End Behavior
5
```

About ActionScript publish settings

You can edit ActionScript in two ways. You can edit ActionScript that is embedded into a Flash document by using the Actions panel. Or you can edit ActionScript that is in a separate script file, external to the Flash document, using the Script window. Because the Actions panel and the Script window are essentially two different views that use the same ActionScript editor, ActionScript settings and preferences within Flash apply to both views.

You edit the Flash document's publish settings to change the version of ActionScript that will be used when the document is published. You can also set the classpath for the current document by passing the global ActionScript classpath.

For more information about modifying the ActionScript publish settings, see "Modifying ActionScript publish settings" on page 64. For more information about setting a document-level or the global level classpath, see "Modifying the classpath" on page 65.

Modifying ActionScript publish settings

When you publish a Flash document, the ActionScript version is set to 2.0 by default and the classpath is inherited from the global classpath setting. If you need to change the version of ActionScript or to specify a document-level classpath, you can do so by editing the publish settings.

To change the ActionScript version:

1. Select File > Publish Settings and then select the Flash tab.

2. Select the ActionScript version from the pop-up menu.

   ActionScript 2.0 is selected by default. If you write your scripts in ActionScript 1.0 instead of 2.0, change this setting before you publish your Flash document.

The ActionScript 2.0 compiler compiles all ActionScript 1.0 code, with the following exception: the slash (/) syntax used to indicate movie clip paths (for example, `parentClip/testMC:varName= "hello world"`) generates compilation errors if you select ActionScript 2.0 as the ActionScript version. To resolve this problem, either rewrite your code using dot (.) notation in place of slashes, or select the ActionScript 1.0 compiler.

You use the Settings button (next to the ActionScript version pop-up menu) to modify the document-level classpath. For more information, see "Modifying the classpath" on page 65.

Modifying the classpath

When you use ActionScript 2.0, you can also set a document-level classpath. This is useful when you create your own classes and you want to override the global ActionScript classpath that is set in the ActionScript preferences.

Changing the classpath in the publish settings only applies to the current Flash file.

You can use the Preferences dialog box to modify the global classpath. To modify the document-level classpath setting, you use the Publish Settings dialog box for the FLA file. In both cases, you can add absolute directory paths (for example, C:/my_classes) and relative directory paths (for example, ../my_classes or ".").

To modify the global classpath:

1. Select Edit > Preferences (Windows) or Flash > Preferences (Macintosh) to open the Preferences dialog box.

2. Click ActionScript in the Category list, and then click ActionScript 2.0 Settings.

3. Do one of the following:

   - To add a directory to the classpath, click Browse to Path, browse to the directory you want to add, and click OK.

     Alternatively, click Add New Path (+) to add a new line to the Classpath list. Double-click the new line, type a relative or absolute path, and click OK.

   - To edit an existing classpath directory, select the path in the Classpath list, click Browse to Path, browse to the directory you want to add, and click OK.

     Alternatively, double-click the path in the Classpath list, type the desired path, and click OK.

   - To delete a directory from the classpath, select the path in the Classpath list and click Remove from Path.

> **NOTE** Do not delete the absolute global classpath (see Global and document-level classpaths). Flash uses this classpath to access built-in classes. If you accidentally delete this classpath, reinstate it by adding $(LocalData)/Classes as a new classpath.

To modify the document-level classpath:

1. Select File > Publish Settings to open the Publish Settings dialog box.

2. Click the Flash tab.

3. Click Settings next to the ActionScript Version pop-up menu.

4. Do one of the following:

   - To add a directory to the classpath, click Browse to Path, browse to the directory you want to add, and click OK.

     Alternatively, click Add New Path (+) to add a new line to the Classpath list. Double-click the new line, type a relative or absolute path, and click OK.

   - To edit an existing classpath directory, select the path in the Classpath list, click Browse to Path, browse to the directory you want to add, and click OK.

     Alternatively, double-click the path in the Classpath list, type the desired path, and click OK.

   - To delete a directory from the classpath, select the path in the Classpath list, and click Remove from Path.

For more information on setting and modifying classpaths, see "About setting and modifying the classpath" on page 246.

Configuration files that install with Flash 8

When you install Flash Basic 8 or Flash Professional 8, several ActionScript-related configuration folders and files are placed on your system. You might use these files to make certain configurations to the authoring environment. As always, modify carefully and save a back up of files that you modify.

ActionScript classes folder   Contain all of the ActionScript classes (AS files) that are included in Flash Professional 8 or Flash Basic 8. Typical paths to this folder are as follows:

- Windows: Hard Disk\Documents and Settings*user*\Local Settings\Application Data\ Macromedia\Flash 8*language*\Configuration\Classes.

- Macintosh: Hard Disk/Users/*user*/Library/Application Support/Macromedia/Flash 8/ *language*/Configuration/Classes.

  The Classes folder is organized into folders that contain directories that contain the classes for Flash Player 7 (FP7) and Flash Player 8 (FP8). It also contains a directory for the mx package (mx), that's used in both players and ASO files (aso). For more information on ASO files, see "Using ASO files" on page 288. For more information on the organization of this directory, see the readme file in the Classes folder.

Include classes folder   Contain all of the global ActionScript include files and is located in:

- Windows: Hard Disk\Documents and Settings*user*\Local Settings\Application Data\ Macromedia\Flash 8*language*\Configuration\Include.
- Macintosh: Hard Disk/Users/*user*/Library/Application Support/Macromedia/Flash 8/ *language*/Configuration/Include.

ActionsPanel.xml configuration file   Includes the configuration file for ActionScript code hinting and is located in:

- Windows: Hard Disk\Documents and Settings*user*\Local Settings\Application Data\ Macromedia\Flash 8*language*\Configuration\ActionsPanel\ActionScript_1_2.
- Macintosh: Hard Disk/Users/*user*/Library/Application Support/Macromedia/Flash 8/ *language*/Configuration/ActionsPanel/ActionScript_1_2.

AsColorSyntax.xml configuration file   The configuration file for ActionScript code color syntax highlighting; located in:

- Windows: Hard Disk\Documents and Settings*user*\Local Settings\Application Data\ Macromedia\Flash 8*language*\Configuration\ActionsPanel\.
- Macintosh: Hard Disk/Users/*user*/Library/Application Support/Macromedia/Flash 8/ *language*/Configuration/ActionsPanel.

CHAPTER 3

About ActionScript

The object-oriented programming (OOP) features in ActionScript 2.0 are based on the ECMAScript 4 Draft Proposal currently in development by ECMA TC39-TG1 (see www.mozilla.org/js/language/es4/index.html). Because the ECMA-4 proposal is not yet a standard, and because it is still changing, ActionScript 2.0 is loosely based on this specification.

ActionScript 2.0 supports all the standard elements of the ActionScript language; it lets you write scripts that more closely adhere to standards used in other object-oriented languages, such as Java. ActionScript 2.0 should be of interest primarily to intermediate or advanced Flash developers who are building applications that require the implementation of classes and subclasses. ActionScript 2.0 also lets you declare the object type of a variable when you create it (see "About assigning data types and strict data typing" on page 83) and provides significantly improved compiler errors (see Appendix A, "Error Messages," on page 787).

Key facts about ActionScript 2.0 include the following points:

- Scripts that use ActionScript 2.0 to define classes or interfaces must be stored as external script files, with a single class defined in each script; that is, classes and interfaces cannot be defined in the Actions panel.

- You can import individual class files implicitly (by storing them in a location specified by global or document-specific search paths and then using them in a script) or explicitly (by using the `import` command); you can import packages (collections of class files in a directory) by using wildcards.

- Applications developed with ActionScript 2.0 are supported by Flash Player 6 and later.

> **CAUTION** The default publish setting for new files created in Flash 8 is ActionScript 2.0. If you plan to modify an existing FLA file with ActionScript 1.0 to use ActionScript 2.0 syntax, ensure that the FLA file specifies ActionScript 2.0 in its publish settings. If it does not, your file will compile incorrectly, although Flash will not necessarily generate compiler errors.

For more information on using ActionScript 2.0 to write object-oriented programs in Flash, see Chapter 7, "Classes," on page 231.

Although Macromedia recommends that you use ActionScript 2.0, you can continue to use ActionScript 1.0 syntax, especially if you are doing more traditional Flash work such as simple animation that doesn't require user interaction.

What is ActionScript

The main features of ActionScript 2.0 include the following:

Familiar object-oriented programming (OOP) model   The primary feature of ActionScript 2.0 is a familiar model for creating object-oriented programs. ActionScript 2.0 implements several object-oriented concepts and keywords such as *class*, *interface*, and *packages* that will be familiar to you if you've programmed with Java.

The OOP model provided by ActionScript 2.0 is a "syntactic formalization" of the prototype chaining method used in previous versions of Macromedia Flash to create objects and establish inheritance. With ActionScript 2.0, you can create custom classes and extend Flash's built-in classes.

Strict data typing   ActionScript 2.0 also lets you explicitly specify data types for variables, function parameters, and function return types. For example, the following code declares a variable named userName of type String (a built-in ActionScript data type, or class).

```
var userName:String = "";
```

Compiler warnings and errors   The previous two features (OOP model and strict data typing) enable the authoring tool and compiler to provide compiler warnings and error messages that help you find bugs in your applications faster than was previously possible in Flash.

When you use ActionScript 2.0, make sure that the publish settings for the FLA file specify ActionScript 2.0. This is the default for files created in Flash MX 2004 and Flash 8. However, if you open an older FLA file that uses ActionScript 1.0 and begin rewriting it in ActionScript 2.0, change the publish settings of the FLA file to ActionScript 2.0. If you don't, your FLA file will not compile correctly, and errors won't be generated.

About choosing between ActionScript 1.0 and ActionScript 2.0

When you start a new document or application in Flash, you must decide how to organize its associated files. You might use classes in some projects, such as when you are building applications or complex FLA files, but not all documents use classes. For example, many short examples in the documentation do not use classes. Using classes to store functionality is not the easiest or best solution for small applications or simple FLA files. It is often more efficient to put ActionScript inside the document. In this case, try to put all your code on the Timeline on as few frames as possible, and avoid placing code on or in instances (such as buttons or movie clips) in a FLA file.

When you build a small project, it is often more work and effort to use classes or external code files to organize ActionScript instead of adding ActionScript within the FLA file. Sometimes it is easier to keep all the ActionScript code within the FLA file, rather than placing it within a class that you import. This does not mean that you should necessarily use ActionScript 1.0. You might decide to put your code inside the FLA file by using ActionScript 2.0 with its strict data typing and its new methods and properties. ActionScript 2.0 also offers a syntax that follows standards in other programming languages. This makes the language easier and more valuable to learn. For example, you will feel familiar with ActionScript if you have encountered another language that's based on the same structure and syntax standards. Or, you can apply this knowledge to other languages you learn in the future. ActionScript 2.0 lets you use an object-oriented approach to developing applications by using an additional set of language elements, which can be advantageous to your application development.

In some cases, you cannot choose which version of ActionScript to use. If you are building a SWF file that targets an old version of Flash Player, such as a mobile device application, you must use ActionScript 1.0, which is compatible with Flash Player for a number of devices.

Remember, regardless of the version of ActionScript, you should follow good practices. Many of these practices, such as remaining consistent with case sensitivity, using code completion, enhancing readability, avoiding keywords for instance names, and keeping a consistent naming convention, apply to both versions.

If you plan to update your application in future versions of Flash, or make it larger and more complex, you should use ActionScript 2.0 and classes, to make it easier to update and modify your application.

Understanding ActionScript and Flash Player

If you compile a SWF file that contains ActionScript 2.0 with publish settings set to Flash Player 6 and ActionScript 1.0, your code functions as long as it does not use ActionScript 2.0 classes. No case sensitivity is involved with the code, only Flash Player. Therefore, if you compile your SWF file with Publish Settings set to Flash Player 7 or 8 and ActionScript 1.0, Flash enforces case sensitivity.

Data type annotations (strict data types) are enforced at compile time for Flash Player 7 and 8 when you have publish settings set to ActionScript 2.0.

ActionScript 2.0 compiles to ActionScript 1.0 bytecode when you publish your applications, so you can target Flash Player 6, 7, or 8 while working with ActionScript 2.0.

CHAPTER 4

Data and Data Types

4

This chapter is the first of several chapters that outline and demonstrate some fundamental concepts of ActionScript. You'll practice some basic coding techniques to learn how to create complex applications. In this chapter, you'll also learn about how to work with data in a FLA file, and what kinds of data you can work with. In the next chapter, Chapter 5, "Syntax and Language Fundamentals," you'll discover how to use ActionScript syntax and form statements. Following this, Chapter 6, "Functions and Methods" demonstrates how to use functions and methods in the ActionScript language.

For more information about data and data types, see the following sections:

About data

Data refers to the numbers, strings, and other information that you can manipulate within Flash. Using data is usually essential when you create applications or websites. You also use data when you create advanced graphics and script-generated animation, and you might have to manipulate values that you use to drive your effects.

You can define data in *variables* within Flash, or you can load data from external files or sites using XML, web services, built-in ActionScript classes, and so on. You can store data in a database, and then represent that information in several ways in a SWF file. This can include displaying the information in text fields or components, or displaying images in movie clip instances.

Some of the most common kinds of data include strings (a sequence of characters, such as names and passages of text), numbers, objects (such as movie clips), Boolean values (`true` and `false`), and so on. In this chapter, you'll also learn about the data types in Flash and how to use them.

For information on types of data, see "About data types" on page 74. For information on variables, see "About variables" on page 89.

About data types

A *data type* describes a piece of data and the kinds of operations that you can perform on it. You store data in a variable. You use data types when creating variables, object instances, and function definitions to assign the type of data you're working with. You use many different data types when you write ActionScript.

ActionScript 2.0 defines several commonly used data types. Data types describe the kind of value that a variable or ActionScript element can contain. A variable that is assigned a data type can only hold a value within that data type's set of values. For information on variables, see "About variables" on page 89.

ActionScript has numerous basic data types that you will probably use frequently in your applications. See the table in "About primitive and complex data types" on page 75 for more information.

ActionScript also has core classes, such as Array and Date, that are considered complex or reference data types. For more info on complex and reference data types, see "About primitive and complex data types" on page 75. In addition, all data types and classes are fully defined in *ActionScript 2.0 Language Reference* in Flash Help.

You can also create custom classes for your applications. Any class that you define using the class declaration is also considered a data type. For more information on core and other built-in classes, see "About top-level and built-in classes" on page 292. For more information on creating custom classes, see Chapter 7, "Classes," on page 231.

In ActionScript 2.0, you can assign data types to variables when you declare them. The data types you assign can be any of the core types or can represent a custom class that you created. For more information, see "About assigning data types and strict data typing" on page 83.

When you debug scripts, you might need to determine the data type of an expression or variable to understand why it is behaving a certain way. You can do this with the `instanceof` and `typeof` operators (see "About determining data type" on page 88).

You can convert one data type to another at runtime using one of the following conversion functions: `Array()`, `Boolean()`, `Number()`, `Object()`, `String()`.

You can find a sample source file, datatypes.fla, in the Samples folder on your hard disk, which shows you how to use data types in an application.

- In Windows, browse to *boot drive*\Program Files\Macromedia\Flash 8\Samples and Tutorials\Samples\ActionScript\DataTypes.
- On the Macintosh, browse to *Macintosh HD*/Applications/Macromedia Flash 8/Samples and Tutorials/Samples/ActionScript/DataTypes.

About primitive and complex data types

You can divide all the different data type values into two main categories: *primitive* or *complex*.

A *primitive value* (or primitive data type) is a value that ActionScript stores at the lowest level of abstraction, which means that operations on the primitive data types are generally faster and more efficient than operations carried out on complex data types. The following data types all define a set of one or more primitive values: Boolean, null, Number, String, and undefined.

A *complex value* (or complex data type) is a value that is not a primitive value and that references the primitive values. Often, these are called *reference* data types. Complex values belong to the Object data type or a data type that is based on the Object data type. Data types that define sets of complex values include Array, Date, Error, Function, and XML. For more information on these complex data types, see their entries in the *ActionScript 2.0 Language Reference* in Flash Help.

Variables that contain primitive data types behave differently in certain situations than those containing complex types. For more information, see "Using variables in a project" on page 108.

ActionScript has the following basic data types that you can use in your applications:

Data type	Description
Boolean	Primitive. The Boolean data type consists of two values: `true` and `false`. No other values are valid for variables of this type. The default value of Boolean variable that has been declared but not initialized is `false`. For more information, see "Boolean data type" on page 77.
MovieClip	Complex. The MovieClip data type lets you control movie clip symbols using the methods of the MovieClip class. For more information, see "MovieClip data type" on page 78.
null	Primitive. The null data type contains the value `null`. This value means no value—that is, a lack of data. You can assign the `null` value in a variety of situations to indicate that a property or variable does not have a value assigned to it. The null data type is the default data type for all classes that define complex data types. An exception to this rule is the Object class, which defaults to `undefined`. For more information, see "null data type" on page 80.
Number	Primitive. This data type can represent integers, unsigned integers, and floating point numbers. To store a floating point number, you should include a decimal point in the number. Without the decimal point, the number is stored as an integer. The Number data type can store values from `Number.MAX_VALUE` (very high) to `Number.MIN_VALUE` (very low). For more information, see *ActionScript 2.0 Language Reference* in Flash Help and "Number data type" on page 80.
Object	Complex. The Object data type is defined by the Object class. The Object class serves as the base class for all class definitions in ActionScript, and it lets you arrange objects inside each other (nested objects). For more information, see "Object data type" on page 81.
String	Primitive. The String data type represents a sequence of 16-bit characters that might include letters, numbers, and punctuation marks. Strings are stored as Unicode characters, using the UTF-16 format. An operation on a String value returns a new instance of the string. For more information, see "String data type" on page 82.
undefined	Primitive. The undefined data type contains one value: `undefined`. This is the default value for instances of the Object class. You can only assign a value of `undefined` to variables that belong to the Object class. For more information, see "undefined data type" on page 83.
Void	Complex. The Void data type contains only one value: `void`. You use this data type to designate functions that don't return a value. Void is a complex data type that references the primitive Void data type. For more information, see "Void data type" on page 83.

You can find a sample source file, datatypes.fla, in the Samples folder on your hard disk, which shows you how to use data types in an application.

■ In Windows, browse to *boot drive*\Program Files\Macromedia\Flash 8\Samples and Tutorials\Samples\ActionScript\DataTypes.

■ On the Macintosh, browse to *Macintosh HD*/Applications/Macromedia Flash 8/Samples and Tutorials/Samples/ActionScript/DataTypes.

Boolean data type

A Boolean value is one that is either `true` or `false`. ActionScript also converts the values `true` and `false` to 1 and 0 when appropriate. Boolean values are most often used with logical operators in ActionScript statements that make comparisons to control the flow of a script.

The following example loads a text file into a SWF file, and displays a message in the Output panel if the text file does not load correctly, or the parameters if it does load successfully. See the comments in the code example for more details.

```
var my_lv:LoadVars = new LoadVars();
//success is a Boolean value
my_lv.onload = function(success:Boolean) {
  //if success is true, trace monthNames
  if (success) {
    trace(my_lv.monthNames);
  //if success is false, trace a message
  } else {
    trace("unable to load text file");
  }
};
my_lv.load("http://www.helpexamples.com/flash/params.txt");
```

The following example checks that users enter values into two TextInput component instances. Two Boolean variables are created, `userNameEntered` and `isPasswordCorrect`, and if both variables evaluate to `true`, a welcome message is assigned to the `titleMessage` String variable.

```
// Add two TextInput components, a Label, and a Button component on the
   Stage.
// Strict data type the three component instances
var userName_ti:mx.controls.TextInput;
var password_ti:mx.controls.TextInput;
var submit_button:mx.controls.Button;
var welcome_lbl:mx.controls.Label;

//Hide the label
welcome_lbl.visible = false;

// Create a listener object, which is used with the Button component.
// When the Button is clicked, checks for a user name and password.
var btnListener:Object = new Object();
btnListener.click = function(evt:Object) {
  // Checks that the user enters at least one character in the TextInput
  // instances and returns a Boolean true/false.
  var userNameEntered:Boolean = (userName_ti.text.length > 0);
  var isPasswordCorrect:Boolean = (password_ti.text == "vertigo");
  if (userNameEntered && isPasswordCorrect) {
    var titleMessage:String = "Welcome " + userName_ti.text + "!";
    welcome_lbl.text = titleMessage;
    //display the label
    welcome_lbl.visible = true;
  }
};
submit_button.addEventListener("click", btnListener);
```

For more information, see "Using functions in Flash" on page 219 and "About logical operators" on page 198.

MovieClip data type

Movie clips are symbols that can play animation in a Flash application. They are the only data type that refers to a graphic element. The MovieClip data type lets you control movie clip symbols using the methods of the MovieClip class.

You do not use a constructor to call the methods of the MovieClip class. You can create a movie clip instance on the Stage or create an instance dynamically. Then you simply call the methods of the MovieClip class using the dot (.) operator.

Working with movie clips on the Stage   The following example calls the `startDrag()` and `getURL()` methods for different movie clip instances that are on the Stage:

```
my_mc.startDrag(true);
parent_mc.getURL("http://www.macromedia.com/support/" + product);
```

The second example returns the width of a movie clip called `my_mc` on the Stage. The targeted instance must be a movie clip, and the returned value must be a numeric value.

```
function getMCWidth(target_mc:MovieClip):Number {
  return target_mc._width;
}
trace(getMCWidth(my_mc));
```

Creating movie clips dynamically   Using ActionScript to create movie clips dynamically is useful when you want to avoid manually creating movie clips on the Stage or attaching them from the library. For example, you might create an image gallery with a large number of thumbnail images that you want to organize on the Stage. Using `MovieClip.createEmptyMovieClip()` lets you create an application entirely using ActionScript.

To dynamically create a movie clip, use `MovieClip.createEmptyMovieClip()`, as shown in the following example:

```
// Creates a movie clip to hold the container.
this.createEmptyMovieClip("image_mc", 9);
// Loads an image into image_mc.
image_mc.loadMovie("http://www.helpexamples.com/flash/images/image1.jpg");
```

The second example creates a movie clip called `square_mc` that uses the Drawing API to draw a rectangle. Event handlers and the `startDrag()` and `stopDrag()` methods of the MovieClip class are added to make the rectangle draggable.

```
this.createEmptyMovieClip("square_mc", 1);
square_mc.lineStyle(1, 0x000000, 100);
square_mc.beginFill(0xFF0000, 100);
square_mc.moveTo(100, 100);
square_mc.lineTo(200, 100);
square_mc.lineTo(200, 200);
square_mc.lineTo(100, 200);
square_mc.lineTo(100, 100);
square_mc.endFill();
square_mc.onPress = function() {
  this.startDrag();
};
square_mc.onRelease = function() {
  this.stopDrag();
};
```

For more information, see Chapter 11, "Working with Movie Clips," on page 357 and the %{MovieClip}% entry in the *ActionScript 2.0 Language Reference* in Flash Help.

null data type

The null data type has only one value, null. This value means *no value*—that is, a lack of data. You can assign the null value in a variety of situations to indicate that a property or variable does not yet have a value assigned to it. For example, you can assign the null value in the following situations:

- To indicate that a variable exists but has not yet received a value
- To indicate that a variable exists but no longer contains a value
- As the return value of a function, to indicate that no value was available to be returned by the function
- As a parameter to a function, to indicate that a parameter is being omitted

Several methods and functions return null if no value has been set. The following example demonstrates how you can use null to test if form fields currently have form focus:

```
if (Selection.getFocus() == null) {
  trace("no selection");
}
```

Number data type

The Number data type is a double-precision floating-point number. The minimum value of a number object is approximately 5e-324. The maximum is approximately 1.79E+308.

You can manipulate numbers using the arithmetic operators addition (+), subtraction (-), multiplication (*), division (/), modulo (%), increment (++), and decrement (--). For more information, see "Using numeric operators" on page 192.

You can also use methods of the built-in Math and Number classes to manipulate numbers. For more information on the methods and properties of these classes, see the %{Math}% and %{Number}% entries in *ActionScript 2.0 Language Reference* in Flash Help.

The following example uses the sqrt() (square root) method of the Math class to return the square root of the number 100:

```
Math.sqrt(100);
```

The following example traces a random integer between 10 and 17 (inclusive):

```
var bottles:Number = 0;
bottles = 10 + Math.floor(Math.random() * 7);
trace("There are " + bottles + " bottles");
```

The following example finds the percent of the intro_mc movie clip that is loaded and represents it as an integer:

```
var percentLoaded:Number = Math.round((intro_mc.getBytesLoaded() /
  intro_mc.getBytesTotal()) * 100);
```

Object data type

An object is a collection of properties. A *property* is an attribute that describes the object. For example, the transparency of an object (such as a movie clip) is an attribute that describes its appearance. Therefore, _alpha (transparency) is a property. Each property has a name and a value. The value of a property can be any Flash data type—even the Object data type. This lets you arrange objects inside each other, or *nest* them.

To specify objects and their properties, you use the dot (.) operator. For example, in the following code, hoursWorked is a property of weeklyStats, which is a property of employee:

```
employee.weeklyStats.hoursWorked
```

The ActionScript MovieClip object has methods that let you control movie clip symbol instances on the Stage. This example uses the play() and nextFrame() methods:

```
mcInstanceName.play();
mc2InstanceName.nextFrame();
```

You can also create custom objects to organize information in your Flash application. To add interactivity to an application with ActionScript, you need many pieces of information: for example, you might need a user's name, age, and phone number; the speed of a ball; the names of items in a shopping cart; the number of frames loaded; or the key that the user pressed last. Creating custom objects lets you organize this information into groups, simplify your scripting, and reuse your scripts.

The following ActionScript code shows an example of using custom objects to organize information. It creates a new object called user and creates three properties, name, age, and phone, which are String and Numeric data types.

```
var user:Object = new Object();
user.name = "Irving";
user.age = 32;
user.phone = "555 1234";
```

For more information, see "Example: Writing custom classes" on page 269.

String data type

A string is a sequence of characters such as letters, numbers, and punctuation marks. You enter strings in an ActionScript statement by enclosing them in single (') or double (") quotation marks.

A common way that you use the string type is to assign a string to a variable. For example, in the following statement, `"L7"` is a string assigned to the variable `favoriteBand_str`:

```
var favoriteBand_str:String = "L7";
```

You can use the addition (+) operator to *concatenate*, or join, two strings. ActionScript treats spaces at the beginning or end of a string as a literal part of the string. The following expression includes a space after the comma:

```
var greeting_str:String = "Welcome, " + firstName;
```

To include a quotation mark in a string, precede it with a backslash character (\). This is called *escaping* a character. There are other characters that cannot be represented in ActionScript except by special escape sequences. The following table lists all the ActionScript escape characters:

Escape sequence	Character
\b	Backspace character (ASCII 8)
\f	Form-feed character (ASCII 12)
\n	Line-feed character (ASCII 10)
\r	Carriage return character (ASCII 13)
\t	Tab character (ASCII 9)
\"	Double quotation mark
\'	Single quotation mark
\\	Backslash
\000 - \377	A byte specified in octal
\x00 - \xFF	A byte specified in hexadecimal
\u0000 - \uFFFF	A 16-bit Unicode character specified in hexadecimal

Strings in ActionScript are immutable, just as they are in Java. Any operation that modifies a string returns a new string.

The String class is a built-in ActionScript class. For information on the methods and properties of the String class, see the %{String}% entry in the *ActionScript 2.0 Language Reference* in Flash Help.

undefined data type

The undefined data type has one value, undefined, and is automatically assigned to a variable to which a value hasn't been assigned, either by your code or user interaction.

The value undefined is automatically assigned; unlike null, you don't assign undefined to a variable or property. You use the undefined data type to check if a variable is set or defined. This data type lets you write code that executes only when the application is running, as shown in the following example:

```
if (init == undefined) {
  trace("initializing app");
  init = true;
}
```

If your application has multiple frames, the code does not execute a second time because the init variable is no longer undefined.

Void data type

The Void data type has one value, void, and is used in a function definition to indicate that the function does not return a value, as shown in the following example:

```
//Creates a function with a return type Void
function displayFromURL(url:String):Void {}
```

About assigning data types and strict data typing

You use variables in Flash to hold values in your code. You can explicitly declare the object type of a variable when you create the variable, which is called *strict data typing*.

If you do not explicitly define an item as holding either a number, a string, or another data type, at runtime Flash Player will try to determine the data type of an item when it is assigned. If you assign a value to a variable, as shown in the following example, Flash Player evaluates at runtime the element on the right side of the operator and determines that it is of the Number data type:

```
var x = 3;
```

Because x was not declared using strict data typing, the compiler cannot determine the type; to the compiler, the variable *x* can have a value of any type. (See "Assigning a data type" on page 84.) A later assignment might change the type of x; for example, the statement x = "hello" changes the type of x to String.

ActionScript always converts primitive data types (such as Boolean, Number, String, null, or undefined) automatically when an expression requires the conversion and the variables aren't strictly typed.

Strict data typing offers several benefits at compile time. Declaring data types (strict data typing) can help prevent or diagnose errors in your code at compile time. To declare a variable using strict data typing, use the following format:

```
var variableName:datatype;
```

 Strict data typing is sometimes called *strong typing* a variable.

Because data type mismatches trigger compiler errors, strict data typing helps you find bugs in your code at compile time and prevents you from assigning the wrong type of data to an existing variable. During authoring, strict data typing activates code hinting in the ActionScript editor (but you should still use instance name suffixes for visual elements).

Using strict data typing helps ensure that you don't inadvertently assign an incorrect type of value to a variable. Flash checks for typing mismatch errors at compile time, and displays an error message if you use the wrong type of value. Therefore, using strict typing also helps to ensure that you do not attempt to access properties or methods that are not part of an object's type. Strict data typing means the ActionScript editor automatically shows code hints for objects.

For more information on creating variables, see "About variables" on page 89. For information on naming variables, see "About naming variables" on page 94. For more information on assigning data types, and the types you can assign, see "Assigning a data type" on page 84.

You can find a sample source file, datatypes.fla, in the Samples folder on your hard disk, which shows you how to use data types in an application.

- In Windows, browse to *boot drive*\Program Files\Macromedia\Flash 8\Samples and Tutorials\Samples\ActionScript\DataTypes.
- On the Macintosh, browse to *Macintosh HD*/Applications/Macromedia Flash 8/Samples and Tutorials/Samples/ActionScript/DataTypes.

Assigning a data type

You need to assign data types whenever you define a variable, whether you declare a variable using the `var` keyword, create a function argument, set function return type, or define a variable to use within a `for` or `for..in` loop. To assign a data type, you use *post-colon syntax*, which means you follow the variable name with a colon and then the data type:

```
var my_mc:MovieClip;
```

There are many possibilities for data types, ranging from the native data types such as Number, String, Boolean, or built-in classes that are included in Flash Player 8, such as BitmapData, FileReference, or even custom classes that you or other developers have written. The most common types of data types you might need to specify are the built-in data types such as Number, String, Boolean, Array, or Object, which are shown in the following code examples.

To assign a specific data type to an item, specify its type using the `var` keyword and post-colon syntax, as shown in the following example:

```
// Strict typing of variable or object
var myNum:Number = 7;
var birthday:Date = new Date();

// Strict typing of parameters
function welcome(firstName:String, age:Number) {
}

// Strict typing of parameter and return value
function square(myNum:Number):Number {
  var squared:Number = myNum * myNum;
  return squared;
}
```

You can declare the data type of objects based on built-in classes (Button, Date, and so on) as well as classes and interfaces that you create. In the following example, if you have a file named Student.as in which you define the Student class, you can specify that objects you create are of type Student:

```
var myStudent:Student = new Student();
```

For this example, suppose you type the following code:

```
// in the Student.as class file
class Student {
  public var status:Boolean; // property of Student objects
}
// in the FLA file
var studentMaryLago:Student = new Student();
studentMaryLago.status = "enrolled"; /* Type mismatch in assignment
  statement: found String where Boolean is required. */
```

When Flash compiles this script, a type mismatch error is generated because the SWF file expects a Boolean value.

If you write a function that doesn't have a return type, you can specify a return type of Void for that function. Or if you create a shortcut to a function, you can assign a data type of Function to the new variable. To specify that objects are of type Function or Void, see the following example:

```
function sayHello(name_str:String):Void {
  trace("Hello, " + name_str);
}
sayHello("world"); // Hello, world
var greeting:Function = sayHello;
greeting("Augustus"); // Hello, Augustus
```

Another advantage of strict data typing is that Flash automatically shows code hints for built-in objects when they are strictly typed. For more information, see "About assigning data types and strict data typing" on page 83.

Files published using ActionScript 1.0 do not respect strict data typing assignments at compile time, so assigning the wrong type of value to a variable that you have strictly typed doesn't generate a compiler error.

```
var myNum:String = "abc";
myNum = 12;
/* No error in ActionScript 1.0, but type mismatch error in ActionScript 2.0
  */
```

The reason for this is that when you publish a file for ActionScript 1.0, Flash interprets a statement such as `var myNum:String = "abc"` as slash syntax rather than as strict typing. (ActionScript 2.0 doesn't support slash syntax.) This behavior can result in an object that is assigned to a variable of the wrong type, causing the compiler to let illegal method calls and undefined property references pass through unreported.

Files published using ActionScript 2.0 can optionally use data typing. Therefore, if you implement strict data typing in your code, make sure you set your publish settings to ActionScript 2.0. You can specify the publish settings and define which version of ActionScript you want to publish your files as by modifying the publish settings from the main menu (File > Publish Settings) or by clicking the Settings button in the Property inspector (make sure no instances are selected). To use a specific version of ActionScript or the Flash Player, select the Flash tab in the Publish Settings dialog box, and make a selection from the ActionScript version pop-up menu.

For information on type checking, see "About type checking" on page 87.

About type checking

Type checking refers to verifying that the type of a variable and an expression are compatible. Therefore, Flash checks that the type you specify for a variable matches the value(s) that you assign to it. For more information on strict data types and assigning data types, see "About assigning data types and strict data typing" on page 83 and "Assigning a data type" on page 84.

Type checking can occur at either compile time or runtime. If you use strict data typing, type checking occurs at compile time. Because ActionScript is a dynamically typed language, ActionScript can also type checking at runtime.

For example, the following code does not specify the data type of the parameter xParam. At runtime, you use the parameter to hold a value of type Number and then a value of type String. The dynamicTest() function then uses the typeof operator to test whether the parameter is of type String or Number.

```
function dynamicTest(xParam) {
  if (typeof(xParam) == "string") {
    var myStr:String = xParam;
    trace("String: " + myStr);
  } else if (typeof(xParam) == "number") {
    var myNum:Number = xParam;
    trace("Number: " + myNum);
  }
}
dynamicTest(100);
dynamicTest("one hundred");
```

You do not need to explicitly add data type information in your ActionScript. The ActionScript compiler lets you use properties and invoke methods that do not exist at compile time. This lets you create properties or assign dynamically methods at runtime.

An example of the flexibility afforded by dynamic type checking involves the use of properties and methods that are not known at compile time. Because the code is less restrictive, it can lead to benefits in some coding situations. For example, the following code creates a function named runtimeTest() that invokes a method and returns a property, neither of which is known to the compiler. The code will not generate a compile-time error, but if the property or method is not accessible at runtime, then a runtime error will occur.

```
function runtimeTest(myParam) {
  myParam.someMethod();
  return myParam.someProperty;
}
```

About determining data type

While testing and debugging your programs, you might discover problems that seem to be related to the data types of different items. Or if you use variables that are not explicitly associated with a data type, you might find it useful to know the data type of a given variable. Using ActionScript, you can determine an item's data type. You can use the typeof operator to return information about data.

Use the typeof operator to get the data types, but remember that typeof does not return information about the class to which an instance belongs.

The following example shows how you can use the typeof operator to return the kind of object that you trace:

```
// Create a new instance of LoadVars class.
var my_lv:LoadVars = new LoadVars();

/* typeof operator doesn't specify class, only specifies that my_lv is an
   object */
var typeResult:String = typeof(my_lv);
trace(typeResult); // object
```

In this example, you create a new String variable named myName, and then convert it into a Number data type:

```
var myName:String = new String("17");
trace(myName instanceof String); // true
var myNumber:Number = new Number(myName);
trace(myNumber instanceof Number); // true
```

For more information about these operators, see %{typeof operator}% and %{instanceof operator}% in the *ActionScript 2.0 Language Reference* in Flash Help. For more information on testing and debugging, see Chapter 18, "Debugging Applications," on page 725 For more information on inheritance and interfaces, see Chapter 8, "Inheritance," on page 307. For more information on classes, see Chapter 7, "Classes," on page 231.

About variables

A *variable* is a container that holds information. The following ActionScript shows what a variable looks like in ActionScript:

```
var myVariable:Number = 10;
```

This variable holds a numerical value. The use of `:Number` in the previous code assigns the type of value that variable holds, called *data typing*. For more information on data typing, see "About assigning data types and strict data typing" on page 83 and "Assigning a data type" on page 84.

The container (represented by the variable name) is always the same throughout your ActionScript, but the contents (the *value*) can change. You can change the value of a variable in a script as many times as you want. When you change the value of a variable while the SWF file plays, you can record and save information about what the user has done, record values that change as the SWF file plays, or evaluate whether a condition is `true` or `false`. You might need the variable to continually update while the SWF file plays, such as when a player's score changes in a Flash game. Variables are essential when you create and handle user interaction in a SWF file.

It's a good idea to assign a value to a variable the first time you declare the variable. Assigning an initial value is called *initializing* the variable, and it's often done on Frame 1 of the Timeline or from within a class that loads when the SWF file begins to play. There are different kinds of variables, which are affected by scope. For more information on different kinds of variables and scope, see "About variables and scope" on page 99.

 Initializing a variable helps you track and compare the variable's value as the SWF file plays.

 Flash Player 7 and later evaluate uninitialized variables differently than Flash Player 6 and earlier. If you have written scripts for Flash Player 6 and plan to write or port scripts for Flash Player 7 or later, you should be understand these differences to avoid unexpected behavior.

Variables can hold different types of data; for more information, see "About data types" on page 74. The type of data that a variable contains affects how the variable's value changes when you assign that value in a script.

Typical types of information that you can store in a variable include a URL (String type), a user's name (String type), the result of a mathematical operation (Number type), the number of times an event occurred (Number type), or whether a user has clicked a particular button (Boolean type). Each SWF file and object instance (such as a movie clip) has a set of variables, with each variable having a value independent of variables in other SWF files or movie clips.

To view the value of a variable, use the `trace()` statement to send the value to the Output panel. Then, the value displays in the Output panel when you test the SWF file in the test environment. For example, `trace(hoursWorked)` sends the value of the variable `hoursWorked` to the Output panel in the test environment. You can also check and set the variable values in the Debugger in the test environment.

For more information on variables, see the following topics:

About declaring variables

You can declare variables on a frame in the timeline, directly on an object, or within an external class file.

Define variables using the `var` keyword and follow the variable naming conventions. You can declare a variable called `firstName`, as shown in the following example:

```
var firstName:String;
```

When you declare a variable, you assign a data type to the variable. In this case, you assign the String data type to the `firstName` variable. For more information on assigning data types, see "About assigning data types and strict data typing" on page 83.

About default values

A *default value* is the value that a variable contains before you set its value. You *initialize* a variable when you set its value for the first time. If you declare a variable, but do not set its value, that variable is *uninitialized*. The value of an uninitialized variable defaults to the value `undefined`. For more information on creating and using variables, see "About variables" on page 89.

About assigning values

You can define a *value* as the current contents of a variable. The value can be a strings, numbers, arrays, objects, XML, dates, or even custom classes that you create. Remember, you declare a variable in Flash using the `var` keyword. When you declare the variable, you also assign a data type to the variable. You can also assign a value to a variable, as long as the value matches the data type you assign to the variable.

The following example shows how you might create a variable called `catName`:

```
var catName:String;
```

After you declare the variable, you can assign a value to it. You might follow the previous line of ActionScript with this line:

```
catName = "Pirate Eye";
```

 NOTE Because `Pirate Eye` is a string, the value needs to be enclosed in straight quotes (quotation marks).

This example assigns the value of `Pirate Eye` to the `catName` variable. When you declare the variable, you can also assign a value to it instead of assigning it afterwards (as in the previous examples). You could set the `catName` variable when you declare it, as shown in the following example:

```
var catName:String = "Pirate Eye";
```

If you want to display the value of the `catName` variable in the test environment, you can use the `trace()` statement. This statement sends the value to the Output panel. You can trace the value of the `catName` variable and see that the actual value doesn't include the quotation marks by using the following ActionScript:

```
var catName:String = "Pirate Eye";
trace(catName); // Pirate Eye
```

Remember that the value you assign must match the data type that you assign to it (in this case, String). If you later try to assign a number to the `catName` variable, such as `catName = 10`, you will see the following error in the Output panel when you test the SWF file:

```
Type mismatch in assignment statement: found Number where String is
    required.
```

This error tells you that you attempted to set the wrong data type to a specified variable.

When you assign a numeric value to a variable, the quotation marks aren't necessary, as shown in the following code:

```
var numWrinkles:Number = 55;
```

If you want to change the value of numWrinkles later in your code, you can assign a new value using the following ActionScript:

```
numWrinkles = 60;
```

When you reassign a value to an existing variable, you don't need to use the var keyword or define the variable's data type (in this case, :Number).

If the value is numeric or Boolean (true or false), the value doesn't use straight quotes (quotation marks). Examples of numeric and Boolean values are shown in the following snippet:

```
var age:Number = 38;
var married:Boolean = true;
var hasChildren:Boolean = false;
```

In the previous example, the variable age contains an integer (nondecimal) value, although you could also use a decimal or floating-point value such as 38.4. Boolean variables (such as married or hasChildren) have only two possible values, true or false.

If you want to create an array and assign values to it, the format is slightly different, as shown in the following code:

```
var childrenArr:Array = new Array("Pylon", "Smithers", "Gil");
```

There is an alternative (shorthand) syntax for creating an array using array access operators, which use the bracket ([ ]) punctuators. You can rewrite the previous example as follows:

```
var childrenArr:Array = ["Pylon", "Smithers", "Gil"];
```

For more information on creating arrays and the array access operators, see "About arrays" on page 167 and "About using dot syntax to target an instance" on page 122.

Similarly, you can create a new object called myObj. You can use either of the following ways to create a new object. The first (and longer) way to code an array is as follows:

```
var myObj:Object = new Object();
myObj.firstName = "Steve";
myObj.age = 50;
myObj.childrenArr = new Array("Mike", "Robbie", "Chip");
```

The second, shorthand way you can code the myObj array is as follows:

```
var myObj:Object = {firstName:"Steve", age:50, childrenArr:["Mike",
    "Robbie", "Chip"]};
```

As you see in this example, using the shorthand method can save a lot of typing and time, especially when you define instances of objects. It is important to be familiar with this alternate syntax because you will encounter it if you work in teams or when you work with third-party ActionScript code that you find, for example, on the Internet or in books.

 NOTE Not all variables need to be explicitly defined. Some variables are created by Flash automatically for you. For example, to find the dimensions of the Stage, you could use the values of the following two predefined values: `Stage.width` and `Stage.height`.

About operators and variables

You might wonder about the mathematical symbols in your code. These symbols are called *operators* in ActionScript. Operators calculate a new value from one or more values, and you use an operator to assign a value to a variable in your code. You use the equality (=) operator to assign a value to a variable:

```
var username:String = "Gus";
```

Another example is the addition (+) operator, which you use to add two or more numeric values to produce a new value. If you use the + operator on two or more string values, the strings will be concatenated. The values that operators manipulate are called *operands*.

When you assign a value, you use an operator to define a value to a variable. For example, the following script uses the assignment operator to assign a value of 7 to the variable `numChildren`:

```
var numChildren:Number = 7;
```

If you want to change the value of the `numChildren` variable, use the following code:

```
numChildren = 8;
```

 NOTE You don't need to use `var` because the variable has previously been defined.

For more information on using operators in your ActionScript, see "About operators" on page 180.

About naming variables

Be careful when you start naming variables, because although they can have nearly any name, there are some rules. A variable's name must follow these rules:

- A variable must be an identifier.

> **NOTE** An *identifier* is the name of a variable, property, object, function, or method. The first character of an indentifier must be a letter, underscore (_), or dollar sign ($). Each subsequent character can be a number, letter, underscore, or dollar sign.

- A variable cannot be a keyword or an ActionScript literal such as `true`, `false`, `null`, or `undefined`. For more information on literals, see "About literals" on page 134.

- A variable must be unique within its scope (see "About variables and scope" on page 99).

- A variable should not be any element in the ActionScript language, such as a class name.

If you don't follow the rules when you name a variable, you might experience syntax errors or unexpected results. In the following example, if you name a variable `new` and then test your document, Flash will generate a compiler error:

```
// This code works as expected.
var helloStr:String = new String();
trace(helloStr.length); // 0
// But if you give a variable the same name as a built-in class...
var new:String = "hello"; //error: Identifier expected
var helloStr:String = new String();
trace(helloStr.length); // undefined
```

The ActionScript editor supports code hints for built-in classes and for variables that are based on these classes. If you want Flash to provide code hints for a particular object type that you assign to a variable, you can strictly type the variable. Code hints provide tooltip-style syntax hints and a pop-up menu that helps you write your code quickly.

For example, type the following code:

```
var members:Array = new Array();
members.
```

As soon as you type the period (.) in the Actions panel, Flash displays a list of methods and properties available for Array objects.

For recommended coding conventions for naming variables, see "Naming variables" on page 750.

Using variables in an application

In this section, you use variables in short code snippets of ActionScript. You need to declare and initialize a variable in a script before you can use it in an expression. Expressions are combinations of operands and operators that represent a value. For example, in the expression i+2, i and 2 are operands, and + is an operator.

If you do not initialize a variable before you use it in an expression, the variable is undefined and may cause unexpected results. For more information on writing expressions, see Chapter 5, "Syntax and Language Fundamentals," on page 117.

If you use an undefined variable, as shown in the following example, the variable's value in Flash Player 7 and later will be NaN, and your script might produce unintended results:

```
var squared:Number = myNum * myNum;
trace(squared); // NaN
var myNum:Number = 6;
```

In the following example, the statement that declares and initializes the variable myNum comes first, so squared can be replaced with a value:

```
var myNum:Number = 6;
var squared:Number = myNum * myNum;
trace(squared); // 36
```

Similar behavior occurs when you pass an undefined variable to a method or function, as shown next.

To compare undefined and defined variables being passed to a function:

1. Drag a Button component to the Stage from the Components panel.

2. Open the Property inspector and type **bad_button** into the Instance Name text box.

3. Type the following code on Frame 1 of the Timeline.

```
// Does not work
function badClickListener(evt:Object):Void {
  getURL(targetUrl);
  var targetUrl:String = "http://www.macromedia.com";
}
bad_button.addEventListener("click", badClickListener);
```

4. Select Control > Test Movie, and notice that the button does not work (it doesn't open the web page).

5. Drag another Button component onto the Stage. Select the button.

6. Open the Property inspector, and type **good_button** into the Instance Name text box.

7. Add the following ActionScript to Frame 1 of the Timeline (following the previous ActionScript you added):

```
// Works
function goodClickListener(evt:Object):Void {
  var targetUrl:String = "http://www.macromedia.com";
  getURL(targetUrl);
}
good_button.addEventListener("click", goodClickListener);
```

8. Select Control > Test Movie and click the second button you added to the Stage.

This button properly opens the web page.

The type of data that a variable contains affects how and when the variable's value changes. Primitive data types, such as strings and numbers, are *passed by value*, which means the current value of the variable is used rather than a reference to that value. Examples of complex data types include the Array and Object data types.

In the following example, you set myNum to 15 and copy the value into otherNum. When you change myNum to 30 (in line 3 of the code), the value of otherNum remains 15 because otherNum doesn't look to myNum for its value. The otherNum variable contains the value of myNum that it receives (in line 2 of the code).

To use variables in your ActionScript:

1. Create a new Flash document, and save it as **var_example.fla**.

2. Select Frame 1 of the Timeline, and type the following code into the Actions panel:

```
var myNum:Number = 15;
var otherNum:Number = myNum;
myNum = 30;
trace(myNum); // 30
trace(otherNum); // 15
```

When you change myNum to 30 (in line 3 of the code), the value of otherNum remains 15 because otherNum doesn't look to myNum for its value. The otherNum variable contains the value of myNum that it receives (in line 2 of the code).

3. Select Control > Test Movie to see the values display in the Output panel.

4. Now add the following ActionScript after the code you added in step 2:

```
function sqr(myNum:Number):Number {
  myNum *= myNum;
  return myNum;
}
var inValue:Number = 3;
var outValue:Number = sqr(inValue);
trace(inValue); // 3
trace(outValue); // 9
```

In the this code, the variable `inValue` contains a primitive value, 3, so the value passes to the `sqr()` function, and the returned value is 9. The value of the variable `inValue` does not change, although the value of `myNum` in the function changes.

5. Select Control > Test Movie to see the values display in the Output panel.

The Object data type can contain such a large amount of complex information that a variable with this type doesn't hold an actual value; it holds a reference to a value. This reference is similar to an alias that points to the contents of the variable. When the variable needs to know its value, the reference asks for the contents and returns the answer without transferring the value to the variable.

For information on passing a variable by reference, see "Passing a variable by reference" on page 97.

Passing a variable by reference

Because the Array and Object data types hold a reference to a value instead of containing its actual value, you need be careful when you work with arrays and objects.

The following example shows how to pass an object by reference. When you create a copy of the array, you actually create only a copy of the reference (or *alias*) to the array's contents. When you edit the contents in the second array, you modify both the contents of the first and second array because they both point to the same value.

To pass an object by reference:

1. Select File > New and then select Flash Document to create a new FLA file, and save it as **copybyref.fla**.

2. Select Frame 1 of the Timeline, and type the following code into the Actions panel:

```
var myArray:Array = new Array("tom", "josie");
var newArray:Array = myArray;
myArray[1] = "jack";
trace(myArray); // tom,jack
trace(newArray); // tom,jack
```

3. Select Control > Test Movie to test the ActionScript.

This ActionScript creates an Array object called `myArray` that has two elements. You create the variable `newArray` and pass a reference to `myArray`. When you change the second element of `myArray` to `jack`, it affects every variable with a reference to it. The `trace()` statement sends `tom,jack` to the Output panel.

> **NOTE** Flash uses a zero-based index, which means that 0 is the first item in the array, 1 is the second, and so on.

In the following example, `myArray` contains an Array object, so you pass the array to function `zeroArray()` by reference. The function `zeroArray()` accepts an Array object as a parameter and sets all the elements of that array to 0. It can modify the array because the array is passed by reference.

To pass an array by reference:

1. Select File > New and then select Flash Document to create a new FLA file, and save it as **arraybyref.fla**.

2. Add the following ActionScript to Frame 1 of the Timeline:

```
function zeroArray (theArr:Array):Void {
  var i:Number;
  for (i = 0; i < theArr.length; i++) {
    theArr[i] = 0;
  }
}

var myArr:Array = new Array();
myArr[0] = 1;
myArr[1] = 2;
myArr[2] = 3;
trace(myArr); // 1,2,3
zeroArray(myArr);
trace(myArr); // 0,0,0
```

3. Select Control > Test Movie to test your ActionScript.

The first `trace()` statement in this ActionScript displays the original contents of the `myArray` array (1,2,3). After you call the `zeroArray()` function and pass a reference to the `myArray` array, each of the array's values are overwritten and set to zero. The subsequent `trace()` statement displays the new contents of the `myArray` array (0,0,0). Because you pass the array by reference and not by value, you don't need to return the updated contents of the array from within the `zeroArray()` function.

For more information on arrays, see "About arrays" on page 167.

About variables and scope

A variable's scope refers to the area in which the variable is known (*defined*) and can be referenced. The area in which the variable is known might be within a certain timeline or inside a function, or it might be globally known throughout the entire application. For more information about scope, see "About scope and targeting" on page 127.

Understanding variable scope is important when you develop Flash applications with ActionScript. Scope indicates not only when and where you can refer to variables but also for how long a particular variable exists in an application. When you define variables in the body of a function, they cease to exist as soon as the specified function ends. If you try to refer to objects in the wrong scope or to variables that have expired, you get errors in your Flash documents, which lead to unexpected behavior or broken functionality.

There are three types of variable scopes in ActionScript:

■ Global variables and functions are visible to every timeline and scope in your document. Therefore, a global variable is defined in all areas of your code.

■ Timeline variables are available to any script on that timeline.

■ Local variables are available within the function body in which they are declared (delineated by curly braces). Therefore, local variables are only defined in a part of your code.

For guidelines on using scope and variables, see Chapter 5, "About scope and targeting," on page 127.

> **NOTE**
> ActionScript 2.0 classes that you create support public, private, and static variable scopes. For more information, see "About class members" on page 256 and "Controlling member access in your classes" on page 278.

You cannot strict type global variables. For information and a workaround, see "Global variables" on page 99.

Global variables

Global variables and functions are visible to every timeline and scope in your document. To declare (or *create*) a variable with global scope, use the _global identifier before the variable name and do not use the var = syntax. For example, the following code creates the global variable myName:

```
var _global.myName = "George"; // Incorrect syntax for global variable
_global.myName = "George"; // Correct syntax for global variable
```

However, if you initialize a local variable with the same name as a global variable, you don't have access to the global variable while you are in the scope of the local variable, as shown in the following example:

```
_global.counter = 100; // Declares global variable
trace(counter); // Accesses the global variable and displays 100
function count():Void {
  for (var counter:Number = 0; counter <= 2; counter++) { // Local variable
    trace(counter); // Accesses local variable and displays 0 through 2
  }
}
count();
trace(counter); // Accesses global variable and displays 100
```

This example simply shows that the global variable is not accessed in the scope of the `count()` function. However, you could access the global-scoped variable if you prefix it with _global. For example, you could access it if you prefix the counter with `_global` as shown in the following code:

```
trace(_global.counter);
```

You cannot assign strict data types to variables that you create in the _global scope, because you have to use the var keyword when you assign a data type. For example, you couldn't do:

```
_global.foo:String = "foo";  //syntax error
var _global.foo:String = "foo"; //syntax error
```

The Flash Player version 7 and later security sandbox enforces restrictions when accessing global variables from SWF files loaded from separate security domains. For more information, see Chapter 17, "Understanding Security," on page 691.

Timeline variables

Timeline variables are available to any script on that particular timeline. To declare timeline variables, use the `var` statement and initialize them in any frame in the timeline. The variable is available to that frame and all following frames, as shown in the following example.

To use timeline variables in a document:

1. Create a new Flash document, and name it **timelinevar.fla**.
2. Add the following ActionScript to Frame 1 of the Timeline:
   ```
   var myNum:Number = 15; /* initialized in Frame 1, so it's available to
     all frames */
   ```
3. Select Frame 20 of the Timeline.
4. Select Insert > Timeline > Blank Keyframe.
5. With the new keyframe selected, type the following ActionScript into the Actions panel:
   ```
   trace(myNum);
   ```

6. Select Control > Test Movie to test the new document.

The value 15 appears in the Output panel after approximately a second. Because Flash documents loop by default, the value 15 continually traces in the Output panel every time the playhead reaches Frame 20 in the Timeline. To stop the looping action, add `stop();` after the `trace()` statement.

You must declare a timeline variable before trying to access it in a script. For example, if you put the code `var myNum:Number = 15;` in Frame 20, any scripts attached to a frame before Frame 20 cannot access `myNum` and are undefined instead of containing the value 15.

Local variables

When you use the `var` statement inside a function block, you declare *local variables*. When you declare a local variable within a function block (also called *function definition*), it is defined within the scope of the function block, and expires at the end of the function block. Therefore, the local variable only exists within that function.

For example, if you declare a variable named `myStr` within a function named `localScope`, that variable will not be available outside of the function.

```
function localScope():Void {
  var myStr:String = "local";
}
localScope();
trace(myStr); // Undefined, because myStr is not defined globally
```

If the variable name you use for your local variable is already declared as a timeline variable, the local definition takes precedence over the timeline definition while the local variable is in scope. The timeline variable will still exist outside of the function. For example, the following code creates a timeline string variable named `str1`, and then creates a local variable of the same name inside the `scopeTest()` function. The `trace` statement inside the function generates the local definition of the variable, but the `trace` statement outside the function generates the timeline definition of the variable.

```
var str1:String = "Timeline";
function scopeTest():Void {
  var str1:String = "Local";
  trace(str1); // Local
}
scopeTest();
trace(str1); // Timeline
```

In the next example, you can see how certain variables live only for the life of a specific function and can generate errors if you try to refer to the variable outside the scope of that function.

To use local variables in an application:

1. Create a new Flash document.

2. Open the Actions panel (Window > Actions) and add the following ActionScript to Frame 1 of the Timeline:

```
function sayHello(nameStr:String):Void {
  var greetingStr:String = "Hello, " + nameStr;
  trace(greetingStr);
}
sayHello("world"); // Hello, world
trace(nameStr); // undefined
trace(greetingStr); // undefined
```

3. Select Control > Test Movie to test the document.

   Flash displays the string "Hello, world" in the Output panel and displays `undefined` for the values of `nameStr` and `greetingStr` because the variables are no longer available in the current scope. You can only reference `nameStr` and `greetingStr` in the execution of the `sayHello` function. When the function exits, the variables cease to exist.

The variables `i` and `j` are often used as loop counters. In the following example, you use `i` as a local variable; it exists only inside the `initArray()` function:

```
var myArr:Array = new Array();
function initArray(arrayLength:Number):Void {
  var i:Number;
  for(i = 0; i < arrayLength; i++) {
    myArr[i] = i + 1;
  }
}
trace(myArr); // <blank>
initArray(3);
trace(myArr); // 1,2,3
trace(i); // undefined
```

> **NOTE**
>
> It's also common to see the following syntax for a `for` loop: `for (var i:Number = 0; i < arrayLength; i++) {...}`.

This example displays `undefined` in the Flash test environment because the variable `i` isn't defined in the main timeline. It exists only in the `initArray()` function.

You can use local variables to help prevent name conflicts, which can cause unexpected results in your application. For example, if you use `age` as a local variable, you could use it to store a person's age in one context and the age of a person's child in another context. There is no conflict in this situation because you are using these variables in separate scopes.

It's good practice to use local variables in the body of a function so the function can act as an independent piece of code. You can change a local variable only within its own block of code. If an expression in a function uses a global variable, code or events outside the function can change its value, which changes the function.

You can assign a data type to a local variable when you declare it, which helps prevent assigning the wrong type of data to an existing variable. For more information, see "About assigning data types and strict data typing" on page 83.

About loading variables

In the following sections, you load variables from the server in different ways or into a document from a URL string or FlashVars (you can use FlashVars to pass variables into Flash) in your HTML code. These practices demonstrate that there are several ways to use variables outside a SWF file.

You can find more information on loading variables (such as name/value pairs) in Chapter 16, "Working with External Data," on page 647.

You can use variables in different ways in a SWF file, depending on what you need the variables for. For more information, see the following topics:

- "Using variables from the URL" on page 103
- "Using FlashVars in an application" on page 106
- "Loading variables from a server" on page 107

Using variables from the URL

When you develop an application or simple example in Flash, you might want to pass values from an HTML page into your Flash document. The passed values are sometimes known as the *query string*, or *URL-encoded variables*. URL variables are useful if you want to create a menu in Flash, for example. You can initialize the menu to show the correct navigation by default. Or you can build an image viewer in Flash and define a default image to show on the website.

To use URL variables in a document:

1. Create a Flash document, and name it **urlvariables.fla**.
2. Select File > Save As, and save the document on your desktop.

3. Select Frame 1 of the Timeline, and add the following code in the Actions panel:

```
this.createTextField("myTxt", 100, 0, 0, 100, 20);
myTxt.autoSize = "left";
myTxt.text = _level0.myURL;
```

4. Select Control > Test Movie to test the SWF file in Flash Player.

The text field displays undefined. If you want to make sure the variables are properly defined before you proceed, you need to check for the existence of the variables in Flash. You can do this by checking to see if they are undefined.

5. To check to see if the variable is defined, modify the ActionScript you added to the Actions panel in step 3 to match the following code. Add the code that appears in **bold**:

```
this.createTextField("myTxt", 100, 0, 0, 100, 20);
myTxt.autoSize = "left";
if (_level0.myURL == undefined) {
  myTxt.text = "myURL is not defined";
} else {
  myTxt.text = _level0.myURL;
}
```

When you publish your Flash document, an HTML document is created by default in the same directory as the SWF file. If an HTML file was not created, select File > Publish settings, and make sure you select HTML in the Formats tab. Then publish your document again.

The following code demonstrates the HTML in the document that is responsible for embedding a Flash document in an HTML page. You need to look at this HTML to understand how URL variables work in the following step (where you add additional code for URL variables).

```
<object classid="clsid:d27cdb6e-ae6d-11cf-96b8-444553540000"
  codebase="http://fpdownload.macromedia.com/pub/shockwave/cabs/flash/
  swflash.cab#version=8,0,0,0" width="550" height="400"
  id="urlvariables" align="middle">
<param name="allowScriptAccess" value="sameDomain" />
<param name="movie" value="urlvariables.swf" />
<param name="quality" value="high" />
<param name="bgcolor" value="#ffffff" />
<embed src="urlvariables.swf" quality="high" bgcolor="#ffffff"
  width="550" height="400" name="urlvariables" align="middle"
  allowScriptAccess="sameDomain" type="application/x-shockwave-flash"
  pluginspage="http://www.macromedia.com/go/getflashplayer" />
</object>
```

6. To pass variables from the generated HTML document to your Flash document, you can pass variables after the path and filename (urlvariables.swf). Add the **bold text** to the HTML file that was generated on your desktop.

```
<object classid="clsid:d27cdb6e-ae6d-11cf-96b8-444553540000"
  codebase="http://fpdownload.macromedia.com/pub/shockwave/cabs/flash/
  swflash.cab#version=8,0,0,0" width="550" height="400"
  id="urlvariables" align="middle">
<param name="allowScriptAccess" value="sameDomain" />
<param name="movie" value="urlvariables.swf?myURL=http://
  weblogs.macromedia.com" />
<param name="quality" value="high" />
<param name="bgcolor" value="#ffffff" />
<embed src="urlvariables.swf?myURL=http://weblogs.macromedia.com"
  quality="high" bgcolor="#ffffff" width="550" height="400"
  name="urlvariables" align="middle" allowScriptAccess="sameDomain"
  type="application/x-shockwave-flash" pluginspage="http://
  www.macromedia.com/go/getflashplayer" />
</object>
```

7. If you want to pass multiple variables to Flash, you need to separate the name/values pairs with an ampersand (&). Find the following code from step 6:

```
?myURL=http://weblogs.macromedia.com
```

Replace it with the following text:

```
?myURL=http://weblogs.macromedia.com&myTitle=Macromedia+News+Aggregator
```

Remember, you need to make the same changes to both the `object` tag and the `embed` tag to maintain consistency between all browsers. You might notice that the words are separated by + punctuators. The words are separated this way because the values are URL-encoded and the + punctuator represents a single blank space.

 NOTE For a list of common URL-encoded special characters, see the Flash TechNote, URL Encoding: Reading special characters from a text file.

Because the ampersand (&) serves as a delimiter for different name/value pairs, if the values you are passing contain ampersands, unexpected results might occur. Given the nature of name/value pairs and parsing, if you had the following values being passed to Flash:

```
my.swf?name=Ben+&+Jerry&flavor=Half+Baked
```

Flash would build the following variables (and values) into the root scope:

```
'name': 'Ben ' (note space at end of value)
' Jerry': '' (note space at beginning of variable name and an empty
  value)
'flavor': 'Half Baked'
```

To avoid this, you need to *escape* the ampersand (&) character in the name/value pair with its URL-encoded equivalent (%26).

8. Open the urlvariables.html document, and find the following code:

```
?myURL=http://weblogs.macromedia.com&myTitle=Macromedia+News+Aggregator
```

Replace it with the following code:

```
?myURL=Ben+%26+Jerry&flavor=Half+Baked
```

9. Save the revised HTML, and test your Flash document again.

You see that Flash created the following name/value pairs.

```
'name': 'Ben & Jerry'
'flavor': 'Half Baked'
```

> **NOTE** All browsers will support string sizes as large as **64K (65535 bytes)** in length. FlashVars must be assigned in both the `object` and `embed` tags in order to work on all browsers.

Using FlashVars in an application

Using FlashVars to pass variables into Flash is similar to passing variables along the URL in the HTML code. With FlashVars, instead of passing variables after the filename, variables are passed in a separate `param` tag as well as in the `embed` tag.

To use FlashVars in a document:

1. Create a new Flash document, and name it **myflashvars.fla**.

2. Select File > Publish Settings and make sure that HTML is selected, and then click OK to close the dialog box.

3. Add the following ActionScript to Frame 1 of the main Timeline:

```
this.createTextField("myTxt", 100, 0, 0, 100, 20);
myTxt.autoSize = "left";
if (_level0.myURL == undefined) {
  myTxt.text = "myURL is not defined";
} else {
  myTxt.text = _level0.myURL;
}
```

> **NOTE** By default, HTML code publishes to the same location as myflashvars.fla.

4. Select File > Publish to publish the SWF and HTML files.

5. Open the directory containing the published files (where you saved myflashvars.fla on your hard drive) and open the HTML document (myflashvars.html by default) in an HTML editor such as Dreamweaver or Notepad.

6. Add the code that appears in **bold** below, so your HTML document matches the following:

```
<object classid="clsid:d27cdb6e-ae6d-11cf-96b8-444553540000"
    codebase="http://fpdownload.macromedia.com/pub/shockwave/cabs/flash/
    swflash.cab#version=8,0,0,0" width="550" height="400" id="myflashvars"
    align="middle">
<param name="allowScriptAccess" value="sameDomain" />
<param name="movie" value="myflashvars.swf" />
<param name="FlashVars" value="myURL=http://weblogs.macromedia.com/">
<param name="quality" value="high" />
<param name="bgcolor" value="#ffffff" />
<embed src="myflashvars.swf" FlashVars="myURL=http://
    weblogs.macromedia.com/" quality="high" bgcolor="#ffffff" width="550"
    height="400" name="myflashvars" align="middle"
    allowScriptAccess="sameDomain" type="application/x-shockwave-flash"
    pluginspage="http://www.macromedia.com/go/getflashplayer" />
</object>
```

This code passes a single variable called `myURL`, which contains the string `http://weblogs.macromedia.com`. When the SWF file loads, a property named `myURL` is created in the _level0 scope. One of the advantages of using FlashVars or passing variables along the URL is that the variables are immediately available in Flash when the SWF file loads. This means you don't have to write any functions to check if the variables have finished loading, which you would need to do if you loaded variables using LoadVars or XML.

7. Save your changes to the HTML document, and then close it.

8. Double click myflashvars.html to test the application.

The text `http://weblogs.macromedia.com`, a variable in the HTML file, appears in the SWF file.

>
> All browsers will support string sizes as large as 64K (65,535 bytes) in length. FlashVars must be assigned in both the `object` and `embed` tags in order to work on all browsers.

Loading variables from a server

There are several ways to load variables into Flash from external sources (such as text files, XML documents, and so on). You can find much more information on loading variables, including name/value pairs, in Chapter 16, "Working with External Data," on page 647.

In Flash, you can easily load variables using the LoadVars class, as shown in the next example.

To load variables from a server:

1. Create a new Flash document.

2. Select Frame 1 of the Timeline, and add the following ActionScript in the Actions panel:

```
var my_lv:LoadVars = new LoadVars();
my_lv.onLoad = function(success:Boolean):Void {
   if (success) {
      trace(this.dayNames); // Sunday,Monday,Tuesday,...
   } else {
      trace("Error");
   }
}
my_lv.load("http://www.helpexamples.com/flash/params.txt");
```

This code loads a text file from a remote server and parses its name/value pairs.

> Download or view the text file (www.helpexamples.com/flash/params.txt) in a browser if you want to know how the variables are formatted.

3. Select Control > Test Movie to test the document.

If the file successfully loads, the `complete` event is called and the Output panel displays the value of `dayNames`. If the text file cannot be downloaded, the `success` argument is set to `false` and the Output panel displays the text `Error`.

Using variables in a project

When you build animations or applications with Flash, there are very few situations in which you don't need to use any kind of variable in your project. For example, if you build a login system, you might need variables to determine whether the user name and password are valid, or whether they are filled in at all.

You can find more information on loading variables (such as name/value pairs) in Chapter 16, "Working with External Data," on page 647.

In the following example, you use variables to store the path of an image you are loading with the Loader class, a variable for the instance of the Loader class, and a couple of functions that are called depending on whether the file is successfully loaded or not.

To use variables in a project:

1. Create a new Flash document, and save it as **imgloader.fla**.

2. Select Frame 1 of the Timeline, and add the following ActionScript to the Actions panel:

```
/* Specify default image in case there wasn't a value passed using
    FlashVars. */
var imgUrl:String = "http://www.helpexamples.com/flash/images/
    image1.jpg";
if (_level0.imgURL != undefined) {
    // If image was specified, overwrite default value.
    imgUrl = _level0.imgURL;
}

this.createEmptyMovieClip("img_mc", 10);
var mclListener:Object = new Object();
mclListener.onLoadInit = function(target_mc:MovieClip):Void {
    target_mc._x = (Stage.width - target_mc._width) / 2;
    target_mc._y = (Stage.height - target_mc._height) / 2;
}
mclListener.onLoadError = function(target_mc:MovieClip):Void {
    target_mc.createTextField("error_txt", 1, 0, 0, 100, 20);
    target_mc.error_txt.autoSize = "left";
    target_mc.error_txt.text = "Error downloading specified image;\n\t" +
    target_mc._url;
}
var myMCL:MovieClipLoader = new MovieClipLoader();
myMCL.addListener(mclListener);
myMCL.loadClip(imgUrl, img_mc);
```

The first line of code specifies the image that you want to dynamically load into your Flash document. Next, you check whether a new value for imgURL was specified using FlashVars or URL-encoded variables. If a new value was specified, the default image URL is overwritten with the new value. For information on using URL variables, see "Using variables from the URL" on page 103. For information on FlashVars, see "Using FlashVars in an application" on page 106.

The next couple of lines of code define the MovieClip instance, and a Listener object for the future MovieClipLoader instance. The MovieClipLoader's Listener object defines two event handlers, onLoadInit and onLoadError. The handlers are invoked when the image successfully loads and initializes on the Stage, or if the image fails to load. Then you create a MovieClipLoader instance, and use the addListener() method to add the previously defined listener object to the MovieClipLoader. Finally, the image is downloaded and triggered when you call the MovieClipLoader.loadClip() method, which specifies the image file to load and the target movie clip to load the image into.

3. Select Control > Test Movie to test the document.

 Because you're testing the Flash document in the authoring tool, no value for `imgUrl` will be passed by FlashVars or along the URL, and therefore the default image displays.

4. Save the Flash document and select File > Publish to publish the file as a SWF and HTML document.

> **NOTE** Make sure that Flash and HTML are both selected in the Publish Settings dialog box. Select File › Publish Settings and then click the Formats tab. Then, select both options.

5. If you test your document in the Flash tool (select Control > Test Movie) or in a local browser (File > Publish Preview > HTML), you will see that the image centers itself both vertically and horizontally on the Stage.

6. Edit the generated HTML document in an editor (such as Dreamweaver or Notepad), and modify the default HTML to match the following text:

```
<object classid="clsid:d27cdb6e-ae6d-11cf-96b8-444553540000"
   codebase="http://fpdownload.macromedia.com/pub/shockwave/cabs/flash/
   swflash.cab#version=8,0,0,0" width="550" height="400"
   id="urlvariables" align="middle">
<param name="allowScriptAccess" value="sameDomain" />
<param name="movie" value="urlvariables.swf" />
<param name="FlashVars" value="imgURL=http://www.helpexamples.com/flash/
   images/image2.jpg">
<param name="quality" value="high" />
<param name="bgcolor" value="#ffffff" />
<embed src="urlvariables.swf" quality="high" FlashVars="imgURL=http://
   www.helpexamples.com/flash/images/image2.jpg" bgcolor="#ffffff"
   width="550" height="400" name="urlvariables" align="middle"
   allowScriptAccess="sameDomain" type="application/x-shockwave-flash"
   pluginspage="http://www.macromedia.com/go/getflashplayer" />
</object>
```

7. Test the HTML document to see the changes. An image that you specify in the HTML code appears in the SWF file.

 To modify this example to use your own images, you would modify the FlashVars value (the string inside the double quotes).

Organizing data in objects

You might already be used to objects that you place on the Stage. For example, you might have a MovieClip object on the Stage, and this object contains other movie clips inside it. Text fields, movie clips, and buttons are often called objects when you place them on the Stage.

Objects, in ActionScript, are collections of properties and methods. Each object has its own name, and it is an instance of a particular class. Built-in objects are from classes that are predefined in ActionScript. For example, the built-in Date class provides information from the system clock on the user's computer. You can use the built-in LoadVars class to load variables into your SWF file.

You can also create objects and classes using ActionScript. You might create an object to hold a collection of data, such as a person's name, address, and telephone number. You might create an object to hold color information for an image. Organizing data in objects can help keep your Flash documents more organized. For general information on creating a custom class to hold a collection of methods and properties, see "Writing custom class files" on page 241. For detailed information on both built-in and custom classes, see Chapter 7, "Classes," on page 231.

There are several ways to create an object in ActionScript. The next example creates simple objects in two different ways, and then loops over the contents of those objects.

To create simple objects in Flash:

1. Create a new Flash document, and save it as **simpleObjects.fla**.

2. Select Frame 1 of the Timeline, and type the following ActionScript into the Actions panel:

    ```
    // The first way
    var firstObj:Object = new Object();
    firstObj.firstVar = "hello world";
    firstObj.secondVar = 28;
    firstObj.thirdVar = new Date(1980, 0, 1); // January 1, 1980
    ```

    This code, which is one way to create a simple object, creates a new object instance and defines a few properties within the object.

3. Now enter the following ActionScript after the code you entered in step 2.

    ```
    // The second way
    var secondObj:Object = {firstVar:"hello world", secondVar:28,
      thirdVar:new Date(1980, 0, 1)};
    ```

    This is another way of creating an object. Both objects are equivalent. This code above creates a new object and initializes some properties using the object shorthand notation.

4. To loop over each of the previous objects and display the contents of objects, add the following ActionScript on Frame 1 of the Timeline (after the code you've already entered):

```
var i:String;
for (i in firstObj) {
   trace(i + ": " + firstObj[i]);
}
```

5. Select Control > Test Movie, and the following text appears in the Output panel:

```
firstVar: hello world
secondVar: 28
thirdVar: Tue Jan 1 00:00:00 GMT-0800 1980
```

You can also use arrays to create objects. Instead of having a series of variables such as firstname1, firstname2, and firstname3 to represent a collection of variables, you can make an array of objects to represent the same data. This technique is demonstrated next.

To use an array to create an object:

1. Create a new Flash document, and save it as **arrayObject.fla**.

2. Select Frame 1 of the Timeline, and type the following ActionScript into the Actions panel:

```
var usersArr:Array = new Array();
usersArr.push({firstname:"George"});
usersArr.push({firstname:"John"});
usersArr.push({firstname:"Thomas"});
```

The benefit of organizing variables into arrays and objects is that it becomes much easier to loop over the variables and see the values, as shown in the following step.

3. Type the following code after the ActionScript you added in step 2.

```
var i:Number;
for (i = 0; i < usersArr.length; i++) {
   trace(usersArr[i].firstname); // George, John, Thomas
}
```

4. Select Control > Test Movie, and the following text appears in the Output panel:

```
George
John
Thomas
```

The following example presents another way to loop over objects. In this example, an object is created and looped over using a `for..in` loop, and each property appears in the Output panel:

```
var myObj:Object = {var1:"One", var2:"Two", var3:18, var4:1987};
var 1:String;
for (i in myObj) {
  trace(i + ": " + myObj[i]);
}
//outputs the following:
/*
    var1: One
    var2: Two
    var3: 18
    var4: 1987
*/
```

For information on creating for loops, see Chapter 5, "Using for loops," on page 161. For information on for..in loops, see "Using for..in loops" on page 162. For more information on objects, see Chapter 7, "Classes," on page 231.

About casting

ActionScript 2.0 lets you cast one data type to another. Casting an object to a different type means you convert the value that the object or variable holds to a different type.

The results of a type cast vary depending on the data types involved. To cast an object to a different type, you wrap the object name in parentheses (( )) and precede it with the name of the new type. For example, the following code takes a Boolean value and casts it to an integer.

```
var myBoolean:Boolean = true;
var myNumber:Number = Number(myBoolean);
```

For more information on casting, see the following topics:

■ "About casting objects" on page 113

About casting objects

The syntax for casting is `type(item)`, where you want the compiler to behave as if the data type of the item is `type`. Casting is essentially a function call, and the function call returns `null` if the cast fails at runtime (this occurs in files published for Flash Player 7 or later; files published for Flash Player 6 do not have runtime support for failed casts). If the cast succeeds, the function call returns the original object. However, the compiler cannot determine whether a cast will fail at runtime and won't generate compile-time errors in those cases.

The following code shows an example:

```
// Both the Cat and Dog classes are subclasses of the Animal class
function bark(myAnimal:Animal) {
  var foo:Dog = Dog(myAnimal);
  foo.bark();
}
var curAnimal:Animal = new Dog();
bark(curAnimal); // Will work
curAnimal = new Cat();
bark(curAnimal); // Won't work
```

In this example, you asserted to the compiler that foo is a Dog object, and therefore the compiler assumes that foo.bark(); is a legal statement. However, the compiler doesn't know that the cast will fail (that is, that you tried to cast a Cat object to an Animal type), so no compile-time error occurs. However, if you include a check in your script to make sure that the cast succeeds, you can find casting errors at runtime, as shown in the following example.

```
function bark(myAnimal:Animal) {
  var foo:Dog = Dog(myAnimal);
  if (foo) {
    foo.bark();
  }
}
```

You can cast an expression to an interface. If the expression is an object that implements the interface or has a base class that implements the interface, the cast succeeds. If not, the cast fails.

 NOTE Casting to null or undefined returns undefined.

You can't override primitive data types that have a corresponding global conversion function with a cast operator of the same name. This is because the global conversion functions have precedence over the cast operators. For example, you can't cast to Array because the Array() conversion function takes precedence over the cast operator.

This example defines two string variables (firstNum and secondNum), which are added together. The initial result is that the numbers are concatenated instead of added because they are a String data type. The second trace statement converts both numbers to a Number data type before performing the addition that yields the proper result. Data conversion is important when working with data loaded using XML or FlashVars, as shown in the following example:

```
var firstNum:String = "17";
var secondNum:String = "29";
trace(firstNum + secondNum); // 1729
trace(Number(firstNum) + Number(secondNum)); // 46
```

For more information on data conversion functions, see the entry for each conversion function in *ActionScript 2.0 Language Reference* in Flash Help: `%{Array function}%`, `%{Boolean function}%`, `%{Number function}%`, `%{Object function}%`, and `%{String function}%`.

CHAPTER 5

Syntax and Language Fundamentals

5

Learning ActionScript syntax and statements is like learning how to put together words to make sentences, which you can then put together into paragraphs. ActionScript can be as simple. For example, in English, a period ends a sentence; in ActionScript, a semicolon ends a statement. In the ActionScript language, you can type a `stop()` action to stop the playhead of a movie clip instance or a SWF file from looping. Or you can write thousands of lines of code to power an interactive banking application. As you can see, ActionScript can do very simple or very complex things.

In Chapter 4, "Data and Data Types," you learned how the ActionScript language uses data, and how you can format it in your code. This chapter demonstrates how you can form statements in ActionScript using *syntax*. It contains many short code snippets and some examples to demonstrate fundamental language concepts. Upcoming chapters contain longer and increasingly involved code examples that combine and facilitate the fundamentals you learn in this chapter.

The general rules described in this section apply to all ActionScript. Most ActionScript terms also have individual requirements; for the rules for a specific term, see its entry in the *ActionScript 2.0 Language Reference* in Flash Help.

Applying the basics of ActionScript in a way that creates elegant programs can be a challenge for users who are new to ActionScript. For more information on how to apply the rules described in this section, see Chapter 19, "Best Practices and Coding Conventions for ActionScript 2.0," on page 745.

 NOTE You add ActionScript directly to a frame on the Timeline within this chapter. In later chapters, you use classes to separate your ActionScript from the FLA file.

For more information on working with ActionScript syntax and language fundamentals, see the following topics:

About syntax, statements, and expressions

The ActionScript language is made up of the built-in classes that make up the ActionScript language. You need to use correct ActionScript *syntax* to form statements so the code compiles and runs correctly in Flash. In this case, syntax refers to the grammar and spelling of a language that you program with. The compiler cannot understand incorrect syntax, so you see errors or warnings displayed in the Output panel when you try to test the document in the test environment. Therefore, syntax is a collection of rules and guidelines that help you form correct ActionScript.

A *statement* is an instruction you give the FLA file to do something, such as to perform a particular action. For example, you can use a conditional statement to determine whether something is true or exists. Then you might execute actions that you specify, such as functions or expressions, based on whether the condition is true or not. The if statement is a conditional statement and evaluates a condition to determine the next action that should occur in your code.

```
// if statement
if (condition) {
  // statements;
}
```

For more information on statements, see "About statements" on page 145.

Expressions, different from statements, are any legal combination of ActionScript symbols that represent a value. Expressions have *values*, while values and properties have *types*. An expression can consist of operators and operands, values, functions, and procedures. The expression follows ActionScript rules of precedence and of association. Typically, Flash Player interprets the expression and then returns a value that you can use in your application.

For example, the following code is an expression:

```
x + 2
```

In the previous expression, x and 2 are operands and + is an operator. For more information on operators and operands, see "About operators" on page 180. For more information on objects and properties, see "Object data type" on page 81.

The way you format your ActionScript also determines how maintainable your code is. For example, it's difficult to read the logic of a FLA file that doesn't contain indents or comments, or contains inconsistent formatting and naming conventions. When you indent blocks of ActionScript (such as loops and if statements), the code is easier to read and debug if you encounter problems. For more information about formatting ActionScript, see "Formatting ActionScript syntax" on page 777. You can also see proper formatting of ActionScript in these sections.

For more information on syntax and language fundamentals, see the following topics:

- "Differences between ActionScript and JavaScript"
- "About case sensitivity"

Differences between ActionScript and JavaScript

ActionScript is similar to the core JavaScript programming language. You don't need to know JavaScript to use and learn ActionScript; however, if you know JavaScript, ActionScript will seem familiar.

This manual does not attempt to teach general programming. There are many resources that provide more information about general programming concepts and the JavaScript language.

- The ECMAScript (ECMA-262) edition 3 language specification is derived from JavaScript and serves as the international standard for the JavaScript language. ActionScript is based on this specification. For more information, see www.ecma-international.org/publications/standards/Ecma-262.htm.
- The Java Technology site has tutorials on object-oriented programming (http://java.sun.com/docs/books/tutorial/java/index.html) that are targeted for the Java language but are useful for understanding concepts that you can apply to ActionScript.

Some of the differences between ActionScript and JavaScript are described in the following list:

■ ActionScript does not support browser-specific objects such as Document, Window, and Anchor.

■ ActionScript does not completely support all the JavaScript built-in objects.

■ ActionScript does not support some JavaScript syntax constructs, such as statement labels.

■ In ActionScript, the eval() function can perform only variable references.

■ ActionScript 2.0 supports several features that are not in the ECMA-262 specification, such as classes and strong typing. Many of these features are modeled after the ECMAScript (ECMA-262) edition 3 language specification (see www.ecma-international.org/publications/standards/Ecma-262.htm).

■ ActionScript does not support regular expressions using the RegExp object. However, Macromedia Central does support the RegExp object. For more information on Macromedia Central, see www.macromedia.com/software/central.

About case sensitivity

When you write ActionScript for Flash Player 7 and later, your code is case-sensitive. This means that variables with slightly different capitalization are considered different from each other. The following ActionScript code shows this:

```
// use mixed capitalization
var firstName:String = "Jimmy";
// use all lower case
trace(firstname); // undefined
```

Or you could write the following:

```
// In file targeting Flash Player 8
// and either ActionScript 1.0 or ActionScript 2.0
//
// Sets properties of two different objects
cat.hilite = true;
CAT.hilite = true;

// Creates three different variables
var myVar:Number = 10;
var myvar:Number = 10;
var mYvAr:Number = 10;
```

> **NOTE**
> It is not a good practice to differentiate between variables, or any identifier, using different case. For more information on naming variables, see Chapter 19, "Best Practices and Coding Conventions for ActionScript 2.0," on page 745.

When you publish for versions of Flash Player (Flash Player 6 and earlier), Flash traces the string `Jimmy` in the Output panel. Because Flash Player 7 and later versions are case-sensitive, `firstName` and `firstname` are two separate variables (when you use either ActionScript 1.0 or ActionScript 2.0). This is an important concept to understand. If you created FLA files for Flash Player 6 or earlier with nonmatching capitalization in your variables, your functionality and files might break during conversion of the file or application that targets a newer version of the Flash Player.

Therefore, it's good practice to follow consistent capitalization conventions, such as those used in this manual. Doing so also makes it easier to differentiate between variables, classes, and function names. Do not use case to make two identifiers differ. Change the instance, variable, or class name—not just the case. For more information on coding conventions, see Chapter 19, "Best Practices and Coding Conventions for ActionScript 2.0," on page 745.

Case sensitivity can have a large impact when you work with a web service that uses its own rules for variable naming and for the case that variables are in when they are returned to the SWF file from the server. For example, if you use a ColdFusion web service, property names from a structure or object might be all uppercase, such as `FIRSTNAME`. Unless you use the same case in Flash, you might experience unexpected results.

> **NOTE**
> Case sensitivity also affects external variables that you load into a SWF file, such as those loaded with `LoadVars.load()`.

Case sensitivity is implemented for external scripts, such as ActionScript 2.0 class files, scripts that you import using the `#include` command, and scripts in a FLA file. If you encounter runtime errors and are exporting to more than one version of Flash Player, you should review both external script files and scripts in FLA files to confirm that you used consistent capitalization.

Case sensitivity is implemented on a per-SWF file basis. If a strict (case-sensitive) Flash Player 8 application calls a nonstrict Flash Player 6 SWF file, ActionScript executed in the Player 6 SWF file is nonstrict. For example, if you use `loadMovie()` to load a Flash Player 6 SWF file into a Flash Player 8 SWF file, the version 6 SWF file remains case-insensitive, while the version 8 SWF file is treated as case-sensitive.

When syntax coloring is enabled, language elements written with correct capitalization are blue by default. For more information, see "About reserved words" on page 143.

About dot syntax and target paths

In ActionScript, you use a dot (.) operator (*dot syntax*) to access properties or methods that belong to an object or instance on the Stage. You also use the dot operator to identify the target path to an instance (such as a movie clip), variable, function, or object.

A dot syntax expression begins with the name of the object or movie clip, followed by a dot, and it ends with the element you want to specify. The following sections demonstrate how to write dot syntax expressions.

To control a movie clip, loaded SWF file, or button, you must specify a *target path*. Target paths are hierarchical addresses of movie clip instance names, variables, and objects in a SWF file. In order to specify a target path for a movie clip or button, you must assign an instance name to the movie clip or button. You name a movie clip instance by selecting the instance and typing the instance name in the Property inspector. Or you can specify the instance name with code if you create the instance using ActionScript. You can use the target path to assign an action to a movie clip or to get or set the value of a variable or property.

For more information on assigning an instance name and using dot syntax to target an instance, see the following topics:

- "About using dot syntax to target an instance" on page 122.
- "About scope and targeting" on page 127
- "Using the Target Path button" on page 128
- "About slash syntax" on page 128

For more information on objects and properties, see "Object data type" on page 81.

About using dot syntax to target an instance

To write ActionScript that controls an instance such as a movie clip or manipulates assets in a loaded SWF file, you must specify its name and its address in code. This is called a *target path*. To target (or address) objects in a SWF file, you use dot syntax (also called *dot notation*). For example, you need to target a movie clip or button instance before you can apply an action to it. Dot syntax helps you create a path to the instance you need to target. The path to the instance that you target is sometimes called the target path.

A FLA file has a particular hierarchy. You can create instances on the Stage or you can use ActionScript. You can even create instances that are inside other instances. Or you might have instances that nest within several other instances. You can manipulate any instance as long as you name it.

You name instances using an *instance name*, which you can specify in two different ways (both demonstrated below):

- Manually by selecting an instance and typing an instance name in the Property inspector (when an instance is on the Stage).
- Dynamically by using ActionScript. You create an instance using ActionScript and assign it an instance name when you create it.

To assign the instance an instance name in the Property inspector, type a name into the Instance Name text box.

You can also give an instance name to an object you create using ActionScript. It can be as simple as the following code:

```
this.createEmptyMovieClip("pic_mc", this.getNextHighestDepth());
pic_mc.loadMovie("http://www.helpexamples.com/flash/images/image1.jpg");
```

This code creates a new movie clip and assigns it the instance name pic_mc. Then, you can manipulate the pic_mc instance using code, such as loading an image into it as demonstrated in the previous code.

For more information on working with scope, see "About scope and targeting" on page 127 and "About variables and scope" on page 99.

Targeting an instance

If you want something to work in your SWF file, you need to target that instance and then tell it to do something, such as assigning it an action or changing its properties. You usually need to define where that instance is in the SWF file (for example, what timeline it's on or what instance it's nested within) by creating the target path. Remember that you have given many of the instances in your FLA file instance names, and then you added code to the FLA file that uses those instance names. When you do this, you target that particular instance and then tell it to do something (such as move the playhead or open a web page). For more information on objects and properties, see "Object data type" on page 81.

To target an instance:

1. Select File > New and select Flash Document.
2. Select File > Save As and name the file **target.fla**.
3. Use the Oval tool to draw a shape on the Stage. Draw an oval of any size and color.
4. Use the Selection tool to select the oval on the Stage.

> **TIP** Remember to select the stroke and fill if necessary.

5. Select Modify > Convert to Symbol, select the Movie Clip option, and then click OK to create the symbol.

6. Select the movie clip on the Stage and give it the instance name **myClip** in the Property inspector.

7. Insert a new layer and rename the layer **actions**.

8. Add the following ActionScript to Frame 1 of the actions layer:

```
myClip._xscale = 50;
```

This line of code targets the `myClip` instance on the Stage. The ActionScript scales the instance to half its original width. Because the ActionScript is on the same timeline as the movie clip symbol, you only need to target the instance using the instance name. If the instance was on a different timeline or nested within another instance, you would need to modify the target path accordingly.

Targeting a nested instance

You can also target instances that are nested inside other instances. Perhaps you want to place a second movie clip instance inside of the myClip instance from the exercise in "Targeting an instance" on page 123. You can also target that nested instance using ActionScript. Before you proceed with the following exercise, you need to complete the exercise in "Targeting an instance" on page 123, and then follow these steps to target a nested instance.

To target a nested instance:

1. Open target.fla from the procedure on targeting an instance, and rename it **target2.fla**.

2. Double-click the myClip instance on the Stage.

3. Select the Oval tool and draw another oval inside of the myClip instance.

4. Select the new shape, and then select Modify > Convert to Symbol.

5. Select the Movie Clip option and click OK.

6. Select the new instance, and type **myOtherClip** in the Instance Name text box of the Property inspector.

7. Click Scene 1 in the edit bar to return to the main Timeline.

8. Add the following ActionScript to Frame 1 of the actions layer:

```
myClip.myOtherClip._xscale = 50;
```

This ActionScript resizes the myOtherClip instance to 50% of its current width. Because the target.fla file modified the myClip instances `_xscale` property, and the myOtherClip is a nested symbol, you'll notice that myOtherClip will be 25 percent of the original width.

If you work with nested movie clips that have their own timelines, you can manipulate the playhead in a nested instance's timeline using code similar to the following snippet:

```
myClip.nestedClip.gotoAndPlay(15);
myClip.someOtherClip.gotoAndStop("tweenIn");
```

Notice that the clip that you manipulate (such as nestedClip) appears right before the action. You'll notice this trend in upcoming sections.

You aren't limited to accessing predefined methods and properties of instances on the Stage, as demonstrated in the previous examples. You can also set a variable within a movie clip, as seen in the following code, which sets a variable in the starClip movie clip:

```
starClip.speed = 1.1;
starClip.gravity = 0.8;
```

If either the speed or gravity variables existed previously in the starClip movie clip instance, the previous values would have been overwritten as soon as the new values were set. You are able to add new properties to the starClip movie clip, because the MovieClip class was defined with the dynamic keyword. The dynamic keyword specifies that objects based on the specified class (in this case MovieClip) can add and access dynamic properties at runtime. For more information about the dynamic statement, see %{dynamic statement}% in the *ActionScript 2.0 Language Reference* in Flash Help.

Targeting dynamic instances and loaded content

You can also create an object using ActionScript and target it using a target path afterwards. For example, you can use the following ActionScript to create a movie clip. Then you can change the rotation of that movie clip using ActionScript, as shown in the next example:

To target a dynamically created movie clip instance:

1. Create a new Flash document and save the file as **targetClip.fla**.

2. Insert a new layer and rename the layer **actions**.

3. Add the following ActionScript to Frame 1 of the actions layer:

```
this.createEmptyMovieClip("rotateClip", this.getNextHighestDepth());
trace(rotateClip);
rotateClip._rotation = 50;
```

4. Select Control > Test Movie to test your document.

   You can tell that you created a movie clip because of the trace statement, but you cannot see anything on the Stage. Even though you added code that creates a movie clip instance, you won't see anything on the Stage unless you add something to the movie clip. For example, you might load an image into the movie clip.

5. Return to the authoring environment, and open the Actions panel.

6. Type the following ActionScript after the code you added in step 3:

```
rotateClip.loadMovie("http://www.helpexamples.com/flash/images/
  image1.jpg");
```

This code loads an image into the rotateClip movie clip that you created with code. You're targeting the rotateClip instance with ActionScript.

7. Select Control > Test Movie to test your document.

Now you should see an image on the Stage that rotates 50° clockwise.

You can also target or identify parts of SWF files that you load into a base SWF file.

To identify a loaded SWF file:

■ Use _levelX, where X is the level number specified in the loadMovie() function that loaded the SWF file.

For example, a SWF file loaded into level 99 has the target path _level99. In the following example, you load a SWF file into level 99 and set its visibility to false:

```
//Load the SWF onto level 99.
loadMovieNum("contents.swf", 99);
//Set the visibility of level 99 to false.
loaderClip.onEnterFrame = function(){
  _level99._visible = false;
};
```

 TIP It's generally a good idea to avoid using levels if you can load content into movie clips at different depths instead. Using the MovieClip.getNextHighestDepth() method enables you to create new movie clip instances on the Stage dynamically without having to check whether there is already an instance at a particular depth.

Setting variables using a path

You can set variables for instances that you nest inside of other instances. For example, if you want to set a variable for a form that's inside another form, you can use the following code. The instance submitBtn is inside of formClip on the main timeline:

```
this.formClip.submitBtn.mouseOver = true;
```

You can express a method or property of a particular object (such as a movie clip or text field) using this pattern. For example, the property of an object would be

```
myClip._alpha = 50;
```

About scope and targeting

When you nest instances, the movie clip that nests a second movie clip is known as the *parent* to the nested instance. The nested instance is known as the child instance. The main Stage and main timeline are essentially a movie clip themselves, and can therefore be targeted as such. For more information on scope, see "About variables and scope" on page 99.

You can target parent instances and parent timelines using ActionScript. When you want to target the current timeline, you use the `this` keyword. For example, when you target a movie clip called myClip that's on the current main timeline, you would use

`this.myClip.`

Optionally, you can drop the `this` keyword, and just use

`myClip`

You might choose to add the `this` keyword for readability and consistency. For more information on recommended coding practices, see Chapter 19, "Best Practices and Coding Conventions for ActionScript 2.0," on page 745.

If you trace the movie clip, for either snippet above you see `_level0.myClip` in the Output panel. However, if you have ActionScript that's inside the myClip movie clip but you want to target the main timeline, target the parent of the movie clip (which is the main Stage). Double-click a movie clip, and place the following ActionScript on the movie clip's timeline:

```
trace("me: " + this);
trace("my parent: " + this._parent);
```

Test the SWF file, and you'll see the following message in the Output panel:

```
me: _level0.myClip
my parent: _level0
```

This indicates you targeted the main timeline. You can use `parent` to create a relative path to an object. For example, if the movie clip `dogClip` is nested inside the animating movie clip animalClip, the following statement on the instance dogClip tells animalClip to stop animating:

```
this._parent.stop();
```

If you're familiar with Flash and ActionScript, you've probably noticed people using the `_root` scope. The `_root` scope generally refers to the main timeline of the current Flash document. You should avoid using the `_root` scope unless it's absolutely necessary. You can use relative target paths instead of `_root`.

If you use `_root` in your code, you can encounter errors if you load the SWF file into another Flash document. When the SWF file loads into a different SWF file, `_root` in the loaded file might point to the root scope of the SWF file it loads into, instead of referring to its own root as you intend it to. This can lead to unpredictable results, or break functionality altogether.

Using the Target Path button

Sometimes it takes some time to figure out what a given target path is, or what target path you need for a piece of code. If you target an instance you have on the Stage, you can use the Target Path button to determine what the path is to that instance.

To use the Target Path button:

1. Open the Actions panel (Window > Actions) and click the Insert Target Path button. The movie clips in your current document appear in a dialog box.

2. Select one of the instances from the list in the dialog box.

3. Click OK.

4. The target path for the selected instance appears in the Script pane.

About slash syntax

Slash syntax was used in Flash 3 and 4 to indicate the target path of a movie clip or variable. This syntax is supported by ActionScript 1.0 in Flash Player 7 and earlier, but it's not supported in ActionScript 2.0 and Flash Player 7 or Flash Player 8.

Using slash syntax is not recommended unless you do not have another option, such as when you create content intended specifically for Flash Player 4 or Flash Lite 1.1 (and earlier) where you must use slash syntax. For more information on Flash Lite, see the Flash Lite product page.

About language punctuators

There are several language *punctuators* in Flash. The most common type of punctuators are semicolons (;), colons (:), parentheses [()] and braces ({}). Each of these punctuators has a special meaning in the Flash language and helps define data types, terminate statements or structure ActionScript. The following sections discuss how to use the punctuators in your code.

For more information on language punctuators, see the following topics:

- "Semicolons and colons" on page 129
- "Curly braces" on page 130
- "Parentheses" on page 133
- "About literals" on page 134
- "About comments" on page 135

For more information on the dot (.) operator and array access ([ ]) operators, see "Using dot and array access operators" on page 188. For information on white space and code formatting, see "Formatting ActionScript syntax" on page 777.

Semicolons and colons

ActionScript statements terminate with a semicolon (;) character, as demonstrated in the following two lines of code:

```
var myNum:Number = 50;
myClip._alpha = myNum;
```

You can omit the semicolon character and the ActionScript compiler assumes that each line of code represents a single statement. However, it is good scripting practice to use semicolons because it makes your code more readable. When you click the Auto Format button in the Actions panel or Script window, trailing semicolons are appended to the end of your statements by default.

> **NOTE** Using a semicolon to terminate a statement allows you to place more than one statement on a single line, but doing so usually makes your code more difficult to read.

Another place you use semicolons is in for loops. You use the semicolon to separate parameters, as shown in the following example. The example loops from 0 to 9 and then displays each number in the Output panel:

```
var i:Number;
for (i = 0; i < 10; i++) {
   trace(i); // 0,1,...,9
}
```

You use colons (:) in your code to assign data types to your variables. To assign a specific data type to an item, specify its type using the var keyword and post-colon syntax, as shown in the following example:

```
// strict typing of variable or object
var myNum:Number = 7;
var myDate:Date = new Date();
// strict typing of parameters
function welcome(firstName:String, myAge:Number) {
}
// strict typing of parameter and return value
function square(num:Number):Number {
   var squared:Number = num * num;
   return squared;
}
```

You can declare the data type of objects based on built-in classes (Button, Date, MovieClip, and so on) and on classes and interfaces that you create. In the following snippet, you create a new object of the custom type Student:

```
var firstStudent:Student = new Student();
```

You can also specify that objects are of the Function or the Void data type. For more information on assigning data types, see Chapter 4, "Data and Data Types," on page 73.

Curly braces

You group ActionScript events, class definitions, and functions into blocks using curly brace ({ }) punctuators. You put the opening brace on the same line as the declaration.

> **NOTE**
> You can also put the opening brace on the line that follows the declaration. Coding conventions recommend that you put the opening brace on the same line for consistency. For information on braces and code conventions, see Chapter 19, "Best Practices and Coding Conventions for ActionScript 2.0," on page 745.

Place braces around each statement when it is part of a control structure (such as if..else or for), even if it contains only a single statement. This good practice helps you avoid errors in your ActionScript when you forget to add braces to your code. The following example shows code that is written using poor form:

```
var numUsers:Number;
if (numUsers == 0)
  trace("no users found.");
```

Although this code validates, it is considered poor form because it lacks braces around the statements.

> **TIP**
> Braces are added to this statement if you click the Check Syntax button.

In this case, if you add a second statement after the trace statement, the second statement executes regardless of whether the numUsers variable equals 0, which can lead to unexpected results. For this reason, add braces so the code looks like the following example:

```
var numUsers:Number;
if (numUsers == 0) {
  trace("no users found");
}
```

In the following example, you create both an event listener object and a MovieClipLoader instance.

```
var imgUrl:String = "http://www.helpexamples.com/flash/images/image1.jpg";
this.createEmptyMovieClip("img_mc", 100);
var mclListener:Object = new Object();
mclListener.onLoadStart = function() {
  trace("starting");
};
mclListener.onLoadInit = function(target_mc:MovieClip):Void {
  trace("success");
};
mclListener.onLoadError = function(target_mc:MovieClip):Void {
  trace("failure");
};
var myClip1:MovieClipLoader = new MovieClipLoader();
myClip1.addListener(mclListener);
myClip1.loadClip(imgUrl, img_mc);
```

The next example displays a simple class file that could be used to create a Student object. You learn more about class files in Chapter 7, "Classes," on page 231.

To use curly braces in an ActionScript file:

1. Select File > New and then select ActionScript File.

2. Select File > Save As and save the new document as **Student.as**.

3. Add the following ActionScript to the AS file.

```
// Student.as
class Student {
  private var _id:String;
  private var _firstName:String;
  private var _middleName:String;
  private var _lastName:String;

  public function Student(id:String, firstName:String,
  middleName:String, lastName:String) {
    this._id = id;
    this._firstName = firstName;
    this._middleName = middleName;
    this._lastName = lastName;
  }
  public function get firstName():String {
    return this._firstName;
  }
  public function set firstName(value:String):Void {
    this._firstName = value;
  }
  // ...
}
```

4. Save the class file.

5. Select File > New and click Flash Document to create a new FLA file.

6. Save the new FLA file as **student_test.fla**.

7. Type the following ActionScript on Frame 1 of the main Timeline:

```
// student_test.fla
import Student;
var firstStudent:Student = new Student("cst94121", "John", "H.", "Doe");
trace(firstStudent.firstName); // John
firstStudent.firstName = "Craig";
trace(firstStudent.firstName); // Craig
```

8. Select File > Save to save the changes to student_test.fla.

9. Select Control > Test Movie to test the FLA and AS files.

The next example demonstrates how curly braces are used when you work with functions.

To use curly braces with functions:

1. Select File > New and select Flash Document to create a new FLA file.

2. Select File > Save As and name the new file **checkform.fla**.

3. Drag an instance of the Label component from the Components panel onto the Stage.

4. Open the Property inspector (Window > Properties > Properties) and with the Label component instance selected, type an instance name of **status_lbl** into the Instance Name text box.

5. Type **200** into the W (width) text box to resize the component to 200 pixels wide.

6. Drag an instance of the TextInput component onto the Stage and give it an instance name of **firstName_ti**.

7. Drag an instance of the Button component onto the Stage and give it an instance name of **submit_button**.

8. Select Frame 1 of the Timeline, and add the following ActionScript into the Actions panel:

```
function checkForm():Boolean {
  status_lbl.text = "";
  if (firstName_ti.text.length == 0) {
    status_lbl.text = "Please enter a first name.";
    return false;
  }
  return true;
}
function clickListener(evt_obj:Object):Void {
  var success:Boolean = checkForm();
};
submit_button.addEventListener("click", clickListener);
```

9. Select File > Save to save the Flash document.

10. Select Control > Test Movie to test the code in the authoring environment.

In the SWF file, an error message is displayed if you click the Button instance on the Stage when you do not have text in the `firstName_ti` TextInput component. This error appears in the Label component and informs users that they need to enter a first name.

The next example using curly braces shows how to create and define properties within an object. In this example, properties are defined in the object by specifying the variable names within the curly brace ({}) punctuators:

```
var myObject:Object = {id:"cst94121", firstName:"John", middleName:"H.",
  lastName:"Doe"};
var i:String;
for (i in myObject) {
  trace(i + ": " + myObject[i]);
}
/*
  id: cst94121
  firstName: John
  middleName: H.
  lastName: Doe
*/
```

You can also use empty curly braces as a syntax shortcut for the `new Object()` function. For example, the following code creates an empty Object instance:

```
var myObject:Object = {};
```

 Remember to make sure each opening curly brace has a matching closing brace.

Parentheses

When you define a function in ActionScript, you place parameters inside parentheses [()] punctuators, as shown in the following lines of code:

```
function myFunction(myName:String, myAge:Number, happy:Boolean):Void {
  // Your code goes here.
}
```

When you call a function, you also include any of the parameters you pass to the function in parentheses, as shown in the following example:

```
myFunction("Carl", 78, true);
```

You can use parentheses to override the ActionScript order of precedence or to make your ActionScript statements easier to read. This means you can change the order in which values are computed by placing brackets around certain values, as seen in the following example:

```
var computedValue:Number = (circleClip._x + 20) * 0.8;
```

Because of order of precedence, if you didn't use parentheses or use two separate statements, the multiplication would be computed first, meaning that the first operation would be 20 * 0.8. The result, 16, would then be added to the current value of circleClip._x and finally assigned to the computedValue variable.

If you don't use parentheses, you must add a statement to evaluate the expression, as shown in the following example:

```
var tempValue:Number = circleClip._x + 20;
var computedValue:Number = tempValue * 0.8;
```

As with brackets and braces, you need to make sure each opening parentheses has a closing parentheses.

About literals

A *literal* is a value that appears directly in your code. Literals are constant (unchanging) values within your Flash documents. Examples of a literal include true, false, 0, 1, 52, or even the string "foo".

The following examples are all literals:

```
17
"hello"
-3
9.4
null
undefined
true
false
```

Literals can also be grouped to form compound literals. Array literals are enclosed in bracket punctuators ([]) and use the comma punctuator (,) to separate array elements. An array literal can be used to initialize an array. The following examples show two arrays that are initialized using array literals. You can use the new statement and pass the compound literal as a parameter to the Array class constructor, but you can also assign literal values directly when instantiating instances of any built-in ActionScript class.

```
// using new statement
var myStrings:Array = new Array("alpha", "beta", "gamma");
var myNums:Array = new Array(1, 2, 3, 5, 8);

// assigning literal directly
var myStrings:Array = ["alpha", "beta", "gamma"];
var myNums:Array = [1, 2, 3, 5, 8];
```

Literals can also be used to initialize a generic object. A generic object is an instance of the Object class. Object literals are enclosed in curly braces ({ }) and use the comma punctuator (,) to separate object properties. Each property is declared with the colon punctuator (:), which separates the name of the property from the value of the property.

You can create a generic object using the new statement and pass the object literal as a parameter to the Object class constructor, or you can assign the object literal directly to the instance you are declaring. The following example creates a new generic object and initializes the object with three properties, propA, propB, and propC, each with values set to 1, 2, and 3, respectively.

```
// using new statement
var myObject:Object = new Object({propA:1, propB:2, propC:3});

// assigning literal directly
var myObject:Object = {propA:1, propB:2, propC:3};
```

Do not confuse a string literal with a String object. In the following example, the first line of code creates the string literal firstStr, and the second line of code creates the String object secondStr:

```
var firstStr:String = "foo"
var secondStr:String = new String("foo")
```

Use string literals unless you specifically need to use a String object for better performance. For more information on strings, see "About strings and the String class" on page 459.

About comments

Comments are a way of annotating your code with plain-English descriptions that do not get evaluated by the compiler. You can use comments within your code to describe what the code is doing or to describe which data returns to the document. Using comments can help you remember important coding decisions, and it can be helpful to anyone else who reads your code. Comments must clearly explain the intent of the code and not just translate the code. If something is not readily obvious in the code, you should add comments to it.

Using comments to add notes to scripts is highly recommended. Comments document the decisions you make in the code, answering both how and why. They make ActionScript easier to understand. For example, you might describe a work-around in comments. Therefore, you or another developer can easily find sections of code to update or fix. Or, if the issue is fixed or improved in a future version of Flash or Flash Player, you could improve the ActionScript by removing the work-around.

Avoid using cluttered comments. An example of cluttered comments is a line of equal signs (=) or asterisks (*) used to create a block or separation around your comments. Instead, use white space to separate your comments from the ActionScript. If you format your ActionScript using the Auto Format button in the Actions panel or Script window, this removes the white space. Remember to add white space back into your code, or use single comment lines (//) to maintain spacing; these lines are easier to remove after you format your code than trying to determine where white space once was.

Before you deploy your project, remove any superfluous comments from the code, such as "define the x and y variables" or other comments that are immediately obvious to other developers. If you find that you have many extra comments in the ActionScript, consider whether you need to rewrite some of the code. If you need to include many comments about how the code works, it is usually a sign that the ActionScript is inelegant and not intuitive.

When you enable syntax coloring, comments are gray by default. Comments can be any length without affecting the size of the exported file, and they do not need to follow rules for ActionScript syntax or keywords.

> **NOTE** Using comments is most important in ActionScript that is intended to teach an audience. Add comments to your code if you are creating sample applications for the purpose of teaching Flash or if you are writing articles or tutorials on ActionScript.

Single-line comments

You use single-line comments to add a comment to a single line in your code. You might comment out a single line of code, or add a short description of what a piece of code accomplishes. To indicate that a line or portion of a line is a comment, precede the comment with two forward slashes (//), as shown in the following code:

```
// The following sets a local variable for age.
var myAge:Number = 26;
```

Single-line comments are typically used to explain a small code snippet. You can use single-line comments for any short comments that fit on a single line. The following example includes a single-line comment:

```
while (condition) {
  // handle condition with statements
}
```

Multiline comments

Use multiline comments, also called block comments, for comments that are several lines in length. Developers commonly use multiline comments to describe files, data structures, methods, and descriptions of files. They are usually placed at the beginning of a file and before or within a method.

To create a comment block, place /* at the beginning of the commented lines and */ at the end of the comment block. This technique lets you create lengthy comments without adding // at the beginning of each line. Using // for numerous sequential lines can lead to some problems when you modify the comments.

The format for a multiline comment is as follows.

```
/*
  The following ActionScript initializes variables used in the main and
  sub-menu systems. Variables are used to track what options are clicked.
*/
```

> **TIP** If you place the comment characters (/* and */) on separate lines at the beginning and end of the comment, you can easily comment them out by placing double slash characters (//) in front of them (for example, ///* and //*/). These let you quickly and easily comment and uncomment your code.

By placing large chunks of script in a comment block, called *commenting out* a portion of your script, you can test specific parts of a script. For example, when the following script runs, none of the code in the comment block executes:

```
// The following code runs.
var x:Number = 15;
var y:Number = 20;

// The following code is commented out and will not run.
/*
// create new Date object
var myDate:Date = new Date();
var currentMonth:Number = myDate.getMonth();
// convert month number to month name
var monthName:String = calcMonth(currentMonth);
var year:Number = myDate.getFullYear();
var currentDate:Number = myDate.getDate();
*/

// The code below runs.
var namePrefix:String = "My name is";
var age:Number = 20;
```

> **TIP** It's good practice to place a blank line before a block comment.

Trailing comments

You use trailing comments to add a comment on the same line as your code. These comments appear on the same line as your ActionScript code. Developers commonly use trailing comments to indicate what a variable contains or to describe or note the value that returns from a line of ActionScript. Format trailing comments as follows:

```
var myAge:Number = 26; // variable for my age
trace(myAge); // 26
```

Space the comments to the right so readers can distinguish them from the code. Try to have the comments line up with each other, if possible, as shown in the following code.

```
var myAge:Number = 28;              // my age
var myCountry:String = "Canada";    // my country
var myCoffee:String = "Hortons";    // my coffee preference
```

If you use autoformatting (click the Auto Format button in the Actions panel), trailing comments move to the next line. Add these comments after you format your code, or you must modify their placement after using the Auto Format button.

Comments inside classes

You use comments in your classes and interfaces to document them to help developers understand the contents of your class. You might start all your class files with a comment that provides the class name, its version number, the date, and your copyright. For example, you might create documentation for your class that is similar to the following comment:

```
/**
   Pelican class
   version 1.2
   10/10/2005
   copyright Macromedia, Inc.
*/
```

Use block comments to describe files, data structures, methods, and descriptions of files. They are usually placed at the beginning of a file and before or within a method.

There are two kinds of comments in a typical class or interface file: documentation comments and implementation comments. Documentation comments are used to describe the code's specifications and do not describe the implementation. You use documentation comments to describe interfaces, classes, methods, and constructors. Implementation comments are used to comment out code or to comment on the implementation of particular sections of code.

Include one documentation comment per class, interface, or member, and place it directly before the declaration. If you have additional information to document that does not fit into the documentation comments, use implementation comments (in the format of block comments or single-line comments). Implementation comments directly follow the declaration.

The two kinds of comments use slightly different delimiters. Documentation comments are delimited with /** and */, and implementation comments are delimited with /* and */.

 Don't include comments that do not directly relate to the class being read. For example, do not include comments that describe the corresponding package.

You can also use single-line comments, block comments, and trailing comments in class files. For more information on these kinds of comments, see the following sections:

- "Single-line comments" on page 136
- "Multiline comments" on page 137
- "Trailing comments" on page 138

About constants and keywords

Constants and keywords are the backbone of ActionScript syntax. Constants are properties with a fixed value that cannot be altered, so they are values that don't change throughout an application.

Flash includes several predefined constants, which can help simplify application development. An example of constants can be found in the Key class, which includes many properties, such as Key.ENTER or Key.PGDN. If you rely on constants, you never have to remember that the key code values for the Enter and Page Down keys are 13 and 34. Using constant values not only makes development and debugging easier, but it also makes your code easier to read by your fellow developers.

Keywords in ActionScript are used to perform specific kinds of actions. They are also reserved words because of this, so you can't use them as identifiers (such as variable, function, or label names). Examples of some reserved keywords are if, else, this, function, and return.

For more information on constants and keywords, see the following topics:

- "Using constants" on page 140
- "About keywords" on page 142
- "About reserved words" on page 143

For more information on objects and properties, see "Object data type" on page 81. For a list of constants in the language (such as `false` and `NaN`), see the ActionScript Language Elements > Constants category in the *ActionScript 2.0 Language Reference* in Flash Help.

Using constants

Constants are properties with a fixed value that cannot be altered; in other words, they are values that don't change throughout an application. The ActionScript language contains many predefined constants. For example, the constants `BACKSPACE`, `ENTER`, `SPACE`, and `TAB` are properties of the Key class and refer to keyboard keys. The constant `Key.TAB` always has the same meaning: it indicates the Tab key on a keyboard. Constants are useful for comparing values and for using values in your application that do not change.

To test whether the user is pressing the Enter key, you could use the following statement:

```
var keyListener:Object = new Object();
keyListener.onKeyDown = function() {
  if (Key.getCode() == Key.ENTER) {
    trace("Are you ready to play?");
  }
};
Key.addListener(keyListener);
```

For the previous ActionScript to work, it may be necessary to disable keyboard shortcuts in the authoring environment. Select Control > Test Movie from the main menu, then while previewing the SWF file in the player, select Control > Disable Keyboard Shortcuts from the SWF file's preview window.

In Flash there is no way to create your own constant values except when you create your own custom classes with private member variables. You cannot create a "read-only" variable within Flash.

Variables should be lowercase or mixed-case letters; however, constants (variables that do not change) should be uppercase. Separate words with underscores, as the following ActionScript shows:

```
var BASE_URL:String = "http://www.macromedia.com"; //constant
var MAX_WIDTH:Number = 10;                          //constant
```

Write static constants in uppercase, and separate words with an underscore. Do not directly code numerical constants unless the constant is 1, 0, or -1, which you might use in a `for` loop as a counter value.

You can use constants for situations in which you need to refer to a property whose value never changes. This helps you find typographical mistakes in your code that you might not find if you use literals. It also lets you change the value in a single place. For more information on literals, see "About literals" on page 134.

For example, the class definition in the next example creates three constants that follow the naming convention used by ActionScript 2.0.

To use constants in an application:

1. Select File > New and then select ActionScript File to create an AS file.

2. Name the new file **ConstExample.as**.

3. Type the following code into the Script window:

```
class ConstExample {
   public static var EXAMPLE_STATIC:String = "Global access";
   public var EXAMPLE_PUBLIC:String = "Public access";
   private var EXAMPLE_PRIVATE:String = "Class access";
}
```

The EXAMPLE_STATIC property is a static property, which means that the property applies to the class as a whole instead of to a particular instance of the class. You must access a static property of a class using the name of the class instead of the name of an instance. You cannot access a static property through a class instance.

4. Create a new Flash document and save it as **const.fla**.

5. Open the Actions panel, and type the following code on Frame 1 of the Timeline:

```
trace(ConstExample.EXAMPLE_STATIC); // output: Global access
```

When you declare the EXAMPLE_STATIC property as static, you use this code to access the value of the property.

6. Select Control > Test Movie to test your document.

You will see Global access in the Output panel.

7. In the Actions panel, type this code following the code you added in step 5.

```
trace(ConstExample.EXAMPLE_PUBLIC); // error
trace(ConstExample.EXAMPLE_PRIVATE); // error
```

8. Select Control > Test Movie to test your document.

The EXAMPLE_PUBLIC and EXAMPLE_PRIVATE properties are not static properties. When you try to access the values through the class, you see the error message:

```
The property being referenced does not have the static attribute.
```

To access a property that is not static, you must access the value through an instance of the class. Because the EXAMPLE_PUBLIC property is a public property, it is available to code outside of the class definition.

9. In the Actions panel, delete the trace statements that you added in steps 5 and 7.

10. Type the following code into the Actions panel:

```
var myExample:ConstExample = new ConstExample();
trace(myExample.EXAMPLE_PUBLIC); // output: Public access
```

This code instantiates the myExample instance and accesses the `EXAMPLE_PUBLIC` property.

11. Select Control > Test Movie to test your document.

You see `Public access` in the Output panel.

12. In the Actions panel, delete the trace statement that you added in step 10.

13. Type the following code into the Actions panel.

```
trace(myExample.EXAMPLE_PRIVATE); // error
```

The `EXAMPLE_PRIVATE` property is a private property, so it is available only within the class definition.

14. Select Control > Test Movie to test your document.

You see `The member is private and cannot be accessed` in the Output panel.

For more information on built-in classes and creating custom classes, see Chapter 7, "Classes," on page 231.

About keywords

Keywords are words in ActionScript that do one specific thing. For example, you use the `var` keyword to declare a variable. The `var` keyword is shown in the following line of code:

```
var myAge:Number = 26;
```

A keyword is a reserved word that has a specific meaning: for example, you use the `class` keyword to define new a new ActionScript class; and you use the `var` keyword to declare local variables. Other examples of reserved keywords are: `if`, `else`, `this`, `function`, and `return`.

Keywords cannot be used as identifiers (such as variable, function, or label names), and you should not use them elsewhere in your FLA files for other things (such as instance names). You have already used the `var` keyword a lot, particularly if you read Chapter 4, "Data and Data Types," on page 73. ActionScript reserves words in the language for specific use. Therefore, you can't use keywords as identifiers (such as variable, function, or label names). You can find a list of these keywords in "About reserved words" on page 143.

About reserved words

Reserved words are words that you cannot use as identifiers in your code because the words are reserved for use by ActionScript. Reserved words include *keywords*, which are ActionScript statements, and words that are reserved for future use. That means you should not use them for naming your variables, instances, custom classes, and so on; doing so can lead to technical problems in your work.

The following table lists reserved keywords in Flash that cause errors in your scripts:

add	and	break	case
catch	class	continue	default
delete	do	dynamic	else
eq	extends	finally	for
function	ge	get	gt
if	ifFrameLoaded	implements	import
in	instanceof	interface	intrinsic
le	lt	ne	new
not	on	onClipEvent	or
private	public	return	set
static	switch	tellTarget	this
throw	try	typeof	var
void	while	with	

The following table lists keywords that are reserved for future use by ActionScript or the ECMAScript (ECMA-262) edition 4 draft language specification. You should also avoid using these keywords in your code:

abstract	enum	export	short
byte	long	synchronized	char
debugger	protected	double	volatile
float	throws	transient	goto

All built-in class names, component class names, and interface names are reserved words, and should not be used as identifiers in your code:

Accessibility	Accordion	Alert	Array
Binding	Boolean	Button	Camera
CellRenderer	CheckBox	Collection	Color
ComboBox	ComponentMixins	ContextMenu	ContextMenuItem
CustomActions	CustomFormatter	CustomValidator	DataGrid
DataHolder	DataProvider	DataSet	DataType
Date	DateChooser	DateField	Delta
DeltaItem	DeltaPacket	DepthManager	EndPoint
Error	FocusManager	Form	Function
Iterator	Key	Label	List
Loader	LoadVars	LocalConnection	Log
Math	Media	Menu	MenuBar
Microphone	Mouse	MovieClip	MovieClipLoader
NetConnection	NetStream	Number	NumericStepper
Object	PendingCall	PopUpManager	PrintJob
ProgressBar	RadioButton	RDBMSResolver	Screen
ScrollPane	Selection	SharedObject	Slide
SOAPCall	Sound	Stage	String
StyleManager	System	TextArea	TextField
TextFormat	TextInput	TextSnapshot	TransferObject
Tree	TreeDataProvider	TypedValue	UIComponent
UIEventDispatcher	UIObject	Video	WebService
WebServiceConnector	Window	XML	XMLConnector
XUpdateResolver			

Several words, although they are not reserved words, should not be used as identifiers (such as variable or instance names) in your ActionScript code. These are words that are used by the built-in classes that make up the ActionScript language. Therefore, do not use the names of properties, methods, classes, interfaces, component class names, and values as names in your code (such as when you name variables, classes, or instances).

To learn what these names are, refer to the *ActionScript 2.0 Language Reference* in Flash Help, and search the Help panel for additional instructional and usage sections in this book (*Learning ActionScript 2.0 in Flash*).

About statements

A *statement* is an instruction you give the FLA file to do something, such as to perform a particular action. For example, you can use a conditional statement to determine whether something is true or exists. Then your code might execute actions that you specify, such as functions or expressions, based on whether the condition is true or not.

For example, the `if` statement is a conditional statement and evaluates a condition to determine the next action that should occur in your code.

```
// if statement
if (condition) {
  // statements;
}
```

Another example is the `return` statement, which returns a result as a value of the function in which it executes.

There are many different ways for you to format or write ActionScript. You might differ from someone else who writes ActionScript in the way you form syntax, such as the way you space out your statements or where you put curly braces ({ }) in your code. Even though there are several different ways you can form statements without breaking your code, there are some general guidelines you can follow to write well-formed ActionScript.

Place only one statement on a line to increase the readability of your ActionScript   The following example shows the recommended and not recommended statement usage:

```
theNum++;        // recommended
theOtherNum++;   // recommended
aNum++; anOtherNum++;  // not recommended
```

Assign variables as separate statements   Consider the following ActionScript example:

```
var myNum:Number = (a = b + c) + d;
```

This ActionScript embeds an assignment within the code, which is difficult to read. If you assign variables as separate statements, it improves readability, as the following example shows:

```
var a:Number = b + c;
var myNum:Number = a + d;
```

The following sections show you how to form specific statements in ActionScript. For information on writing and formatting events, see Chapter 10, "Handling Events," on page 335.

For more information on each statement, see the following topics:

- "About compound statements" on page 146
- "About conditions" on page 146
- "Repeating actions using loops" on page 157

About compound statements

A compound statement contains numerous statements that you enclose within curly brace ({ }) punctuators. The statements inside a compound statement can be any kind of ActionScript statement. A typical compound statement is shown below.

The statements within the curly brace punctuators are indented from the compound statement, as the following ActionScript shows:

```
var a:Number = 10;
var b:Number = 10;
if (a == b) {
  // This code is indented.
  trace("a == b");
  trace(a);
  trace(b);
}
```

This compound statement contains several statements, but acts like a single statement in your ActionScript code. The opening brace is placed at the end of the compound statement. The closing brace begins a line, and aligns with the beginning of the compound statement.

For more information on using braces, see "Curly braces" on page 130.

About conditions

You use conditions to determine whether something is true or exists, and then you can optionally repeat an action (using loops), or execute actions that you specify, such as functions or expressions, based on whether the condition is true or not. For example, you can determine whether a certain variable is defined or has a certain value and execute a block of code based on the result. Also, you could change the graphics within your Flash document based on what time the user's system clock is set to or on the weather in the user's current location.

To perform an action depending on whether a condition exists, or to repeat an action (create loop statements), you can use if, else, else if, for, while, do while, for..in, or switch statements.

For more information on conditions that you can use, and how to write them, see the following topics:

- "About writing conditions" on page 147
- "Using the if statement" on page 148
- "Using the if..else statement" on page 149
- "Using the if..else if statement" on page 150
- "Using a switch statement" on page 151
- "Using try..catch and try..catch..finally statements" on page 153
- "About the conditional operator and alternative syntax" on page 156

About writing conditions

Statements that check whether a condition is true or false begin with the term `if`. If the condition evaluates to `true`, ActionScript executes the next statement. If the condition evaluates to `false`, ActionScript skips to the next statement outside the block of code.

 To optimize your code's performance, check for the most likely conditions first.

The following statements test three conditions. The term `else if` specifies alternative tests to perform if previous conditions are false.

```
if ((passwordTxt.text.length == 0) || (emailTxt.text.length == 0)) {
  gotoAndStop("invalidLogin");
} else if (passwordTxt.text == userID){
  gotoAndPlay("startProgram");
}
```

In this code snippet, if the length of the passwordTxt or emailTxt text fields is 0 (for example, the user hasn't entered a value), the Flash document redirects to the `invalidLogin` frame label. If both the passwordTxt and emailTxt text fields contain values and the passwordTxt text field's contents match the `userID` variable, the SWF file redirects to the `startProgram` frame label.

If you want to check for one of several conditions, you can use the `switch` statement rather than multiple `else if` statements. For more information on `switch` statements, see "Using a switch statement" on page 151.

Refer to the following sections to learn how to write different kinds of conditions in your ActionScript applications.

Using the if statement

Use the `if` statement when you want to execute a series of statements based on a whether a certain condition is true.

```
// if statement
if (condition) {
  // statements;
}
```

There are several times when you'll use `if` statements when you work on a Flash project. For example, if you are building a Flash site that requires users to log in before they can access certain sections of a website, you can use an `if` statement to validate that the user enters some text in the username and password fields.

If you need to validate user names and passwords using an external database, you probably want to verify that the username/password combination a user submits matches a record in the database. You also want to check whether the user has permission to access the specified part of the site.

If you script animations in Flash, you might want to use the `if` statement to test whether an instance on the Stage is still within the boundaries of the Stage. For example, if a ball moves downward along the y-axis, you might need to detect when the ball collides with the bottom edge of the Stage, so you can change the direction so that the ball appears to bounce upwards.

To use an if statement:

1. Select File > New and then select Flash Document.

2. Select Frame 1 of the Timeline, and then type the following ActionScript in the Actions panel:

```
// create a string to hold AM and PM
var amPm:String = "AM";
// no parameters pass to Date, so returns current date/time
var current_date:Date = new Date();
// if current hour is greater than/equal to 12, sets amPm string to "PM".
if (current_date.getHours() >= 12) {
  amPm = "PM";
}
trace(amPm);
```

3. Select Control > Test Movie to test the ActionScript.

   In this code, you create a string that holds AM or PM based on the current time of day. If the current hour is greater than or equal to 12 the amPM string sets to PM. Finally, you trace the amPm string, and if the hour is greater than or equal to 12, PM is displayed. Otherwise, you'll see AM.

Using the if..else statement

The `if..else` conditional statement lets you test a condition and then execute a block of code if that condition exists or execute an alternative block of code if the condition does not exist.

For example, the following code tests whether the value of x exceeds 20, generates a `trace()` statement if it does, or generates a different `trace()` statement if it does not:

```
if (x > 20) {
  trace("x is > 20");
} else {
  trace("x is <= 20");
}
```

If you do not want to execute an alternative block of code, you can use the `if` statement without the `else` statement.

The `if..else` statement in Flash is similar to the `if` statement. For example, if you use the `if` statement to validate that a user's supplied user name and password matches a value stored in a database, then you might want to redirect the user based on whether the user name and password are correct. If the login is valid, you can redirect the user to a welcome page using the `if` block. However, if the login was invalid, you can redirect the user to the login form and display an error message using the `else` block.

To use an if..else statement in a document:

1. Select File > New and then select Flash Document to create a new FLA file.

2. Select Frame 1 of the Timeline, and then type the following ActionScript in the Actions panel:

```
// create a string that holds AM/PM based on the time of day.
var amPm:String;
// no parameters pass to Date, so returns current date/time.
var current_date:Date = new Date();
// if current hour is greater than/equal to 12, sets amPm string to "PM".
if (current_date.getHours() >= 12) {
  amPm = "PM";
} else {
  amPm = "AM";
}
trace(amPm);
```

3. Select Control > Test Movie to test the ActionScript.

   In this code, you create a string that holds AM or PM based on the current time of day. If the current hour is greater than or equal to 12, the amPM string sets to PM. Finally, you trace the amPm string, and if the hour is greater than or equal to 12, PM is displayed. Otherwise, you'll see AM in the Output panel.

Using the if..else if statement

You can test for more than one condition using the `if..else if` conditional statement. You use the following syntax in an `if..else if` statement:

```
// else-if statement
if (condition) {
  // statements;
} else if (condition) {
  // statements;
} else {
  // statements;
}
```

You want to use an `if..else if` block in your Flash projects when you need to check a series of conditions. For example, if you want to display a different image on the screen based on the time of the day the user is visiting, you can create a series of `if` statements that determine if it's early morning, afternoon, evening, or night time. Then you can display an appropriate graphic.

The following code not only tests whether the value of x exceeds 20 but also tests whether the value of x is negative:

```
if (x > 20) {
  trace("x is > 20");
} else if (x < 0) {
  trace("x is negative");
}
```

To use an if..else if statement in a document:

1. Select File > New and then select Flash Document.

2. Select Frame 1 of the Timeline, and then type the following ActionScript in the Actions panel:

    ```
    var now_date:Date = new Date();
    var currentHour:Number = now_date.getHours();
    // if the current hour is less than 11AM...
    if (currentHour < 11) {
      trace("Good morning");
      // else..if the current hour is less than 3PM...
    } else if (currentHour < 15) {
      trace("Good afternoon");
      // else..if the current hour is less than 8PM...
    } else if (currentHour < 20) {
      trace("Good evening");
      // else the current hour is between 8PM and 11:59PM
    } else {
      trace("Good night");
    }
    ```

3. Select Control > Test Movie to test the ActionScript.

In this code, you create a string called `currentHour` that holds the current hour number (for example, if it's 6:19 pm, `currentHour` holds the number 10). You use the `getHours()` method of the Date class to get the current hour. Then you can use the `if..else if` statement to trace information to the Output panel, based on the number that returns. For more information, see the comments in the previous code snippet.

Using a switch statement

The `switch` statement creates a branching structure for ActionScript statements. Similar to the `if` statement, the `switch` statement tests a condition and executes statements if the condition returns a value of `true`.

When you use a `switch` statement, the `break` statement instructs Flash to skip the rest of the statements in that case block and jump to the first statement that follows the enclosing `switch` statement. If a case block doesn't contain a break statement, a condition called "fall through" occurs. In this situation, the following case statement also executes until a break statement is encountered or the `switch` statement ends. This behavior is demonstrated in the following example, where the first case statement doesn't contain a break statement and therefore both of the code blocks for the first two cases (A and B) execute.

All `switch` statements should include a `default` case. The `default` case should always be the last case on a `switch` statement and should also include a `break` statement to prevent a fall-through error if another case is added. For example, if the condition in the following example evaluates to A, both the statements for case A and B execute, because case A lacks a `break` statement. When a case falls through, it does not have a break statement, but includes a comment in the `break` statement's place, which you can see in the following example after case A. Use the following format when you write `switch` statements:

```
switch (condition) {
case A :
  // statements
  // falls through
case B :
  // statements
  break;
case Z :
  // statements
  break;
default :
  // statements
  break;
}
```

To use a switch statement in a document:

1. Select File > New and then select Flash Document.

2. Select Frame 1 of the Timeline, and then type the following ActionScript in the Actions panel:

```
var listenerObj:Object = new Object();
listenerObj.onKeyDown = function() {
  // Use the String.fromCharCode() method to return a string.
  switch (String.fromCharCode(Key.getAscii())) {
  case "A" :
    trace("you pressed A");
    break;
  case "a" :
    trace("you pressed a");
    break;
  case "E" :
  case "e" :
    /* E doesn't have a break statement, so this block executes if you
    press e or E. */
    trace("you pressed E or e");
    break;
  case "I" :
  case "i" :
    trace("you pressed I or i");
    break;
  default :
    /* If the key pressed isn't caught by any of the above cases,
    execute the default case here. */
    trace("you pressed some other key");
  }
};
Key.addListener(listenerObj);
```

3. Select Control > Test Movie to test the ActionScript.

   Type letters using the keyboard, including the a, e, or i key. When you type those three keys, you'll see the `trace` statements in the preceding ActionScript. The line of code creates a new object that you use as a listener for the Key class. You use this object to notify the `onKeyDown()` event when the user presses a key. The `Key.getAscii()` method returns the ASCII code of the last key that the user presses or releases, so you need to use the `String.fromCharCode()` method to return a string that contains the characters represented by the ASCII values in the parameters. Because "E" doesn't have a `break` statement, the block executes if the user presses the *e* or *E* key. If the user presses a key that isn't caught by any of the first three cases, the default case executes.

Using try..catch and try..catch..finally statements

Using try..catch..finally blocks lets you add error handling to your Flash applications. The try..catch..finally keywords let you enclose a block of code where an error can occur and respond to that error. If any code within the try code block throws an error (using the throw statement), control passes to the catch block, if one exists. Then control passes to the finally code block, if one exists. The optional finally block always executes, regardless of whether an error was thrown.

If code within the try block doesn't throw an error (that is, the try block completes normally), the code in the finally block still executes.

> **NOTE** The finally block executes even if the try block exits using a return statement

You write try..catch and try..catch..finally statements using the following format:

```
// try-catch
try {
  // statements
} catch (myError) {
  // statements
}

// try-catch-finally
try {
  // statements
} catch (myError) {
  // statements
} finally {
  // statements
}
```

Any time your code throws an error, you can write custom handlers to handle the error gracefully and take appropriate actions. You might need to try loading external data from a web service or text file or to display an error message to the end user. You can even use the catch block to try to connect to a web service that alerts an administrator that a particular error occurred, so he or she can make sure the application works properly.

To use the try..catch..finally block for data validation before dividing some numbers:

1. Select File > New and then select Flash Document.

2. Select Frame 1 of the Timeline, and then type the following ActionScript in the Actions panel:

```
var n1:Number = 7;
var n2:Number = 0;
try {
   if (n2 == 0) {
      throw new Error("Unable to divide by zero");
   }
   trace(n1/n2);
} catch (err:Error) {
   trace("ERROR! " + err.toString());
} finally {
   delete n1;
   delete n2;
}
```

3. Select Control > Test Movie to test the document.

4. The Output panel displays `Unable to divide by zero`.

5. Return to the authoring environment and change the following line of code:

```
var n2:Number = 0;
```

to

```
var n2:Number = 2;
```

6. Select Control > Enter to test the document again.

   If the value of n2 equals zero, an error is thrown and is caught by the `catch` block, which displays a message in the Output panel. If the value of y is not equal to zero, the Output panel displays the result of n1 divided by n2. The `finally` block executes regardless of whether an error occurs and deletes the values of the n1 and n2 variables from the Flash document.

You aren't limited to throwing new instances of the Error class when an error occurs. You could also extend the Error class to create your own custom errors, as demonstrated in the following example.

To create a custom error:

1. Select File > New and create a new ActionScript file.

2. Select File > Save As and name the file **DivideByZeroException.as**.

3. Type the following ActionScript into the Script pane:

```
// In DivideByZeroException.as:
class DivideByZeroException extends Error {
    var message:String = "Divide By Zero error";
}
```

4. Save the ActionScript file.

5. Create a new Flash document named **exception_test.fla** in the same directory as the ActionScript file, and then save the file.

6. Type the following ActionScript into the Actions panel in Frame 1 of the main Timeline:

```
var n1:Number = 7;
var n2:Number = 0;
try {
    if (n2 == 0) {
        throw new DivideByZeroException();
    } else if (n2 < 0) {
        throw new Error("n2 cannot be less than zero");
    } else {
        trace(n1/n2);
    }
} catch (err:DivideByZeroException) {
    trace(err.toString());
} catch (err:Error) {
    trace("An unknown error occurred; " + err.toString());
}
```

7. Save the Flash document and select Control > Test Movie to test the file in the test environment.

Because the value of n2 equals 0, Flash throws your custom DivideByZeroException error class and displays Divide By Zero error in the Output panel. If you change the value of n2 in line two from 0 to -1, and retest the Flash document, you would see An unknown error occurred; n2 cannot be less than zero in the Output panel. Setting the value of n2 to any number greater than 0 causes the result of the division to appear in the Output panel. For more information on creating custom classes, see Chapter 7, "Classes," on page 231.

About the conditional operator and alternative syntax

If you like shortcuts, you can use the conditional (?:) operator, also called *conditional expressions*. The conditional operator lets you convert simple if..else statements into a single line of code. The operator helps decrease the amount of code you write while accomplishing the same thing, but it also tends to make your ActionScript more difficult to read.

The following condition is written in long hand, and checks whether the variable numTwo is greater than zero, and returns the result of numOne/numTwo or a string of carrot:

```
var numOne:Number = 8;
var numTwo:Number = 5;
if (numTwo > 0) {
  trace(numOne / numTwo); // 1.6
} else {
  trace("carrot");
}
```

Using a conditional expression, you would write the same code using this format:

```
var numOne:Number = 8;
var numTwo:Number = 0;
trace((numTwo > 0) ? numOne/numTwo : "carrot");
```

As you can see, the shortened syntax reduces readability, and so it is not preferable. If you must use conditional operators, place the leading condition (before the question mark [?]) inside parentheses. This helps improve the readability of your ActionScript. The following code is an example of ActionScript with improved readability:

```
var numOne:Number;
(numOne >= 5) ? numOne : -numOne;
```

You can write a conditional statement that returns a Boolean value, as the following example shows:

```
if (cartArr.length > 0) {
  return true;
} else {
  return false;
}
```

However, compared with the previous code, the ActionScript in the following example is preferable:

```
return (cartArr.length > 0);
```

The second snippet is shorter and has fewer expressions to evaluate. It's easier to read and understand.

When you write complex conditions, it is good form to use parentheses [( )] to group conditions. If you do not use parentheses, you (or others working with your ActionScript) might run into operator precedence errors. For more information on operator precedence, see "About operator precedence and associativity" on page 183.

For example, the following code does not use parentheses around the condition:

```
if (fruit -- "apple" && veggie == "leek") {}
```

The following code uses good form by adding parentheses around conditions:

```
if ((fruit == "apple") && (veggie == "leek")) {}
```

Repeating actions using loops

ActionScript can repeat an action a specified number of times or while a specific condition exists. Loops let you repeat a series of statements when a particular condition is true. There are four types of loops in ActionScript: for loops, for..in loops, while loops, and do..while loops. Each type of loop behaves somewhat differently, and each one is useful for different purposes.

Most loops use some kind of counter to control how many times the loop executes. Each execution of a loop is called an *iteration*. You can declare a variable and write a statement that increases or decreases the variable each time the loop executes. In the for action, the counter and the statement that increments the counter are part of the action.

Loop	Description
for loops	Repeat an action using a built-in counter.
for..in loops	Iterate over the children of a movie clip or object.
while loops	Repeat an action while a condition exists.
do..while loops	Similar to while loops, except the expression evaluates at the bottom of the code block, so the loop always runs at least once.

The most common type of loop is the `for` loop, which loops over a block of code a predefined number of times. For example, if you have an array of items, and you want to perform a series of statements on each item in the array, you would use a `for` loop and loop from 0 to the number of items in the array. Another type of loop is the `for..in` loop, which can be very useful when you want to loop over each name/value pair within an object and then perform some type of action. This can be very useful when you are debugging your Flash projects and want to display the values that load from external sources, such as web services or external text/XML files. The final two types of loops (`while` and `do..while`) are useful when you want to loop over a series of statements but you don't necessarily know how many times you need to loop. In this case you can use a `while` loop that loops as long as a certain condition is true.

ActionScript can repeat an action a specified number of times or while a specific condition exists. Use the `while`, `do..while`, `for`, and `for..in` actions to create loops. This section contains general information on these loops. See the following procedures for more information on each of these loops.

To repeat an action while a condition exists:

- Use the `while` statement.

  A `while` loop evaluates an expression and executes the code in the body of the loop if the expression is `true`. After each statement in the body is executed, the expression is evaluated again. In the following example, the loop executes four times:

  ```
  var i:Number = 4;
  while (i > 0) {
      myClip.duplicateMovieClip("newMC" + i, i, {_x:i*20, _y:i*20});
      i--;
  }
  ```

  You can use the `do..while` statement to create the same kind of loop as a `while` loop. In a `do..while` loop, the expression is evaluated at the bottom of the code block so that the loop always runs at least once.

  This is shown in the following example:

  ```
  var i:Number = 4;
  do {
      myClip.duplicateMovieClip("newMC" + i, i, {_x:i*20, _y:i*20});
      i--;
  } while (i > 0);
  ```

  For more information on the `while` statement, see "Using while loops" on page 164.

To repeat an action using a built-in counter:

■ Use the for statement.

Most loops use some kind of counter to control how many times the loop executes. Each execution of a loop is called an *iteration*. You can declare a variable and write a statement that increases or decreases the variable each time the loop executes. In the for action, the counter and the statement that increments the counter are part of the action.

In the following example, the first expression (var i:Number = 4) is the initial expression that is evaluated before the first iteration. The second expression (i > 0) is the condition that is checked each time before the loop runs. The third expression (i--) is called the *post expression* and is evaluated each time after the loop runs.

```
for (var i:Number = 4; i > 0; i--) {
  myClip.duplicateMovieClip("newMC" + i, i, {_x:i*20, _y:i*20});
}
```

For more information on the for statement, see "Using for loops" on page 161.

To loop through the children of a movie clip or an object:

■ Use the for..in statement.

Children include other movie clips, functions, objects, and variables. The following example uses the trace statement to print its results in the Output panel:

```
var myObject:Object = {name:'Joe', age:25, city:'San Francisco'};
var propertyName:String;
for (propertyName in myObject) {
  trace("myObject has the property: " + propertyName + ", with the
  value: " + myObject[propertyName]);
}
```

This example produces the following results in the Output panel:

```
myObject has the property: name, with the value: Joe
myObject has the property: age, with the value: 25
myObject has the property: city, with the value: San Francisco
```

You might want your script to iterate over a particular type of child—for example, over only movie clip children. You can do this using for..in with the typeof operator. In the following example, a child movie clip instance (called instance2) is inside a movie clip instance on the Stage. Add the following ActionScript to Frame 1 of the Timeline:

```
for (var myName in this) {
  if (typeof (this[myName]) == "movieclip") {
    trace("I have a movie clip child named " + myName);
  }
}
```

For more information on the `for..in` statement, see "Using for..in loops" on page 162.

> **WARNING**
> Iterations in Flash execute very quickly in the Flash Player, but loops depend heavily on the processor. The more iterations a loop has and the more statements executed within each block, the more processor resources will be consumed. Poorly written loops can cause performance problems and stability issues.

For more information on each statement, see the individual sections that follow in this chapter, such as "Using while loops" on page 164, and their respective entries in the *ActionScript 2.0 Language Reference* in Flash Help.

About creating and ending loops

The following example shows a simple array of month names. A `for` loop iterates from 0 to the number of items in the array and displays each item in the Output panel.

```
var monthArr:Array = new Array("Jan", "Feb", "Mar", "Apr", "May", "Jun",
  "Jul", "Aug", "Sep", "Oct", "Nov", "Dec");
var i:Number;
for (i = 0; i < monthArr.length; i++) {
  trace(monthArr[i]);
}
```

When you work with arrays, whether they're simple or complex, you need to be aware of a condition called an *infinite loop*. An infinite loop, as its name suggests, is a loop with no end condition. This causes real problems—crashing your Flash application, causing your Flash document to stop responding in a web browser, or causing very inconsistent behavior of your Flash document. The following code is an example of an infinite loop:

```
// BAD CODE- creates an infinite loop
// USE AT OWN RISK!
var i:Number;
for (i = 0; i < 10; i--) {
  trace(i);
}
```

The value of i is initialized to 0 and the end condition is met when i is greater than or equal to 10 and after each iteration the value of i is decremented. You can probably see the obvious error immediately: if the value of i decreases after each loop iteration, the end condition is never met. The results vary on each computer you run it on, and the speed at which the code fails depends on the speed of the CPU and other factors. For example, the loop executes about 142,620 times before displaying an error message on a given computer.

The following error message is displayed in a dialog box:

```
A script in this movie is causing Flash Player to run slowly. If it
  continues to run, your computer may become unresponsive. Do you want to
  abort the script?
```

When you work with loops (and especially `while` and `do..while` loops), always make sure that the loop can exit properly and does not end up in an infinite loop.

For more information on controlling loops, see "Using a switch statement" on page 151.

Using for loops

The `for` loop lets you iterate over a variable for a specific range of values. A `for` loop is useful when you know exactly how many times you need to repeat a series of ActionScript statements. This can be useful if you want to duplicate a movie clip on the Stage a certain number of times or to loop over an array and perform a task on each item in that array. A `for` loop repeats an action using a built-in counter. In a `for` statement, the counter and the statement that increments the counter are all part of the `for` statement. You write the `for` statement using the following basic format:

```
for (init; condition; update) {
  // statements;
}
```

You must supply three expressions to a `for` statement: a variable that is set to an initial value, a conditional statement that determines when the looping ends, and an expression that changes the value of the variable with each loop. For example, the following code loops five times. The value of the variable `i` starts at 0 and ends at 4, and the output are the numbers 0 through 4, each on its own line.

```
var i:Number;
for (i = 0; i < 5; i++) {
  trace(i);
}
```

In the next example, the first expression (`i = 0`) is the initial expression that evaluates before the first iteration. The second expression (`i < 5`) is the condition that you check each time before the loop runs. The third expression (`i++`) is called the *post expression* and is evaluated each time after the loop runs.

To create a for loop:

1. Select File > New and then select Flash Document.

2. Create a movie clip on the Stage.

3. Right-click the movie clip symbol in the Library panel and select Linkage from the context menu.

4. Select the Export for ActionScript check box, and type **libraryLinkageClassName** in the Class text input field. Click OK.

5. Select Frame 1 of the Timeline, and then type the following ActionScript in the Actions panel:

```
var i:Number;
for (i = 0; i < 5; i++) {
  this.attachMovie("libraryLinkageClassName", "clip" + i + "_mc", i,
  {_x:(i * 100)});
}
```

6. Select Control > Test Movie to test the code in Flash Player.

Notice how five movie clips duplicate across the top of the Stage. This ActionScript duplicates the movie clip symbol in the library and repositions the clips on the Stage at *x* coordinates of 0, 100, 200, 300 and 400 pixels. The loop executes five times, with the variable i assigned a value of 0 through 4. On the last iteration of the loop, the value of i increments to 4 and the second expression (i < 5) is no longer true, which causes the loop to exit.

Remember to include a space following each expression in a `for` statement. For more information, see the %{for statement}% in the *ActionScript 2.0 Language Reference* in Flash Help.

Using for..in loops

Use the `for..in` statement to loop through (or *iterate* through) the children of a movie clip, properties of an object, or elements of an array. Children, referenced previously, include other movie clips, functions, objects, and variables. Common uses of the `for..in` loop include looping over instances on a timeline or looping over the key/value pairs within an object. Looping over objects can be an effective way to debug applications because it lets you see what data returns from web services or external documents such as text or XML files.

For example, you can use a `for...in` loop to iterate through the properties of a generic object (object properties are not kept in any particular order, so properties appear in an unpredictable order):

```
var myObj:Object = {x:20, y:30};
for (var i:String in myObj) {
  trace(i + ": " + myObj[i]);
}
```

This code outputs the following in the Output panel:

```
x: 20
y: 30
```

You can also iterate through the elements of an array:

```
var myArray:Array = ["one", "two", "three"];
for (var i:String in myArray) {
  trace(myArray[i]);
}
```

This code outputs the following in the Output panel:

```
three
two
one
```

For more information on objects and properties, see "Object data type" on page 81.

| NOTE | You cannot iterate through the properties of an object if it is an instance of a custom class, unless the class is a dynamic class. Even with instances of dynamic classes, you are able to iterate only through properties that are added dynamically. |

| NOTE | The curly braces ({ }) used to enclose the block of statements to be executed by the `for..in` statement are not necessary if only one statement executes. |

The following example uses `for..in` to iterate over the properties of an object:

To create a for loop:

1. Select File > New and then select Flash Document.

2. Select Frame 1 of the Timeline, and then type the following ActionScript in the Actions panel:

```
var myObj:Object = {name:"Tara", age:27, city:"San Francisco"};
var i:String;
for (i in myObj) {
  trace("myObj." + i + " = " + myObj[i]);
}
```

3. Select Control > Test Movie to test the code in Flash Player.

When you test the SWF file, you should see the following text in the Output panel:

```
myObj.name = Tara
myObj.age = 27
myObj.city = San Francisco
```

If you write a `for..in` loop in a class file (an external ActionScript file), instance members are not available within the loop, but static members are. However, if you write a `for..in` loop in a FLA file for an instance of the class, instance members are available but static members are not. For more information on writing class files, see Chapter 7, "Classes," on page 231. For more information, see the %{for..in statement}% in the *ActionScript 2.0 Language Reference* in Flash Help.

Using while loops

Use the `while` statement to repeat an action while a condition exists, similar to an `if` statement that repeats as long as the condition is `true`.

A `while` loop evaluates an expression and executes the code in the body of the loop if the expression is `true`. If the condition evaluates to `true`, a statement or series of statements runs before looping back to evaluate the condition again. When the condition evaluates to `false`, the statement or series of statements is skipped and the loop ends. Using `while` loops can be very useful when you aren't sure of how many times you'll need to loop over a block of code.

For example, the following code traces numbers to the Output panel:

```
var i:Number = 0;
while (i < 5) {
    trace(i);
    i++;
}
```

You see the following numbers traced to the Output panel:

```
0
1
2
3
4
```

One disadvantage of using a `while` loop instead of a `for` loop is that infinite loops are easier to write with `while` loops. The `for` loop example code does not compile if you omit the expression that increments the counter variable, but the `while` loop example does compile if you omit that step. Without the expression that increments `i`, the loop becomes an infinite loop.

To create and use a `while` loop in a FLA file, follow this example.

To create a while loop:

1. Select File > New and then select Flash Document.

2. Open the Components panel and drag a DataSet component onto the Stage.

3. Open the Property inspector (Window > Properties > Properties) and type the instance name **users_ds**.

4. Select Frame 1 of the Timeline, and then type the following ActionScript in the Actions panel:

```
var users_ds:mx.data.components.DataSet;
//
users_ds.addItem({name:"Irving", age:34});
users_ds.addItem({name:"Christopher", age:48});
users_ds.addItem({name:"Walter", age:23});
//
users_ds.first();
while (users_ds.hasNext()) {
  trace("name:" + users_ds.currentItem["name"] + ", age:" +
  users_ds.currentItem["age"]);
  users_ds.next();
}
```

5. Select Control > Test Movie to test the document.

The following information is displayed in the Output panel:

```
name:Irving, age:34
name:Christopher, age:48
name:Walter, age:23
```

For more information, see the %{while statement}% in the *ActionScript 2.0 Language Reference* in Flash Help.

About do..while loops

You can use the do..while statement to create the same kind of loop as a while loop. However, the expression is evaluated at the bottom of the code block in a do..while loop (it's checked after the code block executes), so the loop always runs at least one time. The statements execute only if the condition evaluates to true.

The following code shows a simple example of a do..while loop that generates output even though the condition is not met.

```
var i:Number = 5;
do {
  trace(i);
  i++;
} while (i < 5);
// Output: 5
```

When you use loops, you need to avoid writing infinite loops. If the condition in a do..while loop continuously evaluates to true, you create an infinite loop that displays a warning or crashes Flash Player. Use a for loop instead if you know how many times you want to loop. For more information on and examples of %{do..while statement}%, see the *ActionScript 2.0 Language Reference* in Flash Help.

Using nested loops in your ActionScript

The following example demonstrates how to make an array of objects and display each of the values in the nested structure. This example shows you how to use the `for` loop to loop through each item in the array and how to use the `for..in` loop to iterate through each key/value pair in the nested objects.

Nesting a loop within another loop:

1. Create a new Flash document.

2. Select File > Save As and name the document **loops.fla**.

3. Add the following code to Frame 1 of the Timeline:

```
var myArr:Array = new Array();
myArr[0] = {name:"One", value:1};
myArr[1] = {name:"Two", value:2};
//
var i:Number;
var item:String;
for (i = 0; i < myArr.length; i++) {
  trace(i);
  for (item in myArr[i]) {
    trace(item + ": " + myArr[i][item]);
  }
  trace("");
}
```

4. Select Control > Test Movie to test your code.

   The following is displayed in the Output panel.

```
0
name: One
value: 1

1
name: Two
value: 2
```

   You know how many items are in the array, so you can loop over each item using a simple `for` loop. Because each object in the array can have different name/value pairs, you can use a `for..in` loop to iterate over each value and display the results in the Output panel.

About arrays

An *array* is an object whose properties are identified by numbers representing their positions in the structure. Essentially, an array is a list of items. It's important to remember that each element in an array doesn't have to be the same data type. You can mix numbers, dates, strings, and objects and even add a nested array at each array index.

The following example is a simple array of month names.

```
var myArr:Array = new Array();
myArr[0] = "January";
myArr[1] = "February";
myArr[2] = "March";
myArr[3] = "April";
```

The previous array of month names can also be rewritten as follows:

```
var myArr:Array = new Array("January", "February", "March", "April");
```

Or, you can use shorthand syntax, as follows:

```
var myArr:Array = ["January", "February", "March", "April"];
```

An array is like a structure for data. An array is like an office building, where each floor contains a different piece of data (such as *accounting* on floor 3, and *engineering* on floor 5). As such, you can store different kinds of data in a single array, including other arrays. Each floor of this building can contain multiple kinds of content (*executives* and *accounting* might share floor 3).

An array contains *elements*, which are equivalent to each floor of the building. Each element has a numeric position (the *index*), which is how you refer to each element's position in the array. This is similar to how each floor in a building has a floor number. Each element can either hold a piece of data (which could be a number, string, Boolean value, or even an array or object) or be empty.

You can also control and modify the array itself. For example, you might want to move the engineering department to the basement of the building. Arrays let you move values around, and they let you change the size of the array (say, renovate the building and add more floors or remove floors). As such, you can add or remove elements and move values to different elements.

Therefore, the building (the array) contains floors (the elements), which are numbered floors (the index), and each floor contains one or more departments (the values).

For more information on modifying arrays, see "About modifying arrays" on page 170. For information on using arrays and about indexes, see "Using arrays" on page 168. For information on adding and removing elements, see "About adding and removing elements" on page 172. For information on the array access operator, see "Using dot and array access operators" on page 188.

You can find a sample source file, array.fla, in the Samples folder on your hard disk. This sample illustrates array manipulation using ActionScript. The code in the sample creates an array and sorts, adds, and removes items of two List components. Find the sample file in the following directories:

■ In Windows, browse to *boot drive*\Program Files\Macromedia\Flash 8\Samples and Tutorials\Samples\ActionScript\Arrays.

■ On the Macintosh, browse to *Macintosh HD*/Applications/Macromedia Flash 8/Samples and Tutorials/Samples/ActionScript/Arrays.

Using arrays

There are several different ways you can use arrays in your work. You can use them to store lists of objects, such as a bunch of returned items. If you load data from remote web servers, you might even receive data as an array of nested objects. Often, arrays contain data in a similar format. For example, if you build an audio application in Flash, you might have a user's playlist stored as an array of song information, stored in objects. Each object contains the song name, artist name, song duration, location of a sound file (such as an MP3), or any other information that you might need to associate with a particular file.

The location of an item in an array is called the *index*. All arrays are zero-based, which means that the first element in the array is [0], the second element is [1], and so on.

There are different kinds of arrays, which you'll discover in the following sections. The most common arrays use a numerical index to look up a particular item in an *indexed array*. The second kind of array is called an *associative array* and uses a text index instead of a numerical index to look up information. For more information on common arrays, see "About arrays" on page 167. For more information on associative arrays, see "Creating associative arrays" on page 176. For more information on multidimensional arrays, see "Creating multidimensional arrays" on page 173. For information on the array access operator, see "Using dot and array access operators" on page 188.

The built-in Array class lets you access and manipulate arrays. To create an Array object, you use the constructor `new Array()` or the array access operator (`[]`). To access the elements of an array, you also use the array access (`[]`) operator. The next example uses an indexed array.

To use arrays in your code:

1. Create a new Flash document, and save it as **basicArrays.fla**.

2. Add the following ActionScript to Frame 1 of the Timeline:

```
// define a new array
var myArr:Array = new Array();
// define values at two indexes
myArr[1] = "value1";
myArr[0] = "value0";
// iterate over the items in the array
var i:String;
for (i in myArr) {
  // trace the key/value pairs
  trace("key: " + i + ", value: " + myArr[i]);
}
```

In the first line of ActionScript, you define a new array to hold the values. Then, you define data (value0 and value1) at two indexes of the array. You use a for..in loop to iterate over each of the items in that array and display the key/value pairs in the Output panel using a trace statement.

3. Select Control > Test Movie to test your code.

The following text is displayed in the Output panel:

```
key: 0, value: value0
key: 1, value: value1
```

For more information on for..in loops, see "Using for..in loops" on page 162.

For information on how to create different kinds of arrays, see the following sections:

- "Creating indexed arrays" on page 172
- "Creating multidimensional arrays" on page 173
- "Creating associative arrays" on page 176

You can find a sample source file, array.fla, in the Samples folder on your hard disk. This sample illustrates array manipulation using ActionScript. The code in the sample creates an array and sorts, adds, and removes items of two List components. Find the sample file in the following directories:

- In Windows, browse to *boot drive*\Program Files\Macromedia\Flash 8\Samples and Tutorials\Samples\ActionScript\Arrays.
- On the Macintosh, browse to *Macintosh HD*/Applications/Macromedia Flash 8/Samples and Tutorials/Samples/ActionScript/Arrays.

About modifying arrays

You can also control and modify the array using ActionScript. You can move values around an array, or you can change the size of the array. For example, if you want to exchange data at two indexes in an array, you can use the following code:

```
var buildingArr:Array = new Array();
buildingArr[2] = "Accounting";
buildingArr[4] = "Engineering";
trace(buildingArr); // undefined,undefined,Accounting,undefined,Engineering

var temp_item:String = buildingArr[2];
buildingArr[2] = buildingArr[4];
buildingArr[4] = temp_item;
trace(buildingArr); // undefined,undefined,Engineering,undefined,Accounting
```

You might wonder why you need to create a temporary variable in the previous example. If you copied the contents of array index 4 into array index 2 and vice versa, the original contents of array index 2 would be lost. When you copy the value from one of the array indexes into a temporary variable, you can save the value and safely copy it back later in your code. For example, if you use the following code instead, you can see that the value of array index 2 (Accounting) has been lost. Now you have two engineering teams but no accountants.

```
// wrong way (no temporary variable)
buildingArr[2] = buildingArr[4];
buildingArr[4] = buildingArr[2];
trace(buildingArr); //
  undefined,undefined,Engineering,undefined,Engineering
```

You can find a sample source file, array.fla, in the Samples folder on your hard disk. This sample illustrates array manipulation using ActionScript. The code in the sample creates an array and sorts, adds, and removes items of two List components. Find the sample file in the following directories:

- In Windows, browse to *boot drive*\Program Files\Macromedia\Flash 8\Samples and Tutorials\Samples\ActionScript\Arrays.

- On the Macintosh, browse to *Macintosh HD*/Applications/Macromedia Flash 8/Samples and Tutorials/Samples/ActionScript/Arrays.

About referencing and finding length

When you work with arrays, you often need to know how many items exist in the array. This can be very useful when writing `for` loops that iterate through every element in the array and execute a series of statements. You can see an example in the following snippet:

```
var monthArr:Array = new Array("Jan", "Feb", "Mar", "Apr", "May", "Jun",
  "Jul", "Aug", "Sep", "Oct", "Nov", "Dec");
trace(monthArr); // Jan,Feb,Mar,Apr,May,Jun,Jul,Aug,Sep,Oct,Nov,Dec
trace(monthArr.length); // 12
var i:Number;
for (i = 0; i < monthArr.length; i++) {
  monthArr[i] = monthArr[i].toUpperCase();
}
trace(monthArr); // JAN,FEB,MAR,APR,MAY,JUN,JUL,AUG,SEP,OCT,NOV,DEC
```

In the previous example, you create an array and populate it with month names. The contents are displayed, and also the array's length. A `for` loop iterates over each item in the array and converts the value to uppercase, and the array contents are displayed again.

In the following ActionScript, if you create an element at array index 5 in an array, the length of the array returns 6 (because the array is zero based), and not the actual number of items in the array as you might expect:

```
var myArr:Array = new Array();
myArr[5] = "five";
trace(myArr.length); // 6
trace(myArr); // undefined,undefined,undefined,undefined,undefined,five
```

For more information on `for` loops, see "Using for loops" on page 161. For information on the array access operator, see "Using dot and array access operators" on page 188.

You can find a sample source file, array.fla, in the Samples folder on your hard disk. This sample illustrates array manipulation using ActionScript. The code in the sample creates an array and sorts, adds, and removes items of two List components. Find the sample file in the following directories:

- In Windows, browse to *boot drive*\Program Files\Macromedia\Flash 8\Samples and Tutorials\Samples\ActionScript\Arrays.

- On the Macintosh, browse to *Macintosh HD*/Applications/Macromedia Flash 8/Samples and Tutorials/Samples/ActionScript/Arrays.

About adding and removing elements

An array contains elements and each element has a numeric position (the index), which is how you refer to each element's position in the array. Each element can either hold a piece of data or be empty. An element can hold the following data: a number, string, Boolean, or even an array or object.

When you create elements in an array, you should create the indexes sequentially whenever possible. This helps you when you debug your applications. In "About referencing and finding length" on page 171, you saw that if you assign a single value in an array at index 5, the array length returns as 6. This causes five undefined values to be inserted into the array.

The following example demonstrates how to create a new array, delete an item at a particular index, and add and replace data at an index in an array:

```
var monthArr:Array = new Array("Jan", "Feb", "Mar", "Apr", "May", "Jun",
  "Jul", "Aug", "Sep", "Oct", "Nov", "Dec");
delete monthArr[5];
trace(monthArr); // Jan,Feb,Mar,Apr,May,undefined,Jul,Aug,Sep,Oct,Nov,Dec
trace(monthArr.length); // 12
monthArr[5] = "JUN";
trace(monthArr); // Jan,Feb,Mar,Apr,May,JUN,Jul,Aug,Sep,Oct,Nov,Dec
```

Even though you deleted the item at array index 5, the array length is still 12, and the item at array index 5 changed to a blank string instead of disappearing completely.

You can find a sample source file, array.fla, in the Samples folder on your hard disk. This sample illustrates array manipulation using ActionScript. The code in the sample creates an array and sorts, adds, and removes items of two List components. Find the sample file in the following directories:

- In Windows, browse to *boot drive*\Program Files\Macromedia\Flash 8\Samples and Tutorials\Samples\ActionScript\Arrays.

- On the Macintosh, browse to *Macintosh HD*/Applications/Macromedia Flash 8/Samples and Tutorials/Samples/ActionScript/Arrays.

Creating indexed arrays

Indexed arrays store a series of one or more values. You can look up items by their position in the array, which you might have done in earlier sections. The first index is always the number 0, and the index increments by one for each subsequent element that you add to the array. You can create an indexed array by calling the Array class constructor or by initializing the array with an array literal. You create arrays using the Array constructor and an array literal in the next example.

To create an indexed array:

1. Create a new Flash document, and save it as **indexArray.fla**.

2. Add the following ActionScript to Frame 1 of the Timeline:

```
var myArray:Array = new Array();
myArray.push("one");
myArray.push("two");
myArray.push("three");
trace(myArray); // one,two,three
```

In the first line of ActionScript, you define a new array to hold the values.

3. Select Control > Test Movie to test your code.

The following text is displayed in the Output panel:

```
one,two,three
```

4. Return to the authoring tool, and delete the code in the Actions panel.

5. Add the following ActionScript to Frame 1 of the Timeline:

```
var myArray:Array = ["one", "two", "three"];
trace(myArray); // one,two,three
```

In this code you use the array literal to define a new array for your code. This code is the equivalent of the ActionScript you wrote in step 2. When you test the code, you see the same output appear in the Output panel.

Creating multidimensional arrays

In ActionScript, you can implement arrays as *nested arrays* that are essentially arrays of arrays. Nested arrays, also known as *multidimensional arrays*, can be thought of as matrices or grids. Therefore, when you are programming, you might use multidimensional arrays to model these kinds of structures. For example, a chess board is a grid of eight columns and rows; you could model the chess board as an array that contains eight elements, each of which is also an array that contains eight elements.

For example, consider a list of tasks that is stored as an indexed array of strings:

```
var tasks:Array = ["wash dishes", "take out trash"];
```

If you want to store a separate list of tasks for each day of the week, you can create a multidimensional array with one element for each day of the week. Each element contains an indexed array that stores the list of tasks.

> **CAUTION**
>
> When you use the array access operator, the ActionScript compiler cannot check whether the accessed element is a valid property of the object.

To create a basic multidimensional array and retrieve elements from the array:

1. Create a new Flash document, and save it as **multiArray1.fla**.

2. Add the following ActionScript to Frame 1 of the Timeline:

```
var twoDArray:Array = new Array(new Array("one","two"), new
  Array("three", "four"));
trace(twoDArray);
```

   This array, twoDArray, consists of two array elements. These elements are themselves arrays consisting of two elements. In this case, twoDArray is the main array that contains two nested arrays.

3. Select Control > Test Movie to test the code. You see the following display in the Output panel.

```
one,two,three,four
```

4. Return to the authoring tool and open the Actions panel. Comment out the trace statement, as shown below:

```
// trace(twoDArray);
```

5. Add the following ActionScript at the end of your code on Frame 1 of the Timeline:

```
trace(twoDArray[0][0]); // one
trace(twoDArray[1][1]); // four
```

   To retrieve elements of a multidimensional array, you use multiple array access ([]) operators after the name of the top-level array. The first [] refers to the index of the top-level array. Subsequent array access operators refer to elements of nested arrays.

6. Select Control > Test Movie to test the code. You see the following display in the Output panel.

```
one
four
```

You can use nested for loops to create multidimensional arrays. The next example shows you how.

To create a multidimensional array using a for loop:

1. Create a new Flash document, and save it as **multiArray2.fla**.

2. Add the following ActionScript to Frame 1 of the Timeline:

```
var gridSize:Number = 3;
var mainArr:Array = new Array(gridSize);
var i:Number;
var j:Number;
for (i = 0; i < gridSize; i++) {
  mainArr[i] = new Array(gridSize);
  for (j = 0; j < gridSize; j++) {
    mainArr[i][j] = "[" + i + "][" + j + "]";
  }
}
trace(mainArr);
```

This ActionScript creates a 3 x 3 array and sets the value of each array node to its index. Then you trace the array (mainArr).

3. Select Control > Test Movie to test the code.

You see the following display in the Output panel:

```
[0][0],[0][1],[0][2],[1][0],[1][1],[1][2],[2][0],[2][1],[2][2]
```

You can also use nested for loops to iterate through the elements of a multidimensional array, as shown in the next example.

To use a for loop to iterate a multidimensional array:

1. Create a new Flash document, and save it as **multiArray3.fla**.

2. Add the following ActionScript to Frame 1 of the Timeline:

```
// from previous example
var gridSize:Number = 3;
var mainArr:Array = new Array(gridSize);
var i:Number;
var j:Number;
for (i = 0; i < gridSize; i++) {
  mainArr[i] = new Array(gridSize);
  for (j = 0; j < gridSize; j++) {
    mainArr[i][j] = "[" + i + "][" + j + "]";
  }
}
```

In this code, seen in the previous example, the outer loop iterates through each element of mainArray. The inner loop iterates through each nested array and outputs each array node.

3. Add the following ActionScript to Frame 1 of the Timeline, following the code you entered in step 2:

```
// iterate through elements
var outerArrayLength:Number = mainArr.length;
for (i = 0; i < outerArrayLength; i++) {
  var innerArrayLength:Number = mainArr[i].length;
  for (j = 0; j < innerArrayLength; j++) {
    trace(mainArr[i][j]);
  }
}
```

This ActionScript iterates through the elements of the array. You use the `length` property of each array as the loop condition.

4. Select Control > Test Movie to view the elements that are displayed in the Output panel. You will see the following in the Output panel:

```
[0][0]
[0][1]
[0][2]
[1][0]
[1][1]
[1][2]
[2][0]
[2][1]
[2][2]
```

For information on using arrays, see "Using arrays" on page 168. For information on array elements, see "About adding and removing elements" on page 172. For information on the array access operator, see "Using dot and array access operators" on page 188.

Creating associative arrays

An associative array, which is like an object, is made of unordered *keys* and *values*. Associative arrays use keys instead of a numeric index to organize stored values. Each key is a unique string, and it is associated with and used to access one value. That value can be a data type such as Number, Array, Object, and so on. When you create code to find a value that's associated with a key, you are indexing or performing a *lookup*. This is what you will probably use associative arrays for most often.

The association between a key and value is commonly referred to as its *binding;* the key and value are *mapped* to each other. For example, a contact book might be considered an associative array, where the names are the keys and email addresses are the values

> **NOTE** Associative arrays are unordered collections of key and value pairs. Your code should not expect the keys of an associative array to be in a specific order.

When you use associative arrays, you can call the array element you need using a string rather than a number, which is often easier to remember. The downside is that these arrays aren't as useful in a loop because they do not use numbers as the index value. They *are* useful when you need to look up by key values frequently. For example, if you had an array of names and ages that you needed to refer to a lot, you might use an associative array.

The following example demonstrates how to create an object and define a series of properties in an associative array.

To create a simple associative array:

1. Create a new Flash document.

2. Type the following ActionScript on Frame 1 of the Timeline:

```
// Define the object to use as an associative array.
var someObj:Object = new Object();
// Define a series of properties.
someObj.myShape = "Rectangle";
someObj.myW = 480;
someObj.myH = 360;
someObj.myX = 100;
someObj.myY = 200;
someObj.myAlpha = 72;
someObj.myColor = 0xDFDFDF;
// Display a property using dot operator and array access syntax.
trace(someObj.myAlpha); // 72
trace(someObj["myAlpha"]); // 72
```

The first line of ActionScript defines a new object (someObj) that you use as the associative array. Following this, you define a series of properties in someObj. Finally, you display a property that you select using both dot operator and array access syntax.

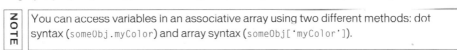

NOTE: You can access variables in an associative array using two different methods: dot syntax (someObj.myColor) and array syntax (someObj['myColor']).

3. Select Control > Test Movie to test your ActionScript.

The Output panel displays the number 72 twice, which represents both of the alpha levels that you traced.

There are two ways to create associative arrays in ActionScript 2.0:

■ Use an Object constructor

■ Use an Array constructor

Both of these ways are demonstrated in upcoming examples.

NOTE: The previous example used an Object constructor to create an associative array.

If you use the Object constructor to create an associative array, you can take advantage of initializing your array with an object literal. An instance of the Object class, also called a generic object, is functionally identical to an associative array. In fact, Object instances are essentially associative arrays. You might use associative arrays for dictionary-like functionality, when it's more convenient to have string keys rather than numerical indices. Each property name of the generic object serves as the key that provides access to a stored value. For more information on literals, see "About literals" on page 134. For more information on classes, see Chapter 7, "Classes," on page 231.

To create an associative array using an Object constructor:

1. Create a new Flash document, and save it as **assocArray.fla**.

2. Add the following ActionScript to Frame 1 of the Timeline:

```
var monitorInfo:Object = {type:"Flat Panel", resolution:"1600 x 1200"};
trace(monitorInfo["type"] + ", " + monitorInfo["resolution"]);
```

This code creates an associative array called monitorInfo, and uses an object literal to initialize the array with two key/value pairs.

> **NOTE** If you do not need to initialize the array at declaration time, you can use the Object constructor to create the array:

```
var monitorInfo:Object = new Object();
```

3. Select Control > Test Movie.

The Output panel displays the following text:

```
Flat Panel, 1600 x 1200
```

4. Add the following ActionScript to Frame 1 of the Timeline, following the code you entered previously:

```
monitorInfo["aspectRatio"] = "16:10";
monitorInfo.colors = "16.7 million";
trace(monitorInfo["aspectRatio"] + ", " + monitorInfo.colors);
```

After you use using either an object literal or the Object class constructor to create the array, you can add new values to the array using either the bracket operator ([ ]) or the dot operator (.), as demonstrated in this code. The code you just typed adds two new values to monitorInfo array.

5. Select Control > Test Movie.

The Output panel displays the following text:

```
16:10, 16.7 million
```

Note that a key can contain a space character. This is possible with the bracket operator, but generates an error if you attempt this with the dot operator. Using spaces in your key names is not recommended. For more information on bracket operators and dot operators, see "About operators" on page 180. For more information on well-formatted code, see "Formatting ActionScript syntax" on page 777.

The second way to create an associative array is to use the Array constructor and then use either the bracket operator ([ ]) or the dot operator (.) to add key and value pairs to the array. If you declare your associative array to be of type Array, you cannot use an object literal to initialize the array.

 There is no advantage to using the Array constructor to create an associative array. The Array constructor is best for creating indexed arrays.

The next example demonstrates how to use the Array constructor to create an associative array.

To create an associative array using the Array constructor:

1. Create a new Flash document, and save it as **assocArray2.fla**.

2. Add the following ActionScript to Frame 1 of the Timeline:

```
var monitorInfo:Array = new Array();
monitorInfo["type"] = "Flat Panel";
monitorInfo["resolution"] = "1600 x 1200";
trace(monitorInfo["type"] + ", " + monitorInfo["resolution"]);
```

This code creates an associative array named monitorInfo using the Array constructor and adds a key called type and a key called resolution, along with their values.

3. Select Control > Test Movie.

The Output panel displays the following text:

```
Flat Panel, 1600 x 1200
```

 There is no advantage to using the Array constructor to create an associative array. The Array constructor is best for creating indexed arrays.

Associative arrays are essentially instances of the Object class, and there is no advantage of creating associative arrays using the Array constructor. Even though you create an associative array using the `new Array()` constructor, you cannot use any of the Array class's methods and properties (such as `sort()` or `length`) when using an associative array. If you want to use key/value pairs instead of a numeric index, you should use the Object class instead of an associative array.

About operators

This section describes general rules about common types of operators, operator precedence, and operator associativity.

Operators are characters that specify how to combine, compare, or change values in an expression. An expression is any statement that Flash can evaluate and that returns a value. You can create an expression by combining operators and values or by calling a function. For more information on expressions, see "About syntax, statements, and expressions" on page 118.

For example, a mathematical expression uses numerical operators to manipulate the values you use. Examples of operator characters are +, <, *, and =. An expression consists of operators and *operands*, and they are any legal combination of ActionScript symbols that represent a value. An operand is the part of your code that the operator performs actions on. For example, in the expression $x + 2$, x and 2 are operands and + is an operator.

You use expressions and operators frequently throughout your code. You can combine operators and values to create an expression, or you can call a function.

 NOTE | This section describes how to use each type of operator; however, there isn't space to cover each one. For information on every operator, including special operators that don't fall into the following categories, see the *ActionScript 2.0 Language Reference* in Flash Help.

The parts of your code that the operator performs actions on are called *operands*. For example, you can use the addition (+) operator to add values of a numeric literal. You could do this to add the value of a variable called `myNum`.

```
myNum + 3;
```

In this example, `myNum` and 3 are operands.

This section describes general rules about common types of operators, operator precedence, and operator associativity:

- "Using operators to manipulate values" on page 181
- "About operator precedence and associativity" on page 183

- "About using operators with strings" on page 186
- "Using dot and array access operators" on page 188
- "About postfix operators" on page 190
- "About unary operators" on page 190
- "About multiplicative operators" on page 191
- "About additive operators" on page 191
- "Using numeric operators" on page 192
- "About relational operators" on page 193
- "About equality operators" on page 193
- "Using relational and equality operators" on page 193
- "About assignment operators" on page 197
- "Using assignment operators" on page 198
- "About logical operators" on page 198
- "Using logical operators" on page 199
- "About bitwise shift operators" on page 200
- "About bitwise logical operators" on page 201
- "Using bitwise operators" on page 201
- "About the conditional operator" on page 203
- "Using operators in a document" on page 203

For information on operators, that do not fall into these categories, see the *ActionScript 2.0 Language Reference* in Flash Help, which contains information about all the operators you can use.

The following sections show you some common uses for operators. For more information on using many operators in a single code sample, see "Using operators in a document" on page 203.

Using operators to manipulate values

Operators are commonly used to manipulate values in Flash. For example, you might want to create a game in Flash where the score changes depending on the user's interaction with instances on the Stage. You can use a variable to hold the value and operators to manipulate the value of the variable.

For example, you might want to increase the value of a variable called myScore. The following example demonstrates how to use the + (addition) and += (addition assignment) operators to add and increment values in your code.

To manipulate values using operators:

1. Create a new Flash document.

2. Open the Actions panel (Window > Actions) and type the following code into the Script pane:

```
// example one
var myScore:Number = 0;
myScore = myScore + 1;
trace("Example one: " + myScore); // 1

// example two
var secondScore:Number = 1;
secondScore += 3;
trace("Example two: " + secondScore); // 4
```

3. Select Control > Test Movie.

The Output panel displays the following text:

```
Example one: 1
Example two: 4
```

The addition operator is fairly straightforward, because it adds two values together. In the first code example, it adds the current value of myScore and the number 1, and then stores the result into the variable myScore.

The second code example uses the addition assignment operator to add and assign a new value in a single step. You can rewrite the line myScore = myScore + 1 (from the previous exercise) as myScore++ or even myScore += 1. The increment operator (++) is a simplified way of saying myScore = myScore + 1, because it handles an increment and assignment simultaneously. You can see an example of the increment operator in the following ActionScript:

```
var myNum:Number = 0;
myNum++;
trace(myNum); // 1
myNum++;
trace(myNum); // 2
```

Notice that the previous code snippet doesn't have assignment operators. It relies on the increment operator instead.

You can manipulate the value of a variable using operators while a condition is true. For example, you can use the increment operator (++) to increment the variable i while the condition is true. In the following code, the condition is true while i is less than the value of 10. While that is true, you increment i one number higher using i++.

```
var i:Number;
for (i = 1; i < 10; i++) {
  trace(i);
}
```

The Output panel displays the numbers 1 through 9, which is i incrementing in value until it reaches the end condition (i is equal to 10), when it stops. The last value displayed is 9. Therefore, the value of i is 1 when the SWF file starts playing, and 9 after the trace completes.

For more information on conditions and loops, see "About statements" on page 145.

About operator precedence and associativity

When you use two or more operators in a statement, some operators take precedence over other operators. Operator precedence and associativity determine the order in which operators are processed. ActionScript has a hierarchy that determines which operators execute before others. There is a table that outlines this hierarchy at the end of this section.

Although it may seem natural to those familiar with arithmetic or basic programming that the compiler processes the multiplication (*) operator before the addition (+) operator, the compiler needs explicit instructions about which operators to process first. Such instructions are collectively referred to as *operator precedence*.

You can see an example of operator precedence when you work with the multiplication and addition operators:

```
var mySum:Number;
mySum = 2 + 4 * 3;
trace(mySum); // 14
```

You see the output of this statement is 14, because multiplication has a higher operator precedence. Therefore, 4 * 3 is evaluated first and the result is added to 2.

You can control what happens by enclosing expressions in parentheses. ActionScript defines a default operator precedence that you can alter using the parentheses (( )) operator. When you put parentheses around the addition expression, ActionScript performs the addition first:

```
var mySum:Number;
mySum = (2 + 4) * 3;
trace(mySum); // 18
```

Now the output of this statement is 18.

It's also possible for operators to have the same precedence. In this case, the associativity determines the order in which the operators perform. You can either have left-to-right associativity or right-to-left associativity.

Take a look at the multiplication operator again. It has left-to-right associativity, so the following two statements are the same.

```
var mySum:Number;
var myOtherSum:Number;
mySum = 2 * 4 * 3;
myOtherSum = (2 * 4) * 3;
trace(mySum); // 24
trace(myOtherSum); // 24
```

You might encounter situations in which two or more operators of the same precedence appear in the same expression. In these cases, the compiler uses the rules of *associativity* to determine which operator to process first. All of the binary operators, except the assignment operators, are *left-associative*, which means that operators on the left are processed before operators on the right. The assignment operators and the conditional (?:) operator are *right-associative*, which means that the operators on the right are processed before operators on the left. For more information on assignment operators, see "Using assignment operators" on page 198. For more information on the conditional (?:) operator, see "About the conditional operator" on page 203.

For example, consider the less than (<) and greater than (>) operators, which have the same precedence. If both operators are used in the same expression, the operator on the left is processed first because both operators are left-associative. This means that the following two statements produce the same output:

```
trace(3 > 2 < 1);   // false
trace((3 > 2) < 1); // false
```

The greater than (>) operator is processed first, which results in a value of true because the operand 3 is greater than the operand 2. The value true is then passed to the less than (<) operator, along with the operand 1. The less than (<) operator converts the value true to the numeric value 1 and compares that numeric value to the second operand 1 to return the value false (the value 1 is not less than 1).

Consider the order of operands in your ActionScript, particularly when you set up complex conditions and you know how often one of those conditions is true. For example, if you know that i will be greater than 50 in your condition, you need to write i<50 first. Therefore, it's checked first, and the second condition that you write doesn't need to be checked as often.

The following table lists all the ActionScript operators and their associativity, from highest to lowest precedence. For more information and guidelines on using operators and parentheses, see Chapter 19, "Formatting ActionScript syntax," on page 777.

Operator	Description	Associativity
Highest precedence		
x++	Post-increment	Left to right
x--	Post-decrement	Left to right
	Object property access	Left to right
[ ]	Array element	Left to right
( )	Parentheses	Left to right
function ( )	Function call	Left to right
++*x*	Pre-increment	Right to left
x	Pre-decrement	Right to left
	Unary negation, such as x = -1	Left to right
~	Bitwise NOT	Right to left
!	Logical NOT	Right to left
new	Allocate object	Right to left
delete	Deallocate object	Right to left
typeof	Type of object	Right to left
void	Returns undefined value	Right to left
*	Multiply	Left to right
/	Divide	Left to right
%	Modulo	Left to right
+	Unary plus	Right to left
-	Unary minus	Right to left
<<	Bitwise left shift	Left to right
>>	Bitwise right shift	Left to right
>>>	Bitwise right shift (unsigned)	Left to right
instanceof	Instance of (finds the class of which the object is an instance) Requires Flash Player 6 or later	Left to right
<	Less than	Left to right

Operator	Description	Associativity
<=	Less than or equal to	Left to right
>	Greater than	Left to right
>=	Greater than or equal to	Left to right
==	Equal	Left to right
!=	Not equal	Left to right
&	Bitwise AND	Left to right
^	Bitwise XOR	Left to right
|	Bitwise OR	Left to right
&&	Logical AND	Left to right
||	Logical OR	Left to right
?:	Conditional	Right to left
=	Assignment	Right to left
*=, /=, %=, +=, -=, &=, |=, ^=, <<=, >>=, >>>=	Compound assignment	Right to left
,	Comma	Left to right

Lowest precedence

About using operators with strings

Comparison operators compare strings only if both operands are strings. An exception to this rule is the strict equality (===) operator. If only one operand is a string, ActionScript converts both operands to numbers and performs a numeric comparison on them. For more information on numeric operators, see "Using numeric operators" on page 192.

Except for the equality operator (==), comparison operators (>, >=, <, and <=) affect strings differently than when they operate on other values.

Comparison operators compare strings to determine which is first alphabetically. Strings with uppercase characters precede strings that are lowercase. That means that "Egg" comes before "chicken".

```
var c:String = "chicken";
var e:String = "Egg";
trace(c < e); // false
var riddleArr:Array = new Array(c, e);
trace(riddleArr); // chicken,Egg
trace(riddleArr.sort()); // Egg,chicken
```

In this ActionScript, the sort() method of the Array class reorders the contents of the array alphabetically. You can see that the value "Egg" comes before the value "chicken" because uppercase E comes before a lowercase c. If you want to compare the strings regardless of case, you need to convert the strings to uppercase or lowercase before you compare them. For more information on comparison operators, see "About equality operators" on page 193 and "Using relational and equality operators" on page 193.

You can use the toLowerCase() or toUpperCase() methods to convert strings to a similar case before you compare them. In the following example, both strings convert to lowercase strings and compare, and now the chicken comes before the egg:

```
var c:String = "chicken";
var e:String = "Egg";
trace(c.toLowerCase() < e.toLowerCase()); // true
```

 NOTE Comparison operators compare only two strings. For example, the operators do not compare the values if one operand is a numerical value. If one of the operands is a string, ActionScript converts both operands to numbers and then compares them numerically.

You can use operators to manipulate strings. You can use the addition (+) operator to concatenate string operands. You might have already used the addition operator to concatenate strings when you write trace statements. For example, you might write the following:

```
var myNum:Number = 10;
trace("The variable is " + myNum + ".");
```

When you test this code, the Output panel displays the following:

```
The variable is 10.
```

In the previous example, the trace statement uses the + operator to concatenate instead of add. When you deal with strings and numbers, Flash sometimes concatenates instead of adding numerically.

For example, you might concatenate two strings from different variables in a single text field. In the following ActionScript code, the variable myNum concatenates with a string, and the string is displayed in the myTxt text field on the Stage.

```
this.createTextField("myTxt", 11, 0, 0, 100, 20);
myTxt.autoSize = "left";
var myNum:Number = 10;
myTxt.text = "One carrot. " + myNum + " large eggplants.";
myTxt.text += " Lots of vegetable broth.";
```

This code outputs the following in a text field with the instance name myTxt:

```
One carrot. 10 large eggplants. Lots of vegetable broth.
```

The previous example shows how you can use the addition (+) and addition assignment (+=) operators to concatenate strings. Notice how the third line of code uses the addition operator to concatenate the value of the myNum variable into the text field, and the fourth line of code uses the addition assignment operator to concatenate a string onto the existing value of the text field.

If only one of the text string operands is actually a string, Flash converts the other operand into a string. Therefore, the value of myNum converts to a string in the previous example.

> **NOTE** ActionScript treats spaces at the beginning or end of a string as a literal part of the string.

Using dot and array access operators

You can use the dot operator (.) and the array access operator ([ ]) to access built-in or custom ActionScript properties. You use dot operators to target certain indexes in an object. For example, if you have an object that contains some user information, you can specify a certain key name in the array access operator to retrieve a user's name, as demonstrated in the following ActionScript:

```
var someUser:Object = {name:"Hal", id:2001};
trace("User's name is: " + someUser["name"]); // User's name is: Hal
trace("User's id is: " + someUser["id"]); // User's id is: 2001
```

For example, the following ActionScript uses the dot operator to set certain properties within objects:

```
myTextField.border = true;
year.month.day = 9;
myTextField.text = "My text";
```

The dot operator and the array access operator are very similar. The dot operator takes an identifier as its property, but the array access operator evaluates the contents to a name and then accesses the value of that named property. The array access operator lets you dynamically set and retrieve instance names and variables.

The array access operator is useful if you don't know exactly what keys are in an object. When this occurs, you can use a for..in loop to iterate through an object or movie clip and display its contents.

To use dot and array access operators:

1. In a new Flash document, create a movie clip on the main Timeline.

2. Select the movie clip and open the Property inspector.

3. Type in an instance name of myClip.

4. Add the following ActionScript to Frame 1 of the Timeline:

```
myClip.spam = 5;
trace(myClip.spam); // 5
```

If you want to set a value in the myClip instance on the current timeline you can use the dot or array access operators, as demonstrated in this ActionScript. If you write an expression inside the array access operator, it evaluates that expression first and uses the result as the variable name.

5. Select Control > Test Movie to test the document.

The Output panel displays 5.

6. Return to the authoring environment, and replace the first line of ActionScript with the following:

```
myClip["spam"] = 10;
```

7. Select Control > Test Movie to test the document.

The Output panel displays 10.

8. Return to the authoring environment, and double-click the myClip instance.

9. Add four new instances inside the myClip instance.

10. Use the Property inspector to add the following instance names to each of the four new instances: **nestedClip1**, **nestedClip2**, **nestedClip3**, **nestedClip4**.

11. Add the following code to Frame 1 of the main Timeline:

```
var i:Number;
for (i = 1; i <= 4; i++) {
   myClip["nestedClip" + i]._visible = false;
}
```

This ActionScript toggles the visibility of each of the nested movie clips.

12. Select Control > Test Movie to test the ActionScript you just added.

Now the four nested instances are invisible. You're using the array access operator to iterate over each nested movie clip in the myClip instance and set its visible property dynamically. You save time, because you don't have to specifically target each instance.

You can also use the array access operator on the left side of an assignment, which lets you set instance, variable, and object names dynamically:

```
myNum[i] = 10;
```

In ActionScript 2.0, you can use the bracket operator to access properties on an object that are created dynamically, in case the class definition for that object is not given the `dynamic` attribute. You can also create multidimensional arrays using this operator. For more information on creating multidimensional arrays using array access operators, see "Creating multidimensional arrays" on page 173.

About postfix operators

The postfix operators take one operator and either increment or decrement the operator's value. Although these operators are unary operators, they are classified separately from the rest of the unary operators because of their higher precedence and special behavior. For information on unary operators, see "About unary operators" on page 190.

When you use a postfix operator as part of a larger expression, the expression's value is returned before the postfix operator is processed. For example, the following code shows how the value of the expression xNum++ is returned before the value is incremented.

```
var xNum:Number = 0;
trace(xNum++); // 0
trace(xNum); // 1
```

When you trace this code, the text in the Output panel reads:

```
0
1
```

The operators in this table have equal precedence:

Operator	Operation performed
++	Increment (postfix)
--	Decrement (postfix)

About unary operators

Unary operators take one operand. The increment (++) and decrement (--) operators in this group are *prefix* operators, which means that they appear before the operand in an expression. They can also appear after the operand, in which case they are *postfix* operators. For information on postfix operators, see "About postfix operators" on page 190.

The prefix operators differ from the postfix counterparts because the increment or decrement operation completes before the value of the overall expression is returned. For example, the following code shows how the value of the expression xNum++ is returned after the value is incremented.

```
var xNum:Number = 0;
trace(++xNum); // 1
trace(xNum); // 1
```

All of the operators in this table have equal precedence:

Operator	Operation performed
++	Increment (prefix)
- -	Decrement (prefix)
+	Unary +
!	Unary - (negation)
typeof	Returns type information
void	Returns undefined value

About multiplicative operators

The multiplicative operators take two operands and perform multiplication, division, or modulo calculations. Other numeric operators include additive operators. For information on additive operators, see "About additive operators" on page 191.

All of the operators in this table have equal precedence:

Operator	Operation performed
*	Multiplication
/	Division
%	Modulo

For information on using multiplicative operators, see "Using numeric operators" on page 192.

About additive operators

The additive operators take two operands and perform addition or subtraction calculations. Other numeric operators include multiplicative operators. For information on multiplicative operators, see "About multiplicative operators" on page 191.

The operators in this table have equal precedence:

Operator	Operation performed
+	Addition
-	Subtraction

For information on using additive operators, see "Using numeric operators" on page 192.

Using numeric operators

You use numeric operators to add, subtract, divide, and multiply values in ActionScript. You can perform different kinds of arithmetic operations. One of the most common operators is the increment operator, commonly formed as i++. There are more things you can do with this operator. For more information on the increment operator, see "Using operators to manipulate values" on page 181.

You can add the increment before (*preincrement*) or after (*postincrement*) an operand.

To understand numeric operators in ActionScript:

1. Create a new Flash document.

2. Type the following ActionScript into Frame 1 of the Timeline:

```
// example one
var firstScore:Number = 29;
if (++firstScore >= 30) {
  // should trace
  trace("Success! ++firstScore is >= 30");
}
// example two
var secondScore:Number = 29;
if (secondScore++ >= 30) {
  // shouldn't trace
  trace("Success! secondScore++ is >= 30");
}
```

3. Select Control > Test Movie to test the ActionScript

   The "Example one" code block traces, but the "Example two" code block does not. The first example uses a preincrement (++firstScore) to increment and calculate firstScore before it's tested against 30. Therefore, firstScore increments to 30 and then tests against 30.

   However, Example two uses a postincrement (secondScore++), which evaluates after the test is performed. Therefore, 29 compares against 30, and then increments to 30 after the evaluation.

For more information on operator precedence, see "About operator precedence and associativity" on page 183.

When you load data from external sources (such as XML files, FlashVars, web services, and so on), you need to be very careful when you work with numeric operators. Sometimes Flash treats the numbers like strings because the SWF file isn't aware of the number's data type. In this case, you could add 3 and 7 with a result of 37 because both numbers are concatenated like strings instead of adding numerically. In this situation, you need to manually convert the data from strings to numbers using the Number() function.

About relational operators

The relational operators take two operands, compare their values, and return a Boolean value. All of the operators in this table have equal precedence:

Operator	Operation performed
<	Less than
>	Greater than
<=	Less than or equal to
>=	Greater than or equal to
instanceof	Checks prototype chain
in	Checks for object properties

For information on using relational operators, see "Using relational and equality operators" on page 193.

About equality operators

The equality operators take two operands, compare their values, and return a Boolean value. All of the operators in this table have equal precedence:

Operator	Operation performed
==	Equality
!=	Inequality
===	Strict equality
!==	Strict inequality

For information on using equality operators, see "Using relational and equality operators" on page 193.

Using relational and equality operators

Relational and equality operators, also called *comparison operators*, compare values of expressions, and they return either `true` or `false` (a Boolean value). You frequently use comparison operators in conditional statements and loops to specify the condition for when the loop should stop.

You can use the equality (==) operator to figure out whether the values or references of two operands are equal, and this comparison returns a Boolean value. String, number, or Boolean operand values compare using a value. Object and array operands are compared by a reference.

In this example, you can see how to use the equality operator to test the array's length and display a message in the Output panel if there are no items in the array.

```
var myArr:Array = new Array();
if (myArr.length == 0) {
  trace("the array is empty.");
}
```

When you select Control > Test Movie, the string the array is empty appears in the Output panel.

You can use the equality operator to compare values, but you cannot use the equality operator to set values. You might try to use the assignment operator (=) to check for equality.

To use relational and equality operators in your code:

1. Create a new Flash document.

2. Type the following ActionScript into Frame 1 of the Timeline:

```
var myNum:Number = 2;
if (myNum == 2) {
  // do something
  trace("It equals 2");
}
```

In this ActionScript, you use the equality operator (==) to check for equality. You check whether the variable myNum equals 2.

3. Select Control > Test Movie.

The string It equals 2 appears in the Output panel.

4. Return to the authoring environment and change:

```
var myNum:Number = 2;
```

to:

```
var myNum:Number = 4;
```

5. Select Control > Test Movie again.

The string It equals 2 doesn't appear in the Output panel.

6. Return to the authoring environment and change:

```
if (myNum == 2) {
```

to

```
if (myNum = 2) {
```

7. Select Control > Test Movie again.

The string It equals 2 appears in the Output panel again.

In step 6, you assign the value of 2 to myNum, instead of comparing myNum to 2. In this case, the if statement executes regardless of the previous value of myNum, which can cause unexpected results when you test the Flash document.

For more information on correctly using the assignment operator, see "Using assignment operators" on page 198.

The strict equality operator (===) is similar to the equality operator, except it doesn't perform type conversion. If two operands are different types, the equality operator returns false. The strict inequality operator (!==) returns the opposite of the strict equality operator.

The following ActionScript demonstrates the key difference between the equality operator (==) and the strict equality operator (===):

```
var num1:Number = 32;
var num2:String = new String("32");
trace(num1 == num2); // true
trace(num1 === num2); // false
```

First, you define numeric variables: num1, and num2. If you compare the variables using the equality operator, Flash tries to convert the values to the same data type and then compare the values to see whether they are equal. When you use the strict equality operator (===) Flash doesn't attempt to do any data type conversion before it compares the values. As a result, Flash sees the variables as two separate values.

In the following example, you'll use the greater than or equal to (>=) operator to compare values and execute code based on the value a user enters into a text field.

To use the greater than or equal to operator in your code:

1. Select File > New and then select Flash Document to create a new FLA file.

2. Add the following code to Frame 1 of the main Timeline:

```
this.createTextField("myTxt", 20, 0, 0, 100, 20);
myTxt.type = "input";
myTxt.border = true;
myTxt.restrict = "0-9";

this.createEmptyMovieClip("submit_mc", 30);
submit_mc.beginFill(0xFF0000);
submit_mc.moveTo(0, 0);
submit_mc.lineTo(100, 0);
submit_mc.lineTo(100, 20);
submit_mc.lineTo(0, 20);
submit_mc.lineTo(0, 0);
submit_mc.endFill();
submit_mc._x = 110;

submit_mc.onRelease = function(evt_obj:Object):Void {
  var myNum:Number = Number(myTxt.text);
  if (isNaN(myNum)) {
    trace("Please enter a number");
    return;
  }
  if (myNum >= 10) {
    trace("Your number is greater than or equal to 10");
  } else {
    trace("Your number is less than 10");
  }
};
```

3. Select Control > Test Movie to test the ActionScript.

   You can also check whether certain conditions are true and execute an alternative block if the condition is not true.

4. Change the condition in your ActionScript to the following.

```
if (myNum == 10) {
  trace("Your number is 10");
} else {
    trace("Your number is not 10");
}
```

5. Select Control > Test Movie to test the ActionScript again.

Except for the strict equality (===) operator, the comparison operators compare strings only if both operands are strings. If only one of the operands is a string, both operands convert to numbers and perform a numeric comparison. For more information on strings and operators, see "About using operators with strings" on page 186. For information on how order and operator precedence affect your ActionScript, see "About operator precedence and associativity" on page 183.

About assignment operators

The assignment operators take two operands and assign a value to one operand based on the value of the other operand. All of the operators in this table have equal precedence:

Operator	Operation performed
=	Assignment
*=	Multiplication assignment
/=	Division assignment
%=	Modulo assignment
+=	Addition assignment
-=	Subtraction assignment
<<=	Bitwise left shift assignment
>>=	Bitwise right shift assignment
>>>=	Bitwise unsigned right shift assignment
&=	Bitwise AND assignment
^=	Bitwise XOR assignment
|=	Bitwise OR assignment

For information on using assignment operators, see "Using assignment operators" on page 198.

Using assignment operators

You can use the assignment operator (=) to assign a given value to a variable. You might assign a string to a variable, as follows:

```
var myText:String = "ScratchyCat";
```

You can also use the assignment operator to assign several variables in the same expression. In the following statement, the value of 10 is assigned the variables numOne, numTwo, and numThree.

```
var numOne:Number;
var numTwo:Number;
var numThree:Number;
numOne = numTwo = numThree = 10;
```

You can also use compound assignment operators to combine operations. These operators perform the operation on both operands, and then they assign the new value to the first operand. For example, both of these statements do the same thing:

```
var myNum:Number = 0;
myNum += 15;
myNum = myNum + 15;
```

When you work with the assignment operator, you can have problems if you try to add values in an expression, as you can see in the following example:

```
trace("the sum of 5 + 2 is: " + 5 + 2); // the sum of 5 + 2 is: 52
```

Flash concatenates the values 5 and 2 instead of adding them. To work around this, you can wrap the expression 5+2 in a pair of parentheses, as shown in the following code:

```
trace("the sum of 5 + 2 is: " + (5 + 2)); // the sum of 5 + 2 is: 7
```

About logical operators

You use logical operators to compare Boolean values (true and false) and then return a Boolean value based on the comparison. For example, if you have two operands that evaluate to true, the logical AND (&&) operator returns true. Or if one or both of the operands evaluate to true, the logical OR (||) operator returns true.

The logical operators take two operands and return a Boolean result. The logical operators differ in precedence and are listed in the table in order of decreasing precedence:

Operator	Operation performed
&&	Logical AND
||	Logical OR

For information on using logical operators, see "Using logical operators" on page 199.

Using logical operators

You often use logical operators with comparison operators to determine the condition of an if statement. This is demonstrated by the next example.

To use logical operators in your code:

1. Select File > New and create a new Flash document.

2. Open the Actions panel and type the following ActionScript on Frame 1 of the Timeline:

```
this.createTextField("myTxt", 20, 0, 0, 100, 20);
myTxt.type = "input";
myTxt.border = true;
myTxt.restrict = "0-9";

this.createEmptyMovieClip("submit_mc", 30);
submit_mc.beginFill(0xFF0000);
submit_mc.moveTo(0, 0);
submit_mc.lineTo(100, 0);
submit_mc.lineTo(100, 20);
submit_mc.lineTo(0, 20);
submit_mc.lineTo(0, 0);
submit_mc.endFill();
submit_mc._x = 110;

submit_mc.onRelease = function():Void {
  var myNum:Number = Number(myTxt.text);
  if (isNaN(myNum)) {
    trace("Please enter a number");
    return;
  }
  if ((myNum > 10) && (myNum < 20)) {
    trace("Your number is between 10 and 20");
  } else {
    trace("Your number is NOT between 10 and 20");
  }
};
```

In this ActionScript, you create a text field at runtime. If you type a number into the text field and click the button on the Stage, Flash uses the logical operator to display a message in the Output panel. The message depends on the value of the number you type into the text field.

When you use operands, you need to be careful of the order. This is particularly the case when you use complex conditions. In the following snippet, you can see how you use the logical AND operator to check that a number is between 10 and 20. Based on the result, you display an appropriate message. If the number is less than 10 or greater than 20, an alternate message is displayed in the Output panel.

```
submit_mc.onRelease = function():Void {
  var myNum:Number = Number(myTxt.text);
  if (isNaN(myNum)) {
    trace("Please enter a number");
    return;
  }
  if ((myNum > 10) && (myNum < 20)) {
    trace("Your number is between 10 and 20");
  } else {
    trace("Your number is NOT between 10 and 20");
  }
};
```

About bitwise shift operators

The bitwise shift operators take two operands and shift the bits of the first operand to the extent specified by the second operand. All of the operators in this table have equal precedence:

Operator	Operation performed
<<	Bitwise left shift
>>	Bitwise right shift
>>>	Bitwise unsigned right shift

For information on using bitwise operators, see "Using bitwise operators" on page 201. For specific information on each bitwise operator, see its entry in the *ActionScript 2.0 Language Reference* in Flash Help.

About bitwise logical operators

The bitwise logical operators take two operands and perform bit-level logical operations. The bitwise logical operators differ in precedence and are listed in the table in order of decreasing precedence:

Operator	Operation performed
&	Bitwise AND
^	Bitwise XOR
|	Bitwise OR

For information on using bitwise operators, see "Using bitwise operators" on page 201. For specific information on each bitwise operator, see its entry in the *ActionScript 2.0 Language Reference* in Flash Help.

Using bitwise operators

Bitwise operators internally manipulate floating-point numbers to change them into 32-bit integers. The exact operation performed depends on the operator, but all bitwise operations evaluate each binary digit (bit) of the 32-bit integer individually to compute a new value. For a list of bitwise shift operators, see "About bitwise shift operators" on page 200. For a list of bitwise logical operators, see "About bitwise logical operators" on page 201.

Using bitwise operators in Flash isn't very common, but can be useful in some circumstances. For example, you might want to build a permissions matrix for a Flash project, but you don't want to create separate variables for each type of permission. In this case, you might use bitwise operators.

The following example shows how you can use the bitwise OR operator with the `Array.sort()` method to specify sort options.

To use the bitwise OR operator:

1. Select File > New and create a new Flash document.

2. Type the following ActionScript into the Actions panel:

```
var myArr:Array = new Array("Bob", "Dan", "doug", "bill", "Hank",
    "tom");
trace(myArr); // Bob,Dan,doug,bill,Hank,tom
myArr.sort(Array.CASEINSENSITIVE | Array.DESCENDING);
trace(myArr); // tom,Hank,doug,Dan,Bob,bill
```

The first line defines an array of random names and traces them to the Output panel. Then you call the `Array.sort()` method and specify two sort options using the constant values `Array.CASEINSENSITIVE` and `Array.DESCENDING`. The result of the sort method causes the items in the array to be sorted in reverse order (z to a). The search is case-insensitive; a and A are treated the same, instead of having a case-sensitive search where Z comes before a.

3. Select Control > Test Movie to test your ActionScript. The following text is displayed in the Output panel:

```
Bob,Dan,doug,bill,Hank,tom
tom,Hank,doug,Dan,Bob,bill
```

There are five options available in the sort method:

- 1 or Array.CASEINSENSITIVE (binary = 1)
- 2 or Array.DESCENDING (binary = 10)
- 4 or Array.UNIQUESORT (binary = 100)
- 8 or Array.RETURNINDEXEDARRAY (binary = 1000)
- 16 or Array.NUMERIC (binary = 10000)

There are three different ways you can define the sort options for an array:

```
my_array.sort(Array.CASEINSENSITIVE | Array.DESCENDING); // constants
my_array.sort(1 | 2); // numbers
my_array.sort(3); // adding the numbers
```

Although it might not be immediately obvious, the number values for the sort options are actually bitwise digits (binary or base 2). The constant value `Array.CASEINSENSITIVE` equals the numeric value of 1, which also happens to be the binary value of 1. The constant value `Array.DECENDING` has a numeric value of 2 or a binary value of 10.

Working with binary numbers can get confusing. Binary only has two possible values, 1 or 0, which is why the value 2 is represented as 10. If you want to display the number 3 in binary, it would be 11 (1+10). The number 4 represented in binary is 100, representing 5 in binary is 101, and so on.

The following ActionScript demonstrates how to sort an array of numeric values in descending order by using the bitwise AND operator to add the `Array.DESCENDING` and `Array.NUMERIC` constants together.

```
var scores:Array = new Array(100,40,20,202,1,198);
trace(scores); // 100,40,20,202,1,198
trace(scores.sort()); // 1,100,198,20,202,40
var flags:Number = Array.NUMERIC|Array.DESCENDING;
trace(flags); // 18 (base 10)
trace(flags.toString(2)); // 10010 (binary -- base2)
trace(scores.sort(flags)); // 202,198,100,40,20,1
```

About the conditional operator

The conditional operator is a ternary operator, which means that it take three operands. The conditional operator is a short-hand method of applying the `if..else` conditional statement:

Operator	Operation performed
?:	Conditional

For information on using the conditional operator and an example, see "About the conditional operator and alternative syntax" on page 156.

Using operators in a document

In the following example, you use the `Math.round()` method to round calculations to an arbitrary number of decimal places. This method rounds the value of the x parameter up or down to the nearest integer, and then returns the value. After you slightly modify the ActionScript, you can make Flash round numbers to a certain number of decimal places instead.

In the next example, you also use the division and multiplication operators to calculate a user's score based on the number of correct answers divided by the total number of questions that are asked. The user's score can multiply by a number and display to get a score between 0% and 100%. Then you use the addition operator to concatenate the user's score into a string that is displayed in the Output panel.

To use operators in ActionScript:

1. Create a new Flash document.

2. Type the following ActionScript on Frame 1 of the main Timeline:

```
var correctAnswers:Number = 11;
var totalQuestions:Number = 13;
//round to the nearest integer
//var score:Number = Math.round(correctAnswers / totalQuestions * 100);
//round to two decimal places
var score:Number = Math.round(correctAnswers / totalQuestions * 100 *
   100) / 100;
trace("You got " + correctAnswers + " out of " + totalQuestions + "
   answers correct, for a score of " + score + "%.");
```

3. Select Control > Test Movie.

   The Output panel displays the following text:

   ```
   You got 11 out of 13 answers correct, for a score of 84.62%.
   ```

   When you call `Math.round()` in this example, the score rounds to the nearest integer (85) and is displayed in the Output panel. If you multiply the number by an additional 100, before you call `Math.round()`, and then divide by 100, you can make Flash round the number to 2 decimal places. This results in a more accurate score.

4. Try changing the `correctAnswers` variable to 3 and select Control > Test Movie to test the SWF file again.

If you are building a testing application, you might want to create a series of true/false or multiple choice questions using the RadioButton and Label components. After users finish answering each of the questions and click the submit button, you can compare their answers to an answer key and then calculate their score.

CHAPTER 6

Functions and Methods

Understanding functions is important when you're writing ActionScript, creating classes, and using methods. There are several different kinds of functions that you'll work with. In this chapter, you learn about functions and methods: how to use them in your applications when you use built-in classes, and how to write them. In Chapter 7, "Classes," you'll create custom classes in which you'll write functions regularly. You'll also learn how to write functions in ActionScript class files.

You can use functions in your code to add interactivity, animations, and other effects to your applications. This chapter covers the kinds of functions that you can write in your Flash applications. For information on what functions and methods are, as well as exercises in which you write and use functions and methods in Flash, see the following topics:

About functions and methods

Methods and functions are blocks of ActionScript code that you can reuse anywhere in a SWF file. You might write your functions in the FLA file or in an external ActionScript file and then call the function from anywhere within your documents. Methods are merely functions that are located within an ActionScript class definition. You can define functions to execute a series of statements on passed values. Your functions can also return values. After a function is defined, it can be called from any timeline, including a timeline of a loaded SWF file.

If you pass values as parameters to a function, the function can perform calculations using the supplied values. Each function has individual characteristics, and some functions require that you pass certain types or numbers of values. If you pass more parameters than the function requires, the function ignores the extra values. If you don't pass a required parameter, the function assigns the undefined data type to the empty parameters. This can cause errors during runtime. A function can also return values (see "Returning values from functions" on page 225).

> **NOTE**
> To call a function, that function's definition must be in a frame that the playhead has reached.

You can think of a well-written function as a "black box." If the function contains carefully placed comments about its input, output, and purpose, a person using the function does not need to understand exactly how it works internally.

The basic syntax for a simple *named function* is:

```
function traceMe() {
  trace("your message");
}
traceMe();
```

For information on writing named functions, see "Writing named functions" on page 211.

The basic syntax for a simple named function that builds on the previous example by passing a parameter, yourMessage, is:

```
function traceMe(yourMessage:String) {
  trace(yourMessage);
}
traceMe("How you doing?");
```

Alternatively, if you want to pass multiple parameters, you could use the following code:

```
var yourName:String = "Ester";
var yourAge:String = "65";
var favSoftware:String = "Flash";
function traceMe(favSoftware:String, yourName:String, yourAge:String) {
  trace("I'm " + yourName + ", I like " + favSoftware + ", and I'm " +
  yourAge + ".");
}
traceMe(favSoftware,yourName,yourAge);
```

For more information on passing parameters, see "Passing parameters to a function" on page 223.

There are numerous kinds of functions that you can write. For more information on writing functions, as well as links to sections on writing specific kinds of functions, see "About types of methods and functions" on page 207. For an example that compares methods and functions, see "Understanding methods" on page 227.

 NOTE
For information on writing code using Script Assist, see "Using Script Assist to write ActionScript," "Creating a startDrag/stopDrag event using Script Assist," and the ActionScript: Use Script Assist Mode tutorial (which begins with "Open the starter document") in Flash Help.

For more information about functions and methods, see the following topics:

- "About types of methods and functions" on page 207

About types of methods and functions

Functions that belong to a class are called the *methods* of that class. There are several types of functions that you can use in your applications, including built-in functions, named and user-defined functions, anonymous functions, callback functions, constructor functions, and function literals. The following sections contain information on how to define these functions.

You can also write functions in an ActionScript class file. You use these functions as methods in your scripts. In the following example, the Person class displays a constructor method, class methods, instance methods, and accessor methods (getters and setters). The comments in this code sample show where these methods occur in the code.

> **NOTE** For information on writing class files, such as the following, see Chapter 7, "Classes," on page 231.

```
class Person {
  public static var numPeople:Number = 0;

  // instance members
  private var _speed:Number;

  // constructor
  public function Person(speed:Number) {
    Person.numPeople++;
    this._speed = speed;
  }

  // static methods
  public static function getPeople():Number {
    return Person.numPeople;
  }

  // instance methods
  public function walk(speed:Number):Void {
    this._speed = speed;
  }
  public function run():Void {
    this._speed *= 2;
  }
  public function rest():Void {
    this._speed = 0;
  }

  // getters/setters (accessor methods)
  public function get speed():Number {
    return this._speed;
  }
}
```

For a full demonstration of how to write methods like the ones in the previous code sample, see Chapter 7, "Classes," on page 231. The methods that you use in your code might belong to a class that is built into the ActionScript language. MovieClip and Math are examples of top-level classes that you might use in an application. When you use methods from these classes in your code, they are functions written in the built-in class (similar to the previous code sample). Alternatively, you could use methods from a custom class that you wrote yourself.

Functions that don't belong to a class are called *top-level functions* (sometimes called *predefined* or *built-in functions*), meaning that you can call them without a constructor. Examples of functions that are built in to the top level of the ActionScript language are trace() and setInterval().

To add a top-level function call to your code, just add a single line of code in the Script pane of the Actions panel. For example, type the following:

```
trace("my message");
```

When you test the SWF file with this single line of code, the top-level trace() function is called, and text appears in the Output panel.

Remember: when you want to assign a method to a property, you omit the parentheses after the method name because you're passing a reference to the function:

```
my_mc.myMethod = aFunction;
```

However, when you want to invoke a method in your code, you need to include the parentheses following the method name:

```
my_mc.myMethod();
```

 For more information on top-level functions, see "About built-in and top-level functions" on page 210.

You can also define functions in numerous other ways. For more information on each kind of function, see the following sections:

- "About built-in and top-level functions" on page 210
- "Writing named functions" on page 211
- "Writing anonymous and callback functions" on page 212
- "About function literals" on page 215
- "Targeting and calling user-defined functions" on page 217
- "About constructor functions" on page 215

For information on writing and using functions and methods, see the following related sections. For information on using functions, see "Using functions in Flash" on page 219. For information on using methods, see "Understanding methods" on page 227.

 NOTE For information on writing code using Script Assist, see "Using Script Assist to write ActionScript," "Creating a startDrag/stopDrag event using Script Assist," and the ActionScript: Use Script Assist Mode tutorial (which begins with "Open the starter document") in Flash Help.

About built-in and top-level functions

As discussed in "About functions and methods" on page 206, a function is a block of ActionScript code that can be reused anywhere in a SWF file. If you pass values as parameters to a function, the function operates on those values. A function can also return values.

You can use functions that are built into the ActionScript language. They might be top level, as described in "About types of methods and functions" on page 207; or the function might be in a built-in class, such as Math or MovieClip, which you use as a method in your application.

You use built-in functions in ActionScript to perform certain tasks and to access information. For example, you can get the number of milliseconds the SWF file has been playing by using getTimer(). Or you can get the version number of Flash Player that hosts the file by using getVersion(). Functions that belong to an object are called *methods*. Functions that don't belong to an object are called *top-level functions* and are found in subcategories of the Global Functions category of the Actions panel.

Some built-in functions require you to pass certain values. If you pass more parameters than the function requires, the extra values are ignored. If you don't pass a required parameter, the empty parameters are assigned the undefined data type, which can cause errors during runtime.

NOTE To call a function, that function's definition must be in a frame that the playhead has reached.

Top-level functions are easy to use. To call a function, simply use the function name and pass any parameters required by that function. (For information on required parameters, see the entry for the function in the *ActionScript 2.0 Language Reference* in Flash Help). For example, add the following ActionScript to Frame 1 of the Timeline:

```
trace("my message");
```

When you test the SWF file, my message appears in the Output panel. Two other examples of top-level functions are setInterval() and getTimer(). The next example shows how to use both of these functions together. Add the following code to Frame 1 of the Timeline:

```
function myTimer():Void {
  trace(getTimer());
}
var intervalID:Number = setInterval(myTimer, 100);
```

This code creates a simple timer using getTimer(), and uses the setInterval() and trace() top-level functions to display the number of milliseconds since the SWF file began to play in Flash Player.

Calling a top-level function is like calling a *user defined function*. For more information, see "Targeting and calling user-defined functions" on page 217. For information on each function, see its entry in *ActionScript 2.0 Language Reference* in Flash Help.

Writing named functions

A named function is a kind of function that you commonly create in your ActionScript code to carry out all kinds of actions. When you create a SWF file, the named functions are compiled first, which means that you can reference the function anywhere in your code, as long as the function has been defined in the current or a previous frame. For example, if a function is defined in Frame 2 of a timeline, you cannot access that function in Frame 1 of the timeline.

The standard format for named functions is as follows:

```
function functionName(parameters) {
  // function block
}
```

This piece of code contains the following parts:

- functionName is the unique name of the function. All function names in a document must be unique.

- parameters contains one or more parameters that you pass to the function. Parameters are sometimes called *arguments*. For more information on parameters, see "Passing parameters to a function" on page 223.

- // function block contains all of the ActionScript code that's carried out by the function. This part contains the statements that "do stuff." You can put the code that you want to execute here. The // function block comment is a placeholder for where your code for the function block would go.

To use a named function:

1. Create a new document called **namedFunc.fla**.

2. Import a short sound file into the library by selecting File > Import > Import to Library and selecting a sound file.

3. Right-click the sound file and select Linkage.

4. Type **mySoundID** in the Identifier text box.

5. Select Frame 1 of the Timeline and add the following code to the Actions panel:

    ```
    function myMessage() {
      trace("mySoundID completed");
    }
    var my_sound:Sound = new Sound();
    my_sound.attachSound("mySoundID");
    my_sound.onSoundComplete = myMessage;
    my_sound.start();
    ```

    In this code you create a named function called `myMessage`, which you use later in the script to call a `trace()` function.

6. Select Control > Test Movie to test the SWF file.

You use the `function` statement to create your own function in ActionScript. Remember that parameters are optional; however, if you don't have parameters, you still need to include the brackets. The content between the curly braces ({ }) is called the *function block*.

You can write functions on the main timeline or within external ActionScript files, including class files.

You also write constructor functions in class files using this format (however, the name of the function matches the class). For more information on constructor functions, see "Writing the constructor function" on page 274. Also see Chapter 7, "Classes," on page 231 for information on and examples of writing functions in classes.

Writing anonymous and callback functions

A named function is a function that you reference in your script before or after you define it, whereas an *anonymous function* is an unnamed function that references itself; you reference the anonymous function when you create it. When you write ActionScript code, you will create many anonymous functions.

Anonymous functions are commonly used when you work with event handlers. To write an anonymous function, you could store a function literal inside a variable. Therefore, you can reference the function later in your code. The next example shows you how to write an anonymous function.

To write an anonymous function:

1. Create a movie clip on the Stage, and then select the clip.

2. Open the Property inspector, and type **my_mc** into the Instance Name text box.

3. Select Frame 1 of the Timeline, and type the following code into the Actions panel:

```
var myWidth = function () {
   trace(my_mc._width);
};
//later in code you can add
myWidth();
```

4. Select Control > Test Movie.

   The width of the movie clip is displayed in the Output panel.

You can also create a function inside an object, such as an XML or LoadVars instance. You can associate an anonymous function with a certain event to create a *callback function*. A function calls a callback function after a specific event occurs, such as after something finishes loading (onLoad()) or finishes animating (onMotionFinished()).

For example, sometimes you need to write ActionScript to handle data that loads into a SWF file from the server. After you finish loading data into a SWF file, you can access the data from that location. It's important to use ActionScript to check whether the data has been fully loaded. You can use callback functions to send a signal that the data has been loaded into the document.

In the following callback function, in which you load a remote XML document, you associate an anonymous function with the onLoad() event. You use XML.load() and the callback function, as shown in the following example. Type the following code on Frame 1 of the Timeline:

```
var my_xml:XML = new XML();
my_xml.onLoad = function(success:Boolean):Void {
   trace(success);
};
my_xml.load("http://www.helpexamples.com/crossdomain.xml");
```

You can see from the previous code snippet that the onLoad() event handler uses an anonymous function to handle the onLoad() event.

For more information on callback functions, see Chapter 10, "Handling Events," on page 335.

You could also use anonymous functions with the setInterval() function, as seen in the following code, which uses setInterval() to call the anonymous function approximately every 1000 milliseconds (1 second):

```
setInterval(function() {trace("interval");}, 1000);
```

You can use named functions instead of anonymous functions. Named functions are often easier to read and understand (except in some circumstances, such as callback functions). You can also forward-reference a named function, which means you reference it before the function exists on a timeline.

You cannot reference an anonymous function anywhere in your code (unless you assign it to a variable), as you can when you use a named function. For example, suppose that you have anonymous functions on Frame 5 of your FLA file, such as the following:

```
//with a movie clip called my_mc that spans the timeline
stop();
var myWidth = function () {
  trace(my_mc._width);
};
```

If you place the following code on Frame 1, it cannot reference the function:

```
myWidth();
```

Similarly, the following code placed on any frame does not work:

```
myWidth();
var myWidth:Function = function () {
  trace(my_mc._width);
};
```

However, this code works properly:

```
var myWidth:Function = function () {
  trace(my_mc._width);
};
myWidth();
```

> **NOTE** You could also place `myWidth()` on any frame that is after the frame that contains the `myWidth` function.

When defining a named function, calling it in a frame script works, even though the equivalent code with an anonymous function does not work:

```
// the following does work because you are calling a named function:
myWidth();
function myWidth() {
  trace("foo");
}

// the following does not work because you are calling an anonymous
    function:
myWidth();
var myWidth:Function = function () {
  trace("foo");
};
```

For more information, see "Writing named functions" on page 211.

NOTE

For information on writing code using Script Assist, see "Using Script Assist to write ActionScript," "Creating a startDrag/stopDrag event using Script Assist," and the ActionScript: Use Script Assist Mode tutorial (which begins with "Open the starter document") in Flash Help.

About function literals

A *function literal* is an unnamed function that you declare in an expression instead of in a statement. Function literals are useful when you need to use a function temporarily or to use a function in your code where you might use an expression instead. The syntax for a function literal is:

```
function (param1, param2, etc) {
  // statements
};
```

For example, the following code uses a function literal as an expression:

```
var yourName:String = "Ester";
setInterval(function() {trace(yourName);}, 200);
```

NOTE

When you redefine a function literal, the new function definition replaces the old definition.

You can store a function literal in a variable to access it later in your code. To do so, you use an *anonymous function*. For more information, see "Writing anonymous and callback functions" on page 212.

About constructor functions

The constructor of a class is a special function that is called automatically when you create an instance of a class by using the new keyword (such as, `var my_xml:XML = new XML();`). The constructor function has the same name as the class that contains it. For example, a custom Person class that you create would contain the following constructor function:

```
public function Person(speed:Number) {
  Person.numPeople++;
  this._speed = speed;
}
```

Then you could create a new instance by using:

```
var myPerson:Person = new Person();
```

 NOTE If you do not explicitly declare a constructor function in your class file—that is, if you don't create a function whose name matches that of the class—the compiler automatically creates an empty constructor function for you.

A class can contain only one constructor function; overloaded constructor functions are not allowed in ActionScript 2.0. Also, a constructor function cannot have a return type. For more information on writing constructor functions in class files, "Writing the constructor function" on page 274.

Defining global and timeline functions

In "About functions and methods" on page 206, you explored the different kinds of functions that are available in Flash. As with variables, functions are attached to the timeline of the movie clip that defines them, and you must use a target path to call them. As with variables, you can use the _global identifier to declare a global function that is available to all timelines and scopes without using a target path. To define a global function, precede the function name with the identifier _global, as shown in the following example:

```
_global.myFunction = function(myNum:Number):Number {
    return (myNum * 2) + 3;
};
trace(myFunction(5)) // 13
```

For information on _global and scope, "About variables and scope" on page 99.

To define a timeline function, use the function statement followed by the name of the function, any parameters to be passed to the function, and the ActionScript statements that indicate what the function does.

The following example is a function named areaOfCircle with the parameter radius:

```
function areaOfCircle(radius:Number):Number {
  return (Math.PI * radius * radius);
}
trace(areaOfCircle(8));
```

You can also define functions in numerous other ways. For more information on each kind of function, see the following sections:

- "About built-in and top-level functions" on page 210
- "Writing named functions" on page 211
- "Writing anonymous and callback functions" on page 212
- "About function literals" on page 215

- "About constructor functions" on page 215
- "Targeting and calling user-defined functions" on page 217

For information on naming functions, see "Naming functions" on page 218. For a detailed example of using functions in an external class file, see "Using functions in Flash" on page 219 and Chapter 7, "Classes," on page 231.

> **NOTE**
>
> For information on writing code using Script Assist, see "Using Script Assist to write ActionScript," "Creating a startDrag/stopDrag event using Script Assist," and the ActionScript: Use Script Assist Mode tutorial (which begins with "Open the starter document") in Flash Help.

Targeting and calling user-defined functions

User-defined functions are simply functions that you create yourself to use in applications, as opposed to functions in built-in classes that perform predefined functions. You name the functions yourself and add statements in the function block. Previous sections cover writing functions such as named, unnamed, and callback functions. For information on naming functions, see "Naming functions" on page 218, and for information on using functions, see "Using functions in Flash" on page 219.

You can use a target path to call a function in any timeline from any timeline, including from a timeline of a loaded SWF file. To call a function, type the target path to the name of the function, if necessary, and pass any required parameters inside parentheses. There are several forms of syntax for user-defined functions. The following code uses a path to call the `initialize()` function, which was defined on the current timeline and requires no parameters:

```
this.initialize();
```

The following example uses a relative path to call the `list()` function, which was defined in the `functionsClip` movie clip:

```
this._parent.functionsClip.list(6);
```

For information on writing named functions, see "Writing named functions" on page 211. For more information on parameters, see "Passing parameters to a function" on page 223.

You can also define your own named functions. For example, the following named function `helloWorld()` is user defined:

```
function helloWorld() {
  trace("Hello world!");
};
```

The following example shows you how to use a user-defined function in a FLA file.

To create and call a simple user-defined function:

1. Create a new Flash document and save it as **udf.fla.**

2. Add the following ActionScript to Frame 1 of the main Timeline:

```
function traceHello(name:String):Void {
  trace("hello, " + name + "!");
}
traceHello("world"); // hello, world!
```

The previous code creates a user-defined function named `traceHello()` that takes one argument, `name`, and traces a greeting message. To call the user-defined function, you can call `traceHello` from the same timeline as the function definition and pass a single string value.

3. Select Control > Test Movie to test the Flash document.

For more information on named functions, see "Writing named functions" on page 211. Classes contain many user-defined functions. For information on writing functions in class files, see "Using functions in Flash" on page 219. Also see the following sections in Chapter 7, "Classes": "Using methods and properties from a class file" on page 251, "About public, private, and static methods and properties (members)" on page 253, and "About class members" on page 256.

Naming functions

Function names should start with a lowercase letter. Your function names should describe the value the function returns, if any. For example, if the function returns the title of a song, you might name it `getCurrentSong()`.

Establish a standard for grouping similar functions (functions that relate to each other based on functionality), because ActionScript does not permit overloading. In the context of object-oriented programming (OOP), *overloading* refers to the ability to make your functions behave differently depending on what data types are passed into them.

As with variables, you cannot use special characters, and the method name cannot start with a number. For more information, see "Naming conventions" on page 746. For information on naming methods, see "Naming methods" on page 229.

Using functions in Flash

This section shows you how to use functions in an application. Some of the following code examples use ActionScript that resides in the FLA file, and other code examples place functions in a class file for comparison. For more information and examples on using functions in a class file, see Chapter 7, "Classes," on page 231. For detailed information and instruction on how to write functions for a class file, see "Example: Writing custom classes" on page 269.

To reduce the amount of work you have to do, as well as the size of your SWF file, try to reuse blocks of code whenever possible. One way you can reuse code is by calling a function multiple times instead of creating different code each time. Functions can be generic pieces of code; you can use the same blocks of code for slightly different purposes in a SWF file. Reusing code lets you create efficient applications and minimizes the ActionScript code that you must write, which reduces development time.

You can create functions in a FLA file or a class file or write ActionScript code that resides in a code-based component. The following examples show you how to create functions on a timeline and in a class file.

 By packing your code into class files or code-based components, you can easily share, distribute, or reuse blocks of code. Users can install your component, drag it onto the Stage, and use the code that you store in the file, such as the workflow for code-based components available in Flash (Window > Common Libraries > Classes).

The following example shows you how to create and call a function in a FLA file.

To create and call a function in a FLA file:

1. Create a new Flash document and save it as **basicFunction.fla**.

2. Select Window > Actions to open the Actions panel.

3. Type the following ActionScript code into the Script pane:

```
function helloWorld(){
  // statements here
  trace("Hello world!");
};
```

This ActionScript defines the (user-defined, named) function called `helloWorld()`. If you test your SWF file at this time, nothing happens. For example, you don't see the `trace` statement in the Output panel. To see the `trace` statement, you have to call the `helloWorld()` function.

4. Type the following line of ActionScript code after the function:

```
helloWorld();
```

This code calls the `helloWorld()` function.

5. Select Control > Test Movie to test the FLA file.

The following text is displayed in the Output panel: `Hello world!`

For information on passing values (parameters) to a function, see "Passing parameters to a function" on page 223.

There are several different ways that you can write functions on the main timeline. Most notably, you can use named functions and anonymous functions. For example, you can use the following syntax when you create functions:

```
function myCircle(radius:Number):Number {
    return (Math.PI * radius * radius);
}
trace(myCircle(5));
```

Anonymous functions are often more difficult to read. Compare the following code to the preceding code.

```
var myCircle:Function = function(radius:Number):Number {
    // function block here
    return (Math.PI * radius * radius);
};
trace(myCircle(5));
```

You can also place functions in class files when you use ActionScript 2.0, as the following example shows:

```
class Circle {
    public function area(radius:Number):Number {
        return (Math.PI * Math.pow(radius, 2));
    }
    public function perimeter(radius:Number):Number {
        return (2 * Math.PI * radius);
    }
    public function diameter(radius:Number):Number {
        return (radius * 2);
    }
}
```

For more information on writing functions in a class file, see Chapter 7, "Classes," on page 231.

As you can see in the previous code sample, you don't need to place functions on a timeline. The following example also puts functions in a class file. This is a good practice to adopt when you create large applications by using ActionScript 2.0, because it lets you reuse your code easily in several applications. When you want to reuse the functions in other applications, you can import the existing class rather than rewrite the code from scratch or duplicate the functions in the new application.

To create functions in a class file:

1. Create a new ActionScript document and save it as **Utils.as**.

2. Type the following ActionScript into the Script pane:

```
class Utils {
  public static function randomRange(min:Number, max:Number):Number {
    if (min > max) {
      var temp:Number = min;
      min = max;
      max = temp;
    }
    return (Math.floor(Math.random() * (max - min + 1)) + min);
  }
  public static function arrayMin(num_array:Array):Number {
    if (num_array.length == 0) {
      return Number.NaN;
    }
    num_array.sort(Array.NUMERIC | Array.DESCENDING);
    var min:Number = Number(num_array.pop());
    return min;
  }
  public static function arrayMax(num_array:Array):Number {
    if (num_array.length == 0) {
      return undefined;
    }
    num_array.sort(Array.NUMERIC);
    var max:Number = Number(num_array.pop());
    return max;
  }
}
```

3. Select File > Save to save the ActionScript file.

4. Create a new Flash document and save it as **classFunctions.fla** in the same directory as Utils.as.

5. Select Window > Actions to open the Actions panel.

6. Type the following ActionScript into the Script pane:

```
var randomMonth:Number = Utils.randomRange(0, 11);
var min:Number = Utils.arrayMin([3, 3, 5, 34, 2, 1, 1, -3]);
var max:Number = Utils.arrayMax([3, 3, 5, 34, 2, 1, 1, -3]);
trace("month: " + randomMonth);
trace("min: " + min); // -3
trace("max: " + max); // 34
```

7. Select Control > Test Movie to test the documents. The following text is displayed in the Output panel:

```
month: 7
min: -3
max: 34
```

> **NOTE** For information on writing code using Script Assist, see "Using Script Assist to write ActionScript," "Creating a startDrag/stopDrag event using Script Assist," and the ActionScript: Use Script Assist Mode tutorial (which begins with "Open the starter document") in Flash Help.

Using variables in functions

Local variables are valuable tools for organizing code and making it easy to understand. When a function uses local variables, it can hide its variables from all other scripts in the SWF file; local variables are invoked in the scope of the body of the function and cease to exist when the function exits. Flash also treats any parameters passed to a function as local variables.

> **NOTE** You can also use regular variables in a function. However, if you modify regular variables, it is good practice to use script comments to document these modifications.

To use variables in functions:

1. Create a new Flash document and save it as **flashvariables.fla**.

2. Add the following ActionScript to Frame 1 of the main Timeline:

```
var myName:String = "Ester";
var myAge:String = "65";
var myFavSoftware:String = "Flash";
function traceMe(yourFavSoftware:String, yourName:String,
  yourAge:String) {
  trace("I'm " + yourName + ", I like " + yourFavSoftware + ", and I'm "
  + yourAge + ".");
}
traceMe(myFavSoftware, myName, myAge);
```

3. Select Control > Test Movie to test the Flash document.

For more information on passing parameters, see "Passing parameters to a function" on page 223. For more information on variables and data, see Chapter 4, "Data and Data Types," on page 73

Passing parameters to a function

Parameters, also referred to as *arguments*, are the elements on which a function executes its code. (In this book, the terms *parameter* and *argument* are interchangeable.) You can pass parameters (values) to a function. You can then use these parameters for processing the function. You use the values within the function block (statements within the function).

Sometimes parameters are required, and sometimes they are optional. You might even have some required and some optional parameters in a single function. If you do not pass enough parameters to a function, Flash sets the missing parameter values to undefined, which may cause unexpected results in your SWF file.

The following function called myFunc() takes the parameter someText:

```
function myFunc(someText:String):Void {
    trace(someText);
}
```

After passing the parameter, you can pass a value to the function when you call the function. This value traces in the Output panel, as follows:

```
myFunc("This is what traces");
```

When you call the function, you should always pass the specified number of parameters unless your function checks for undefined values and sets default values accordingly. The function substitutes the passed values for the parameters in the function definition; if any parameters are missing, Flash sets their value to undefined. You regularly pass parameters into functions when you write ActionScript code.

You can also pass multiple parameters to a function, which can be as simple as the following:

```
var birthday:Date = new Date(1901, 2, 3);
trace(birthday);
```

Each parameter is separated by a comma delimiter. Many built-in functions in the ActionScript language have multiple parameters. For example, the startDrag() method of the MovieClip class takes five parameters, lockCenter, left, top, right, and bottom:

```
startDrag(lockCenter:Boolean, left:Number, top:Number, right:Number,
    bottom:Number):Void
```

To pass a parameter to a function:

1. Create a new Flash document and save it as **parameters.fla**.

2. Add the following code to Frame 1 of the Timeline:

```
function traceMe(yourMessage:String):Void {
  trace(yourMessage);
}
traceMe("How are you doing?");
```

The first few lines of code create a user-defined function called `traceMe()`, which takes a single parameter, `yourMessage`. The last line of code calls the `traceMe()` function and passes the string value "`How are you doing?`".

3. Select Control > Test Movie to test the Flash document.

The next example demonstrates how to pass multiple parameters to a function.

To pass multiple parameters to a function:

1. Create a new Flash document and save it as **functionTest.fla**.

2. Add the following code to Frame 1 of the main Timeline:

```
function getArea(width:Number, height:Number):Number {
    return width * height;
}
```

The `getArea()` function takes two parameters, `width` and `height`.

3. Type the following code after the function:

```
var area:Number = getArea(10, 12);
trace(area); // 120
```

The `getArea()` function call assigns the values 10 and 12 to the width and height, respectively, and you save the return value in the `area` instance. Then you trace the values that you save in the `area` instance.

4. Select Control > Test Movie to test the SWF file.

You see `120` in the Output panel.

The parameters in the `getArea()` function are similar to values in a local variable; they exist while the function is called and cease to exist when the function exits.

In the next example, the ActionScript returns the value `NaN` (not a number) if you don't pass enough parameters to the `addNumbers()` function.

To pass a variable number of parameters to a function:

1. Create a new Flash document and save it as **functionTest2.fla**.

2. Add the following code to Frame 1 of the main Timeline:

```
function addNumbers(a:Number, b:Number, c:Number):Number {
    return (a + b + c);
}
trace(addNumbers(1, 4, 6)); // 11
trace(addNumbers(1, 4)); // NaN (Not a Number), c equals undefined
trace(addNumbers(1, 4, 6, 8)); // 11
```

If you don't pass enough parameters to the addNumbers function, the missing arguments are assigned a default value of undefined. If you pass too many parameters, the excess parameters are ignored.

3. Select Control > Test Movie to test the Flash document.

Flash displays the following values: 11, NaN, 11.

Returning values from functions

You use the return statement to return values from functions. The return statement specifies the value that is returned by a function. The return statement returns the result of an evaluation as a value of the function in which an expression executes. The return statement returns its result immediately to the calling code.

For more information, see %{return statement}% in the *ActionScript 2.0 Language Reference* in Flash Help.

The following rules govern how to use the return statement in functions:

- If you specify a return type other than Void for a function, you must include a return statement and it must be followed by the returned value in the function.

- If you specify a return type of Void, you do not need to include a return statement, but if you do, it must not be followed by any value.

- Regardless of the return type, you can use a return statement to exit from the middle of a function.

- If you don't specify a return type, including a return statement is optional.

For example, the following function returns the square of the parameter myNum and specifies that the returned value must be a Number data type:

```
function sqr(myNum:Number):Number {
    return myNum * myNum;
}
```

Some functions perform a series of tasks without returning a value. The next example returns the processed value. You are capturing that value in a variable, and then you can use that variable within your application.

To return a value and capture it in a variable:

1. Create a new Flash document and save it as **return.fla**.

2. Add the following code to Frame 1 of the main Timeline:

```
function getArea(width:Number, height:Number):Number {
    return width * height;
}
```

The getArea() function takes two parameters, width and height.

3. Type the following code after the function:

```
var area:Number = getArea(10, 12);
trace(area); // 120
```

The getArea() function call assigns the values 10 and 12 to the width and height, respectively, and you save the return value in the area instance. Then you trace the values that you save in the area instance.

4. Select Control > Test Movie to test the SWF file.

   You see 120 in the Output panel.

   The parameters in the getArea() function are similar to values in a local variable; they exist while the function is called and cease to exist when the function exits.

About nested functions

You can call a function from inside another function. This lets you nest functions so that you can have them perform specific tasks in Flash.

For example, you can nest functions on a timeline to perform specific tasks on a string. Type the following code on Frame 1 of the Timeline:

```
var myStr:String = "My marshmallow chicken is yellow.";
trace("Original string: " + myStr);
function formatText():Void {
  changeString("Put chicken in microwave.");
  trace("Changed string: " + myStr);
}
function changeString(newtext:String):Void {
  myStr = newtext;
}
// Call the function.
formatText();
```

Select Control > Test Movie to test the nested function. The formatText() and changeString() functions are both applied to the string when you call the formatText() function.

Understanding methods

Methods are functions that are associated with a class. The class could be a custom class or built-in classes that are part of the ActionScript language. For information on comparing methods to functions, see "About functions and methods" on page 206 and "About types of methods and functions" on page 207.

For example, sortOn() is a built-in method associated with the Array class (sortOn is a function of the predefined Array class built into Flash).

To use the sortOn() method in a FLA file:

1. Create a new Flash document and save it as **methods.fla**.

2. Add the following code to Frame 1 of the Timeline:

```
var userArr:Array = new Array();
userArr.push({firstname:"George", age:39});
userArr.push({firstname:"Dan", age:43});
userArr.push({firstname:"Socks", age:2});
userArr.sortOn("firstname");
var userArrayLenth:Number = userArr.length;
var i:Number;
for (i = 0; i < userArrayLenth; i++) {
  trace(userArr[i].firstname);
}
```

You use the sortOn() method of the Array class to create a new Array object named userArr. The array is populated by three objects that contain a first name and age, and then the array is sorted based on the value of each object's firstname property. Finally, you loop over each item in the array and display the first name in the Output panel and sort the names alphabetically by first letter.

3. Select Control > Test Movie to test the SWF file.

This code displays the following in the Output panel:

```
Dan
George
Socks
```

As demonstrated in "Writing named functions" on page 211, when you write the following code on Frame 1 of the Timeline, your ActionScript code defines a function called eatCabbage().

```
function eatCabbage() {
    trace("tastes bad");
}
eatCabbage();
```

However, if you write the eatCabbage() function within a class file and, for example, call eatCabbage() in the FLA file, then eatCabbage() is considered to be a method.

The next examples show you how to create methods within a class.

To compare methods and functions:

1. Create a new ActionScript file, select File > Save As, and save it as **EatingHabits.as**.

2. Type the following ActionScript code in the Script window:

```
class EatingHabits {
  public function eatCabbage():Void {
    trace("tastes bad");
  }
}
```

3. Save your changes to EatingHabits.as.

4. Create a new Flash document, select File > Save As, name it **methodTest.fla**, and save this file in the same directory as EatingHabits.as.

5. Type the following ActionScript code onto Frame 1 of the Timeline:

```
var myHabits:EatingHabits = new EatingHabits();
myHabits.eatCabbage();
```

When you use this ActionScript, you are calling the eatCabbage() method of the EatingHabits class.

 NOTE When you use methods of any built-in class (in addition to the custom class you wrote earlier in this procedure), you are using a *method* on a timeline.

6. After the previous line of ActionScript, add the following code:

```
function eatCarrots():Void {
    trace("tastes good");
}
eatCarrots();
```

In this code, you write and call the eatCarrots() function.

7. Select Control > Test Movie to test the SWF file.

Naming methods

You should use verbs to name methods, and words with mixed cases for concatenated words, making sure that the first letter is lowercase. For example, you might name methods in the following ways:

```
sing();
boogie();
singLoud();
danceFast();
```

You use verbs for most method names because methods perform an operation on an object. As with variables, you cannot use special characters, and the method name cannot start with a number. For more information, see "Naming conventions" on page 746.

CHAPTER 7

Classes

This chapter introduces you to using and writing classes using ActionScript 2.0. Classes are the backbone of ActionScript 2.0, and are more important than they were in earlier versions of Macromedia Flash. You will learn how important classes are in Flash throughout this chapter.

This chapter begins by explaining some fundamental terminology and how it relates to classes and object-oriented programming (OOP). Next you walk through a sample class file and understand how each section of the class file works and how the class is organized. The rest of the chapter shows you how to create your own custom classes and how to use them within your Flash documents. You learn about the Flash classpath and how a class should be documented so that other people who read or use your code can easily understand the code and the class's overall purpose.

This section contains code examples that you can use to become familiar with creating classes in ActionScript 2.0. By the end of this chapter, you should be able to write a typical class file, understand and recognize Flash classes, and also feel comfortable reading other people's class files.

If you're not familiar with ActionScript 2.0 scripting, see Chapter 5, "Syntax and Language Fundamentals," on page 117 and Chapter 19, "Best Practices and Coding Conventions for ActionScript 2.0," on page 745.

For more information on working with custom and built-in classes, see the following topics:

About object-oriented programming and Flash

ActionScript 2.0 is an object-oriented language. Like ActionScript, OOP languages are based on the concept of *classes* and *instances*. A class defines all of the properties that distinguish a series of objects. For example, a User class represents a bunch of users who are using your application. Then, you have an *instantiation* of the class, which, for the User class, is one of the individual users—one of its members. The instantiation produces an *instance* of the User class, and that instance has all of the properties of the User class.

Classes are also considered like *data types* or *templates* that you can create to define a new type of object. For example, if you need a data type of Lettuce in your application, you might write the Lettuce class. This defines the Lettuce object, and then you can assign your Lettuce methods (`wash()`) and properties (`leafy` or `bugs`). To define a class, you use the `class` keyword in an external script file. You can create an external script file in the Flash authoring tool by selecting File > New and then selecting ActionScript File.

Flash Player 8, available in both Flash Basic 8 and Flash Professional 8, adds several new features to the ActionScript language such as filter effects, file upload and download, and the External API. As always, ActionScript 2.0 provides several powerful and familiar OOP concepts and keywords (such as `class`, `interface`, and `package`) found in other programming languages, such as Java. The programming language lets you build program structures that are reusable, scalable, robust, and maintainable. It can also decrease development time by providing users with thorough coding assistance and debugging information. You can use ActionScript 2.0 to create objects and establish inheritance and to create custom classes and extend the Flash top-level and built-in classes. You learn how to create classes and use custom classes in this chapter.

Flash Basic 8 and Flash Professional 8 include approximately 65 top-level and built-in classes that provide everything from basic, or "primitive," data types (Array, Boolean, Date, and so on), to custom errors and events, as well as several ways to load external content (XML, images, raw binary data, and more). You can also write your own custom classes and integrate them into your Flash documents or even extend the top-level classes and add your own functionality or modify existing functionality. For example, "About class members" on page 256 in this chapter shows you how to make a custom Person class that contains custom properties for the person's name and age. You can then treat this custom class as a new data type in your documents and create a new instance of the class using the `new` operator.

For more information on working with OOP, see the following topics:

- "The benefits of using classes" on page 233
- "About packages" on page 234
- "About values and data types" on page 237
- "Object-oriented programming fundamentals" on page 237

The benefits of using classes

In OOP, a class defines a category of object. A class describes the properties (data) and methods (behaviors) for an object, much like an architectural blueprint describes the characteristics of a building. You write a custom class in an external ActionScript (AS) file and you can import it into your application when you compile the FLA file.

Classes can be very useful when you build larger Flash applications because you can organize a lot of the application's complexity in external class files. When you move a lot of the logic into a custom class, you can not only make the code easier to reuse, but you can also "hide" some of the methods and properties from other parts of the ActionScript code. This helps you prevent people from accessing sensitive information or changing data that shouldn't be changed.

When you use a class, you can also extend existing classes and add new functionality or modify existing functionality. For example, if you create three very similar classes, you can write a base class and then write two other classes that extend the base class. These two classes can add additional methods and properties, so that you don't need to create three class files that all duplicate the same code and logic.

Another benefit of using classes is code reusability. For example, if you create a custom class that creates a custom progress bar using the Drawing application programming interface (API), you could save the progress bar class in your classpath and reuse the same code in all of your Flash documents by importing the custom class. For more information on setting the classpath, see "About importing class files" on page 245 and "About setting and modifying the classpath" on page 246.

About packages

When you are creating classes, you organize your ActionScript class files in *packages*. A package is a directory that contains one or more class files and that resides in a designated classpath directory (see "About importing class files" on page 245 and "About setting and modifying the classpath" on page 246). A package can, in turn, contain other packages, called *subpackages*, each with its own class files.

Like variables, package names must be identifiers; that is, the first character can be a letter, underscore (_), or dollar sign ($), and each subsequent character can be a letter, number, underscore, or dollar sign. There are preferred ways to name packages, which for example recommend that you avoid using underscores or dollar sign characters. For more information on naming packages, see "Naming packages" on page 755.

Packages are commonly used to organize related classes. For example, you might have three related classes, Square, Circle, and Triangle, that are defined in Square.as, Circle.as, and Triangle.as. Assume that you've saved the ActionScript files to a directory specified in the classpath, as shown in the following example:

```
// In Square.as:
class Square {}

// In Circle.as:
class Circle {}

// In Triangle.as:
class Triangle {}
```

Because these three class files are related, you might decide to put them in a package (directory) called Shapes. In this case, the fully qualified class name would contain the package path, as well as the simple class name. Package paths are denoted with dot (.) syntax, where each dot indicates a subdirectory.

For example, if you placed each ActionScript file that defines a shape in the Shapes directory, you would need to change the name of each class file to reflect the new location, as follows:

```
// In Shapes/Square.as:
class Shapes.Square {}

// In Shapes/Circle.as:
class Shapes.Circle {}

// In Shapes/Triangle.as:
class Shapes.Triangle {}
```

To reference a class that resides in a package directory, you can either specify its fully qualified class name or import the package by using the import statement. For more information, see "Working with packages" on page 236.

A comparison of classes and packages

In OOP, a class defines a category of object. Classes are essentially data types that you can create if you want to define a new type of object in your application. A class describes the *properties* (data) and *behaviors* (methods) for an object, much like an architectural blueprint describes the characteristics of a building. The properties (variables defined within a class) and methods of a class are collectively called the class's *members*. To use the properties and methods defined by a class, you generally first create an instance of that class (except for classes that have all static members (see "About class (static) members" on page 304, such as the top-level Math class, and "Static methods and properties" on page 255). The relationship between an instance and its class is similar to the relationship between a house and its blueprints.

Packages in Flash are directories that contain one or more class files and reside in a designated file path. You might place related custom class files within a single directory. For example, you might have three related classes called SteelWidget, PlasticWidget, and WoodWidget that are defined in SteelWidget.as, PlasticWidget.as, and WoodWidget.as. You would organize these classes in the Widget package. For more information on packages, see "Working with packages" on page 236 and "Creating and packaging your class files" on page 272.

Working with packages

Packages are directories that contain one or more class files and reside in a designated classpath directory. For example, the flash.filters package is a directory on your hard disk that contains several class files for each filter type (such as BevelFilter, BlurFilter, DropShadowFilter, and so on) in Flash 8.

> **NOTE**
>
> To use the `import` statement, you must specify ActionScript 2.0 and Flash Player 6 or later in the Flash tab of your FLA file's Publish Settings dialog box.

The `import` statement lets you access classes without specifying their fully qualified names. For example, if you want to use the BlurFilter class in a script, you must refer to it by its fully qualified name (flash.filters.BlurFilter) or import it; if you import it, you can refer to it by its class name (BlurFilter). The following ActionScript code demonstrates the differences between using the `import` statement and using fully qualified class names.

If you don't import the BlurFilter class, your code needs to use the fully qualified class name (package name followed by class name) in order to use the filter:

```
// without importing
var myBlur:flash.filters.BlurFilter = new flash.filters.BlurFilter(10, 10,
    3);
```

The same code, written with an `import` statement, lets you access the BlurFilter using only the class name instead of always having to use the fully qualified name. This can save typing and reduce the chance of making typing mistakes:

```
// with importing
import flash.filters.BlurFilter;
var myBlur:BlurFilter = new BlurFilter(10, 10, 3);
```

If you were importing several classes within a package (such as the BlurFilter, DropShadowFilter, and GlowFilter) you could use one of two methods of importing each class. The first method of importing multiple classes is to import each class using a separate `import` statement, as seen in the following snippet:

```
import flash.filters.BlurFilter;
import flash.filters.DropShadowFilter;
import flash.filters.GlowFilter;
```

Using individual `import` statements for each class within a package can quickly become very time consuming and prone to typing mistakes. The second method of importing classes within a package is to use a wildcard import that imports all classes within a certain level of a package. The following ActionScript shows an example of using a wildcard import:

```
import flash.filters.*; // imports each class within flash.filters package
```

The `import` statement applies only to the current script (frame or object) in which it's called. For example, suppose on Frame 1 of a Flash document you import all the classes in the macr.util package. On that frame, you can reference classes in that package by their class names instead of their fully qualified names. If you wanted to use the class name on another frame script, however, you would need to reference classes in that package by their fully qualified names or add an `import` statement to the other frame that imports the classes in that package.

When using `import` statements, it's also important to note that classes are imported only for the level specified. For example, if you imported all classes in the mx.transitions package, only those classes within the /transitions/ directory are imported, not all classes within subdirectories (such as the classes in the mx.transitions.easing package).

 TIP If you import a class but don't use it in your script, the class isn't exported as part of the SWF file. This means you can import large packages without being concerned about the size of the SWF file; the bytecode associated with a class is included in a SWF file only if that class is actually used.

About values and data types

Data, values, and types are important when you start writing classes and using them. You learned about data and types in Chapter 4, "Data and Data Types," on page 73. When you work with classes, remember that data types describe the kind of information a variable or ActionScript element can contain, such as Boolean, Number, and String. For more information, see "About data types" on page 74.

Expressions have values, while values and properties have *types*. The values that you can set and get to and from a property in your class must be compatible with that property. Type compatibility means the type of a value is compatible with the type that is in use, such as the following example:

```
var myNum:Number = 10;
```

For more information on strict data typing, see "About assigning data types and strict data typing" on page 83.

Object-oriented programming fundamentals

In the following sections, you will examine some of the terminology used throughout this chapter before you start writing ActionScript code. This brief introduction to principles involved in developing object-oriented programs helps you follow the examples and sections within this chapter and the rest of this book. These principles are described in more depth in the rest of this chapter, along with details on how they are implemented in Flash 8.

The following sections use the analogy of a cat, demonstrating how cats might compare to OOP concepts.

Objects

Think of a real-world object, such as a cat. A cat could be said to have *properties* (or states), such as name, age, and color; a cat also has behaviors such as sleeping, eating, and purring. In the world of OOP, objects also have properties and behaviors. Using object-oriented techniques, you can model a real-world object (such as a cat) or a more abstract object (such as a chemical process).

 NOTE The word *behaviors* is used generically here and does not refer to the Behaviors panel in the Flash authoring environment.

For more information on objects, see "Object data type" on page 81.

Instances and class members

Continuing with the real-world analogy of a cat, consider that there are cats of different colors, ages, and names, with different ways of eating and purring. But despite their individual differences, all cats are members of the same category, or in OOP terms, the same class: the class of cats. In OOP terminology, each individual cat is said to be an *instance* of the Cat class.

Likewise in OOP, a class defines a blueprint for a type of object. The characteristics and behaviors that belong to a class are jointly referred to as *members* of that class. The characteristics (in the cat example, the name, age, and color) are called *properties* of the class and are represented as variables; the behaviors (play, sleep) are called *methods* of the class and are represented as functions.

For more information on instances and class members, see "About class members" on page 256 and "Using class members" on page 260.

Inheritance

One of the primary benefits of OOP is that you can create *subclasses* of (or *extend*) a class; the subclass then inherits all the properties and methods of the class. The subclass typically defines additional methods and properties or overrides methods or properties defined in the superclass. Subclasses can also override (provide their own definitions for) methods defined in a superclass.

One of the major benefits of using a superclass/subclass structure is that it is easier to reuse similar code between various classes. For example, you could build a superclass called Animal, which contains common characteristics and behaviors of all animals. Next you could build several subclasses that inherit from the Animal superclass and add characteristics and behaviors specific to that type of animal.

You might create a Cat class that inherits from another class. For example, you might create a Mammal class that defines certain properties and behaviors common to all mammals. You could then create a Cat subclass that extends the Mammal class. Another subclass, say, the Siamese class, could extend (*subclass*) the Cat class, and so on.

Writing subclasses lets you reuse code. Instead of recreating all the code common to both classes, you can simply extend an existing class.

 TIP In a complex application, determining how to structure the hierarchy of your classes is an important part of the design process. Make sure you determine this hierarchy before you begin to program.

For more information on inheritance and subclasses, see Chapter 8, "Inheritance," on page 307.

Interfaces

Interfaces in OOP can be described as templates of class definitions, and classes that implement interfaces are required to implement that template of methods. Using the cat analogy, an interface is similar to a blueprint of a cat: the blueprint tells you which parts you need, but not necessarily how those parts are assembled, or how the parts work.

You can use interfaces to add structure and ease of maintenance to your applications. Because ActionScript 2.0 supports extending only from a single superclass, you can use interfaces as a form of limited multiple inheritance.

You can also think of an interface as a "programming contract" that you can use to enforce relationships between otherwise unrelated classes. For example, suppose you are working with a team of programmers, each of whom is working on a different part (class) of the same application. While designing the application, you agree on a set of methods that the different classes use to communicate. So you create an interface that declares these methods, their parameters, and their return types. Any class that implements this interface must provide definitions for those methods; otherwise, a compiler error results.

For more information on inheritance, see Chapter 8, "Inheritance," on page 307. For more information on interfaces, see Chapter 9, "Interfaces," on page 319.

Encapsulation

In elegant object-oriented design, objects are seen as "black boxes" that contain, or *encapsulate*, functionality. A programmer should be able to interact with an object by knowing only its properties, methods, and events (its programming interface), without knowing the details of its implementation. This approach enables programmers to think at higher levels of abstraction and provides an organizing framework for building complex systems.

Encapsulation is why ActionScript 2.0 includes, for example, member access control, so details of the implementation can be made private and invisible to code outside an object. The code outside the object is forced to interact with the object's programming interface rather than with the implementation details (which can be hidden in private methods and properties). This approach provides some important benefits; for example, it lets the creator of the object change the object's implementation without requiring any changes to code outside of the object—that is, as long as the programming interface doesn't change.

For more information on encapsulation, see "About using encapsulation" on page 267.

Polymorphism

OOP lets you express differences between individual classes using a technique called *polymorphism*, by which classes can override methods of their superclasses and define specialized implementations of those methods. In Flash, subclasses can define specialized implementations of methods inherited from its superclass but cannot access the superclass's implementation as in other programming languages.

For example, you might start with a class called Mammal that has `play()` and `sleep()` methods. You then create Cat, Monkey, and Dog subclasses to extend the Mammal class. The subclasses override the `play()` method from the Mammal class to reflect the habits of those particular kinds of animals. Monkey implements the `play()` method to swing from trees; Cat implements the `play()` method to pounce at a ball of yarn; Dog implements the `play()` method to fetch a ball. Because the `sleep()` functionality is similar among the animals, you would use the superclass implementation.

For more information on polymorphism, see Chapter 8, "Inheritance," on page 307 and "Using polymorphism in an application" on page 314.

Writing custom class files

The following example examines the parts of a class file. You learn how to write a class, and how you can modify the class to extend the ways that you can use it with Flash. You learn about the parts of a class and how to import them as well as related information about working with custom class files in Flash.

You begin by looking at a very simple class. The following example shows the organization of a simple class called UserClass.

To define a class, you use the `class` keyword in an external script file (that is, not in a script you are writing in the Actions panel). The class structure is also pertinent for interface files. This structure is illustrated below, and following this illustration you create a class.

- The class file begins with documentation comments that include a general description of the code as well as author and version information.
- Add your `import` statements (if applicable).
- Write a package statement, class declaration, or interface declaration, as follows:
  `class UserClass {...}`
- Include any necessary class or interface implementation comments. In these comments, add information that is pertinent for the entire class or interface.
- Add all your static variables. Write the public class variables first and follow them with private class variables.
- Add instance variables. Write the public member variables first, and follow them with private member variables.
- Add the constructor statement, such as the one in the following example:
  `public function UserClass(username:String, password:String) {...}`
- Write your methods. Group methods by their functionality, not by their accessibility or scope. Organizing methods this way helps improve the readability and clarity of your code.
- Write the getter/setter methods into the class file.

The following example looks at a simple ActionScript class named User.

To create class files:

1. Select File > New and then select ActionScript File, and then click OK.

2. Select File > Save As and name the new file **User.as**.

3. Type the following ActionScript code into the Script window:

```
/**
    User class
    author: John Doe
    version: 0.8
    modified: 08/21/2005
    copyright: Macromedia, Inc.

    This code defines a custom User class that allows you to create new
    users and specify user login information.
*/

class User {
    // private instance variables
    private var __username:String;
    private var __password:String;

    // constructor statement
    public function User(p_username:String, p_password:String) {
        this.__username = p_username;
        this.__password = p_password;
    }

    public function get username():String {
        return this.__username;
    }
    public function set username(value:String):Void {
        this.__username = value;
    }

    public function get password():String {
        return this.__password;
    }
    public function set password(value:String):Void {
        this.__password = value;
    }
}
```

4. Save your changes to the class file.

The previous code snippet begins with a standardized *documentation comment*, which specifies the class name, author, version, date the class was last modified, copyright information, and a brief description of what the class does.

The User class's constructor statement takes two parameters: p_username and p_password, which are copied into the class's private instance variables __username and __password. The remainder of the code in the class defines the getter and setter properties for the private instance variables. If you want to create a read-only property, then you would define a getter function, but not a setter function. For example, if you want to make sure a user name cannot be changed after it has been defined, you would delete the username setter function in the User class file.

5. Select File > New and then select Flash Document.

6. Select File > Save As and name the file **user_test.fla**. Save the file in the same directory as User.as.

7. Type the following ActionScript into Frame 1 of the Timeline:

```
import User;
var user1:User = new User("un1", "pw1");
trace("Before:");
trace("\t username = " + user1.username); // un1
trace("\t password = " + user1.password); // pw1
user1.username = "1nu";
user1.password = "1wp";
trace("After:");
trace("\t username = " + user1.username); // 1nu
trace("\t password = " + user1.password); // 1wp
```

Because the User class you created previously is very basic, the ActionScript in the Flash document is also very straightforward. The first line of code imports the custom User class into your Flash document. Importing the User class lets you use the class as a custom data type.

A single instance of the User class is defined and assigned to a variable named user1. You assign the user1 User object a value and define a username of un1 and a password of pw1. The following two trace statements display the current value of user1.username and user1.password using the User class's getter functions, which both return strings. The next two lines use the User class's setter functions to set new values for the username and password variables. Finally, you trace the values for username and password to the Output panel. The trace statements display the modified values that you set using the setter functions.

8. Save the FLA file, and then select Control > Test Movie to test the files.

You see the results of the `trace` statements in the Output panel. In the next examples, you use these files in an application.

A sample file on your hard disk demonstrates how to create a dynamic menu with XML data and a custom class file. The sample calls the ActionScript `XmlMenu()` constructor and passes it two parameters: the path to the XML menu file and a reference to the current timeline. The rest of the functionality resides in a custom class file, XmlMenu.as.

You can find the sample source file, xmlmenu.fla, in the Samples folder on your hard disk.

■ On Windows, browse to *boot drive*\Program Files\Macromedia\Flash 8\Samples and Tutorials\Samples\ActionScript\XML_Menu.

■ On the Macintosh, browse to *Macintosh HD*/Applications/Macromedia Flash 8/Samples and Tutorials/Samples/ActionScript/XML_Menu.

About working with custom classes in an application

In "Writing custom class files" on page 241, you created a custom class file. In the following sections, you use that class file in an application. At the minimum, the workflow for creating classes involves the following steps:

1. Define a class in an external ActionScript class file. For information on defining and writing a class file, see "Writing custom class files" on page 241.

2. Save the class file to a designated classpath directory (a location where Flash looks for classes), or in the same directory as the application's FLA file. For more information on setting the classpath, see "About setting and modifying the classpath" on page 246. For a comparison and more information on importing class files, see "About importing class files" on page 245.

3. Create an instance of the class in another script, either in a FLA document or an external script file or by creating a subclass based on the original class. For more information on creating an instance of a class, see "Creating instances of classes in an example" on page 284.

The following sections in this chapter contain code examples that you can use to become familiar with creating classes in ActionScript 2.0. If you're not familiar with ActionScript 2.0, please read Chapter 4, "Data and Data Types," on page 73 and Chapter 5, "Syntax and Language Fundamentals," on page 117.

For more information on working with custom classes, see the following topics:

- "About importing class files" on page 245
- "Using a class file in Flash" on page 250
- "Using methods and properties from a class file" on page 251
- "About class members" on page 256
- "About getter and setter methods" on page 261
- "How the compiler resolves class references" on page 249
- "About dynamic classes" on page 265
- "About using encapsulation" on page 267
- "About using the this keyword in classes" on page 268

A sample file on your hard disk demonstrates how to create a dynamic menu with XML data and a custom class file. The sample calls the ActionScript XmlMenu() constructor and passes it two parameters: the path to the XML menu file and a reference to the current timeline. The rest of the functionality resides in a custom class file, XmlMenu.as.

You can find the sample source file, xmlmenu.fla, in the Samples folder on your hard disk.

- On Windows, browse to *boot drive*\Program Files\Macromedia\Flash 8\Samples and Tutorials\Samples\ActionScript\XML_Menu.
- On the Macintosh, browse to *Macintosh HD*/Applications/Macromedia Flash 8/Samples and Tutorials/Samples/ActionScript/XML_Menu.

About importing class files

In order to use a class or interface that you've defined, Flash must locate the external ActionScript files that contain the class or interface definition so that it can import the file. The list of directories in which Flash searches for class, interface, function, and variable definitions is called the *classpath*. Flash has two classpath settings—a global classpath and a document-level classpath:

- **Global classpath** is a classpath that's shared by all Flash documents. You set it in the Preferences dialog box (Edit > Preferences (Windows) or Flash > Preferences (Macintosh), click ActionScript in the Category list, and then click ActionScript 2.0 Settings).
- **Document-level classpath** is a classpath that you specifically define for a single Flash document. It is set in the Publish Settings dialog box (File > Publish Settings, select the Flash tab, and then click the Settings button).

When you import class files, the following rules apply:

- The `import` statements can exist in the following locations:
    - Anywhere before the class definition in class files
    - Anywhere in frame or object scripts
    - Anywhere in ActionScript files that you include in an application (using the `#include` statement).
- You import individual, packaged definitions using this syntax:

  `import flash.display.BitmapData;`
- You can import entire packages using the wildcard syntax:

  `import flash.display.*;`

You can also include ActionScript code in a Flash document (FLA) file using an `include` statement. The following rules apply to the `include` statement:

- `include` statements are essentially a copy and paste of the content inside the included ActionScript file.
- `include` statements inside ActionScript class files are relative to the subdirectory that contains the file.
- An `include` statement in a FLA file can only bring in code that is valid inside FLA files, and the same goes for other places that `include` statements can live. For example, if you have an `include` statement inside a class definition, only property and method definitions can exist in the included ActionScript file:

```
// Foo.as
class Foo {
   #include "FooDef.as"
}

// FooDef.as:
var fooProp;
function fooMethod() {}
trace("Foo"); // This statement is not permitted in a class definition.
```

For more information on the `include` statement, see %{#include directive}% in the *ActionScript 2.0 Language Reference* in Flash Help. For more information on classpaths, see "About setting and modifying the classpath" on page 246.

About setting and modifying the classpath

In order to use a class or interface that you've defined, Flash must locate the external ActionScript files that contain the class or interface definition. The list of directories in which Flash searches for class and interface definitions is called the *classpath*.

When you create an ActionScript class file, you need to save the file to one of the directories specified in the classpath or a subdirectory therein. (You can modify the classpath to include the desired directory path). Otherwise, Flash won't be able to resolve, that is, locate, the class or interface specified in the script. Subdirectories that you create within a classpath directory are called packages and let you organize your classes. (For more information on packages, see "Creating and packaging your class files" on page 272.)

Flash has two classpath settings: a *global classpath* and a *document-level classpath*. The global classpath is a classpath that's shared by all of your Flash documents. The document-level classpath is a classpath that you specifically define for a single Flash document.

The global classpath applies to external ActionScript files and to FLA files, and you set it in the Preferences dialog box (Windows: Edit > Preferences (Windows) or Flash > Preferences (Macintosh), select ActionScript from the Category list, and then click ActionScript 2.0 Settings). You can set the document-level classpath in the Flash document's Publish Settings dialog box (File > Publish Settings, select the Flash tab, and then click the Settings button).

<table>
<tr><td></td><td>When you click the Check Syntax button above the Script pane while editing an ActionScript file, the compiler looks only in the global classpath. ActionScript files aren't associated with FLA files in Edit mode and don't have their own classpath.</td></tr>
</table>

Using a global classpath

The global classpath is a classpath that's shared by all of your Flash documents.

You can modify the global classpath using the Preferences dialog box. To modify the document-level classpath setting, you use the Publish Settings dialog box for the FLA file. In both cases, you can add absolute directory paths (for example, C:/my_classes) and relative directory paths (for example, ../my_classes or "."). The order of directories in the dialog box reflects the order in which they are searched.

By default, the global classpath contains one absolute path and one relative path. The absolute path is denoted by $(LocalData)/Classes in the Preferences dialog box. The location of the absolute path is shown here:

- Windows: Hard Disk\Documents and Settings*user*\Local Settings\ Application Data\Macromedia\Flash 8*language*\Configuration\Classes.
- Macintosh: Hard Disk/Users/*user*/Library/Application Support/Macromedia/Flash 8/ *language*/Configuration/Classes.

<table>
<tr><td></td><td>Do not delete the absolute global classpath. Flash uses this classpath to access built-in classes. If you accidentally delete this classpath, reinstate it by adding $(LocalData)/Classes as a new classpath.</td></tr>
</table>

The relative path portion of the global classpath is denoted by a single dot (.) and points to the current document directory. Be aware that relative classpaths can point to different directories, depending on the location of the document being compiled or published.

You can use the following steps to add a global classpath or edit an existing classpath.

To modify the global classpath:

1. Select Edit > Preferences (Windows) or Flash > Preferences (Macintosh) to open the Preferences dialog box.

2. Click the ActionScript in the left column, and then click the ActionScript 2.0 Settings button.

3. Click the Browse to Path button to browse to the directory you want to add.

4. Browse to the path that you want to add and click OK.

To delete a directory from the classpath:

1. Select the path in the Classpath list.

2. Click the Remove from Path button.

> **NOTE**
>
> Do not delete the absolute global classpath. Flash uses this classpath to access built-in classes. If you accidentally delete this classpath, you can reinstate it by adding $(LocalData)/Classes as a new classpath.

For information on importing packages, see "Working with packages" on page 236.

Using a document-level classpath

The document-level classpath applies only to FLA files. You set the document-level classpath in the Publish Settings dialog box for a particular FLA file (File > Publish Settings, then click the Flash tab, and then click ActionScript 2.0 Settings). The document-level classpath is empty by default. When you create and save a FLA file in a directory, that directory becomes a designated classpath directory.

When you create classes, in some cases you might want to store them in a directory that you then add to the list of global classpath directories in the following situations:

■ If you have a set of utility classes that all your projects use

■ If you want to check the syntax of your code (click the Check Syntax button) that's within the external ActionScript file

Creating a directory prevents the loss of custom classes if you ever uninstall and reinstall Flash, especially if the default global classpath directory is deleted and overwritten, because you would lose any classes that you stored in that directory.

For example, you might create a directory such as the following for your custom classes:

- Windows: Hard Disk\Documents and Settings*user*\custom classes.
- Macintosh: Hard Disk/Users/*user*/custom classes.

Then, you would add this path to the list of global classpaths (see "Using a global classpath" on page 247).

When Flash attempts to resolve class references in a FLA script, it first searches the document-level classpath specified for that FLA file. If Flash doesn't find the class in that classpath, or if that classpath is empty, it searches the global classpath. If Flash doesn't find the class in the global classpath, a compiler error occurs.

To modify the document-level classpath:

1. Select File > Publish Settings to open the Publish Settings dialog box.
2. Click the Flash tab.
3. Click the Settings button next to the ActionScript Version pop-up menu.
4. You can either manually type a file path or you can click the Browse to Path button to browse to the directory you want to add to the classpath.

> **NOTE** To edit an existing classpath directory, select the path in the Classpath list, click the Browse to Path button, browse to the directory you want to add, and click OK.

> **NOTE** To delete a directory from the classpath, select the path in the Classpath list, and click the Remove Selected Path (-) button.

For more information on packages, see "About packages" on page 234.

How the compiler resolves class references

When Flash attempts to resolve class references in a FLA script, it first searches the document-level classpath specified for that FLA file. If the class is not found in that classpath, or if that classpath is empty, Flash searches the global classpath. If the class is not found in the global classpath, a compiler error occurs.

In Flash Professional, when you click the Check Syntax button while editing an ActionScript file, the compiler looks only in the global classpath; ActionScript files aren't associated with FLA files in Edit mode and don't have their own classpath.

Using a class file in Flash

To create an instance of an ActionScript class, use the `new` operator to invoke the class's constructor function. The constructor function always has the same name as the class and returns an instance of the class, which you typically assign to a variable. For example, if you were using the User class from "Writing custom class files" on page 241, you would write the following code to create a new User object:

```
var firstUser:User = new User();
```

> In some cases, you don't need to create an instance of a class to use its properties and methods. For more information on class (static) members, see "About class (static) members" on page 304 and "Static methods and properties" on page 255.

Use the dot (.) operator to access the value of a property in an instance. Type the name of the instance on the left side of the dot, and the name of the property on the right side. For example, in the following statement, `firstUser` is the instance and `username` is the property:

```
firstUser.username
```

You can also use the top-level or built-in classes that make up the ActionScript language in a Flash document. For example, the following code creates a new Array object and then shows its `length` property:

```
var myArray:Array = new Array("apples", "oranges", "bananas");
trace(myArray.length); // 3
```

For more information on using custom classes in Flash, see "Example: Using custom class files in Flash" on page 282. For information on the constructor function, see "Writing the constructor function" on page 274.

Using methods and properties from a class file

In OOP, members (properties or methods) of a class can be instance members or class members. Instance members are created for each instance of the class; they are defined to the prototype of the class when they are initialized in the class definition. In contrast, class members are created once per class. (Class members are also known as static members.)

Properties are attributes that define an object. For example, `length` is a property of all arrays that specifies the number of elements in the array. Methods are functions that you associate with a class. For more information on functions and methods, see Chapter 6, "Functions and Methods," on page 205.

The following example shows you how you would create a method in a class file:

```
class Sample {
  public function myMethod():Void {
    trace("myMethod");
  }
}
```

Next you could invoke that method in your document. To invoke an instance method or access an instance property, you reference an instance of the class. In the following example, `picture01`, an instance of the custom Picture class (available in the following exercise), invokes the `showInfo()` method:

```
var img1:Picture = new Picture("http://www.helpexamples.com/flash/images/
    image1.jpg");
// Invoke the showInfo() method.
img1.showInfo();
```

The next example demonstrates how you can write a custom Picture class to hold various pieces of information about a photo.

To use the Picture and PictureClass classes in a FLA file:

1. Select File > New and then select ActionScript File. Save the document as **Picture.as** and then click OK.

   You write your custom Picture class in this document.

2. Type the following ActionScript code into the Script window:

```
/**
  Picture class
  author: John Doe
  version: 0.53
  modified: 6/24/2005
  copyright: Macromedia, Inc.

  The Picture class is used as a container for an image and its URL.
*/

class Picture {
  private var __infoObj:Object;

  public function Picture(src:String) {
    this.__infoObj = new Object();
    this.__infoObj.src = src;
  }

  public function showInfo():Void {
    trace(this.toString());
  }
  private function toString():String {
    return "[Picture src=" + this.__infoObj.src + "]";
  }

  public function get src():String {
    return this.__infoObj.src;
  }
  public function set src(value:String):Void {
    this.__infoObj.src = value;
  }
}
```

3. Save the ActionScript file.

4. Select File > New and then select Flash Document to create a new FLA file. Save it as **picture_test.fla** in the same directory as you saved the Picture class file.

5. Type the following ActionScript code into Frame 1 of the Timeline:

```
var picture1:Picture = new Picture("http://www.helpexamples.com/flash/
  images/image1.jpg");
picture1.showInfo();
this.createEmptyMovieClip("img_mc", 9);
img_mc.loadMovie(picture1.src);
```

6. Save the Flash document.

7. Select Control > Test Movie to test the document.

The following text is displayed in the Output panel:

```
[Picture src=http://www.helpexamples.com/flash/images/image1.jpg]
```

A sample file on your hard disk demonstrates how to create a dynamic menu with XML data and a custom class file. The sample calls the ActionScript `XmlMenu()` constructor and passes it two parameters: the path to the XML menu file and a reference to the current timeline. The rest of the functionality resides in a custom class file, XmlMenu.as.

You can find the sample source file, xmlmenu.fla, in the Samples folder on your hard disk.

- On Windows, browse to *boot drive*\Program Files\Macromedia\Flash 8\Samples and Tutorials\Samples\ActionScript\XML_Menu.

- On the Macintosh, browse to *Macintosh HD*/Applications/Macromedia Flash 8/Samples and Tutorials/Samples/ActionScript/XML_Menu.

About public, private, and static methods and properties (members)

When you write ActionScript class files in an external script file, there are four types of methods and properties that you can create: public methods and properties, private methods and properties, public static methods and properties, and private static methods and properties. These methods and properties define how Flash can access variables, and they allow you to specify what parts of your code can access certain methods or properties.

When you are building class-based applications, whether the application is small or large, it is especially important to consider whether a method or property should be private or public. Considering this ensures that your code is as secure as possible. For example, if you were building a User class, you might not want to allow people using the class to be able to change a user's ID. By setting the class property (sometimes referred to as an *instance member*) to `private`, you can limit access to the property to code within the class or subclasses of that class, meaning that no users can change that property directly.

Public methods and properties

The `public` keyword specifies that a variable or function is available to any caller. Because variables and functions are public by default, the `this` keyword is used primarily for stylistic and readability benefits, indicating that the variable exists in the current scope. For example, you might want to use the `this` keyword for consistency in a block of code that also contains private or static variables. The `this` keyword can be used with either the public or private keyword.

The following Sample class already has a public method named `myMethod()`:

```
class Sample {
  private var ID:Number;
  public function myMethod():Void {
    this.ID = 15;
    trace(this.ID); // 15
    trace("myMethod");
  }
}
```

If you want to add a `public` property, you use the word "public" instead of "private," as you can see in the following sample code:

```
class Sample {
  private var ID:Number;
  public var email:String;
  public function myMethod():Void {
    trace("myMethod");
  }
}
```

Because the `email` property is public, you can change it within the Sample class, or directly within a FLA.

Private methods and properties

The `private` keyword specifies that a variable or function is available only to the class that declares or defines it or to subclasses of that class. By default, a variable or function is public, and available to any caller. Use the `this` keyword if you want to restrict access to a variable or function, as you can see in the following example:

```
class Sample {
  private var ID:Number;
  public function myMethod():Void {
    this.ID = 15;
    trace(this.ID); // 15
    trace("myMethod");
  }
}
```

If you want to add a private property to the previous class, you simply use the keyword `private` before the `var` keyword.

If you attempt to access the private `ID` property from outside the Sample class, you get a compiler error and a message in the Output panel. The message indicates that the member is private and cannot be accessed.

Static methods and properties

The static keyword specifies that a variable or function is created only once per class rather than in every object based on that class. You can access a static class member without creating an instance of the class. Static methods and properties can be set in either the public or private scope.

Static members, also called *class members*, are assigned to the class, not to any instance of the class. To invoke a class method or access a class property, you reference the class name, rather than a specific instance of the class, as shown in the following code:

```
trace(Math.PI / 8); // 0.392699081698724
```

If you type this single line of code in the script pane of the Actions panel, you see a result trace in the Output panel.

For example, in the previous Sample class example, you could create a static variable to keep track of how many instances of the class have been created, as demonstrated in the following code:

```
class Sample {
   public static var count:Number = 0;
   private var ID:Number;
   public var email:String;
   public function Sample() {
     Sample.count++;
     trace("count updated: " + Sample.count);
   }
   public function myMethod():Void {
     trace("myMethod");
   }
}
```

Every time you create a new instance of the Sample class, the constructor method traces the total number of Sample class instances that have been defined so far.

Some of the top-level ActionScript classes have class members (or static members), as you saw earlier in this section when you called the Math.PI property. Class members (properties and methods) are accessed or invoked on the class name, not on an instance of the class. Therefore, you don't create an instance of the class to use those properties and methods.

For example, the top-level Math class consists only of static methods and properties. To call any of its methods, you don't create an instance of the Math class. Instead, you simply call the methods on the Math class itself. The following code calls the sqrt() method of the Math class:

```
var squareRoot:Number = Math.sqrt(4);
trace(squareRoot); // 2
```

The following code invokes the `max()` method of the Math class, which determines the larger of two numbers:

```
var largerNumber:Number = Math.max(10, 20);
trace(largerNumber); // 20
```

For more information on creating class members, see "About class members" on page 256 and "Using class members" on page 260.

A sample file on your hard disk demonstrates how to create a dynamic menu with XML data and a custom class file. The sample calls the ActionScript `XmlMenu()` constructor and passes it two parameters: the path to the XML menu file and a reference to the current timeline. The rest of the functionality resides in a custom class file, XmlMenu.as.

You can find the sample source file, xmlmenu.fla, in the Samples folder on your hard disk.

- On Windows, browse to *boot drive*\Program Files\Macromedia\Flash 8\Samples and Tutorials\Samples\ActionScript\XML_Menu.

- On the Macintosh, browse to *Macintosh HD*/Applications/Macromedia Flash 8/Samples and Tutorials/Samples/ActionScript/XML_Menu.

About class members

Most of the members (methods and properties) discussed so far in this chapter are of a type called *instance members*. For each instance member, there's a unique copy of that member in every instance of the class. For example, the `email` member variable of the Sample class has an instance member, because each person has a different e-mail address.

Another type of member is a *class member*. There is only one copy of a class member, and you use it for the entire class. Any variable declared within a class, but outside a function, is a property of the class. In the following example, the Person class has two properties, `age` and `username`, of type Number and String, respectively:

```
class Person {
  public var age:Number;
  public var username:String;
}
```

Similarly, any function declared within a class is considered a method of the class. In the Person class example, you can create a method called getInfo():

```
class Person {
  public var age:Number;
  public var username:String;
  public function getInfo():String {
    // getInfo() method definition
  }
}
```

In the previous code snippet the Person class's getInfo() method, as well as the age and username properties, are all public instance members. The age property would not be a good class member, because each person has a different age. Only properties and methods that are shared by all individuals of the class should be class members.

Suppose that you want every class to have a species variable that indicates the proper Latin name for the species that the class represents. For every Person object, the species is *Homo sapiens*. It would be wasteful to store a unique copy of the string "Homo sapiens" for every instance of the class, so this member should be a class member.

Class members are declared with the static keyword. For example, you could declare the species class member with the following code:

```
class Person {
  public static var species:String = "Homo sapiens";
  // ...
}
```

You can also declare methods of a class to be static, as shown in the following code:

```
public static function getSpecies():String {
  return Person.species;
}
```

Static methods can access only static properties, not instance properties. For example, the following code results in a compiler error because the class method getAge() references the instance variable age:

```
class Person {
  public var age:Number = 15;
  // ...
  public static function getAge():Number {
    return age; /* **Error**: Instance variables cannot be accessed in
    static functions. */
  }
}
```

To solve this problem, you could either make the method an instance method or make the variable a class variable.

For more information on class members (also called static properties), see "Static methods and properties" on page 255.

A sample file on your hard disk demonstrates how to create a dynamic menu with XML data and a custom class file. The sample calls the ActionScript `XmlMenu()` constructor and passes it two parameters: the path to the XML menu file and a reference to the current timeline. The rest of the functionality resides in a custom class file, XmlMenu.as.

You can find the sample source file, xmlmenu.fla, in the Samples folder on your hard disk.

- On Windows, browse to *boot drive*\Program Files\Macromedia\Flash 8\Samples and Tutorials\Samples\ActionScript\XML_Menu.

- On the Macintosh, browse to *Macintosh HD*/Applications/Macromedia Flash 8/Samples and Tutorials/Samples/ActionScript/XML_Menu.

Using the Singleton design pattern

A common way to use class members is with the Singleton design pattern. A *design pattern* defines a formal approach for structuring your code. Typically, you might structure a design pattern as a solution for a common programming problem. There are many established design patterns, such as Singleton. The Singleton design pattern makes sure that a class has only one instance and provides a way of globally accessing the instance. For detailed information on the Singleton design pattern, see www.macromedia.com/devnet/mx/coldfusion/articles/design_patterns.html.

Often you encounter situations when you need exactly one object of a particular type in a system. For example, in a chess game, there is only one chessboard, and in a country, there is only one capital city. Even though there is only one object, you should encapsulate the functionality of this object in a class. However, you might need to manage and access the one instance of that object. Using a global variable is one way to do this, but global variables are not desirable for most projects. A better approach is to make the class manage the single instance of the object itself using class members. The following example shows a typical Singleton design pattern usage, where the Singleton instance is created only once.

To use the Singleton design pattern:

1. Select File > New and then select ActionScript File. Save the document as **Singleton.as**.

2. Type the following ActionScript code into the Script window:

```
/**
    Singleton class
    author: John Doe
    version: 0.53
    modified: 6/24/2008
    copyright: Macromedia, Inc.
*/

class Singleton {
  private static var instance:Singleton = null;
  public function trackChanges():Void {
    trace("tracking changes.");
  }
  public static function getInstance():Singleton {
    if (Singleton.instance == null) {
      trace("creating new Singleton.");
      Singleton.instance = new Singleton();
    }
    return Singleton.instance;
  }
}
```

3. Save the Singleton.as document.

4. Select File > New and then select Flash Document to create a new FLA file, and save it as **singleton_test.fla** in the same directory as you saved the Singleton class file.

5. Type the following ActionScript code into Frame 1 of the Timeline:

```
Singleton.getInstance().trackChanges(); // tracking changes.

var s:Singleton = Singleton.getInstance(); // tracking changes.
s.trackChanges();
```

6. Save the Flash document.

7. Select Control > Test Movie to test the document.

The Singleton object is not created until you need it—that is, until some other code asks for it by calling the getInstance() method. This is typically called *lazy creation*, and it can help make your code more efficient in many circumstances.

Remember not to use too few or too many class files for your application, because doing so can lead to poorly designed class files, which are not beneficial to the application's performance or to your workflow. You should always attempt to use class files instead of placing code in other places (such as timelines); however, avoid creating many classes that have only a small amount of functionality or only a few classes that handle a lot of functionality. Both of these scenarios might indicate poor design.

Using class members

One use of class (static) members is to maintain state information about a class and its instances. For example, suppose you want to keep track of the number of instances that have been created from a particular class. An easy way to do this is to use a class property that increments each time a new instance is created.

In the following example, you'll create a class called Widget that defines a single, static instance counter named `widgetCount`. Each time a new instance of the class is created, the value of `widgetCount` increments by 1 and the current value of `widgetCount` is displayed in the Output panel.

To create an instance counter using a class variable:

1. Select File > New and then select ActionScript File, and then click OK.

2. Type the following code into the Script window:

```
class Widget {
    //Initialize the class variable
    public static var widgetCount:Number = 0;
    public function Widget() {
        Widget.widgetCount++;
        trace("Creating widget #" + Widget.widgetCount);
    }
}
```

   The `widgetCount` variable is declared as static, so it initializes to 0 only once. Each time the Widget class's constructor statement is called, it adds 1 to `widgetCount` and then shows the number of the current instance that's being created.

3. Save your file as **Widget.as**.

4. Select File > New and then select Flash Document to create a new FLA, and save it as **widget_test.fla** in the same directory as Widget.as.

5. In widget_test.fla, type the following code into Frame 1 of the Timeline:

```
// Before you create any instances of the class,
// Widget.widgetCount is zero (0).
trace("Widget count at start: " + Widget.widgetCount); // 0
var widget1:Widget = new Widget(); // 1
var widget2:Widget = new Widget(); // 2
var widget3:Widget = new Widget(); // 3
trace("Widget count at end: " + Widget.widgetCount); // 3
```

6. Save the changes to widget_test.fla.

7. Select Control > Test Movie to test the file.

Flash displays the following information in the Output panel:

```
Widget count at start: 0
Creating widget # 1
Creating widget # 2
Creating widget # 3
Widget count at end: 3
```

About getter and setter methods

Getter and setter methods are accessor methods, meaning that they are generally a public interface to change private class members. You use getter and setter methods to define a property. You access getter and setter methods as properties outside the class, even though you define them within the class as methods. Those properties outside the class can have a different name from the property name in the class.

There are some advantages to using getter and setter methods, such as the ability to let you create members with sophisticated functionality that you can access like properties. They also let you create read-only and write-only properties.

Even though getter and setter methods are useful, you should be careful not to *overuse* them because, among other issues, they can make code maintenance more difficult in certain situations. Also, they provide access to your class implementation, like public members. OOP practice discourages direct access to properties within a class.

When you write classes, you are always encouraged to make as many as possible of your instance variables private and add getter and setter methods accordingly. This is because there are several times when you may not want to let users change certain variables within your classes. For example, if you have a private static method that tracks the number of instances created for a specific class, you don't want a user to modify that counter using code. Only the constructor statement should increment that variable whenever it's called. In this situation, you might create a private instance variable and allow a getter method only for the counter variable, which means users are able to retrieve the current value only by using the getter method, and they won't be able to set new values using the setter method. Creating a getter without a setter is a simple way of making certain variables in your class read-only.

Using getter and setter methods

The syntax for getter and setter methods is as follows:

- A getter method does not take any parameters and always returns a value.
- A setter method always takes a parameter and never returns a value.

Classes typically define getter methods that provide read access and setter methods that provide write access to a given property. For example, imagine a class that contains a property called userName:

```
private var userName:String;
```

Instead of allowing instances of the class to directly access this property (user.userName = "Buster", for example), the class might have two methods, getUserName() and setUserName(), that would be implemented as shown in the next example.

To use getter and setter methods:

1. Select File > New and then select ActionScript File, and then click OK.

2. Type the following code into the Script window:

```
class Login {
  private var __username:String;
  public function Login(username:String) {
    this.__username = username;
  }
  public function getUserName():String {
    return this.__username;
  }
  public function setUserName(value:String):Void {
    this.__username = value;
  }
}
```

3. Save the ActionScript document as **Login.as**.

   As you can see, `getUserName()` returns the current value of `userName`, and
   `setUserName()` sets the value of `userName` to the string parameter passed to the method.

4. Select File > New and then select Flash Document to create a new FLA, and save it as
   login_test.fla in the same directory as Login.as.

5. Add the following ActionScript to Frame 1 of the main Timeline:

```
var user:Login = new Login("RickyM");

// calling getUserName() method
var userName:String = user.getUserName();
trace(userName); // RickyM

// calling setUserName() method
user.setUserName("EnriqueI");
trace(user.getUserName()); // EnriqueI
```

6. Select Control > Test Movie to test the file.

   Flash displays the following information in the Output panel:

```
RickyM
EnriqueI
```

However, if you want to use a more concise syntax, you can use implicit getter and setter
methods. Implicit getter and setter methods let you access class properties in a direct manner,
while maintaining good OOP practice.

To define these methods, use the `get` and `set` method attributes. You create methods that get
or set the value of a property, and add the keyword `get` or `set` before the method name, as
shown in the next example.

> **NOTE**
> Implicit getter and setter methods are syntactic shorthand for the `Object.addProperty()`
> method found in ActionScript 1.0.

To use implicit getter and setter methods:

1. Select File > New and then select ActionScript File, and then click OK.

2. Type the following code into the Script window:

```
class Login2 {
  private var __username:String;
  public function Login2(username:String) {
    this.__username = username;
  }
  public function get userName():String {
    return this.__username;
  }
  public function set userName(value:String):Void {
    this.__username = value;
  }
}
```

3. Save the ActionScript document **as Login2.as**.

   Remember that a getter method does not take any parameters. A setter method must take exactly one required parameter. A setter method can have the same name as a getter method in the same scope. Getter and setter methods cannot have the same names as other properties. For example, in the previous example code you defined getter and setter methods named userName; in this case you could not also have a property named userName in the same class.

4. Select File > New and then select Flash Document to create a new FLA, and save it as **login2_test.fla** in the same directory as Login2.as.

5. Add the following ActionScript to Frame 1 of the main Timeline:

```
var user:Login2 = new Login2("RickyM");

// calling "get" method
var userNameStr:String = user.userName;
trace(userNameStr); // RickyM

// calling "set" method
user.userName = "EnriqueI";
trace(user.userName); // EnriqueI
```

   Unlike ordinary methods, you invoke getter and setter methods without any parentheses or arguments. You invoke getter and setter methods as you would a property by the same name.

6. Save the Flash document and select Control > Test Movie to test the file.

Flash displays the following information in the Output panel:

```
RickyM
EnriqueI
```

 NOTE | You cannot use getter and setter method attributes in interface method declarations.

About dynamic classes

Adding the `dynamic` keyword to a class definition specifies that objects based on the specified class can add and access dynamic properties at runtime. You should create dynamic classes only if you specifically require this functionality.

Type checking on dynamic classes is less strict than type checking on nondynamic classes, because members accessed inside the class definition and on class instances are not compared with those defined in the class scope. Class member functions, however, can still be type checked for return types and parameter types.

For information on creating dynamic classes, see "Creating dynamic classes" on page 265.

Creating dynamic classes

By default, the properties and methods of a class are fixed. That is, an instance of a class can't create or access properties or methods that weren't originally declared or defined by the class. For example, consider a Person class that defines two properties, `userName` and `age`.

To create a class that is not dynamic:

1. Select File > New and then select ActionScript File, and then click OK.

2. Type the following ActionScript into the Script window:

```
class Person {
    public var userName:String;
    public var age:Number;
}
```

If, in another script, you create an instance of the Person class and try to access a property of the class that doesn't exist, the compiler generates an error.

3. Save the file on your hard disk as **Person.as**.

4. Select File > New and then select Flash Document to create a new FLA file, and then click OK.

5. Select File > Save As, name the file **person_test.fla**, and save the file in the same directory as the Person class you created earlier.

6. Add the following code to create a new instance of the Person class (firstPerson), and try to assign a value to a property called hairColor (which doesn't exist in the Person class):

```
var firstPerson:Person = new Person();
firstPerson.hairColor = "blue"; // Error. There is no property with the
    name 'hairColor'.
```

7. Save the Flash document.

8. Select Control > Test Movie to test the code.

   This code causes a compiler error because the Person class doesn't declare a property named hairColor. In most cases, this is exactly what you want to happen. Compiler errors might not seem desirable, but they are very beneficial to programmers: good error messages help you to write correct code by pointing out mistakes early in the coding process.

In some cases, however, you might want to add and access properties or methods of a class at runtime that aren't defined in the original class definition. The dynamic class modifier lets you do just that.

To create a dynamic class:

1. Select File > New and then select ActionScript File, and then click OK.

2. Select File > Save As and name the file **Person2.as**. Save the file on your hard disk.

3. Type the following code into the Script window:

```
dynamic class Person2 {
    public var userName:String;
    public var age:Number;
}
```

   This ActionScript adds the dynamic keyword to the Person class in the previous example. Instances of the Person2 class can add and access properties and methods that are not defined in this class.

4. Save your changes to the ActionScript file.

5. Select File > New and then select Flash Document to create a new FLA file, and then click OK.

6. Select File > Save As and name the new file **person2_test.fla**. Save it in the same directory as Person2.as.

7. Type the following code to create a new instance of the Person2 class (firstPerson), and assign a value to a property called hairColor (which doesn't exist in the Person2 class).

```
var firstPerson:Person2 = new Person2();
firstPerson.hairColor = "blue";
trace(firstPerson.hairColor); // blue
```

8. Save your changes to the person2_test.fla file.

9. Select Control > Test Movie to test the code.

    Because the custom Flash class is dynamic, you can add methods and properties to the class at runtime (when the SWF file plays). When you test the code the text blue should be displayed in the Output panel.

When you develop applications, you wouldn't want to make classes dynamic unless you needed to. One reason not to use dynamic classes is that type checking on dynamic classes is less strict than type checking on nondynamic classes, because members accessed inside the class definition and on class instances are not compared with those defined in the class scope. Class member functions, however, can still be type checked for return types and parameter types.

Subclasses of dynamic classes are also dynamic, with one exception. Subclasses of the MovieClip class are not dynamic by default, even though the MovieClip class itself is dynamic. This implementation provides you with more control over subclasses of the MovieClip class, because you can choose to make your subclasses dynamic or not:

```
class A extends MovieClip {}          // A is not dynamic
dynamic class B extends A {}          // B is dynamic
class C extends B {}                  // C is dynamic
class D extends A {}                  // D is not dynamic
dynamic class E extends MovieClip{}   // E is dynamic
```

For information on subclasses, see Chapter 8, "Inheritance," on page 307.

About using encapsulation

In elegant object-oriented design, objects are seen as "black boxes" that contain, or *encapsulate*, functionality. A programmer should be able to interact with an object by knowing only its properties, methods, and events (its programming interface), without knowing the details of its implementation. This approach enables programmers to think at higher levels of abstraction and provides an organizing framework for building complex systems.

Encapsulation is why ActionScript 2.0 includes, for example, member access control, so that details of the implementation can be made private and invisible to code outside an object. The code outside the object is forced to interact with the object's programming interface rather than with the implementation details. This approach provides some important benefits; for example, it lets the creator of the object change the object's implementation without requiring any changes to code outside of the object, as long as the programming interface doesn't change.

An example of encapsulation in Flash would be setting all your member and class variables to private and forcing people who implement your classes to access these variables using getter and setter methods. Performing encapsulation this way ensures that if you ever need to change the structure of the variables in the future, you would need only to change the behavior of the getter and setter functions rather than force every developer to change the way he or she accesses the class's variables.

The following code shows how you could modify the Person class from earlier examples, set its instance members to private, and define getter and setter methods for the private instance members:

```
class Person {
  private var __userName:String;
  private var __age:Number;
  public function get userName():String {
    return this.__userName;
  }
  public function set userName(value:String):Void {
    this.__userName = value;
  }
  public function get age():Number {
    return this.__age;
  }
  public function set age(value:Number):Void {
    this.__age = value;
  }
}
```

About using the this keyword in classes

Use the `this` keyword as a prefix within your classes for methods and member variables. Although it is not necessary, the `this` keyword makes it easy to tell that a property or method belongs to a class when it has a prefix; without the keyword, you cannot tell whether the property or method belongs to the superclass.

You can also use a class name prefix for static variables and methods, even within a class. This helps qualify the references you make, which makes code readable. Depending on the coding environment you use, adding prefixes might also trigger code hints.

> **NOTE**
> You do not have to add these prefixes, and some developers feel it is unnecessary. Macromedia recommends adding the `this` keyword as a prefix, because it can aid readability and helps you write clean code by providing context for your methods and variables.

Example: Writing custom classes

Now that you've explored the basics of a class file, and what kinds of things it contains, it's time to learn some of the general guidelines for creating a class file. The first example in this chapter shows you how to write classes and package them. The second example shows you how to use those class files with a FLA file.

<table>
<tr><td>C A U T I O N</td><td>ActionScript code in external files is compiled into a SWF file when you publish, export, test, or debug a FLA file. Therefore, if you make any changes to an external file, you must save the file and recompile any FLA files that use it.</td></tr>
</table>

As discussed in "Writing custom class files" on page 241, a class consists of two main parts: the *declaration* and the *body*. The class declaration consists minimally of the class statement, followed by an identifier for the class name, and then left and right curly braces ({ }). Everything inside the braces is the class body, as shown in the following example:

```
class className {
  // class body
}
```

Remember: you can define classes only in external ActionScript files. For example, you can't define a class in a frame script in a FLA file. Therefore, you create a new file for this example.

In its most basic form, a class declaration consists of the class keyword, followed by the class name (Person, in this case), and then left and right curly braces ({ }). Everything between the braces is called the class body and is where the class's properties and methods are defined.

By the end of this example, the basic ordering of your class files is as follows:

- Documentation comments
- Class declaration
- Constructor function
- Class body

You do not write subclasses in this chapter. For more information on inheritance and subclassing, see Chapter 8, "Inheritance," on page 307.

This example includes the following topics:

- "About general guidelines for creating a class" on page 270
- "Creating and packaging your class files" on page 272
- "Writing the constructor function" on page 274
- "Adding methods and properties" on page 276
- "Controlling member access in your classes" on page 278
- "Documenting the classes" on page 280

A sample file on your hard disk demonstrates how to create a dynamic menu with XML data and a custom class file. The sample calls the ActionScript `XmlMenu()` constructor and passes it two parameters: the path to the XML menu file and a reference to the current timeline. The rest of the functionality resides in a custom class file, XmlMenu.as.

You can find the sample source file, xmlmenu.fla, in the Samples folder on your hard disk.

- On Windows, browse to *boot drive*\Program Files\Macromedia\Flash 8\ Samples and Tutorials\Samples\ActionScript\XML_Menu.

- On the Macintosh, browse to *Macintosh HD*/Applications/Macromedia Flash 8/ Samples and Tutorials/Samples/ActionScript/XML_Menu.

About general guidelines for creating a class

The following points are guidelines to follow when you write custom class files. They help you write correct and well-formed classes. You practice these guidelines in upcoming examples.

- In general, place only one declaration per line, and do not place either the same or different types of declarations on a single line. Format your declarations as the following example shows:

```
private var SKU:Number; // product SKU (identifying) number
private var quantity:Number; // quantity of product
```

- Initialize local variables when you declare them, unless that initial value is determined by a calculation. For information on initializing variables, see "Adding methods and properties" on page 276.

- Declare variables before you first use them (including loops). For example, the following code predeclares the loop iterator variable (i) before using it in the `for` loop:

```
var my_array:Array = new Array("one", "two", "three");
var i:Number;
for (i = 0 ; i < my_array.length; i++) {
  trace(i + " = " + my_array[i]);
}
```

- Avoid using local declarations that hide higher-level declarations. For example, do not declare a variable twice, as the following example shows:

```
// bad code
var counter:Number = 0;
function myMethod() {
  var counter:Number;
  for (counter = 0; counter <= 4; counter++) {
    // statements;
  }
}
```

This code declares the same variable inside an inner block.

- Do not assign many variables to a single value in a statement, because it is difficult to read, as you can see in the following ActionScript code samples:

```
// bad form
xPos = yPos = 15;
```

or

```
// bad form
class User {
   private var m_username:String, m_password:String;
}
```

- Have a good reason for making public instance variables, or public static, class, or member variables. Make sure that these variables are explicitly public before you create them this way.

- Set most member variables to private unless there is a good reason to make them public. It is much better from a design standpoint to make member variables private and allow access only to those variables through a small group of getter and setter functions.

About naming class files

Class names must be identifiers—that is, the first character must be a letter, underscore (_), or dollar sign ($), and each subsequent character must be a letter, number, underscore, or dollar sign. As a preferred practice, try to always limit class names to letters.

The class name must exactly match the name of the ActionScript file that contains it, including capitalization. In the following example, if you create a class called Rock, the ActionScript file that contains the class definition must be named Rock.as:

```
// In file Rock.as
class Rock {
  // Rock class body
}
```

You name and create a class definition in the following section. See the section "Creating and packaging your class files" on page 272 to create, name, and package the class files. For more information on naming class files, see "Naming classes and objects" on page 753.

Creating and packaging your class files

In this section, you create, name, and package your class files for this example ("Example: Writing custom classes" on page 269). The following sections show you how to write complete (yet simple) class files. For detailed information on packages, see "About packages" on page 234, "A comparison of classes and packages" on page 235, and "Working with packages" on page 236.

When you create a class file, decide where you want to store the file. In the following steps, you'll save the class file and the application FLA file that uses the class file in the same directory for simplicity. However, if you want to check syntax, you also need to tell Flash how it can find the file. Typically, when you create an application, you add the directory in which you store your application and class files to the Flash classpath. For information about classpaths, see "About setting and modifying the classpath" on page 246.

Class files are also called ActionScript (AS) files. You create AS files in the Flash authoring tool or by using an external editor. Several external editors, such as Macromedia Dreamweaver and Macromedia Flex Builder, can create AS files.

> **NOTE**
>
> The name of a class (ClassA) must exactly match the name of the AS file that contains it (ClassA.as). This is very important; if these two names don't match exactly, including capitalization, the class won't compile.

To create a class file and class declaration:

1. Select File > New and then select Flash Document to create a new FLA document, and then click OK.

2. Select File > Save As, name the new file **package_test.fla**, and save the Flash document to the current directory.

   You'll add content to this Flash document in a future step.

3. Select File > New and then select ActionScript File, and then click OK.

4. Select File > Save As and create a new subdirectory named **com**, and then do the following:

   a. In the com subdirectory, create a new subdirectory named **macromedia**.

   b. in the macromedia subdirectory, create an new subdirectory named **utils**.

   c. Save the current ActionScript document in the utils directory and name the file **ClassA.as**.

5. Type the following code into the Script window:

   ```
   class com.macromedia.utils.ClassA {
   }
   ```

   The preceding code creates a new class named ClassA in the com.macromedia.utils package.

6. Save the ClassA.as ActionScript document.

7. Select File > New and then select ActionScript File, and then click OK.

8. Select File > Save As, name the new file **ClassB.as**, and save it in the same directory as ClassA.as created in an earlier step.

9. Type the following code into the Script window:

```
class com.macromedia.utils.ClassB {
}
```

The previous code creates a new class named ClassB in the com.macromedia.utils package.

10. Save your changes to both the ClassA.as and ClassB.as class files.

The class files you use in a FLA file import into a SWF file when you compile it. The code you write in a class file should have a certain methodology and ordering, which are discussed in the following sections.

If you are creating multiple custom classes, use packages to organize your class files. A package is a directory that contains one or more class files and resides in a designated classpath directory. A class name must be fully qualified within the file in which it is declared—that is, it must reflect the directory (package) in which it is stored. For more information on classpaths, see "About setting and modifying the classpath" on page 246.

For example, a class named com.macromedia.docs.YourClass is stored in the com/macromedia/docs directory. The class declaration in the YourClass.as file looks like this:

```
class com.macromedia.docs.YourClass {
  // your class
}
```

 NOTE You write the class declaration that reflects the package directory in the following section, "Example: Writing custom classes" on page 269.

For this reason, it's good practice to plan your package structure before you begin creating classes. Otherwise, if you decide to move class files after you create them, you will have to modify the class declaration statements to reflect their new location.

To package your class files:

1. Decide on the package name you'd like to use.

   Package names should be intuitive and easily identifiable by fellow developers. Remember that the package name also matches a specific directory structure. For example, any classes in the com.macromedia.utils package needs to be placed in a com/macromedia/utils folder on your hard drive.

2. Create the required directory structure after you've chosen a package name.

For example, if your package was named `com.macromedia.utils`, you would need to create a directory structure of com/macromedia/utils and place your classes in the utils folder.

3. Use the com.macromedia.utils prefix for any class you create in this package.

For example, if your class name was ClassA, the full class name would need to be `com.macromedia.utils.ClassA` within the `com/macromedia/utils/ClassA.as` class file.

4. If you change your package structure at a future point, remember to modify not only the directory structure, but the package name within each class file, as well as every import statement or reference to a class within that package.

To continue writing the class files, see "Writing the constructor function" on page 274.

Writing the constructor function

You have already learned how to write the class declaration in "Creating and packaging your class files" on page 272. In this part of the chapter, you write what's called the class file's *constructor function*.

> **NOTE**
> You learn how to write the comments, statements, and declarations in later sections.

Constructors are functions that you use to initialize (*define*) the properties and methods of a class. By definition, constructors are functions within a class definition that have the same name as the class. For example, the following code defines a Person class and implements a constructor function. In OOP, the constructor function initializes each new instance of a class.

A class's constructor is a special function that is called automatically when you create an instance of a class using the `new` operator. The constructor function has the same name as the class that contains it. For example, the Person class you created contained the following constructor function:

```
// Person class constructor function
public function Person (uname:String, age:Number) {
  this.__name = uname;
  this.__age = age;
}
```

Consider the following points when you write constructor functions:

- If no constructor function is explicitly declared—that is, if you don't create a function whose name matches that of the class—the compiler automatically creates an empty constructor function for you.

- A class can contain only one constructor function; overloaded constructor functions are not allowed in ActionScript 2.0.

- A constructor function should have no return type.

The term *constructor* is also typically used when you create (instantiate) an object based on a particular class. The following statements are calls to the constructor functions for the top-level Array class and the custom Person class:

```
var day_array:Array = new Array("Sun", "Mon", "Tue", "Wed", "Thu", "Fri",
    "Sat");
var somePerson:Person = new Person("Tom", 30);
```

Next you'll add a special function called a constructor function.

> **NOTE**
>
> The following exercise is part of "Example: Writing custom classes" on page 269. If you do not wish to progress through the example, you can download the class files from www.helpexamples.com/flash/learnas/classes/.

To add the constructor functions to your class files:

1. Open the ClassA.as class file in the Flash authoring tool.

2. Modify the existing class file so it matches the following code (the changes to make appear in boldface):

```
class com.macromedia.utils.ClassA {
    function ClassA() {
        trace("ClassA constructor");
    }
}
```

The previous code defines a constructor method for the ClassA class. This constructor traces a simple string to the Output panel, which will let you know when a new instance of the class has been created.

3. Open the ClassB.as class file in the Flash authoring tool.

4. Modify the class file so it matches the following code (the changes to make appear in boldface):

```
class com.macromedia.utils.ClassB {
    function ClassB() {
        trace("ClassB constructor");
    }
}
```

5. Save both ActionScript files before you proceed.

To continue writing your class file, see "Adding methods and properties" on page 276.

Adding methods and properties

To create the properties for the ClassA and ClassB classes, use the `var` keyword to define variables.

NOTE

The following three exercises are part of "Example: Writing custom classes" on page 269. If you do not wish to progress through the example, you can download the class files from www.helpexamples.com/flash/learnas/classes/.

To add properties to the ClassA and ClassB classes:

1. Open ClassA.as and ClassB.as in the Flash authoring tool.

2. Modify the ClassA.as ActionScript file to match the following code (the changes to make appear in boldface):

```
class com.macromedia.utils.ClassA {
  static var _className:String;
  function ClassA() {
    trace("ClassA constructor");
  }
}
```

   The previous block of code adds a single new static variable, `_className`, which contains the name of the current class.

3. Modify the ClassB class and add the static variable so it is similar to the previous code.

4. Save both ActionScript files before you proceed.

> TIP
>
> By convention, class properties are defined at the top of the class body. Defining them at the top makes the code easier to understand, but isn't required.

You use the post-colon syntax (for example, `var username:String` and `var age:Number`) in the variable declarations. This is an example of strict data typing. When you type a variable using the `var variableName:variableType` format, the ActionScript compiler ensures that any values assigned to that variable match the specified type. If the correct data type is not used in the FLA file importing this class, the compiler throws an error. For more information on strict data typing, see "About assigning data types and strict data typing" on page 83.

A class's members consist of properties (variable declarations) and methods (function definitions). You must declare and define all properties and methods inside the class body (the curly braces [{ }]); otherwise, an error occurs during compilation. For information on members, see "About public, private, and static methods and properties (members)" on page 253.

To add methods to the ClassA and ClassB classes:

1. Open ClassA.as and ClassB.as in the Flash authoring tool.

2. Modify the ClassA class file so it matches the following code (the changes to make appear in boldface):

```
class com.macromedia.utils.ClassA {
    static var _className:String;

    function ClassA() {
      trace("ClassA constructor");
    }
    function doSomething():Void {
      trace("ClassA - doSomething()");
    }
}
```

The block of code in boldface creates a new method in the class, which traces a string to the Output panel.

3. In ClassA.as, select Tools > Check Syntax to check the syntax of your ActionScript file.

If any errors are reported in the Output panel, compare the ActionScript in your script to the complete code written in the previous step. If you cannot fix the code errors, copy and paste the complete code into the Script window before you proceed.

4. Check the syntax of ClassB.as as you did in ClassA.as.

If any errors appear in the Output panel, copy and paste the complete code into the Script window before you proceed:

```
class com.macromedia.utils.ClassB {
    static var _className:String;

    function ClassB() {
      trace("ClassB constructor");
    }
    function doSomething():Void {
      trace("ClassB - doSomething()");
    }
}
```

5. Save both ActionScript files before you proceed.

You can initialize properties inline—that is, when you declare them—with default values, as shown in the following example:

```
class Person {
  var age:Number = 50;
  var username:String = "John Doe";
}
```

When you initialize properties inline, the expression on the right side of an assignment must be a compile-time constant. That is, the expression cannot refer to anything that is set or defined at runtime. Compile-time constants include string literals, numbers, Boolean values, null, and undefined, as well as constructor functions for the following top-level classes: Array, Boolean, Number, Object, and String.

To initialize properties inline:

1. Open ClassA.as and ClassB.as in the Flash authoring tool.

2. Modify the ClassA class file so the code matches the following ActionScript (the changes to make appear in boldface):

```
class com.macromedia.utils.ClassA {
  static var _className:String = "ClassA";

  function ClassA() {
    trace("ClassA constructor");
  }
  function doSomething():Void {
    trace("ClassA - doSomething()");
  }
}
```

   The only difference between the existing class file and the previous block of code is there is now a value defined for the static _className variable, "ClassA".

3. Modify the ClassB class file and add the inline property, changing the value to "ClassB".

4. Save both ActionScript files before you proceed.

This rule applies only to instance variables (variables that are copied into each instance of a class), not class variables (variables that belong to the class).

> **NOTE** When you initialize arrays inline, only one array is created for all instances of the class.

To continue writing your class file, see "Controlling member access in your classes" on page 278.

Controlling member access in your classes

By default, any property or method of a class can be accessed by any other class: all members of a class are public by default. However, in some cases you might want to protect data or methods of a class from access by other classes. You need to make those members private (available only to the class that declares or defines them).

You specify public or private members using the public or private member attribute. For example, the following code declares a private variable (a property) and a private method (a function). The following class (LoginClass) defines a private property named `userName` and a private method named `getUserName()`:

```
class LoginClass {
  private var userName:String;
  private function getUserName():String {
    return this.userName;
  }
  // Constructor:
  public function LoginClass(user:String) {
    this.userName = user;
  }
}
```

Private members (properties and methods) are accessible only to the class that defines those members and to subclasses of that original class. Instances of the original class, or instances of subclasses of that class, cannot access privately declared properties and methods; that is, private members are accessible only within class definitions, not at the instance level. In the following example, you change member access in your class files.

> **NOTE**
>
> This exercise is part of "Example: Writing custom classes" on page 269. If you do not wish to progress through the example, you can download the class files from www.helpexamples.com/flash/learnas/classes/.

To control member access:

1. Open ClassA.as and ClassB.as in the Flash authoring tool.

2. Modify the ClassA.as ActionScript file so its contents match the following ActionScript (the changes to make appear in boldface):

```
class com.macromedia.utils.ClassA {
  private static var _className:String = "ClassA";

  public function ClassA() {
    trace("ClassA constructor");
  }
  public function doSomething():Void {
    trace("ClassA - doSomething()");
  }
}
```

This previous code sets both methods (the ClassA constructor and the `doSomething()` method) as public, meaning that they can be accessed by external scripts. The static `_className` variable is set as private, meaning the variable can be accessed only from within the class and not from external scripts.

3. Modify the ClassB.as ActionScript file and add the same method and property access as the ClassA class.

4. Save both ActionScript files before you proceed.

An instance of ClassA or ClassB cannot access the private members. For example, the following code, added to Frame 1 of the Timeline in a FLA file, would result in a compiler error indicating that the method is private and can't be accessed:

```
import com.macromedia.utils.ClassA;
var a:ClassA = new ClassA();
trace(a._className); // Error. The member is private and cannot be accessed.
```

Member access control is a compile-time-only feature; at runtime, Flash Player does not distinguish between private or public members.

To continue writing your class file, see "Documenting the classes" on page 280.

Documenting the classes

Using comments in your classes and interfaces is an important part of documenting them for other users. For example, you might want to distribute your class files into the Flash community, or you might be working with a team of designers or developers who will use your class files in their work or as part of a project you're working on. Documentation helps other users understand the purpose and origins of the class.

There are two kinds of comments in a typical class or interface file: *documentation comments* and *implementation comments*. You use documentation comments to describe the code's specifications, but not the implementation. You use implementation comments to comment out code or to comment on the implementation of particular sections of code. The two kinds of comments use slightly different delimiters. Documentation comments are delimited with /** and */, and implementation comments are delimited with /* and */.

 Documentation comments are not a language construct in ActionScript 2.0. However, they are a common way of structuring comments in a class file that you can use in your AS files.

Use documentation comments to describe interfaces, classes, methods, and constructors. Include one documentation comment per class, interface, or member, and place it directly before the declaration.

If you have to document additional information that does not fit into the documentation comments, use implementation comments (in the format of block comments or single-line comments, as described in "About comments" on page 135). Implementation comments, if you add them, directly follow the declaration.

<table>
<tr><td>NOTE</td><td>Do not include comments that do not directly relate to the class being read. For example, do not include comments that describe the corresponding package.</td></tr>
</table>

<table>
<tr><td>NOTE</td><td>The following exercise is part of "Example: Writing custom classes" on page 269. If you do not wish to progress through the example, you can download the class files from www.helpexamples.com/flash/learnas/classes/.</td></tr>
</table>

To document your class files:

1. Open ClassA.as and ClassB.as in the Flash authoring tool.

2. Modify the ClassA class file and add the new code to the top of the class file (the changes to make appear in boldface):

```
/**
   ClassA class
   version 1.1
   6/21/2005
   copyright Macromedia, Inc.
 */
class com.macromedia.utils.ClassA {
   private static var _className:String = "ClassA";

   public function ClassA() {
      trace("ClassA constructor");
   }
   public function doSomething():Void {
      trace("ClassA - doSomething()");
   }
}
```

The code above added a comment to the top of the class file. It's always a good idea to add comments to your ActionScript and Flash files so that you can add useful information such as the author of the class, date last modified, copyright information, or any potential issues/bugs that may be present in the file.

3. Add a similar comment to the top of the ClassB.as ActionScript file, changing the class name and any other information as you see fit.

4. Save both ActionScript files before you proceed.

You might also add the block, single-line, or trailing comments within the class's code. For information on writing good comments within your code, see "Writing good comments" on page 757. For general information about comments, see "Single-line comments" on page 136, "Multiline comments" on page 137, and "Trailing comments" on page 138.

To learn how to use these custom class files in a SWF file, see "Example: Using custom class files in Flash" on page 282.

Example: Using custom class files in Flash

This example uses class files that are written in the example called "Example: Writing custom classes" on page 269, or you can download them from www.helpexamples.com/flash/learnas/classes/. If you completed "Example: Writing custom classes" on page 269, locate ClassA.as and ClassB.as on your hard disk.

Since the package name of the ClassA class file is `com.macromedia.utils.ClassA`, you'll need to make sure that you save the class files in the proper directory structure. Create a subfolder named com in the current directory. Within the com folder, add a new folder named macromedia. Add a third, and final, subdirectory within the macromedia folder named utils. Save both the ClassA.as and ClassB.as class files within this utils folder. Now you are ready to proceed with this example.

You can use the custom classes written in "Example: Writing custom classes" on page 269 with a FLA file. In this example, you use the custom classes to create a small application in Flash. Your classes compile into the SWF file when you publish the document, and then everything works together. In the following exercises, you learn how classpaths work, how to use class files in your application, as well as how to import classes and packages.

To continue this example, proceed to "Importing classes and packages" on page 282.

Importing classes and packages

To reference a class in another script, you must prefix the class name with the class's package name. The combination of a class's name and its package path is the class's fully qualified class name. If a class resides in a top-level classpath directory—not in a subdirectory in the classpath directory—then its class name is also its fully qualified class name.

To specify package paths, use dot (.) notation to separate package directory names. Package paths are hierarchical; that is, each dot represents a nested directory. For example, suppose you create a class named ClassName that resides in a `com/macromedia/docs/learnAs2` package in your classpath. To create an instance of that class, you could specify the fully qualified class name.

You can also use the fully qualified class name to type your variables, as shown in the following example:

```
var myInstance:com.macromedia.docs.learnAs2.ClassName = new
    com.macromedia.docs.learnAs2.ClassName();
```

You can use the `import` statement to import packages into a script, which lets you use a class's abbreviated name rather than its fully qualified name. You can also use the wildcard character (*) to import all the classes in a package. If you use the wildcard character, you don't need to use the fully qualified class name each time you use the class.

For example, suppose that in a script you imported the above class using the `import` statement, as shown in the following example:

```
import com.macromedia.docs.learnAs2.util.UserClass;
```

Later, in the same script, you could reference that class by its abbreviated name, as shown in the following example:

```
var myUser:UserClass = new UserClass();
```

You can use the wildcard character (*) to import all the classes in a given package. Suppose you have a package named `com.macromedia.utils` that contains two ActionScript class files, ClassA.as and ClassB.as. In another script, you could import both classes in that package using the wildcard character, as shown in the following code:

```
import com.macromedia.utils.*;
```

The following example shows that you can then reference either of the classes directly in the same script:

```
var myA:ClassA = new ClassA();
var myB:ClassB = new ClassB();
```

The `import` statement applies only to the current script (frame or object) in which it's called. If an imported class is not used in a script, the class is not included in the resulting SWF file's bytecode, and the class isn't available to any SWF files that the FLA file containing the `import` statement might load.

> **NOTE**
> The following exercise is part of "Example: Using custom class files in Flash" on page 282 which continues the examples "Example: Writing custom classes". If you need ClassA and ClassB, you can download the class files from www.helpexamples.com/flash/learnas/classes/.

To import a class or package:

1. Open the file called package_test.fla.

2. Type the following code into the Script window:

```
import com.macromedia.utils.*;
var a = new ClassA(); // ClassA constructor
var b = new ClassB(); // ClassB constructor
```

The previous block of code begins by importing each of the classes within the com.macromedia.utils package by using the wildcard (*) character. Next, you create a new instance of the ClassA class, which causes the constructor method to trace a message to the Output panel. An instance of the ClassB class is also created, which sends debugging messages to the Output panel.

3. Save your changes to the Flash document before you proceed.

To continue using these class files in a Flash file, see "Creating instances of classes in an example" on page 284.

Creating instances of classes in an example

Instances are objects that contain all the properties and methods of a particular class. For example, arrays are instances of the Array class, so you can use any of the methods or properties of the Array class with any array instance. Or you can create you own class, such as UserSettings, and then create an instance of the UserSettings class.

Continuing the example you started in "Example: Using custom class files in Flash" on page 282, you modified FLA file to import the classes you wrote so that you don't have to always refer to them by their fully qualified names.

The next step in this example ("Example: Using custom class files in Flash" on page 282) is to create an instance of the ClassA and ClassB classes in a script, such as a frame script in a package_test.fla Flash document, and assign it to a variable. To create an instance of a custom class, you use the new operator in the same way you would when creating an instance of a top-level ActionScript class (such as the Date or Array class). You refer to the class using its fully qualified class name, or import the class (as demonstrated in "Importing classes and packages" on page 282.)

 The following exercise is part of "Example: Using custom class files in Flash" on page 282 which continues the examples "Example: Writing custom classes".

To create a new instance of the ClassA and ClassB classes:

1. Open the file called **package_test.fla**.

2. Type the following boldface code into the Script window:

```
import com.macromedia.utils.*;
var a:ClassA = new ClassA(); // ClassA constructor
a.doSomething(); // call the ClassA's doSomething() method
var b:ClassB = new ClassB(); // ClassB constructor
b.doSomething(); // call the ClassB's doSomething() method
```

Data typing your objects in this code example enables the compiler to ensure that you don't try to access properties or methods that aren't defined in your custom class. For more information on strict data typing, see "About assigning data types and strict data typing" on page 83. The exception to data typing your objects is if you declare the class to be dynamic using the `dynamic` keyword. See "Creating dynamic classes" on page 265.

3. Save your changes to the FLA file before you proceed.

You should now have a basic understanding of how to create and use classes in your Flash documents. Remember that you can also create instances of top-level ActionScript or built-in classes (see "About working with built-in classes" on page 302).

To continue using these class files in a Flash file, see "Assigning a class to symbols in Flash" on page 285.

Assigning a class to symbols in Flash

You can also assign a class to symbols that you might use in a Flash file, such as a movie clip object on the Stage.

To assign a class to a movie clip symbol:

1. Select File > New and then select ActionScript File, and then click OK.

2. Select File > Save As, name the file **Animal.as**, and save the file on your hard disk.

3. Type the following code into the Script window:

```
class Animal {
  public function Animal() {
    trace("Animal::constructor");
  }
}
```

This ActionScript creates a new class called Animal that has a constructor method that traces a string to the Output panel.

4. Save your changes to the ActionScript file.

5. Select File > New and then select Flash Document to create a new FLA file, and then click OK.

6. Select File > Save As, name the file **animal_test.fla**, and save the file to the same folder as the Animal.as file you created in step 2.

7. Select Insert > New Symbol to launch the Create New Symbol dialog box.

8. Enter a symbol name of **animal**, and select the Movie Clip option.

9. Click the Advanced button in the lower-right corner of the Create New Symbol dialog box to enable more options.

   The Advanced button is available when you are in the basic mode of the Create New Symbol dialog box.

10. Click the Export for ActionScript check box in the Linkage section.

    Enabling this option allows you to dynamically attach instances of this symbol to your Flash documents during runtime.

11. Enter an identifier value of **animal_id**, and set the ActionScript 2.0 Class to **Animal** (to match the class name specified in step 3).

12. Select the Export in First Frame check box and click OK to apply your changes and close the dialog box.

13. Save the Flash document and select Control > Test Movie.

    The Output panel displays the text from your Animal class's constructor function.

 NOTE If you need to modify the Movie Clip's Linkage properties, you can right-click the symbol in the document's library and select Properties or Linkage from the context menu.

Compiling and exporting classes

By default, classes used by a SWF file are packaged and exported in the SWF file's first frame. You can also specify a different frame where your classes are packaged and exported. This is useful, for example, if a SWF file uses many classes that require a long time to download (such as components). If the classes are exported in the first frame, the user has to wait until all the class code has downloaded before that frame appears. By specifying a later frame in the timeline, you could display a short-loading animation in the first few frames of the timeline while the class code in the later frame downloads.

To specify the export frame for classes for a Flash document:

1. Select File > New and then select Flash Document. Save the new document as **exportClasses.fla**.

2. Rename the default layer to **content**, drag a ProgressBar component from the Components panel to the Stage, and give it an instance name of **my_pb**.

3. Create a new layer, drag it above the content layer, and rename it **actions**.

4. Add the following ActionScript code to Frame 1 of the actions layer on the main Timeline:

   ```
   my_pb.indeterminate = true;
   ```

5. Create a new keyframe on Frame 2 of the actions layer and add the following ActionScript code:

   ```
   var classesFrame:Number = 10;
   if (_framesloaded < classesFrame) {
      trace(this.getBytesLoaded() + " of " + this.getBytesTotal() + " bytes
      loaded");
      gotoAndPlay(1);
   } else {
      gotoAndStop(classesFrame);
   }
   ```

6. Create a new keyframe on Frame 10 of the actions layer and add the following ActionScript:

   ```
   stop();
   ```

7. Create a new keyframe on Frame 10 of the content layer and drag several components onto the Stage.

8. Right-click each component (except the ProgressBar) in the Library panel and select Linkage from the context menu to launch the Linkage Properties dialog box.

9. In the Linkage Properties dialog box, make sure that Export for ActionScript is selected, deselect the Export in First Frame check box, and click OK.

10. Select File > Publish Settings.

11. In the Publish Settings dialog box, select the Flash tab.

12. Click the Settings button next to the ActionScript version pop-up menu to open the ActionScript Settings dialog box.

13. In the Export Frame for Classes text box, enter the number of the frame where you want to export your class code (Frame 10).

    If the frame specified does not exist in the timeline, you get an error message when you publish your SWF file.

14. Click OK to close the ActionScript Settings dialog box, and then click OK to close the Publish Settings dialog box.

15. Select Control > Test Movie to test the Flash document. If the Components load too quickly, select View > Simulate Download from the SWF file. Flash simulates downloading the Flash document at a lower speed, which allows you to see the progress bar component animate as the class files download.

For more information on ASO files, see "Using ASO files" on page 288.

Using ASO files

During compilation, Flash sometimes creates files with .aso extensions in the /aso subdirectory of the default global classpath directory (see "About setting and modifying the classpath" on page 246). The .aso extension stands for *ActionScript object* (ASO). For each ActionScript 2.0 file that is implicitly or explicitly imported and successfully compiled, Flash generates an ASO file. The file contains the bytecode that's produced from the associated ActionScript (AS) file. Therefore, these files contain the compiled form (the *bytecode*) of a class file.

Flash needs to regenerate an ASO file only when the following scenarios occur:

■ The corresponding AS file has been modified.

■ ActionScript files that contain definitions imported or used by the corresponding ActionScript file have been modified.

■ ActionScript files included by the corresponding ActionScript file have been modified.

The compiler creates ASO files for caching purposes. You might notice that your first compilation is slower than subsequent compilations. This is because only the AS files that have changed are recompiled into ASO files. For unchanged AS files, the compiler reads the already-compiled bytecode directly out of the ASO file instead of recompiling the AS file.

The ASO file format is an intermediate format developed for internal use only. It is not a documented file format and is not intended to be redistributed.

If you experience problems in which Flash appears to be compiling older versions of a file you have edited, delete the ASO files and then recompile. If you plan to delete ASO files, delete them when Flash is not performing other operations, such as checking syntax or exporting SWFs.

To delete ASO files:

If you are editing a FLA file, and you want to delete an ASO file, select one of the following in the authoring environment:

- Select Control > Delete ASO Files to delete ASO files and continue editing.
- Select Control > Delete ASO Files and Test Movie to delete ASO files and test the application.

If you are editing an ActionScript document in the Script window:

- Select Control > Delete ASO Files to delete ASO files and continue editing.
- Select Control > Delete ASO Files and Test Project to delete ASO files and then test the application.

There is a limit to how much code you can place in a single class: the bytecode for a class definition in an exported SWF file cannot be larger than 32,767 bytes. If the bytecode is larger than that limit, a warning message appears.

You can't predict the size of the bytecode representation of a given class, but classes up to 1,500 lines usually don't go over the limit.

If your class goes over the limit, move some of the code into another class. In general, it is good OOP practice to keep classes relatively short.

Understanding classes and scope

When you move ActionScript code into classes, you might have to change how you use the this keyword. For example, if you have a class method that uses a callback function (such as the LoadVars class's onLoad() method), it can be difficult to know whether the this keyword refers to the class or to the LoadVars object. In this situation, it might be necessary to create a pointer to the current class, as the next example shows.

To understand scope and external class files:

1. Select File > New and then select ActionScript File, and then click OK.

2. Type or paste the following code into the Script window:

```
/**
   Product class
   Product.as
*/
class Product {
  private var productsXml:XML;
  // constructor
  // targetXmlStr - string, contains the path to an XML file
  function Product(targetXmlStr:String) {
    /* Create a local reference to the current class.
       Even if you are within the XML's onLoad event handler, you
       can reference the current class instead of only the XML packet.
    */
    var thisObj:Product = this;
    // Create a local variable, which is used to load the XML file.
    var prodXml:XML = new XML();
    prodXml.ignoreWhite = true;
    prodXml.onLoad = function(success:Boolean) {
      if (success) {
        /* If the XML successfully loads and parses,
           set the class's productsXml variable to the parsed
           XML document and call the init function.
        */
        thisObj.productsXml = this;
        thisObj.init();
      } else {
        /* There was an error loading the XML file. */
        trace("error loading XML");
      }
    };
    // Begin loading the XML document.
    prodXml.load(targetXmlStr);
  }
  public function init():Void {
    // Display the XML packet.
    trace(this.productsXml);
  }
}
```

Because you are trying to reference the private member variable within an onLoad handler, the this keyword actually refers to the prodXml instance and not the Product class, which you might expect. For this reason, you must create a pointer to the local class file so that you can directly reference the class from the onLoad handler. You can now use this class with a Flash document.

3. Save the previous ActionScript code as **Product.as**.

4. Create a new Flash document named **testProduct.fla** in the same directory.

5. Select Frame 1 of the main Timeline.

6. Type the following ActionScript into the Actions panel:

```
var myProduct:Product - new Product("http://www.helpexamples.com/
   crossdomain.xml");
```

7. Select Control > Test Movie to test this code in the test environment.

The contents of the specified XML document appear in the Output panel.

Another type of scope you encounter when working with these classes is static variables and static functions. The static keyword specifies that a variable or function is created only once per class rather than being created in every instance of that class. You can access a static class member without creating an instance of the class by using the syntax someClassName.username. For more information on static variables and functions, see "About public, private, and static methods and properties (members)" on page 253 and "Using class members" on page 260.

Another benefit of static variables is that static variables don't lose their values after the variable's scope has ended. The following example demonstrates how you can use the static keyword to create a counter that tracks how many instances of the class Flash has created. Because the numInstances variable is static, the variable is created only once for the entire class, not for every single instance.

To use the static keyword:

1. Select File > New and then select ActionScript File, and then click OK.

2. Type the following code into the Script window:

```
class User {
  private static var numInstances:Number = 0;
  public function User() {
    User.numInstances++;
  }
  public static function get instances():Number {
    return User.numInstances;
  }
}
```

The previous code defines a User class that tracks the number of times the constructor has been called. A private, static variable (User.numInstances) is incremented within the constructor method.

3. Save the document as **User.as**.

4. Select File > New and then select Flash Document to create a new FLA file, and save the FLA file in the same directory as User.as.

5. Type the following ActionScript code in Frame 1 of the Timeline:

```
trace(User.instances); // 0
var user1:User = new User();
trace(User.instances); // 1
var user2:User = new User();
trace(User.instances); // 2
```

The first line of code calls the static `instances()` getter method, which returns the value of the private static `numInstances` variable. The rest of the code creates new instances of the User class and displays the current value returned by the `instances()` getter method.

6. Select Control > Test Movie to test the documents.

For information on using the `this` keyword in classes, see "About using the this keyword in classes" on page 268.

About top-level and built-in classes

In addition to the ActionScript core language elements and constructs (`for` and `while` loops, for example) and primitive data types (numbers, strings, and Booleans) described earlier in this manual (see Chapter 4, "Data and Data Types," on page 73 and Chapter 5, "Syntax and Language Fundamentals," on page 117), ActionScript also provides several built-in classes (*complex data types*). These classes provide a variety of scripting features and functionality. You have used top-level classes and other built-in classes that are part of the ActionScript language in earlier chapters, and you will use them throughout the remaining chapters. There are many classes that ship with Flash that you use to create interactivity and functionality in your SWF files, and you can even build complex applications using them. For example, you can use the Math class to perform equations in your applications. Or you might use the BitmapData class to create pixels and scripted animations.

Top-level classes, listed in "Top-level classes" on page 294, are written into Flash Player. In the Actions toolbox, these classes are located in the ActionScript 2.0 Classes directory. Some of the top-level classes are based on the ECMAScript (ECMA-262) edition 3 language specification and are called *core ActionScript classes*. Examples of core classes are the Array, Boolean, Date, and Math classes. For more information on packages, see "Working with packages" on page 236.

You can find the ActionScript classes installed on your hard disk. You can find the classes folders here:

- Windows: Hard Disk\Documents and Settings*user*\Local Settings\ Application Data\Macromedia\Flash 8*language*\Configuration\Classes.

- Macintosh: Hard Disk/Users/*user*/Library/Application Support/Macromedia/Flash 8/ *language*/Configuration/Classes.

Do note the Read Me document located in this directory for more information about its structure.

To understand the distinction between core ActionScript classes and those specific to Flash, consider the distinction between core and client-side JavaScript. The client-side JavaScript classes provide control over the client environment (the web browser and web page content), and the classes specific to Flash provide runtime control over the appearance and behavior of a Flash application.

The rest of the built-in ActionScript classes are specific to Macromedia Flash and the Flash Player object model. Examples of these classes are the Camera, MovieClip, and LoadVars classes. Other classes are organized into packages, such as flash.display. All of these classes are sometimes referred to as *built-in* classes (predefined classes that you can use for adding functionality to your applications).

The following sections introduce the built-in ActionScript classes, and describe the fundamental tasks you perform with these built-in classes. For an overview of working with classes and objects in object-oriented programming, see "About working with built-in classes" on page 302. Code examples using these classes are included throughout the entire *Learning ActionScript 2.0 in Flash* manual.

For information on language elements (such as constants, operators, and directives), see Chapter 5, "Syntax and Language Fundamentals," on page 117.

For more information on top-level and built-in classes, see the following topics:

- "Top-level classes" on page 294
- "The flash.display package" on page 298
- "The flash.external package" on page 298
- "The flash.filters package" on page 299
- "The flash.geom package" on page 300
- "The flash.net package" on page 300
- "The flash.text package" on page 301
- "The mx.lang package" on page 301
- "The System and TextField packages" on page 301

Other language elements

There are other language elements that make up ActionScript, outside of classes. These include directives, constants, global functions, global properties, operators, and statements. For information on how to use each of these language elements, see the following topics:

- Chapter 5, "Syntax and Language Fundamentals"
- Chapter 6, "Functions and Methods"

You can find a list of these language elements in the following sections of the *ActionScript 2.0 Language Reference* in Flash Help:

- %{Compiler Directives}%
- %{Constants}%
- %{Global Functions}%
- %{Global Properties}%
- %{Operators}%
- %{Statements}%

Top-level classes

The top level contains the ActionScript classes and global functions, many of which provide core functionality for your applications. *Core classes*, borrowed directly from ECMAScript, include Array, Boolean, Date, Error, Function, Math, Number, Object, String, and System. To find more information on each class, see the following table.

> **NOTE**
> The CustomActions and XMLUI classes are available only in the Flash authoring environment.

Class	Description
Accessibility	The Accessibility class manages communication between SWF files and screen reader applications. You use the methods of this class with the global `_accProps` property to control accessible properties for movie clips, buttons, and text fields at runtime. See %{Accessibility}%.
Array	The Array class represents arrays in ActionScript and all array objects are instances of this class. The Array class contains methods and properties for working with array objects. See %{Array}%.
AsBroadcaster	Provides event notification and listener management capabilities that can be added to other objects. See %{AsBroadcaster}%.
Boolean	The Boolean class is a wrapper for Boolean (`true` or `false`) values. See %{Boolean}%.›.

Class	Description
Button	The Button class provides methods, properties, and event handlers for working with buttons. See %{Button}%. Note that the built-in Button class is different from the Button component class, associated with the version 2 component, Button.
Camera	The Camera class provides access to the user's camera, if one is installed. When used with Flash Communication Server, your SWF file can capture, broadcast, and record images and video from a user's camera. See %{Camera}%.
Color	The Color class lets you set the RGB color value and color transform of movie clip instances and retrieve those values after you set them. The Color class is deprecated in Flash Player 8 in favor of the ColorTransform class. For information on color transforms, see %{ColorTransform (flash.geom.ColorTransform)}%.
ContextMenu	The ContextMenu class lets you control the contents of the Flash Player context menu at runtime. You can associate separate ContextMenu objects with MovieClip, Button, or TextField objects by using the menu property available to those classes. You can also add custom menu items to a ContextMenu object by using the ContextMenuItem class. See %{ContextMenu}%.
ContextMenuItem	The ContextMenuItem class lets you create new menu items that appear in the Flash Player context menu. You add new menu items that you create with this class to the Flash Player context menu by using the ContextMenu class. See %{ContextMenuItem}%.
CustomActions	The CustomActions class lets you manage any custom actions that are registered with the authoring tool. See %{CustomActions}%.
Date	The Date class shows how dates and times are represented in ActionScript, and it supports operations for manipulating dates and times. The Date class also provides the means for obtaining the current date and time from the operating system. See %{Date}%.
Error	The Error class contains information about runtime errors that occur in your scripts. You typically use the `throw` statement to generate an error condition, which you can handle using a `try..catch..finally` statement. See %{Error}%.
Function	The Function class is the class representation of all ActionScript functions, including those native to ActionScript and those that you define. See %{Function}%.
Key	The Key class provides methods and properties for getting information about the keyboard and key presses. See %{Key}%.

Class	Description
LoadVars	The LoadVars class lets you transfer variables between a SWF file and a server in name-value pairs. See %{LoadVars}%.
LocalConnection	The LocalConnection class lets you develop SWF files that send instructions to each other without using the `fscommand()` method or JavaScript. See %{LocalConnection}%.
Math	The Math class provides convenient access to common mathematical constants and provides several common mathematical functions. All the properties and methods of the Math class are static and must be called with the syntax `Math.method(parameter)` or `Math.constant`. See %{Math}%.
Microphone	The Microphone class provides access to the user's microphone, if one is installed. When used with Flash Communication Server, your SWF file can broadcast and record audio from a user's microphone. See %{Microphone}%.
Mouse	The Mouse class provides control over the mouse in a SWF file; for example, this class lets you hide or show the mouse pointer. See %{Mouse}%.
MovieClip	Every movie clip in a SWF file is an instance of the MovieClip class. You use the methods and properties of this class to control movie clip objects. See %{MovieClip}%.
MovieClipLoader	This class lets you implement listener callbacks that provide status information while SWF, JPEG, GIF, and PNG files load into movie clip instances. See %{MovieClipLoader}%.
NetConnection	The NetConnection class establishes a local streaming connection for playing a Flash Video (FLV) file from an HTTP address or from the local file system. See %{NetConnection}%.
NetStream	The NetStream class controls playback of FLV files from a local file system or HTTP address. See %{NetStream}%.
Number	The Number class is a wrapper for the primitive number data type. See %{Number}%.
Object	The Object class is at the root of the ActionScript class hierarchy; all other classes inherit its methods and properties. See %{Object}%.
PrintJob	The PrintJob class lets you print content from a SWF file, including content that is rendered dynamically, and multipage documents. See %{PrintJob}%.
Selection	The Selection class lets you set and control the text field in which the insertion point is located (the text field that has focus). See %{Selection}%.

Class	Description
SharedObject	The SharedObject class offers persistent local data storage on the client computer, similar to cookies. This class offers real-time data sharing between objects on the client's computer. See %{SharedObject}%.
Sound	The Sound class provides control over sounds in a SWF file. See %{Sound}%.
Stage	The Stage class provides information about a SWF file's dimensions, alignment, and scale mode. It also reports Stage resize events. See %{Stage}%.
String	The String class is a wrapper for the string primitive data type, which lets you use the methods and properties of the String object to manipulate primitive string value types. See %{String}%.
System	The System class provides information about Flash Player and the system on which Flash Player is running (for example, screen resolution and current system language). It also lets you show or hide the Flash Player Settings panel and modify SWF file security settings. See %{System}%.
TextField	The TextField class provides control over dynamic and input text fields, such as retrieving formatting information, invoking event handlers, and changing properties such as alpha or background color. See %{TextField}%.
TextFormat	The TextFormat class lets you apply formatting styles to characters or paragraphs in a TextField object. See %{TextFormat}%.
TextSnapshot	The TextSnapshot object lets you access and lay out static text inside a movie clip. See %{TextSnapshot}%.
Video	The Video class lets you show video objects in a SWF file. You can use this class with Flash Communication Server to display live streaming video in a SWF file, or within Flash to display a Flash Video (FLV) file. See %{Video}%.
XML	This class contains methods and properties for working with XML objects. See %{XML}%.
XMLNode	The XMLNode class represents a single node in an XML document tree. It is the XML class's superclass. See %{XMLNode}%.

Class	Description
XMLSocket	The XMLSocket class lets you create a persistent socket connection between a server computer and client running Flash Player. Client sockets enable low-latency data transfer, such as that which is required for real-time chat applications. See %{XMLSocket}%.
XMLUI	The XMLUI object enables communication with SWF files that are used as a custom user interface for the Flash authoring tool's extensibility features (such as Behaviors, Commands, Effects, and Tools). See %{XMLUI}%.

The flash.display package

The flash.display package contains the BitmapData class that you can use to build visual displays.

Class	Description
BitmapData	The BitmapData class lets you create arbitrarily sized transparent or opaque bitmap images in the document and manipulate them in various ways at runtime. See %{BitmapData (flash.display.BitmapData)}%.

The flash.external package

The flash.external package lets you communicate with the Flash Player container using ActionScript code. For example, if you embed a SWF file in an HTML page, that HTML page is the container. You would be able to communicate with the HTML page using the ExternalInterface class and JavaScript. Also called the External API.

Class	Description
ExternalInterface	The ExternalInterface class is the External API, a subsystem that enables communications between ActionScript and the Flash Player container (such as an HTML page using JavaScript) or a desktop application that uses Flash Player. See %{ExternalInterface (flash.external.ExternalInterface)}%.

The flash.filters package

The flash.filters package contains classes for the bitmap filter effects available in Flash Player 8. Filters let you apply rich visual effects, such as blur, bevel, glow, and drop shadows, to Image and MovieClip instances. For more information on each class, see the cross references provided in the following table.

Class	Description
BevelFilter	*The BevelFilter class lets you add a bevel effect to a movie clip instance.* See %{BevelFilter (flash.filters.BevelFilter)}%.
BitmapFilter	The BitmapFilter class is a base class for all filter effects. See %{BitmapFilter (flash.filters.BitmapFilter)}%.
BlurFilter	*The* BlurFilter *class lets you apply a blur effect to movie clip instances.* See %{BlurFilter (flash.filters.BlurFilter)}%.
ColorMatrixFilter	The ColorMatrixFilter class lets you apply a 4 x 5 matrix transformation on the ARGB color and alpha values of every pixel on the input image. After applying the transformation, you can produce a result with a new set of ARGB color and alpha values. See %{ColorMatrixFilter (flash.filters.ColorMatrixFilter)}%.
ConvolutionFilter	The ConvolutionFilter class lets you apply a matrix convolution filter effect. See %{ConvolutionFilter (flash.filters.ConvolutionFilter)}%.
DisplacementMapFilter	The DisplacementMapFilter class lets you use the pixel values from a specified image (the displacement map image) to spatially displace the original instance (a movie clip) that you apply the filter to. See %{DisplacementMapFilter (flash.filters.DisplacementMapFilter)}%.
DropShadowFilter	The DropShadowFilter class lets you add a drop shadow to a movie clip. See %{DropShadowFilter (flash.filters.DropShadowFilter)}%.
GlowFilter	The GlowFilter class lets you add a glow effect to a movie clip. See %{GlowFilter (flash.filters.GlowFilter)}%.
GradientBevelFilter	The GradientBevelFilter class lets you apply a gradient bevel effect to a movie clip. See %{GradientBevelFilter (flash.filters.GradientBevelFilter)}%.
GradientGlowFilter	The GradientGlowFilter class lets you apply a gradient glow effect to a movie clip. See %{GradientGlowFilter (flash.filters.GradientGlowFilter)}%.

The flash.geom package

The flash.geom package contains geometry classes, such as points, rectangles, and transformation matrices. These classes support the BitmapData class and the bitmap caching feature. For more information on each class, see the cross references provided in the following table.

Class	Description
ColorTransform	The ColorTransform class lets you mathematically set the RGB color value and color transform of an instance. You can retrieve these values after they have been set. See %{ColorTransform (flash.geom.ColorTransform)}%.
Matrix	Represents a transformation matrix that determines how to map points from one coordinate space to another. See %{Matrix (flash.geom.Matrix)}%.
Point	The Point object represents a location in a two-dimensional coordinate system, where x represents the horizontal axis and y represents the vertical axis. See %{Point (flash.geom.Point)}%.
Rectangle	The Rectangle class is used to create and modify Rectangle objects. See %{Rectangle (flash.geom.Rectangle)}%.
Transform	Collects data about color transformations and coordinate manipulations that are applied to an object instance. See %{Transform (flash.geom.Transform)}%.

The flash.net package

The flash.net package contains classes that let you upload and download one or more files between a user's computer and the server. For more information on each class, see the cross references provided in the following table.

Class	Description
FileReference	The FileReference class lets you upload and download one or more files between a user's computer and a server. See %{FileReference (flash.net.FileReference)}%.
FileReferenceList	The FileReferenceList class lets you upload one or more files from a user's computer to a server. See %{FileReferenceList (flash.net.FileReferenceList)}%.

The flash.text package

The flash.text package contains the TextRenderer class for working with advanced anti-aliasing in available in Flash Player 8.

Class	Description
TextRenderer	This class provides functionality for the advanced anti-aliasing capability in Flash Player 8. See %{TextRenderer (flash.text.TextRenderer)}%.

The mx.lang package

The mx.lang package contains the Locale class for working with multilanguage text.

Class	Description
Locale	This class lets you control how multilanguage text displays in a SWF file. See %{Locale (mx.lang.Locale)}%.

The System and TextField packages

The System package contains the capabilities, IME, and security classes. These classes deal with client settings that might affect your application in Flash Player. For more information on each class, see the cross references provided in the following table.

Class	Description
capabilities	The capabilities class determines the abilities of the system and Flash Player that's hosting the SWF file. This lets you customize content for different formats. See %{capabilities (System.capabilities)}%.
IME	The IME class lets you directly manipulate the operating system's input method editor (IME) that's within the Flash Player application running on a client computer. See %{IME (System.IME)}%.
security	The security class contains methods that specify how SWF files in different domains can communicate with each other. See %{security (System.security)}%.

The TextField package contains the StyleSheet class that you can use to apply CSS styles to text.

Class	Description
StyleSheet	The StyleSheet class lets you create a style sheet object that contains text formatting rules such as font size, color, and other formatting styles. See %{StyleSheet (TextField.StyleSheet)}%.

About working with built-in classes

In object-oriented programming (OOP), a *class* defines a category of object. A class describes the properties (data) and behavior (methods) for an object, much like an architectural blueprint describes the characteristics of a building. For information on classes and other object-oriented programming concepts, see the following sections:

- "Object-oriented programming fundamentals" on page 237
- "Writing custom class files" on page 241

Flash 8 has many built-in classes that you can use in your code (see "About top-level and built-in classes" on page 292), which helps you easily add interactivity to your applications. To use the properties and methods defined by a built-in class, you generally first create an *instance* of that class (except for classes that have static members). The relationship between an instance and its class is similar to the relationship between a house and its architectural blueprints, as discussed in "About top-level and built-in classes" on page 292.

For more information on using classes that are built into Flash 8, see the following topics:

- "About creating a new instance of a built-in class" on page 302
- "Accessing built-in object properties" on page 303
- "About calling built-in object methods" on page 304
- "About class (static) members" on page 304
- "Preloading class files" on page 305
- "Excluding classes" on page 304

About creating a new instance of a built-in class

To create an instance of an ActionScript class, use the new operator to invoke the class's constructor function. The constructor function always has the same name as the class, and returns an instance of the class, which you typically assign to a variable.

For example, the following code creates a new Sound object:

```
var song_sound:Sound = new Sound();
```

In some cases, you don't need to create an instance of a class to use its properties and methods. For more information, see "About class (static) members" on page 304.

Accessing built-in object properties

Use the dot (.) operator to access the value of a property in an object. Put the name of the object on the left side of the dot, and put the name of the property on the right side. For example, in the following statement, my_obj is the object and firstName is the property:

```
my_obj.firstName
```

The following code creates a new Array object and then shows its length property:

```
var my_array:Array = new Array("apples", "oranges", "bananas");
trace(my_array.length); // 3
```

You can also use the array access operator ([]) to access the properties of an object, such as using the array access operator for debugging purposes. The following example loops over an object to display each of its properties.

To loop over the contents of an object:

1. Create a new Flash document and save it as **forin.fla**.

2. Add the following ActionScript to Frame 1 of the main Timeline:

    ```
    var results:Object = {firstName:"Tommy", lastName:"G", age:7, avg:0.336,
        b:"R", t:"L"};
    for (var i:String in results) {
        trace("the value of [" + i + "] is: " + results[i]);
    }
    ```

    The previous code defines a new Object named results and defines values for firstName, lastName, age, avg, b, and t. A for..in loop traces each property in the results object and traces their value to the Output panel.

3. Select Control > Test movie to test the Flash document.

For more information on operators, including dot and array access operators, see "About operators" on page 180. For more information on methods and properties, see Chapter 6, "Functions and Methods," on page 205. For examples of working with properties of the built-in MovieClip class, see Chapter 11, "Working with Movie Clips," on page 357 For examples of working with the properties of the TextField, String, TextRenderer, and TextFormat classes, see Chapter 12, "Working with Text and Strings," on page 389.

About calling built-in object methods

You call an object's method by using the dot (.) operator followed by the method. For example, the following code creates a new Sound object and calls its setVolume() method:

```
var my_sound:Sound = new Sound(this);
my_sound.setVolume(50);
```

For examples of working with methods of the built-in MovieClip class, see Chapter 11, "Working with Movie Clips," on page 357. For examples of working with methods of the built-in TextField, String, TextRenderer, and TextFormat classes, see Chapter 12, "Working with Text and Strings," on page 389.

About class (static) members

Some built-in ActionScript classes have *class members* (*static members*). Class members (properties and methods) are accessed or invoked on the class name, not on an instance of the class. Therefore, you don't create an instance of the class to use those properties and methods.

For example, all the properties of the Math class are static. The following code invokes the max() method of the Math class to determine the larger of two numbers:

```
var largerNumber:Number = Math.max(10, 20);
trace(largerNumber); // 20
```

For more information on static methods of the Math class, and examples of using them, see %{Math}% in the *ActionScript 2.0 Language Reference* in Flash Help.

Excluding classes

To reduce the size of a SWF file, you might want to exclude classes from compilation but still be able to access and use them for type checking. For example, you might want to do this if you are developing an application that uses multiple SWF files or shared libraries, especially those that access many of the same classes. Excluding classes helps you avoid duplicating classes in those files.

For more information on excluding classes, see the following topics:

■ "Preloading class files" on page 305

To exclude classes from compilation:

1. Create a new XML file.

2. Name the XML file *FLA_filename_***exclude.xml**, where *FLA_filename* is the name of your FLA file without the extension.

   For example, if your FLA file is sellStocks.fla, the XML filename must be sellStocks_exclude.xml.

3. Save the file in the same directory as the FLA file.

4. Place the following tags in the XML file:

```
<excludeAssets>
   <asset name="className1" />
   <asset name="className2" />
</excludeAssets>
```

   The values you specify for the name attributes in the `<asset>` tags are the names of classes you want to exclude from the SWF file. Add as many as you require for your application. For example, the following XML file excludes the mx.core.UIObject and mx.screens.Slide classes from the SWF file:

```
<excludeAssets>
   <asset name="mx.core.UIObject" />
   <asset name="mx.screens.Slide" />
</excludeAssets>
```

For information on preloading classes, see "Preloading class files" on page 305.

Preloading class files

This section describes some of the methodologies for preloading and exporting classes in Flash 8 (including the classes that components in version 2 of the Macromedia Component Architecture use). *Preloading* involves loading some of the data for a SWF file before the user starts interacting with it. Flash imports classes on the first frame of a SWF file when you use external classes, and this data is the first element to load into a SWF file. It is similar for the component classes, because the framework for components also loads into the first frame of a SWF file. When you build large applications, the loading time can be lengthy when you must import data, so you must deal with this data intelligently, as the following procedures show.

Because the classes are the first data to load, you might have problems creating a progress bar or loading animation if the classes load before the progress bar, because you probably want the progress bar to reflect the loading progress of all data (including classes). Therefore, you want to load the classes after other parts of the SWF file, but before you use components.

The following procedure shows you how to change the frame in which classes load into a SWF file.

To select a different frame for the classes to load into a SWF file:

1. Select File > Publish Settings.

2. Select the Flash tab, and click the Settings button.

3. In the Export Frame for Classes text box, type the number of a new frame to determine when to load the classes.

4. Click OK.

You cannot use any classes until the playhead reaches the frame you choose to load them into. For example, version 2 components require classes for their functionality, so you must load components after the Export frame for ActionScript 2.0 classes. If you export for Frame 3, you cannot use anything from those classes until the playhead reaches Frame 3 and loads the data.

If you want to preload a file that uses classes, such as version 2 component classes, you must preload the components in the SWF file. To accomplish this, you must set your components to export for a different frame in the SWF file. By default, the UI components export in Frame 1 of the SWF file, so make sure that you deselect Export in First Frame from the component's Linkage dialog box.

If components do not load on the first frame, you can create a custom progress bar for the first frame of the SWF file. Do not reference any components in your ActionScript or include any components on the Stage until you load the classes for the frame you specified in the Export Frame for Classes text box.

CAUTION	You must export components after the ActionScript classes that they use.

CHAPTER 8

Inheritance

In Chapter 7, "Classes," you learned how to write class files and how classes help you organize code into external files. The chapter also demonstrated how you can organize class files into related packages. This chapter aims to show you how to write more advanced classes that extend the functionality of an existing class. This is a useful subject, because you might find yourself extending your own custom classes or existing classes so that you can add new methods and properties.

For more information on inheritance, see "About inheritance" on page 307. For more information on methods and properties, see Chapter 6, "Functions and Methods," on page 205.

For more information on inheritance, see the following topics:

About inheritance

In Chapter 7, "Classes," you saw how you could create a class file to create your own custom data types. Learning how to create custom class files shows you how to move code off the timeline and into external files. Moving code into external files makes it easier to edit your code. Now that you're familiar with the basics of creating your own custom classes, you learn about an object-oriented programming (OOP) technique called *subclassing* or *extending a class*, which lets you create new classes based on an existing class.

One of the benefits of OOP is that you can create *subclasses* of a class. The subclass inherits all the properties and methods of a *superclass*. For example, if you extend (or *subclass*) the MovieClip class, you are creating a custom class that extends the MovieClip class. Your subclass inherits all of the properties and methods of the MovieClip class. Or you might create a set of classes that extends from a custom superclass. For example, the Lettuce class might extend from the Vegetable superclass.

Your subclass typically defines additional methods and properties that you can use in your application, hence it *extends* the superclass. Subclasses can also override (provide their own definitions for) methods inherited from a superclass. If a subclass overrides a method inherited from its superclass, you can no longer access the superclass's definition within the subclass. The only exception to the above rule is that, if you are within the subclass's constructor function, you call the superclass's constructor using the `super` statement. For more information on overriding, see "Overriding methods and properties" on page 312.

For example, you might create a Mammal class that defines certain properties and behaviors that are common to all mammals. You could then create a Cat subclass that extends the Mammal class. Using subclasses lets you reuse code so that instead of re-creating all the code common to both classes you could simply extend an existing class. Another subclass, the Siamese class, could extend the Cat class, and so on. In a complex application, determining how to structure the hierarchy of your classes is a large part of the design process.

Inheritance and subclassing are very useful in larger applications, because they let you create a series of related classes that can share functionality. For example, you could create an Employee class that defines the basic methods and properties of a typical employee within a company. You could then create a new class called Contractor that extends the Employee class and inherits all of its methods and properties. The Contractor class could add its own specific methods and properties, or it could override methods and properties that are defined in the Employee superclass. You could then create a new class called Manager, which also extends the Employee class and defines additional methods and properties such as `hire()`, `fire()`, `raise()`, and `promote()`. You could even extend a subclass, such as Manager, and create a new class called Director, which again adds new methods or overrides existing methods.

Each time that you extend an existing class, the new class inherits all the current methods and properties of the subclass. If each class wasn't related, you'd have to rewrite each method and property in each separate class file, even if the functionality was the same in the fellow classes. You would have to spend a lot more time not only coding, but also debugging your application and maintaining a project if similar logic changed in multiple files.

In ActionScript, you use the `extends` keyword to establish inheritance between a class and its superclass, or to extend an interface. For more information on using the `extends` keyword, see "About writing subclasses in Flash" on page 309 and "About writing a subclass" on page 309. For additional information on the `extends` keyword, see %{extends statement}% in the *ActionScript 2.0 Language Reference* in Flash Help.

About writing subclasses in Flash

In object-oriented programming, a subclass can inherit the properties and methods of another class, called the *superclass*. You can extend your own custom classes as well as many of the core and Flash Player ActionScript classes. You cannot extend the TextField class or static classes, such as the Math, Key, and Mouse classes.

To create this kind of relationship between two classes, you use the class statement's `extends` clause. To specify a superclass, you use the following syntax:

```
class SubClass extends SuperClass {}
```

The class you specify in SubClass inherits all the properties and methods defined in SuperClass.

For example, you might create a Mammal class that defines properties and methods common to all mammals. To create a variation of the Mammal class, such as a Marsupial class, you would extend the Mammal class—that is, create a subclass of the Mammal class, as follows:

```
class Marsupial extends Mammal {}
```

The subclass inherits all the properties and methods of the superclass, including any properties or methods that you have declared to be private using the `private` keyword.

For more information on extending classes, see the following topics:

- "About writing a subclass" on page 309
- "Overriding methods and properties" on page 312

For more information on private members, see "About public, private, and static methods and properties (members)" on page 253. For an example that creates a subclass, see "Example: Extending the Widget class" on page 310.

About writing a subclass

The following code defines the custom class JukeBox, which extends the Sound class. It defines an array called `song_arr` and a method called `playSong()`, which plays a song and invokes the `loadSound()` method that it inherits from the Sound class.

```
class JukeBox extends Sound {
  public var song_arr:Array = new Array("beethoven.mp3", "bach.mp3",
  "mozart.mp3");
  public function playSong(songID:Number):Void {
    super.loadSound(song_arr[songID], true);
  }
}
```

If you don't place a call to super() in the constructor function of a subclass, the compiler automatically generates a call to the constructor of its immediate superclass with no parameters as the first statement of the function. If the superclass doesn't have a constructor, the compiler creates an empty constructor function and then generates a call to it from the subclass. However, if the superclass takes parameters in its definition, you must create a constructor in the subclass and call the superclass with the required parameters.

Multiple inheritance, or inheriting from more than one class, is not allowed in ActionScript 2.0. However, classes can effectively inherit from multiple classes if you use individual extends statements, as shown in the following example:

```
// not allowed
class C extends A, B {} // **Error: A class may not extend more than one
    class.

// allowed
class B extends A {}
class C extends B {}
```

You can also use interfaces to implement a limited form of multiple inheritance. For more information on interfaces, see Chapter 9, "Interfaces," on page 319. For an example that creates a subclass, see "Example: Extending the Widget class" on page 310. For additional information on super, see %{super statement}% in the *ActionScript 2.0 Language Reference* in Flash Help.

Example: Extending the Widget class

Class members propagate to subclasses of the superclass that defines those members. The next example demonstrates how you could create a Widget class, which you extend (subclass) by writing a class named SubWidget.

To create the Widget class and SubWidget subclass:

1. Create a new ActionScript file and save it as **Widget.as**.

2. Add the following code to the new document:

```
class Widget {
    public static var widgetCount:Number = 0;
    public function Widget() {
        Widget.widgetCount++;
    }
}
```

3. Save your changes to the ActionScript file.

4. Create a new ActionScript file and save it as **SubWidget.as** in the same directory as the Widget class.

5. In SubWidget.as, type the following code into the Script window:

```
class SubWidget extends Widget {
  public function SubWidget() {
    trace("Creating subwidget #" + Widget.widgetCount);
  }
}
```

6. Save your changes to SubWidget.as.

7. Create a new FLA file, and save it as **subWidgetTest.fla** in the same directory as the previous ActionScript class files.

8. In the subWidgetTest.fla file, type the following code into Frame 1 of the main Timeline:

```
var sw1:SubWidget = new SubWidget();
var sw2:SubWidget = new SubWidget();
trace("Widget.widgetCount = " + Widget.widgetCount);
trace("SubWidget.widgetCount = " + SubWidget.widgetCount);
```

The previous code creates two instances of the SubWidget class: sw1 and sw2. Each call to the `SubWidget` constructor traces the current value of the static `Widget.widgetCount` property. Because the SubWidget class is a subclass of the Widget class, you can access the `widgetCount` property through the SubWidget class, and the compiler rewrites the reference (in the bytecode, not in your ActionScript file) as `Widget.widgetCount`. If you try to access the static `widgetCount` property off of instances of the Widget or SubWidget class, like sw1 or sw2, the compiler throws an error.

9. Save your changes to the document.

10. Select Control > Test Movie to test the Flash document.

The Output panel displays the following output:

```
Creating subwidget #1
Creating subwidget #2
Widget.widgetCount = 2
SubWidget.widgetCount = 2
```

You see this output because even though the Widget class's constructor is never explicitly called, the SubWidget class's constructor calls it for you. This causes the Widget class's constructor to increment the Widget class's static `widgetCount` variable.

The ActionScript 2.0 compiler can resolve static member references within class definitions.

If you don't specify the class name for the `Widget.widgetCount` property but instead refer only to `widgetCount`, the ActionScript 2.0 compiler resolves the reference to `Widget.widgetCount` and correctly exports that property. Similarly, if you refer to the property as `SubWidget.widgetCount`, the compiler rewrites the reference (in the bytecode, not in your ActionScript file) as `Widget.widgetCount` because SubWidget is a subclass of the Widget class.

> **CAUTION** If you try to access the static `widgetCount` variable from the Widget class using the sw1 or sw2 instances, Flash generates an error telling you that static members can be accessed only directly through classes.

For optimal readability of your code, Macromedia recommends that you always use explicit references to static member variables in your code, as shown in the previous example. Using explicit references means that you can easily identify where the definition of a static member resides.

Overriding methods and properties

When a subclass extends a superclass, the subclass inherits all of the superclass's methods and properties. One of the advantages of working with classes and extending classes is that it allows you not only to provide new functionality to an existing class but also to modify existing functionality. For example, consider the Widget class that you created in "Example: Extending the Widget class" on page 310. You could create a new method in your superclass (Widget) and then either override the method in your subclass (SubWidget) or just use the inherited method from the Widget class. The following example shows how you can override existing methods in your classes.

To override methods in a subclass:

1. Create a new ActionScript document and save it as **Widget.as**.

2. In Widget.as, type the following ActionScript code into the Script window.

   Note: If you created the Widget class in an earlier example, modify the existing code by adding the `doSomething()` method, as follows:

```
class Widget {
  public static var widgetCount:Number = 0;
  public function Widget() {
    Widget.widgetCount++;
  }
  public function doSomething():Void {
    trace("Widget::doSomething()");
  }
}
```

3. Save your changes to the ActionScript document.

The Widget class now defines a constructor and a public method called `doSomething()`.

4. Create a new ActionScript file named **SubWidget.as** and save it in the same directory as Widget.as.

> **NOTE**
> If you created the SubWidget class in "Example: Extending the Widget class" on page 310, you can use this file instead.

5. In SubWidget.as, type the following ActionScript code into the Script window:

```
class SubWidget extends Widget {
  public function SubWidget() {
    trace("Creating subwidget # " + Widget.widgetCount);
    doSomething();
  }
}
```

6. Save your changes to SubWidget.as.

Notice that the SubWidget class's constructor calls the `doSomething()` method that you defined in the superclass.

7. Create a new Flash document and save it as **subWidgetTest.fla** in the same directory as the ActionScript documents.

8. In subWidgetTest.fla, type the following ActionScript into Frame 1 of the main Timeline:

```
var sw1:SubWidget = new SubWidget();
var sw2:SubWidget = new SubWidget();
```

9. Save your changes to the Flash document.

10. Select Control > Test Movie to test the Flash document. You see the following output in the Output panel:

```
Creating subwidget # 1
Widget::doSomething()
Creating subwidget # 2
Widget::doSomething()
```

This output shows that the SubWidget class's constructor calls the constructor of its superclass (Widget), which increments the static `widgetCount` property. The SubWidget's constructor traces the superclass's static property and calls the `doSomething()` method, which inherits from the superclass.

11. Open the SubWidget class and add a new method named `doSomething()`. Modify your class so that it matches the following code (add the code that's in boldface):

```
class SubWidget extends Widget {
  public function SubWidget() {
    trace("Creating subwidget # " + Widget.widgetCount);
    doSomething();
  }
  public function doSomething():Void {
    trace("SubWidget::doSomething()");
  }
}
```

12. Save your changes to the class file, and then open subwidgetTest.fla again.

13. Select Control > Test Movie to test the file. You see the following output in the Output panel:

```
Creating subwidget # 1
SubWidget::doSomething()
Creating subwidget # 2
SubWidget::doSomething()
```

The previous output shows that the `doSomething()` method in the SubWidget class's constructor is calling the `doSomething()` method in the current class instead of the superclass.

Open the SubWidget class again, and modify the SubWidget class's constructor to call the superclass's `doSomething()` method (add the code that's in boldface):

```
  public function SubWidget() {
    trace("Creating subwidget # " + Widget.widgetCount);
    super.doSomething();
  }
```

As demonstrated, you can add the `super` keyword to call the superclass's `doSomething()` method instead of the `doSomething()` method in the current class. For additional information on `super`, see the `super` entry in the *ActionScript 2.0 Language Reference* in Flash Help.

14. Save the SubWidget class file with the modified constructor and select Control > Test Movie to republish the Flash document.

The Output panel displays the contents of the Widget class's `doSomething()` method.

Using polymorphism in an application

Object-oriented programming lets you express differences between individual classes using a technique called polymorphism, by which classes can override methods of their superclasses and define specialized implementations of those methods.

For example, you might start with a class called Mammal that has `play()` and `sleep()` methods. You then create Cat, Monkey, and Dog subclasses to extend the Mammal class. The subclasses override the `play()` method from the Mammal class to reflect the habits of those particular kinds of animals. Monkey implements the `play()` method to swing from trees; Cat implements the `play()` method to pounce at a ball of yarn; Dog implements the `play()` method to fetch a ball. Because the `sleep()` functionality is similar among the animals, you would use the superclass implementation. The following procedure demonstrates this example in Flash.

To use polymorphism in an application:

1. Create a new ActionScript document and save it as **Mammal.as**.

   This document is the base class for a few different animal classes that you create in upcoming steps.

2. In Mammal.as, type the following ActionScript code into the Script window:

```
class Mammal {
  private var _gender:String;
  private var _name:String = "Mammal";

  // constructor
  public function Mammal(gender:String) {
    this._gender = gender;
  }

  public function toString():String {
    return "[object " + speciesName + "]";
  }
  public function play():String {
    return "Chase another of my kind.";
  }
  public function sleep():String {
    return "Close eyes.";
  }

  public function get gender():String {
    return this._gender;
  }
  public function get speciesName():String {
    return this._name;
  }
  public function set speciesName(value:String):Void {
    this._name = value;
  }
}
```

The previous class defines two private variables, _gender and _name, which are used to store the animal's gender and mammal type. Next, the Mammal constructor is defined. The constructor takes a single parameter, gender, which it uses to set the private _gender variable defined earlier. Three additional public methods are also specified: toString(), play(), and sleep(), each of which returns string objects. The final three methods are getter and setter methods for the mammal's _gender and _name properties.

3. Save the ActionScript document.

   This class serves as the superclass for the Cat, Dog, and Monkey classes, which you create shortly. You can use the toString() method of the Mammal class to display a string representation of any Mammal instance (or any instance that extended the Mammal class).

4. Create a new ActionScript file and save it as **Cat.as** in the same directory as the Mammal.as class file you created in step 1.

5. In Cat.as, type the following ActionScript code into the Script window:

```
class Cat extends Mammal {
    // constructor
    public function Cat(gender:String) {
        super(gender);
        speciesName = "Cat";
    }

    public function play():String {
        return "Pounce a ball of yarn.";
    }
}
```

   Notice that you are overriding the play() method in the Mammal superclass. The Cat class defines only two methods, a constructor and a play() method. Since the Cat class extends the Mammal class, the Mammal classes's methods and properties are inherited by the Cat class. For more information on overriding, see "Overriding methods and properties" on page 312.

6. Save your changes to the ActionScript document.

7. Create a new ActionScript document and save it as **Dog.as** in the same directory as the two previous class files.

8. In Dog.as, type the following ActionScript code into the Script window:

```
class Dog extends Mammal {
  // constructor
  public function Dog(gender:String) {
    super(gender);
    speciesName = "Dog";
  }

  public function play():String {
    return "Fetch a stick.";
  }
}
```

Notice that the Dog class is very similar in structure to the Cat class, except that a few of the values have changed. Again, the Dog class extends the Mammal class and inherits all its methods and properties. The Dog constructor takes a single property, gender, which it passes to the Dog class's parent class, Mammal. The speciesName variable is also overridden and set to the string Dog. The play() method is also overridden from the parent class.

9. Save your changes to the ActionScript document.

10. Create another ActionScript document in the same directory as your other files, and save it as **Monkey.as**.

11. In Monkey.as, type the following ActionScript code into the Script window:

```
class Monkey extends Mammal {
  // constructor
  public function Monkey(gender:String) {
    super(gender);
    speciesName = "Monkey";
  }

  public function play():String {
    return "Swing from a tree.";
  }
}
```

Similar to the previous two classes, Cat and Dog, the Monkey class extends the Mammal class. The Monkey class's constructor calls the constructor for the Mammal class, passing the gender to the Mammal's constructor, as well as setting speciesName to the string Monkey. The Monkey class also overrides the behavior of the play() method.

12. Save your changes to the ActionScript document.

13. Now that you've created three subclasses of the Mammal class, create a new Flash document called **mammalTest.fla**.

14. In mammalTest.fla, type the following ActionScript code into Frame 1 of the main Timeline:

```
var mammals_arr:Array = new Array();
this.createTextField("info_txt", 10, 10, 10, 450, 80);
info_txt.html = true;
info_txt.multiline = true;
info_txt.border = true;
info_txt.wordWrap = true;

createMammals()
createReport()

function createMammals():Void {
  mammals_arr.push(new Dog("Female"));
  mammals_arr.push(new Cat("Male"));
  mammals_arr.push(new Monkey("Female"));
  mammals_arr.push(new Mammal("Male"));
}

function createReport():Void {
  var i:Number;
  var len:Number = mammals_arr.length;
  // Display Mammal info in 4 columns of HTML text using tab stops.
  info_txt.htmlText = "<textformat tabstops='[110, 200, 300]'>";
  info_txt.htmlText += "<b>Mammal\tGender\tSleep\tPlay</b>";
  for (i = 0; i < len; i++) {
    info_txt.htmlText += "<p>" + mammals_arr[i].speciesName
        + "\t" + mammals_arr[i].gender
        + "\t" + mammals_arr[i].sleep()
        + "\t" + mammals_arr[i].play() + "</p>";
    // The trace statement calls the Mammal.toString() method.
    trace(mammals_arr[i]);
  }
  info_txt.htmlText += "</textformat>";
}
```

The mammalTest.fla code is a bit more complex than the previous classes. First it imports the three animal classes.

15. Save the Flash document, and then select Control > Test Movie to test the document.

You see the Mammal information displayed in a text field on the Stage, and the following text in the Output panel:

```
[object Dog]
[object Cat]
[object Monkey]
[object Mammal]
```

CHAPTER 9

Interfaces

In object-oriented programming (OOP), an interface is a document that lets you declare (but not define) the methods that must appear within a class. When you work in teams of developers, or build larger applications in Flash, interfaces can be very beneficial during development. Interfaces allow developers to easily identify the base methods in ActionScript classes. These methods must be implemented when developers use each interface.

This chapter walks you through a few sample interfaces, and by the end of the chapter you are able to build your own interface files. If you are not familiar with building classes, make sure that you read Chapter 7, "Classes," before you try the tutorials and examples in this chapter.

For more information on working with interfaces, see the following topics:

About interfaces

In object-oriented programming, interfaces are like classes whose methods are not implemented (defined)—that is, they otherwise don't "do" anything. Therefore, an interface consists of "empty" methods. Another class can then implement the methods declared by the interface. In ActionScript, the distinction between interface and object is only for compile-time error checking and language rule enforcement.

An interface is not a class; however, this is not altogether true in ActionScript at runtime because an interface is abstract. ActionScript interfaces do exist at runtime to allow type casting (changing an existing data type to a different type). The ActionScript 2.0 object model does not support multiple inheritance. Therefore, a class can inherit from a single parent class. This parent class can be either a core or Flash Player class or a user-defined (custom) class. You can use interfaces to implement a limited form of multiple inheritance, by which a class inherits from more than one class.

For example, in C++, the Cat class could extend the Mammal class as well as a Playful class, which has methods `chaseTail()` and `eatCatNip()`. Like Java, ActionScript 2.0 does not allow a class to extend multiple classes directly but does allow a class to extend a single class and implement multiple interfaces. So you could create a Playful interface that declares the `chaseTail()` and `eatCatNip()` methods. A Cat class, or any other class, could then implement this interface and provide definitions for those methods.

You can also think of an interface as a "programming contract" that you can use to enforce relationships between otherwise unrelated classes. For example, suppose you are working with a team of programmers, each of whom is working on a different class within the same application. While designing the application, you agree on a set of methods that the different classes use to communicate. You create an interface that declares these methods, their parameters, and their return types. Any class that implements this interface must provide definitions for those methods; otherwise, a compiler error results. The interface is like a communication protocol to which all the classes must adhere.

One way to do this would be to create a class that defines all these methods and then have each class extend, or inherit from, this superclass. But because the application consists of classes that are unrelated, it doesn't make sense to put them all into a common class hierarchy. A better solution is to create an interface that declares the methods these classes use to communicate, and then have each class implement (provide its own definitions for) those methods.

You can usually program successfully without using interfaces. When used appropriately, however, interfaces can make the design of your applications more elegant, scalable, and maintainable.

ActionScript interfaces exist at runtime to allow type casting; see Chapter 4, "About casting objects," on page 113. An interface is not an object or a class, but the workflow is similar to working with classes. For more information on the class workflow, see "Writing custom class files" on page 241. For a tutorial on creating an application with interfaces, see "Example: Using interfaces" on page 328.

For more information on using interfaces, see the following sections:

- "About the interface keyword" on page 321
- "About naming interfaces" on page 321
- "Defining and implementing interfaces" on page 322

About the interface keyword

The `interface` keyword defines an interface. An interface is similar to a class, with the following important differences:

- Interfaces contain only declarations of methods, not their implementation. That is, every class that implements an interface must provide an implementation for each method declared in the interface.
- Only public members are allowed in an interface definition; static and class members are not permitted.
- The `get` and `set` statements are not allowed in interface definitions.
- To use the `interface` keyword, you must specify ActionScript 2.0 and Flash Player 6 or later in the Flash tab of your FLA file's Publish Settings dialog box.

The `interface` keyword is supported only when used in external script files, not in scripts that you write in the Actions panel.

About naming interfaces

Interface names have an uppercase first letter, the same as class names. Interface names are usually adjectives, such as `Printable`. The following interface name, `IEmployeeRecords`, uses an initial uppercase letter and concatenated words with mixed case:

```
interface IEmployeeRecords {}
```

> **NOTE**
>
> Some developers start interface names with an uppercase "I" to distinguish them from classes. This is a good practice to adopt because it lets you quickly distinguish between interfaces and regular classes.

For more information on naming conventions, see Chapter 19, "Best Practices and Coding Conventions for ActionScript 2.0," on page 745.

Defining and implementing interfaces

The process for creating an interface is the same as for creating a class. Like classes, you can define interfaces only in external ActionScript files. At a minimum, the workflow for creating an interface involves the following steps:

- Defining a interface in an external ActionScript file
- Saving the interface file to a designated classpath directory (a location where Flash looks for classes) or in the same directory as the application's FLA file
- Creating an instance of the class in another script, either in a Flash (FLA) document or an external script file, or subinterfaces based on the original interface
- Creating a class that implements the interface in an external script file

You declare an interface using the `interface` keyword, followed by the interface name, and then left and right curly braces ({ }), which define the body of the interface, as shown in the following example:

```
interface IEmployeeRecords {
  // interface method declarations
}
```

An interface can contain only method (function) declarations, including parameters, parameter types, and function return types.

For more information on conventions for structuring classes and interfaces, see Chapter 19, "Best Practices and Coding Conventions for ActionScript 2.0," on page 745. For a tutorial on creating an application that uses an interface, see "Example: Using interfaces" on page 328.

For example, the following code declares an interface named `IMyInterface` that contains two methods, `method1()` and `method2()`. The first method, `method1()`, has no parameters and specifies a return type of Void (meaning that it does not return a value). The second method, `method2()`, has a single parameter of type String, and specifies a return type of Boolean.

To create a simple interface:

1. Create a new ActionScript file and save it as **IMyInterface.as**.

2. Type the following ActionScript code into the Script window:

```
interface IMyInterface {
  public function method1():Void;
  public function method2(param:String):Boolean;
}
```

3. Save your changes to the ActionScript file.

    In order to use the interface within an application, you first need to create a class that implements your new interface.

4. Create a new ActionScript file and save it as **MyClass.as** in the same directory as the IMyInterface.as.

5. In the MyClass class file, type the following ActionScript code into the Script window:

```
class MyClass {
}
```

In order to instruct the custom class (MyClass) to use your interface (IMyInterface), you need to use the `implements` keyword, which specifies that a class must define all the methods declared in the interface (or interfaces) that you implement.

6. Modify the ActionScript code in MyClass.as (add the boldface code) so it matches the following snippet:

```
class MyClass implements IMyInterface {
}
```

You place the `implements` keyword after the class name.

7. Click the Check Syntax button.

Flash displays an error in the Output panel stating that MyClass must implement method X from interface IMyInterface. You see this error message because any class that extends an interface must define each method that's listed in the interface document.

8. Modify the MyClass document again (add the boldface code), and write ActionScript code for the `method1()` and `method2()` methods, as shown in the following snippet:

```
class MyClass implements IMyInterface {
  public function method1():Void {
    // ...
  };
  public function method2(param:String):Boolean {
    // ...
    return true;
  }
}
```

9. Save the MyClass.as document and click Check Syntax.

The Output panel no longer displays any error messages or warnings because you have now defined the two methods.

The class file that you create is not limited to the public methods that you define in the interface file. The interface file only outlines the minimum methods that you must implement, as well as those methods' properties and return types. Classes that implement a particular interface almost always include additional methods, variables, and getter and setter methods.

Interface files cannot contain any variable declarations or assignments. Functions that you declare in an interface cannot contain curly braces. For example, the following interface does not compile:

```
interface IBadInterface {
  // Compiler error. Variable declarations not allowed in interfaces.
  public var illegalVar:String;

  // Compiler error. Function bodies not allowed in interfaces.
  public function illegalMethod():Void {
  }

  // Compiler error. Private methods are not allowed in interfaces.
  private function illegalPrivateMethod():Void;

  // Compiler error. Getters/setters are not allowed in interfaces.
  public function get illegalGetter():String;
}
```

For a tutorial demonstrating how to create a complex interface, see "Example: Using interfaces" on page 328.

The rules for naming interfaces and storing them in packages are the same as those for classes; see "About naming class files" on page 271.

Creating interfaces as data types

Like a class, an interface defines a new data type. You can consider any class that implements an interface to be of the type that is defined by the interface. This is useful for determining whether a given object implements a given interface. For example, consider the interface IMovable, which you create in the following example.

To create an interface as a data type:

1. Create a new ActionScript document and save it to your hard disk as **IMovable.as**.

2. In IMovable.as, type the following ActionScript code into the Script window:

```
interface IMovable {
  public function moveUp():Void;
  public function moveDown():Void;
}
```

3. Save your changes to the ActionScript file.

4. Create a new ActionScript document and save it as **Box.as** in the same directory as IMovable.as.

   In this document, you create a Box class that implements the IMovable interface that you created in an earlier step.

5. In Box.as, type the following ActionScript code into the Script window:

```
class Box implements IMovable {
   public var xPos:Number;
   public var yPos:Number;

   public function Box() {
   }

   public function moveUp():Void {
     trace("moving up");
     // method definition
   }
   public function moveDown():Void {
     trace("moving down");
     // method definition
   }
}
```

6. Save your changes to the ActionScript document.

7. Create a new Flash document named **boxTest.fla,** and then save it in the same directory as the two previous ActionScript documents.

8. Select Frame 1 of the Timeline, open the ActionScript editor, and then type the following ActionScript code into the Actions panel (or Script window):

```
var newBox:Box = new Box();
```

This ActionScript code creates an instance of the Box class, which you declare as a variable of the Box type.

9. Save your changes to the Flash document, and then select Control > Test Movie to test the SWF file.

In Flash Player 7 and later, you can cast an expression to an interface type or other data type at runtime. Unlike Java interfaces, ActionScript interfaces exist at runtime, which allows type casting. If the expression is an object that implements the interface or has a superclass that implements the interface, the object is returned. Otherwise, null is returned. This is useful if you want to ensure that a particular object implements a certain interface. For more information on type casting, see Chapter 4, "About casting objects," on page 113.

10. Add the following code at the end of the ActionScript code in boxTest.fla:

```
if (IMovable(newBox) != null) {
  newBox.moveUp();
} else {
  trace("box instance is not movable");
}
```

This ActionScript code checks whether the newBox instance implements the IMovable interface before you call the moveUp() method on the object.

11. Save the Flash document, and then select Control > Test Movie to test the SWF file.

Because the Box instance implements the IMovable interface, the Box.moveUp() method is called, and the text "moving up" appears in the Output panel.

For more information about casting, see Chapter 4, "About casting objects," on page 113.

Understanding inheritance and interfaces

You can use the extends keyword to create subclasses of an interface. This can be very useful in larger projects for which you might want to extend (or *subclass*) an existing interface and add additional methods. These methods must be defined by any classes implementing that interface.

One consideration you need to make when extending interfaces is that you receive error messages in Flash if multiple interface files declare functions with the same names but have different parameters or return types.

The following example demonstrates how you can subclass an interface file using the extends keyword.

To extend an interface:

1. Create a new ActionScript file, and then save it as **Ia.as**.

2. In Ia.as, type the following ActionScript code into the Script window:

```
interface Ia {
  public function f1():Void;
  public function f2():Void;
}
```

3. Save your changes to the ActionScript file.

4. Create a new ActionScript file and save it as **Ib.as** in the same folder as the Ia.as file you created in step 1.

5. In Ib.as, type the following ActionScript code into the Script window:

```
interface Ib extends Ia {
  public function f8():Void;
  public function f9():Void;
}
```

6. Save your changes to the ActionScript file.

7. Create a new ActionScript file and save it as **ClassA.as** in the same directory as the two previous files.

8. In ClassA.as, type the following ActionScript code into the Script window:

```
class ClassA implements Ib {
  // f1() and f2() are defined in interface Ia.
  public function f1():Void {
  }
  public function f2():Void {
  }

  // f8() and f9() are defined in interface Ib, which extends Ia.
  public function f8():Void {
  }
  public function f9():Void {
  }
}
```

9. Save your class file and click the Check Syntax button above the Script window.

Flash doesn't generate any error messages as long as all four methods are defined and match the definitions from their respective interface files.

> **NOTE** Classes are only able to extend one class in ActionScript 2.0, although you can use classes to implement as many interfaces as you want.

If you want your ClassA class to implement multiple interfaces in the previous example, you would simply separate the interfaces with commas. Or, if you had a class that extended a superclass and implemented multiple interfaces, you would use code similar to the following:

```
class ClassA extends ClassB implements Ib, Ic, Id {...}.
```

Example: Using interfaces

In this example you create a simple interface that you can reuse between many different classes.

To build an interface:

1. Create a new ActionScript file and save it as **IDocumentation.as**.

2. In IDocumentation.as, type the following ActionScript code into the Script window:

```
interface IDocumentation {
  public function downloadUpdates():Void;
  public function checkForUpdates():Boolean;
  public function searchHelp(keyword:String):Array;
}
```

3. Save the changes that you made to the ActionScript interface file.

4. Create a new ActionScript file in the same directory as the IDocumentation.as file, and save this new file as **FlashPaper.as**.

5. In FlashPaper.as, type the following ActionScript code into the Script window:

```
class FlashPaper implements IDocumentation {
}
```

6. Save the changes that you made to the ActionScript file.

7. Click the Check Syntax button for your ActionScript class.

   You see an error that's similar to the following message:

```
**Error** path\FlashPaper.as: Line 1: The class must implement method
  'checkForUpdates' from interface 'IDocumentation'.

    class FlashPaper implements IDocumentation {

Total ActionScript Errors: 1   Reported Errors: 1
```

   This error appears because the current FlashPaper class doesn't define any of the public methods that you defined in the IDocumentation interface.

8. Open the FlashPaper.as class file again and modify the existing ActionScript code so that it matches the following code:

```
class FlashPaper implements IDocumentation {
  private static var __version:String = "1,2,3,4";
  public function downloadUpdates():Void {
  };
  public function checkForUpdates():Boolean {
    return true;
  };
  public function searchHelp(keyword:String):Array {
    return []
  };
}
```

9. Save your changes to the ActionScript file, and then click Check Syntax again.

This time you don't see any errors appear in the Output panel.

 You can add as many additional static, public, or private variables or methods as you want to the FlashPaper class file. The interface file defines only a set of minimum methods that must appear within any class that implements that interface.

10. Open the IDocumentation interface document again, and add the following boldface line of code (below the `searchHelp()` method):

```
interface IDocumentation {
    public function downloadUpdates():Void;
    public function checkForUpdates():Boolean;
    public function searchHelp(keyword:String):Array;
    public function addComment(username:String, comment:String):Void;
}
```

11. Save your changes to the interface file, and then reopen the FlashPaper.as document.

12. Click the Check Syntax button, and you see a new error message in the Output panel:

```
**Error** path\FlashPaper.as: Line 1: The class must implement method
    'addComment' from interface 'IDocumentation'.
        class FlashPaper implements IDocumentation {
Total ActionScript Errors: 1   Reported Errors: 1
```

You see the previous error because the FlashPaper.as class file no longer defines all the classes that you outlined in the interface file. To fix this error message, you must either add the `addComment()` method to the FlashPaper class or remove the method definition from the IDocumentation interface file.

13. Add the following method in the FlashPaper class:

```
public function addComment(username:String, comment:String):Void {
    /* Send parameters to server-side page, which inserts comment into
    database. */
}
```

14. Save the changes to FlashPaper.as and click the Check Syntax button and you should no longer receive any errors.

In the previous section, you created a class-based on the IDocumentation interface file. In this section you create a new class that also implements the IDocumentation interface, although it adds some additional methods and properties.

This tutorial demonstrates the usefulness of using interfaces because if you want to create another class that extends the IDocumentation interface, you can easily identify the methods that are required within the new class.

Example: Creating a complex interface

The following example shows several ways to define and implement interfaces. In this tutorial you learn how to create a simple interface file and how to write a class that implements multiple interfaces, as well as how to have interfaces extend other interfaces to create more complex data structures.

To create a complex interface:

1. Create a new ActionScript document and save it as **InterfaceA.as**.

2. Create a new folder called **complexInterface** and save InterfaceA.as to this directory.

   You save all of the files you create for this tutorial in this directory.

3. In Interface.as, type the following ActionScript code into the Script window:

```
// filename: InterfaceA.as
interface InterfaceA {
  public function k():Number;
  public function n(z:Number):Number;
}
```

4. Save the ActionScript document and then create a new ActionScript document named **ClassB.as** and save it in the complexInterface directory.

   ClassB.as implements the InterfaceA interface you created previously.

5. In ClassB.as, type the following ActionScript code into the Script window:

```
// filename: ClassB.as
class ClassB implements InterfaceA {
  public function k():Number {
    return 25;
  }
  public function n(z:Number):Number {
    return (z + 5);
  }
}
```

6. Save your changes to the ClassB.as document and then create a new Flash document and save it as **classbTest.fla** in the complexInterface directory.

   This class file tests the ClassB class you created previously.

7. In classbTest.fla, type the following ActionScript code on Frame 1 of the Timeline:

```
// filename: classbTest.fla
import ClassB;
var myB:ClassB = new ClassB();
trace(myB.k()); // 25
trace(myB.n(7)); // 12
```

8. Save your changes to the Flash document, and then select Control >Test Movie to test the Flash document.

The Output panel displays two numbers, 25 and 12, which are the results of the k() and n() methods in the ClassB class.

9. Create a new ActionScript file and save it as **ClassC.as** in the complexInterface directory.

This class file implements the InterfaceA interface that you created in step 1.

10. In ClassC.as, type the following ActionScript code into the Script window:

```
// filename: ClassC.as
class ClassC implements InterfaceA {
  public function k():Number {
    return 25;
  }
  // **Error** The class must also implement method 'n' from interface
  'InterfaceA'.
}
```

If you click the Check Syntax button for the ClassC class file, Flash displays an error message in the Output panel that says the current class must implement the n() method defined in the InterfaceA interface. When you create classes that implement an interface, it is important that you define methods for each entry in the interface.

11. Create a new ActionScript document and save it as **InterfaceB.as** in the complexInterface directory.

12. In InterfaceB.as, type the following ActionScript code into the Script window:

```
// filename: InterfaceB.as
interface InterfaceB {
  public function o():Void;
}
```

13. Save your changes to the InterfaceB.as document, and then create a new ActionScript document and save it in the complexInterface directory as **ClassD.as**.

This class implements both the InterfaceA interface and the InterfaceB interface you created in earlier steps. The ClassD class must include method implementations for each of the methods listed in each of the interface files.

14. In ClassD.as, type the following ActionScript code into the Script window:

```
// filename: ClassD.as
class ClassD implements InterfaceA, InterfaceB {
  public function k():Number {
    return 15;
  }
  public function n(z:Number):Number {
    return (z * z);
  }
  public function o():Void {
    trace("o");
  }
}
```

15. Save your changes to the ClassD.as file, and then create a new Flash document and save it as **classdTest.fla**.

This Flash document tests the ClassD class that you created previously.

16. In classdTest.fla, add the following ActionScript code on Frame 1 of the Timeline:

```
// filename: classdTest.fla
import ClassD;
var myD:ClassD = new ClassD();
trace(myD.k()); // 15
trace(myD.n(7)); // 49
myD.o(); // o
```

17. Save your changes to the classdTest.fla file and then select Control > Test Movie to test the file.

The values 15 and 49 and the letter o should be displayed in the Output panel. These values are the results of the `ClassD.k()` method, `ClassD.n()`, and `ClassD.o()` methods, respectively.

18. Create a new ActionScript document and save it as **InterfaceC.as**.

This interface extends the InterfaceA interface you created earlier, and it adds a new method definition.

19. In InterfaceC.as, type the following ActionScript code into the Script window:

```
// filename: InterfaceC.as
interface InterfaceC extends InterfaceA {
  public function p():Void;
}
```

20. Save your changes to the ActionScript file and then create a new ActionScript file and save it as **ClassE.as** in the complexInterface directory.

This class implements two interfaces, InterfaceB and InterfaceC.

21. In ClassE.as, type the following ActionScript code into the Script window:

```
// filename: ClassE.as
class ClassE implements InterfaceB, InterfaceC {
  public function k():Number {
    return 15;
  }
  public function n(z:Number):Number {
    return (z + 5);
  }
  public function o():Void {
    trace("o");
  }
  public function p():Void {
    trace("p");
  }
}
```

22. Save your changes to the ActionScript document, and then create a new Flash document and save it as **classeTest.fla** in the complexInterface directory.

23. In classeTest.fla, type the following ActionScript code on Frame 1 of the Timeline:

```
// filename: classeTest.fla
import ClassE;
var myE:ClassE = new ClassE();
trace(myE.k()); // 15
trace(myF.n(7)); // 12
myE.o(); // o
myE.p(); // p
```

24. Save the Flash document, and then select Control > Test Movie to test the SWF file.

The values 15, 12, o, and p display in the Output panel. These values are the values that return from the ClassE.k(), ClassE.n(), ClassE.o(), and ClassE.p() methods. Since the ClassE class implemented both the InterfaceB and InterfaceC interfaces, each method from the two interface files must be defined. Although the InterfaceB and InterfaceC interfaces only define the o() and p() methods, InterfaceC extends InterfaceA. This means that all of its defined methods, k() and n(), must also be implemented.

CHAPTER 10

Handling Events

Events are actions that occur while a SWF file is playing. An event such as a mouse click or a keypress is called a *user event* because it occurs as a result of direct user interaction. An event that Flash Player generates automatically, such as the initial appearance of a movie clip on the Stage, is called a *system event* because it isn't generated directly by the user.

In order for your application to react to events, you must use *event handlers*—ActionScript code associated with a particular object and event. For example, when a user clicks a button on the Stage, you might advance the playhead to the next frame. Or when an XML file finishes loading over the network, the contents of that file might appear in a text field.

You can handle events in ActionScript in several ways:

- "Using event handler methods" on page 336
- "Using event listeners" on page 338
- "Using button and movie clip event handlers" on page 343, specifically, %{on handler}% and %{onClipEvent handler}%.
- "Broadcasting events from component instances" on page 348

Using event handlers with %{loadMovie (MovieClip.loadMovie method)}% can be unpredictable. If you attach an event handler to a button using `on()`, or if you create a dynamic handler using an event handler method such as %{onPress (MovieClip.onPress handler)}%, and then you call `loadMovie()`, the event handler is not available after the new content is loaded. However, if you use %{onClipEvent handler}% or %{on handler}% to attach an event handler to a movie clip, and then call `loadMovie()` on that movie clip, the event handler is still available after the new content is loaded.

For more information on handling events, see the following sections:

Using event handler methods

An event handler method is a method of a class that is invoked when an event occurs on an instance of that class. For example, the MovieClip class defines an onPress event handler that is invoked whenever the mouse is pressed on a movie clip object. Unlike other methods of a class, however, you don't invoke an event handler directly; Flash Player invokes it automatically when the appropriate event occurs.

The following ActionScript classes are examples of classes that define event handlers: Button, ContextMenu, ContextMenuItem, Key, LoadVars, LocalConnection, Mouse, MovieClip, MovieClipLoader, Selection, SharedObject, Sound, Stage, TextField, XML and XMLSocket. For more information about the event handlers they provide, see the entries for each class in *ActionScript 2.0 Language Reference* in Flash Help. The word *handler* is added in the title of each event handler.

By default, event handler methods are undefined: when a particular event occurs, its corresponding event handler is invoked, but your application doesn't respond further to the event. To have your application respond to the event, you define a function with the function statement and then assign that function to the appropriate event handler. The function you assign to the event handler is then automatically invoked whenever the event occurs.

An event handler consists of three parts: the object to which the event applies, the name of the object's event handler method, and the function you assign to the event handler. The following example shows the basic structure of an event handler:

```
object.eventMethod = function () {
  // Your code here, responding to event.
}
```

For example, suppose you have a button named next_btn on the Stage. The following code assigns a function to the button's onPress event handler; this function advances the playhead to the next frame in the current timeline:

```
next_btn.onPress = function () {
  nextFrame();
}
```

Assigning a function reference   In the previous code, the nextFrame() function is assigned to an event handler for onPress. You can also assign a function reference (name) to an event handler method and later define the function, as shown in the following example:

```
// Assign a function reference to button's onPress event handler.
next_btn.onPress = goNextFrame;

// Define goNextFrame() function.
function goNextFrame() {
  nextFrame();
}
```

Notice in the following example that you assign the function reference, not the function's return value, to the onPress event handler:

```
// Incorrect!
next_btn.onPress = goNextFrame();
// Correct.
next_btn.onPress = goNextFrame;
```

Receiving passed parameters   Some event handlers receive passed parameters that provide information about the event that occurred. For example, the TextField.onSetFocus event handler is invoked when a text field instance gains keyboard focus. This event handler receives a reference to the text field object that previously had keyboard focus.

For example, the following code inserts some text into a text field that no longer has keyboard focus:

```
this.createTextField("my_txt", 99, 10, 10, 200, 20);
my_txt.border = true;
my_txt.type = "input";
this.createTextField("myOther_txt", 100, 10, 50, 200, 20);
myOther_txt.border = true;
myOther_txt.type = "input";
myOther_txt.onSetFocus = function(my_txt:TextField) {
  my_txt.text = "I just lost keyboard focus";
};
```

Event handlers for runtime objects   You can also assign functions to event handlers for objects you create at runtime. For example, the following code creates a new movie clip instance (`newclip_mc`) and then assigns a function to the clip's `onPress` event handler:

```
this.attachMovie("symbolID", "newclip_mc", 10);
newclip_mc.onPress = function () {
  trace("You pressed me");
}
```

For more information, see "Creating movie clips at runtime" on page 366.

Overriding event handler methods   By creating a class that extends an ActionScript class, you can override event handler methods with the functions that you write. You can define an event handler in a new subclass that you can then reuse for various objects by linking any symbol in the library of the extended class to the new subclass. The following code overrides the MovieClip class's `onPress` event handler with a function that decreases the transparency of the movie clip:

```
// FadeAlpha class -- sets transparency when you click the movie clip.
class FadeAlpha extends MovieClip {
  function onPress() {
    this._alpha -= 10;
  }
}
```

For specific instructions on extending an ActionScript class and linking to a symbol in the library, see the examples in "Assigning a class to symbols in Flash" on page 285. For information on writing and working with custom classes, see Chapter 7, "Classes."

Using event listeners

Event listeners let an object, called a *listener object*, receive events broadcast by another object, called a *broadcaster object*. The broadcaster object registers the listener object to receive events generated by the broadcaster. For example, you can register a movie clip object to receive `onResize` notifications from the Stage, or a button instance could receive `onChanged` notifications from a text field object. You can register multiple listener objects to receive events from a single broadcaster, and you can register a single listener object to receive events from multiple broadcasters.

The listener-broadcaster model for events, unlike event handler methods, lets you have multiple pieces of code listen to the same event without conflict. Event models that do not use the listener/broadcaster model, such as XML.onLoad(), can be problematic when various pieces of code are listening to the same event; the different pieces of code have conflicts over control of that single XML.onLoad callback function reference. With the listener/broadcaster model, you can easily add listeners to the same event without worrying about code bottlenecks.

The following ActionScript classes can broadcast events: %{Key}%, %{Mouse}%, %{MovieClipLoader}%, %{Selection}%, %{Stage}%, and %{TextField}%. To see which listeners are available for a class, see each class entry in the *ActionScript 2.0 Language Reference* in Flash Help.

For more information on event listeners, see the following topics:

- "Event listener model" on page 339
- "Event listener example" on page 340

The Stage class can broadcast events. You can find a sample source file, stagesize.fla, in the Samples folder on your hard disk. This sample demonstrates how the Stage.scaleMode property affects the values of Stage.width and Stage.height when the browser window is resized.

- In Windows, browse to *boot drive*\Program Files\Macromedia\Flash 8\Samples and Tutorials\Samples\ActionScript\StageSize.
- On the Macintosh, browse to *Macintosh HD*/Applications/Macromedia Flash 8/Samples and Tutorials/Samples/ActionScript/StageSize.

Event listener model

The event model for event listeners is similar to the model for event handlers (see "Using event handler methods" on page 336), with two main differences:

- You assign the event handler to the listener object, not the object that broadcasts the event.
- You call a special method of the broadcaster object, addListener(), which registers the listener object to receive its events.

The following code outlines the event listener model:

```
var listenerObject:Object = new Object();
listenerObject.eventName = function(eventObj:Object) {
  // Your code here
};
broadcasterObject.addListener(listenerObject);
```

The code starts with an object, *listenerObject*, with a property *eventName*. Your listener object can be any object, such as an existing object, movie clip, or button instance on the Stage, or it can be an instance of any ActionScript class. For example, a custom movie clip could implement the listener methods for Stage listeners. You could even have one object that listens to several types of listeners.

The *eventName* property is an event that occurs on *broadcasterObject*, which then broadcasts the event to *listenerObject*. You can register multiple listeners to one event broadcaster.

You assign a function to the event listener that responds to the event in some way.

Last, you call the `addListener()` method on the broadcaster object, passing the listener object to the addListener() method.

To unregister a listener object from receiving events, you call the `removeEventListener()` method of the broadcaster object, passing it the name of the event to remove, and the listener object.

```
broadcasterObject.removeListener(listenerObject);
```

Event listener example

The following example shows how to use the `onSetFocus` event listener in the Selection class to create a simple focus manager for a group of input text fields. In this case, the border of the text field that receives keyboard focus is enabled (appears), and the border of the text field that does not have focus is disabled.

To create a simple focus manager with event listeners:

1. Using the Text tool, create a text field on the Stage.

2. Select the text field, and then in the Property inspector, select Input from the Text Type pop-up menu and select the Show Border Around Text option.

3. Create another input text field below the first one.

    Make sure the Show Border Around Text option is not selected for this text field. You can continue to create input text fields.

4. Select Frame 1 in the Timeline and open the Actions panel (Window > Actions).

5. To create an object that listens for focus notification from the Selection class, enter the following code in the Actions panel:

```
// Creates listener object, focusListener.
var focusListener:Object = new Object();
// Defines function for listener object.
focusListener.onSetFocus = function(oldFocus_txt:TextField,
  newFocus_txt:TextField) {
  oldFocus_txt.border = false;
  newFocus_txt.border = true;
}
```

This code creates an object named focusListener that defines an onSetFocus property and assigns a function to the property. The function takes two parameters: a reference to the text field that does not have focus and one to the text field that has focus. The function sets the border property of the text field that does not have focus to false, and sets the border property of the text field that has focus to true.

6. To register the focusListener object to receive events from the Selection object, add the following code to the Actions panel:

```
// Registers focusListener with broadcaster.
Selection.addListener(focusListener);
```

7. Test the application (Control > Test Movie), click in the first text field, and press the Tab key to switch focus between fields.

Using event listeners with components

When you work with components, you have a slightly different event-listener syntax. Components generate events, and you must specifically listen for these events by using either a listener object or a custom function.

The following example shows how you can use event listeners to monitor the download progress of a dynamically loaded image.

To listen for Loader component events:

1. Drag an instance of the Loader component onto the Stage from the Components panel.

2. Select the loader, and type **my_ldr** in the Instance Name text box in the Property inspector.

3. Add the following code to Frame 1 of the main Timeline;

```
System.security.allowDomain("http://www.helpexamples.com");

var loaderListener:Object = new Object();
loaderListener.progress = function(evt_obj:Object):Void {
  trace(evt_obj.type); // progress
  trace("\t" + evt_obj.target.bytesLoaded + " of " +
  evt_obj.target.bytesTotal + " bytes loaded");
}
loaderListener.complete = function(evt_obj:Object):Void {
  trace(evt_obj.type); // complete
}

my_ldr.addEventListener("progress", loaderListener);
my_ldr.addEventListener("complete", loaderListener);
my_ldr.load("http://www.helpexamples.com/flash/images/image1.jpg");
```

This ActionScript code defines a listener object named `loaderListener`, which listens for two events: `progress` and `complete`. When each of these events are dispatched, their code is executed, and debugging text is displayed in the Output panel if you test the SWF file in the authoring tool.

Next you tell the `my_ldr` instance to listen for each of the two specified events (`progress` and `complete`) and specify the listener object or function to execute when the event is dispatched. Finally, the `Loader.load()` method is called, which triggers the image to begin downloading.

4. Select Control > Test Movie to test the SWF file.

The image downloads into the Loader instance on the Stage, and then several messages are displayed in the Output panel. Depending on the size of the image you download, and if the image was cached on the user's local system, the `progress` event might be dispatched numerous times, whereas the complete event is only dispatched after the image is completely downloaded.

When you work with components and dispatch events, the syntax is slightly different from the event listeners in previous examples. Most notably, you must use the `addEventListener()` method instead of calling `addListener()`. Secondly, you must specify the specific event you want to listen for as well as the event listener object or function.

Instead of using a listener object, as in the first procedure under "Using event listeners with components" on page 341, you can use a custom function. The code in the previous example could be rewritten as follows:

```
System.security.allowDomain("http://www.helpexamples.com");

my_ldr.addEventListener("progress", progressListener);
my_ldr.addEventListener("complete", completeListener);
my_ldr.load("http://www.helpexamples.com/flash/images/image1.png");

function progressListener(evt_obj:Object):Void {
  trace(evt_obj.type); // progress
  trace("\t" + evt_obj.target.bytesLoaded + " of " +
  evt_obj.target.bytesTotal + " bytes loaded");
}
function completeListener(evt_obj:Object):Void {
  trace(evt_obj.type); // complete
}
```

> **NOTE**
> In the previous examples, the event listeners are always added before the Loader.load() method is called. If you call the Loader.load() method before you specify the event listeners, the load might complete before the event listeners are fully defined. This means that the content might display and the complete event might not be caught.

Using button and movie clip event handlers

You can attach event handlers directly to a button or movie clip instance on the Stage by using the onClipEvent() and on() event handlers. The onClipEvent() event handler broadcasts movie clip events, and the on() event handler handles button events.

To attach an event handler to a button or movie clip instance, click the button or movie clip instance on the Stage to bring it in focus, and then enter code in the Actions panel. The title of the Actions panel reflects that code will be attached to the button or movie clip: Actions Panel - Button or Actions Panel - Movie Clip. For guidelines about using code that's attached to button or movie clip instances, see "Attaching code to objects" on page 760.

> **NOTE**
> Do not confuse button and movie clip event handlers with component events, such as SimpleButton.click, UIObject.hide, and UIObject.reveal, which must be attached to component instances and are discussed in *Using Components* in Flash Help.

You can attach `onClipEvent()` and `on()` only to movie clip instances that have been placed on the Stage during authoring. You cannot attach `onClipEvent()` or `on()` to movie clip instances that are created at runtime (using the `attachMovie()` method, for example). To attach event handlers to objects created at runtime, use event handler methods or event listeners. (See "Using event handler methods" on page 336 and "Using event listeners" on page 338.)

> **NOTE**
> Attaching `onClipEvent()` and `on()` handlers is not a recommended practice. Instead, you should put your code in frame scripts or in a class file, as demonstrated throughout this manual. For more information, see "Using event handler methods" on page 336 and "Attaching code to objects" on page 760.

For more information on button and movie clip event handlers, see the following topics:

- "Using on and onClipEvent with event handler methods" on page 344
- "Specifying events for on or onClipEvent methods" on page 345
- "Attaching or assigning multiple handlers to one object" on page 347

Using on and onClipEvent with event handler methods

You can, in some cases, use different techniques to handle events without conflict. Using the `on()` and `onClipEvent()` methods doesn't conflict with using event handler methods that you define.

For example, suppose you have a button in a SWF file; the button can have an `on(press)` handler that tells the SWF file to play, and the same button can have an `onPress()` method, for which you define a function that tells an object on the Stage to rotate. When you click the button, the SWF file plays and the object rotates. Depending on when and what kinds of events you want to invoke, you can use the `on()` and `onClipEvent()` methods, event handler methods, or both techniques of event handling.

However, the scope of variables and objects in `on()` and `onClipEvent()` handlers is different than in event handler and event listeners. See "Event handler scope" on page 349.

You can also use `on()` with movie clips to create movie clips that receive button events. For more information, see "Creating movie clips with button states" on page 348. For information on specifying events for `on()` and `onClipEvent()`, see "Specifying events for on or onClipEvent methods" on page 345.

To use an on handler and onPress event handler:

1. Create a new Flash document and save it as **handlers.fla**.

2. Select the Rectangle Tool and draw a large square on the Stage.

3. Select the Selection Tool, double-click the square on the Stage, and press F8 to launch the Convert to Symbol dialog box.

4. Enter a symbol name for the box, set the type to Movie clip and click OK.

5. Give the movie clip on the Stage an instance name of **box_mc**.

6. Add the following ActionScript directly on the movie clip symbol on the Stage:

```
on (press) {
   trace("on (press) {...}");
}
```

7. Add the following ActionScript to Frame 1 of the main Timeline:

```
box_mc.onPress = function() {
   trace("box_mc.onPress = function() {...};");
},
```

8. Select Control > Test Movie to test the Flash document.

   When you click the movie clip symbol on the Stage, the following output is sent to the Output panel:

   on (press) {...}

   box_mc.onPress = function() {...};

> **NOTE**
>
> Attaching `onClipEvent()` and `on()` handlers is not a recommended practice. Instead, you should put your code in frame scripts or in a class file, as demonstrated throughout this manual. For more information, see "Using event handler methods" on page 336 and "Attaching code to objects" on page 760.

Specifying events for on or onClipEvent methods

To use an `on()` or `onClipEvent()` handler, attach it directly to an instance of a button or movie clip on the Stage and specify the event you want to handle for that instance. For a complete list of events supported by the `on()` and `onClipEvent()` event handlers, see %{on handler}% and %{onClipEvent handler}% in the *ActionScript 2.0 Language Reference* in Flash Help.

For example, the following `on()` event handler executes whenever the user clicks the button to which the handler is attached:

```
on (press) {
   trace("Thanks for pressing me.");
}
```

You can specify two or more events for each `on()` handler, separated by commas. The ActionScript in a handler executes when either of the events specified by the handler occurs. For example, the following `on()` handler attached to a button executes whenever the mouse rolls over and then off the button:

```
on (rollOver, rollOut) {
  trace("You rolled over, or rolled out");
}
```

You can also add key press events using `on()` handlers. For example, the following code traces a string when you press the number 3 on the keyboard. Select a button or movie clip instance, and add the following code to the Actions panel:

```
on (keyPress "3") {
  trace("You pressed 3")
}
```

Or, if you want to trace when the Enter key is pressed by a user, you could use the following code format. Select a button or movie clip instance, and add the following code to the Actions panel:

```
on (keyPress "<Enter>") {
  trace("Enter Pressed");
}
```

Select Control > Test Movie, and press the Enter key to see the string trace to the Output panel. If nothing traces, select Control > Disable Keyboard Shortcuts and try again. For more information on adding keypress interactivity to your applications, see %{Key}%.

> **NOTE**
>
> Attaching `onClipEvent()` and `on()` handlers is not a recommended practice. Instead, you should put your code in frame scripts or in a class file, as demonstrated throughout this manual. For more information, see "Using event handler methods" on page 336 and "Attaching code to objects" on page 760.

Attaching or assigning multiple handlers to one object

You can also attach more than one handler to an object if you want different scripts to run when different events occur. For example, you could attach the following `onClipEvent()` handlers to the same movie clip instance. The first executes when the movie clip first loads (or appears on the Stage); the second executes when the movie clip is unloaded from the Stage.

```
on (press) {
  this.unloadMovie()
}
onClipEvent (load) {
  trace("I've loaded");
}
onClipEvent (unload) {
  trace("I've unloaded");
}
```

> **NOTE**
> Attaching `onClipEvent()` and `on()` handlers is not a recommended practice. Instead, you should put your code in frame scripts or in a class file, as demonstrated throughout this manual. For more information, see "Using event handler methods" on page 336 and "Attaching code to objects" on page 760.

To attach multiple handlers to one object using code that's placed on the timeline, see the following example. The code attaches the `onPress` and `onRelease` handlers to a movie clip instance.

To assign multiple handlers to an object:

1. Create a new Flash document, and name it **assignMulti.fla**.

2. Select Frame 1 of the Timeline, and add the following code in the Actions panel:

```
this.createEmptyMovieClip("img_mc", 10);
var mclListener:Object = new Object();
mclListener.onLoadInit = function(target_mc:MovieClip) {
    target_mc.onPress = function() {
        target_mc.startDrag();
    };
    target_mc.onRelease = function() {
        target_mc.stopDrag();
    };
}
mclListener.onLoadError = function(target_mc:MovieClip) {
    trace("error downloading image");
}
var img_mcl:MovieClipLoader = new MovieClipLoader();
img_mcl.addListener(mclListener);
img_mcl.loadClip("http://www.helpexamples.com/flash/images/image1.jpg",
  img_mc);
```

3. Select Control > Test Movie to test the document.

The image loads into the `img_mc` instance, and the `onPress()` and `onRelease()` event handlers let you drag the image around the Stage.

Broadcasting events from component instances

For any component instance, you can specify how an event is handled. Component events are handled differently than events broadcast from native ActionScript objects.

For more information, see "Handling Component Events" in *Using Components* in Flash Help.

Creating movie clips with button states

When you attach an `on()` handler to a movie clip, or assign a function to one of the MovieClip mouse event handlers for a movie clip instance, the movie clip responds to mouse events in the same way as a button. You can also create automatic button states (Up, Over, and Down) in a movie clip by adding the frame labels `_up`, `_over`, and `_down` to the movie clip's timeline.

When the user moves the mouse over the movie clip or clicks it, the playhead is sent to the frame with the appropriate frame label. To designate the hit area that a movie clip uses, you use the %{hitArea (MovieClip.hitArea property)}% property.

To create button states in a movie clip:

1. Create a new Flash document and save it as **mcbutton.fla**.

2. Using the Rectangle Tool, draw a small rectangle (approximately 100 pixels wide by 20 pixels high) on the Stage.

3. Double-click the shape with the Selection tool and press F8 to launch the Convert to Symbol dialog box.

4. Enter a symbol name of **mcbutton**, set the symbol type to movie clip, and click OK.

5. Double-click the movie clip symbol on the Stage to enter symbol-editing mode.

6. Create a new layer in the movie clip's timeline and rename the new layer **labels**.

7. Enter a frame label of `_up` in the Property inspector.

8. Create a new layer above the default layer and labels layer.

9. Rename the new layer **actions** and add the following ActionScript to Frame 1 of the movie clip's timeline:

```
stop();
```

10. Select Frame 10, all three layers, and select Insert > Timeline > Keyframe.

11. Add a stop() action on Frame 10 of the actions layer, and add a frame label of **_over** in frame 10 of the labels layer.

12. Select the rectangle on Frame 10 and use the Property inspector to select a different fill color.

13. Create new keyframes on frame 20 of each of the three layers, and add a frame label of **_down** in the Property inspector.

14. Modify the color of the rectangle in Frame 20 so each of the three button states have a different color.

15. Return to the main timeline.

16. To make the movie clip respond to mouse events, do one of the following:

   ■ Attach an on() event handler to the movie clip instance, as discussed in "Using button and movie clip event handlers" on page 343).

   ■ Assign a function to one of the movie clip object's mouse event handlers (onPress, onRelease, and so forth), as discussed in "Using event handler methods" on page 336.

17. Select Control > Test Movie to test the Flash document.

   Move your mouse pointer over the movie clip instance on the Stage and the movie clip automatically goes to the movie clip's _over state. Click the movie clip instance and the playhead automatically goes to the movie clip's _down state.

Event handler scope

The scope, or *context*, of variables and commands that you declare and execute within an event handler depends on the type of event handler you use: event handlers or event listeners, or on() and onClipEvent() handlers. If you're defining an event handler in a new ActionScript class, the scope also depends on how you define the event handler. This section contains both ActionScript 1.0 and ActionScript 2.0 examples.

ActionScript 1.0 examples   Functions assigned to event handler methods and event listeners (as with all ActionScript functions that you write) define a local variable scope, but on() and onClipEvent() handlers do not.

For example, consider the following two event handlers. The first is an `onPress` event handler associated with a movie clip named `clip_mc`. The second is an `on()` handler attached to the same movie clip instance.

```
// Attached to clip_mc's parent clip timeline:
clip_mc.onPress = function () {
   var shoeColor; // local function variable
   shoeColor = "blue";
}
// on() handler attached to clip_mc:
on (press) {
   var shoeColor; // no local variable scope
   shoeColor = "blue";
}
```

Although both event handlers contain the same code, they have different results. In the first case, the `color` variable is local to the function defined for `onPress`. In the second case, because the `on()` handler doesn't define a local variable scope, the variable is defined in the scope of the timeline of the `clip_mc` movie clip.

For `on()` event handlers attached to buttons, rather than to movie clips, variables (as well as function and method calls) are invoked in the scope of the timeline that contains the button instance.

For instance, the following `on()` event handler produces different results that depend on whether it's attached to a button or movie clip object. In the first case, the `play()` function call starts the playhead of the timeline that contains the button; in the second case, the `play()` function call starts the timeline of the movie clip to which the handler is attached.

```
// Attached to button.
on (press) {
   play(); // Plays parent timeline.
}
// Attached to movie clip.
on (press) {
   play(); // Plays movie clip's timeline.
}
```

When attached to a button object, the `play()` function applies to the timeline that contains the button—that is, the button's parent timeline. But when the `on(press)` handler is attached to a movie clip object, the `play()` function call applies to the movie clip that bears the handler. If you attach the following code to a movie clip, it plays the parent timeline:

```
// Attached to movie clip.
on (press) {
   _parent.play(); // Plays parent timeline.
}
```

Within an event handler or event listener definition, the same `play()` function applies to the timeline that contains the function definition. For example, suppose you declare the following `my_mc.onPress` event handler method on the timeline that contains the `my_mc` movie clip instance:

```
// Function defined on a timeline
my_mc.onPress = function () {
  play(); // plays timeline that it is defined on.
};
```

To play the movie clip that defines the `onPress` event handler, refer explicitly to that clip using the `this` keyword, as follows:

```
// Function defined on root timeline
my_mc.onPress = function () {
  this.play(); // plays timeline of my_mc clip.
};
```

However, the same code placed on the root timeline for a button instance would instead play the root timeline:

```
my_btn.onPress = function () {
  this.play(); // plays root timeline
};
```

For more information about the scope of the `this` keyword in event handlers, see "Scope of the this keyword" on page 353.

ActionScript 2.0 example The following TextLoader class is used to load a text file and display some text after it successfully loads the file.

```
// TextLoader.as
class TextLoader {
  private var params_lv:LoadVars;
  public function TextLoader() {
    params_lv = new LoadVars();
    params_lv.onLoad = onLoadVarsDone;
    params_lv.load("http://www.helpexamples.com/flash/params.txt");
  }
  private function onLoadVarsDone(success:Boolean):Void {
    _level0.createTextField("my_txt", 999, 0, 0, 100, 20);
    _level0.my_txt.autoSize = "left";
    _level0.my_txt.text = params_lv.monthNames; // undefined
  }
}
```

This code cannot work correctly because there is a problem involving scope with the event handlers, and what this refers to is confused between the onLoad event handler and the class. The behavior that you might expect in this example is that the onLoadVarsDone() method will be invoked in the scope of the TextLoader object; but it is invoked in the scope of the LoadVars object because the method was extracted from the TextLoader object and grafted onto the LoadVars object. The LoadVars object then invokes the this.onLoad event handler when the text file is successfully loaded, and the onLoadVarsDone() function is invoked with this set to LoadVars, not TextLoader. The params_lv object resides in the this scope when it is invoked, even though the onLoadVarsDone() function relies on the params_lv object by reference. Therefore, the onLoadVarsDone() function is expecting a params_lv.params_lv instance that does not exist.

To correctly invoke the onLoadVarsDone() method in the scope of the TextLoader object, you can use the following strategy: use a function literal to create an anonymous function that calls the desired function. The owner object is still visible in the scope of the anonymous function, so it can be used to find the calling TextLoader object.

```
// TextLoader.as
class TextLoader {
  private var params_lv:LoadVars;
  public function TextLoader() {
    params_lv = new LoadVars();
    var owner:TextLoader = this;
    params_lv.onLoad = function (success:Boolean):Void {
      owner.onLoadVarsDone(success);
    }
    params_lv.load("http://www.helpexamples.com/flash/params.txt");
  }
  private function onLoadVarsDone(success:Boolean):Void {
    _level0.createTextField("my_txt", 999, 0, 0, 100, 20);
    _level0.my_txt.autoSize = "left";
    _level0.my_txt.text = params_lv.monthNames; //
  January,February,March,...
  }
}
```

Scope of the this keyword

The this keyword refers to the object in the currently executing scope. Depending on what type of event handler technique you use, this can refer to different objects.

Within an event handler or event listener function, this refers to the object that defines the event handler or event listener method. For example, in the following code, this refers to my_mc:

```
// onPress() event handler attached to main timeline:
my_mc.onPress = function () {
  trace(this); // _level0.my_mc
}
```

Within an on() handler attached to a movie clip, this refers to the movie clip to which the on() handler is attached, as shown in the following code:

```
// Attached to movie clip named my_mc on main timeline
on (press) {
  trace(this); // _level0.my_mc
}
```

Within an on() handler attached to a button, this refers to the timeline that contains the button, as shown in the following code:

```
// Attached to button on main timeline
on (press) {
  trace(this); // _level0
}
```

Using the Delegate class

The Delegate class lets you run a function in a specific scope. This class is provided so that you can dispatch the same event to two different functions (see "Delegating events to functions" in *Using Components* in Flash Help), and so that you can call functions within the scope of the containing class.

When you pass a function as a parameter to EventDispatcher.addEventListener(), the function is invoked in the scope of the broadcaster component instance, not the object in which it is declared (see "Delegating the scope of a function" in *Using Components* in Flash Help). You can use Delegate.create() to call the function within the scope of the declaring object.

The following example shows three methods of listening for events for a Button component instance. Each way that you add event listeners to a Button component instance results in the event being dispatched in a different scope.

To use the Delegate class to listen for events:

1. Create a new Flash document and save it as **delegate.fla**.

2. Drag a Button component from the User Interface folder of the Components panel to the library.

   You add and position the button instance on the Stage using ActionScript in a later step.

3. Add the following ActionScript to Frame 1 of the main Timeline:

```
import mx.controls.Button;
import mx.utils.Delegate;

function clickHandler(eventObj:Object):Void {
  trace("[" + eventObj.type + "] event on " + eventObj.target + "
  instance.");
  trace("\t this -> " + this);
}

var buttonListener:Object = new Object();
buttonListener.click = function(eventObj:Object):Void {
  trace("[" + eventObj.type + "] event on " + eventObj.target + "
  instance.");
  trace("\t this -> " + this);
};

this.createClassObject(Button, "one_button", 10, {label:"One"});
one_button.move(10, 10);
one_button.addEventListener("click", clickHandler);

this.createClassObject(Button, "two_button", 20, {label:"Two"});
two_button.move(120, 10);
two_button.addEventListener("click", buttonListener);

this.createClassObject(Button, "three_button", 30, {label:"Three"});
three_button.move(230, 10);
three_button.addEventListener("click", Delegate.create(this,
  clickHandler));
```

The preceding code is separated into six sections (each section is separated by a blank line). The first section imports the Button class (for the Button component) as well as the Delegate class. The second section of code defines a function that you call when the user clicks some of the buttons. The third section of code creates an object that you use as an event listener, and the object listens for a single event, click.

The remaining three sections of code each create a new Button component instance on the Stage, reposition the instance, and add an event listener for the `click` event. The first button adds an event listener for the `click` event and passes a reference to a `click` handler function directly. The second button adds an event listener for the `click` event and passes a reference to a listener object, which contains a handler for the `click` event. Finally, the third function adds an event listener for the `click` event, uses the Delegate class to dispatch the click event in the `this` scope (where `this` equals `_level0`) and passes a reference to the `click` handler function.

4. Select Control > Test Movie to test the Flash document.

5. Click each button instance on the Stage to see which scope in which the event is handled.

   a. Click the first button on the Stage to trace the following text in the Output panel:

   ```
   [click] event on _level0.one_button instance.
       this -> _level0.one_button
   ```

   When you click `one_button` instance, the `this` scope refers to the button instance itself.

   b. Click the second button on the Stage to trace the following text in the Output panel:

   ```
   [click] event on _level0.two_button instance.
       this -> [object Object]
   ```

   When you click the `two_button` instance, the `this` scope refers to the `buttonListener` object.

   c. Click the third button on the Stage to trace the following text in the Output panel:

   ```
   [click] event on _level0.three_button instance.
       this -> _level0
   ```

   When you click the `three_button` instance, the `this` scope refers to the scope that you specify in the `Delegate.create()` method call, or in this case, `_level0`.

CHAPTER 11

Working with Movie Clips

Movie clips are like self-contained SWF files that run independently of each other and the timeline that contains them. For example, if the main timeline has only one frame and a movie clip in that frame has ten frames, each frame in the movie clip plays when you play the main SWF file. A movie clip can, in turn, contain other movie clips, or *nested clips*. Movie clips nested in this way have a hierarchical relationship, where the *parent clip* contains one or more *child clips*.

You can name movie clip instances to uniquely identify them as objects that can be controlled with ActionScript. When you give a movie clip instance an *instance name*, the instance name identifies it as an object of the MovieClip class type. You use the properties and methods of the MovieClip class to control the appearance and behavior of movie clips at runtime.

You can think of movie clips as autonomous objects that can respond to events, send messages to other movie clip objects, maintain their state, and manage their child clips. In this way, movie clips provide the foundation of *component-based architecture* in Macromedia Flash Basic 8 and Macromedia Flash Professional 8. In fact, the components available in the Components panel (Window > Components) are sophisticated movie clips that are designed and programmed to look and behave in certain ways.

For information on using the Drawing API (drawing methods of the MovieClip class), filters, blends, scripted animation and more, see Chapter 13, "Animation, Filters, and Drawings."

For more information on movie clips, see the following topics:

About controlling movie clips with ActionScript

You can use global ActionScript functions or the methods of the MovieClip class to perform tasks on movie clips. Some methods of the MovieClip class perform the same tasks as functions of the same name; other MovieClip methods, such as `hitTest()` and `swapDepths()`, don't have corresponding function names.

The following example shows the difference between using a method and using a function. Each statement duplicates the instance `my_mc`, names the new clip `new_mc`, and places it at a depth of 5.

```
my_mc.duplicateMovieClip("new_mc", 5);
duplicateMovieClip(my_mc, "new_mc", 5);
```

When a function and a method offer similar behaviors, you can select to control movie clips by using either one. The choice depends on your preference and your familiarity with writing scripts in ActionScript. Whether you use a function or a method, the target timeline must be loaded in Flash Player when the function or method is called.

To use a method, activate it by using the target path of the instance name, a dot (.), and then the method name and parameters, as shown in the following statements:

```
myMovieClip.play();
parentClip.childClip.gotoAndPlay(3);
```

In the first statement, `play()` moves the playhead in the `myMovieClip` instance. In the second statement, `gotoAndPlay()` sends the playhead in `childClip` (which is a child of the instance `parentClip`) to Frame 3 and continues to move the playhead.

Global functions that control a timeline have a *target* parameter that let you specify the target path to the instance that you want to control. For example, in the following script `startDrag()` targets the instance the code is placed on and makes it draggable:

```
my_mc.onPress = function() {
  startDrag(this);
};
my_mc.onRelease = function() {
  stopDrag();
};
```

The following functions target movie clips: `loadMovie()`, `unloadMovie()`, `loadVariables()`, `setProperty()`, `startDrag()`, `duplicateMovieClip()`, and `removeMovieClip()`. To use these functions, you must enter a target path for the function's *target* parameter to indicate the target of the function.

The following MovieClip methods can control movie clips or loaded levels and do not have equivalent functions: `MovieClip.attachMovie()`, `MovieClip.createEmptyMovieClip()`, `MovieClip.createTextField()`, `MovieClip.getBounds()`, `MovieClip.getBytesLoaded()`, `MovieClip.getBytesTotal()`, `MovieClip.getDepth()`, `MovieClip.getInstanceAtDepth()`, `MovieClip.getNextHighestDepth()`, `MovieClip.globalToLocal()`, `MovieClip.localToGlobal()`, `MovieClip.hitTest()`, `MovieClip.setMask()`, `MovieClip.swapDepths()`.

For more information about these functions and methods, see their entries in the *ActionScript 2.0 Language Reference* in Flash Help.

For an example of scripted animation in Flash, you can find a sample source file, animation.fla, in the Samples folder on your hard disk.

- In Windows, browse to *boot drive*\Program Files\Macromedia\Flash 8\ Samples and Tutorials\Samples\ActionScript\Animation.

- On the Macintosh, browse to *Macintosh HD*/Applications/Macromedia Flash 8/ Samples and Tutorials/Samples/ActionScript/Animation.

You can find samples of photo gallery applications on your hard disk. These files provide examples of how to use ActionScript to control movie clips dynamically while loading image files into a SWF file, which includes scripted animation. You can find the sample source files, gallery_tree.fla and gallery_tween.fla, in the Samples folder on your hard disk.

- In Windows, browse to *boot drive*\Program Files\Macromedia\Flash 8\ Samples and Tutorials\Samples\ActionScript\Galleries.

- On the Macintosh, browse to *Macintosh HD*/Applications/Macromedia Flash 8/ Samples and Tutorials/Samples/ActionScript/Galleries.

Calling multiple methods on a single movie clip

You can use the `with` statement to address a movie clip once and then execute a series of methods on that clip. The `with` statement works on all ActionScript objects (for example, Array, Color, and Sound)—not only movie clips.

The `with` statement takes a movie clip as a parameter. The object you specify is added to the end of the current target path. All actions nested inside a `with` statement are carried out inside the new target path, or scope. For example, in the following script, the `donut.hole` object passes to the `with` statement to change the properties of `hole`:

```
with (donut.hole) {
  _alpha = 20;
  _xscale = 150;
  _yscale = 150;
}
```

The script behaves as if the statements inside the `with` statement were called from the timeline of the `hole` instance. The preceding code is equivalent to the following example:

```
donut.hole._alpha = 20;
donut.hole._xscale = 150;
donut.hole._yscale = 150;
```

The preceding code is also equivalent to the following example:

```
with (donut) {
  hole._alpha = 20;
  hole._xscale = 150;
  hole._yscale = 150;
}
```

Loading and unloading SWF files

To play additional SWF files without closing Flash Player, or to switch SWF files without loading another HTML page, you can use one of the following options:

- The global `loadMovie()` function or `loadMovie()` method of the MovieClip class.
- The `loadClip()` method of the MovieClipLoader class. For more information on the MovieClipLoader class, see %{MovieClipLoader}% in the *ActionScript 2.0 Language Reference* in Flash Help.

You can also use the `loadMovie()` method to send variables to a CGI script, which generates a SWF file as its CGI output. For example, you might use this procedure to load dynamic SWF or image files based on specified variables within a movie clip. When you load a SWF file, you can specify a level or movie clip target into which the SWF file loads. If you load a SWF file into a target, the loaded SWF file inherits the properties of the targeted movie clip. After the Flash movie is loaded, you can change those properties.

The `unloadMovie()` method removes a SWF file previously loaded by the `loadMovie()` method. Explicitly unloading SWF files with `unloadMovie()` ensures a smooth transition between SWF files and can decrease the memory that Flash Player requires. It can be more efficient in some situations to set the movie clip's `_visible` property to `false` instead of unloading the clip. If you might reuse the clip at a later time, set the `_visible` property to `false` and then set to `true` when necessary.

Use `loadMovie()` to do any of the following:

- Play a sequence of banner ads that are SWF files by placing a `loadMovie()` function in a container SWF file that sequentially loads and unloads SWF banner files.
- Develop a branching interface with links that lets the user select among several SWF files that are used to display a site's content.
- Build a navigation interface with navigation controls in level 0 that loads content into other levels. Loading content into levels helps produce smoother transitions between pages of content than loading new HTML pages in a browser.

For more information on loading SWF files, see "Loading external SWF and image files" on page 607.

For more information, see the following topics:

- "Specifying a root timeline for loaded SWF files" on page 362
- "Loading image files into movie clips" on page 363

Specifying a root timeline for loaded SWF files

The _root ActionScript property specifies or contains a reference to the root timeline of a SWF file. If a SWF file has multiple levels, the root timeline is on the level that contains the currently executing script. For example, if a script in level 1 evaluates _root, _level1 is returned. However, the timeline that _root specifies can change, depending on whether a SWF file is running independently (in its own level) or was loaded into a movie clip instance by a loadMovie() call.

In the following example, consider a file named container.swf that has a movie clip instance named target_mc on its main timeline. The container.swf file declares a variable named userName on its main timeline; the same script then loads another file called contents.swf into the target_mc movie clip:

```
// In container.swf:
_root.userName = "Tim";
target_mc.loadMovie("contents.swf");
my_btn.onRelease = function():Void {
  trace(_root.userName);
};
```

In the following example, the loaded SWF file, contents.swf, also declares a variable named userName on its root timeline:

```
// In contents.swf:
_root.userName = "Mary";
```

After contents.swf loads into the movie clip in container.swf, the value of userName that's attached to the root timeline of the hosting SWF file (container.swf) would be set to "Mary" instead of "Tim". This could cause code in container.swf (as well as contents.swf) to malfunction.

To force _root to always evaluate to the timeline of the loaded SWF file, rather than the actual root timeline, use the _lockroot property. You can set this property either by the loading the SWF file or by the SWF file being loaded. When _lockroot is set to true on a movie clip instance, that movie clip acts as _root for any SWF file loaded into it. When _lockroot is set to true within a SWF file, that SWF file acts as its own root, no matter what other SWF file loads it. Any movie clip, and any number of movie clips, can set _lockroot to true. By default, this property is false.

For example, the author of container.swf could put the following code on Frame 1 of the main Timeline:

```
// Added to Frame 1 in container.swf:
target_mc._lockroot = true;
```

This step ensures that any references to _root in contents.swf—or any SWF file loaded into target_mc—refers to its own timeline, not to the actual root timeline of container.swf. Now when you click the button, "Tim" appears.

Alternatively, the author of contents.swf could add the following code to its main timeline:

```
// Added to Frame 1 in contents.swf:
this._lockroot = true;
```

This would ensure that no matter where contents.swf is loaded, any reference it makes to _root refers to its own main timeline, not to that of the hosting SWF file.

For more information, see %{_lockroot (MovieClip._lockroot property)}%.

Loading image files into movie clips

You can use the loadMovie() function, or the MovieClip method of the same name, to load image files into a movie clip instance. You can also use the loadMovieNum() function to load an image file into a level.

When you load an image into a movie clip, the upper left corner of the image is placed at the registration point of the movie clip. Because this registration point is often the center of the movie clip, the loaded image might not appear centered. Also, when you load an image to a root timeline, the upper-left corner of the image is placed on the upper-left corner of the Stage. The loaded image inherits rotation and scaling from the movie clip, but the original content of the movie clip is removed.

For more information, see %{loadMovie function}%, %{loadMovie (MovieClip.loadMovie method)}%, and %{loadMovieNum function}% in the *ActionScript 2.0 Language Reference* in Flash Help and "Loading external SWF and image files" on page 607.

Changing movie clip position and appearance

To change the properties of a movie clip as it plays, write a statement that assigns a value to a property or use the setProperty() function. For example, the following code sets the rotation of instance mc to 45:

```
my_mc._rotation = 45;
```

This is equivalent to the following code, which uses the setProperty() function:

```
setProperty("my_mc", _rotation, 45);
```

Some properties, called *read-only properties,* have values that you can read but cannot set. (These properties are specified as read-only in their *ActionScript 2.0 Language Reference* entries.) The following are read-only properties: `_currentframe`, `_droptarget`, `_framesloaded`, `_parent`, `_target`, `_totalframes`, `_url`, `_xmouse`, and `_ymouse`.

You can write statements to set any property that is not read-only. The following statement sets the `_alpha` property of the `wheel_mc` movie clip instance, which is a child of the `car_mc` instance:

```
car_mc.wheel_mc._alpha = 50;
```

In addition, you can write statements that get the value of a movie clip property. For example, the following statement gets the value of the `_xmouse` property on the current level's timeline and sets the `_x` property of the `my_mc` instance to that value:

```
this.onEnterFrame = function() {
  my_mc._x = _root._xmouse;
};
```

This is equivalent to the following code, which uses the `getProperty()` function:

```
this.onEnterFrame = function() {
  my_mc._x = getProperty(_root, _xmouse);
};
```

The `_x`, `_y`, `_rotation`, `_xscale`, `_yscale`, `_height`, `_width`, `_alpha`, and `_visible` properties are affected by transformations on the movie clip's parent, and transform the movie clip and any of the clip's children. The `_focusrect`, `_highquality`, `_quality`, and `_soundbuftime` properties are global; they belong only to the level 0 main timeline. All other properties belong to each movie clip or loaded level.

For a list of movie clip properties, see the property summary for the %{MovieClip}% class in the *ActionScript 2.0 Language Reference* in Flash Help.

For an example of scripted animation in Flash, you can find a sample source file, animation.fla, in the Samples folder on your hard disk.

- In Windows, browse to *boot drive*\Program Files\Macromedia\Flash 8\Samples and Tutorials\Samples\ActionScript\Animation.

- On the Macintosh, browse to *Macintosh HD*/Applications/Macromedia Flash 8/Samples and Tutorials/Samples/ActionScript/Animation.

You can find samples of photo gallery applications on your hard disk. These files provide examples of how to use ActionScript to control movie clips dynamically while loading image files into a SWF file, which includes scripted animation. You can find the sample source files, gallery_tree.fla and gallery_tween.fla, in the Samples folder on your hard disk.

- In Windows, browse to *boot drive*\Program Files\Macromedia\Flash 8\ Samples and Tutorials\Samples\ActionScript\Galleries.

- On the Macintosh, browse to *Macintosh HD*/Applications/Macromedia Flash 8/ Samples and Tutorials/Samples/ActionScript/Galleries.

Dragging movie clips

You can use the global `startDrag()` function or the `MovieClip.startDrag()` method to make a movie clip draggable. For example, you can make a draggable movie clip for games, drag-and-drop functions, customizable interfaces, scroll bars, and sliders.

A movie clip remains draggable until explicitly stopped by `stopDrag()` or until another movie clip is targeted with `startDrag()`. Only one movie clip at a time can be dragged in a SWF file.

To create more complicated drag-and-drop behavior, you can evaluate the `_droptarget` property of the movie clip being dragged. For example, you might examine the `_droptarget` property to see if the movie clip was dragged onto a specific movie clip (such as a "trash can" movie clip) and then trigger another action, as shown in the following example:

```
// Drag a piece of garbage.
garbage_mc.onPress = function() {
  this.startDrag(false);
};
// When the garbage is dragged over the trashcan, make it invisible.
garbage_mc.onRelease = function() {
  this.stopDrag();
  // Convert the slash notation to dot notation using eval.
  if (eval(this._droptarget) == trashcan_mc) {
    garbage_mc._visible = false;
  }
};
```

For more information, see %{startDrag function}% or %{startDrag (MovieClip.startDrag method)}% in the *ActionScript 2.0 Language Reference* in Flash Help.

You can a sample photo gallery application on your hard disk. This file provides an example of how to use ActionScript to control movie clips dynamically while loading image files into a SWF file, which includes making each movie clip draggable. You can find the sample source file, gallery_tween.fla, in the Samples folder on your hard disk.

- In Windows, browse to *boot drive*\Program Files\Macromedia\Flash 8\ Samples and Tutorials\Samples\ActionScript\Galleries.

- On the Macintosh, browse to *Macintosh HD*/Applications/Macromedia Flash 8/ Samples and Tutorials/Samples/ActionScript/Galleries.

Creating movie clips at runtime

In addition to creating movie clip instances in the Flash authoring environment, you can also create movie clip instances at runtime in the following ways:

- "Creating an empty movie clip" on page 366
- "Duplicating or removing a movie clip" on page 368
- "Attaching a movie clip symbol to the Stage" on page 368

Each movie clip instance you create at runtime must have an instance name and a depth (stacking, or z-order) value. The depth you specify determines how the new clip overlaps with other clips on the same timeline. It also lets you overwrite movie clips that reside at the same depth. (See "Managing movie clip depths" on page 372.)

You can a sample photo gallery application on your hard disk. This file provides an example of how to use ActionScript to control movie clips dynamically while loading image files into a SWF file, which includes creating movie clips at runtime. You can find the sample source file, gallery_tween.fla, in the Samples folder on your hard disk.

- In Windows, browse to *boot drive*\Program Files\Macromedia\Flash 8\Samples and Tutorials\Samples\ActionScript\Galleries.
- On the Macintosh, browse to *Macintosh HD*/Applications/Macromedia Flash 8/Samples and Tutorials/Samples/ActionScript/Galleries.

For an example source file that creates and removes numerous movie clips at runtime, you can find a sample source file, animation.fla, in the Samples folder on your hard disk

- In Windows, browse to *boot drive*\Program Files\Macromedia\Flash 8\Samples and Tutorials\Samples\ActionScript\Animation.
- On the Macintosh, browse to *Macintosh HD*/Applications/Macromedia Flash 8/Samples and Tutorials/Samples/ActionScript/Animation.

For more information, see the following topics:

- "Creating an empty movie clip" on page 366
- "Duplicating or removing a movie clip" on page 368
- "Attaching a movie clip symbol to the Stage" on page 368

Creating an empty movie clip

To create a new, empty movie clip instance on the Stage, use the `createEmptyMovieClip()` method of the MovieClip class. This method creates a movie clip as a child of the clip that calls the method. The registration point for a newly created empty movie clip is the upper-left corner.

For example, the following code creates a new child movie clip named `new_mc` at a depth of 10 in the movie clip named `parent_mc`:

```
parent_mc.createEmptyMovieClip("new_mc", 10);
```

The following code creates a new movie clip named `canvas_mc` on the root timeline of the SWF file in which the script is run, and then activates `loadMovie()` to load an external JPEG file into itself:

```
this.createEmptyMovieClip("canvas_mc", 10);
canvas_mc.loadMovie("http://www.helpexamples.com/flash/images/image1.jpg");
```

As shown in the following example, you can load the image2.jpg image into a movie clip and use the `MovieClip.onPress()` method to make the image act like a button. Loading an image using `loadMovie()` replaces the movie clip with the image but doesn't give you access to movie clip methods. To get access to movie clip methods, you must create an empty parent movie clip and a container child movie clip. Load the image into the container and place the event handler on the parent movie clip.

```
// Creates a parent movie clip to hold the container.
this.createEmptyMovieClip("my_mc", 0);

// Creates a child movie clip inside of "my_mc".
// This is the movie clip the image will replace.
my_mc.createEmptyMovieClip("container_mc",99);

// Use MovieClipLoader to load the image.
var my_mcl:MovieClipLoader = new MovieClipLoader();
my_mcl.loadClip("http://www.helpexamples.com/flash/images/image2.jpg",
  my_mc.container_mc);

// Put event handler on the my_mc parent movie clip.
my_mc.onPress = function():Void {
  trace("It works");
};
```

For more information, see %{createEmptyMovieClip (`MovieClip.createEmptyMovieClip` method)}% in the *ActionScript 2.0 Language Reference* in Flash Help.

For an example source file that creates and removes numerous movie clips at runtime, you can find a sample source file, animation.fla, in the Samples folder on your hard disk

- In Windows, browse to *boot drive*\Program Files\Macromedia\Flash 8\ Samples and Tutorials\Samples\ActionScript\Animation.

- On the Macintosh, browse to *Macintosh HD*/Applications/Macromedia Flash 8/ Samples and Tutorials/Samples/ActionScript/Animation.

Duplicating or removing a movie clip

To duplicate or remove movie clip instances, use the `duplicateMovieClip()` or `removeMovieClip()` global functions, or the MovieClip class methods of the same name. The `duplicateMovieClip()` method creates a new instance of an existing movie clip instance, assigns it a new instance name, and gives it a depth, or z-order. A duplicated movie clip always starts at Frame 1, even if the original movie clip was on another frame when duplicated and is always in front of all previously defined movie clips placed on the timeline.

To delete a movie clip you created with `duplicateMovieClip()`, use `removeMovieClip()`. Duplicated movie clips are also removed if the parent movie clip is deleted.

For more information, see %{duplicateMovieClip function}% and %{removeMovieClip function}% in the *ActionScript 2.0 Language Reference* in Flash Help.

For an example source file that creates and removes numerous movie clips at runtime, you can find a sample source file, animation.fla, in the Samples folder on your hard disk

- In Windows, browse to *boot drive*\Program Files\Macromedia\Flash 8\Samples and Tutorials\Samples\ActionScript\Animation.
- On the Macintosh, browse to *Macintosh HD*/Applications/Macromedia Flash 8/Samples and Tutorials/Samples/ActionScript/Animation.

Attaching a movie clip symbol to the Stage

The last way to create movie clip instances at runtime is to use the `attachMovie()` method. The `attachMovie()` method attaches to the Stage an instance of a movie clip symbol in the SWF file's library. The new clip becomes a child clip of the clip that attached it.

To use ActionScript to attach a movie clip symbol from the library, you must export the symbol for ActionScript and assign it a unique linkage identifier. To do this, you use the Linkage Properties dialog box.

By default, all movie clips that are exported for use with ActionScript load before the first frame of the SWF file that contains them. This can create a delay before the first frame plays. When you assign a linkage identifier to an element, you can also specify whether this content should be added before the first frame. If it isn't added in the first frame, you must include an instance of it in some other frame of the SWF file; if you don't, the element is not exported to the SWF file.

To assign a linkage identifier to a movie clip:

1. Select Window > Library to open the Library panel.
2. Select a movie clip in the Library panel.

3. In the Library panel, select Linkage from the Library panel pop-up menu.

    The Linkage Properties dialog box appears.

4. For Linkage, select Export for ActionScript.

5. For Identifier, enter an ID for the movie clip.

    By default, the identifier is the same as the symbol name.

    You can optionally assign an ActionScript class to the movie clip symbol. This lets the movie clip inherit the methods and properties of a specified class. (See "Assigning a class to a movie clip symbol" on page 384.)

6. If you don't want the movie clip to load before the first frame, deselect the Export in First Frame option.

    If you deselect this option, place an instance of the movie clip on the frame of the timeline where you want it to be available. For example, if the script you're writing doesn't reference the movie clip until Frame 10, place an instance of the symbol at or before Frame 10 on the Timeline.

7. Click OK.

After you've assigned a linkage identifier to a movie clip, you can attach an instance of the symbol to the Stage at runtime by using `attachMovie()`.

To attach a movie clip to another movie clip:

1. Assign a linkage identifier to a movie clip library symbol, as described in the previous example.

2. With the Actions panel open (Window > Actions), select a frame in the Timeline.

3. In the Actions panel's Script pane, type the name of the movie clip or level to which you want to attach the new movie clip.

    For example, to attach the movie clip to the root timeline, type **this**.

4. In the Actions toolbox (at the left of the Actions panel), select ActionScript 2.0 Classes > Movie > MovieClip > Methods, and select `attachMovie()`.

5. Using the code hints that appear as a guide, enter values for the following parameters:

    - For `idName`, specify the identifier you entered in the Linkage Properties dialog box.

    - For `newName`, enter an instance name for the attached clip so that you can target it.

    - For `depth`, enter the level at which the duplicate movie clip will be attached to the movie clip. Each attached movie clip has its own stacking order, with level 0 as the level of the originating movie clip. Attached movie clips are always on top of the original movie clip, as shown in the following example:

    ```
    this.attachMovie("calif_id", "california_mc", 10);
    ```

For more information, see %{attachMovie (`MovieClip.attachMovie method`)}% in the
ActionScript 2.0 Language Reference in Flash Help.

Adding parameters to dynamically created movie clips

When you use `MovieClip.attachMovie()` and `MovieClip.duplicateMovie()` to create or
duplicate a movie clip dynamically, you can populate the movie clip with parameters from
another object. The *initObject* parameter of `attachMovie()` and `duplicateMovie()`
allows dynamically created movie clips to receive clip parameters.

For more information, see %{attachMovie (MovieClip.attachMovie method)}% and
%{duplicateMovieClip (`MovieClip.duplicateMovieClip method`)}% in the
ActionScript 2.0 Language Reference in Flash Help.

To populate a dynamically created movie clip with parameters from a specified object:

Do one of the following:

- Use the following syntax with `attachMovie()`:

  `myMovieClip.attachMovie(idName, newName, depth [, initObject]);`

- Use the following syntax with `duplicateMovie()`:

  `myMovieClip.duplicateMovie(idName, newName, depth [, initObject]);`

The *initObject* parameter specifies the name of the object whose parameters you want to
use to populate the dynamically created movie clip.

To populate a movie clip with parameters by using attachMovie():

1. In a new Flash document, create a movie clip symbol by selecting Insert > New Symbol.

2. Type **dynamic_mc** in the Symbol Name text box, and select the Movie Clip behavior.

3. Inside the symbol, create a dynamic text field on the Stage with an instance name of
   name_txt.

   Make sure this text field is below and to the right of the registration point.

4. Select Frame 1 of the movie clip's Timeline, and open the Actions panel (Window >
   Actions).

5. Create a new variable called `name_str`, and assign its value to the `text` property of
   `name_txt`, as shown in the following example:

   ```
   var name_str:String;
   name_txt.text = name_str;
   ```

6. Select Edit > Edit Document to return to the main Timeline.

7. Select the movie clip symbol in the library, and select Linkage from the Library pop-up menu.

   The Linkage Properties dialog box appears.

8. Select the Export for ActionScript option, and Export in first frame.

9. Type **dynamic_id** into the Indentifier text box, and click OK.

10. Select the first frame of the main Timeline, and add the following code to the Actions panel's Script pane:

```
/* Attaches a new movie clip and moves it to an x and y coordinate of 50
   */

this.attachMovie("dynamic_id", "newClip_mc", 99, {name_str:"Erick",
   _x:50, _y:50});
```

11. Test the Flash document(Control > Test Movie).

   The name you specified in the attachMovie() call appears inside the new movie clip's text field.

You can find a sample photo gallery application on your hard disk. This file provides an example of how to use ActionScript to control movie clips dynamically while loading image files into a SWF file, which includes creating movie clips at runtime. You can find the sample source file, gallery_tween.fla, in the Samples folder on your hard disk.

- In Windows, browse to *boot drive*\Program Files\Macromedia\Flash 8\Samples and Tutorials\Samples\ActionScript\Galleries.

- On the Macintosh, browse to *Macintosh HD*/Applications/Macromedia Flash 8/Samples and Tutorials/Samples/ActionScript/Galleries.

For an example source file that creates and removes numerous movie clips at runtime, you can find a sample source file, animation.fla, in the Samples folder on your hard disk

- In Windows, browse to *boot drive*\Program Files\Macromedia\Flash 8\Samples and Tutorials\Samples\ActionScript\Animation.

- On the Macintosh, browse to *Macintosh HD*/Applications/Macromedia Flash 8/Samples and Tutorials/Samples/ActionScript/Animation.

Managing movie clip depths

Every movie clip has its own *z*-order space that determines how objects overlap within its parent SWF file or movie clip. Every movie clip has an associated depth value, which determines if it renders in front of or behind other movie clips in the same movie clip timeline. When you create a movie clip at runtime by using %{attachMovie (MovieClip.attachMovie method)}%, %{duplicateMovieClip (MovieClip.duplicateMovieClip method)}%, or %{createEmptyMovieClip (MovieClip.createEmptyMovieClip method)}%, you always specify a depth for the new clip as a method parameter. For example, the following code attaches a new movie clip to the timeline of a movie clip named container_mc with a depth value of 10.

```
container_mc.attachMovie("symbolID", "clip1_mc", 10);
```

This example creates a new movie clip with a depth of 10 within the *z*-order space of container_mc.

The following code attaches two new movie clips to container_mc. The first clip, named clip1_mc, is rendered behind clip2_mc because it was assigned a lower depth value.

```
container_mc.attachMovie("symbolID", "clip1_mc", 10);
container_mc.attachMovie("symbolID", "clip2_mc", 15);
```

Depth values for movie clips can range from -16384 to 1048575. If you create or attach a new movie clip on a depth that already has a movie clip, the new or attached clip overwrites the existing content. To avoid this problem, use the MovieClip.getNextHighestDepth() method; however, do not use this method with components that use a different depth-management system. Instead, use "DepthManager class" with component instances.

The MovieClip class provides several methods for managing movie clip depths; for more information, see %{getNextHighestDepth (MovieClip.getNextHighestDepth method)}%, %{getInstanceAtDepth (MovieClip.getInstanceAtDepth method)}%, %{getDepth (MovieClip.getDepth method)}%, and %{swapDepths (MovieClip.swapDepths method)}% in the *ActionScript 2.0 Language Reference* in Flash Help.

For more information on movie clip depths, see the following topics:

- "Determining the next highest available depth" on page 373
- "Determining the instance at a particular depth" on page 373
- "Determining the depth of an instance" on page 374
- "Swapping movie clip depths" on page 374

Determining the next highest available depth

To determine the next highest available depth within a movie clip, use
`MovieClip.getNextHighestDepth()`. The integer value returned by this method indicates
the next available depth that will render in front of all other objects in the movie clip.

The following code attaches a new movie clip, with a depth value of 10, on the root timeline
named `file_mc`. It then determines the next highest available depth in that same movie clip
and creates a new movie clip called `edit_mc` at that depth.

```
this.attachMovie("menuClip","file_mc", 10, {_x:0, _y:0});
trace(file_mc.getDepth()); // 10
var nextDepth:Number = this.getNextHighestDepth();
this.attachMovie("menuClip", "edit_mc", nextDepth, {_x:200, _y:0});
trace(edit_mc.getDepth()); // 11
```

In this case, the variable named `nextDepth` contains the value 11 because that's the next
highest available depth for the `edit_mc` movie clip.

Do not use `MovieClip.getNextHighestDepth()` with components; instead, use the depth
manager. For more information, see "DepthManager class" in the *Component Language
Reference* in Flash Help. For more information on `MovieClip.getNextHighestDepth()`, see
%{getNextHighestDepth (MovieClip.getNextHighestDepth method)}%.

To obtain the current highest occupied depth, subtract 1 from the value that
`getNextHighestDepth()` returns, as shown in the next section.

Determining the instance at a particular depth

To determine the instance at a particular depth, use `MovieClip.getInstanceAtDepth()`.
This method returns a reference to the MovieClip instance at the specified depth.

The following code combines `getNextHighestDepth()` and `getInstanceAtDepth()` to
determine the movie clip at the (current) highest occupied depth on the root timeline.

```
var highestOccupiedDepth:Number = this.getNextHighestDepth() - 1;
var instanceAtHighestDepth:MovieClip =
    this.getInstanceAtDepth(highestOccupiedDepth);
```

For more information, see %{getInstanceAtDepth (MovieClip.getInstanceAtDepth
method)}% in the *ActionScript 2.0 Language Reference* in Flash Help.

Determining the depth of an instance

To determine the depth of a movie clip instance, use `MovieClip.getDepth()`.

The following code iterates over all the movie clips on a SWF file's main timeline and shows each clip's instance name and depth value in the Output panel:

```
for (var item:String in _root) {
  var obj:Object = _root[item];
  if (obj instanceof MovieClip) {
    var objDepth:Number = obj.getDepth();
    trace(obj._name + ":" + objDepth)
  }
}
```

For more information, see %{getDepth (MovieClip.getDepth method)}% in the *ActionScript 2.0 Language Reference* in Flash Help.

Swapping movie clip depths

To swap the depths of two movie clips on the same timeline, use `MovieClip.swapDepths()`. The following examples show how two movie clip instances can swap depths at runtime.

To swap movie clip depths:

1. Create a new Flash document called **swap.fla**.
2. Draw a blue circle on the Stage.
3. Select the blue circle, and then select Modify > Convert to Symbol.
4. Select the Movie clip option, and then click OK.
5. Select the instance on the Stage, and then type **first_mc** into the Instance Name text box in the Property inspector.
6. Draw a red circle on the Stage, and then select Modify > Convert to Symbol.
7. Select the Movie clip option, and then click OK.
8. Select the instance on the Stage, and then type **second_mc** into the Instance Name text box in the Property inspector.
9. Drag the two instances so that they overlap slightly on the Stage.
10. Select Frame 1 of the Timeline, and then type the following code into the Actions panel:

```
first_mc.onRelease = function() {
    this.swapDepths(second_mc);
};
second_mc.onRelease = function() {
  this.swapDepths(first_mc);
};
```

11. Select Control > Test Movie to test the document.

When you click the instances on the Stage, they swap depths. You'll see the two instances change which clip is on top of the other clip.

For more information, see %{swapDepths (MovieClip.swapDepths method)}% in the *ActionScript 2.0 Language Reference* in Flash Help.

About caching and scrolling movie clips with ActionScript

As your designs in Flash grow in size, whether you are creating an application or complex scripted animations, you need to consider performance and optimization. When you have content that remains static (such as a rectangle movie clip), Flash does not optimize the content. Therefore, when you change the position of the rectangle movie clip, Flash redraws the entire rectangle in Flash Player 7 and earlier.

In Flash Player 8, you can cache specified movie clips and buttons to improve the performance of your SWF file. The movie clip or button is a *surface*, essentially a bitmap version of the instance's vector data, which is data that you do not intend to change much over the course of your SWF file. Therefore, instances with caching turned on are not continually redrawn as the SWF file plays, which lets the SWF file render quickly.

> You can update the vector data, at which time the surface is recreated. Therefore, the vector data cached in the surface does not need to remain the same for the entire SWF file.

You can use ActionScript to enable caching or scrolling and to control backgrounds. You can use the Property inspector to enable caching for a movie clip instance. To cache movie clips or buttons without using ActionScript, you can select the Use runtime bitmap caching option in the Property inspector instead.

The following table contains brief descriptions of the new properties for movie clip instances:

Property	Description
cacheAsBitmap	Makes the movie clip instance cache a bitmap representation of itself. Flash creates a surface object for the instance, which is a cached bitmap instead of vector data. If you change the bounds of the movie clip, the surface is recreated instead of resized. For more information and an example, see "Caching a movie clip" on page 379.
opaqueBackground	Lets you specify a background color for the opaque movie clip instance. If you set this property to a numeric value, the movie clip instance has an opaque (nontransparent) surface. An opaque bitmap does not have an alpha channel (transparency), and renders faster. For more information and an example, see "Setting the background of a movie clip" on page 381.
scrollRect	Lets you quickly scroll movie clip content and have a window for viewing larger content. The movie clip's contents are cropped, and the instance scrolls with a specified width, height, and scroll offsets. This lets the user quickly scroll movie clip content and have a window that displays larger content than the Stage area. Text fields and complex content that you display in the instance can scroll faster because Flash does not regenerate the entire movie clip vector data. For more information and an example, see %{scrollRect (MovieClip.scrollRect property)}%.

These three properties are independent of each other, however, the opaqueBackground and scrollRect properties work best when an object is cached as a bitmap. You only see performance benefits for the opaqueBackground and scrollRect properties when you set cacheAsBitmap to true.

To create a surface that's also scrollable, you must set the cacheAsBitmap and scrollRect properties for the movie clip instance. Surfaces can nest within other surfaces. The surface copies the bitmap onto its parent surface.

For information on alpha channel masking, which requires you to set the cacheAsBitmap property to true, see "About alpha channel masking" on page 383.

 NOTE You cannot apply caching directly to text fields. You need to place text within a movie clip to take advantage of this feature. For an example, see the sample file in *Flash install directory*\Samples and Tutorials\Samples\ActionScript\FlashType.

You can find a sample source file that shows you how bitmap caching can be applied to an instance. Find the file called cacheBitmap.fla, in the Samples folder on your hard disk.

- In Windows, browse to boot drive\Program Files\Macromedia\Flash 8\ Samples and Tutorials\Samples\ActionScript\CacheBitmap.

- On the Macintosh, browse to Macintosh HD/Applications/Macromedia Flash 8/ Samples and Tutorials/Samples/ActionScript/CacheBitmap.

You can also find a sample source file that shows you how to apply bitmap caching to scrolling text. Find the sample source file, flashtype.fla, in the Samples folder on your hard disk.

- In Windows, browse to boot drive\Program Files\Macromedia\Flash 8\Samples and Tutorials\Samples\ActionScript\FlashType.

- On the Macintosh, browse to Macintosh HD/Applications/Macromedia Flash 8/Samples and Tutorials/Samples/ActionScript/FlashType.

When to enable caching

Enabling caching for a movie clip creates a surface, which has several advantages, such as helping complex vector animations to render fast. There are several scenarios in which you will want to enable caching. It might seem as though you will always want to enable caching to improve the performance of your SWF files; however, there are situations in which enabling caching does not improve performance, or even decrease it. This section describes scenarios in which caching should be used, and when to use regular movie clips.

Overall performance of cached data depends on how complex the vector data of your instances are, how much of the data you change, and whether or not you set the opaqueBackground property. If you are changing small regions, the difference between using a surface and using vector data could be negligible. You might want to test both scenarios with your work before you deploy the application.

For information on alpha channel masking, which requires you to set the cacheAsBitmap property to true, see "About alpha channel masking" on page 383.

When to use bitmap caching

The following are typical scenarios in which you might see significant benefits when you enable bitmap caching.

Complex background image An application that contains a detailed and complex background image of vector data (perhaps an image where you applied the trace bitmap command, or artwork that you created in Adobe Illustrator). You might animate characters over the background, which slows the animation because the background needs to continuously regenerate the vector data. To improve performance, you can select the content, store it in a movie clip, and set the opaqueBackground property to true. The background is rendered as a bitmap and can be redrawn quickly, so that your animation plays much faster.

Scrolling text field　An application that displays a large amount of text in a scrolling text field. You can place the text field in a movie clip that you set as scrollable with scrolling bounds (the `scrollRect` property). This enables fast pixel scrolling for the specified instance. When a user scrolls the movie clip instance, Flash shifts the scrolled pixels up and generates the newly exposed region instead of regenerating the entire text field.

Windowing system　An application with a complex system of overlapping windows. Each window can be open or closed (for example, web browser windows). If you mark each window as a surface (set the `cacheAsBitmap` property to `true`), each window is isolated and cached. Users can drag the windows so that they overlap each other, and each window doesn't need to regenerate the vector content.

All of these scenarios improve the responsiveness and interactivity of the application by optimizing the vector graphics.

You can find a sample source file that shows you how bitmap caching can be applied to an instance. Find the file called cacheBitmap.fla, in the Samples folder on your hard disk.

- In Windows, browse to boot drive\Program Files\Macromedia\Flash 8\ Samples and Tutorials\Samples\ActionScript\CacheBitmap.

- On the Macintosh, browse to Macintosh HD/Applications/Macromedia Flash 8/ Samples and Tutorials/Samples/ActionScript/CacheBitmap.

You can also find a sample source file that shows you how to apply bitmap caching to scrolling text. Find the sample source file, flashtype.fla, in the Samples folder on your hard disk.

- In Windows, browse to boot drive\Program Files\Macromedia\Flash 8\Samples and Tutorials\Samples\ActionScript\FlashType.

- On the Macintosh, browse to Macintosh HD/Applications/Macromedia Flash 8/Samples and Tutorials/Samples/ActionScript/FlashType.

When to avoid using bitmap caching

Misusing this feature could negatively affect your SWF file. When you develop a FLA file that uses surfaces, remember the following guidelines:

- Do not overuse surfaces (movie clips with caching enabled). Each surface uses more memory than a regular movie clip, which means that you should only enable surfaces when you need to improve rendering performance.

  A cached bitmap can use significantly more memory than a regular movie clip instance. For example, if the movie clip on Stage is 250 pixels by 250 pixels in size, when cached it might use 250 KB instead of 1 KB when it's a regular (uncached) movie clip instance.

- Avoid zooming into cached surfaces. If you overuse bitmap caching, a large amount of memory is consumed (see previous bullet), especially if you zoom in on the content.

- Use surfaces for movie clip instances that are largely static (nonanimating). You can drag or move the instance, but the contents of the instance should not animate or change a lot. For example, if you rotate or transform an instance, the instance changes between the surface and vector data, which is difficult to process and negatively affects your SWF file.

- If you mix surfaces with vector data, it increases the amount of processing that Flash Player (and sometimes the computer) needs to do. Group surfaces together as much as possible; for example, when you create windowing applications.

Caching a movie clip

To cache a movie clip instance, you need to set the `cacheAsBitmap` property to `true`. After you set the `cacheAsBitmap` property to `true`, you might notice that the movie clip instance automatically pixel-snaps to whole coordinates. When you test the SWF file, you should notice that any complex vector animation renders much faster.

A surface (cached bitmap) is not created, even if `cacheAsBitmap` is set to `true`, if one or more of the following occurs:

- The bitmap is greater than 2880 pixels in height or width.
- The bitmap fails to allocate (out of memory error).

To cache a movie clip:

1. Create a new Flash document, and name the file **cachebitmap.fla**.
2. Type 24 into the fps text box in the Property inspector (Window > Properties > Properties).
3. Create or import a complex vector graphic into the FLA file.

   You can find a complex vector graphic in the finished source file for this example in the following directory:

   - In Windows, browse to *boot drive*\Program Files\Macromedia\Flash 8\Samples and Tutorials\Samples\ActionScript\CacheBitmap.
   - On the Macintosh, browse to *Macintosh HD*/Applications/Macromedia Flash 8/ Samples and Tutorials/Samples/ActionScript/CacheBitmap.

4. Select the vector graphic, and select Modify > Convert to Symbol.
5. Type **star** into the Name text box, and then click Advanced (if the dialog box is not already expanded).
6. Select Export for ActionScript (which also selects Export in first frame).
7. Type **star_id** into the Identifier text box.
8. Click OK to create the movie clip symbol, with the linkage identifier of Star.

9. Select Frame 1 of the Timeline, and then add the following ActionScript to the Actions panel:

```
import mx.transitions.Tween;

var star_array:Array = new Array();
for (var i:Number = 0; i < 20; i++) {
  makeStar();
}
function makeStar():Void {
  var depth:Number = this.getNextHighestDepth();
  var star_mc:MovieClip = this.attachMovie("star_id", "star" + depth,
  depth);
  star_mc.onEnterFrame = function() {
    star_mc._rotation += 5;
  }
  star_mc._y = Math.round(Math.random() * Stage.height - star_mc._height
  / 2);
  var star_tween:Tween = new Tween(star_mc, "_x", null, 0, Stage.width,
  (Math.random() * 5) + 5, true);
  star_tween.onMotionFinished = function():Void  {
    star_tween.yoyo();
  };
  star_array.push(star_mc);
}
var mouseListener:Object = new Object();
mouseListener.onMouseDown = function():Void {
  var star_mc:MovieClip;
  for (var i:Number = 0; i < star_array.length; i++) {
    star_mc = star_array[i];
    star_mc.cacheAsBitmap = !star_mc.cacheAsBitmap;
  }
}
Mouse.addListener(mouseListener);
```

10. Select Control > Test Movie to test the document.

11. Click anywhere on the Stage to enable bitmap caching.

You'll notice that the animation changes from appearing to animate at 1 frame per second, to a smooth animation where the instances animate back and forth across the Stage. When you click the Stage, it toggles the `cacheAsBitmap` setting between `true` and `false`.

If you toggle caching on and off, as demonstrated in the previous example, it frees the data that is cached. You can also apply this code for a Button instance. See `%{cacheAsBitmap (Button.cacheAsBitmap property)}%` in the *ActionScript 2.0 Language Reference* in Flash Help.

For examples of scrolling movie clips, see `%{scrollRect (MovieClip.scrollRect property)}%` in the *ActionScript 2.0 Language Reference* in Flash Help. For information on alpha channel masking, which requires you to set the `cacheAsBitmap` property to `true`, see "About alpha channel masking" on page 383.

You can find a sample source file that shows you how bitmap caching can be applied to an instance. Find the file called cacheBitmap.fla, in the Samples folder on your hard disk.

- In Windows, browse to boot drive\Program Files\Macromedia\Flash 8\Samples and Tutorials\Samples\ActionScript\CacheBitmap.

- On the Macintosh, browse to Macintosh HD/Applications/Macromedia Flash 8/Samples and Tutorials/Samples/ActionScript/CacheBitmap.

You can also find a sample source file that shows you how to apply bitmap caching to scrolling text. Find the sample source file, flashtype.fla, in the Samples folder on your hard disk.

- In Windows, browse to boot drive\Program Files\Macromedia\Flash 8\Samples and Tutorials\Samples\ActionScript\FlashType.

- On the Macintosh, browse to Macintosh HD/Applications/Macromedia Flash 8/Samples and Tutorials/Samples/ActionScript/FlashType.

Setting the background of a movie clip

You can set an opaque background for a movie clip. For example, when you have a background that contains complex vector art, you can set the `opaqueBackground` property to a specified color (typically the same color as the Stage). The background is then treated as a bitmap, which helps optimize performance.

When you set `cacheAsBitmap` to `true`, and also set the `opaqueBackground` property to a specified color, the opaqueBackground property allows the internal bitmap to be opaque and rendered faster. If you do not set `cacheAsBitmap` to `true`, the `opaqueBackground` property adds an opaque vector-square shape to the background of the movie clip instance. It does not create a bitmap automatically.

The following example shows how to set the background of a movie clip to optimize performance.

To set the background of a movie clip:

1. Create a new Flash document called **background.fla**.

2. Draw a blue circle on the Stage.

3. Select the blue circle, and then select Modify > Convert to Symbol.

4. Select the Movie clip option, and then click OK.

5. Select the instance on the Stage, and then type **my_mc** into the Instance Name text box in the Property inspector.

6. Select Frame 1 of the Timeline, and then type the following code into the Actions panel:

```
/* When you set cacheAsBitmap, the internal bitmap is opaque and renders
   faster. */
my_mc.cacheAsBitmap = true;
my_mc.opaqueBackground = 0xFF0000;
```

7. Select Control > Test Movie to test the document.

   The movie clip appears on the Stage with the background color that you specified.

For more information on this property, see `%{opaqueBackground (MovieClip.opaqueBackground property)}%` in the *ActionScript 2.0 Language Reference* in Flash Help.

Using movie clips as masks

You can use a movie clip as a mask to create a hole through which the contents of another movie clip are visible. The mask movie clip plays all the frames in its timeline, the same as a regular movie clip. You can make the mask movie clip draggable, animate it along a motion guide, use separate shapes within a single mask, or resize a mask dynamically. You can also use ActionScript to turn a mask on and off.

You cannot use a mask to mask another mask. You cannot set the _alpha property of a mask movie clip. Only fills are used in a movie clip that is used as a mask; strokes are ignored.

To create a mask:

1. Create a square on the Stage with the Rectangle tool.

2. Select the square and press F8 to convert it into a movie clip.

   This instance is your mask.

3. In the Property inspector, type **mask_mc** in the Instance Name text box.

   The masked movie clip is revealed under all opaque (nontransparent) areas of the movie clip acting as the mask.

4. Select Frame 1 in the Timeline.

5. Open the Actions panel (Window > Actions) if it isn't already open.

6. In the Actions panel, enter the following code:

```
System.security.allowDomain("http://www.helpexamples.com");

this.createEmptyMovieClip("img_mc", 10);
var mclListener:Object = new Object();
mclListener.onLoadInit = function(target_mc:MovieClip):Void {
   target_mc.setMask(mask_mc);
}
var my_mcl:MovieClipLoader = new MovieClipLoader();
my_mcl.addListener(mclListener);
my_mcl.loadClip("http://www.helpexamples.com/flash/images/image1.jpg",
   img_mc);
```

7. Select Control > Test Movie to test the document.

An external JPEG image loads into the SWF file at runtime, and is masked by the shape you drew previously on the Stage.

For detailed information, see %{setMask (`MovieClip.setMask method`)}% in the *ActionScript 2.0 Language Reference* in Flash Help.

About masking device fonts

You can use a movie clip to mask text that is set in a device font. In order for a movie clip mask on a device font to work properly, the user must have Flash Player 6 (6.0.40.0) or later.

When you use a movie clip to mask text set in a device font, the rectangular bounding box of the mask is used as the masking shape. That is, if you create a nonrectangular movie clip mask for device font text in the Flash authoring environment, the mask that appears in the SWF file is the shape of the rectangular bounding box of the mask, not the shape of the mask itself.

You can mask device fonts only by using a movie clip as a mask. You cannot mask device fonts by using a mask layer on the Stage.

About alpha channel masking

Alpha channel masking is supported if both the mask and the maskee movie clips use bitmap caching. This support also lets you use a filter on the mask independently of the filter that is applied to the maskee itself.

To see an example of alpha masking, download the alpha masking sample file from www.macromedia.com/go/flash_samples.

In this sample file, the mask is an oval (`oval_mask`) that has alpha of 50% and a blur filter applied to it. The maskee (`flower_maskee`) has alpha of 100% and no filter applied on it. Both movie clips have runtime bitmap caching applied in the Property inspector.

In the Actions panel, the following code is placed on Frame 1 of the Timeline:

```
flower_maskee.setMask(oval_mask);
```

When you test the document (Control > Test Movie), the maskee is alpha blended by using the mask.

> **NOTE** Mask layers do not support alpha channel masking. You must use ActionScript code to apply a mask, and use runtime bitmap caching.

Handling movie clip events

Movie clips can respond to user events, such as mouse clicks and keypresses, as well as system-level events, such as the initial loading of a movie clip on the Stage. ActionScript provides two ways to handle movie clip events: through event handler methods and `onClipEvent()` and `on()` event handlers. For more information on handling movie clip events, see Chapter 10, "Handling Events.".

Assigning a class to a movie clip symbol

Using ActionScript 2.0, you can create a class that extends the behavior of the built-in MovieClip class and then use the Linkage Properties dialog box to assign that class to a movie clip library symbol. Whenever you create an instance of the movie clip to which the class is assigned, it assumes the properties and behaviors defined by the class assigned to it. (For more information about ActionScript 2.0, see "Example: Writing custom classes" on page 269.)

In a subclass of the MovieClip class, you can provide method definitions for the built-in MovieClip methods and event handlers, such as `onEnterFrame` and `onRelease`. In the following procedure, you'll create a class called MoveRight that extends the MovieClip class; MoveRight defines an `onPress` handler that moves the clip 20 pixels to the right whenever the user clicks the movie clip. In the second procedure, you'll create a movie clip symbol in a new Flash (FLA) document and assign the MoveRight class to that symbol.

To create a movie clip subclass:

1. Create a new directory called **BallTest**.

2. Select File > New, and select ActionScript file from the list of document types to create a new ActionScript file.

3. Enter the following code in your script file:

```
// MoveRight class -- moves clip to the right 20 pixels when clicked
class MoveRight extends MovieClip {
   public function onPress() {
      this._x += 20;
   }
}
```

4. Save the document as MoveRight.as in the BallTest directory.

To assign the class to a movie clip symbol:

1. In Flash, select File > New, select Flash Document from the list of file types, and click OK.

2. Using the Oval tool, draw a circle on the Stage.

3. Select the circle, and select Modify > Convert to Symbol.

4. In the Convert to Symbol dialog box, select Movie Clip as the symbol's behavior, and enter **ball_mc** in the Name text box.

5. Select Advanced to show the options for Linkage, if they aren't already showing.

6. Select the Export for ActionScript option, and type **MoveRight** in the Class text box. Click OK.

7. Save the file as ball.fla in the BallTest directory (the same directory that contains the MoveRight.as file).

8. Test the Flash document(Control > Test Movie).

   Each time you click the ball movie clip, it moves 20 pixels to the right.

If you create component properties for a class and want a movie clip to inherit those component properties, you need to take an additional step: with the movie clip symbol selected in the Library panel, select Component Definition from the Library pop-up menu and enter the new class name in the Class box.

Initializing class properties

In the example presented in the second procedure under "Assigning a class to a movie clip symbol", you added the instance of the Ball symbol to the Stage while authoring. As discussed in "Adding parameters to dynamically created movie clips" on page 370, you can assign parameters to clips you create at runtime by using the *initObject* parameter of attachMovie() and duplicateMovie(). You can use this feature to initialize properties of the class you're assigning to a movie clip.

For example, the following class named MoveRightDistance is a variation of the MoveRight class (see "Assigning a class to a movie clip symbol" on page 384). The difference is a new property named distance, whose value determines how many pixels a movie clip moves each time it is clicked.

To pass arguments to a custom class:

1. Create a new ActionScript document and save it as **MoveRightDistance.as**.

2. Type the following ActionScript into the Script window:

```
// MoveRightDistance class -- moves clip to the right 5 pixels every
   frame.
class MoveRightDistance extends MovieClip {
   // Distance property determines how many
   // pixels to move clip for each mouse press.
   var distance:Number;
   function onPress() {
      this._x += this.distance;
   }
}
```

3. Save your progress.

4. Create a new Flash document, and save it as **MoveRightDistance.fla** in the same directory as the class file.

5. Create a movie clip symbol that contains a vector shape, such as an oval, and then delete any content from the Stage.

   You only need a movie clip symbol in the library for this example.

6. In the Library panel, right-click (Windows) or Control-click (Macintosh) the symbol and select Linkage from the context menu.

7. Assign the linkage identifier **Ball** to the symbol.

8. Type **MoveRightDistance** into the AS 2.0 Class text box.

9. Add the following code to Frame 1 of the Timeline:

```
this.attachMovie("Ball", "ball50_mc", 10, {distance:50});
this.attachMovie("Ball", "ball125_mc", 20, {distance:125});
```

This code creates two new instances of the symbol on the root timeline of the SWF file. The first instance, named ball50_mc, moves 50 pixels each time it is clicked; the second, named ball125_mc, moves 125 pixels each time it is clicked.

10. Select Control > Test Movie to test the SWF file.

CHAPTER 12

Working with Text and Strings

Many of the applications, presentations, and graphics that you create with Macromedia Flash Professional 8 or Macromedia Flash Basic 8 include some kind of text. You can use many different kinds of text. You might use static text in your layouts, but dynamic text for longer passages of text. Or you might use input text to capture user input, and text in an image for your background design. You can create text fields with the Flash authoring tool, or use ActionScript.

One way to display text is to use code to manipulate how strings appear before they are loaded and displayed on the Stage at runtime. You can work with strings in an application in several ways, such as sending them to a server and retrieving a response, parsing strings in an array, or validating strings that the user types into a text field.

This chapter describes several ways to use text and strings in your applications, focusing on using code to manipulate text.

The following list describes terminology used in this chapter.

Alias   Aliased text does not use color variations to make its jagged edges appear smoother, unlike anti-aliased text (see following definition).

Anti-alias   You use anti-aliasing to smooth text so the edges of characters that appear onscreen look less jagged. The Anti-Alias option in Flash makes text more legible by aligning text outlines along pixel boundaries, and is particularly effective for clearly rendering smaller font sizes.

Characters   Characters are letters, numerals, and punctuation that you combine to make up strings.

Device fonts   Device fonts are special fonts in Flash that are not embedded in a SWF file. Instead, Flash Player uses whatever font on the local computer that most closely resembles the device font. Because font outlines are not embedded, a SWF file size is smaller than using embedded font outlines. However, because device fonts are not embedded, the text that you create with these fonts looks different than expected on computer systems that do not have a font installed that corresponds to the device font. Flash includes three device fonts: _sans (similar to Helvetica and Arial), _serif (similar to Times Roman), and _typewriter (similar to Courier).

Fonts   Sets of characters with a similar font face, style, and size.

String   A sequence of characters.

Text   A series of one or more strings that can be displayed in a text field, or within a user interface component.

Text fields   A visual element on the Stage that lets you display text to a user. Similar to an input text field or text area form control in HTML, Flash lets you set text fields as editable (read-only), allow HTML formatting, enable multiline support, password masking, or apply a CSS stylesheet to your HTML formatted text.

Text formatting   You can apply formatting to a text field, or certain characters within a text field. Some examples of text formatting options that can be applied to text are: alignment, indenting, bold, color, font size, margin widths, italics, and letter spacing.

For more information on text, see the following topics:

About text fields

A dynamic or input text field is a TextField object (an instance of the TextField class). When you create a text field in the authoring environment, you can assign it an instance name in the Property inspector. You can use the instance name in ActionScript statements to set, change, and format the text field and its content by using the TextField and TextFormat classes.

You can use the user interface to create several kinds of text fields, or you can use ActionScript to create text fields. You can create the following kinds of text fields in Flash:

Static text   Use static text to display characters that do not need to change, to display small amounts of text, or to display special fonts that are not available on most computers. You can also display uncommon fonts by embedding characters for dynamic text fields.

Dynamic text   Use dynamic text fields when you need to display characters that are updated or that change at runtime. Also, you can load text into dynamic text fields.

Input text   Use input text fields when you need to capture user input. Users can type in these text fields.

Text components   You can use TextArea or TextInput components to display or capture text in your applications. The TextArea component is similar to a dynamic text field with built-in scroll bars. The TextInput component is similar to an input text field. Both components have additional functionality over their text field equivalents; however, they add more file size to your application.

> **NOTE**
> All text fields support Unicode. For information on Unicode, see "About strings and the String class" on page 459

The methods of the TextField class let you set, select, and manipulate text in a dynamic or input text field that you create during authoring or at runtime. For more information, see "Using the TextField class" on page 392. For information on debugging text fields at runtime, see "About displaying text field properties for debugging" on page 742.

ActionScript also provides several ways to format your text at runtime. The TextFormat class lets you set character and paragraph formatting for TextField objects (see "Using the TextFormat class" on page 428). Flash Player also supports a subset of HTML tags that you can use to format text (see "Using HTML-formatted text" on page 445). Flash Player 7 and later supports the img HTML tag, which lets you embed not just external images but also external SWF files as well as movie clips that reside in the library (see "Image tag" on page 448).

In Flash Player 7 and later, you can apply Cascading Style Sheet (CSS) styles to text fields using the TextField.StyleSheet class. You can use CSS styles to style built-in HTML tags, define new formatting tags, or apply styles. For more information on using CSS, see "Formatting text with Cascading Style Sheet styles" on page 430.

You can also assign HTML formatted text, which might optionally use CSS styles, directly to a text field. In Flash Player 7 and later, HTML text that you assign to a text field can contain embedded media (movie clips, SWF files, and JPEG files). In Flash Player 8, you can also dynamically load PNG, GIF, and *progressive* JPEG images (Flash Player 7 does not support progressive JPEG images). The text wraps around the embedded media similar to how a web browser wraps text around media embedded in an HTML document. For more information, see "Image tag" on page 448.

For information on the terminology that compares text, strings, and more, see the introduction for this chapter, "Working with Text and Strings" on page 389.

Using the TextField class

The TextField class represents any dynamic or input (editable) text field you create using the Text tool in Flash. You use the methods and properties of this class to control text fields at runtime. TextField objects support the same properties as MovieClip objects, with the exception of the `_currentframe`, `_droptarget`, `_framesloaded`, and `_totalframes` properties. You can get and set properties and invoke methods for text fields dynamically.

To use ActionScript to control a dynamic or input text field, you must assign the text field an instance name in the Property inspector. You can then reference the text field with the instance name, and use the methods and properties of the TextField class to control the contents or basic appearance of the text field.

You can also create TextField objects at runtime, and assign them instance names, using the `MovieClip.createTextField()` method. For more information, see "Creating text fields at runtime" on page 395.

For more information on using the TextField class, see the following topics:

- "Assigning text to a text field at runtime" on page 393
- "About text field instance and variable names" on page 394

You can find sample source files that demonstrate how to work with text fields using ActionScript. The source files are called textfieldsA.fla and textfieldsB.fla, and you can find them in the Samples folder on your hard disk:

- In Windows, browse to *boot drive*\Program Files\Macromedia\Flash 8\ Samples and Tutorials\Samples\ActionScript\TextFields.

- On the Macintosh, browse to *Macintosh HD*/Applications/Macromedia Flash 8/ Samples and Tutorials/Samples/ActionScript/TextFields.

Assigning text to a text field at runtime

When you build applications with Flash, you may want to load text from an external source, such as a text file, an XML file, or even a remote web service. Flash provides a great deal of control over how you create and display text on the Stage, such as supporting text that is HTML formatted, plain text, XML formatted text, and external style sheets. Or you can use ActionScript to define a stylesheet.

To assign text to a text field, you can use the `TextField.text` or the `TextField.htmlText` property. Or, if you entered a value in the variable text field in the Property inspector, you can assign a value to the text field by creating a variable with the specified name. If you use version 2 of Macromedia Components Architecture in your Flash document, you can also assign values by creating bindings between components.

The following exercise assigns text to a text field at runtime.

To assign text to a text field at runtime:

1. Using the Text tool, create a text field on the Stage.

2. With the text field selected, in the Property inspector (Window > Properties > Properties), select Input Text from the Text Type pop-up menu, and enter **headline_txt** in the Instance Name text box.

   Instance names must consist only of letters, numbers, underscores (_), and dollar signs ($).

3. Select Frame 1 of the Timeline, and open the Actions panel (Window > Actions).

4. Type the following code in the Actions panel:

   ```
   headline_txt.text = "New articles available on Developer Center";
   ```

5. Select Control > Test Movie to test the Flash document.

You can also create a text field with ActionScript, and then assign text to it. Type the following ActionScript on Frame 1 of the Timeline:

```
this.createTextField("headline_txt", this.getNextHighestDepth(), 100, 100,
   300, 20);
headline_txt.text = "New articles available on Developer Center";
```

This code creates a new text field with the instance name `headline_txt`. The text field is created at the next highest depth, at the *x* and *y* coordinates of 100, 100, with a text field width of 200 pixels and a height of 20 pixels. When you test the SWF file (Control > Test Movie), the text "New articles available on Developer Center" appears on the Stage.

To create an HTML-formatted text field:

Use one of the following two steps to enable HTML formatting for the text field:

- Select a text field and click Render Text as HTML in the Property inspector.
- Set the text field's `html` property to `true` by using ActionScript (see the following code sample).

To apply HTML formatting to a text field by using ActionScript, type the following ActionScript on Frame 1 of the Timeline:

```
this.createTextField("headline_txt", this.getNextHighestDepth(), 100, 100,
    300, 20);
headline_txt.html = true;
headline_txt.htmlText = "New articles available on <i>Developer Center</
    i>.";
```

The preceding code dynamically creates a new text field, enables HTML formatting, and displays the text "New articles available on Developer Center" on the Stage, with the word "Developer Center" appearing in italics.

> **CAUTION**
> When you use HTML formatted text with a text field (not components) on the Stage, you must assign the text to the text field's `htmlText` property instead of the text property.

You can find sample source files that demonstrate how to work with text fields using ActionScript. The source files are called textfieldsA.fla and textfieldsB.fla, and you can find them in the Samples folder on your hard disk:

- In Windows, browse to *boot drive*\Program Files\Macromedia\Flash 8\Samples and Tutorials\Samples\ActionScript\TextFields.
- On the Macintosh, browse to *Macintosh HD*/Applications/Macromedia Flash 8/Samples and Tutorials/Samples/ActionScript/TextFields.

About text field instance and variable names

In the Instance Name text box in the Property inspector, you must assign an instance name to a text field to invoke methods and get and set properties on that text field.

In the Var text box in the Property inspector, you can assign a variable name to a dynamic or input text field. You can then assign values to the variable. This is a deprecated functionality that you might use when you create applications for older versions of Flash Player (such as Flash Player 4). When you target newer players, target the text of a text field by using its instance name and ActionScript.

Do not confuse a text field's instance name with its variable name, however. A text field's variable name is a variable reference to the text contained by that text field; it is not a reference to an object.

For example, if you assigned a text field the variable name myTextVar, you can use the following code to set the contents of the text field:

```
var myTextVar:String = "This is what will appear in the text field";
```

However, you can't use the variable name myTextVar to set the text field's text property. You have to use the instance name, as shown in the following code:

```
// This won't work.
myTextVar.text = "A text field variable is not an object reference";

// For input text field with instance name "myField", this will work.
myField.text = "This sets the text property of the myField object";
```

Use the TextField.text property to control the contents of a text field, unless you're targeting a version of Flash Player that doesn't support the TextField class. This reduces the chances of a variable name conflict, which could result in unexpected behavior at runtime.

You can find sample source files that demonstrate how to work with text fields using ActionScript. The source files are called textfieldsA.fla and textfieldsB.fla, and you can find them in the Samples folder on your hard disk:

- In Windows, browse to *boot drive*\Program Files\Macromedia\Flash 8\ Samples and Tutorials\Samples\ActionScript\TextFields.
- On the Macintosh, browse to *Macintosh HD*/Applications/Macromedia Flash 8/ Samples and Tutorials/Samples/ActionScript/TextFields.

Creating text fields at runtime

You can use the createTextField() method of the MovieClip class to create an empty text field on the Stage at runtime. The new text field is attached to the timeline of the movie clip that calls the method.

To dynamically create a text field using ActionScript:

1. Select File > New and then select Flash Document to create a new FLA file.

2. Type the following ActionScript on Frame 1 of the Timeline:

```
this.createTextField("test_txt", 10, 0, 0, 300, 100);
```

This code creates a 300 x 100-pixel text field named test_txt with a location of (0, 0) and a depth (z-order) of 10.

3. To access the methods and properties of the newly created text field, use the instance name specified in the first parameter of the `createTextField()` method.

   For example, the following code creates a new text field named `test_txt`, and modifies its properties to make it a multiline, word-wrapping text field that expands to fit inserted text. Then it assigns some text using the text field's `text` property:

   ```
   test_txt.multiline = true;
   test_txt.wordWrap = true;
   test_txt.autoSize = "left";
   test_txt.text = "Create new text fields with the
       MovieClip.createTextField() method.";
   ```

4. Select Control > Test Movie to see the text field.

   The text is created at runtime and appears on the Stage.

You can use the `TextField.removeTextField()` method to remove a text field created with `createTextField()`. The `removeTextField()` method does not work on a text field placed by the timeline during authoring.

For more information, see %{createTextField (MovieClip.createTextField method)}% and %{removeTextField (TextField.removeTextField method)}% in the *ActionScript 2.0 Language Reference* in Flash Help.

 NOTE Some TextField properties, such as `_rotation`, are not available when you create text fields at runtime. You can rotate a text field only if it uses embedded fonts. See "To embed a font symbol:" on page 408.

You can find sample source files that demonstrate how to work with text fields using ActionScript. The source files are called textfieldsA.fla and textfieldsB.fla, and you can find them in the Samples folder on your hard disk:

- In Windows, browse to *boot drive*\Program Files\Macromedia\Flash 8\ Samples and Tutorials\Samples\ActionScript\TextFields.

- On the Macintosh, browse to *Macintosh HD*/Applications/Macromedia Flash 8/ Samples and Tutorials/Samples/ActionScript/TextFields.

About manipulating text fields

You can manipulate text fields that you create in a FLA file in several ways. You can manipulate a text field as long as you assign an instance name in the Property inspector, or you can assign one with code if you use code to create the field. The following simple example creates a text field, assigns text to it, and changes the border property of the field:

```
this.createTextField("pigeon_txt", this.getNextHighestDepth(), 100, 100,
    200, 20);
pigeon_txt.text = "I like seeds";
pigeon_txt.border = true;
```

For a complete list of properties in the TextField class, see the *ActionScript 2.0 Language Reference* in Flash Help.

For examples of how to manipulate text fields, see the following sections:

- "Changing a text field's position" on page 397
- "Changing a text field's dimensions at runtime" on page 398

You can find sample source files that demonstrate how to work with text fields using ActionScript. The source files are called textfieldsA.fla and textfieldsB.fla, and you can find them in the Samples folder on your hard disk:

- In Windows, browse to *boot drive*\Program Files\Macromedia\Flash 8\ Samples and Tutorials\Samples\ActionScript\TextFields.
- On the Macintosh, browse to *Macintosh HD*/Applications/Macromedia Flash 8/ Samples and Tutorials/Samples/ActionScript/TextFields.

Changing a text field's position

You can change a text field's position on the Stage at runtime. You need to set new values for the text field's _x and _y properties, as shown in the following example.

To reposition a text field by using ActionScript:

1. Create a new FLA file and save it as **positionText.fla**.

2. Add the following ActionScript to Frame 1 of the Timeline:

```
this.createTextField("my_txt", 10, 0, 0, 300, 200);
my_txt.border = true;
my_txt.text = "Hello world";
my_txt._x = (Stage.width - my_txt._width) / 2;
my_txt._y = (Stage.height - my_txt._height) / 2;
```

3. Save the Flash document and select Control > Test Movie to see the text field centered on the Stage.

You can find sample source files that demonstrate how to work with text fields using ActionScript. The source files are called textfieldsA.fla and textfieldsB.fla, and you can find them in the Samples folder on your hard disk:

- In Windows, browse to *boot drive*\Program Files\Macromedia\Flash 8\ Samples and Tutorials\Samples\ActionScript\TextFields.

- On the Macintosh, browse to *Macintosh HD*/Applications/Macromedia Flash 8/ Samples and Tutorials/Samples/ActionScript/TextFields.

Changing a text field's dimensions at runtime

You may need to get or set a text field's dimensions dynamically at runtime, rather than in the authoring environment. The next example creates a text field on a timeline and sets its initial dimensions to 100 pixels wide by 21 pixels high. Later, the text field is resized to 300 pixels wide by 200 pixels high, and it is repositioned to the center of the Stage.

To resize a text field using ActionScript:

1. Create a new Flash document and save it as **resizeText.fla**.

2. Add the following ActionScript to Frame 1 of the Timeline:

```
this.createTextField("my_txt", 10, 0, 0, 100, 21);
my_txt.border = true;
my_txt.multiline = true;
my_txt.text = "Hello world";
my_txt.wordWrap = true;
my_txt._width = 300;
my_txt._height = 200;
my_txt._x = (Stage.width - my_txt._width) / 2;
my_txt._y = (Stage.height - my_txt._height) / 2;
```

3. Save the Flash document and select Control > Test Movie to see the results in the authoring environment.

The previous example resized a dynamically created text field to 300 pixels by 200 pixels at runtime, but when you load content from an external website and are not sure how much content will be returned, this technique may not be suitable for your needs. Fortunately, Flash includes a `TextField.autoSize` property, which you can use to automatically resize a text field to fit its contents. The following example demonstrates how you can use the `TextField.autoSize` property to resize the text field after text is added to the text field.

To automatically resize text fields based on content:

1. Create a new Flash document and save it as **resizeTextAuto.fla**.

2. Add the following code to Frame 1 of the main Timeline:

```
this.createTextField("my_txt", 10, 10, 10, 160, 120);
my_txt.autoSize = "left";
my_txt.border = true;
my_txt.multiline = true;
my_txt.text = "Lorem ipsum dolor sit amet, consectetur adipisicing elit,
    sed do eiusmod tempor incididunt ut labore et dolore magna aliqua. Ut
    enim ad minim veniam, quis nostrud exercitation ullamco laboris nisi
    ut aliquip ex ea commodo consequat. Duis aute irure dolor in
    reprehenderit in voluptate velit esse cillum dolore eu fugiat nulla
    pariatur. Excepteur sint occaecat cupidatat non proident, sunt in
    culpa qui officia deserunt mollit anim id est laborum.";
my_txt.wordWrap = true;
```

> **NOTE**
> If you paste this code directly into the Actions panel from some versions of Flash Help, you may encounter line breaks in the long text string. In this case, the code won't compile. If you encounter this situation, enable Hidden Characters on the pop-up menu of the Actions panel, and then remove the line break characters in the long text string.

3. Save the Flash document and select Control > Test Movie to view the Flash document in the authoring environment.

   Flash resizes the text field vertically so that all the content can be displayed without being cropped by the text field boundaries. If you set the `my_txt.wordWrap` property to `false`, the text field resizes horizontally to accommodate the text.

   To enforce a maximum height on the auto-sized text field (so that the text field height doesn't exceed the boundaries of the Stage), use the following code.

```
if (my_txt._height > 160) {
  my_txt.autoSize = "none";
  my_txt._height = 160;
}
```

You must add some scrolling functionality, such as a scroll bar, to allow users to view the remainder of the text. Alternatively, you can roll the mouse pointer over the text; this method is often adequate while testing this code.

You can find sample source files that demonstrate how to work with text fields using ActionScript. The source files are called textfieldsA.fla and textfieldsB.fla, and you can find them in the Samples folder on your hard disk:

- In Windows, browse to *boot drive*\Program Files\Macromedia\Flash 8\ Samples and Tutorials\Samples\ActionScript\TextFields.

- On the Macintosh, browse to *Macintosh HD*/Applications/Macromedia Flash 8/ Samples and Tutorials/Samples/ActionScript/TextFields.

About loading text and variables into text fields

You can load text into a Flash document several ways, including (but certainly not limited to) using FlashVars, LoadVars, XML, or web services. Perhaps the simplest method of passing text into a Flash document is to use the FlashVars property, which passes short strings of text into a Flash document through the `object` and `embed` tags in the HTML code that you use to embed the SWF file in an HTML page. Another easy way to load text or variables into a Flash document is to use the LoadVars class, which can load large blocks of text or load a series of URL encoded variables from a text file.

As you can see from the previous examples in this section, some ways of loading text into a SWF file are easier than others. However, if you syndicate data from external sites, you might not have a choice for the format of the data that you need to load.

Each way of loading and/or sending data to and from a SWF file has its pros and cons. XML, web services, and Flash Remoting are the most versatile for loading external data, but they are also the most difficult to learn. For information on Flash Remoting, see www.macromedia.com/support/flashremoting.

FlashVars and LoadVars are much simpler, as demonstrated in "Using FlashVars to load and display text" on page 401 and "Using LoadVars to load and display text" on page 402, but they can be much more limited in the types and formats of data that you can load. Also, you must follow security restrictions when you send and load data. For information on security, see Chapter 17, "Understanding Security." For more information on loading external data, see Chapter 16, "Working with External Data."

The following sections show you different ways to load text and variables into your documents:

- "Using FlashVars to load and display text" on page 401
- "Using LoadVars to load and display text" on page 402
- "Loading variables by using LoadVars" on page 404
- "Loading and displaying text from an XML document" on page 405

You can find sample source files that demonstrate how to work with text fields using ActionScript. The source files are called loadText.fla and formattedText.fla, and you can find them in the Samples folder on your hard disk:

- In Windows, browse to *boot drive*\Program Files\Macromedia\Flash 8\ Samples and Tutorials\Samples\ActionScript\LoadText.
- On the Macintosh, browse to *Macintosh HD*/Applications/Macromedia Flash 8/ Samples and Tutorials/Samples/ActionScript/LoadText.

You can also find a source file that loads text and applies anti-alias formatting in addition to bitmap caching. The sample source file is called flashtype.fla in the Samples folder on your hard disk:

- In Windows, browse to *boot drive*\Program Files\Macromedia\Flash 8\ Samples and Tutorials\Samples\ActionScript\FlashType.
- On the Macintosh, browse to *Macintosh HD*/Applications/Macromedia Flash 8/ Samples and Tutorials/Samples/ActionScript/FlashType.

Using FlashVars to load and display text

Using FlashVars is simple, but requires you to publish your SWF files along with HTML documents. You modify the generated HTML code and include the FlashVars properties in both the `object` and `embed` tags. You can then test the Flash document by viewing the modified HTML document in your web browser.

To use FlashVars to pass variables from HTML to your Flash document:

1. Create a new Flash document and save it as **flashvars.fla**.

2. Add the following ActionScript to Frame 1 of the Timeline:
   ```
   this.createTextField("my_txt", 10, 10, 10, 100, 21);
   my_txt.text = _level0.username;
   ```

3. Save the Flash document and select File > Publish to generate the HTML and SWF files.

    An HTML document publishes, by default, to the same directory as your FLA file. If an HTML document does not publish, select File > Publish Settings and then select the Formats tab. Make sure that you select HTML.

4. Open up the flashvars.html document in a text or HTML editor.

5. In the HTML document, modify the code inside the `object` tag to match the following. The code you need to add is in **boldface**.

```
<object classid="clsid:d27cdb6e-ae6d-11cf-96b8-444553540000"
    codebase="http://fpdownload.macromedia.com/pub/shockwave/cabs/flash/
    swflash.cab#version=8,0,0,0" width="550" height="400" id="flashvars"
    align="middle">
<param name="allowScriptAccess" value="sameDomain" />
<param name="movie" value="flashvars.swf" />
<param name="FlashVars" value="username=Thomas" />
<param name="quality" value="high" />
<param name="bgcolor" value="#ffffff" />
<embed src="flashvars.swf" FlashVars="username=Thomas" quality="high"
    bgcolor="#ffffff" width="550" height="400" name="flashvars"
    align="middle" allowScriptAccess="sameDomain" type="application/x-
    shockwave-flash" pluginspage="http://www.macromedia.com/go/
    getflashplayer" />
</object>
```

6. Save your changes to the HTML document.

7. Open the modified HTML in a web browser.

The SWF file displays the name "Thomas" in the dynamically created text field on the Stage.

For information on security, see Chapter 17, "Understanding Security."

Using LoadVars to load and display text

You can also use the LoadVars class to load content into a SWF file, which loads text or variables from an external file on the same server, or even content from a different server. The next example demonstrates how to dynamically create a text field and populate it with the contents of a remote text file.

To use LoadVars to populate a text field with external text:

1. Create a new Flash document and save it as **loadvarsText.fla**.

2. Add the following ActionScript to Frame 1 of the Timeline:

```
this.createTextField("my_txt", 10, 10, 10, 320, 100);
my_txt.autoSize = "left";
my_txt.border = true;
my_txt.multiline = true;
my_txt.wordWrap = true;

var lorem_lv:LoadVars = new LoadVars();
lorem_lv.onData = function (src:String):Void {
  if (src != undefined) {
    my_txt.text = src;
  } else {
    my_txt.text = "Unable to load external file.";
  }
}
lorem_lv.load("http://www.helpexamples.com/flash/lorem.txt");
```

The first block of code in the previous snippet creates a new text field on the Stage and enables multiline and word wrapping. The second block of code defines a new LoadVars object that is used to load a text file (lorem.txt) from a remote web server and display its contents into the my_txt text field created earlier.

3. Save the Flash document and select Control > Test Movie to test the SWF file.

After a slight delay, Flash displays the contents of the remote file in the text field on the Stage.

For information on security, see Chapter 17, "Understanding Security."

Loading variables by using LoadVars

The LoadVars class also lets you load variables in a URL-encoded format, similar to passing variables in the query string in a web browser. The following example demonstrates how to load a remote text file into a SWF file and display its variables, monthNames and dayNames.

To load variables from a text file by using LoadVars:

1. Create a new Flash document and save it as **loadvarsVariables.fla**.

2. Add the following code to Frame 1 of the Timeline:

```
this.createTextField("my_txt", 10, 10, 10, 320, 100);
my_txt.autoSize = "left";
my_txt.border = true;
my_txt.multiline = true;
my_txt.wordWrap = true;

var lorem_lv:LoadVars = new LoadVars();
lorem_lv.onLoad = function (success:Boolean):Void {
  if (success) {
    my_txt.text = "dayNames: " + lorem_lv.dayNames + "\n\n";
    my_txt.text += "monthNames: " + lorem_lv.monthNames;
  } else {
    my_txt.text = "Unable to load external file.";
  }
}
/* contents of params.txt:
  &monthNames=January,February,...&dayNames=Sunday,Monday,...
*/
lorem_lv.load("http://www.helpexamples.com/flash/params.txt");
```

3. Save the Flash document and select Control > Test Movie from the main menu.

   Because you are using the LoadVars.onLoad() method instead of LoadVars.onData(), Flash parses out the variables and creates variables within the LoadVars object instance. The external text file contains two variables, monthNames and dayNames, which both contain strings.

For information on security, see Chapter 17, "Understanding Security."

Loading and displaying text from an XML document

XML data is a popular way to distribute content on the Internet, in part because it is a widely accepted standard for organizing and parsing data. As such, XML is an excellent choice for sending and receiving data from Flash; however, XML is slightly more difficult to learn than using LoadVars and FlashVars to load data and display text.

To load text into Flash from an external XML document:

1. Create a new Flash document and save it as **xmlReviews.fla**.

2. Add the following code to Frame 1 of the Timeline:

```
this.createTextField("my_txt", 10, 10, 10, 320, 100);
my_txt.autoSize = "left";
my_txt.border = true;
my_txt.multiline = true;
my_txt.wordWrap = true;

var reviews_xml:XML = new XML();
reviews_xml.ignoreWhite = true;
reviews_xml.onLoad = function (success:Boolean):Void {
   if (success) {
      var childItems:Array = reviews_xml.firstChild.childNodes;
      for (var i:Number = 0; i < childItems.length; i++) {
         my_txt.text += childItems[i].firstChild.firstChild.nodeValue +
   "\n";
      }
   } else {
      my_txt.text = "Unable to load external file.";
   }
}
reviews_xml.load("http://www.helpexamples.com/flash/xml/reviews.xml");
```

The first block of code in the preceding snippet creates a new text field on the Stage. This text field is used to display various parts of the XML document that is loaded later. The second block of code handles creating an XML object that will be used to load the XML content. Once the date is completely loaded and parsed by Flash, the `XML.onLoad()` event handler is invoked and displays the contents of the XML packet in the text field.

3. Save the Flash document and select Control > Test Movie to test the SWF file.

   Flash displays the following output in the text field on the Stage:

```
Item 1
Item 2
...
Item 8
```

For information on security, see Chapter 17, "Understanding Security."

Using fonts

Fonts are sets of characters with a similar font face, style, and size. No matter what you create using Flash Basic 8 or Flash Professional 8, you will probably use text with at least one or two fonts in your Flash applications. If you build animations, and you are not sure if your end users will have a specific font installed on their systems, you need to understand the basics about embedding fonts.

The following sections show you how to embed characters, entire fonts, shared fonts, and other techniques for working with fonts in Flash 8.

For more information on fonts, see the following sections:

- "Embedding characters" on page 407
- "Embedding fonts" on page 408
- "Creating custom character sets" on page 410
- "Using TextField methods with embedded fonts" on page 413
- "About sharing fonts" on page 415

The following example shows you how to add and remove embedded characters and character sets in a Flash document.

To add and remove embedded characters and character sets:

1. Create a new Flash document and save it as **embedding.fla**.

2. Create a dynamic text field on the Stage by using the Text tool.

3. Click Embed to launch the Character Embedding dialog box.

4. Select a specific character set to embed by clicking it with your mouse pointer.

   To select multiple character sets, you can use the Shift or Control key while selecting items with your mouse pointer. To select a block of character sets, select a character set with your mouse pointer, press and hold Shift, and click a new character set. Using Shift selects every character set between the two selected character sets. To select multiple non-sequential character sets, press and hold the Control key while you select character sets. You can also quickly select multiple character sets by selecting a character set with your mouse, and with the mouse button still held down, drag your mouse over multiple character sets.

5. To remove a specific character set that you added earlier, press and hold the Control key and deselect the character set by clicking it with your mouse pointer.

6. To remove every selected character set and any specified characters in the Include these characters text input field, click Don't Embed.

Don't Embed clears any previously specified individual characters or character sets.

> **CAUTION**
>
> Clicking Don't Embed in the Character Embedding dialog box removes any specified embedded characters and character sets that were previously chosen without asking you to confirm.

Embedding characters

If you're working with embedded fonts and know exactly what characters you need, you can reduce file size by embedding only the characters that you need instead of including additional, unused font outlines. To embed certain characters within a text field and not embed a whole character set, use the Character Embedding dialog box to specify which specific characters you want to embed.

To embed specific characters for use in a text field:

1. Create a new Flash document and save it as **charembed.fla**.

2. Using the Text tool, create a text field on the Stage and set the text field's text type to either dynamic or input.

3. With the text field still selected on the Stage, click Embed in the Property inspector to open the Character Embedding dialog box.

   The Character Embedding dialog box lets you set which character sets will embed in the Flash document (as well as how many glyphs per character set), specify specific characters to embed, and tells you the total number of glyphs being embedded for this text field.

4. Type the string **hello world** into the Include these characters text box.

   The dialog box tells you that a total of 8 glyphs will be embedded for this text field. Even though the string "hello world" contains 11 characters, Flash only embeds unique glyphs, so the letters l and o are embedded once instead of multiple times.

5. Click OK to apply the changes and return to your document.

6. Using the Text tool, create a new text field on the Stage.

7. Set the text field's text type to dynamic in the Property inspector.

8. Type the string **hello world** into the text field on the Stage.

9. Click Embed in the Property inspector to open the Character Embedding dialog box again.

10. Click Auto Fill to automatically populate the Include These Characters text box.

You will see the string "helo wrd". Instead of having to tell Flash which characters you want to include, Flash can determine all unique characters in the specified text field for you.

> **TIP**
>
> Flash can determine characters to embed automatically only if the text field contains text on the Stage. If the text field is populated by using ActionScript, you must specify which characters you want to embed for the text field.

11. Click OK.

Embedding fonts

When you embed fonts, Flash stores all of the font information in the SWF file so the font is displayed properly even if it's not installed on the user's computer. If you use a font in your FLA file that isn't installed on a user's system, and you don't embed the font in the SWF file, Flash Player automatically selects a substitute font to use instead.

> **NOTE**
>
> You need to embed a font only if you're using dynamic or input text fields. If you use a static text field, you don't need to embed the font.

To embed a font symbol:

1. Select Window > Library to open the current FLA file's library.

   Open the library that you want to add the font symbol to.

2. Select New Font from the library's pop-up menu (upper-right corner of the Library panel).

3. Type a name for the font symbol in the Name text box of the Font Symbol Properties dialog box.

4. Select a font from the Font menu or type the name of a font in the Font text box.

5. Select Bold, Italic, or Alias text if you want to apply a style to the font.

6. Enter the font size to embed, and then click OK to apply the changes and return to your document.

   Your font now appears in the current document's library.

After you've embedded a font in your library, you can use it with a text field on the Stage.

To use an embedded font symbol in your Flash document:

1. Follow the steps in the procedure under "Embedding fonts" on page 408 to embed a font in your library.

2. Use the Text tool to create a text field on the Stage.

3. Type some text in the text field.

4. Select the text field, and open the Property inspector.

   a. Set the text field to single-line.

   b. Select the name of the embedded font by using the Font drop-down menu.

   Embedded fonts have an asterisk (*) after the font name.

5. Click Embed in the Property inspector to launch the Character Embedding dialog box.

   The Character Embedding dialog box lets you select the individual characters or character sets that you want to embed for the selected text field. To specify what characters to embed, either type the characters into the text box in the dialog box, or click Auto Fill to automatically populate the text field with the unique characters currently in the text field. If you aren't sure which characters you will need (for example, because your text loads from an external file or a web service), you can select entire sets of characters to embed, such as Uppercase [A..Z], Lowercase [a..z], Numerals [0..9], Punctuation [!@#%...], and character sets for several different languages.

   > **NOTE** Each character set you select increases the final size of the SWF file because Flash has to store all of the font information for each character set that you use.

6. Select the individual characters or character sets you want to embed, and then click OK to apply the changes and return to your document.

7. Select Control > Test Movie to test the Flash document in the authoring environment.

   The embedded font is displayed in the text field on the Stage. To properly test that the font is embedded, you might need to test on a separate computer without the embedded font installed.

   Or you can set the `TextField._alpha` or `TextField._rotation` properties for the text field with embedded fonts, because these properties work only on embedded fonts (see the following steps).

8. Close the SWF file and return to the authoring tool.

9. Select the text field on the Stage, and open the Property inspector.

   a. Set the text field's Text type to Dynamic Text.

   b. Type **font_txt** into the Instance Name text box.

10. Add the following code to Frame 1 of the Timeline:

```
font_txt._rotation = 45;
```

11. Select Control > Test Movie again to view the changes in the authoring environment.

The embedded font rotates 45° clockwise, and you can still see the text because it's embedded in the SWF file.

> **CAUTION**
>
> If you don't embed a font within your Flash document and Flash Player automatically chooses a font substitute on the user's computer, the TextField.font property returns the original font used within the FLA, not the name of the substituted font.

> **NOTE**
>
> If you use embedded fonts with a variety of styles in your text fields, you must embed the style that you want to use. For example, if you're using an embedded font called Times, and then want a word to be italic, you must make sure to embed both the normal and italic character outlines. Otherwise, the text won't appear in the text field.

Creating custom character sets

In addition to using the Flash default character sets, you can also create your own character sets and add them to the Character Embedding dialog box. For example, you might need to allow some fields to include Extended Latin, to support various accented characters. However, perhaps you don't need the numerals and punctuation, or perhaps you only need uppercase characters. Rather than embedding entire character sets, you can create a custom character set that contains only the characters that you need. This way you can keep the size of your SWF file as small as possible, because you don't store any extra font information for the characters that you don't need.

To create a custom character set, you must edit the UnicodeTable.xml file, located in the C:\Program Files\Macromedia\Flash 8*<language>*\First Run\FontEmbedding\ directory. This file defines the default character sets and the character ranges and characters that they contain.

Before you create a custom character set, you should understand the necessary XML structure. The following XML nodes define the Uppercase [A..Z] character set:

```
<glyphRange name="Uppercase [A..Z] " id="1" >
  <range min="0x0020" max ="0x0020" />
  <range min="0x0041" max ="0x005A" />
</glyphRange>
```

Notice that the glyphRange node includes name, Uppercase [A..Z], and id. A glyphRange node can have as many *range* child nodes as you need. A range can be a single character, such as 0x0020 (the space character), seen in the previous snippet, or a range of characters, such as the second range child node. To embed only a single character, set the min value and the max value to the same unicode character value.

Another example of an XML glyphRange node is the Numerals [0..9] node:

```
<glyphRange name="Numerals [0..9] " id="3" >
  <range min="0x0030" max ="0x0039" />
  <range min="0x002E" max ="0x002E" />
</glyphRange>
```

This range of characters includes the Unicode values 0x0030 (zero) through 0x0039 (9), as well as 0x002E (.).

Before you create a custom character set, you need to know the characters and their corresponding Unicode values. The best place to find Unicode values is the Unicode Standards web site, www.unicode.org, which contains the Unicode Character Code chart for dozens of languages.

> **CAUTION**
>
> To add custom character sets, you need to edit an XML file in the Flash installation folder. Before you edit this file, you should make a backup copy in case you want to revert to the original Unicode table.

> **CAUTION**
>
> Macromedia recommends that you do not modify the existing character sets that are installed with Flash, and that you instead make your own custom character sets that include the characters and punctuation that you require.

To create and use a custom character set:

1. Open the UnicodeTable.xml document, located in the *<Flash install directory>**<language>*\First Run\FontEmbedding\ directory, using an XML or text editor such as Notepad or TextEdit.

 Remember to save a backup of this document, in case you want to revert to the original file that is installed with Flash.

2. Scroll to the bottom of the XML document and add the following XML code directly before the closing `</fontEmbeddingTable>` node:

```
<glyphRange name="Uppercase and Numerals [A..Z,0..9] " id="100" >
    <range min="0x0020" max ="0x0020" />
    <range min="0x002E" max ="0x002E" />
    <range min="0x0030" max ="0x0039" />
    <range min="0x0041" max ="0x005A" />
</glyphRange>
```

3. Save your changes to UnicodeTable.xml.

    If you have Flash open, you must restart the application before you can use the new character set.

4. Open or restart Flash and then create a new Flash document.

5. Add a new TextField instance on the Stage by using the Text tool.

6. Set the Text type of the TextField to Dynamic in the Property inspector, and then click Embed Character Options to open the Character Embedding dialog box.

7. Scroll to the bottom of the Character Embedding dialog box and select your new custom character set, Uppercase and Numerals [A..Z,0..9] (38 glyphs).

8. Select any other character sets and click OK.

If you select your custom character set, Uppercase and Numerals [A..Z,0..9], as well as the default Uppercase [A..Z] or Numerals [0..9] character set, notice that the number of glyphs that are embedded doesn't change. This is because all of the uppercase characters are included in your custom character set, and Flash doesn't include duplicate characters, which keeps the file size as small as possible. If you select the Punctuation character set, which includes 52 glyphs, as well as your custom character set, which includes 38 glyphs, Flash stores information for only 88 glyphs instead of 90. This happens because two overlapping characters, the space and the period, are already included in your custom character set.

> **TIP**
> The position of a character set in the Character Embedding dialog box is determined by its location in the XML document. You can reorder the character sets, including your custom character sets, by moving ‹glyphRange› packets in the XML file.

Using TextField methods with embedded fonts

Methods of the TextField class provide useful functionality for your applications. For example, you can control the thickness of a text field by using ActionScript as demonstrated in the following example.

To set a text field's thickness using ActionScript:

1. Create a new Flash document and save it as **textfieldThickness.fla**.

2. Open the Library panel, and select New Font from the pop-up menu (in the upper-right corner of the Library panel).

   The Font Symbol Properties dialog box opens. This dialog box lets you select a font to embed in the SWF file (including a font style and font size). You can also assign a font name that appears in the document's library and the font drop-down menu in the Property inspector (if you have a text field selected on the Stage).

   a. Select the Times New Roman font from the Font drop-down menu.

   b. Make sure that you deselect the Bold and Italic options.

   c. Set the size to 30 pixels.

   d. Enter a font name of **Times (embedded)**.

   e. Click OK.

3. In the library, right-click the font symbol, and then select Linkage from the context menu.

   Flash opens the Linkage Properties dialog box.

4. Select the Export for ActionScript and Export in first frame options and click OK.

5. Add the following ActionScript to Frame 1 of the Timeline:

```
// 1
this.createTextField("thickness_txt", 10, 0, 0, Stage.width, 22);
this.createTextField("lorem_txt", 20, 0, 20, Stage.width, 0);
lorem_txt.autoSize = "left";
lorem_txt.embedFonts = true;
lorem_txt.antiAliasType = "advanced";
lorem_txt.text = "Lorem ipsum dolor sit amet, consectetur adipisicing
   elit, sed do eiusmod tempor incididunt ut labore et dolore magna
   aliqua. Ut enim ad minim veniam, quis nostrud exercitation ullamco
   laboris nisi ut aliquip ex ea commodo consequat. Duis aute irure dolor
   in reprehenderit in voluptate velit esse cillum dolore eu fugiat nulla
   pariatur. Excepteur sint occaecat cupidatat non proident, sunt in
   culpa qui officia deserunt mollit anim id est laborum.";
lorem_txt.wordWrap = true;

// 2
var style_fmt:TextFormat = new TextFormat();
style_fmt.font = "Times (embedded)";
style_fmt.size = 30;
lorem_txt.setTextFormat(style_fmt);

// 3
var mouseListener:Object = new Object();
mouseListener.onMouseMove = function():Void {
   // Values for TextField.thickness can range from -200 to +200.
   lorem_txt.thickness = Math.round(_xmouse * (400 / Stage.width) - 200);
   thickness_txt.text = "TextField.thickness = " + lorem_txt.thickness;
};
Mouse.addListener(mouseListener);
```

The first block of code creates two text fields, `thickness_txt` and `lorem_txt`, and positions them on the Stage. The `lorem_txt` text field sets its `embedFonts` property to `true` and populates the text field with a block of text.

The second block of code defines a text format with the font face Times New Roman, sets the font size to 30 pixels, and applies the text format to the `lorem_txt` text field.

The third, and final, block of code defines and assigns a mouse listener for the `onMouseMove` event. When the mouse pointer moves horizontally across the Stage, the `TextField.thickness` property changes between -200 and +200, depending on the current value of `_xmouse`.

6. Save your changes to the FLA file.

7. Select Control > Test Movie to test your Flash document.

When you move the mouse pointer to the left half of the Stage, the font thickness decreases. When you move the mouse pointer to the right half of the Stage, the font thickness increases.

About sharing fonts

To use a font as a shared library item, you can create a font symbol in the Library panel, and then assign the following attributes to the font symbol:

- An identifier string
- A URL where the document containing the font symbol will be posted

In this way, you can link to the font and use it in a Flash application without the font being stored in the FLA file.

About font rendering and anti-alias text

Font rendering in Flash controls the way that your text appears in a SWF file; that is, how it is rendered (or *drawn*) at runtime. The advanced font rendering technology used in Flash Player 8, called FlashType. FlashType uses advanced rendering technology to help make text appear legible and clear at small to regular font sizes, such as when you apply advanced anti-aliasing to your text fields. This technology is discussed in more detail later in this section.

Anti-aliasing lets you smooth text so that the edges of characters displayed onscreen look less jagged, which can be particularly helpful when you want to display text using small text sizes. The Anti-Alias option for text makes characters more legible by aligning text outlines along pixel boundaries, and is particularly effective for more clearly rendering small font sizes. You can apply anti-aliasing for each text field in your application, rather than for individual characters.

Anti-aliasing is supported for static, dynamic, and input text if the user has Flash Player 7 or later. It is supported only for static text if the user has an earlier version of Flash Player. Advanced anti-aliasing options are available for Flash Player 8.

Flash Basic 8 and Flash Professional 8 include a significantly improved font rasterization and rendering technology, called FlashType, for working with anti-aliased fonts. Flash 8 includes five font rendering methods, which are available only when you publish SWF files for Flash Player 8. If you are publishing files for use with Flash Player 7 or earlier versions, only the Anti-Alias for Animation option is available for use with your text fields.

FlashType is a high-quality font rendering technology that you can enable by using either the Flash 8 authoring tool or ActionScript. The FlashType technology lets you render font faces with high-quality output at small sizes, with more control. You can apply FlashType to embedded font rendering for static, dynamic, and input text fields. The improved capabilities mean that embedded text appears at the same level of quality as device text, and fonts appear the same on different platforms.

The font rendering methods available for Flash Player 8 are Device Fonts, Bitmap Text (no anti-alias), Anti-Alias for Animation, Anti-Alias for Readability, and Custom Anti-Alias, which lets you define a custom value for thickness and sharpness. For more information on these options, see "Font rendering options in Flash" on page 416.

> **NOTE**
> When you open existing FLA files in Flash 8, your text is not automatically updated to the Anti-Alias for Readability option; you must select individual text fields and manually change the anti-aliasing settings to take advantage of the FlashType rendering technology.

Advanced and custom anti-alias features support the following:

- Scaled and rotated text
- All fonts (plain, bold, or italic) up to 255 pt size
- File exporting to most formats (such as JPEG or GIF files)

Advanced and custom anti-alias features do not support the following:

- Flash Player 7 or earlier
- Skewed or flipped text
- Printing
- File exporting to the PNG file format

> **NOTE**
> When text is animated, the player turns off advanced anti-alias to improve the appearance of your text while it's moving. After the animation is complete, anti-alias is turned back on.

A sample file on your hard disk shows how to apply and manipulate anti-aliased text in an application. You use the FlashType rendering technology to create small text that's highly legible. This sample also demonstrates how text fields can scroll quickly and smoothly when you use the `cacheAsBitmap` property.

You can find the sample source file, flashtype.fla, in the Samples folder on your hard disk.

In Windows, browse to *boot drive*\Program Files\Macromedia\Flash 8\Samples and Tutorials\Samples\ActionScript\FlashType.

On the Macintosh, browse to *Macintosh HD*/Applications/Macromedia Flash 8/Samples and Tutorials/Samples/ActionScript/FlashType.

Font rendering options in Flash

Five different font rendering options are available in Flash 8. To select an option, select the text field and open the Property inspector. Select an option from the Font rendering method pop-up menu.

Device Fonts   Produces a smaller SWF file size. The option renders using fonts that are currently installed on the end user's computer.

Bitmap Text (no anti-alias)   Produces sharp text edges, without anti-aliasing. This option produces a larger SWF file size, because font outlines are included in the SWF file.

Anti-Alias for Animation   Produces anti-alias text that animates smoothly. The text also animates faster in some situations, because alignment and anti-alias are not applied while the text animates. You do not see a performance improvement when you use big fonts with lots of letters, or scaled fonts. This option produces a larger SWF file size, because font outlines are included in the SWF file.

Anti-Alias for Readability   The advanced anti-aliasing engine is used for this option. This option offers the highest-quality text, with the most legible text. This option produces the largest SWF file size, because it includes font outlines, and also special anti-aliasing information.

Custom Anti-Alias   The same as Anti-Alias for Readability, but you can visually manipulate the anti-aliasing parameters to produce a specific appearance. This option is useful to produce the best possible appearance for new or uncommon fonts.

For an example of how to use anti-alias with ActionScript, see "Setting anti-alias with ActionScript" on page 417.

About continuous stroke modulation

The FlashType font rendering technology exploits the inherent properties of distance fields to provide continuos stroke modulation (CSM); for example, continuous modulation of both the stroke weight and the edge sharpness of the text. CSM uses two rendering parameters to control the mapping of adaptively sampled distance field (ADF) distances to glyph density values. Optimal values for these parameters are highly subjective; they can depend on user preferences, lighting conditions, display properties, typeface, foreground and background colors, and point size. The function that maps ADF distances to density values has an outside cutoff, below which values are set to 0, and an inside cutoff, above which values are set to a maximum density value, such as 255.

Setting anti-alias with ActionScript

Flash 8 offers two types of anti-aliasing: normal and advanced. Advanced anti-aliasing is available only in Flash Player 8 and later, and can be used only if you embed the font in the library and have the text field's `embedFonts` property set to `true`. For Flash Player 8, the default setting for text fields created using ActionScript is `normal`.

To set values for the `TextField.antiAliasType` property, use the following string values:

normal Applies the regular text anti-aliasing. This matches the type of anti-aliasing that Flash Player used in version 7 and earlier.

advanced Applies advanced anti-aliasing for improved text readability, which is available in Flash Player 8. Advanced anti-aliasing allows font faces to be rendered at very high quality at small sizes. It is best used with applications that have a lot of small text.

> **TIP** Macromedia does not recommend advanced anti-aliasing for fonts larger than 48 points.

To use ActionScript to set anti-alias text, see the following example.

To use advanced anti-aliasing:

1. Create a new Flash document and save it as **antialiastype.fla**.

2. Create two movie clips on the Stage and give them instances names of **normal_mc** and **advanced_mc**.

   You will use these movie clips to toggle between the two types of anti-aliasing: normal and advanced.

3. Open the Library panel and select New Font from the pop-up menu in the upper-right corner of the Library panel.

   The Font Symbol Properties dialog box opens, in which you can select a font to embed in the SWF file (including a font style and font size). You can also assign a font name that appears in the document's library and in the Font drop-down menu in the Property inspector (if you have a text field selected on the Stage).

   a. Select the Arial font from the Font drop-down menu.

   b. Make sure that the Bold and Italic options are not selected.

   c. Set the size to 10 pixels.

   d. Enter the font name of **Arial-10 (embedded)**.

   e. Click OK.

4. In the library, right-click the font symbol and select Linkage from the context menu.

   The Linkage Properties dialog box appears.

5. Select the Export for ActionScript and Export in First Frame options, enter the linkage identifier **Arial-10**, and click OK.

6. Add the following ActionScript to Frame 1 of the main Timeline:

```
var text_fmt:TextFormat = new TextFormat();
text_fmt.font = "Arial-10";
text_fmt.size = 10;

this.createTextField("my_txt", 10, 20, 20, 320, 240);
my_txt.autoSize = "left";
my_txt.embedFonts = true;
my_txt.selectable = false;
my_txt.setNewTextFormat(text_fmt);
my_txt.multiline = true;
my_txt.wordWrap = true;

var lorem_lv:LoadVars = new LoadVars();
lorem_lv.onData = function(src:String) {
  if (src != undefined) {
    my_txt.text = src;
  } else {
    my_txt.text = "unable to load text file.";
  }
};
lorem_lv.load("http://www.helpexamples.com/flash/lorem.txt");

normal_mc.onRelease = function() {
  my_txt.antiAliasType = "normal";
};
advanced_mc.onRelease = function() {
  my_txt.antiAliasType = "advanced";
};
```

The preceding code is separated into four key areas. The first block of code creates a new TextFormat object, which specifies a font and font size to be used for a text field that will be created shortly. The specified font, Arial-10, is the linkage identifier for the font symbol that you embedded in a previous step.

The second block of code creates a new text field with the instance name my_txt. In order for the font to be properly embedded, you must set embedFonts to true for the text field instance. The code also sets the text formatting for the new text field to the TextFormat object that you created earlier.

The third block of code defines a LoadVars instance that populates the text field on the Stage with the contents of an external text file. After the document is fully loaded (but not parsed), the entire contents of the file are copied into the my_txt.text property, so that they are displayed on the Stage.

The fourth, and final, block of code defines onRelease event handlers for both the normal_mc movie clip and the advanced_mc movie clip. When the user clicks and releases either one of these options, the anti-alias type for the text field on the Stage changes.

7. Save your changes to the FLA file.

8. Select Control > Test Movie to test your Flash document.

9. Click the `advanced_mc` movie clip on the Stage.

   Clicking the movie clip switches the anti-alias type from normal (the default) to advanced. When you are dealing with text fields with a smaller font size, setting the anti-aliasing to advanced can dramatically improve the readability of the text.

    TIP Advanced anti-aliasing allows font faces to be rendered at high quality at small sizes. It is best used with applications that have a lot of small text. Macromedia does not recommend advanced anti-aliasing for fonts larger than 48 points.

For information on formatting anti-alias text, see "Using a grid fit type" on page 426 and "About formatting anti-alias text" on page 423.

A sample file on your hard disk shows how to apply and manipulate anti-aliased text in an application. You use the FlashType rendering technology to create small text that's highly legible. This sample also demonstrates how text fields can scroll quickly and smoothly when you use the `cacheAsBitmap` property.

You can find the sample source file, flashtype.fla, in the Samples folder on your hard disk.

In Windows, browse to *boot drive*\Program Files\Macromedia\Flash 8\Samples and Tutorials\Samples\ActionScript\FlashType.

On the Macintosh, browse to *Macintosh HD*/Applications/Macromedia Flash 8/Samples and Tutorials/Samples/ActionScript/FlashType.

Setting tables for fonts

If you create fonts for use in SWF files or for distribution to Flash developers, you may need to set tables for fonts to control how they render on the Stage.

Advanced anti-aliasing uses adaptively sampled distance fields (ADFs) to represent the outlines that determine a glyph (a character). Flash uses two values:

- An outside cutoff value, below which densities are set to 0.
- An inside cutoff value, above which densities are set to a maximum density value, such as 255.

Between these two cutoff values, the mapping function is a linear curve ranging from 0 at the outside cutoff to the maximum density at the inside cutoff.

Adjusting the outside and inside cutoff values affects stroke weight and edge sharpness. The spacing between these two parameters is comparable to twice the filter radius of classic anti-aliasing methods; a narrow spacing provides a sharper edge, while a wider spacing provides a softer, more filtered edge. When the spacing is 0, the resulting density image is a bilevel bitmap. When the spacing is very wide, the resulting density image has a watercolor-like edge.

Typically, users prefer sharp, high contrast edges at small point sizes and softer edges for animated text and larger point sizes.

The outside cutoff typically has a negative value, the inside cutoff has a positive value, and their midpoint lies near 0. Adjusting these parameters to shift the midpoint toward negative infinity increases the stroke weight; shifting the midpoint toward positive infinity decreases the stroke weight.

> **NOTE** The outside cutoff should always be less than or equal to the inside cutoff.

Flash Player includes advanced anti-aliasing settings for ten basic fonts; and for these fonts, advanced anti-aliasing settings are provided only for the font sizes from 6 to 20. For these fonts, all sizes below 6 use the settings for 6, and all sizes above 20 use the settings for 20. Other fonts map to the supplied font data. The `setAdvancedAntialiasingTable()` method lets you set custom anti-aliasing data for other fonts and font sizes, or to override the default settings for the provided fonts. For more information on creating an anti-aliasing table, see the following example:

To create an advanced anti-aliasing table for an embedded font:

1. Create a new Flash document and save it as **advancedaatable.fla**.

2. Select New Font from the Library panel pop-up menu.

3. Select Arial from the Font pop-up menu, and then set the font size to 32 points.

4. Select both the Bold and Italics options.

5. Enter the font name **Arial (embedded)** in the Name text box and click OK.

6. Right-click (Windows) or Control-click (Macintosh) the font symbol in the library, and select Linkage.

7. In the Linkage Properties dialog box:

   a. Type **Arial-embedded** in the Identifier text box.

   b. Select Export for ActionScript and Export in First Frame.

   c. Click OK.

8. Select Frame 1 of the main Timeline, and add the following ActionScript in the
Actions panel:

```
import flash.text.TextRenderer;
var arialTable:Array = new Array();
arialTable.push({fontSize:16.0, insideCutoff:0.516,
  outsideCutoff:0.416});
arialTable.push({fontSize:32.0, insideCutoff:2.8, outsideCutoff:-2.8});
TextRenderer.setAdvancedAntialiasingTable("Arial", "bolditalic", "dark",
  arialTable);

var my_fmt:TextFormat = new TextFormat();
my_fmt.align = "justify";
my_fmt.font = "Arial-embedded";
my_fmt.size = 32;

this.createTextField("my_txt", 999, 10, 10, Stage.width-20,
  Stage.height-20);
my_txt.antiAliasType = "advanced";
my_txt.embedFonts = true;
my_txt.multiline = true;
my_txt.setNewTextFormat(my_fmt);
my_txt.sharpness = 0;
my_txt.thickness = 0;
my_txt.wordWrap = true;

var lorem_lv:LoadVars = new LoadVars();
lorem_lv.onData = function(src:String):Void {
  if (src != undefined) {
    my_txt.text = src + "\n\n" + src;
  } else {
    trace("error downloading text file");
  }
};
lorem_lv.load("http://www.helpexamples.com/flash/lorem.txt");
```

The preceding code is separated into four sections. The first section of code imports the
TextRenderer class and defines a new anti-aliasing table for two different sizes of the Arial
font. The second section of code defines a new TextFormat object, which you use to apply
text formatting to the text field (that you create in the next section of code). The next
section of code creates a new text field with a my_txt instance name, enables advanced
anti-aliasing, applies the text format object (created earlier), and enables multiline text and
word wrapping. The final block of code defines a LoadVars object that you use to load text
from an external text file, and populate the text field on the Stage.

9. Select Control > Test movie to test the Flash document.

   After the text loads from the remote server, Flash displays some text in the text field, and you can see the advanced anti-aliasing table properties applied to your text field. The embedded font on the Stage should appear like it has a slight blur effect because of the current `insideCutoff` and `outsideCutoff` values.

About text layout and formatting

You can control text layout and formatting by using ActionScript. The TextFormat class provides a great deal of control over how the text appears at runtime, in addition to other forms of formatting such as style sheets (see "Formatting text with Cascading Style Sheet styles" on page 430) and HTML text (see "Using HTML-formatted text" on page 445).

You can also control how characters fit on the grid by using ActionScript when you use anti-alias text in a SWF file. This helps you to control the appearance of the characters at runtime. For an example of how to use a grid fit type in your applications, see "Using a grid fit type" on page 426.

For general information on text fields, see "About text fields" on page 391. For information on formatting text, see "About formatting anti-alias text" on page 423. For more information on the TextFormat class, see "Using the TextFormat class" on page 428 and `%{TextFormat}%` in the *ActionScript 2.0 Language Reference* in Flash Help.

For more information on text layout and text formatting using the TextFormat class, see the following sections:

- "About formatting anti-alias text" on page 423
- "Using a grid fit type" on page 426
- "Using the TextFormat class" on page 428
- "Default properties of new text fields" on page 430

About formatting anti-alias text

Flash 8 introduces two new properties that you can use when you format text fields with advanced anti-aliasing enabled: `sharpness` and `thickness`. Sharpness refers to the amount of aliasing that is applied to the text field instance. A high value for sharpness makes the embedded font edge appear jagged and sharp. Setting sharpness to a lower value makes the font appear softer, with more blurring. Setting a font's thickness is similar to enabling bold formatting for a text field. The higher the thickness, the bolder the font appears.

The following example dynamically loads a text file and displays text on the Stage. Moving the mouse pointer along the *x* axis sets the sharpness between -400 and 400. Moving the mouse pointer along the *y* axis sets the thickness between -200 and 200.

To modify a text field's sharpness and thickness:

1. Create a new Flash document and save it as **sharpness.fla**.
2. Select New Font from the pop-up menu in the upper-right corner of the Library panel.
3. Select Arial from the Font drop-down menu and set the font size to 24 points.
4. Enter the font name of **Arial-24 (embedded)** in the Name text box and click OK.
5. Right-click the font symbol in the library and select Linkage to open the Linkage Properties dialog box.
6. Set the linkage identifier to Arial-24, select the Export for ActionScript and Export in First Frame check boxes, and click OK.
7. Add the following code to Frame 1 of the main Timeline:

```
var my_fmt:TextFormat = new TextFormat();
my_fmt.size = 24;
my_fmt.font = "Arial-24";

this.createTextField("lorem_txt", 10, 0, 20, Stage.width, (Stage.height
    - 20));
lorem_txt.setNewTextFormat(my_fmt);
lorem_txt.text = "loading...";
lorem_txt.wordWrap = true;
lorem_txt.autoSize = "left";
lorem_txt.embedFonts = true;
lorem_txt.antiAliasType = "advanced";

this.createTextField("debug_txt", 100, 0, 0, Stage.width, 20);
debug_txt.autoSize = "left";
debug_txt.background = 0xFFFFFF;

var lorem_lv:LoadVars = new LoadVars();
lorem_lv.onData = function(src:String) {
   lorem_txt.text = src;
}
lorem_lv.load("http://www.helpexamples.com/flash/lorem.txt");

var mouseListener:Object = new Object();
mouseListener.onMouseMove = function():Void {
   lorem_txt.sharpness = (_xmouse * (800 / Stage.width)) - 400;
   lorem_txt.thickness = (_ymouse * (400 / Stage.height)) - 200;
   debug_txt.text = "sharpness=" + Math.round(lorem_txt.sharpness) +
      ", thickness=" + Math.round(lorem_txt.thickness);
};
Mouse.addListener(mouseListener);
```

This ActionScript code can be separated into five key sections. The first section of code defines a new TextFormat instance that will be applied to a dynamically created text field. The next two sections create two new text fields on the Stage. The first text field, `lorem_txt`, applies the custom text formatting object created earlier, enables embedded fonts, and sets the `antiAliasType` property to `true`. The second text field, `debug_txt`, displays the current sharpness and thickness values for the `lorem_txt` text field. The fourth section of code creates a LoadVars object, which is responsible for loading the external text file and populating the `lorem_txt` text field. The fifth, and final, section of code defines a mouse listener that is called whenever the mouse pointer moves on the Stage. The current values for `sharpness` and `thickness` are calculated based on the current position of the mouse pointer on the Stage. The `sharpness` and `thickness` properties are set for the `lorem_txt` text field, and the current values are displayed in the `debug_txt` text field.

8. Select Control > Test Movie to test the document.

   Move the mouse pointer along the *x* axis to change the text field's sharpness. Move the mouse pointer from left to right to cause the sharpness to increase and appear more jagged. Move the mouse pointer along the *y* axis to cause the text field's thickness to change.

For more information on using anti-alias text in a SWF file, see "Setting anti-alias with ActionScript" on page 417, "Font rendering options in Flash" on page 416, and "Using a grid fit type" on page 426.

A sample file on your hard disk shows how to apply and manipulate anti-aliased text in an application. You use the FlashType rendering technology to create small text that's highly legible. This sample also demonstrates how text fields can scroll quickly and smoothly when you use the `cacheAsBitmap` property.

You can find the sample source file, flashtype.fla, in the Samples folder on your hard disk.

In Windows, browse to *boot drive*\Program Files\Macromedia\Flash 8\Samples and Tutorials\Samples\ActionScript\FlashType.

On the Macintosh, browse to *Macintosh HD*/Applications/Macromedia Flash 8/Samples and Tutorials/Samples/ActionScript/FlashType.

Using a grid fit type

When you use advanced anti-aliasing on a text field, three types of grid fitting are available:

none   Specifies no grid fitting. Horizontal and vertical lines in the glyphs are not forced to the pixel grid. This setting is usually good for animation and for large font sizes.

pixel   Specifies that strong horizontal and vertical lines are fit to the pixel grid. This setting works only for left-aligned text fields. This setting generally provides the best legibility for left-aligned text.

subpixel   Specifies that strong horizontal and vertical lines are fit to the subpixel grid on an LCD monitor. The subpixel setting is generally good for right-aligned and center-aligned dynamic text, and it is sometimes a useful trade-off for animation versus text quality.

The following example shows how to set a grid fit type on a text field by using ActionScript.

To set a grid fit type on a text field:

1. Create a new Flash document and save it as **gridfittype.fla**.
2. Select New Font from the pop-up menu in the upper-right corner of the Library panel.
3. Select Arial font from the Font drop-down menu and set the font size to 10 points.
4. Type the font name **Arial-10 (embedded)** in the Name text box and click OK.
5. Right-click the font symbol in the library and select Linkage to open the Linkage Properties dialog box.
6. Set the linkage identifier to Arial-10, and then select the Export for ActionScript and Export in First Frame check boxes.
7. Click OK.

8. Add the following code to Frame 1 of the main Timeline:

```
var my_fmt:TextFormat = new TextFormat();
my_fmt.size = 10;
my_fmt.font = "Arial-10";
var h:Number = Math.floor(Stage.height / 3);

this.createTextField("none_txt", 10, 0, 0, Stage.width, h);
none_txt.antiAliasType = "advanced";
none_txt.embedFonts = true;
none_txt.gridFitType = "none";
none_txt.multiline = true;
none_txt.setNewTextFormat(my_fmt);
none_txt.text = "loading...";
none_txt.wordWrap = true;

this.createTextField("pixel_txt", 20, 0, h, Stage.width, h);
pixel_txt.antiAliasType = "advanced";
pixel_txt.embedFonts = true;
pixel_txt.gridFitType = "pixel";
pixel_txt.multiline = true;
pixel_txt.selectable = false;
pixel_txt.setNewTextFormat(my_fmt);
pixel_txt.text = "loading...";
pixel_txt.wordWrap = true;

this.createTextField("subpixel_txt", 30, 0, h*2, Stage.width, h);
subpixel_txt.antiAliasType = "advanced";
subpixel_txt.embedFonts = true;
subpixel_txt.gridFitType = "subpixel";
subpixel_txt.multiline = true;
subpixel_txt.setNewTextFormat(my_fmt);
subpixel_txt.text = "loading...";
subpixel_txt.wordWrap = true;

var lorem_lv:LoadVars = new LoadVars();
lorem_lv.onData = function(src:String):Void {
  if (src != undefined) {
    none_txt.text = "[antiAliasType=none]\n" + src;
    pixel_txt.text = "[antiAliasType=pixel]\n" + src;
    subpixel_txt.text = "[antiAliasType=subpixel]\n" + src;
  } else {
    trace("unable to load text file");
  }
};
lorem_lv.load("http://www.helpexamples.com/flash/lorem.txt");
```

The preceding ActionScript code can be separated into five sections. The first section defines a new text format object that specifies two properties, `size` and `font`. The `font` property refers to the linkage identifier of the font symbol currently in the document library. The second, third, and fourth sections of code each create a new dynamic text field on the Stage and set some common properties: `antiAliasType` (which must be set to `advanced`), `embedFonts` (set to `true`), `multiline`, and `wordWrap`. Each section also applies the text format object created in an earlier section, and sets the grid fit type to `normal`, `pixel`, or `subpixel`. The fifth, and final, section creates a LoadVars instance, which loads the contents of an external text file into each of the text fields that you created with code.

9. Save the document and select Control > Test movie to test the SWF file.

Each text field should be initialized with the value "`loading...`". After the external text file is successfully loaded, each text field displays some formatted sample text using a different grid-fit type.

 The FlashType rendering technology uses grid fitting only at 0º rotation.

Using the TextFormat class

You can use the TextFormat class to set the formatting properties of a text field. The TextFormat class incorporates character and paragraph formatting information. Character formatting information describes the appearance of individual characters: font name, point size, color, and an associated URL. Paragraph formatting information describes the appearance of a paragraph: left margin, right margin, indentation of the first line, and left, right, or center alignment.

To use the TextFormat class, you first create a TextFormat object and set its character and paragraph formatting styles. You then apply the TextFormat object to a text field using the `TextField.setTextFormat()` or `TextField.setNewTextFormat()` method.

The `setTextFormat()` method changes the text format that is applied to individual characters, to groups of characters, or to the entire body of text in a text field. Newly inserted text, however—such as text entered by a user or inserted with ActionScript—does not assume the formatting specified by a `setTextFormat()` call. To specify the default formatting for newly inserted text, use `TextField.setNewTextFormat()`. For more information, see %{setTextFormat (TextField.setTextFormat method)}% and %{setNewTextFormat (TextField.setNewTextFormat method)}% in the *ActionScript 2.0 Language Reference* in Flash Help.

To format a text field with the TextFormat class:

1. In a new Flash document, create a text field on the Stage using the Text tool.

   Type some text in the text field on the Stage, such as **Bold, italic, 24 point text.**

2. In the Property inspector, type **myText_txt** in the Instance Name text box, select Dynamic from the Text Type pop-up menu, and select Multiline from the Line Type pop-up menu.

3. Select Frame 1 on the Timeline and open the Actions panel (Window > Actions).

4. Enter the following code in the Actions panel to create a TextFormat object, set the `bold` and `italic` properties to `true`, and set the `size` property to 24:

   ```
   // Create a TextFormat object.
   var txt_fmt:TextFormat = new TextFormat();
   // Specify paragraph and character formatting.
   txt_fmt.bold = true;
   txt_fmt.italic = true;
   txt_fmt.size = 24;
   ```

5. Apply the TextFormat object to the text field you created in step 1 by using `TextField.setTextFormat()`:

   ```
   myText_txt.setTextFormat(txt_fmt);
   ```

   This version of `setTextFormat()` applies the specified formatting to the entire text field. Two other versions of this method let you apply formatting to individual characters or groups of characters. For example, the following code applies bold, italic, 24-point formatting to the first three characters you entered in the text field:

   ```
   myText_txt.setTextFormat(0, 3, txt_fmt);
   ```

   For more information, see %{setTextFormat (TextField.setTextFormat method)}% in the *ActionScript 2.0 Language Reference* in Flash Help.

6. Select Control > Test Movie to test the application.

For more information on using the TextFormat class, see the following topics:

- "Default properties of new text fields" on page 430
- "Formatting text with Cascading Style Sheet styles" on page 430

Default properties of new text fields

Text fields created at runtime with `createTextField()` receive a default TextFormat object with the following properties:

```
align = "left"
blockIndent = 0
bold = false
bullet = false
color = 0x000000
font = "Times New Roman" (default font is Times on Mac OS X)
indent = 0
italic = false
kerning = false
leading = 0
leftMargin = 0
letterSpacing = 0
rightMargin = 0
size = 12
tabStops = [] (empty array)
target = ""
underline = false
url = ""
```

> **NOTE** The default font property on the Mac OS X is Times.

For a complete list of TextFormat methods and their descriptions, see `%{TextFormat}%` in the *ActionScript 2.0 Language Reference* in Flash Help.

Formatting text with Cascading Style Sheet styles

Cascading Style Sheet (CSS) styles are a way to work with text styles that can be applied to HTML or XML documents. A style sheet is a collection of formatting rules that specify how to format HTML or XML elements. Each rule associates a style name, or *selector*, with one or more style properties and their values. For example, the following style defines a selector named `bodyText`:

```
.bodyText {
  text-align: left
}
```

You can create styles that redefine built-in HTML formatting tags that Flash Player uses (such as `<p>` and `<li>`). You can also create style *classes* that can be applied to specific HTML elements using the `<p>` or `<span>` tag's `class` attribute, or define new tags.

You use the TextField.StyleSheet class to work with text style sheets. Although the TextField class can be used with Flash Player 6, the TextField.StyleSheet class requires that SWF files target Flash Player 7 or later. You can load styles from an external CSS file or create them natively using ActionScript. To apply a style sheet to a text field that contains HTML- or XML-formatted text, you use the `TextField.styleSheet` property. The styles defined in the style sheet are mapped automatically to the tags defined in the HTML or XML document.

Using styles sheets involves the following three basic steps:

- Create a style sheet object from the TextField.StyleSheet class (for more information see %{StyleSheet (TextField.StyleSheet)}% in the *ActionScript 2.0 Language Reference* in Flash Help).

- Add styles to the style sheet object, either by loading them from an external CSS file or by creating new styles with ActionScript.

- Assign the style sheet to a TextField object that contains HTML- or XML-formatted text.

For more information, see the following topics:

- "Supported CSS properties" on page 432
- "Creating a style sheet object" on page 433
- "Loading external CSS files" on page 434
- "Creating new styles with ActionScript" on page 435
- "Applying styles to a TextField object" on page 436
- "Applying a style sheet to a TextArea component" on page 436
- "Combining styles" on page 438
- "Using style classes" on page 438
- "Styling built-in HTML tags" on page 439
- "An example of using styles with HTML" on page 439
- "Using styles to define new tags" on page 442
- "An example of using styles with XML" on page 443

You can find a sample source file, formattedText.fla, in the Samples folder on your hard disk, which shows you how to apply CSS formatting to text that you load into a SWF file at runtime.

In Windows, browse to *boot drive*\Program Files\Macromedia\Flash 8\ Samples and Tutorials\Samples\ActionScript\LoadText.

On the Macintosh, browse to *Macintosh HD*/Applications/Macromedia Flash 8/ Samples and Tutorials/Samples/ActionScript/LoadText.

Supported CSS properties

Flash Player supports a subset of properties in the original CSS1 specification (www.w3.org/TR/REC-CSS1). The following table shows the supported CSS properties and values as well as their corresponding ActionScript property names. (Each ActionScript property name is derived from the corresponding CSS property name; the hyphen is omitted and the subsequent character is capitalized.)

CSS property	ActionScript property	Usage and supported values
text-align	textAlign	Recognized values are `left`, `center`, right, and `justify`.
font-size	fontSize	Only the numeric part of the value is used. Units (px, pt) are not parsed; pixels and points are equivalent.
text-decoration	textDecoration	Recognized values are `none` and `underline`.
margin-left	marginLeft	Only the numeric part of the value is used. Units (px, pt) are not parsed; pixels and points are equivalent.
margin-right	marginRight	Only the numeric part of the value is used. Units (px, pt) are not parsed; pixels and points are equivalent.
font-weight	fontWeight	Recognized values are `normal` and `bold`.
kerning	kerning	Recognized values are `true` and `false`.
font-style	fontStyle	Recognized values are `normal` and `italic`.
letterSpacing	letterSpacing	Only the numeric part of the value is used. Units (px, pt) are not parsed; pixels and points are equivalent.
text-indent	textIndent	Only the numeric part of the value is used. Units (px, pt) are not parsed; pixels and points are equivalent.

CSS property	ActionScript property	Usage and supported values
font-family	fontFamily	A comma-separated list of fonts to use, in descending order of desirability. Any font family name can be used. If you specify a generic font name, it is converted to an appropriate device font. The following font conversions are available: mono is converted to _typewriter, sans-serif is converted to _sans, and serif is converted to _serif.
color	color	Only hexadecimal color values are supported. Named colors (such as blue) are not supported. Colors are written in the following format: #FF0000.

Creating a style sheet object

CSSs are represented in ActionScript by the TextField.StyleSheet class. This class is available only for SWF files that target Flash Player 7 or later. To create a style sheet object, call the constructor function of the TextField.StyleSheet class:

```
var newStyle:TextField.StyleSheet = new TextField.StyleSheet();
```

To add styles to a style sheet object, you can either load an external CSS file into the object or define the styles in ActionScript. See "Loading external CSS files" on page 434 and "Creating new styles with ActionScript" on page 435.

You can find a sample source file, formattedText.fla, in the Samples folder on your hard disk, which shows you how to apply CSS formatting to text that you load into a SWF file at runtime.

In Windows, browse to *boot drive*\Program Files\Macromedia\Flash 8\ Samples and Tutorials\Samples\ActionScript\LoadText.

On the Macintosh, browse to *Macintosh HD*/Applications/Macromedia Flash 8/ Samples and Tutorials/Samples/ActionScript/LoadText.

Loading external CSS files

You can define styles in an external CSS file and then load that file into a style sheet object. The styles defined in the CSS file are added to the style sheet object. To load an external CSS file, you use the load() method of the TextField.StyleSheet class. To determine when the CSS file has finished loading, use the style sheet object's onLoad event handler.

In the following example, you create and load an external CSS file and use the TextField.StyleSheet.getStyleNames() method to retrieve the names of the loaded styles.

To load an external style sheet:

1. In your preferred text or CSS editor, create a new file.

2. Add the following style definitions to the file:

```
.bodyText {
    font-family: Arial,Helvetica,sans-serif;
    font-size: 12px;
}

.headline {
    font-family: Arial,Helvetica,sans-serif;
    font-size: 24px;
}
```

3. Save the CSS file as styles.css.

4. In Flash, create a new FLA file.

5. In the Timeline (Window > Timeline), select Layer 1.

6. Open the Actions panel (Window > Actions).

7. Add the following code to the Actions panel:

```
var styles:TextField.StyleSheet = new TextField.StyleSheet();
styles.onLoad = function(success:Boolean):Void {
    if (success) {
        // display style names.
        trace(this.getStyleNames());
    } else {
        trace("Error loading CSS file.");
    }
};
styles.load("styles.css");
```

> **NOTE**
> In the previous code snippet, this.getStyleNames() refers to the styles object you constructed in the first line of ActionScript.

8. Save the FLA file to the same directory that contains styles.css.

9. Test the Flash document (Control > Test Movie).

   You should see the names of the two styles in the Output panel.

   ```
   .bodyText,.headline
   ```

   If you see "Error loading CSS file." in the Output panel, make sure the FLA file and the CSS file are in the same directory and that you typed the name of the CSS file correctly.

As with all other ActionScript methods that load data over the network, the CSS file must reside in the same domain as the SWF file that is loading the file. (See "Cross-domain and subdomain access between SWF files" on page 710.) For more information on using CSS with Flash, see %{StyleSheet (TextField.StyleSheet)}% in the *ActionScript 2.0 Language Reference* in Flash Help.

You can find a sample source file, formattedText.fla, in the Samples folder on your hard disk, which shows you how to apply CSS formatting to text that you load into a SWF file at runtime.

In Windows, browse to *boot drive*\Program Files\Macromedia\Flash 8\Samples and Tutorials\Samples\ActionScript\LoadText.

On the Macintosh, browse to *Macintosh HD*/Applications/Macromedia Flash 8/Samples and Tutorials/Samples/ActionScript/LoadText.

Creating new styles with ActionScript

You can create new text styles with ActionScript by using the setStyle() method of the TextField.StyleSheet class. This method takes two parameters: the name of the style and an object that defines that style's properties.

For example, the following code creates a style sheet object named styles that defines two styles that are identical to the ones you already imported (see "Loading external CSS files" on page 434):

```
var styles:TextField.StyleSheet = new TextField.StyleSheet();
styles.setStyle("bodyText",
  {fontFamily: 'Arial,Helvetica,sans-serif',
   fontSize: '12px'}
);
styles.setStyle("headline",
  {fontFamily: 'Arial,Helvetica,sans-serif',
   fontSize: '24px'}
);
```

Applying styles to a TextField object

To apply a style sheet object to a TextField object, you assign the style sheet object to the text field's `styleSheet` property.

```
textObj_txt.styleSheet = styles;
```

When you assign a style sheet object to a TextField object, the following changes occur to the text field's normal behavior:

- The text field's `text` and `htmlText` properties, and any variable associated with the text field, always contain the same value and behave identically.
- The text field becomes read-only and cannot be edited by the user.
- The `setTextFormat()` and `replaceSel()` methods of the TextField class no longer function with the text field. The only way to change the field is by altering the text field's `text` or `htmlText` property or by changing the text field's associated variable.
- Any text assigned to the text field's `text` property, `htmlText` property, or associated variable is stored verbatim; anything written to one of these properties can be retrieved in the text's original form.

Applying a style sheet to a TextArea component

To apply a style sheet to a TextArea component, you create a style sheet object and assign it HTML styles using the TextField.StyleSheet class. You then assign the style sheet to the TextArea component's `styleSheet` property.

The following examples create a style sheet object, `styles`, and assign it to the `myTextArea` component instance.

Using a style sheet with a TextArea component:

1. Create a new Flash document and save it as **textareastyle.fla**.
2. Drag a TextArea component from the User Interface folder of the Components panel to the Stage and give it an instance name of **myTextArea**.

3. Add the following ActionScript to Frame 1 of the main Timeline:

```
// Create a new style sheet object and set styles for it.
var styles:TextField.StyleSheet = new TextField.StyleSheet();
styles.setStyle("html", {fontFamily:'Arial,Helvetica,sans-serif',
          fontSize:'12px',
          color:'#0000FF'});
styles.setStyle("body", {color:'#00CCFF',
          textDecoration:'underline'});
styles.setStyle("h1",{fontFamily:'Arial,Helvetica,sans-serif',
          fontSize:'24px',
          color:'#006600'});

/* Assign the style sheet object to myTextArea component. Set html
   property to true, set styleSheet property to the style sheet object.
   */
myTextArea.styleSheet = styles;
myTextArea.html = true;

var myVars:LoadVars = new LoadVars();
// Define onData handler and load text to be displayed.
myVars.onData = function(myStr:String):Void {
   if (myStr != undefined) {
     myTextArea.text = myStr;
   } else {
     trace("Unable to load text file.");
   }
};
myVars.load("http://www.helpexamples.com/flash/myText.htm");
```

The preceding block of code creates a new TextField.StyleSheet instance that defines three styles: for the html, body, and h1 HTML tags. Next, the style sheet object is applied to the TextArea component and HTML formatting is enabled. The remaining ActionScript defines a LoadVars object that loads an external HTML file and populates the text area with the loaded text.

4. Select Control > Test Movie to test the Flash document.

Combining styles

CSS styles in Flash Player are additive; that is, when styles are nested, each level of nesting can contribute style information, which is added together to result in the final formatting.

The following example shows some XML data assigned to a text field:

```
<sectionHeading>This is a section</sectionHeading>
<mainBody>This is some main body text, with one
<emphasized>emphatic</emphasized> word.</mainBody>
```

For the word *emphatic* in the above text, the emphasized style is nested within the mainBody style. The mainBody style contributes color, font-size, and decoration rules. The emphasized style adds a font-weight rule to these rules. The word *emphatic* will be formatted using a combination of the rules specified by mainBody and emphasized.

Using style classes

You can create style "classes" (not true ActionScript 2.0 classes) that you can apply to a <p> or <span> tag using either tag's class attribute. When applied to a <p> tag, the style affects the entire paragraph. You can also style a span of text that uses a style class using the <span> tag.

For example, the following style sheet defines two style classes: mainBody and emphasis:

```
.mainBody {
  font-family: Arial,Helvetica,sans-serif;
  font-size: 24px;
}
.emphasis {
  color: #666666;
  font-style: italic;
}
```

Within HTML text you assign to a text field, you can apply these styles to <p> and <span> tags, as shown in the following snippet:

```
<p class='mainBody'>This is <span class='emphasis'>really exciting!</
  span></p>
```

Styling built-in HTML tags

Flash Player supports a subset of HTML tags. (For more information, see "Using HTML-formatted text" on page 445.) You can assign a CSS style to every instance of a built-in HTML tag that appears in a text field. For example, the following code defines a style for the built-in `<p>` HTML tag. All instances of that tag are styled in the manner specified by the style rule.

```
p {
  font-family: Arial,Helvetica,sans-serif;
  font-size: 12px;
  display: inline;
}
```

The following table shows which built-in HTML tags can be styled and how each style is applied:

Style name	How the style is applied
p	Affects all `<p>` tags.
body	Affects all `<body>` tags. The p style, if specified, takes precedence over the body style.
li	Affects all `<li>` bullet tags.
a	Affects all `<a>` anchor tags.
a:link	Affects all `<a>` anchor tags. This style is applied after any a style.
a:hover	Applied to an `<a>` anchor tag when the mouse pointer is over the link. This style is applied after any a and a:link style. After the mouse pointer moves off the link, the a:hover style is removed from the link.
a:active	Applied to an `<a>` anchor tag when the user clicks the link. This style is applied after any a and a:link style. After the mouse button is released, the a:active style is removed from the link.

An example of using styles with HTML

This section presents an example of using styles with HTML tags. You can create a style sheet that styles some built-in tags and defines some style classes. Then, you can apply that style sheet to a TextField object that contains HTML-formatted text.

To format HTML with a style sheet:

1. Create a new file in your preferred text or CSS editor.

2. Add the following style sheet definition to the file:

```
p {
   color: #000000;
   font-family: Arial,Helvetica,sans-serif;
   font-size: 12px;
   display: inline;
}

a:link {
   color: #FF0000;
}

a:hover{
   text-decoration: underline;
}

.headline {
   color: #000000;
   font-family: Arial,Helvetica,sans-serif;
   font-size: 18px;
   font-weight: bold;
   display: block;
}

.byline {
   color: #666600;
   font-style: italic;
   font-weight: bold;
   display: inline;
}
```

This style sheet defines styles for two built-in HTML tags (`<p>` and `<a>`) that will be applied to all instances of those tags. It also defines two style classes (`.headline` and `.byline`) that will be applied to specific paragraphs and text spans.

3. Save the file as **html_styles.css**.

4. Create a new text file in a text or HTML editor, and save the document as **myText.htm**.

   Add the following text to the file:

```
<p class='headline'>Flash adds FlashType rendering technology!</
p><p><span class='byline'>San Francisco, CA</span>--Macromedia Inc.
announced today a new version of Flash that features a brand new font
rendering technology called FlashType. Most excellent at rendering
small text with incredible clarity and consistency across platforms.
For more information, visit the <a href='http://
www.macromedia.com'>Macromedia Flash web site.</a></p>
```

> **NOTE** If you copy and paste this text string, make sure that you remove any line breaks that might have been added to the text string.

5. Create a new Flash document in the Flash authoring tool.

6. Select the first frame in Layer 1 in the Timeline (Window > Timeline).

7. Open the Actions panel (Window > Actions), and add the following code to the Actions panel:

```
this.createTextField("news_txt", 99, 50, 50, 450, 300);
news_txt.border = true;
news_txt.html = true;
news_txt.multiline = true;
news_txt.wordWrap = true;
// Create a new style sheet and LoadVars object.
var myVars_lv:LoadVars = new LoadVars();
var styles:TextField.StyleSheet = new TextField.StyleSheet();
// Location of CSS and text files to load.
var txt_url:String = "myText.htm";
var css_url:String = "html_styles.css";
// Define onData handler and load text to display.
myVars_lv.onData = function(src:String):Void {
  if (src != undefined) {
    news_txt.htmlText = src;
  } else {
    trace("Unable to load HTML file");
  }
};
myVars_lv.load(txt_url);

// Define onLoad handler and Load CSS file.
styles.onLoad = function(success:Boolean):Void {
  if (success) {
    /* If the style sheet loaded without error,
       then assign it to the text object,
       and assign the HTML text to the text field. */
    news_txt.styleSheet = styles;
    news_txt.text = storyText;
```

```
      } else {
        trace("Unable to load CSS file.");
      }
    };
    styles.load(css_url);
```

> **NOTE** In this ActionScript, you are loading the text from an external file. For information on loading external data, see Chapter 15, "Working with Images, Sound, and Video."

8. Save the file as **news_html.fla** in the same directory that contains the CSS file you created in step 3.

9. Select Control > Test Movie to see the styles applied to the HTML text automatically.

Using styles to define new tags

If you define a new style in a style sheet, that style can be used as a tag, in the same way as you would use a built-in HTML tag. For example, if a style sheet defines a CSS style named `sectionHeading`, you can use `<sectionHeading>` as an element in any text field associated with the style sheet. This feature lets you assign arbitrary XML-formatted text directly to a text field, so that the text is automatically formatted using the rules in the style sheet.

For example, the following style sheet creates the new styles `sectionHeading`, `mainBody`, and `emphasized`:

```
.sectionHeading {
  font-family: Verdana, Arial, Helvetica, sans-serif;
  font-size: 18px;
  display: block
}
.mainBody {
  color: #000099;
  text-decoration: underline;
  font-size: 12px;
  display: block
}
.emphasized {
  font-weight: bold;
  display: inline
}
```

You could then populate a text field associated with that style sheet with the following XML-formatted text:

```
<sectionHeading>This is a section</sectionHeading>
<mainBody>This is some main body text,
with one <emphasized>emphatic</emphasized> word.
</mainBody>
```

An example of using styles with XML

In this section, you create a FLA file that has XML-formatted text. You'll create a style sheet using ActionScript, rather than importing styles from a CSS file as shown in "An example of using styles with HTML" on page 439

To format XML with a style sheet:

1. In Flash, create a FLA file.

2. Using the Text tool, create a text field approximately 400 pixels wide and 300 pixels high.

3. Open the Property inspector (Window > Properties > Properties), and select the text field.

4. In the Property inspector, select Dynamic Text from the Text Type menu, select Multiline from the Line Type menu, select the Render Text as HTML option, and type **news_txt** in the Instance Name text box.

5. On Layer 1 in the Timeline (Window > Timeline), select the first frame.

6. To create the style sheet object, open the Actions panel (Window > Actions), and add the following code to the Actions panel:

```
var styles:TextField.StyleSheet = new TextField.StyleSheet();
styles.setStyle("mainBody", {
    color:'#000000',
    fontFamily:'Arial,Helvetica,sans-serif',
    fontSize:'12',
    display:'block'
});
styles.setStyle("title", {
    color:'#000000',
    fontFamily:'Arial,Helvetica,sans-serif',
    fontSize:'18',
    display:'block',
    fontWeight:'bold'
});
styles.setStyle("byline", {
    color:'#666600',
    fontWeight:'bold',
    fontStyle:'italic',
    display:'inline'
});
styles.setStyle("a:link", {
    color:'#FF0000'
});
styles.setStyle("a:hover", {
    textDecoration:'underline'
});
```

This code creates a new style sheet object named `styles` that defines styles by using the `setStyle()` method. The styles exactly match the ones you created in an external CSS file earlier in this chapter.

7. To create the XML text to assign to the text field, open a text editor and enter the following text into a new document:

```
<story><title>Flash now has FlashType</title><mainBody><byline>San
    Francisco, CA</byline>--Macromedia Inc. announced today a new version
    of Flash that features the new FlashType rendering technology. For
    more information, visit the <a href="http://
    www.macromedia.com">Macromedia Flash website</a></mainBody></story>
```

> **NOTE**
> If you copy and paste this text string, make sure that you remove any line breaks that might have been added to the text string. Select Hidden Characters from the pop-up menu in the Actions panel to see and remove any extra line breaks.

8. Save the text file as **story.xml**.

9. In Flash, add the following code in the Actions panel, following the code in step 6.

   This code loads the story.xml document, assigns the style sheet object to the text field's `styleSheet` property, and assigns the XML text to the text field:

```
var my_xml:XML = new XML();
my_xml.ignoreWhite = true;
my_xml.onLoad = function(success:Boolean):Void {
   if (success) {
      news_txt.styleSheet = styles;
      news_txt.text = my_xml;
   } else {
      trace("Error loading XML.");
   }
};
my_xml.load("story.xml");
```

> **NOTE**
> You are loading XML data from an external file in this ActionScript. For information on loading external data, see Chapter 15, "Working with Images, Sound, and Video."

10. Save the file as **news_xml.fla** in the same folder as story.xml.

11. Run the SWF file (Control > Test Movie) to see the styles automatically applied to the text in the text field.

Using HTML-formatted text

Flash Player supports a subset of standard HTML tags such as `<p>` and `<li>` that you can use to style text in any dynamic or input text field. Text fields in Flash Player 7 and later also support the `<img>` tag, which lets you embed image files (JPEG, GIF, PNG), SWF files, and movie clips in a text field. Flash Player automatically wraps text around images embedded in text fields in much the same way that a web browser wraps text around embedded images in an HTML page. For more information, see "About embedding images, SWF files, and movie clips in text fields" on page 454.

Flash Player also supports the `<textformat>` tag, which lets you apply paragraph formatting styles of the TextFormat class to HTML-enabled text fields. For more information, see "Using the TextFormat class" on page 428.

For more information on HTML-formatted text, see the following topics:

- "Required properties and syntax for using HTML-formatted text" on page 445
- "About supported HTML tags" on page 446
- "About supported HTML entities" on page 453
- "About embedding images, SWF files, and movie clips in text fields" on page 454

Required properties and syntax for using HTML-formatted text

To use HTML in a text field, you must set several properties of the text field, either in the Property inspector or by using ActionScript:

- Enable the text field's HTML formatting by selecting the Render Text as HTML option in the Property inspector or by setting the text field's `html` property to `true`.
- To use HTML tags such as `<p>`, `<br>`, and `<img>`, you must make the text field a multiline text field by selecting the Multiline option in the Property inspector or by setting the text field's `multiline` property to `true`.
- In ActionScript, set the value of `TextField.htmlText` to the HTML-formatted text string you want to display.

For example, the following code enables HTML formatting for a text field named `headline_txt` and then assigns some HTML to the text field:

```
this.createTextField("headline_txt", 1, 10, 10, 500, 300);
headline_txt.html = true;
headline_txt.wordWrap = true;
headline_txt.multiline = true;
headline_txt.htmlText = "<font face='Times New Roman' size='25'>This is how
  you assign HTML text to a text field.</font><br>It's very useful.</br>";
```

To render HTML correctly, you must use the correct syntax. Attributes of HTML tags must be enclosed in double (") or single (') quotation marks. Attribute values without quotation marks can produce unexpected results, such as improper rendering of text. For example, the following HTML snippet *cannot* be rendered properly by Flash Player because the value assigned to the `align` attribute (`left`) is not enclosed in quotation marks:

```
this.createTextField("myField_txt", 10, 10, 10, 400, 200);
myField_txt.html = true;
myField_txt.htmlText = "<p align=left>This is left-aligned text</p>";
```

If you enclose attribute values in double quotation marks, you must *escape* the quotation marks (\"). Either of the following ways of doing this is acceptable:

```
myField_txt.htmlText = "<p align='left'>This uses single quotes</p>";
myField_txt.htmlText = "<p align=\"left\">This uses escaped double quotes</
    p>";
myField_txt.htmlText = '<p align="left">This uses outer single quotes</p>';
myField_txt.htmlText = '<p align=\'left\'>This uses escaped single quotes</
    p>';
```

It's not necessary to escape double quotation marks if you're loading text from an external file; it's necessary only if you're assigning a string of text in ActionScript.

About supported HTML tags

This section lists the built-in HTML tags that Flash Player supports. You can also create new styles and tags by using CSS; see "Formatting text with Cascading Style Sheet styles" on page 430.

For more information on supported HTML tags, see the following topics:

- "Anchor tag" on page 447
- "Bold tag" on page 447
- "Break tag" on page 447
- "Font tag" on page 448
- "Image tag" on page 448
- "Italic tag" on page 449
- "List item tag" on page 450
- "Paragraph tag" on page 450
- "Span tag" on page 451
- "Text format tag" on page 451
- "Underline tag" on page 452

Anchor tag

The `<a>` tag creates a hypertext link and supports the following attributes:

- `href`   A string of up to 128 characters that specifies the URL of the page to load in the browser. The URL can be either absolute or relative to the location of the SWF file that is loading the page. An example of an absolute reference to a URL is http://www.macromedia.com; an example of a relative reference is `/index.html`.

- `target`   Specifies the name of the target window where you load the page. Options include `_self`, `_blank`, `_parent`, and `_top`. The `_self` option specifies the current frame in the current window, `_blank` specifies a new window, `_parent` specifies the parent of the current frame, and `_top` specifies the top-level frame in the current window.

For example, the following HTML code creates the link "Go home," which opens www.macromedia.com in a new browser window:

```
urlText_txt.htmlText = "<a href='http://www.macromedia.com'
  target='_blank'>Go home</a>";
```

You can use the special `asfunction` protocol to cause the link to execute an ActionScript function in a SWF file instead of opening a URL. For more information on the `asfunction` protocol, see %{asfunction protocol}% in the *ActionScript 2.0 Language Reference* in Flash Help.

You can also define `a:link`, `a:hover`, and `a:active` styles for anchor tags by using style sheets. See "Styling built-in HTML tags" on page 439.

 NOTE   Absolute URLs must be prefixed with `http://`; otherwise, Flash treats them as relative URLs.

Bold tag

The `<b>` tag renders text as bold, as shown in the following example:

```
text3_txt.htmlText = "He was <b>ready</b> to leave!";
```

A bold typeface must be available for the font used to display the text.

Break tag

The `<br>` tag creates a line break in the text field. You must set the text field to be a multiline text field to use this tag.

In the following example, the line breaks between sentences:

```
this.createTextField("text1_txt", 1, 10, 10, 200, 100);
text1_txt.html = true;
text1_txt.multiline = true;
text1_txt.htmlText = "The boy put on his coat.<br />His coat was <font
  color='#FF0033'>red</font> plaid.";
```

Font tag

The `<font>` tag specifies a font or list of fonts to display the text.

The font tag supports the following attributes:

- `color`   Only hexadecimal color (#FFFFFF) values are supported. For example, the following HTML code creates red text:

  ```
  myText_txt.htmlText = "<font color='#FF0000'>This is red text</font>";
  ```

- `face`   Specifies the name of the font to use. As shown in the following example, you can specify a list of comma-delimited font names, in which case Flash Player selects the first available font:

  ```
  myText_txt.htmlText = "<font face='Times, Times New Roman'>Displays as
      either Times or Times New Roman...</font>";
  ```

  If the specified font is not installed on the user's computer system or isn't embedded in the SWF file, Flash Player selects a substitute font.

  For more information on embedding fonts in Flash applications, see %{embedFonts (TextField.embedFonts property)}% in the *ActionScript 2.0 Language Reference* in Flash Help and "Setting dynamic and input text options" in Flash Help.

- `size`   Specifies the size of the font, in pixels, as shown in the following example:

  ```
  myText_txt.htmlText = "<font size='24' color='#0000FF'>This is blue, 24-
      point text</font>";
  ```

  You can also use relative point sizes instead of a pixel size, such as +2 or -4.

Image tag

The `<img>` tag lets you embed external image files (JPEG, GIF, PNG), SWF files, and movie clips inside text fields and TextArea component instances. Text automatically flows around images you embed in text fields or components. To use this tag, you must set your dynamic or input text field to be multiline and to wrap text.

To create a multiline text field with word wrapping, do one of the following:

- In the Flash authoring environment, select a text field on the Stage and then, in the Property inspector, select Multiline from the Text Type menu.

- For a text field created at runtime with %{createTextField (MovieClip.createTextField method)}%, set the new text field instance's %{multiline (TextField.multiline property)}% and %{multiline (TextField.multiline property)}% properties to true.

The `<img>` tag has one required attribute, src, which specifies the path to an image file, a SWF file, or the linkage identifier of a movie clip symbol in the library. All other attributes are optional.

The `<img>` tag supports the following attributes:

- src   Specifies the URL to an image or SWF file, or the linkage identifier for a movie clip symbol in the library. This attribute is required; all other attributes are optional. External files (JPEG, GIF, PNG, and SWF files) do not show until they are downloaded completely.

- id   Specifies the name for the movie clip instance (created by Flash Player) that contains the embedded image file, SWF file, or movie clip. This is useful if you want to control the embedded content with ActionScript.

- width   The width of the image, SWF file, or movie clip being inserted, in pixels.

- height   The height of the image, SWF file, or movie clip being inserted, in pixels.

- align   Specifies the horizontal alignment of the embedded image within the text field. Valid values are left and right. The default value is left.

- hspace   Specifies the amount of horizontal space that surrounds the image where no text appears. The default value is 8.

- vspace   Specifies the amount of vertical space that surrounds the image where no text appears. The default value is 8.

For more information and examples of using the `<img>` tag, see "About embedding images, SWF files, and movie clips in text fields" on page 454.

Italic tag

The `<i>` tag displays the tagged text in italics, as shown in the following code:

```
That is very <i>interesting</i>.
```

This code example would render as follows:

That is very *interesting*.

An italic typeface must be available for the font used.

List item tag

The `<li>` tag places a bullet in front of the text that it encloses, as shown in the following code:

```
Grocery list:
<li>Apples</li>
<li>Oranges</li>
<li>Lemons</li>
```

This code example would render as follows:

Grocery list:

- Apples
- Oranges
- Lemons

> Ordered and unordered lists (`<ol>` and `<ul>` tags) are not recognized by Flash Player, so they do not modify how your list is rendered. All list items use bullets.

Paragraph tag

The `<p>` tag creates a new paragraph. You must set the text field to be a multiline text field to use this tag.

The `<p>` tag supports the following attributes:

- `align`   Specifies alignment of text within the paragraph; valid values are `left`, `right`, `justify`, and `center`.
- `class`   Specifies a CSS style class defined by a TextField.StyleSheet object. (For more information, see "Using style classes" on page 438.)

  The following example uses the `align` attribute to align text on the right side of a text field.

  ```
  this.createTextField("myText_txt", 1, 10, 10, 400, 100);
  myText_txt.html = true;
  myText_txt.multiline = true;
  myText_txt.htmlText = "<p align='right'>This text is aligned on the
    right side of the text field</p>";
  ```

  The following example uses the `class` attribute to assign a text style class to a `<p>` tag:

  ```
  var myStyleSheet:TextField.StyleSheet = new TextField.StyleSheet();
  myStyleSheet.setStyle(".blue", {color:'#99CCFF', fontSize:18});
  this.createTextField("test_txt", 10, 0, 0, 300, 100);
  test_txt.html = true;
  test_txt.styleSheet = myStyleSheet;
  test_txt.htmlText = "<p class='blue'>This is some body-styled text.</
    p>.";
  ```

Span tag

The `<span>` tag is available only for use with CSS text styles. (For more information, see "Formatting text with Cascading Style Sheet styles" on page 430.) It supports the following attribute:

- `class`   Specifies a CSS style class defined by a TextField.StyleSheet object. For more information on creating text style classes, see "Using style classes" on page 438.

Text format tag

The `<textformat>` tag lets you use a subset of paragraph formatting properties of the TextFormat class within HTML text fields, including line leading, indentation, margins, and tab stops. You can combine `<textformat>` tags with the built-in HTML tags.

The `<textformat>` tag has the following attributes:

- `blockindent`   Specifies the block indentation in points; corresponds to `TextFormat.blockIndent`. (See %{blockIndent (TextFormat.blockIndent property)}% in the *ActionScript 2.0 Language Reference* in Flash Help.)

- `indent`   Specifies the indentation from the left margin to the first character in the paragraph; corresponds to `TextFormat.indent`. Lets you use negative integers. (See %{indent (TextFormat.indent property)}% in the *ActionScript 2.0 Language Reference* in Flash Help.)

- `leading`   Specifies the amount of leading (vertical space) between lines; corresponds to `TextFormat.leading`. Lets you use negative integers. (See %{leading (TextFormat.leading property)}% in the *ActionScript 2.0 Language Reference* in Flash Help.)

- `leftmargin`   Specifies the left margin of the paragraph, in points; corresponds to `TextFormat.leftMargin`. (See %{leftMargin (TextFormat.leftMargin property)}% in the *ActionScript 2.0 Language Reference* in Flash Help.)

- `rightmargin`   Specifies the right margin of the paragraph, in points; corresponds to `TextFormat.rightMargin`. (See %{rightMargin (TextFormat.rightMargin property)}% in the *ActionScript 2.0 Language Reference* in Flash Help.)

- `tabstops`   Specifies custom tab stops as an array of non-negative integers; corresponds to `TextFormat.tabStops`. (See %{tabStops (TextFormat.tabStops property)}% in the *ActionScript 2.0 Language Reference* in Flash Help.)

The following table of data with boldfaced row headers is the result of the code example in the procedure that follows:

Name	Age	Occupation
Rick	33	Detective
AJ	34	Detective

To create a formatted table of data using tab stops:

1. Create a new Flash document, and save it as **tabstops.fla**.

2. In the Timeline, select the first frame on Layer 1.

3. Open the Actions panel (Window > Actions), and enter the following code in the Actions panel:

```
// Create a new text field.
this.createTextField("table_txt", 99, 50, 50, 450, 100);
table_txt.multiline = true;
table_txt.html = true;
// Creates column headers, formatted in bold, separated by tabs.
var rowHeaders:String = "<b>Name\tAge\tOccupation</b>";

// Creates rows with data.
var row_1:String = "Rick\t33\tDetective";
var row_2:String = "AJ\t34\tDetective";

// Sets two tabstops, at 50 and 100 points.
table_txt.htmlText = "<textformat tabstops='[50,100]'>";
table_txt.htmlText += rowHeaders;
table_txt.htmlText += row_1;
table_txt.htmlText += row_2 ;
table_txt.htmlText += "</textformat>";
```

The use of the tab character escape sequence (\t) adds tabs between each column in the table. You append text using the += operator.

4. Select Control > Test Movie to view the formatted table.

Underline tag

The <u> tag underlines the tagged text, as shown in the following code:

```
This is <u>underlined</u> text.
```

This code would render as follows:

This is <u>underlined</u> text.

About supported HTML entities

HTML entities help you display certain characters in HTML formatted text fields, so that they are not interpreted as HTML. For example, you use less-than (<) and greater-than (>) characters to enclose HTML tags, such as <img> and <span>. To display less-than or greater-than characters in HTML formatted text fields in Flash, you need to substitute HTML entities for those characters. The following ActionScript creates an HTML formatted text field on the Stage and uses HTML entities to display the string "<b>" without having the text appear in bold:

```
this.createTextField("my_txt", 10, 100, 100, 100, 19);
my_txt.autoSize = "left";
my_txt.html = true;
my_txt.htmlText = "The &lt;b&gt; tag makes text appear <b>bold</b>.";
```

At runtime, the previous code example in Flash displays the following text on the Stage:

The <b> tag makes text appear **bold**.

In addition to the greater-than and less-than symbols, Flash also recognizes other HTML entities that are listed in the following table.

Entity	Description
&lt;	< (less than)
&gt;	> (greater than)
&amp;	& (ampersand)
&quot;	" (double quotes)
&apos;	' (apostrophe, single quote)

Flash also supports explicit character codes, such as ' (ampersand - ASCII) and & (ampersand - Unicode).

The following ActionScript demonstrates how you can use ASCII or Unicode character codes to embed a tilde (~) character:

```
this.createTextField("my_txt", 10, 100, 100, 100, 19);
my_txt.autoSize = "left";
my_txt.html = true;
my_txt.htmlText = "&#126;"; // tilde (ASCII)
my_txt.htmlText += "\t"
my_txt.htmlText += "&#x007E;"; // tilde (Unicode)
```

About embedding images, SWF files, and movie clips in text fields

In Flash Player 7 and later, you can use the `<img>` tag to embed image files (JPEG, GIF, PNG), SWF files, and movie clips inside dynamic and input text fields, and TextArea component instances. (For a full list of attributes for the `<img>` tag, see "Image tag" on page 448.)

Flash displays media embedded in a text field at full size. To specify the dimensions of the media you are embedding, use the `<img>` tag's `height` and `width` attributes. (See "About specifying height and width values" on page 456.)

In general, an image embedded in a text field appears on the line following the `<img>` tag. However, when the `<img>` tag is the first character in the text field, the image appears on the first line of the text field.

Embedding SWF and image files

To embed an image or SWF file in a text field, specify the absolute or relative path to the image (GIF, JPEG, or PNG) or SWF file in the `<img>` tag's `src` attribute. For example, the following example inserts a GIF file that's located in the same directory as the SWF file (a relative address, on or offline).

Embedding an image in a text field:

1. Create a new Flash document, and save it as **embedding.fla**.

2. Add the following ActionScript to Frame 1 of the main Timeline:

```
this.createTextField("image1_txt", 10, 50, 50, 450, 150);
image1_txt.html = true;
image1_txt.htmlText = "<p>Here's a picture from my vacation:<img
  src='beach.gif'>";
```

The preceding code creates a new dynamic text field on the Stage, enables HTML formatting, and adds some text and a local image to the text field.

3. Add the following ActionScript below the code added in the previous step:

```
this.createTextField("image2_txt", 20, 50, 200, 400, 150);
image2_txt.html = true;
image2_txt.htmlText = "<p>Here's a picture from my garden:<img
  src='http://www.helpexamples.com/flash/images/image2.jpg'>";
```

You can also insert an image by using an absolute address. The preceding code inserts a JPEG file that's located in a directory that's on a server. The SWF file that contains this code might be on your hard disk or on a server.

4. Save the document and select Control > Test Movie to test the document.

The upper text field should have a sentence of text and most likely an error message in the Output panel saying that Flash was unable to locate a file named beach.gif in the current directory. The lower text field should have a sentence of text and an image of a flower that was loaded from the remote server.

Copy a GIF image to the same directory as the FLA and rename the image to beach.gif and select Control > Test Movie to retest the Flash document.

> **NOTE**
> When using absolute URLs, you must make sure that your URL is prefixed with `http://`.

Embedding movie clip symbols

To embed a movie clip symbol in a text field, you specify the symbol's linkage identifier for the <img> tag's src attribute. (For information on defining a linkage identifier, see "Attaching a movie clip symbol to the Stage" on page 368.)

For example, the following code inserts a movie clip symbol with the linkage identifier symbol_ID into a dynamic text field with the instance name textField_txt.

To embed a movie clip into a text field:

1. Create a new Flash document and save it as **embeddedmc.fla**.

2. Draw a new shape on the Stage, or select File > Import > Import to Stage and select an image that is roughly 100 pixels wide by 100 pixels high.

3. Convert the shape or image imported in the previous step by selecting it on the Stage and pressing F8 to open the Convert to Symbol dialog box.

4. Set the behavior to Movie Clip and enter a descriptive symbol name. Select the upper-left square of the registration point grid, and click Advanced to switch to advanced mode if you haven't already done so.

5. Select the Export of ActionScript and Export in First Frame check boxes.

6. Enter the linkage identifier **img_id** in the Identifier text box and then click OK.

7. Add the following ActionScript to Frame 1 of the main Timeline:
```
this.createTextField("textField_txt", 10, 0, 0, 300, 200);
textField_txt.html = true;
textField_txt.htmlText = "<p>Here's a movie clip symbol:<img
  src='img_id'>";
```

For an embedded movie clip to be displayed properly and completely, the registration point for its symbol should be at point (0,0).

8. Save your changes to the Flash document.

9. Select Control > Test Movie to test the Flash document.

About specifying height and width values

If you specify `width` and `height` attributes for an `<img>` tag, space is reserved in the text field for the image file, SWF file, or movie clip. After an image or SWF file is downloaded completely, it appears in the reserved space. Flash scales the media up or down, according to the values you specify for `height` and `width`. You must enter values for both the `height` and `width` attributes to scale the image.

If you don't specify values for `height` and `width`, no space is reserved for the embedded media. After an image or SWF file has downloaded completely, Flash inserts it into the text field at full size and rebreaks text around it.

 NOTE If you are dynamically loading your images into a text field containing text, it is good practice to specify the width and height of the original image so the text properly wraps around the space you reserve for your image.

Controlling embedded media with ActionScript

Flash creates a new movie clip for each `<img>` tag and embeds that movie clip within the TextField object. The `<img>` tag's `id` attribute lets you assign an instance name to the movie clip that is created. This lets you control that movie clip with ActionScript.

The movie clip that Flash creates is added as a child movie clip to the text field that contains the image.

For example, the following example embeds a SWF file in a text field.

To embed a SWF file in a text field:

1. Create a new Flash document.
2. Resize the document's Stage size to 100 pixels by 100 pixels.
3. Use the Rectangle tool to draw a red square on the Stage.
4. Resize the square to 80 pixels by 80 pixels by using the Property inspector, and then move the shape to the center of the Stage.
5. Select Frame 20 on the Timeline and then press F7 (Windows or Macintosh) to insert a new blank keyframe.
6. Use the Oval tool to draw a blue circle on the Stage on Frame 20.
7. Resize the circle to 80 pixels by 80 pixels by using the Property inspector, and then move it to the center of the Stage.
8. Click a blank frame between Frame 1 and 20, and set the tween type to Shape in the Property inspector.
9. Save the current document as **animation.fla**.

10. Select Control > Test Movie to preview the animation.

The SWF file is created in the same directory as the FLA. For this exercise to work correctly, you need the SWF file to generate so that you can load it into a separate FLA file.

11. Create a new FLA file and save it as **animationholder.fla**.

Save the file in the same folder as the animation.fla file you created previously.

12. Add the following ActionScript code to Frame 1 of the main Timeline:

```
this.createTextField("textField_txt", 10, 0, 0, 300, 200);
textField_txt.html = true;
textField_txt.htmlText = "Here's an interesting animation: <img
  src='animation.swf' id='animation_mc'>";
```

In this case, the fully qualified path to the newly created movie clip is `textField_txt.animation_mc`.

13. Save your changes to the Flash document and then select Control > Test Movie to preview the animation within the text field.

To control the SWF file as it plays in a text field, complete the next exercise.

To control a SWF file that plays in a text field:

1. Follow the steps in the first procedure under "Controlling embedded media with ActionScript" on page 456.

2. Create a button instance on the Stage and give it the instance name **stop_btn** in the Property inspector.

3. Add the following ActionScript code beneath the existing code in Frame 1 of the main Timeline:

```
stop_btn.onRelease = function() {
  textField_txt.animation_mc.stop();
};
```

4. Select Control > Test Movie to test the application.

Now, whenever you click the `stop_btn` button instance, the timeline of the animation nested within the text field stops.

For information on making your embedded media into a hyperlink, see "About making hypertext links out of embedded media" on page 458.

About making hypertext links out of embedded media

To make a hypertext link out of an embedded image file, SWF file, or movie clip, enclose the `<img>` tag in an `<a>` tag:

```
textField_txt.htmlText = "Click the image to return home<a
  href='home.htm'><img src='home.jpg'></a>";
```

When the mouse pointer is over an image, SWF file, or movie clip that is enclosed by `<a>` tags, the mouse pointer turns into a "pointing hand" icon, the same as it does with standard hypertext links. Interactivity, such as mouse clicks and keypresses, does not register in SWF files and movie clips that are enclosed by `<a>` tags.

For information on embedding media, see "About making hypertext links out of embedded media" on page 458.

Example: Creating scrolling text

You can use several methods to create scrolling text in Flash. You can make dynamic and input text fields scrollable by selecting the Scrollable option from the Text menu or the context menu, or by pressing Shift and double-clicking the text field handle.

You can use the `scroll` and `maxscroll` properties of the TextField object to control vertical scrolling and the `hscroll` and `maxhscroll` properties to control horizontal scrolling in a text field. The `scroll` and `hscroll` properties specify the current vertical and horizontal scrolling positions, respectively; you can read and write these properties. The `maxscroll` and `maxhscroll` properties specify the maximum vertical and horizontal scrolling positions, respectively; you can only read these properties.

The TextArea component provides an easy way to create scrolling text fields with a minimum amount of scripting. For more information, see "TextArea component" in the *Components Language Reference* in Flash Help.

To create a scrollable dynamic text field:

Do one of the following:

- Shift-double-click the handle on the dynamic text field.
- Select the dynamic text field with the Selection tool, and select Text > Scrollable.
- Select the dynamic text field with the Selection tool. Right-click (Windows) or Control-click (Macintosh) the dynamic text field, and select Text > Scrollable.

To use the scroll property to create scrolling text:

1. Do one of the following:

   ▪ Use the Text tool to drag a text field on the Stage. Assign the text field the instance name **textField_txt** in the Property inspector.

   ▪ Use ActionScript to create a text field dynamically with the `MovieClip.createTextField()` method. Assign the text field the instance name **textField_txt** as a parameter of the method.

    If you are *not* dynamically loading text into the SWF file, select Text > Scrollable from the main menu.

2. Create an Up button and a Down button, or select Window > Common Libraries > Buttons, and drag buttons to the Stage.

   You will use these buttons to scroll the text up and down.

3. Select the Down button on the Stage and type **down_btn** into the Instance Name text box.

4. Select the Up button on the Stage and type **up_btn** into the Instance Name text box.

5. Select Frame 1 on the Timeline, and, in the Actions panel (Window > Actions), enter the following code to scroll the text down in the text field:

```
down_btn.onPress = function() {
   textField_txt.scroll += 1;
};
```

6. Following the ActionScript in step 5, enter the following code to scroll the text up:

```
up_btn.onPress = function() {
   textField_txt.scroll -= 1;
};
```

   Any text that loads into the `textField_txt` text field can be scrolled using the up and down buttons.

About strings and the String class

In programming, a string is an ordered series of characters. You use strings often in your Flash documents and class files to display text in applications, such as within text fields. Also, you can store values as strings that you can use in an application for a variety of purposes. You can put strings directly in your ActionScript code by placing quotation marks around the characters of data. For more information on creating strings, see "Creating strings" on page 468. For information on using text fields, see "Using the TextField class" on page 392.

You can associate each character with a specified character code, which you can also optionally use to display text. For example, the character "A" is represented by the Unicode character code 0041, or 65 in ASCII (American Standard Code for Information Interchange). For more information on character codes and code charts, see www.unicode.org/charts. As you can see, the way you represent strings in a Flash document depends a lot on the character set you choose, and the way you encode characters.

Character encoding refers to the code, or method, for representing a set of characters in a language to representative codes, such as numeric values. The *character code* (as mentioned in the previous paragraph) is the table of mapped values (such as the ASCII table, where A equals 65). The encoding method deciphers it in a computer program.

For example, each letter in the English language would have a representative numerical code in a character encoding. ASCII encodes each letter, number, and some symbols to 7-bit binary versions of each integer. ASCII is a character set consisting of 95 printable characters and numerous control characters; ASCII is used by computers to represent text.

Like ASCII, *Unicode* is another way to associate a code with each letter of the alphabet. Because ASCII cannot support large character sets, such as Chinese, the Unicode Standard is a valuable standard to encode languages. Unicode is the standard for character sets that can represent any language set. It is a standard that exists to help development in multiple languages. The character code designates what character it represents, and the standard attempts to provide a universal way to encode characters that are part of any language. Strings could be displayed on any computer system, or platform, or software used. Then, it is up to the program involved (such as Flash or a web browser) to display the character glyph (its visual appearance).

Over the years, the number of characters that Unicode supports has expanded to add support for more (and larger) languages. The character encodings are called Unicode Transformation Format (UTF) and Universal Character Set (UCS), which include UTF-8, UTF-16, and UTF-32. The numbers in UTF encoding represent the number of bits in a unit, and the numbers in a UCS encoding represent bytes.

- UTF-8 is the standard encoding for exchanging text, such as online mail systems. UTF is an 8-bit system.
- UTF-16 is commonly used for internal processing.

Strings can be of various lengths in your applications. You can determine the length of your string, although this might vary, depending on what language you're using. Also, you might encounter a terminating character at the end of a string, and this null character doesn't have a value. This terminating character is not an actual character, but you can use it to determine when a string ends. For example, if you're working with socket connections, you might watch for the terminating character to know the end of a string (such as in a chat program).

You can find a sample source file, strings.fla, in the Samples folder on your hard disk. This file shows you how to build a simple word processor that compares and retrieves string and substring selections.

- In Windows, browse to *boot drive*\Program Files\Macromedia\Flash 8\ Samples and Tutorials\Samples\ActionScript\Strings.
- On the Macintosh, browse to *Macintosh HD*/Applications/Macromedia Flash 8/ Samples and Tutorials/Samples/ActionScript/Strings.

For more information on Strings and the String Class, see the following topics:

- "About the Strings panel" on page 461
- "Using the Locale class" on page 462
- "Using an input method editor" on page 464
- "About the String class" on page 467
- "Creating strings" on page 468
- "About the escape character" on page 469
- "Analyzing and comparing characters in strings" on page 470
- "Converting and concatenating strings" on page 473
- "Returning substrings" on page 476

About the Strings panel

The Strings panel lets you create and update multilingual content. You can specify content for text fields that span multiple languages, and have Flash automatically determine the content that should appear in a certain language based on the language of the computer that is running Flash Player.

For general information on the Strings panel, and how to use it in your applications, see the following topics in Flash Help:

- "Authoring multilanguage text with the Strings panel"
- "About editing strings in the Strings panel"
- "Translating text in the Strings panel or an XML file"
- "Importing an XML file into the Strings panel"

You can use the Locale class to control how multilanguage text is displayed. For more information, see "Using the Locale class" on page 462 and `%{Locale (mx.lang.Locale)}%` in the *ActionScript 2.0 Language Reference* in Flash Help.

Using the Locale class

The Locale class (mx.lang.Locale) allows you to control how multilanguage text is displayed in a Flash application at runtime. With the Strings panel, you can use string IDs instead of string literals in dynamic text fields, which allows you to create a SWF file that displays text loaded from a language-specific XML file. You can use the following methods to display the language-specific strings contained in the XML Localization Interchange File Format (XLIFF) files.

Automatically at runtime   Flash Player replaces string IDs with strings from the XML file, which matches the default system language code that is returned by `%{language (capabilities.language property)}%`.

Manually using stage language   String IDs are replaced by strings when the SWF file compiles, and cannot be changed by Flash Player.

Using ActionScript at runtime   You can control string ID replacement by using ActionScript, which is controlled at runtime. This option gives you control over both the timing and the language of string ID replacement.

You can use the properties and methods of the Locale class when you want to replace the string IDs by using ActionScript to control the application when it plays in Flash Player. For a demonstration of how to use the Locale class, see the following procedure.

To use the Locale class to create multilanguage sites:

1. Create a new Flash document and save it as **locale.fla**.

2. Open the Strings panel (Window > Other Panels > Strings) and click Settings.

3. Select two languages, en (English) and fr (French), and click Add to add the languages to the Active languages pane.

4. Select the Via ActionScript at Runtime option, set the default runtime language to French, and click OK.

5. Drag a ComboBox component from the User Interface folder of the Components panel (Window > Components) onto the Stage and give it the instance name **lang_cb**.

6. Create a dynamic text field on the Stage using the Text tool and give the text field the instance name **greeting_txt**.

7. With the text field selected on the Stage, type a string identifier of **greeting** in the ID text box of the Strings panel and click Apply.

   You'll notice that Flash converts the greeting string into IDS_GREETING.

8. In the String panel's grid, type the string **hello** in the en column.

9. Type the string **bonjour** in the fr column.

You use these strings when you use the `lang_cb` combo box to change the language on the Stage.

10. Add the following ActionScript to Frame 1 of the main Timeline:

```
import mx.lang.Locale;
Locale.setLoadCallback(localeListener);
lang_cb.dataProvider = Locale.languageCodeArray.sort();
lang_cb.addEventListener("change", langListener);
greeting_txt.autoSize = "left";
Locale.loadLanguageXML(lang_cb.value);

function langListener(eventObj:Object):Void {
  Locale.loadLanguageXML(eventObj.target.value);
}
function localeListener(success:Boolean):Void {
  if (success) {
    greeting_txt.text = Locale.loadString("IDS_GREETING");
  } else {
    greeting_txt.text = "unable to load language XML file.";
  }
}
```

The preceding ActionScript is split into two sections. The first section of code imports the Locale class and specifies a callback listener that is called whenever a language XML file is finished loading. Next, the `lang_cb` combo box is populated with a sorted array of available languages. Whenever the `lang_cb` value changes, Flash's event dispatcher triggers the `langListener()` function, which loads the specified-language XML file. The second section of code defines two functions, `langListener()`, and `localeListener()`. The first function, `langListener()`, is called whenever the `lang_cb` combo box's value is changed by the user. The second function, `localeListener()`, is called whenever a language XML file is finished loading. The function checks if the load was successful, and if so, sets the `text` property of the `greeting_txt` instance to the greeting for the selected language.

11. Select Control > Test Movie to test the Flash document.

| TIP | The XML file that you use must use the XML Localization Interchange File Format (XLIFF). |

| CAUTION | The Locale class is different from the other classes in the *ActionScript 2.0 Language Reference* in Flash Help, since it is not part of the Flash Player. Because this class installed in the Flash Authoring classpath, it is automatically compiled into your SWF files. Using the Locale class increases the SWF file size slightly, because the class must be compiled into the SWF file. |

For more information, see %{Locale (mx.lang.Locale)}% in the *ActionScript 2.0 Language Reference* in Flash Help.

Using an input method editor

An input method editor (IME) lets users type non-ASCII text characters in Asian languages such as Chinese, Japanese, and Korean. The IME class in ActionScript lets you directly manipulate the operating system's IME in the Flash Player application that is running on a client computer.

Using ActionScript, you can determine the following:

- Whether an IME is installed on the user's computer.
- Whether the IME is enabled or disabled on the user's computer.
- Which conversion mode the current IME is using.

The IME class can determine which conversion mode the current IME is using: for example, if the Japanese IME is active, you can determine if the conversion mode is Hiragana, Katakana (and so on) using the System.IME.getConversionMode() method. You can set it with the System.IME.setConversionMode() method.

> **NOTE** Curently, you cannot tell *which* IME is active (if any), or change from one IME to another (for instance, English to Japanese or Korean to Chinese)

You can also disable or enable the IME by using your application at runtime, and perform other functions, depending on the user's operating system. You can check whether a system has an IME by using the System.capabilities.hasIME property. The next example shows how to determine whether the user has an IME installed and active.

To determine whether the user has an IME installed and active:

1. Create a new Flash document and save it as **ime.fla**.

2. Add the following ActionScript to Frame 1 of the main Timeline:

```
if (System.capabilities.hasIME) {
  if (System.IME.getEnabled()) {
    trace("You have an IME installed and enabled.");
  } else {
    trace("You have an IME installed but not enabled.");
  }
} else {
  trace("Please install an IME and try again.");
}
```

The preceding code first checks whether the current system has an IME installed. If an IME is installed, Flash checks whether it is currently enabled.

3. Select Control > Test Movie to test the document.

A message appears in the Output panel stating whether you have an IME installed and currently active.

You can also use the IME class to enable and disable the IME in Flash at runtime. The following example requires that you have an IME installed on your system. For more information on installing an IME on your specific platform, see the following links:

- www.microsoft.com/globaldev/default.mspx
- http://developer.apple.com/documentation/
- http://java.sun.com

You can enable and disable an IME while the SWF file plays, as shown in the following example.

To enable and disable an input method editor at runtime:

1. Create a new Flash document and save it as **ime2.fla**.

2. Create two button symbol instances on the Stage and give them the instance names **enable_btn** and **disable_btn**.

3. Add the following ActionScript to Frame 1 of the main Timeline:

```
checkIME();

var my_fmt:TextFormat = new TextFormat();
my_fmt.font = "_sans";

this.createTextField("ime_txt", 10, 100, 10, 320, 240);
ime_txt.border = true;
ime_txt.multiline = true;
ime_txt.setNewTextFormat(my_fmt);
ime_txt.type = "input";
ime_txt.wordWrap = true;

enable_btn.onRelease = function() {
  System.IME.setEnabled(true);
};
disable_btn.onRelease = function() {
  System.IME.setEnabled(false);
};

function checkIME():Boolean {
  if (System.capabilities.hasIME) {
    if (System.IME.getEnabled()) {
      trace("You have an IME installed and enabled.");
      return true;
    } else {
      trace("You have an IME installed but not enabled.");
      return false;
    }
  } else {
    trace("Please install an IME and try again.");
    return false;
  }
}
```

The preceding code is separated into five sections. The first section calls the checkIME() method, which displays a message in the Output panel if the system has an IME installed or active. The second section defines a custom text-format object, which sets the font to _sans. The third section creates an input text field and applies the custom text format. The fourth section creates some event handlers for the enable_btn and disable_btn instances created in an earlier step. The fifth, and final, section of code defines the custom checkIME() function, which checks whether the current system has an IME installed and if so, whether or not the IME is active.

4. Save the FLA file and select Control > Test Movie to test the document.

> **NOTE**
> This example requires that you have an IME installed on your system. For information on installing an IME, see the links that precede this example.

Type some text into the input text field on the Stage. Switch your IME to a different language and type in the input text field again. Flash Player inputs characters by using the new IME. If you click the `disable_btn` button on the Stage, Flash reverts to using the previous language and ignores the current IME settings.

For information on `System.capabilities.hasIME`, see `%{hasIME (capabilities.hasIME property)}%` in the *ActionScript 2.0 Language Reference* in Flash Help.

About the String class

A string is also a class and data type in the core ActionScript language. The String data type represents a sequence of 16-bit characters that might include letters, numbers, and punctuation marks. Strings are stored as Unicode characters, using the UTF-16 format. An operation on a String value returns a new instance of the string. The default value for a variable declared with the String data type is `null`.

For more information on strings, data, and values, see Chapter 4, "Data and Data Types."

The String class contains methods that let you work with text strings. Strings are important in working with many objects, and the methods described in this chapter are useful in working with strings used in many objects, such as TextField, XML, ContextMenu, and FileReference instances.

The String class is a wrapper for the String primitive data type, and provides methods and properties that let you manipulate primitive string values. You can convert the value of any object into a string by using the `String()` function. All the methods of the String class, except for `concat()`, `fromCharCode()`, `slice()`, and `substr()`, are generic, which means the methods call the `toString()` function before they perform their operations, and you can use these methods with other non-String objects.

Because all string indexes are zero-based, the index of the last character for any `myStr` string is `myStr.length - 1`.

You can find a sample source file, strings.fla, in the Samples folder on your hard disk. This file shows you how to build a simple word processor that compares and retrieves string and substring selections.

■ In Windows, browse to *boot drive*\Program Files\Macromedia\Flash 8\ Samples and Tutorials\Samples\ActionScript\Strings.

- On the Macintosh, browse to *Macintosh HD*/Applications/Macromedia Flash 8/ Samples and Tutorials/Samples/ActionScript/Strings.

Creating strings

You can call any of the methods of the String class by using the `new String()` constructor method or by using a string literal value. If you specify a string literal, the ActionScript interpreter automatically converts it to a temporary String object, calls the method, and discards the temporary String object. You can also use the `String.length` property with a string literal.

Do not confuse a string *literal* with a String *object*. For more information on string literals and the String object, see Chapter 5, "About literals," on page 134.

In the following example, the line of code creates the `firstStr` string literal. To declare a string literal, use single straight quotation mark (`'`) or double straight quotation mark (`"`) delimiters.

To create and use strings:

1. Create a new Flash document and save it as **strings.fla**.

2. Add the following ActionScript to Frame 1 of the main Timeline:

```
var firstStr:String = "foo";
var secondStr:String = new String("foo");
trace(firstStr == secondStr); // true
var thirdStr:String;
trace(thirdStr); // undefined
```

This code defines three String objects, one that uses a string literal, one that uses the `new` operator, and the other without an initial value. Strings can be compared by using the equality (==) operator, as shown in the third line of code. When referring to variables, you specify the data type only when the variable is being defined.

3. Select Control > Test Movie to test the document.

Always use string literals unless you specifically need to use a String object. For more information on string literals and the String object, see Chapter 5, "About literals," on page 134.

To use single straight quotation mark (`'`) and double straight quotation mark (`"`) delimiters within a single string literal, use the backslash character (\) to escape the character. The following two strings are equivalent:

```
var firstStr:String = "That's \"fine\"";
var secondStr:String = 'That\'s "fine"';
```

For more information on using the backslash character in strings, see "About the escape character" on page 469.

Remember that you cannot use "curly quotation mark" or "special quotation mark" characters within your ActionScript code; they are different from the straight quotation marks (') and (") that you can use in your code. When you paste text from another source into ActionScript, such as the web or a Word document, be sure to use straight quote delimiters.

You can find a sample source file, strings.fla, in the Samples folder on your hard disk. This file shows you how to build a simple word processor that compares and retrieves string and substring selections.

- In Windows, browse to *boot drive*\Program Files\Macromedia\Flash 8\Samples and Tutorials\Samples\ActionScript\Strings.
- On the Macintosh, browse to *Macintosh HD*/Applications/Macromedia Flash 8/Samples and Tutorials/Samples/ActionScript/Strings.

About the escape character

You can use the backslash escape character (\), to define other characters in string literals.

Escape sequence	Description
\b	The backspace character.
\f	The form feed character.
\n	The newline character.
\r	The carriage return.
\t	The tab character.
\u*nnnn*	The Unicode character with the character code specified by the hexidecimal number *nnnn*. For example, \u263a is the smile character.
\x*nn*	The ASCII character with the character code specified by the hexidecimal number *nn*.
\'	A single quotation mark.
\"	A double quotation mark.
\\	A single backslash character.

For more information on string literals, see Chapter 5, "About literals," on page 134 and "Creating strings" on page 468.

Analyzing and comparing characters in strings

Every character in a string has an index position in the string (an integer). The index position of the first character is 0. For example, in the string yellow, the character y is in position 0 and the character w is in position 5.

Every string has a length property, which is equal to the number of characters in the string:

```
var companyStr:String = "macromedia";
trace(companyStr.length); // 10
```

An empty string and a null string both have a length of zero:

```
var firstStr:String = new String();
trace(firstStr.length); // 0

var secondStr:String = "";
trace(secondStr.length); // 0
```

If a string doesn't contain a value, its length is set to undefined:

```
var thirdStr:String;
trace(thirdStr.length); // undefined
```

> **WARNING**
>
> If your string contains a null byte character (\0), the string value will be truncated.

You can also use character codes to define a string. For more information on character codes and character encoding, see "About strings and the String class" on page 459.

The following example creates a variable named myStr and sets the string's value based on ASCII values passed to the String.fromCharCode() method:

```
var myStr:String =
   String.fromCharCode(104,101,108,108,111,32,119,111,114,108,100,33);
trace(myStr); // hello world!
```

Each number listed in the fromCharCode() method in the previous code represents a single character. For example, the ASCII value 104 represents a lowercase h, and the ASCII value 32 represents the space character.

You can also use the String.fromCharCode() method to convert Unicode values, although the unicode value must be converted from hexidecimal to decimal values, as shown in the following ActionScript:

```
// Unicode 0068 == "h"
var letter:Number = Number(new Number(0x0068).toString(10));
trace(String.fromCharCode(letter)); // h
```

You can examine the characters in various positions in a string, as in the following example.

To loop over a string:

1. Create a new Flash document.

2. Add the following ActionScript to Frame 1 of the main Timeline:

```
var myStr:String = "hello world!";
for (var i:Number = 0; i < myStr.length; i++) {
  trace(myStr.charAt(i));
}
```

3. Select Control > Test Movie to preview your Flash document. You should see each character traced to the Output panel on a separate line.

4. Modify the existing ActionScript code so that it traces the ASCII value for each character:

```
var myStr:String = "hello world!";
for (var i:Number = 0; i < myStr.length; i++) {
  trace(myStr.charAt(i) + " - ASCII=" + myStr.charCodeAt(i));
}
```

5. Save the current Flash document and select Control > Test Movie to preview the SWF file.

   When you run this code, the following is displayed in the Output panel:

```
h - ASCII=104
e - ASCII=101
l - ASCII=108
l - ASCII=108
o - ASCII=111
  - ASCII=32
w - ASCII=119
o - ASCII=111
r - ASCII=114
l - ASCII=108
d - ASCII=100
! - ASCII=33
```

 You can also split a string into an array of characters by using the String.split() method and entering an `empty string ("")` as a delimiter; for example, `var charArray:Array = myStr.split("");`

You can use operators to compare strings. For information on using operators with strings, see "About using operators with strings" on page 186.

You can use these operators with conditional statements, such as `if` and `while`. The following example uses operators and strings to make a comparison.

To compare two strings:

1. Create a new Flash document and save it as **comparestr.fla**.

2. Add the following ActionScript to Frame 1 of the main Timeline:

```
var str1:String = "Apple";
var str2:String = "apple";
if (str1 < str2) {
  trace("Uppercase letters sort first.");
}
```

3. Save the Flash document and select Control > Test Movie to test the SWF file.

You can use the equality (==) and inequality (!=) operators to compare strings with other types of objects, as shown in the following example.

To compare strings to other data types:

1. Create a new Flash document and save it as **comparenum.fla**.

2. Add the following ActionScript to Frame 1 of the main Timeline:

```
var myStr:String = "4";
var total:Number = 4;
if (myStr == total) {
  trace("Types are converted.");
}
```

3. Save the Flash document and select Control > Test Movie to test the SWF file.

    When comparing two different data types (such as strings and numbers), Flash tries to convert the data types so that a comparison can be made.

Use the strict equality (===) and strict inequality (!==) operators to verify that both comparison objects are of the same type. The following example uses strict comparison operators to ensure that Flash doesn't try to convert data types while trying to compare values.

To force strict data type comparisons:

1. Create a new Flash document and save it as **comparestrict.fla**.

2. Add the following ActionScript to Frame 1 of the main Timeline:

```
var str1:String = "4";
var str2:String = "5";
var total:Number = 4;
if (str1 !== total) {
  trace("Types are not converted.");
}
if (str1 !== str2) {
  trace("Same type, but the strings don't match.");
}
```

3. Save the Flash document and select Control > Test Movie.

For more information on using operators with strings, see "About using operators with strings" on page 186.

You can find a sample source file, strings.fla, in the Samples folder on your hard disk. This file shows you how to build a simple word processor that compares and retrieves string and substring selections.

- In Windows, browse to *boot drive*\Program Files\Macromedia\Flash 8\ Samples and Tutorials\Samples\ActionScript\Strings.

- On the Macintosh, browse to *Macintosh HD*/Applications/Macromedia Flash 8/ Samples and Tutorials/Samples/ActionScript/Strings.

Converting and concatenating strings

You can use the toString() method to convert many objects to strings. Most built-in objects have a toString() method for this purpose:

```
var n:Number = 0.470;
trace(typeof(n.toString())); // string
```

When you use the addition (+) operator with a combination of string and nonstring instances, you don't need to use the toString() method. For details on concatenation, see the second procedure in this section.

The toLowerCase() method and the toUpperCase() method convert alphabetical characters in the string to lowercase and uppercase, respectively. The following example demonstrates how to convert a string from lowercase to uppercase characters.

To convert a string from lowercase to uppercase:

1. Create a new Flash document and save it as **convert.fla**.

2. Type the following code on Frame 1 of the Timeline:

```
var myStr:String = "Dr. Bob Roberts, #9.";
trace(myStr.toLowerCase()); // dr. bob roberts, #9.
trace(myStr.toUpperCase()); // DR. BOB ROBERTS, #9.
trace(myStr); // Dr. Bob Roberts, #9.
```

3. Save the Flash document and select Control > Test Movie.

> **NOTE**
> After these methods are executed, the source string remains unchanged. To transform the source string, use the following:

```
myStr = myStr.toUpperCase();
```

When you concatenate strings, you take two strings and join them sequentially into one string. For example, you can use the addition (+) operator to concatenate two strings. The next example shows you how to concatenate two strings.

To concatenate two strings:

1. Create a new Flash document and save it as **concat.fla**.

2. Add the following code to Frame 1 of the Timeline:

```
var str1:String = "green";
var str2:String = str1 + "ish";
trace(str2); // greenish
//
var str3:String = "yellow";
str3 += "ish";
trace(str3); // yellowish
```

The preceding code shows two methods of concatenating strings. The first method uses the addition (+) operator to join the str1 string with the string "ish". The second method uses the addition and assignment (+=) operator to concatenate the string "ish" with the current value of str3.

3. Save the Flash document and select Control > Test Movie.

You can also use the concat() method of the String class to concatenate strings. This method is demonstrated in the following example.

To concatenate two strings with the concat() method:

1. Create a new Flash document and save it as **concat2.fla**.

2. Add the following code to Frame 1 of the Timeline:

```
var str1:String = "Bonjour";
var str2:String = "from";
var str3:String = "Paris";
var str4:String = str1.concat(" ", str2, " ", str3);
trace(str4); // Bonjour from Paris
```

3. Select Control > Test Movie to test the Flash document.

If you use the addition (+) operator (or the addition and assignment [+=] operator) with a string and a nonstring object, ActionScript automatically converts nonstring objects to strings in order to evaluate the expression. This conversion is demonstrated in the following code example:

```
var version:String = "Flash Player ";
var rel:Number = 8;
version = version + rel;
trace(version); // Flash Player 8
```

However, you can use parentheses to force the addition (+) operator to evaluate arithmetically, as demonstrated in the following ActionScript code:

```
trace("Total: $" + 4.55 + 1.46); // Total: $4.551.46
trace("Total: $" + (4.55 + 1.46)); // Total: $6.01
```

You can use the `split()` method to create an array of substrings of a string, which is divided based on a delimiter character. For example, you could segment a comma- or tab-delimited string into multiple strings.

For example, the following code shows how you can split an array into substrings by using the ampersand (&) character as a delimiter.

To create an array of substrings segmented by delimiter:

1. Create a new Flash document and save it as **strsplit.fla**.

2. Add the following ActionScript to Frame 1 of the main Timeline:

```
var queryStr:String = "first=joe&last=cheng&title=manager&startDate=3/6/
   65";
var params:Array = queryStr.split("&", 2);
trace(params); // first=joe,last=cheng
    /* params is set to an array with two elements:
       params[0] == "first=joe"
       params[1] == "last=cheng"
    */
```

3. Select Control > Test Movie to test the Flash document.

The second parameter of the `split()` method defines the maximum size of the array. If you don't want to limit the size of the array created by the `split()` method, you can omit the second parameter.

The easiest way to parse a query string (a string delimited with & and = characters) is to use the `LoadVars.decode()` method, as shown in the following ActionScript:

```
var queryStr:String = "first=joe&last=cheng&title=manager&startDate=3/6/
   65";
var my_lv:LoadVars = new LoadVars();
my_lv.decode(queryStr);
trace(my_lv.first); // joe
```

For more information on using operators with strings, see "About using operators with strings" on page 186.

You can find a sample source file, strings.fla, in the Samples folder on your hard disk. This file shows you how to build a simple word processor that compares and retrieves string and substring selections.

- In Windows, browse to *boot drive*\Program Files\Macromedia\Flash 8\ Samples and Tutorials\Samples\ActionScript\Strings.

- On the Macintosh, browse to *Macintosh HD*/Applications/Macromedia Flash 8/ Samples and Tutorials/Samples/ActionScript/Strings.

Returning substrings

The `substr()` and `substring()` methods of the String class are similar. Both return a substring of a string and both take two parameters. In both methods, the first parameter is the position of the starting character in the given string. However, in the `substr()` method, the second parameter is the *length* of the substring to return, and in the `substring()` method the second parameter is the position of the character at the *end* of the substring (which is not included in the returned string). This example shows the difference between these two methods:

To find a substring by character position:

1. Create a new Flash document and save it as **substring.fla**.

2. Add the following ActionScript to Frame 1 of the main Timeline:

```
var myStr:String = "Hello from Paris, Texas!!!";
trace(myStr.substr(11,15)); // Paris, Texas!!!
trace(myStr.substring(11,15)); // Pari
```

   The first method, `substr()`, returns a string 15 characters long starting from the eleventh character. The second method, `substring()`, returns a string four characters long by grabbing all characters between the eleventh and fifteenth index.

3. Add the following ActionScript below the code added in the preceding step:

```
trace(myStr.slice(11, 15)); // Pari
trace(myStr.slice(-3, -1)); // !!
trace(myStr.slice(-3, 26)); // !!!
trace(myStr.slice(-3, myStr.length)); // !!!
trace(myStr.slice(-8, -3)); // Texas
```

   The `slice()` method functions similarly to the `substring()` method. When given two non-negative integers as parameters, it works exactly the same. However, the `slice()` method can take negative integers as parameters.

4. Select Control > Test Movie to test the Flash document.

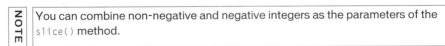

> **NOTE** You can combine non-negative and negative integers as the parameters of the `slice()` method.

You can use the `indexOf()` and `lastIndexOf()` methods to locate matching substrings within a string, as shown in the following example.

To find the character position of a matching substring:

1. Create a new Flash document and save it as **indexof.fla**.

2. Add the following ActionScript to Frame 1 of the main Timeline:

```
var myStr:String = "The moon, the stars, the sea, the land";
trace(myStr.indexOf("the")); // 10
trace(myStr.indexOf("the", 11)); // 21
```

The first index of the word *the* begins at the 10th character because the indexOf() method is case sensitive; therefore the first instance of *The* isn't considered. You can also specify a second parameter to the indexOf() method to indicate the index position in the string from which to start the search. In the preceding code, Flash searches for the first index of the word *the* that occurs after the 11th character.

3. Add the following ActionScript below the code that you added in the previous step:

```
trace(myStr.lastIndexOf("the")); // 30
trace(myStr.lastIndexOf("the", 29)); // 21
```

The lastIndexOf() method finds the last occurrence of a substring in the string. For example, instead searching for a character or substring from the beginning of a string, lastIndexOf() starts from the end of a string and works backward. Similarly to the indexOf() method, if you include a second parameter with the lastIndexOf() method, the search is conducted from that index position, although with lastIndexOf() the string is searched backward (from right to left).

4. Select Control > Test Movie to test your Flash document.

TIP · The indexOf() and lastIndexOf() methods are case sensitive.

You can find a sample source file, strings.fla, in the Samples folder on your hard disk. This file shows you how to build a simple word processor that compares and retrieves string and substring selections.

- In Windows, browse to *boot drive*\Program Files\Macromedia\Flash 8\ Samples and Tutorials\Samples\ActionScript\Strings.

- On the Macintosh, browse to *Macintosh HD*/Applications/Macromedia Flash 8/ Samples and Tutorials/Samples/ActionScript/Strings.

CHAPTER 13

Animation, Filters, and Drawings

13

This chapter describes how to add animation to your Macromedia Flash Basic 8 and Macromedia Flash Professional 8 applications using ActionScript instead of (or in addition to) timeline-based animations that use motion or shape tweens. Using code to create animation and effects often reduces the file size of your finished application, and can also improve the performance and consistency of the animation itself. At times, ActionScript-based animations might even reduce your workload: code can be faster to write, and it's easy to apply to many instances at once or reuse in other applications. This chapter also shows you how to animate by using fundamental ActionScript basics, the Tween and TransitionManager classes, the Drawing API, filter classes, and blend modes.

You can use the Drawing API, which consists of the drawing methods in the MovieClip class, to add animation and draw. These methods let you use code to create lines, fills, and shapes, instead of using the drawing tools in the authoring tool.

Filters and other expressive effects are also important in many Flash applications, to quickly apply an effect and animate it. You can use code to add and animate filter effects, blend modes, and bitmap images.

This chapter contains the following sections, which describe using ActionScript to create animation and add effects, as well as using the Drawing API to draw in ActionScript:

Scripting animation with ActionScript 2.0

You can use ActionScript 2.0 to add animation to your Flash applications, instead of using motion or shape tweens on a timeline. The following sections show you how to use code to animate instances, such as changing the transparency and appearance of the instance, and moving the instance around the Stage.

For information on using the Tween and TransitionManager classes to further automate code-based animations, see "TransitionManager class" and "Tween class" in the *Components Language Reference* in Flash Help. These classes help you add advanced easing equations and transition animations to movie clip instances in your application. Many of these effects are difficult to recreate using ActionScript without these prebuilt classes, because the code you need to use involves writing complex mathematical equations to achieve the effect.

For more information about how to animate drawings that you create with code, see "Drawing with ActionScript" on page 552.

The following sections describe how to script animations:

- "About animation and frame rate" on page 481
- "Fading objects with code" on page 481
- "Adding color and brightness effects with code" on page 484
- "Moving objects with code" on page 487
- "Panning an image with code" on page 488

For an example of scripted animation in Flash, you can find a sample source file, animation.fla, in the Samples folder on your hard disk.

- In Windows, browse to *boot drive*\Program Files\Macromedia\Flash 8\Samples and Tutorials\Samples\ActionScript\Animation.
- On the Macintosh, browse to *Macintosh HD*/Applications/Macromedia Flash 8/Samples and Tutorials/Samples/ActionScript/Animation.

You can find samples of photo gallery applications on your hard disk. These files provide examples of how to use ActionScript to control movie clips dynamically while loading image files into a SWF file, which includes scripted animation. You can find the sample source files, gallery_tree.fla and gallery_tween.fla, in the Samples folder on your hard disk.

- In Windows, browse to *boot drive*\Program Files\Macromedia\Flash 8\ Samples and Tutorials\Samples\ActionScript\Galleries.
- On the Macintosh, browse to *Macintosh HD*/Applications/Macromedia Flash 8/ Samples and Tutorials/Samples/ActionScript/Galleries.

About animation and frame rate

When you add animation to an application, consider the frame rate that you set your FLA file to. You need to think about frame rate when working with animations because it can affect the performance of your SWF file and the computer that plays it. Setting a frame rate too high can lead to processor problems, especially when you use many assets or use ActionScript to create animation.

However, you also need to consider the frame rate setting, because it affects how smoothly your animation plays. For example, an animation set to 12 frames per second (fps) in the Property inspector plays 12 frames each second. If the document's frame rate is set to 24 fps, the animation appears to animate more smoothly than if it ran at 12 fps. However, your animation at 24 fps also plays much faster than it does at 12 fps, so the total duration (in seconds) is shorter. Therefore, if you need to make a 5-second animation using a higher frame rate, it means you need to add additional frames to fill those five seconds than at a lower frame rate (and thus, this raises the total file size of your animation). A 5-second animation at 24 fps typically has a higher file size than a 5-second animation at 12 fps.

> **NOTE** When you use an `onEnterFrame` event handler to create scripted animations, the animation runs at the document's frame rate, similar to if you created a motion tween on a timeline. An alternative to the `onEnterFrame` event handler is `setInterval` (see %{setInterval function}% in the *ActionScript 2.0 Language Reference* in Flash Help). Instead of depending on frame rate, you call functions at a specified interval. Like `onEnterFrame`, the more frequently you use `setInterval` to call a function, the more resource intensive the animation is on your processor.

Use the lowest possible frame rate that makes your animation appear to play smoothly at runtime, which helps reduce the strain on the end-user's processor. Try not to use a frame rate that's more than 30 to 40 fps; high frame rates put a lot of stress on processors, and do not change the appearance of the animation much or at all at runtime.

Also, especially if you're working with timeline-based animation, select a frame rate for your animation as early as possible in the development process. When you test the SWF file, check the duration, and the SWF file size, of your animation. The frame rate greatly affects the speed of the animation.

Fading objects with code

When you work with movie clips on the Stage, you might want to fade the movie clip in or out instead of toggling its `_visible` property. The following procedure demonstrates how to use an `onEnterFrame` event handler to animate a movie clip.

To fade a movie clip by using code:

1. Create a new Flash document called **fade1.fla**.

2. Draw some graphics on the Stage using the drawing tools, or import an image to the Stage (File > Import > Import to Stage).

3. Select the content on the Stage and select Modify > Convert to Symbol.

4. Select the Movie clip option and click OK to create the symbol.

5. Select the movie clip instance on the Stage and type **img1_mc** in the Instance Name text box in the Property inspector.

6. Select Frame 1 of the Timeline, and add the following code to the Actions panel:

```
img1_mc.onEnterFrame = function() {
  img1_mc._alpha -= 5;
  if (img1_mc._alpha <= 0) {
    img1_mc._visible = false;
    delete img1_mc.onEnterFrame;
  }
};
```

This code uses an `onEnterFrame` event handler, which is invoked repeatedly at the frame rate of the SWF file. The number of times per second that the event handler is called depends on the frame rate at which the Flash document is set. If the frame rate is 12 frames per second (fps), the `onEnterFrame` event handler is invoked 12 times per second. Likewise, if the Flash document's frame rate is 30 fps, the event handler is invoked 30 times per second.

7. Select Control > Test Movie to test the document.

The movie clip you added to the Stage slowly fades out.

You can modify the `_alpha` property by using the `setInterval()` function instead of an `onEnterFrame` event handler, as the next procedure shows.

To fade an object by using the setInterval() function:

1. Create a new Flash document called **fade2.fla**.

2. Draw some graphics on the Stage, or import an image to the Stage (File > Import > Import to Stage).

3. Select the content on the Stage and select Modify > Convert to Symbol.

4. Select the Movie clip option and click OK to create the symbol.

5. Select the movie clip instance on the Stage and type **img1_mc** in the Instance Name text box in the Property inspector.

6. Select Frame 1 of the Timeline and add the following code to the Actions panel:

```
var alpha_interval:Number = setInterval(fadeImage, 50, img1_mc);
function fadeImage(target_mc:MovieClip):Void {
  target_mc._alpha -= 5;
  if (target_mc._alpha <= 0) {
    target_mc._visible = false;
    clearInterval(alpha_interval);
  }
}
```

The `setInterval()` function behaves slightly differently than the `onEnterFrame` event handler, because the `setInterval()` function tells Flash precisely how frequently the code should call a particular function. In this code example, the user-defined `fadeImage()` function is called every 50 milliseconds (20 times per second). The `fadeImage()` function decrements the value of the current movie clip's `_alpha` property. When the `_alpha` value is equal to or less than 0, the interval is cleared, which causes the `fadeImage()` function to stop executing.

7. Select Control > Test Movie to test the document.

The movie clip you added to the Stage slowly fades out.

For more information on user-defined functions, see "Defining global and timeline functions" on page 216. For more information on the `onEnterFrame` event handler, see %{onEnterFrame (MovieClip.onEnterFrame handler)}% in the *ActionScript 2.0 Language Reference* in Flash Help. For more information on the `setInterval()` function, see %{setInterval function}% in the *ActionScript 2.0 Language Reference* in Flash Help.

For an example of scripted animation in Flash, you can find a sample source file, animation.fla, in the Samples folder on your hard disk

- In Windows, browse to *boot drive*\Program Files\Macromedia\Flash 8\Samples and Tutorials\Samples\ActionScript\Animation.

- On the Macintosh, browse to *Macintosh HD*/Applications/Macromedia Flash 8/Samples and Tutorials/Samples/ActionScript/Animation.

Adding color and brightness effects with code

In addition to using ActionScript to set and animate alpha fades (see "Fading objects with code" on page 481), you can animate various color and brightness effects by using code instead of using the Filters panel in the Property inspector.

The following procedure loads a JPEG image and applies a color transform filter, which modifies the red and green channels as the mouse pointer moves along the *x*-axis and *y*-axis.

To change an object's color channels by using ActionScript:

1. Create a new Flash document called **colorTrans.fla**.

2. Select Frame 1 of the Timeline, and add the following code to the Actions panel:

```
import flash.geom.Transform;
import flash.geom.ColorTransform;

var imageClip:MovieClip = this.createEmptyMovieClip("imageClip", 1);
var clipLoader:MovieClipLoader = new MovieClipLoader();
clipLoader.loadClip("http://www.helpexamples.com/flash/images/
   image1.jpg", imageClip);

var mouseListener:Object = new Object();
mouseListener.onMouseMove = function():Void {
  var transformer:Transform = new Transform(imageClip);
  var colorTransformer:ColorTransform = transformer.colorTransform;
  colorTransformer.redMultiplier = (_xmouse / Stage.width) * 1;
  colorTransformer.greenMultiplier = (_ymouse / Stage.height) * 1;
  transformer.colorTransform = colorTransformer;
}
Mouse.addListener(mouseListener);
```

3. Select Control > Test Movie to test the document, and then move the mouse pointer around the Stage.

   The image file that loads transforms colors as you move the mouse.

You can also use the ColorMatrixFilter class to convert a color image to a black and white image, as the following procedure shows.

To use the ColorMatrixFilter class to change an image to a grayscale image:

1. Create a new Flash document called **grayscale.fla**.

2. Select Frame 1 of the Timeline, and add the following code to the Actions panel:

```
import flash.filters.ColorMatrixFilter;
System.security.allowDomain("http://www.helpexamples.com");
var mcl_obj:Object = new Object();
mcl_obj.onLoadInit = function(target_mc:MovieClip):Void {
    var myElements_array:Array = [0.3, 0.59, 0.11, 0, 0,
        0.3, 0.59, 0.11, 0, 0,
        0.3, 0.59, 0.11, 0, 0,
        0, 0, 0, 1, 0];
    var myColorMatrix_filter:ColorMatrixFilter = new
    ColorMatrixFilter(myElements_array);
    target_mc.filters = [myColorMatrix_filter];
}
this.createEmptyMovieClip("img_mc", this.getNextHighestDepth());
var img_mcl:MovieClipLoader = new MovieClipLoader();
img_mcl.addListener(mcl_obj);
img_mcl.loadClip("http://www.helpexamples.com/flash/images/image1.jpg",
    img_mc);
```

The preceding code begins by importing the ColorMatrixFilter class, and creates a listener object that will be used with a new MovieClipLoader instance created in some later code. Next, a new movie clip instance is created with the instance name img_mc, as well as a new movie clip loader instance with the instance name img_mcl. Finally, the source movie clip is loaded into the img_mc movie clip on the Stage. When the image is successfully loaded, the onLoadInit event handler is called and attaches a ColorMatrixFilter to the loaded image.

3. Select Control > Test Movie to test the document.

The image that you load onto the Stage changes to a grayscale image. View the image online (www.helpexamples.com/flash/images/image1.jpg) to see the original color of the image.

You can also set an image's brightness by using the ActionScript code in the following procedure.

To change an image's brightness:

1. Create a new Flash document called **brightness.fla**.

2. Select Frame 1 of the Timeline and add the following code to the Actions panel:

```
import flash.filters.ColorMatrixFilter;
System.security.allowDomain("http://www.helpexamples.com/");
var mcl_obj:Object = new Object();
mcl_obj.onLoadInit = function(target_mc:MovieClip):Void {
    var myElements_array:Array = [1, 0, 0, 0, 100,
        0, 1, 0, 0, 100,
        0, 0, 1, 0, 100,
        0, 0, 0, 1, 0];
    var myColorMatrix_filter:ColorMatrixFilter = new
    ColorMatrixFilter(myElements_array);
    target_mc.filters = [myColorMatrix_filter];
}
this.createEmptyMovieClip("img_mc", this.getNextHighestDepth());
var img_mcl:MovieClipLoader = new MovieClipLoader();
img_mcl.addListener(mcl_obj);
img_mcl.loadClip("http://www.helpexamples.com/flash/images/image2.jpg",
    img_mc);
```

This block of code uses the MovieClipLoader class to load an external JPEG. When the image successfully loads, the MovieClipLoader class onLoadInit event handler is called and modifies the image brightness to 100 using the ColorMatrixFilter filter.

3. Select Control > Test Movie to test the document.

The image that you load into the SWF file changes its brightness when you test the SWF file. View the image online (`http://www.helpexamples.com/flash/images/image2.jpg`) to see the original appearance of the image.

For an example of scripted animation in Flash, you can find a sample source file, animation.fla, in the Samples folder on your hard disk.

- In Windows, browse to *boot drive*\Program Files\Macromedia\Flash 8\Samples and Tutorials\Samples\ActionScript\Animation.

- On the Macintosh, browse to *Macintosh HD*/Applications/Macromedia Flash 8/Samples and Tutorials/Samples/ActionScript/Animation.

You can also find samples of photo gallery applications on your hard disk. These files provide examples of how to use ActionScript to control movie clips dynamically while loading image files into a SWF file, which includes scripted animation. You can find the sample source files, gallery_tree.fla and gallery_tween.fla, in the Samples folder on your hard disk.

- In Windows, browse to *boot drive*\Program Files\Macromedia\Flash 8\ Samples and Tutorials\Samples\ActionScript\Galleries.

- On the Macintosh, browse to *Macintosh HD*/Applications/Macromedia Flash 8/ Samples and Tutorials/Samples/ActionScript/Galleries.

Moving objects with code

Using ActionScript to move an object is similar to modifying an object's _alpha property, except that you instead modify the object's _x or _y property.

The following procedure animates a dynamically loaded JPEG image and slides it horizontally across the Stage.

To move an instance on the Stage by using code:

1. Create a new Flash document called **moveClip.fla**.

2. Change the frame rate of the document to 24 fps in the Property inspector.

   The animation is much smoother if you use a higher frame rate, such as 24 fps.

3. Select Frame 1 of the Timeline, and add the following code to the Actions panel:

```
// Create a movie clip instance.
this.createEmptyMovieClip("img1_mc", 10);
var mc1_obj:Object = new Object();
mc1_obj.onLoadInit = function (target_mc:MovieClip):Void {
   target_mc._x = Stage.width;
   target_mc.onEnterFrame = function() {
      target_mc._x -= 3; // decrease current _x position by 3 pixels
      if (target_mc._x <= 0) {
         target_mc._x = 0;
         delete target_mc.onEnterFrame;
      }
   };
};
var img_mcl:MovieClipLoader = new MovieClipLoader();
img_mcl.addListener(mc1_obj);
// Load an image into the movie clip
img_mcl.loadClip("http://www.helpexamples.com/flash/images/image1.jpg",
   img1_mc);
```

   This code example loads an external image from a remote web server and, when the image is fully loaded, animates it horizontally across the Stage. Instead of using an onEnterFrame event handler, you could use the setInterval() function to animate the image.

4. Select Control > Test Movie to test the document.

   The image loads and then animates from the right side of the Stage to the upper-left corner of the Stage.

For information on using an `onEnterFrame` event handler or `setInterval()` function to animate the image, see "Fading objects with code" on page 481.

For an example of scripted animation in Flash, you can find a sample source file, animation.fla, in the Samples folder on your hard disk.

- In Windows, browse to *boot drive*\Program Files\Macromedia\Flash 8\ Samples and Tutorials\Samples\ActionScript\Animation.

- On the Macintosh, browse to *Macintosh HD*/Applications/Macromedia Flash 8/ Samples and Tutorials/Samples/ActionScript/Animation.

You can also find samples of photo gallery applications on your hard disk. These files provide examples of how to use ActionScript to control movie clips dynamically while loading image files into a SWF file, which includes scripted animation. You can find the sample source files, gallery_tree.fla and gallery_tween.fla, in the Samples folder on your hard disk.

- In Windows, browse to *boot drive*\Program Files\Macromedia\Flash 8\ Samples and Tutorials\Samples\ActionScript\Galleries.

- On the Macintosh, browse to *Macintosh HD*/Applications/Macromedia Flash 8/ Samples and Tutorials/Samples/ActionScript/Galleries.

Panning an image with code

Using ActionScript, you can easily pan large images within your Flash documents. This is useful when your image doesn't fit on the Stage, or you want to create an animation effect in which you pan a movie clip from one side of the Stage to the other. For example, if you have a large panoramic image that is larger than your Stage size, but you don't want to reduce the dimensions of your image or increase the dimensions of your Stage, you can create a movie clip that acts as a mask for the larger image.

The following procedure demonstrates how you can dynamically mask a movie clip and use an `onEnterFrame` event handler to animate an image behind the mask.

To pan an instance on the Stage using code:

1. Create a new Flash document called **pan.fla**.

2. Change the frame rate of the document to 24 fps in the Property inspector.

   The animation is much smoother if you use a higher frame rate, such as 24 fps.

3. Select Frame 1 of the Timeline, and add the following code to the Actions panel:

```
System.security.allowDomain("http://www.helpexamples.com/");
// initialize variables
var direction:Number = -1;
var speed:Number = 5;
// create clip to load an image into
this.createEmptyMovieClip("img_mc", 10);
// create a clip to use as a mask
this.createEmptyMovieClip("mask_mc", 20);
// use the Drawing API to draw/create a mask
with (mask_mc) {
   beginFill(0xFF0000, 0);
   moveTo(0, 0);
   lineTo(300, 0);
   lineTo(300, 100);
   lineTo(0, 100);
   lineTo(0, 0);
   endFill();
}

var mcl_obj:Object = new Object();
mcl_obj.onLoadInit = function(target_mc:MovieClip) {
   // set the target movie clip's mask to mask_mc
   target_mc.setMask(mask_mc);
   target_mc.onEnterFrame = function() {
      target_mc._x += speed * direction;
      // if the target_mc is at an edge, reverse the animation direction
      if ((target_mc._x <= -(target_mc._width-mask_mc._width)) ||
   (target_mc._x >= 0)) {
         direction *= -1;
      }
   };
};

var my_mcl:MovieClipLoader = new MovieClipLoader();
my_mcl.addListener(mcl_obj);
my_mcl.loadClip("http://www.helpexamples.com/flash/images/image1.jpg",
   img_mc);
```

The first section of code in this code example defines two variables: direction and speed. The direction variable controls whether the masked image scrolls from left to right (1) or right to left (-1). The speed variable controls how many pixels are moved each time the onEnterFrame event handler is called. Larger numbers cause the animation to move more quickly, although the animation appears a bit less smooth.

The next section of code creates two empty movie clips: img_mc and mask_mc. A 300 pixel by 100 pixel rectangle is drawn inside the mark_mc movie clip using the Drawing API. Next, a new object (mcl_obj) is created, which you use as a listener for a MovieClipLoader instance created in the final block of code. This object defines an event listener for the onLoadInit event, masks the dynamically loaded image, and sets up the scrolling animation. After the image reaches the left or right edge of the mask, the animation reverses.

The final block of code defines a MovieClipLoader instance, specifies the listener object you created earlier, and begins loading the JPEG image into the img_mc movie clip.

4. Select Control > Test Movie to test the document.

The image loads and then animates back and forth in a panning motion (side to side motion). The image is masked at runtime. To see the original image, you can view it online (www.helpexamples.com/flash/images/image1.jpg).

About bitmap caching, scrolling, and performance

Flash Player 8 introduces bitmap caching, which helps you enhance the performance of nonchanging movie clips in your applications. When you set the MovieClip.cacheAsBitmap or Button.cacheAsBitmap property to true, Flash Player caches an internal bitmap representation of the movie clip or button instance. This can improve performance for movie clips that contain complex vector content. All of the vector data for a movie clip that has a cached bitmap is drawn to the bitmap, instead of to the main Stage.

 NOTE The bitmap is copied to the main Stage as unstretched, unrotated pixels snapped to the nearest pixel boundaries. Pixels are mapped one-to-one with the parent object. If the bounds of the bitmap change, the bitmap is re-created instead of being stretched.

For detailed information on caching button or movie clip instances see the following sections in Chapter 11, "Working with Movie Clips":

- "About caching and scrolling movie clips with ActionScript" on page 375
- "Caching a movie clip" on page 379
- "Setting the background of a movie clip" on page 381

It's ideal to use the `cacheAsBitmap` property with movie clips that have mostly static content and that do not scale and rotate frequently. With such movie clips, using the `cacheAsBitmap` property can lead to performance improvements when the movie clip is translated (when its *x* and *y* position is changed). For detailed information about when to use this feature, see "When to enable caching" on page 377.

You can find a sample source file that shows you how bitmap caching can be applied to an instance. Find the file called cacheBitmap.fla, in the Samples folder on your hard disk.

- In Windows, browse to *boot drive*\Program Files\Macromedia\Flash 8\ Samples and Tutorials\Samples\ActionScript\CacheBitmap.

- On the Macintosh, browse to *Macintosh IID*/Applications/Macromedia Flash 8/ Samples and Tutorials/Samples/ActionScript/CacheBitmap.

You can also find a sample source file that shows you how to apply bitmap caching to scrolling text. Find the sample source file, flashtype.fla, in the Samples folder on your hard disk.

- In Windows, browse to *boot drive*\Program Files\Macromedia\Flash 8\ Samples and Tutorials\Samples\ActionScript\FlashType.

- On the Macintosh, browse to *Macintosh HD*/Applications/Macromedia Flash 8/ Samples and Tutorials/Samples/ActionScript/FlashType.

About the Tween and TransitionManager classes

When you install Flash Basic 8 or Flash Professional 8, you also install two powerful classes: the Tween and TransitionManager classes. This section describes how to use these classes with movie clips and Macromedia V2 components (included with Flash MX 2004 and Flash 8) to add animation easily to your SWF files.

If you create a slide presentation or form application with Flash Professional 8 (ActionScript 2.0 only), you can select behaviors that add different kinds of transitions between slides, which is similar to when you create a PowerPoint presentation. You add this functionality into a screen application by using the Tween and TransitionManager classes, which generate ActionScript that animates the screens depending on the behavior that you choose.

You can also use the Tween and TransitionManager classes outside of a screen-based document, in either Flash Basic 8 or Flash Professional 8. For example, you can use the classes with the component set of version 2 of the Macromedia Component Architecture, or with movie clips. If you want to change the way a ComboBox component animates, you can use the TransitionManager class to add some *easing* when the menu opens. Easing refers to gradual acceleration or deceleration during an animation, which helps your animations appear more realistic. You can also use the Tween and TransitionManager classes, instead of creating motion tweens on the timeline or writing custom code, to create your own animated menu system.

> **NOTE** The Tween and TransitionManager classes are available only in ActionScript 2.0, but these classes are available in both Flash Basic 8 and Flash Professional 8.

For information on each method and property of the Tween class, see "Tween class" in the *Components Language Reference* in Flash Help. For information on each method and property of the TransitionManager class, see "TransitionManager class" in the *Components Language Reference* in Flash Help. For information on working with packages, see "Working with filter packages" on page 509.

You can find a sample source file that uses these classes to add scripted animation. Find tweenProgress.fla in the Samples folder on your hard disk.

- In Windows, browse to *boot drive*\Program Files\Macromedia\Flash 8\Samples and Tutorials\Samples\ActionScript\Tween ProgressBar.
- On the Macintosh, browse to *Macintosh HD*/Applications/Macromedia Flash 8/Samples and Tutorials/Samples/ActionScript/Tween ProgressBar.

For more information on the Tween and TransitionManager classes, see the following topics:

- "Adding tweens and transitions to a file in Flash Professional 8 (Flash Professional 8 only)" on page 493
- "Animating with the TransitionManager and Tween classes" on page 495
- "About easing classes and methods" on page 498
- "About the Tween class" on page 499
- "Using the Tween class" on page 500
- "Combining the TransitionManager and Tween classes" on page 506

Adding tweens and transitions to a file in Flash Professional 8 (Flash Professional 8 only)

The Tween and TransitionManager classes are designed to let you use simple ActionScript to add animations to parts of your SWF file. The Flash authoring environment contains behaviors that let you use these prebuilt classes for transitions in a screen-based application. To create a slide presentation or form application, you can select behaviors that add different kinds of transitions between slides.

Before you start to use these transitions with movie clips in Flash, you should see what they do when you use a screen-based application.

To view the ActionScript that creates a transition in a slide presentation:

1. Select File > New to create a new slide presentation in Flash Professional 8.

2. Select Flash Slide Presentation from the General tab and click OK.

3. Select Window > Behaviors to open the Behaviors panel.

4. Click Add Behavior (+).

5. Select Screen > Transition from the pop-up menu to open the Transitions dialog box.

6. Select the Zoom transition.

7. Type 1 into the Duration text box.

8. Select Bounce from the Easing pop-up menu.

9. Click OK to apply the settings and close the dialog box.

    This adds about 15 lines of ActionScript directly onto the slide. The following snippet shows the relevant transition code:

    ```
    mx.transitions.TransitionManager.start(eventObj.target,
        {type:mx.transitions.Zoom, direction:0, duration:1,
        easing:mx.transitions.easing.Bounce.easeOut, param1:empty,
        param2:empty});
    ```

This code calls the TransitionManager class and then applies the Zoom transition with the specified `mx.transitions.easing.Bounce.easeOut` easing method. In this case, the transition applies to the selected slide. To apply this effect to a movie clip, you can modify the ActionScript to use in your Flash animations. Modifying the code to work with a movie clip symbol is easy: change the first parameter from `eventObj.target` to the desired movie clip's instance name.

Flash comes with ten transitions, which you can customize by using the easing methods and several optional parameters. Remember, easing refers to gradual acceleration or deceleration during an animation, which helps your animations appear more realistic. For example, a ball might gradually increase its speed near the beginning of an animation, but slow down before it arrives at a full stop at the end of the animation. There are many equations for this acceleration and deceleration, which change the easing animation accordingly.

The following table describes the transitions included in Flash Basic 8 (using code) and Flash Professional 8 (using code or behaviors):

Transition	Description
Iris	Reveals the screen or movie clip by using an animated mask of a shape that zooms in.
Wipe	Reveals the screen or movie clip by using an animated mask of a shape that moves horizontally.
Pixel Dissolve	Masks the screen or movie clip by using disappearing or appearing rectangles.
Blinds	Reveals the next screen or movie clip by using disappearing or appearing rectangles.
Fade	Fades the screen or movie clip in or out.
Fly	Slides in the screen or movie clip from a particular direction.
Zoom	Zooms the screen or movie clip in or out.
Squeeze	Scales the current screen or movie clip horizontally or vertically.
Rotate	Rotates the current screen or movie clip.
Photo	Has the screen or movie clip appear like a photographic flash.

Each transition has slightly different customizations that you can apply to the animation. The Transitions dialog box lets you preview a sample animation before you apply the effect to the slide or form.

> **TIP**
>
> To preview how each transition works with the different methods in the easing classes, you can double-click Transition.swf in boot drive\Program Files\Macromedia\Flash 8\language\First Run\Behaviors\ folder or *Macintosh HD*:Applications:Macromedia Flash 8:First Run:Behaviors: to open the SWF file in the stand-alone player.

Animating with the TransitionManager and Tween classes

You can use the TransitionManager and Tween classes in Flash Basic 8 and Flash Professional 8 to add animations to movie clips, components, and frames using ActionScript. If you don't use the TransitionManager or the Tween class, you have to write custom code to animate movie clips or modify their level of transparency (alpha) and coordinates (location). If you add easing to the animation, the ActionScript (and mathematics) can become complex quickly. However, if you want to change the easing on a particular animation and you use these prebuilt classes, you can select a different class instead of trying to figure out the new mathematical equations you need to create a smooth animation.

The following procedure animates a movie clip so that it uses the TransitionManager class to zoom in on the Stage.

To animate a movie clip using the TransitionManager class:

1. Select File > New and select Flash Document.

2. Click OK to create the new FLA file.

3. Save the FLA file as **zoom.fla**.

4. Select File > Import > Import to Stage, and select an image on your hard disk to import into the FLA file.

   The image is imported into your file as a bitmap image, so you need to convert the image manually into a movie clip symbol.

5. Click Open to import the image.

6. Select the imported image on the Stage and select Modify > Convert to Symbol

7. Name the symbol **img1**, and make sure you set the behavior to Movie Clip.

   By default, the registration point of the symbol is in the upper-left corner of the symbol.

8. Click OK to convert the bitmap image into a movie clip.

9. With the image still selected, open the Property inspector (Window > Properties > Properties), and assign the movie clip the instance name **img1_mc**.

10. Select Frame 1 of the main Timeline and add the following ActionScript to the Actions panel:

```
mx.transitions.TransitionManager.start(img1_mc,
    {type:mx.transitions.Zoom, direction:0, duration:1,
    easing:mx.transitions.easing.Bounce.easeOut, param1:empty,
    param2:empty});
```

>
> For information on working with packages, see "Working with filter packages" on page 509.

11. Select Control > Test Movie to test the animation.

The image grows and has a slight bouncing effect before it returns to its original size. If the animation moves too quickly, increase the animation's duration (in the previous code snippet) from one second to two or three seconds (for example, `duration:3`).

You might notice that the image is anchored in the upper-left corner and grows toward the lower-right corner. This is different from the preview you see in the Transitions dialog box.

Creating complex animations is easy using the Tween and TransitionManager classes and doesn't require you to create motion or shape tweens on the timeline. Most importantly, you don't need to write complex math to create easing methods. If you want images to zoom in from the center instead of anchoring on a corner, modify the symbol's registration point when you convert the image from a bitmap into a symbol.

To zoom images in from the center of the image:

1. Complete the steps in the previous procedure.

2. Open the zoom.fla file, and select File > Save As to save a new copy of the document.

Save the file as **zoom2.fla**.

3. Drag a copy of the bitmap symbol from the Library panel onto the Stage beside the current movie clip symbol.

4. With the bitmap image still selected on the Stage, press F8 to convert the symbol into a movie clip.

Name the symbol **img2**.

5. In the Convert to Symbol dialog box, click the center of the 3 x 3 grid to set the registration point to the center of the bitmap and click OK.

6. Select the new movie clip on the Stage and use the Property inspector to give it an instance name of **img2_mc**.

7. Select Frame 1 of the main Timeline and add the following ActionScript to the existing code:

```
mx.transitions.TransitionManager.start(img2_mc,
    {type:mx.transitions.Zoom, direction:mx.transitions.Transition.IN,
    duration:1, easing:mx.transitions.easing.Bounce.easeOut});
```

8. Select Control > Test Movie to test the animation.

   The second movie clip grows from the center of the symbol instead of the corner.

> **NOTE**
>
> Some transitions are sensitive to where you locate the registration point. Changing the registration point can have a dramatic effect on how the animation looks in a SWF file. For example, if the registration point is in the upper-left corner (default) when you use the Zoom transition, the transition begins from that location.

For information on each method and property of the Tween class, see "Tween class" in the *Components Language Reference* in Flash Help. For information on each method and property of the TransitionManager class, see "TransitionManager class" in the *Components Language Reference* in Flash Help.

You can find a sample source file that uses these classes to add scripted animation. Find tweenProgress.fla in the Samples folder on your hard disk.

- In Windows, browse to *boot drive*\Program Files\Macromedia\Flash 8\ Samples and Tutorials\Samples\ActionScript\Tween ProgressBar.
- On the Macintosh, browse to *Macintosh IID*/Applications/Macromedia Flash 8/ Samples and Tutorials/Samples/ActionScript/Tween ProgressBar.

About easing classes and methods

"Adding tweens and transitions to a file in Flash Professional 8 (Flash Professional 8 only)" on page 493 describes how to use the Bounce easing class to add a bouncing effect to the movie clip. In addition to Bounce, Flash 8 offers five additional easing classes, which are described in the following table:

Transition	Description
Back	Extends the animation beyond the transition range at one or both ends once to resemble an overflow effect.
Bounce	Adds a bouncing effect within the transition range at one or both ends. The number of bounces relates to the duration—longer durations produce more bounces.
Elastic	Adds an elastic effect that falls outside the transition range at one or both ends. The amount of elasticity is unaffected by the duration.
Regular	Adds slower movement at one or both ends. This feature lets you add a speeding up effect, a slowing down effect, or both.
Strong	Adds slower movement at one or both ends. This effect is similar to Regular easing, but it's more pronounced.
None	Adds an equal movement from start to end without effects, slowing down, or speeding up. This transition is also called a linear transition.

These six easing classes each have three easing methods, which are described in the following table:

Method	Description
easeIn	Provides the easing effect at the beginning of the transition.
easeOut	Provides the easing effect at the end of the transition.
easeInOut	Provides the easing effect at the beginning and end of the transition.

To open these classes in Flash or your ActionScript editor, browse to *Hard Disk*\Program Files\Macromedia\Flash 8*language*\First Run\Classes\mx\transitions\easing\ folder on Windows (assumes a default installation), or *Macintosh HD*:Applications:Macromedia Flash 8:First Run:Classes:mx:transitions:easing.

The procedure on zooming images under "Animating with the TransitionManager and Tween classes" on page 495 used the mx.transitions.easing.Bounce.easeOut easing class and method. In the folder on your hard disk, the ActionScript refers to the easeOut() method within the Bounce.as class. This ActionScript file is in the easing folder.

For information on each method and property of the Tween class, see "Tween class" in the *Components Language Reference* in Flash Help. For information on each method and property of the TransitionManager class, see "TransitionManager class" in the *Components Language Reference* in Flash Help.

 To preview how each transition works with the different methods in the easing classes, you can double-click Transition.swf in *boot drive*\Program Files\Macromedia\Flash 8*language*\First Run\Behaviors\ or *Macintosh HD*:Applications:Macromedia Flash 8:First Run:Behaviors: to open the SWF file in the stand-alone player.

You can find a sample source file that adds scripted animation using these classes. Find tweenProgress.fla in the Samples folder on your hard disk.

- In Windows, browse to *boot drive*\Program Files\Macromedia\Flash 8\ Samples and Tutorials\Samples\ActionScript\Tween ProgressBar.

- On the Macintosh, browse to *Macintosh HD*/Applications/Macromedia Flash 8/ Samples and Tutorials/Samples/ActionScript/Tween ProgressBar.

About the Tween class

The Tween class lets you move, resize, and fade movie clips easily on the Stage. The constructor for the mx.transitions.Tween class has the following parameter names and types:

```
function Tween(obj, prop, func, begin, finish, duration, useSeconds) {
    // code ...
}
```

obj   The movie clip object that the Tween instance targets.

prop   A string name of a property in obj to which the values are to be tweened.

func   The easing method that calculates an easing effect for the tweened object's property values.

begin   A number that indicates the starting value of prop (the target object property to be tweened).

finish   A number that indicates the ending value of prop (the target object property to be tweened).

duration   A number that indicates the length of time of the tween motion. If omitted, the duration is set to infinity by default.

useSeconds   A Boolean value related to the value you specify in the duration parameter, which indicates to use seconds if true, or frames if false.

For example, imagine that you want to move a movie clip across the Stage. You can add keyframes to a timeline and insert a motion or shape tween between them, you can write some code in an `onEnterFrame` event handler, or you can use the `setInterval()` function to call a function at periodic intervals. If you use the Tween class, you have another option that lets you modify a movie clip's _x and _y properties. You can also add the previously described easing methods. To take advantage of the Tween class, you can use the following ActionScript:

```
new mx.transitions.Tween(ball_mc, "_x",
  mx.transitions.easing.Elastic.easeOut, 0, 300, 3, true);
```

This ActionScript snippet creates a new instance of the Tween class, which animates the `ball_mc` movie clip on the Stage along the x-axis (left to right). The movie clip animates from 0 pixels to 300 pixels in three seconds, and the ActionScript applies an elastic easing method. This means that the ball extends past 300 pixels on the x-axis before using a fluid motion effect to animating back.

You can find a sample source file that adds scripted animation using these classes. Find tweenProgress.fla in the Samples folder on your hard disk.

- In Windows, browse to *boot drive*\Program Files\Macromedia\Flash 8\ Samples and Tutorials\Samples\ActionScript\Tween ProgressBar.
- On the Macintosh, browse to *Macintosh HD*/Applications/Macromedia Flash 8/ Samples and Tutorials/Samples/ActionScript/Tween ProgressBar.

Using the Tween class

If you use the Tween class in more than one place in your Flash document, you might opt to use an `import` statement. This lets you import the Tween class and easing methods rather than give the fully qualified class names each time you use them, as the following procedure shows.

To import and use the Tween class:

1. Create a new document and call it **easeTween.fla**.
2. Create a movie clip on the Stage.
3. Select the movie clip instance and type **ball_mc** into the Instance Name text box in the Property inspector.
4. Select Frame 1 of the Timeline and add the following code in the Actions panel:

```
import mx.transitions.Tween;
import mx.transitions.easing.*;
new Tween(ball_mc, "_x", Elastic.easeOut, Stage.width, 0, 3, true);
```

This code example uses two `import` statements. The first statement imports the mx.transitions.Tween class only, and the second `import` statement uses the wildcard (*) shortcut to import each of the six easing classes by using a single line of code. The second statement imports an entire package of classes.

> **NOTE**
> For information on working with packages, see "Working with filter packages" on page 509.

5. Select Control > Test Movie to see the animation.

Flash documentation defines *package* as directories that contain one or more class files and that reside in a designated classpath directory. In this case, the package resides in the C:\Program Files\Macromedia\Flash 8*language*\First Run\Classes\mx\transitions\ easing folder (Windows), or HD:Applications:Macromedia Flash 8:First Run:Classes:mx:transitions:easing (Macintosh). You might agree that importing an entire package is much better than having to import the six classes separately. Instead of referring to the mx.transitions.Tween class, your ActionScript directly refers to the Tween class. Likewise, instead of using the fully qualified class name for the easing classes, mx.transitions.easing.Elastic.easeOut for example, you can type **Elastic.easeOut** in your ActionScript code. For more information, see "Working with filter packages" on page 509.

Using similar code, you set the `_alpha` property to fade instances in and out, instead of the `_x` property, as the next procedure shows.

To fade instances using the Tween class:

1. Create a new document, and call it **fadeTween.fla**.

2. Create a movie clip on the Stage.

3. Select the movie clip instance, and type **ball_mc** into the Instance Name text box in the Property inspector.

4. Select Frame 1 of the Timeline and add the following code in the Actions panel:

```
import mx.transitions.Tween;
import mx.transitions.easing.*;
new Tween(ball_mc, "_alpha", Strong.easeIn, 100, 0, 3, true);
```

Instead of moving around the Stage, now `ball_mc` fades from 100% visible to completely transparent in three seconds. To make the symbol fade out more quickly, change the duration parameter from 3 to 1 or 2.

5. Select Control > Test Movie to see the animation.

If you change the document's frame rate, the animation appears to play more smoothly. For information on animation and frame rate, see "About animation and frame rate" on page 481.

Instead of using seconds, you can fade the symbol over a few frames. To set the duration in frames instead of seconds in the Tween class, you change the final parameter, useSeconds, from true to false. When you set the parameter to true, you tell Flash that the specified duration is in seconds. If you set the parameter to false, the duration is the number of frames you want to use for the tween. The next procedure shows how to set a tween to frames instead of seconds.

To set a duration of frames instead of seconds:

1. Create a new document, and call it **framesTween.fla**.

2. Create a movie clip on the Stage.

3. Select the movie clip instance, and type **ball_mc** into the Instance Name text box in the Property inspector.

4. Select Frame 1 of the Timeline, and add the following code in the Actions panel:
   ```
   import mx.transitions.Tween;
   import mx.transitions.easing.*;
   new Tween(ball_mc, "_alpha", Strong.easeIn, 100, 0, 24, false);
   ```
   This code fades out the ball_mc instance using the Strong.easeIn easing method. Instead of fading the instance for three seconds, it fades the instance across 24 frames.

5. Select Control > Test Movie to see the animation.

   Wait a moment, then the instance fades out across 24 frames.

6. Return to the authoring environment and open the Property inspector.

7. Change the document's frame rate to 24 fps.

   If you increase the frame rate of your FLA file, you see the instance fade out sooner. For information on animation and frame rate, see "About animation and frame rate" on page 481.

Using frames instead of seconds offers more flexibility, but remember that the duration relates to the frame rate of the current Flash document. If your Flash document uses a frame rate of 12 frames per second (fps), the previous code snippet fades the instance over two seconds (24 frames/12 fps = 2 seconds). However, if your frame rate is 24 fps, the same code fades the instance over one second (24 frames/24 fps = 1 second). If you use frames to measure duration, you can significantly change the speed of your animation when you change the document's frame rate, without modifying your ActionScript.

The Tween class has several more useful features. For example, you can write an event handler that triggers when the animation completes, as the next procedure shows.

To trigger code when an animation is completed:

1. Create a new document, and call it **triggerTween.fla**.

2. Create a movie clip on the Stage.

3. Select the movie clip instance and type **ball_mc** into the Instance Name text box in the Property inspector.

4. Select Frame 1 of the Timeline and add the following code in the Actions panel:

```
import mx.transitions.Tween;
import mx.transitions.easing.*;
var tween_handler:Object = new Tween(ball_mc, "_alpha", Strong.easeIn,
  100, 0, 3, true);
tween_handler.onMotionFinished = function() {
  trace("onMotionFinished triggered");
};
```

   If you test this ActionScript in your FLA file, you see the message "onMotionFinished triggered" appear in the Output panel after ball_mc finishes fading on the Stage.

5. Select Control > Test Movie to see the animation.

   Wait for a moment, and then the instance fades out. When it finishes tweening, you see the message appear in the Output panel.

For more information on functions, see Chapter 7, "Classes."

About continuing animations using the continueTo() method

"Using the Tween class" on page 500 demonstrates how to use the Tween class in your applications. However, if you want to move the ball after the initial animation is complete, there are at least two ways you can do it. One solution is to reanimate the ball by using the onMotionFinished event handler. However, the Tween class offers a simpler solution, the continueTo() method. The continueTo() method instructs the tweened animation to continue from its current value to a new value, as the following ActionScript shows:

```
import mx.transitions.Tween;
import mx.transitions.easing.*;
var ball_tween:Object = new Tween(ball_mc, "_x", Regular.easeIn, 0, 300, 3,
  true);
ball_tween.onMotionFinished = function() {
    ball_tween.continueTo(0, 3);
};
```

After the initial tween finishes, the ball_mc movie clip tweens back to its original position at 0 pixels. The following snippet (edited for brevity) shows the function prototype for the continueTo() method:

```
function continueTo(finish:Number, duration:Number):Void {
    /* omitted to save space. */
}
```

Only two arguments pass to the `continueTo()` method, instead of the seven arguments for the Tween constructor method, as the following snippet shows:

```
function Tween (obj, prop, func, begin, finish, duration, useSeconds) {
    /* omitted to save space. */
}
```

The five parameters that aren't required by the `continueTo()` method (`obj`, `prop`, `func`, `begin`, and `useSeconds`) use the arguments that you defined earlier in the call to the Tween class. When you call the `continueTo()` method, you assume that the `obj`, `prop`, `func` (easing type), and `useSeconds` arguments are the same as in the earlier call to the Tween class. The `continueTo()` method uses the `finish` value from the call to the Tween class, instead of specifying a value for the `begin` argument, as the following ActionScript shows:

```
import mx.transitions.Tween;
import mx.transitions.easing.*;
var ball_tween:Object = new Tween(ball_mc, "_x", Regular.easeIn, 0, 300, 3,
    true);
ball_tween.onMotionFinished = function() {
    ball_tween.continueTo(0, 3);
};
```

This code moves the `ball_mc` instance along the *x*-axis from 0 pixels to 300 pixels in three seconds. After the animation finishes, the `onMotionFinished` event handler is triggered and calls the `continueTo()` method. The `continueTo()` method tells the target object (`ball_mc`) to proceed from its current position and animate for three seconds along the *x*-axis to 0 pixels and to use the same easing method. You use the values specified in the call to the Tween constructor method for any parameters that you don't define in the `continueTo()` method. If you don't specify a duration for the `continueTo()` method, it uses the duration you specify in the call to the Tween constructor.

Creating animations that run continuously

You can make an animation continue moving back and forth along the *x*-axis without stopping. The Tween class accommodates this kind of animation with the aptly named `yoyo()` method. The `yoyo()` method waits for the `onMotionFinished` event handler to execute, and then it reverses the `begin` and `finish` parameters. The animation begins again, as the following procedure demonstrates.

To create an animation that continues endlessly:

1. Create a new Flash document called **yoyo.fla.**

2. Open the Actions panel and enter the following ActionScript on Frame 1 of the Timeline:

```
import mx.transitions.Tween;
import mx.transitions.easing.*;

this.createEmptyMovieClip("box_mc", this.getNextHighestDepth());
with (box_mc) {
    beginFill(0xFF0000, 60);
    moveTo(0, 0);
    lineTo(20, 0);
    lineTo(20, Stage.height);
    lineTo(0, Stage.height);
    lineTo(0, 0);
    endFill();
}
```

The first section code begins by importing the Tween class, as well as each class in the easing package. The next section of code creates a new movie clip with an instance name of box_mc and draws a rectangle 20 pixels wide and the same height as the Stage.

3. Add the following ActionScript after the code created in the previous step:

```
var box_tween:Tween = new Tween(box_mc, "_x", Regular.easeInOut, 0,
    Stage.width, 3, true);
box_tween.onMotionFinished = function() {
    box_tween.yoyo();
};
```

This code creates a new tween to animate the box_mc movie clip across the Stage along the *x*-axis over 3 seconds.

4. Select Control > Test Movie to test the animation.

The box animates from left to right and back. If the animation isn't smooth, you might want to increase the document's frame rate from 12 fps to 24 fps.

As the box approaches the right edge of the Stage, it animates outside the boundaries of the Stage. While this might not seem significant, you might not want the rectangle to disappear from view off the side of the Stage and then reappear a second later and animate in the other direction.

To make adjustments, animate the rectangle from 0 pixels to the width of the Stage minus the width of the box_mc movie clip.

5. To stop the rectangle from disappearing, revise the corresponding lines of code from step 3 to match the following code:

```
var box_tween:Tween = new Tween(box_mc, "_x", Regular.easeInOut, 0,
    (Stage.width - box_mc._width), 3, true);
```

6. Test the animation again (Control > Test Movie).

Now, the box stops easing before it goes off the boundaries of the Stage.

Combining the TransitionManager and Tween classes

You can generate interesting effects when you combine the TransitionManager and Tween classes. You can use the TransitionManager class to move a movie clip along the *x*-axis while you adjust the same clip's _alpha property using the Tween class. Each class can use a different easing method, which means you have many animation possibilities for objects in your SWF files. You can take advantage of the continueTo() and yoyo() methods in the Tween class or the onMotionFinished event handler to create a unique effect.

You combine the TransitionManager and Tween classes to animate a dynamically loaded movie clip and fade it in on the Stage after it fully loads from the remote server, as the following procedure shows.

To use the TransitionManager and Tween classes together:

1. Create a new Flash document and save the file as **combination.fla**.

2. Add the following ActionScript on Frame 1 of the Timeline:

```
import mx.transitions.*;
import mx.transitions.easing.*;

var mcl_obj:Object = new Object();
mcl_obj.onLoadInit = function(target_mc:MovieClip) {
    new Tween(target_mc, "_alpha", Strong.easeIn, 0, 100, 2, true);
    TransitionManager.start(target_mc, {type:Fly,
  direction:Transition.IN, duration:3, easing:Elastic.easeInOut,
  startPoint:6});
};

var my_mcl:MovieClipLoader = new MovieClipLoader();
my_mcl.addListener(mcl_obj);
my_mcl.loadClip("http://www.helpexamples.com/flash/images/image1.jpg",
  this.createEmptyMovieClip("img_mc", this.getNextHighestDepth()));
```

This code is separated into three main sections.

The first section of code imports the classes within the transitions package as well as the transitions.easing package. You import the entire transitions package in this example so you do not need to enter the fully qualified class name for the Tween class, TransitionManager class, or the selected transition (in this case, *Fly*). This process can reduce the amount of code you type and save you from potential typographical errors.

The second section of ActionScript creates a listener object for the MovieClipLoader class instance, which you create in the third section of code. When the target movie clip loads into the MovieClipLoader instance, the `onLoadInit` event triggers and executes the block of code, which calls both the Tween class and the TransitionManager class. This event handler fades in the target movie clip because you modify the `_alpha` property in the Tween class, and *flies* the target movie clip along the *x*-axis.

The third section of ActionScript code creates a MovieClipLoader instance and applies the listener object that you created earlier (so the target movie clip loader instance can listen for the `onLoadInit` event). Then you load the target JPEG image into a movie clip that you create dynamically by calling the `createEmptyMovieClip()` method.

3. Save your document and select Control > Test Movie to view the animation in the test environment.

After the external JPEG image finishes downloading from the server, the image fades in gradually and animates from right to left across the Stage.

For information on using the Tween class, see "Using the Tween class" on page 500.

For information on each method and property of the Tween class, see "Tween class" in the *Components Language Reference* in Flash Help. For information on each method and property of the TransitionManager class, see "TransitionManager class" in the *Components Language Reference* in Flash Help.

You can find a sample source file that adds scripted animation using these classes. Find tweenProgress.fla in the Samples folder on your hard disk.

- In Windows, browse to *boot drive*\Program Files\Macromedia\Flash 8\ Samples and Tutorials\Samples\ActionScript\Tween ProgressBar.
- On the Macintosh, browse to *Macintosh HD*/Applications/Macromedia Flash 8/ Samples and Tutorials/Samples/ActionScript/Tween ProgressBar.

Using filter effects

Filters are visual effects that you can apply to objects rendered at runtime by Flash Player, such as movie clip instances. The filters include drop shadow, blur, glow, bevel, gradient glow, and gradient bevel. You can also use an adjust color filter that lets you edit a movie clip's brightness, contrast, saturation, and hue. You can apply filters using the Flash user interface in Flash Professional 8, or using ActionScript in Flash Basic 8 or Flash Professional 8.

You can apply each of these filter effects to movie clips, buttons, or text fields by using either the Filters tab in the Property inspector or by using ActionScript. If you use ActionScript to apply the filters to an instance, you can also use a displacement map filter (see "Using the displacement map filter" on page 539) or a convolution filter (see "Using the convolution filter" on page 538). These filters are applied to the vector definitions, so there is no overhead of storing a bitmap image within the SWF file. You can also write ActionScript that lets you modify an existing filter that you applied to a text field, movie clip, or button.

The following procedure demonstrates how you could use an onEnterFrame event handler to animate a glow filter effect on a movie clip.

To animate a filter effect applied to a movie clip instance:

1. Create a new Flash document and save it as **animFilter.fla**.

2. Add the following ActionScript to Frame 1 of the Timeline:

```
this.createEmptyMovieClip("box_mc", 10);
box_mc.lineStyle(20, 0x000000);
box_mc.beginFill(0x000000);
box_mc.moveTo(0, 0);
box_mc.lineTo(160, 0);
box_mc.lineTo(160, 120);
box_mc.lineTo(0, 120);
box_mc.lineTo(0, 0);
box_mc.endFill();
box_mc._x = 100;
box_mc._y = 100;

box_mc.filters = [new flash.filters.GlowFilter()];
var dir:Number = 1;
box_mc.blur = 10;
box_mc.onEnterFrame = function() {
  box_mc.blur += dir;
  if ((box_mc.blur >= 30) || (box_mc.blur <= 10)) {
    dir *= -1;
  }
  var filter_array:Array = box_mc.filters;
  filter_array[0].blurX = box_mc.blur;
  filter_array[0].blurY = box_mc.blur;
  box_mc.filters = filter_array;
};
```

This code completes two different functionalities. The first section creates and positions a movie clip instance, and draws a black rounded rectangle on the Stage. The second block of code applies a glow filter to the rectangle on the Stage and defines an `onEnterFrame` event handler, which is responsible for animating the filter effect. The `onEnterFrame` event handler animates the glow filter between a blur of 10 and 30 pixels, and after the animation is greater than or equal to 30, or less than or equal to 10, the direction of the animation reverses.

3. Save your changes to the Flash document and select Control > Test Movie to test the SWF file.

For more information on working with filters in an application, see the following topics:

- "Working with filter packages" on page 509
- "Working with filters, caching, and the MovieClip class" on page 511
- "About hit detection, rotating, skewing, and scaling filters" on page 513
- "Applying filters to object instances and BitmapData instances" on page 513
- "About error handling, performance, and filters" on page 514

For an example of using ActionScript to apply filters, you can find a sample source file, Filters.fla, in the Samples folder on your hard disk.

- In Windows, browse to *boot drive*\Program Files\Macromedia\Flash 8\ Samples and Tutorials\Samples\ActionScript\Filters.
- On the Macintosh, browse to *Macintosh HD*/Applications/Macromedia Flash 8/ Samples and Tutorials/Samples/ActionScript/Filters.

Working with filter packages

Packages are directories that contain one or more class files and reside in a designated classpath directory. For example, the flash.filters package is a directory on your hard disk that contains several class files for each filter type (such as BevelFilter, BlurFilter, DropShadowFilter, and so on) in Flash 8. When class files are organized this way, you must access the classes in a specific way. You either *import* the class, or reference it using a *fully qualified name*.

 To use the import statement, you must specify ActionScript 2.0 and Flash Player 6 or later in the Flash tab of your FLA file's Publish Settings dialog box.

The `import` statement lets you access classes without specifying their fully qualified names. For example, to use a BlurFilter in a script, you must refer to it by its fully qualified name (flash.filters.BlurFilter) or import it; if you import it, you can refer to it by its class name (BlurFilter) in your code instead. The following ActionScript code demonstrates the differences between using the import statement and using fully qualified class names.

If you don't import the BlurFilter class, your code needs to use the fully qualified class name (package name followed by class name) in order to use the filter:

```
// without importing
var myBlur:flash.filters.BlurFilter = new flash.filters.BlurFilter(10, 10,
    3);
```

The same code, written with an `import` statement, lets you access the BlurFilter using the class name instead of continually referencing it using the fully qualified name. This can save typing and reduces the chance of making typing mistakes:

```
// with importing
import flash.filters.BlurFilter;
var myBlur:BlurFilter = new BlurFilter(10, 10, 3);
```

To import several classes within a package (such as the BlurFilter, DropShadowFilter, and GlowFilter) you can use one of two ways to import each class. The first way to import multiple classes is to import each class by using a separate `import` statement, as seen in the following snippet:

```
import flash.filters.BlurFilter;
import flash.filters.DropShadowFilter;
import flash.filters.GlowFilter;
```

If you use individual import statements for each class within a package, it becomes time consuming to write and prone to typing mistakes. You can avoid importing individual class files by using a *wildcard* import, which imports all classes within a certain level of a package. The following ActionScript shows an example of using a wildcard import:

```
import flash.filters.*; // imports each class within flash.filters package
```

The `import` statement applies only to the current script (frame or object) in which it's called. For example, suppose on Frame 1 of a Flash document you import all the classes in the `macr.util` package. On that frame, you can reference classes in the package by using their class names instead of their fully qualified name. To use the class name on another frame script, reference classes in that package by their fully qualified names or add an import statement to the other frame that imports the classes in that package.

When you use import statements, remember that classes are only imported for the level that you specify. For example, if you import all classes in the mx.transitions package, only the classes within the /transitions/ directory are imported, not all classes within subdirectories (such as the classes in the mx.transitions.easing package).

> **T** If you import a class but don't use it in your script, the class isn't exported as part of the
> **P** SWF file. This means that you can import large packages without being concerned about the size of the SWF file; the bytecode associated with a class is included in a SWF file only if that class is actually used.

For an example of using ActionScript to apply filters, you can find a sample source file, Filters.fla, in the Samples folder on your hard disk.

- In Windows, browse to *boot drive*\Program Files\Macromedia\Flash 8\ Samples and Tutorials\Samples\ActionScript\Filters.
- On the Macintosh, browse to *Macintosh HD*/Applications/Macromedia Flash 8/ Samples and Tutorials/Samples/ActionScript/Filters.

Working with filters, caching, and the MovieClip class

If a movie clip has an associated filter, it's marked to cache itself as a transparent bitmap when the SWF file loads. As long as the movie clip has at least one filter applied to it, Flash Player caches the movie clip as a bitmap at runtime by forcing the cacheAsBitmap property to be true. The cached bitmap is used as a source image for the filter effects. Each movie clip usually has two bitmaps: one bitmap is the original unfiltered source movie clip, the second bitmap is the final image after filtering. If you do not change the appearance of the movie clip at runtime, the final image does not need to update, which helps improve performance.

You can access filters applied to an instance by calling the MovieClip.filters property. Calling this property returns an array that contains each filter object currently associated with the movie clip instance. A filter itself has a set of properties unique to that filter, such as the following:

```
trace(my_mc.filters[0].angle); // 45.0
trace(my_mc.filters[0].distance); // 4
```

You can access and modify filters as you would a regular array object. Setting and getting the filters by using the property returns a *duplicate* of the filters object, not a *reference*.

To modify an existing filter, you can use code similar to the code in the following procedure.

To modify a filter's properties when applied to a movie clip instance:

1. Create a new Flash document and save the file as **modifyFilter.fla**.

2. Add the following ActionScript to Frame 1 of the Timeline:

```
this.createEmptyMovieClip("my_mc", 10);
// draw square
with (my_mc) {
    beginFill(0xFF0000, 100);
    moveTo(0, 0);
    lineTo(100, 0);
    lineTo(100, 100);
    lineTo(0, 100);
    lineTo(0, 0);
    endFill();
}
my_mc._x = 100;
my_mc._y = 100;

// use default DropShadowFilter values
my_mc.filters = [new flash.filters.DropShadowFilter()];
trace(my_mc.filters[0].distance); // 4
var filter_array:Array = my_mc.filters;
filter_array[0].distance = 10;
my_mc.filters = filter_array;
trace(my_mc.filters[0].distance); // 10
```

The first section of this code uses the Drawing API to create a red square, and positions the shape on the Stage. The second section of code applies a drop shadow filter to the square. Next, the code creates a temporary array to hold the current filters to apply to the red square on the Stage. The distance property of the first filter is set to 10 pixels, and the modified filter is reapplied to the my_mc movie clip instance.

3. Select Control > Test Movie to test the document.

> **NOTE** Currently, no support is available for having any filters perform rotation based upon their parent's rotation or some sort of other rotation. The blur filter always blurs perfectly horizontally or vertically, independently of the rotation or skew of any item in the parent object tree.

> **TIP** Filtered content has the same restrictions on size as content with its cacheAsBitmap property set to true. If the author zooms in too far on the SWF file, the filters are no longer visible when the bitmap representation is greater than 2880 pixels in either direction. When you publish SWF files with filters, it is a good idea to disable the zoom menu options.

For an example of using ActionScript to apply filters, you can find a sample source file, Filters.fla, in the Samples folder on your hard disk.

- In Windows, browse to *boot drive*\Program Files\Macromedia\Flash 8\
  Samples and Tutorials\Samples\ActionScript\Filters.
- On the Macintosh, browse to *Macintosh HD*/Applications/Macromedia Flash 8/
  Samples and Tutorials/Samples/ActionScript/Filters.

About hit detection, rotating, skewing, and scaling filters

No filtered region (drop shadow, for example) outside of a movie clip instance's bounding box rectangle is considered to be part of the surface for hit detection purposes (determining if an instance overlaps or intersects with another instance). Because hit detection is vector-based, you cannot perform a hit detection on the bitmap result. For example, if you apply a bevel filter to a button instance, hit detection is not available on the beveled portion of the instance.

Scaling, rotating, and skewing are not supported by filters; if the instance itself is scaled (_xscale and _yscale are not 100%), the filter effect does not scale with the instance. This means that the original shape of the instance rotates, scales, or skews; however, the filter does not rotate, scale, or skew with the instance.

You can animate an instance with a filter to create realistic effects, or nest instances and use the BitmapData class to animate filters to achieve this effect.

Applying filters to object instances and BitmapData instances

The use of filters depends on the object instance to which you apply the filter. Use the following guidelines when you apply a filter to an object or BitmapData instance:

- To apply filters to movie clips, text fields, and buttons at runtime, use the `filters` property. Setting the `filters` property of an object does not modify the object and can be undone by clearing the `filters` property.
- To apply filters to BitmapData instances, use the `BitmapData.applyFilter()` method. Calling `applyFilter()` on a BitmapData object modifies that BitmapData object and cannot be undone.

> **NOTE** (Flash Professional 8 only) You can also apply filter effects to images and video during authoring using the Filters tab in the Property inspector.

About error handling, performance, and filters

One problem that arises if you use too many filters in an application is the potential to use large amounts of memory and cause Flash Player performance to suffer. Because a movie clip with filters attached has two bitmaps that are both 32-bit, these bitmaps can cause your application to use a significant amount of memory if you use many bitmaps. You might see an out-of-memory error generated by the computer's operating system. On a modern computer, out-of-memory errors should be rare, unless you are using filter effects extensively in an application (for example, you have thousands of bitmaps on the Stage).

However, if you do encounter an out-of-memory error, the following occurs:

- The filters array is ignored.
- The movie clip is drawn using the regular vector renderer.
- No bitmaps are cached for the movie clip.

After you see an out-of-memory error, a movie clip never attempts to use a filters array or a bitmap cache. Another factor that affects player performance is the value that you use for the `quality` parameter for each filter that you apply. Higher values require more CPU and memory for the effect to render, whereas setting the `quality` parameter to a lower value requires less computer resources. Therefore, you should avoid using an excessive number of filters, and use a lower `quality` setting when possible.

> **CAUTION**
>
> If a 100 pixel by 100 pixel object is zoomed in once, it uses four times the memory since the content's dimensions are now 200 pixels by 200 pixels. If you zoom another two times, the shape is drawn as an 800 pixel by 800 pixel object which uses 64 times the memory as the original 100 pixel by 100 pixel object. Whenever you use filters in a SWF file, it is always a good idea to disable the zoom menu options from the SWF file's context menu.

You can also encounter errors if you use invalid parameter types. Some filter parameters also have a particular valid range. If you set a value that's outside of the valid range, the value changes to a valid value that's within the range. For example, `quality` should be a value from 1 to 3 for a standard operation, and can only be set to 0 to 15. Anything higher than 15 is set to 15.

Also, some constructors have restrictions on the length of arrays required as input parameters. If a convolution filter or color matrix filter is created with an invalid array (not the right size), the constructor fails and the filter is not created successfully. If the filter object is then used as an entry on a movie clip's filters array, it is ignored.

> **TIP**
>
> When using a blur filter, using values for blurX and blurY that are powers of 2 (such as 2, 4, 8, 16, and 32) can be computed faster and give a 20% to 30% performance improvement.

Working with filters using ActionScript

The flash.filters package contains classes for the bitmap filter effects that are new in Flash Player 8. Filters let you use ActionScript to apply rich visual effects, such as blur, bevel, glow, and drop shadow, to text, movie clip, and button instances. You can also use the Flash authoring tool to apply filter effects to objects such as text, images, and video. Flash has nine filter effects, although only seven are accessible by using the user interface in Flash Professional 8. The ConvolutionFilter and DisplacementMapFilter filters are only available by using ActionScript code.

> **NOTE**
>
> All filters are availabe by using ActionScript in both Flash Basic 8 and Flash Professional 8.

The following procedure loads a semitransparent PNG image, and applies a GlowFilter effect to the nontransparent portion of the image.

To apply filters to semitransparent images:

1. Create a new Flash document and save it as **transparentImg.fla**.

2. Add the following ActionScript to Frame 1 of the Timeline:

   ```
   import flash.filters.GlowFilter;
   System.security.allowDomain("http://www.helpexamples.com");
   var mclListener:Object = new Object();
   mclListener.onLoadInit = function(target_mc:MovieClip) {
       target_mc._x = (Stage.width - target_mc._width) / 2;
       target_mc._y = (Stage.height - target_mc._height) / 2;
       var glow:GlowFilter = new GlowFilter();
       target_mc.filters = [glow];
   };
   this.createEmptyMovieClip("img_mc", 10);
   var img_mcl:MovieClipLoader = new MovieClipLoader();
   img_mcl.addListener(mclListener);
   img_mcl.loadClip("http://www.helpexamples.com/flash/images/logo.png",
       img_mc);
   ```

   This code uses a movie clip loader instance to load a semi-transparent PNG image. After the image finishes loading, the image moves to the center of the Stage and a glow filter is applied.

3. Select Control > Test Movie to test the document.

   The glow filter effect is only applied to the opaque (nontransparent) area of the PNG image.

The following sections describe how to use the filters:

- "Using the blur filter" on page 517
- "Using the drop shadow filter" on page 519
- "Using the glow filter" on page 523
- "Creating gradient glows" on page 525
- "Using the bevel filter" on page 527
- "Applying a gradient bevel filter" on page 534
- "Using the color matrix filter" on page 536
- "Using the convolution filter" on page 538
- "Using the displacement map filter" on page 539

For an example of using ActionScript to apply filters, you can find a sample source file, Filters.fla, in the Samples folder on your hard disk.

- In Windows, browse to *boot drive*\Program Files\Macromedia\Flash 8\ Samples and Tutorials\Samples\ActionScript\Filters.
- On the Macintosh, browse to *Macintosh HD*/Applications/Macromedia Flash 8/ Samples and Tutorials/Samples/ActionScript/Filters.

Using the blur filter

The BlurFilter class lets you apply a blur visual effect to a variety of objects in Flash. A blur effect softens the details of an image. You can produce blurs that range from creating a softly unfocused look to a Gaussian blur, a hazy appearance like viewing an image through semi-opaque glass. The blur filter is based on a box-pass blur filter. The quality parameter defines how many times the blur should be repeated (three passes approximates a Gaussian blur filter).

> **NOTE** The blur filter scales only when you zoom into the Stage.

For more information on this filter, see %{BlurFilter (flash.filters.BlurFilter)}% in the *ActionScript 2.0 Language Reference* in Flash Help.

The following procedure blurs a dynamically loaded image based on the mouse pointer's current position on the Stage. The further the pointer is from the center of the Stage, the more the image is blurred.

To blur an image based on the mouse pointer's position:

1. Create a new Flash document and save it as **dynamicblur.fla**.

2. Add the following code to Frame 1 of the Timeline:

```
import flash.filters.BlurFilter;
System.security.allowDomain("http://www.helpexamples.com");
var mclListener:Object = new Object();
mclListener.onLoadInit = function(target_mc:MovieClip) {
   // Center the target_mc movie clip on the Stage.
   target_mc._x = (Stage.width - target_mc._width) / 2;
   target_mc._y = (Stage.height - target_mc._height) / 2;
};
this.createEmptyMovieClip("img_mc", 10);
var img_mcl:MovieClipLoader = new MovieClipLoader();
img_mcl.addListener(mclListener);
img_mcl.loadClip("http://www.helpexamples.com/flash/images/image1.jpg",
   img_mc);
var blur:BlurFilter = new BlurFilter(10, 10, 2);

var mouseListener:Object = new Object();
mouseListener.onMouseMove = function():Void {
   /* Moving the pointer to the center of the Stage sets the blurX and
   blurY properties to 0%. */
   blur.blurX = Math.abs(_xmouse - (Stage.width / 2)) / Stage.width * 2 *
   255;
   blur.blurY = Math.abs(_ymouse - (Stage.height / 2)) / Stage.height * 2
   * 255;
   img_mc.filters = [blur];
};
Mouse.addListener(mouseListener);
```

The first section of this code loads and positions a dynamically loaded image on the Stage. The second section defines a listener that is called whenever the mouse moves. You calculate the amount of horizontal and vertical blurring based on the mouse pointer's current position on the Stage. The further you move the pointer away from the center of the Stage, the more blurring is applied to the instance.

3. Select Control > Test Movie to test the Flash document.

    Move the mouse pointer along the *x*-axis to modify the amount of horizontal blurring. The instance blurs more when the pointer moves farther away from the horizontal center of the Stage. Moving the pointer along the *y*-axis causes the vertical blurring to increase or decrease, depending on the distance from the vertical center of the Stage.

When you use a blur filter, using values for blurX and blurY that are powers of two (such as 2, 4, 8, 16, and 32) can be computed faster and give a 20% to 30% performance improvement.

Setting a blur value lower than 1.03125 disables the blur effect.

Using the drop shadow filter

The DropShadowFilter class lets you add a drop shadow to a variety of objects in Flash. The shadow algorithm is based on the same box filter that the blur filter uses (see "Using the blur filter" on page 517). Several options are available for the style of the drop shadow, including inner or outer shadow and knockout mode.

For more information on the drop shadow filter, see %{DropShadowFilter (flash.filters.DropShadowFilter)}% in the *ActionScript 2.0 Language Reference* in Flash Help.

The following procedure uses the Drawing API to draw a square on the Stage. When you move the mouse pointer horizontally along the Stage, this code modifies the distance from the square that the drop shadow appears, whereas moving the cusror vertically modifies how much the drop shadow blurs.

To use the drop shadow filter:

1. Create a new Flash document and save it as **dropshadow.fla.**

2. Add the following ActionScript to Frame 1 of the Timeline:

```
// import the filter classes
import flash.filters.DropShadowFilter;
// create a movie clip called shapeClip
this.createEmptyMovieClip("shapeClip", 1);
// use the Drawing API to draw a shape
with (shapeClip) {
    beginFill(0xFF0000, 100);
    moveTo(0, 0);
    lineTo(100, 0);
    lineTo(100, 100);
    lineTo(0, 100);
    lineTo(0, 0);
    endFill();
}
// position the shape
shapeClip._x = 100;
shapeClip._y = 100;
// click the square, increase shadow strength
shapeClip.onPress = function():Void {
    dropShadow.strength++;
    shapeClip.filters = [dropShadow];
};
// create a filter
var dropShadow:DropShadowFilter = new DropShadowFilter(4, 45, 0x000000,
    0.4, 10, 10, 2, 3);

var mouseListener:Object = new Object();
// create and apply a listener that controls the filter when the mouse
    moves
mouseListener.onMouseMove = function():Void {
    dropShadow.distance = (_xmouse / Stage.width) * 50 - 20;
    dropShadow.blurX = (_ymouse / Stage.height) * 10;
    dropShadow.blurY = dropShadow.blurX;
    shapeClip.filters = [dropShadow];
};
Mouse.addListener(mouseListener);
```

The first section of code creates a new movie clip and uses the Drawing API to draw a red square. The second section of code defines a mouse listener, which is called whenever the mouse moves. The mouse listener calculates the drop shadow's distance and level of blurring based on the current *x* and *y* positions of the mouse pointer, and reapplies the drop shadow filter. If you click the red square, the drop shadow's strength increases.

3. Select Control > Test Movie to test the Flash document.

Move the mouse pointer along the *x*-axis to change the value of the drop shadow's distance, and move the mouse pointer along the *y*-axis to change the amount of blur applied to the movie clip instance.

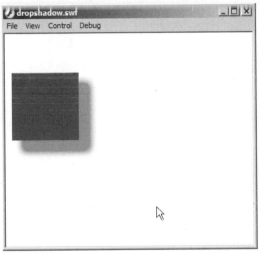

You can also create drop shadows and apply them to dynamically loaded images. The following procedure demonstrates how you can load an external image and apply a drop shadow that follows the mouse pointer. The further the pointer moves away from the image's upper-left corner, the more horizontal and vertical blurring is applied to the image.

To create a drop shadow that follows the mouse pointer:

1. Create a new Flash document and save it as **dropshadowmouse.fla**.

2. Add the following ActionScript to Frame 1 of the Timeline:

```
import flash.filters.DropShadowFilter;
System.security.allowDomain("http://www.helpexamples.com");
var dropShadow:DropShadowFilter = new DropShadowFilter(4, 45, 0x000000,
    0.8, 10, 10, 2, 2);
// Load and position the image on the Stage.
var mclListener:Object = new Object();
mclListener.onLoadInit = function(target_mc:MovieClip):Void {
    target_mc._x = (Stage.width - target_mc._width) / 2;
    target_mc._y = (Stage.height - target_mc._height) / 2;
};
this.createEmptyMovieClip("img_mc", 10);
var img_mcl:MovieClipLoader = new MovieClipLoader();
img_mcl.addListener(mclListener);
img_mcl.loadClip("http://www.helpexamples.com/flash/images/image1.jpg",
    img_mc);

// When mouse moves, recalculate the position of the drop shadow.
var mouseListener:Object = new Object();
mouseListener.onMouseMove = function():Void {
    var p1:Number = img_mc._y - _ymouse;
    var p2:Number = img_mc._x - _xmouse;
    var degrees:Number = Math.atan2(p1, p2) / (Math.PI / 180);
    dropShadow.distance = Math.sqrt(Math.pow(p1, 2) + Math.pow(p2, 2)) *
        0.5;
    dropShadow.blurX = dropShadow.distance;
    dropShadow.blurY = dropShadow.blurX;
    dropShadow.angle = degrees - 180;
    img_mc.filters = [dropShadow];
};
Mouse.addListener(mouseListener);
```

The first section of this code defines a drop shadow instance, loads an external image, and repositions the image at the center of the Stage. The second section of code defines a mouse listener, which you call whenever the user moves the mouse pointer around the Stage. Whenever the mouse moves, the event handler recalculates the distance and angle between the mouse pointer and the upper-left corner of the image. Based on this calculation, the drop shadow filter is reapplied to the movie clip.

3. Select Control > Test Movie to test the Flash document.

When you run the SWF file, the drop shadow follows the mouse pointer. The closer you move the mouse pointer to the upper-left corner of the image on the Stage, the less of a blur effect is applied to the image. As the mouse pointer moves further from the upper-left corner of the image, the drop shadow effect becomes more apparent.

You can also apply drop shadows to dynamically loaded semitransparent PNG images. In the following procedure, the drop shadow filter is applied only to the solid area of the PNG, not the transparency.

To apply a drop shadow to a semitransparent image:

1. Create a new Flash document and save it as **dropshadowTransparent.fla**.

2. Add the following ActionScript to Frame 1 of the Timeline:

```
import flash.filters.DropShadowFilter;
System.security.allowDomain("http://www.helpexamples.com");
var mclListener:Object = new Object();
mclListener.onLoadInit = function(target_mc:MovieClip):Void {
    target_mc._x = (Stage.width - target_mc._width) / 2;
    target_mc._y = (Stage.height - target_mc._height) / 2;
    var dropShadow:DropShadowFilter = new DropShadowFilter(4, 45,
    0x000000, 0.5, 10, 10, 2, 3);
    target_mc.filters = [dropShadow];
};
mclListener.onLoadError = function(target_mc:MovieClip):Void {
    trace("unable to load image.");
};
this.createEmptyMovieClip("logo_mc", 10);
var my_mcl:MovieClipLoader = new MovieClipLoader();
my_mcl.addListener(mclListener);
my_mcl.loadClip("http://www.helpexamples.com/flash/images/logo.png",
    logo_mc);
```

This ActionScript code uses the MovieClipLoader class to load an image and apply a drop shadow filter when the image is completely loaded from the remote server.

3. Select Control > Test Movie to test the Flash document.

Flash loads a PNG image with a transparent background. When you apply the drop shadow filter, only the opaque (nontransparent) portion of the image has the filter applied.

Using the glow filter

The GlowFilter class lets you add a glow effect to various objects in Flash. The glow algorithm is based on the same box filter that is the blur filter uses (see "Using the blur filter" on page 517). You can set the style of the glow in several ways, including inner or outer glow and knockout mode. The glow filter is similar to the drop shadow filter with the `distance` and `angle` properties of the drop shadow set to 0.

For more information on the glow filter, see %{GlowFilter (flash.filters.GlowFilter)}% in the *ActionScript 2.0 Language Reference* in Flash Help.

The following procedure demonstrates how you can apply a glow filter to a dynamically created movie clip on the Stage. Moving your mouse pointer around the Stage causes the movie clip's blur to change, and clicking the dynamically created shape causes the filter's strength to increase.

To use the glow filter:

1. Create a new Flash document and save it as **glowfilter.fla**.

2. Add the following ActionScript code to Frame 1 of the Timeline:

```
import flash.filters.GlowFilter;

this.createEmptyMovieClip("shapeClip", 10);
with (shapeClip) {
   beginFill(0xFF0000, 100);
   moveTo(0, 0);
   lineTo(100, 0);
   lineTo(100, 100);
   lineTo(0, 100);
   lineTo(0, 0);
   endFill();
}
shapeClip._x = 100;
shapeClip._y = 100;
shapeClip.onPress = function():Void {
   glow.strength++;
   shapeClip.filters = [glow];
};
var glow:GlowFilter = new GlowFilter(0xCC0000, 0.5, 10, 10, 2, 3);
var mouseListener:Object = new Object();
mouseListener.onMouseMove = function():Void {
   glow.blurX = (_xmouse / Stage.width) * 255;
   glow.blurY = (_ymouse / Stage.width) * 255;
   shapeClip.filters = [glow];
};
Mouse.addListener(mouseListener);
```

This code uses the Drawing API to draw a square on the Stage, and applies a glow filter to the shape. Whenever the mouse pointer moves along the x-axis or y-axis, the glow filter's blur is calculated and applied to the shape.

3. Select Control > Test Movie to test the document.

The amount of horizontal and vertical blurring is calculated by the mouse pointer's current _xmouse and _ymouse position. As you move the mouse pointer to the upper-left corner of the Stage, the amount of horizontal and vertical blurring decreases. Conversely, as the mouse pointer moves to the lower-right corner of the Stage, the amount of horizontal and vertical blurring increases.

Creating gradient glows

The GradientGlowFilter class lets you create a gradient glow effect for a variety of objects in Flash. A gradient glow is a realistic-looking glow with a color gradient that you can specify. You can apply a gradient glow around the inner or outer edge of an object or on top of an object.

For more information on this filter, see %{GradientBevelFilter (flash.filters.GradientBevelFilter)}% in the *ActionScript 2.0 Language Reference* in Flash Help.

The following procedure uses the Drawing API to draw a square on the Stage, and then applies a gradient glow filter to the shape. Clicking the square on the Stage increases the filter's strength, whereas moving the mouse pointer horizontally or vertically modifies the amount of blurring along the *x*-axis or *y*-axis.

To apply a gradient glow filter:

1. Create a new Flash document and save it as **gradientglow.fla.**

2. Add the following ActionScript to Frame 1 of the Timeline:

```
import flash.filters.GradientGlowFilter;
// create a new shapeClip instance
var shapeClip:MovieClip = this.createEmptyMovieClip("shapeClip", 10);
// use Drawing API to create a shape
with (shapeClip) {
   beginFill(0xFF0000, 100);
   moveTo(0, 0);
   lineTo(100, 0);
   lineTo(100, 100);
   lineTo(0, 100);
   lineTo(0, 0);
   endFill();
}

// position the shape
shapeClip._x = 100;
shapeClip._y = 100;
// define a gradient glow
var gradientGlow:GradientGlowFilter = new GradientGlowFilter(0, 45,
   [0x000000, 0xFF0000], [0, 1], [0, 255], 10, 10, 2, 3, "outer");

// define a mouse listener, listen for two events
var mouseListener:Object = new Object();
mouseListener.onMouseDown = function():Void {
   gradientGlow.strength++;
   shapeClip.filters = [gradientGlow];
};
mouseListener.onMouseMove = function():Void {
   gradientGlow.blurX = (_xmouse / Stage.width) * 255;
   gradientGlow.blurY = (_ymouse / Stage.height) * 255;
   shapeClip.filters = [gradientGlow];
};
Mouse.addListener(mouseListener);
```

The previous code is split into three sections. The first section of code uses the Drawing API to create a square and positions the shape on the Stage. The second section of code defines a new gradient glow filter instance, which creates a glow from red to black. The third section of code defines a mouse listener, which listens for two mouse event handlers. The first event handler is onMouseDown, which causes the strength of the gradient glow to increase. The second event handler is onMouseMove, which is called whenever the mouse pointer moves within the SWF file. The further the mouse pointer moves from the upper-left corner of the Flash document, the stronger the glow effect that is applied.

3. Select Control > Test Movie to test the document.

As you move your mouse pointer around the Stage, the gradient glow filter's blur increases and decreases strength. Click the left mouse button to increase the glow's strength.

Using the bevel filter

The BevelFilter class lets you add a bevel effect to a variety of objects in Flash. A bevel effect gives objects a three-dimensional look. You can customize the look of the bevel with different highlight and shadow colors, the amount of blur on the bevel, the angle of the bevel, the placement of the bevel, and a knockout effect.

For more information on this filter, see %{BevelFilter (flash.filters.BevelFilter)}% in the *ActionScript 2.0 Language Reference* in Flash Help.

The following procedure uses the Drawing API to create a square, and adds a bevel to the shape.

To use the bevel filter:

1. Create a new Flash document and save it as **bevel.fla**.

2. Add the following ActionScript to Frame 1 of the Timeline:

```
import flash.filters.BevelFilter;
// define a bevel filter
var bevel:BevelFilter = new BevelFilter(4, 45, 0xFFFFFF, 1, 0xCC0000, 1,
   10, 10, 2, 3);
// create a new shapeClip instance
var shapeClip:MovieClip = this.createEmptyMovieClip("shapeClip", 1);
// use the Drawing API to create a shape
with (shapeClip) {
   beginFill(0xFF0000, 100);
   moveTo(0, 0);
   lineTo(100, 0);
   lineTo(100, 100);
   lineTo(0, 100);
   lineTo(0, 0);
   endFill();
}
// position the shape on the Stage
shapeClip._x = 100;
shapeClip._y = 100;
// click the mouse to increase the strength
shapeClip.onPress = function():Void {
   bevel.strength += 2;
   shapeClip.filters = [bevel];
};

// define a listener to modify the filter when pointer moves
var mouseListener:Object = new Object();
mouseListener.onMouseMove = function():Void {
   bevel.distance = (_xmouse / Stage.width) * 10;
   bevel.blurX = (_ymouse / Stage.height) * 10;
   bevel.blurY = bevel.blurX;
   shapeClip.filters = [bevel];
};
Mouse.addListener(mouseListener);
```

The first section of code defines a BevelFilter instance, and uses the Drawing API to draw a square on the Stage. When you click the square on the Stage, the current strength value of the bevel increments and gives the bevel a taller, sharper appearance. The second section of code defines a mouse listener, which modifies the bevel's distance and blurring based on the current position of the mouse pointer.

3. Select Control > Test Movie to test the Flash document.

When you move the mouse pointer along the *x*-axis, the offset distance of the bevel increases or decreases. When you move the mouse pointer along the *y*-axis, the mouse pointer's current coordinates modifies the amount of horizontal and vertical blurring.

About the gradient bevel filter

The gradient bevel filter is applied to an object as a rectangle, with the colors of the gradient distributed to three portions of the rectangle: two bevel edges (a *highlight* and a *shadow*) and an area we'll call the *base fill*. The following diagrams depicts the rectangle, with the bevel type set to inner. In the rectangle on the left, the dark gray areas are the bevel edges, and the light gray area is the base fill. In the rectangle on the right, a rainbow gradient bevel, with a four-color bevel on each edge, is applied.

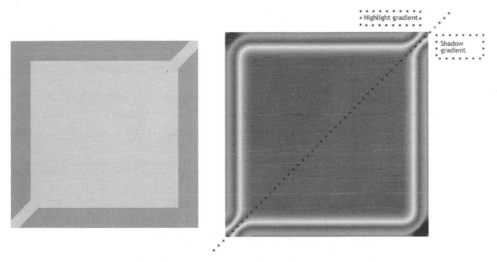

The different properties of the gradient bevel filter control the way the filter is applied. The colors of the gradient bevel are set in the colors array. The actual distribution of colors in each portion of the rectangle is determined by the ratios array. The distance property determines the offset distance, or how many pixels away from the object the bevel edge is applied. The `blurX` and `blurY` properties control the sharpness of the colors in the bevel; higher values effectively make the bevel wider and softer, while lower values make the bevel thinner and sharper. The angle property is the theoretical light source falling on the object, thus causing a highlight and shadow effect on the object's edges. The `strength` property controls the spread of the colors: a lower strength value mutes the colors, as in the example; a higher strength value makes the outer numbers in the array stronger, forcing the middle colors in the array to be less prominent. Finally, `knockout` and `type` properties determine how and where the bevel filter is applied to the whole object: whether the filter knocks out the object and where it is placed.

One of the more complicated concepts to apply in the gradient bevel filter is the color distribution. To understand how the colors in a gradient bevel are distributed, think first of the colors you want in your gradient bevel. Because a simple bevel has the understood concepts of highlight color and shadow color, you can apply the same concepts to understand the gradient bevel filter: you have a highlight gradient and a shadow gradient. The highlight appears on the top left corner, and the shadow appears on the bottom right corner. There are four colors in the highlight and four in the shadow. However, you have to add another color (the base fill color), which appears where the edges of the highlight and shadow meet. There are nine colors for the colors array, which you can see in the previous diagram.

The number of colors in the colors array determine the number of elements in the alphas and ratios array. The first item in the colors array corresponds to the first item in the alphas array and in the ratios array, and so on. Because you have nine colors, you also have nine values in the alphas array and nine in the ratios array. The alpha values set the alpha transparency value of the colors.

The ratio values in the ratios array can range from 0 to 255 pixels. The middle value is 128; 128 is the base fill value. For most usages, to get the bevel effect you want, you should assign the ratio values as follows, using the example of nine colors:

- The first four colors range from 0 through 127, increasing in value so each value is greater than or equal to the previous one. This is the first bevel edge, say, our highlight.

- The fifth color (the middle color) is the base fill, set to 128. The pixel value of 128 sets the base fill, which appears either outside the shape (and around the bevel edges) if type is set to outer; or inside the shape, effectively covering the object's own fill, if the type is set to inner.

- The last four colors range from 129 through 255, increasing in value so each value is greater than or equal to the previous one. This is the second bevel edge, for example, your shadow.

If you think of a gradient as composed of stripes of various colors, blending into each other, each ratio value sets the number of pixels for the associated color, thus setting the width of the color stripe in the gradient. If you want an equal distribution of colors for each edge:

- Use an odd number of colors, where the middle color is the base fill.
- Distribute the values between 0 through 127 and 129 through 255 equally among your colors.
- Adjust the value to change the width of each stripe of color in the gradient.

NOTE   The angle value determines which edge is the highlight and which edge is the shadow.

The angle value determines the angle at which the gradient colors are applied to the object; meaning, where the highlight and shadow appear on the object. The colors are applied in the same order as the array.

The following code takes a pink square (drawn with the Drawing API) and applies a rainbow gradient filter. The colors, in the order in which they are present in the array, are: blue, green, purple, and yellow (highlight); red (base fill); yellow, purple, green, black (shadow). To determine the ratios values, we assign four highlight colors values from 0 to 127, making them roughly equal, and shadow colors from 129 to 255. The colors on the outer edges, blue (16) and black (235).

```
var colors:Array = [0x0000FF, 0x00FF00, 0x9900FF, 0xFFFF00, 0xFF0000,
  0xFFFF00, 0x9900FF, 0x00FF00,0x000000];
var alphas:Array = [1, 1, 1, 1, 1, 1, 1, 1, 1];
var ratios:Array = [16, 32, 64, 96, 128, 160, 192, 224, 235];
var gradientBevel:GradientBevelFilter = new GradientBevelFilter(8, 225,
  colors, alphas, ratios, 16, 16, 1.3, 2, "inner", false);
```

The following figure shows the gradient bevel filter created by the code above, a nine-color rainbow bevel applied to a red rectangle movie clip:

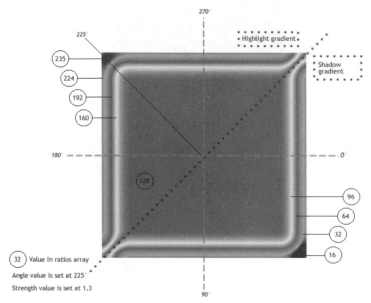

The dashed line shows how angles are determined. The figure shows how the angle of 225° is realized on the filter, and also shows each ratio value for each color. Setting the angle at 225° indicates that the first color in the array begins at 225°, which is in the top left corner (the highlight). The dotted line shows where the highlight gradient is applied and where the shadow gradient is applied.

The original movie clip color is pink, but setting the 128 value to red means the 128-pixel value is the base fill and covers the original movie clip fill. However, when you set the filters property, the original object is not altered; by simply clearing the `filters` property, you can restore the original movie clip fill.

The properties of all filters affect each other, so if you adjust one property to change the effect that you're applying, you might need to adjust another property as well.

The full ActionScript code to create the previous figure is as follows:

```
import flash.filters.GradientBevelFilter;

// draws a filled square shape
this.createEmptyMovieClip("square_mc", this.getNextHighestDepth());
    square_mc.beginFill(0xFF99CC);
    square_mc.moveTo(40, 40);
    square_mc.lineTo(200, 40);
    square_mc.lineTo(200, 200);
    square_mc.lineTo(40, 200);
    square_mc.lineTo(40, 40);
    square_mc.endFill();

/* GradientBevelFilter(distance:Number, angle:Number, colors:Array,
   alphas:Array, ratios:Array, blurX:Number, blurY:Number, strength:Number,
   quality:Number, type:String, knockout:Boolean) */

// create colors, alphas, and ratios arrays
var colors:Array = [0x0000FF, 0x00FF00, 0x9900FF, 0xFFFF00, 0xFF0000,
   0xFFFF00, 0x9900FF, 0x00FF00,0x000000];//blue, green, purple, yellow,
   red, yellow, purple, green, black
var alphas:Array = [1, 1, 1, 1, 1, 1, 1, 1, 1];
var ratios:Array = [16, 32, 64, 96, 128, 160, 192, 224, 235];

// create the filter object
var gradientBevel:GradientBevelFilter = new GradientBevelFilter(8, 225,
   colors, alphas, ratios, 16, 16, 1.3, 2, "inner", false);

// apply the filter to the square movie clip
square_mc.filters = [gradientBevel];
```

Applying a gradient bevel filter

The GradientBevelFilter class lets you apply a gradient bevel effect to objects in Flash. A gradient bevel is a beveled edge that's enhanced with gradient color on the outside, inside, or top of an object. Beveled edges bring a three-dimensional look to objects, and can have colorful results as shown in the following figure.

For more information on this filter, see %{GradientBevelFilter (flash.filters.GradientBevelFilter)}% in the *ActionScript 2.0 Language Reference* in Flash Help.

The following procedure uses the Drawing API to draw a square on the Stage, and applies a gradient bevel filter to the shape.

To use the gradient bevel filter:

1. Create a new Flash document and save it as **gradientbevel.fla**.

2. Add the following ActionScript to Frame 1 of the Timeline:

```
import flash.filters.GradientBevelFilter;
var shapeClip:MovieClip = this.createEmptyMovieClip("shape_mc", 1);
with (shapeClip) {
   beginFill(0xFF0000, 100);
   moveTo(0, 0);
   lineTo(200, 0);
   lineTo(200, 200);
   lineTo(0, 200);
   lineTo(0, 0);
   endFill();
}
shapeClip._x = (Stage.width - shapeClip._width) / 2;
shapeClip._y = (Stage.height - shapeClip._height) / 2;
var colors:Array = new Array(0xFFFFFF, 0xCCCCCC, 0x000000);
var alphas:Array = new Array(1, 0, 1);
var ratios:Array = new Array(0, 128, 255);
var gradientBevel:GradientBevelFilter = new GradientBevelFilter(10, 45,
   colors, alphas, ratios, 4, 4, 5, 3);
var mouseListener:Object = new Object();
mouseListener.onMouseDown = function() {
   gradientBevel.strength++;
   shapeClip.filters = [gradientBevel];
};
mouseListener.onMouseMove = function() {
   gradientBevel.blurX = (_xmouse / Stage.width) * 255;
   gradientBevel.blurY = (_ymouse / Stage.height) * 255;
   shapeClip.filters = [gradientBevel];
};
Mouse.addListener(mouseListener);
```

This code uses the Drawing API to draw a square on the Stage, which is placed at the center of the Stage. When you move the mouse pointer around the Stage, the amount of blurring along the x-axis and y-axis increases or decreases. When you move your pointer towards the left of the Stage, the amount of horizontal blurring decreases. When you move the pointer towards the right of the Stage, the blurring increases. Similarly, the higher the pointer is on the Stage, the smaller the amount of blurring that occurs along the y-axis.

3. Select Control > Test Movie to test the document and view the results.

Using the color matrix filter

The ColorMatrixFilter class lets you apply a 4 x 5 matrix transformation on the ARGB color and alpha values of every pixel on the input image to produce a result with a new set of ARGB color and alpha values. This filter allows hue (distinct color or shade) rotation, saturation (intensity of a specific hue) changes, luminance (brightness or intensity of a color) to alpha, and various other effects. Also, you can animate these filters to create effects in your applications.

> **NOTE** You can apply the color matrix filter to bitmaps and movie clip instances.

For more information on the color matrix filter, see %{ColorMatrixFilter (flash.filters.ColorMatrixFilter)}% in the *ActionScript 2.0 Language Reference* in Flash Help.

You can use the color matrix filter to modify the brightness of an instance, as the following example demonstrates.

To increase the brightness of a movie clip:

1. Create a new Flash document and save it as **brightness.fla**.

2. Add the following ActionScript to Frame 1 of the Timeline:

```
import flash.filters.ColorMatrixFilter;
System.security.allowDomain("http://www.helpexamples.com/");
var mcl_obj:Object = new Object();
mcl_obj.onLoadInit = function(target_mc:MovieClip):Void {
  var myElements_array:Array = [1, 0, 0, 0, 100,
      0, 1, 0, 0, 100,
      0, 0, 1, 0, 100,
      0, 0, 0, 1, 0];
  var myColorMatrix_filter:ColorMatrixFilter = new
  ColorMatrixFilter(myElements_array);
  target_mc.filters = [myColorMatrix_filter];
}
this.createEmptyMovieClip("img_mc", this.getNextHighestDepth());
var img_mcl:MovieClipLoader = new MovieClipLoader();
img_mcl.addListener(mcl_obj);
img_mcl.loadClip("http://www.helpexamples.com/flash/images/image2.jpg",
  img_mc);
```

This code dynamically loads a JPEG image by using a MovieClipLoader instance. After the image is completely loaded and is placed on the Stage, the instance's brightness is set to 100% by using a color matrix filter.

3. Select Control > Test Movie to test the document.

You could also create an animated brightness effect by combining the Tween class with the ColorMatrixFilter class, as the next procedure shows.

To animate the brightness level of an instance by using the Tween class:

1. Create a new Flash document and save it as **brightnesstween.fla**.

2. Add the following ActionScript to Frame 1 of the Timeline:

```
import flash.filters.ColorMatrixFilter;
import mx.transitions.Tween;
import mx.transitions.easing.*;
System.security.allowDomain("http://www.helpexamples.com");
var mclListener:Object = new Object();
mclListener.onLoadInit = function(target_mc:MovieClip):Void {
  // center movie clip instance on Stage
  target_mc._x = (Stage.width - target_mc._width) / 2;
  target_mc._y = (Stage.height - target_mc._height) / 2;
  target_mc.watch("brightness", brightnessWatcher, target_mc);
  // animate the target_mc movie clip between -100 and +100 brightness
  var t:Object = new Tween(target_mc, "brightness", Elastic.easeOut,
    100, -100, 3, true);
  t.onMotionFinished = function() {
    this.yoyo();
  };
};
this.createEmptyMovieClip("img_mc", 10);
var img_mcl:MovieClipLoader = new MovieClipLoader();
img_mcl.addListener(mclListener);
img_mcl.loadClip("http://www.helpexamples.com/flash/images/image1.jpg",
  img_mc);

function brightnessWatcher(prop:String, oldVal:Number, newVal:Number,
  target_mc:MovieClip):Number {
  var brightness_array:Array = [1, 0, 0, 0, newVal,
      0, 1, 0, 0, newVal,
      0, 0, 1, 0, newVal,
      0, 0, 0, 1, 0];
  target_mc.filters = [new ColorMatrixFilter(brightness_array)];
  return newVal;
};
```

The first section of code uses the MovieClipLoader class to load a JPEG image onto the Stage. After the image completely loads, you reposition the image to the center of the Stage. Then you use the Tween class to animate the image brightness level. To animate the brightness, you use the `Object.watch()` method, which registers an event handler that you start when a specified property of an ActionScript object changes. Whenever some ActionScript tries to set the custom brightness property of the `target_mc` instance, you call the `brightnessWatcher` function. The custom `brightnessWatcher` function creates a new array, which uses the color matrix filter to set the target image's brightness to a specified amount.

3. Select Control > Test Movie to test the document.

    After the image loads and is placed on the Stage, the image's brightness animates between -100 and 100. After the brightness tween is complete, the animation is reversed using the `Tween.yoyo()` method, which causes the tween to constantly animate.

Using the convolution filter

The ConvolutionFilter class applies a matrix convolution filter effect. A convolution combines pixels in a source image that you specify with neighboring pixels to produce an image. You can achieve a wide variety of imaging operations by using the convolution filter, which includes blurring, edge detection, sharpening, embossing, and beveling effects.

> **NOTE** You can apply this filter on bitmaps and movie clip instances.

A matrix convolution is based on an n x m matrix, which describes how a given pixel value in the input image is combined with its neighboring pixel values to produce a resulting pixel value. Each resulting pixel is determined by applying the matrix to the corresponding source pixel and its neighboring pixels.

This filter is only available by using ActionScript. For more information on this filter, see %{ConvolutionFilter (flash.filters.ConvolutionFilter)}% in the *ActionScript 2.0 Language Reference* in Flash Help.

The following procedure applies the convolution filter to a dynamically loaded JPEG image.

To use the convolution filter to modify an image's color:

1. Create a new Flash document and save it as **convolution.fla**.

2. Add the following ActionScript to Frame 1 of the Timeline:

```
import flash.filters.ConvolutionFilter;
import flash.display.BitmapData;

this.createEmptyMovieClip("shape_mc", 1);
shape_mc.createEmptyMovieClip("holder_mc", 1);
var imageLoader:MovieClipLoader = new MovieClipLoader();
imageLoader.loadClip("http://www.helpexamples.com/flash/images/
   image1.jpg", shape_mc.holder_mc);
var matrixArr:Array = [1, 4, 6, 4, 1, 4, 16, 24, 16, 4, 16, 6, 24, 36,
   24, 6, 4, 16, 24, 16, 4, 1, 4, 6, 4, 1];
var convolution:ConvolutionFilter = new ConvolutionFilter(5, 5,
   matrixArr);
shape_mc.filters = [convolution];

var mouseListener:Object = new Object();
mouseListener.onMouseMove = function():Void {
   convolution.divisor = (_xmouse / Stage.width) * 271;
   convolution.bias = (_ymouse / Stage.height) * 100;
   shape_mc.filters = [convolution];
};
Mouse.addListener(mouseListener);
```

The preceding code is separated into three sections. The first section imports two classes: ConvolutionFilter and BitmapData. The second section creates a nested movie clip and uses a movie clip loader object to load an image into the nested movie clip. A convolution filter object is created and applied to the shape_mc movie clip. The final section of code defines a mouse listener object that modifies the convolution filter's divisor and bias properties based on the current position of the mouse pointer and reapplies the convolution filter to the shape_mc movie clip.

3. Select Control > Test Movie to test the Flash document.

Moving the mouse pointer along the *x*-axis of the Stage modifies the filter's divisor, whereas moving the mouse pointer along the *y*-axis of the Stage modifies the filter's bias.

Using the displacement map filter

The DisplacementMapFilter class uses the pixel values from the specified BitmapData object (called the *displacement map image*) to perform a displacement of an instance that's on the Stage, such as a movie clip instance or a bitmap data instance. You can use this filter to achieve a warped or mottled effect on a specified instance.

This filter is only available by using ActionScript. For more information on this filter, see %{DisplacementMapFilter (flash.filters.DisplacementMapFilter)}% in the *ActionScript 2.0 Language Reference* in Flash Help.

The following procedure loads a JPEG image and applies a displacement map filter to it, which causes the image to look distorted. Whenever the user moves the mouse, the displacement map is regenerated.

To distort an image with the displacement map filter:

1. Create a new Flash document and save it as **displacement.fla**.

2. Add the following ActionScript to Frame 1 of the Timeline:

```
import flash.filters.DisplacementMapFilter;
import flash.geom.Point;
import flash.display.BitmapData;

var perlinBmp:BitmapData;
var displacementMap:DisplacementMapFilter;
var mclListener:Object = new Object();
mclListener.onLoadInit = function(target_mc:MovieClip):Void {
    target_mc._x = (Stage.width - target_mc._width) / 2;
    target_mc._y = (Stage.height - target_mc._height) / 2;
    perlinBmp = new BitmapData(target_mc._width, target_mc._height);
    perlinBmp.perlinNoise(target_mc._width, target_mc._height, 10,
  Math.round(Math.random() * 100000), false, true, 1, false);
    displacementMap = new DisplacementMapFilter(perlinBmp, new Point(0,
  0), 1, 1, 100, 100, "color");
    shapeClip.filters = [displacementMap];
};
var shapeClip:MovieClip = this.createEmptyMovieClip("shapeClip", 1);
shapeClip.createEmptyMovieClip("holderClip", 1);
var imageLoader:MovieClipLoader = new MovieClipLoader();
imageLoader.addListener(mclListener);
imageLoader.loadClip("http://www.helpexamples.com/flash/images/
  image1.jpg", shapeClip.holderClip);

var mouseListener:Object = new Object();
mouseListener.onMouseMove = function():Void {
  perlinBmp.perlinNoise(shapeClip._width, shapeClip._height, 10,
  Math.round(Math.random() * 100000), false, true, 1, false);
  shapeClip.filters = [displacementMap];
};
Mouse.addListener(mouseListener);
```

This code loads a JPEG image and places it on the Stage. After the image is completely loaded, this code creates a BitmapData instance and uses the `perlinNoise()` method to fill it with randomly placed pixels. The BitmapData instance passes to the displacement map filter, which is applied to the image and causes the image to look distorted.

3. Select Control > Test Movie to test the document.

Move your mouse pointer around the Stage to re-create a displacement map by calling the `perlinNoise()` method, which changes the appearance of the JPEG image.

Manipulating filter effects with code

Flash Basic 8 and Flash Professional 8 let you dynamically add various filters to your movie clips, text fields, and buttons on the Stage, instead of having to add filters in the Flash Professional 8 authoring environment (using the Filters tab in the Property inspector). When you add and manipulate filters during playback, you can add realistic shadows, blurs, and glows that react to mouse movements or user events.

For examples of how to manipulate filters with code, see the following topics:

- "Adjusting filter properties" on page 541
- "Animating a filter by using ActionScript" on page 543
- "Using the clone() method" on page 544

Adjusting filter properties

The array of filters applied to an object can be accessed through standard ActionScript calls by using the `MovieClip.filters` property. This process returns an array that contains each filter object currently associated with the MovieClip. Each filter has a set of properties unique to that filter. The filters can be accessed and modified just like an array object, although getting and setting the filters by using the `filters` property returns a duplicate of the filters object instead of a reference.

Setting the `filters` property duplicates the filters array passed in and does not store it as a reference. When getting the filters property, it returns a new copy of the array. One negative implication of this approach is that the following code does not work:

```
// does not work
my_mc.filters[0].blurX = 20;
```

Because the previous code snippet returns a copy of the filters array, the code modifies the copy instead of the original array. In order to modify the blurX property, you would need to use the following ActionScript code instead:

```
// works
var filterArray:Array = my_mc.filters;
filterArray[0].blurX = 20;
my_mc.filters = filterArray;
```

The following procedure blurs an image based on the current position of the mouse pointer on the Stage. Whenever the mouse pointer moves horizontally or vertically, the `blurX` and `blurY` properties of the blur filter are modified accordingly.

To adjust a movie clip's filter properties:

1. Create a new Flash document and save it as **adjustfilter.fla**.

2. Add the following ActionScript to Frame 1 of the Timeline:

```
import flash.filters.BlurFilter;

this.createEmptyMovieClip("holder_mc", 10);
holder_mc.createEmptyMovieClip("img_mc", 20);
holder_mc.img_mc.loadMovie("http://www.helpexamples.com/flash/images/
    image2.jpg");
holder_mc.filters = [new BlurFilter(10, 10, 2)];
holder_mc._x = 75;
holder_mc._y = 75;

holder_mc.onMouseMove = function() {
    var tempFilter:BlurFilter = holder_mc.filters[0];
    tempFilter.blurX = Math.floor((_xmouse / Stage.width) * 255);
    tempFilter.blurY = Math.floor((_ymouse / Stage.height) * 255);
    holder_mc.filters = [tempFilter];
};
```

The previous code is split into three sections. The first section imports the flash.filters.BlurFilter class so that you don't have to use the fully qualified class name when you refer to the BlurFilter class. The second section of code creates a couple of movie clips and loads an image into one of the nested clips. The third section of code responds to the mouse movement on the Stage and adjusts the blur accordingly.

3. Select Control > Test Movie to test the Flash document.

Moving the mouse pointer along the *x*-axis modifies the blur filter's `blurX` property. Moving the mouse pointer along the *y*-axis modifies the blur filter's `blurY` property. The closer the mouse pointer is to the upper-left corner of the Stage, the less blurring is applied to the movie clip.

Animating a filter by using ActionScript

You can use ActionScript, such as the Tween class, to animate filters at runtime, which lets you apply interesting, animated effects to your Flash applications.

In the following example, you see how to combine the BlurFilter with the Tween class to create an animated blur that modifies the Blur filter between a value of 0 and 10 at runtime.

To animate blurs using the Tween class:

1. Create a new Flash document and save it as **animatedfilter.fla**.

2. Add the following ActionScript to Frame 1 of the Timeline:

```
import flash.filters.BlurFilter;
import mx.transitions.Tween;
import mx.transitions.easing.*;

this.createEmptyMovieClip("holder_mc", 10);
holder_mc.createEmptyMovieClip("img_mc", 20);

var mclListener:Object = new Object();
mclListener.onLoadInit = function(target_mc:MovieClip) {
    target_mc._x = (Stage.width - target_mc._width) / 2;
    target_mc._y = (Stage.height - target_mc._height) / 2;
    var myTween:Tween = new Tween(target_mc, "blur", Strong.easeInOut, 0,
    20, 3, true);
    myTween.onMotionChanged = function() {
        target_mc._parent.filters = [new BlurFilter(target_mc.blur,
    target_mc.blur, 1)];
    };
    myTween.onMotionFinished = function() {
        myTween.yoyo();
    }
};
var my_mcl:MovieClipLoader = new MovieClipLoader();
my_mcl.addListener(mclListener);
my_mcl.loadClip("http://www.helpexamples.com/flash/images/image1.jpg",
    holder_mc.img_mc);
```

The preceding code is separated into three sections. The first section imports the required classes and packages. The second section creates a nested movie clip that is used to load an image and apply filters to the holder movie clip. The final section of code creates a new MovieClipLoader instance and a listener for the movie clip loader. The listener object defines a single event handler function, `onLoadInit`, that is started once the image successfully loads and is available on the Stage. First the image is repositioned to the center of the Stage, then a new Tween object is created that animates the movie clip and applies a blur filter of 0 and 10.

3. Select Control > Test Movie to test the Flash document.

Using the clone() method

The `clone()` method within each filter class returns a new filter instance with all of the same properties as the original filter instance. When you work with filters, you might want to make a copy of a filter, and to do so you need to duplicate the filter using the `clone()` method. If you do not use the clone method to duplicate a filter, Flash creates a reference to the original filter only. If Flash creates a reference to the original filter, any change made to the duplicate filter also modifies the original filter object.

The following procedure creates a new instance of a DropShadowFilter (`greenDropShadow`), calls the `clone()` method to duplicate the green drop shadow filter, and saves a new filter named `redDropShadow`. The cloned filter sets a new drop shadow color, and both filters are applied to a `flower_mc` movie clip instance that's on the Stage.

To use the clone method:

1. Create a new Flash document, and name it **clone.fla**.

2. Create a movie clip on the Stage.

3. Select the movie clip instance, and type **flower_mc** in the Instance Name text box in the Property inspector.

4. Select Frame 1 of the Timeline, and add the following code in the Actions panel:

```
import flash.filters.DropShadowFilter;
var greenDropShadow:DropShadowFilter = new DropShadowFilter();
greenDropShadow.color = 0x00FF00; // green
var redDropShadow:DropShadowFilter = greenDropShadow.clone();
redDropShadow.color = 0xFF0000; // red
flower_mc.filters = [greenDropShadow, redDropShadow];
```

The preceding code creates a new instance of the drop shadow filter and gives it the name `greenDropShadow`. The green drop shadow object is duplicated by using the `DropShadowFilter.clone()` method and creates a new filter object called `redDropShadow`. Both the green drop shadow and red drop shadow filters are applied to the `flower_mc` movie clip instance on the Stage. If you did not call the `clone()` method, both drop shadows would appear red. The reason for this appearance is that setting the `redDropShadow.color` property changes both the red drop shadow and green drop shadow objects because the red drop shadow contains a reference to the green drop shadow.

5. Select Control > Test Movie to test the Flash document.

The filter is duplicated and cloned, and both filters are applied to the `flower_mc` instance.

For more information on the `clone()` method, see %{clone (DropShadowFilter.clone method)}% in the *ActionScript 2.0 Language Reference* in Flash Help. For related information, you can also see the `clone()` method of any filter class.

Creating bitmaps with the BitmapData class

The BitmapData class lets you create arbitrarily sized transparent or opaque bitmap images, then manipulate them in various ways at runtime. When you manipulate a BitmapData instance directly by using ActionScript, you can create very complex images without incurring the overhead of constantly redrawing the content from vector data in Flash Player. The methods of the BitmapData class support a variety of effects that are not available through the Filters tab in the Flash workspace.

A BitmapData object contains an array of pixel data. This data either can represent a fully opaque bitmap or a transparent bitmap that contains alpha channel data. Either type of BitmapData object is stored as a buffer of 32-bit integers. Each 32-bit integer determines the properties of a single pixel in the bitmap. Each 32-bit integer is a combination of four 8-bit *channel* values (from 0 to 255) that describe the alpha transparency and the red, green, and blue (ARGB) values of the pixel.

For information on working with packages, see "Working with filter packages" on page 509.

You can find a sample source file that uses the BitmapData class to manipulate an image. Find the file called BitmapData.fla in the Samples folder on your hard disk.

■ In Windows, browse to *boot drive*\Program Files\Macromedia\Flash 8\ Samples and Tutorials\Samples\ActionScript\BitmapData.

- On the Macintosh, browse to *Macintosh HD*/Applications/Macromedia Flash 8/ Samples and Tutorials/Samples/ActionScript/BitmapData.

The following procedure dynamically loads a JPEG image onto the Stage, and uses the BitmapData class to create a noise effect, similar to static on a television. The noise effect is redrawn with a random pattern every 100 milliseconds (1/10 of a second). Moving the mouse pointer along the *x*-axis and *y*-axis affects how much static is drawn at every interval.

To create a noise effect with the BitmapData class:

1. Create a new Flash document and save it as **noise.fla**.

2. Add the following ActionScript to Frame 1 of the Timeline:

```
import flash.display.BitmapData;
this.createTextField("status_txt", 90, 0, 0, 100, 20);
status_txt.selectable = false;
status_txt.background = 0xFFFFFF;
status_txt.autoSize = "left";
function onMouseMove() {
    status_txt._x = _xmouse;
    status_txt._y = _ymouse-20;
    updateAfterEvent();
}
this.createEmptyMovieClip("img_mc", 10);
img_mc.loadMovie("http://www.helpexamples.com/flash/images/image1.jpg");
var noiseBmp:BitmapData = new BitmapData(Stage.width, Stage.height,
    true);
this.attachBitmap(noiseBmp, 20);
setInterval(updateNoise, 100);
var grayScale:Boolean = true;
function updateNoise():Void {
    var low:Number = 30 * _xmouse / Stage.width;
    var high:Number = 200 * _ymouse / Stage.height;
    status_txt.text = "low:" + Math.round(low) + ", high:" +
    Math.round(high);
    noiseBmp.noise(Math.round(Math.random() * 100000), low, high, 8,
    true);
}
```

This code creates a text field with the instance name status_txt, which follows the mouse pointer and displays the current values for the high and low parameters for the noise() method. The setInterval() function changes the noise effect, which is updated every 100 milliseconds (1/10 of a second), by continuously calling the updateNoise() function. The high and low parameters for the noise() method are determined by calculating the pointer's current position on the Stage.

3. Select Control > Test Movie to test the document.

Moving the mouse pointer along the *x*-axis affects the `low` parameter; moving the mouse pointer along the *y*-axis affects the `high` parameter.

The BitmapData class also lets you distort a dynamically loaded image by using a combination of a `perlinNoise()` method effect and a displacement map filter. The following procedure shows this.

To apply a displacement map filter to an image:

1. Create a new Flash document and save it as **displacement.fla**.

2. Add the following ActionScript to Frame 1 of the Timeline:

```
// Import classes.
import flash.filters.DisplacementMapFilter;
import flash.display.BitmapData;
import flash.geom.Point;
// Create a clip and a nested clip.
var shapeClip:MovieClip = this.createEmptyMovieClip("shapeClip", 1);
shapeClip.createEmptyMovieClip("holderClip", 1);
// Load JPEG.
var imageLoader:MovieClipLoader = new MovieClipLoader();
imageLoader.loadClip("http://www.helpexamples.com/flash/images/
   image4.jpg", shapeClip.holderClip);
// Create BitmapData instance.
var perlinBmp:BitmapData = new BitmapData(Stage.width, Stage.height);
perlinBmp.perlinNoise(Stage.width, Stage.height, 10,
   Math.round(Math.random() * 100000), false, true, 1, false);
// Create and apply the displacement map filter.
var displacementMap:DisplacementMapFilter = new
   DisplacementMapFilter(perlinBmp, new Point(0, 0), 1, 1, 100, 100,
   "color", 1);
shapeClip.filters = [displacementMap];
// Create and apply a listener.
var mouseListener:Object = new Object();
mouseListener.onMouseMove = function():Void {
   perlinBmp.perlinNoise(Stage.width, Stage.height, 10,
   Math.round(Math.random() * 100000), false, true, 1, false);
   shapeClip.filters = [displacementMap];
}
Mouse.addListener(mouseListener);
```

This code example consists of five logical sections. The first section imports the necessary classes for the example. The second block of code creates a nested movie clip and loads a JPEG image from a remote server. The third block of code creates a new BitmapData instance named `perlinBmp`, which is the same size as the dimensions of the Stage. The `perlinBmp` instance contains the results of a Perlin noise effect, and is used later as a parameter for the displacement map filter. The fourth block of code creates and applies the displacement map filter effect to the dynamically loaded image created earlier. The fifth, and final, block of code creates a listener for the mouse that regenerates the Perlin noise that the displacement map filter uses whenever the user moves the mouse pointer.

3. Select Control > Test Movie to test the Flash document.

About blending modes

You can apply blend modes to movie clip objects by using the Flash workspace (Flash Professional 8) or ActionScript (Flash Basic 8 and Flash Professional 8). At runtime, multiple graphics are merged as one shape. For this reason, you cannot apply different blend modes to different graphic symbols.

For more information on using ActionScript to apply blend modes, see "Applying blending modes" on page 549.

Blend modes involve combining the colors of one image (the base image) with the colors of another image (the blend image) to produce a third image. Each pixel value in an image is processed with the corresponding pixel value of the other image to produce a pixel value for that same position in the result.

The `MovieClip.blendMode` property supports the following blend modes:

add   Commonly used to create an animated lightening dissolve effect between two images.

alpha   Commonly used to apply the transparency of the foreground on the background.

darken   Commonly used to superimpose type.

difference   Commonly used to create more vibrant colors.

erase   Commonly used to *cut out* (erase) part of the background using the foreground alpha.

hardlight   Commonly used to create shading effects.

invert   Used to invert the background.

layer   Used to force the creation of a temporary buffer for precomposition for a particular movie clip.

lighten   Commonly used to superimpose type.

multiply   Commonly used to create shadows and depth effects.

normal   Used to specify that the pixel values of the blend image override those of the base image.

overlay   Commonly used to create shading effects.

screen   Commonly used to create highlights and lens flares.

subtract   Commonly used to create an animated darkening dissolve effect between two images.

Applying blending modes

The following procedure loads a dynamic image and lets you apply different blend modes to the image by selecting a blending mode from a combo box on the Stage.

To apply different blending modes to an image:

1. Create a new Flash document and save it as **blendmodes.fla**.

2. Drag a ComboBox component instance onto the Stage and give it an instance name of **blendMode_cb**.

3. Add the following ActionScript to Frame 1 of the Timeline:

```
var blendMode_dp:Array = new Array();
blendMode_dp.push({data:"add", label:"add"});
blendMode_dp.push({data:"alpha", label:"alpha"});
blendMode_dp.push({data:"darken", label:"darken"});
blendMode_dp.push({data:"difference", label:"difference"});
blendMode_dp.push({data:"erase", label:"erase"});
blendMode_dp.push({data:"hardlight", label:"hardlight"});
blendMode_dp.push({data:"invert", label:"invert"});
blendMode_dp.push({data:"layer", label:"layer"});
blendMode_dp.push({data:"lighten", label:"lighten"});
blendMode_dp.push({data:"multiply", label:"multiply"});
blendMode_dp.push({data:"normal", label:"normal"});
blendMode_dp.push({data:"overlay", label:"overlay"});
blendMode_dp.push({data:"screen", label:"screen"});
blendMode_dp.push({data:"subtract", label:"subtract"});
blendMode_cb.dataProvider = blendMode_dp;

var mclListener:Object = new Object();
mclListener.onLoadInit = function(target_mc:MovieClip) {
  var blendModeClip:MovieClip =
  target_mc.createEmptyMovieClip("blendModeType_mc", 20);
  with (blendModeClip) {
    beginFill(0x999999);
    moveTo(0, 0);
    lineTo(target_mc._width / 2, 0);
    lineTo(target_mc._width / 2, target_mc._height);
    lineTo(0, target_mc._height);
    lineTo(0, 0);
    endFill();
  }
  target_mc._x = (Stage.width - target_mc._width) / 2;
  target_mc._y = (Stage.height - target_mc._height) / 2;
  blendModeClip.blendMode = blendMode_cb.value;
};
this.createEmptyMovieClip("img_mc", 10);
var img_mcl:MovieClipLoader = new MovieClipLoader();
img_mcl.addListener(mclListener);
img_mcl.loadClip("http://www.helpexamples.com/flash/images/image1.jpg",
  img_mc);

function cbListener(eventObj:Object):Void {
  img_mc.blendModeType_mc.blendMode = eventObj.target.value;
}
blendMode_cb.addEventListener("change", cbListener);
```

This ActionScript code populates the combo box with each type of blending mode, so the user can view each effect on the dynamically loaded image. A listener object is created, which is used with a MovieClipLoader instance. The listener object defines a single event listener, onLoadInit, which is invoked when the image is completely downloaded and is initialized by Flash. The event listener creates a new movie clip named blendModeType_mc, and uses the Drawing API to draw a rectangular shape over the left half of the image. The currently selected blending mode for the ComboBox instance is then applied to the blendModeType_mc movie clip.

The rest of the code sets up the MovieClipLoader instance, which is responsible for loading the specified image into a movie clip on the Stage. Finally, a listener is defined for the blendMode_cb ComboBox instance, which applies the selected blending mode whenever a new item is selected from the ComboBox instance.

4. Select Control > Test Movie to test the document.

About operation order

The following list is the order of operations in which a filters array, blend modes, color transforms, and mask layers are attached or performed for a movie clip instance:

1. The movie clip's bitmap is updated from vector content (the cacheAsBitmap property is set to true).

2. If you use the setMask() method, and the mask has a bitmap cache, Flash performs an alpha blend between the two images.

3. Filters are then applied (blur, drop shadow, glow, and so on.)

4. If you use the ColorTransform class, the color transform operation is performed and cached as bitmap result.

5. If you apply a blending mode, the blend is then performed (using a vector renderer).

6. If you apply external masking layers, the layers perform masking (using a vector renderer).

Drawing with ActionScript

You can use methods of the MovieClip class to draw lines and fills on the Stage. This lets you create drawing tools for users and draw shapes in the SWF file in response to events. The following are the MovieClip class drawing methods:

- `beginFill()`
- `beginGradientFill()`
- `clear()`
- `curveTo()`
- `endFill()`
- `lineTo()`
- `lineStyle()`
- `moveTo()`

You can use the drawing methods with any movie clip. However, if you use the drawing methods with a movie clip that was created in authoring mode, the drawing methods execute before the clip is drawn. In other words, content that is created in authoring mode is drawn on top of content drawn with the drawing methods.

You can use movie clips with drawing methods as masks; however, as with all movie clip masks, strokes are ignored.

For more information on drawing with ActionScript, see the following topics:

- "Using drawing methods to draw lines, curves, and shapes" on page 553
- "Drawing specific shapes" on page 555
- "Using complex gradient fills" on page 559
- "Using line styles" on page 560
- "Using Drawing API methods and scripting animation" on page 566

You can find a sample source file, drawingapi.fla, in the Samples folder on your hard disk, which shows you how to use the Drawing API in a Flash application.

- In Windows, browse to *boot drive*\Program Files\Macromedia\Flash 8\ Samples and Tutorials\Samples\ActionScript\DrawingAPI.
- On the Macintosh, browse to *Macintosh HD*/Applications/Macromedia Flash 8/ Samples and Tutorials/Samples/ActionScript/DrawingAPI.

Using drawing methods to draw lines, curves, and shapes

You can use the Flash Drawing API to dynamically create shapes on the Stage at runtime. You can use these shapes to dynamically mask content, apply filters to them, or animate them around the Stage. You can also use the Drawing API to create various drawing tools, which let users use the mouse or keyboard to draw shapes on the SWF file.

To draw a line:

1. Create a new Flash document and save it as **line.fla**.

2. Add the following ActionScript to Frame 1 of the Timeline:

```
this.createEmptyMovieClip("line_mc", 10);
line_mc.lineStyle(1, 0x000000, 100);
line_mc.moveTo(0, 0);
line_mc.lineTo(200, 100);
line_mc._x = 100;
line_mc._y = 100;
```

This code draws a line from 0,0 on the Stage to 200,100. The line's _x and _y coordinates are then modified to reposition the line to 100,100 on the Stage.

3. Save your Flash document and select Control > Test Movie to test the SWF file.

To draw a more complex shape, continue calling the `MovieClip.lineTo()` method and draw a rectangle, square, or oval, as the following procedures show.

To draw a curve:

1. Create a new Flash document and save it as **curve.fla**.

2. Add the following ActionScript to Frame 1 of the Timeline:

```
this.createEmptyMovieClip("circle_mc", 1);
with (circle_mc) {
    lineStyle(4, 0x000000, 100);
    beginFill(0xFF0000);
    moveTo(200, 300);
    curveTo(300, 300, 300, 200);
    curveTo(300, 100, 200, 100);
    curveTo(100, 100, 100, 200);
    curveTo(100, 300, 200, 300);
    endFill();
}
```

3. Save your Flash document and select Control > Test Movie to test the Flash document.

   This code uses the Drawing API to draw a circle on the Stage. The circle shape uses only four calls to the `MovieClip.curveTo()` method and therefore can look a little distorted. For another example that uses the Drawing API to create a circle, see the procedure on creating a circle under "Drawing specific shapes" on page 555 for code that uses eight calls to the `MovieClip.curveTo()` method to draw a more realistic circle.

To draw a triangle:

1. Create a new Flash document and save it as **triangle.fla**.

2. Add the following ActionScript to Frame 1 of the Timeline:

   ```
   this.createEmptyMovieClip("triangle_mc", 1);
   ```

   This code uses the `MovieClip.createEmptyMovieClip()` method to create an empty movie clip on the Stage. The new movie clip is a child of an existing movie clip (in this case, the main timeline).

3. Add the following ActionScript to Frame 1 of the Timeline, following the code you added in the preceding step:

   ```
   with (triangle_mc) {
       lineStyle(5, 0xFF00FF, 100);
       moveTo(200, 200);
       lineTo(300, 300);
       lineTo(100, 300);
       lineTo(200, 200);
   }
   ```

   In this code, the empty movie clip (`triangle_mc`) calls drawing methods. This code draws a triangle with 5-pixel purple lines and no fill.

4. Save your Flash document and select Control > Test Movie to test the Flash document.

For detailed information on these methods, see their entries in %{MovieClip}% in the *ActionScript 2.0 Language Reference* in Flash Help.

You can find a sample source file, drawingapi.fla, in the Samples folder on your hard disk, which shows you how to use the Drawing API in a Flash application.

- In Windows, browse to *boot drive*\Program Files\Macromedia\Flash 8\ Samples and Tutorials\Samples\ActionScript\DrawingAPI.

- On the Macintosh, browse to *Macintosh HD*/Applications/Macromedia Flash 8/ Samples and Tutorials/Samples/ActionScript/DrawingAPI.

Drawing specific shapes

This section shows you how to create some more flexible methods that you can use to draw more advanced shapes, such as rounded rectangles and circles.

To create a rectangle:

1. Create a new Flash document and save it as **rect.fla**.

2. Add the following ActionScript code to Frame 1 of the Timeline:

```
this.createEmptyMovieClip("rectangle_mc", 10);
rectangle_mc._x = 100;
rectangle_mc._y = 100;
drawRectangle(rectangle_mc, 240, 180, 0x99FF00, 100);
function drawRectangle(target_mc:MovieClip, boxWidth:Number,
  boxHeight:Number, fillColor:Number, fillAlpha:Number):Void {
  with (target_mc) {
    beginFill(fillColor, fillAlpha);
    moveTo(0, 0);
    lineTo(boxWidth, 0);
    lineTo(boxWidth, boxHeight);
    lineTo(0, boxHeight);
    lineTo(0, 0);
    endFill();
  }
}
```

3. Save your Flash document and select Control > Test Movie to test the Flash document.

   Flash draws a simple green rectangle on the Stage and positions it at 100,100. To change the dimensions of the rectangle, or its fill color or transparency, you can change those values within the call to the drawRectangle() method instead of having to modify the contents of the MovieClip.beginFill() method.

You can also create a rectangle with rounded corners using the Drawing API, as the following procedure shows.

To create a rounded rectangle:

1. Create a new Flash document and save it as **roundrect.fla**.

2. Add the following ActionScript code to Frame 1 of the Timeline:

```
this.createEmptyMovieClip("rectangle_mc", 10);
rectangle_mc._x = 100;
rectangle_mc._y = 100;
drawRoundedRectangle(rectangle_mc, 240, 180, 20, 0x99FF00, 100);
function drawRoundedRectangle(target_mc:MovieClip, boxWidth:Number,
  boxHeight:Number, cornerRadius:Number, fillColor:Number,
  fillAlpha:Number):Void {
  with (target_mc) {
    beginFill(fillColor, fillAlpha);
    moveTo(cornerRadius, 0);
    lineTo(boxWidth - cornerRadius, 0);
    curveTo(boxWidth, 0, boxWidth, cornerRadius);
    lineTo(boxWidth, cornerRadius);
    lineTo(boxWidth, boxHeight - cornerRadius);
    curveTo(boxWidth, boxHeight, boxWidth - cornerRadius, boxHeight);
    lineTo(boxWidth - cornerRadius, boxHeight);
    lineTo(cornerRadius, boxHeight);
    curveTo(0, boxHeight, 0, boxHeight - cornerRadius);
    lineTo(0, boxHeight - cornerRadius);
    lineTo(0, cornerRadius);
    curveTo(0, 0, cornerRadius, 0);
    lineTo(cornerRadius, 0);
    endFill();
  }
}
```

3. Save the Flash document and select Control > Test Movie to test the document.

   A green rectangle appears on the Stage that is 240 pixels wide and 180 pixels high with 20-pixel rounded corners. You can create multiple instances of rounded rectangles by creating new movie clips using `MovieClip.createEmptyMovieClip()` and calling your custom `drawRoundedRectangle()` function.

You can create a perfect circle using the Drawing API, as the following procedure shows.

To create a circle:

1. Create a new Flash document and save as **circle2.fla**.

2. Add the following ActionScript code to Frame 1 of the Timeline:

```
this.createEmptyMovieClip("circle_mc", 10);
circle_mc._x = 100;
circle_mc._y = 100;
drawCircle(circle_mc, 100, 0x99FF00, 100);

function drawCircle(target_mc:MovieClip, radius:Number,
  fillColor:Number, fillAlpha:Number):Void {
  var x:Number = radius;
  var y:Number = radius;
  with (target_mc) {
    beginFill(fillColor, fillAlpha);
    moveTo(x + radius, y);
    curveTo(radius + x, Math.tan(Math.PI / 8) * radius + y,
  Math.sin(Math.PI / 4) * radius + x, Math.sin(Math.PI / 4) * radius +
  y);
    curveTo(Math.tan(Math.PI / 8) * radius + x, radius + y, x, radius +
  y);
    curveTo(-Math.tan(Math.PI / 8) * radius + x, radius+ y, -
  Math.sin(Math.PI / 4) * radius + x, Math.sin(Math.PI / 4) * radius +
  y);
    curveTo(-radius + x, Math.tan(Math.PI / 8) * radius + y, -radius +
  x, y);
    curveTo(-radius + x, -Math.tan(Math.PI / 8) * radius + y, -
  Math.sin(Math.PI / 4) * radius + x, -Math.sin(Math.PI / 4) * radius +
  y);
    curveTo(-Math.tan(Math.PI / 8) * radius + x, -radius + y, x, -radius
  + y);
    curveTo(Math.tan(Math.PI / 8) * radius + x, -radius + y,
  Math.sin(Math.PI / 4) * radius + x, -Math.sin(Math.PI / 4) * radius +
  y);
    curveTo(radius + x, -Math.tan(Math.PI / 8) * radius + y, radius + x,
  y);
    endFill();
  }
}
```

3. Save your Flash document and select Control > Test Movie to test the SWF file.

This code creates a more complex, and realistic, circle than the previous circle example. Instead of only using four calls to the curveTo() method, this example uses eight calls to the curveTo() method, which gives the shape a much rounder appearance.

You can use the Drawing API to create a triangle, as the following procedure shows.

To create a fancy triangle:

1. Create a new Flash document and save it as **fancytriangle.fla**.

2. Add the following ActionScript to Frame 1 of the Timeline:

```
this.createEmptyMovieClip("triangle_mc", 10);
triangle_mc._x = 100;
triangle_mc._y = 100;
drawTriangle(triangle_mc, 100, 0x99FF00, 100);

function drawTriangle(target_mc:MovieClip, sideLength:Number,
  fillColor:Number, fillAlpha:Number):Void {
  var tHeight:Number = sideLength * Math.sqrt(3) / 2;
  with (target_mc) {
    beginFill(fillColor, fillAlpha);
    moveTo(sideLength / 2, 0);
    lineTo(sideLength, tHeight);
    lineTo(0, tHeight);
    lineTo(sideLength / 2, 0);
    endFill();
  }
}
```

The Drawing API draws an equilateral triangle on the Stage and fills it with the specified fill color and amount of alpha (transparency).

3. Save the Flash document and select Control > Test Movie to test the Flash document.

You can find a sample source file, drawingapi.fla, in the Samples folder on your hard disk, which shows you how to use the Drawing API in a Flash application.

- In Windows, browse to *boot drive*\Program Files\Macromedia\Flash 8\
  Samples and Tutorials\Samples\ActionScript\DrawingAPI.

- On the Macintosh, browse to *Macintosh HD*/Applications/Macromedia Flash 8/
  Samples and Tutorials/Samples/ActionScript/DrawingAPI.

Using complex gradient fills

The Flash Drawing API supports gradient fills as well as solid fills. The following procedure creates a new movie clip on the Stage, use the Drawing API to create a square, and then fills the square with a radial red and blue gradient.

To create a complex gradient:

1. Create a new Flash document and save it as **radialgradient.fla**.

2. Add the following ActionScript to Frame 1 of the Timeline:

```
this.createEmptyMovieClip("gradient_mc", 10);
var fillType:String = "radial";
var colors:Array - [0xFF0000, 0x0000FF];
var alphas:Array = [100, 100];
var ratios:Array = [0, 0xFF];
var matrix:Object = {a:200, b:0, c:0, d:0, e:200, f:0, g:200, h:200,
   i:1};
var spreadMethod:String = "reflect";
var interpolationMethod:String = "linearRGB";
var focalPointRatio:Number = 0.9;
with (gradient_mc) {
   beginGradientFill(fillType, colors, alphas, ratios, matrix,
   spreadMethod, interpolationMethod, focalPointRatio);
   moveTo(100, 100);
   lineTo(100, 300);
   lineTo(300, 300);
   lineTo(300, 100);
   lineTo(100, 100);
   endFill();
}
```

The preceding ActionScript code uses the Drawing API to create a square on the Stage and calls the beginGradientFill() method to fill the square with a red and blue circular gradient.

3. Save the Flash document and select Control > Test Movie to view the Flash file.

Using line styles

The Flash Drawing API lets you specify a line style that Flash uses for subsequent calls to `MovieClip.lineTo()` and `MovieClip.curveTo()` until you call `MovieClip.lineStyle()` with different parameters, as follows:

```
lineStyle(thickness:Number, rgb:Number, alpha:Number, pixelHinting:Boolean,
    noScale:String, capsStyle:String, jointStyle:String, miterLimit:Number)
```

You can call `MovieClip.lineStyle()` in the middle of drawing a path to specify different styles for different line segments within a path.

For more information on using ActionScript to set line styles, see the following sections:

- "Setting stroke and caps styles" on page 560
- "Setting parameters of line styles" on page 562

Setting stroke and caps styles

Flash 8 includes several improvements to line drawing. New line parameters added in Flash Player 8 are `pixelHinting`, `noScale`, `capsStyle`, `jointStyle`, and `miterLimit`.

The following procedure demonstrates the difference between the three new caps styles in Flash Player 8: `none`, `round`, and `square`.

To set caps styles using ActionScript:

1. Create a new Flash document and save it as **capstyle.fla**.

2. Add the following ActionScript to Frame 1 of the Timeline:

```
// Set up grid movie clip.
this.createEmptyMovieClip("grid_mc", 50);
grid_mc.lineStyle(0, 0x999999, 100);
grid_mc.moveTo(50, 0);
grid_mc.lineTo(50, Stage.height);
grid_mc.moveTo(250, 0);
grid_mc.lineTo(250, Stage.height);
// line 1 (capsStyle: round)
this.createEmptyMovieClip("line1_mc", 10);
with (line1_mc) {
   createTextField("label_txt", 1, 5, 10, 100, 20);
   label_txt.text = "round";
   lineStyle(20, 0x99FF00, 100, true, "none", "round", "miter", 0.8);
   moveTo(0, 0);
   lineTo(200, 0);
   _x = 50;
   _y = 50;
}
// line 2 (capsStyle: square)
this.createEmptyMovieClip("line2_mc", 20);
with (line2_mc) {
   createTextField("label_txt", 1, 5, 10, 100, 20);
   label_txt.text = "square";
   lineStyle(20, 0x99FF00, 100, true, "none", "square", "miter", 0.8);
   moveTo(0, 0);
   lineTo(200, 0);
   _x = 50;
   _y = 150;
}
// line 3 (capsStyle: none)
this.createEmptyMovieClip("line3_mc", 30);
with (line3_mc) {
   createTextField("label_txt", 1, 5, 10, 100, 20);
   label_txt.text = "none";
   lineStyle(20, 0x99FF00, 100, true, "none", "none", "miter", 0.8);
   moveTo(0, 0);
   lineTo(200, 0);
   _x = 50;
   _y = 250;
}
```

The preceding code dynamically creates four movie clips and uses the Drawing API to create a series of lines on the Stage. The first movie clip contains two vertical lines, one at 50 pixels and the other at 250 pixels on the x-axis. The next three movie clips each draw a green line on the Stage and sets their capsStyle to round, square, or none.

3. Select Control > Test Movie to test the document.

The different caps styles appear on the Stage at runtime.

Setting parameters of line styles

You can set the parameters of line styles to change the appearance of your strokes. You can use parameters to change the thickness, color, alpha, scale, and other attributes of the line style.

Setting line thickness

The `thickness` parameter of the `MovieClip.lineStyle()` method lets you specify the thickness of the line drawn in points as a number. You can draw a line any thickness between 0 and 255 points wide, although setting the thickness to 0 creates what is called a *hairline thickness*, where the stroke is always 1 pixel, regardless of whether the SWF file is zoomed in or resized.

The following procedure demonstrates the difference between a standard 1-pixel thickness line and a hairline thickness line.

To create a hairline stroke:

1. Create a new Flash document and save it as **hairline.fla**.

2. Add the following ActionScript to Frame 1 of your Timeline:

```
this.createEmptyMovieClip("drawing_mc", 10);
// create a red, hairline thickness line
drawing_mc.lineStyle(0, 0xFF0000, 100);
drawing_mc.moveTo(0, 0);
drawing_mc.lineTo(200, 0);
drawing_mc.lineTo(200, 100);
// create a blue line with a 1 pixel thickness
drawing_mc.lineStyle(1, 0x0000FF, 100);
drawing_mc.lineTo(0, 100);
drawing_mc.lineTo(0, 0);
drawing_mc._x = 100;
drawing_mc._y = 100;
```

The preceding code uses the Drawing API to draw two lines on the Stage. The first line is red and has a thickness of 0, indicating a hairline thickness, the second line is blue and has a thickness of 1 pixel.

3. Save the Flash document and select Control > Test Movie to test the SWF file.

Initially, both the red and blue lines look exactly the same. If you right-click in the SWF file and select Zoom In from the context menu, the red line always appears as a 1-pixel line; however, the blue line grows larger each time you zoom in to the SWF file.

Setting line color (rgb)

The second parameter in the `lineStyle()` method, `rgb`, lets you control the color of the current line segment as a number. By default, Flash draws black lines (#000000), although you can specify different colors by setting a new hexidecimal color value using `0xRRGGBB` syntax. In this syntax, RR is a red value (between 00 and FF), GG is a green value (00 to FF), and BB is a blue value (00 to FF).

For example, you represent a red line as `0xFF0000`, a green line as `0x00FF00`, a blue line as `0x0000FF`, a purple line as `0xFF00FF` (red and blue), a white line as #FFFFFF, a gray line as #999999, and so on.

Setting line alpha

The third parameter in the `lineStyle()` method, `alpha`, lets you control the transparency (alpha) level for the line. Transparency is a numerical value between 0 and 100, where 0 represents a completely transparent line, and 100 is completely opaque (visible).

Setting line pixel hinting (pixelHinting)

The pixel hinting for strokes parameter, `pixelHinting`, means that line and curve anchors are set on full pixels. The strokes are on full pixels for any stroke thickness, which means that you never see a blurry vertical or horizontal line. You set the `pixelHinting` parameter to a Boolean value (`true` or `false`).

Setting line scale (noScale)

You set the `noScale` parameter by using a String value, which lets you specify a scaling mode for the line. You can use a nonscaleable stroke in horizontal mode or vertical mode, scale the line (normal), or use no scaling.

> It is useful to enable scaling for user interface elements when users zoom in, but not if a movie clip is only scaled vertically or horizontally.

You can use one of four different modes to specify when scaling should occur and when it shouldn't. The following are the possible values for the `noScale` property:

`normal`   Always scale the thickness (*default*).

`vertical`   Do not scale the thickness if the object is scaled vertically.

`horizontal`   Do not scale the thickness if the object is scaled horizontally.

`none`   Never scale the thickness.

Setting line caps (capsStyle) and joints (jointStyle)

You can set three types of caps styles for the `capsStyle` parameter:

- `round` (*default*)

- `square`

- `none`

The following procedure demonstrates the differences between each of the three caps styles. A visual representation of each cap style appears on the Stage when you test the SWF file.

To set different caps styles:

1. Create a new Flash document and save it as **capsstyle2.fla**.

2. Add the following ActionScript to Frame 1 of the Timeline:

```
var lineLength:Number = 100;
// round
this.createEmptyMovieClip("round_mc", 10);
round_mc.lineStyle(20, 0xFF0000, 100, true, "none", "round");
round_mc.moveTo(0, 0);
round_mc.lineTo(lineLength, 0);
round_mc.lineStyle(0, 0x000000);
round_mc.moveTo(0, 0);
round_mc.lineTo(lineLength, 0);
round_mc._x = 50;
round_mc._y = 50;
var lbl:TextField = round_mc.createTextField("label_txt", 10, 0, 10,
    lineLength, 20);
lbl.text = "round";
var lineLength:Number = 100;
// square
this.createEmptyMovieClip("square_mc", 20);
square_mc.lineStyle(20, 0xFF0000, 100, true, "none", "square");
square_mc.moveTo(0, 0);
square_mc.lineTo(lineLength, 0);
square_mc.lineStyle(0, 0x000000);
square_mc.moveTo(0, 0);
square_mc.lineTo(lineLength, 0);
square_mc._x = 200;
```

```
square_mc._y = 50;
var lbl:TextField = square_mc.createTextField("label_txt", 10, 0, 10,
    lineLength, 20);
lbl.text = "square";
// none
this.createEmptyMovieClip("none_mc", 30);
none_mc.lineStyle(20, 0xFF0000, 100, true, "none", "none");
none_mc.moveTo(0, 0);
none_mc.lineTo(lineLength, 0);
none_mc.lineStyle(0, 0x000000);
none_mc.moveTo(0, 0);
none_mc.lineTo(lineLength, 0);
none_mc._x = 350;
none_mc._y = 50;
var lbl:TextField = none_mc.createTextField("label_txt", 10, 0, 10,
    lineLength, 20);
lbl.text = "none";
```

The preceding code uses the Drawing API to draw three lines, each with a different value for capsStyle.

3. Select Control > Test Movie to test the Flash document.

You can set the following three types of joint styles for the jointStyle parameter:

- round (*default*)

- miter

- bevel

The following example demonstrates the differences between each of the three joint styles.

To set different joint styles:

1. Create a new Flash document and save it as **jointstyles.fla**.

2. Add the following ActionScript to Frame 1 of the Timeline:

```
var lineLength:Number = 100;
// miter
this.createEmptyMovieClip("miter_mc", 10);
miter_mc.lineStyle(25, 0xFF0000, 100, true, "none", "none", "miter",
    25);
miter_mc.moveTo(0, lineLength);
miter_mc.lineTo(lineLength / 2, 0);
miter_mc.lineTo(lineLength, lineLength);
miter_mc.lineTo(0, lineLength);
miter_mc._x = 50;
miter_mc._y = 50;
var lbl:TextField = miter_mc.createTextField("label_txt", 10, 0,
    lineLength + 20, lineLength, 20);
lbl.autoSize = "center";
lbl.text = "miter";
```

```
// round
this.createEmptyMovieClip("round_mc", 20);
round_mc.lineStyle(25, 0xFF0000, 100, true, "none", "none", "round");
round_mc.moveTo(0, lineLength);
round_mc.lineTo(lineLength / 2, 0);
round_mc.lineTo(lineLength, lineLength);
round_mc.lineTo(0, lineLength);
round_mc._x = 200;
round_mc._y = 50;
var lbl:TextField = round_mc.createTextField("label_txt", 10, 0,
    lineLength + 20, lineLength, 20);
lbl.autoSize = "center";
lbl.text = "round";
// bevel
this.createEmptyMovieClip("bevel_mc", 30);
bevel_mc.lineStyle(25, 0xFF0000, 100, true, "none", "none", "bevel");
bevel_mc.moveTo(0, lineLength);
bevel_mc.lineTo(lineLength / 2, 0);
bevel_mc.lineTo(lineLength, lineLength);
bevel_mc.lineTo(0, lineLength);
bevel_mc._x = 350;
bevel_mc._y = 50;
var lbl:TextField = bevel_mc.createTextField("label_txt", 10, 0,
    lineLength + 20, lineLength, 20);
lbl.autoSize = "center";
lbl.text = "bevel";
```

Flash uses the Drawing API to draw three triangles on the Stage. Each triangle has a different value for its joint style.

3. Save the Flash document and select Control > Test Movie to test the document.

Setting line miter (miterLimit)

The miterLimit property is a numerical value that indicates the limit at which a miter joint (see "Setting line caps (capsStyle) and joints (jointStyle)" on page 564) is cut off. The miterLimit value is a general multiplier of a stroke. For example, with a value of 2.5, miterLimit is cut off at 2.5 times the stroke size. Valid values range from 0 to 255 (if a value for miterLimit is undefined, the default value is 3). The miterLimit property is only used if jointStyle is set to miter.

Using Drawing API methods and scripting animation

You can combine the Drawing API with the Tween and TransitionManager classes to create some excellent animated results, and you only have to write a small amount of ActionScript.

The following procedure loads a JPEG image and dynamically masks the image so you can reveal the image slowly after it loads by tweening the image's mask.

To animate dynamic masks:

1. Create a new Flash document and save it as **dynmask.fla**.

2. Add the following ActionScript to Frame 1 of the Timeline:

```
import mx.transitions.Tween;
import mx.transitions.easing.*;
var mclListener:Object = new Object();
mclListener.onLoadInit = function(target_mc:MovieClip) {
  target_mc._visible = false;
  // Center the image on the Stage.
  target_mc._x = (Stage.width - target_mc._width) / 2;
  target_mc._y = (Stage.height - target_mc._height) / 2;
  var maskClip:MovieClip = target_mc.createEmptyMovieClip("mask_mc",
  20);
  with (maskClip) {
    // Draw a mask that is the same size as the loaded image.
    beginFill(0xFF00FF, 100);
    moveTo(0, 0);
    lineTo(target_mc._width, 0);
    lineTo(target_mc._width, target_mc._height);
    lineTo(0, target_mc._height);
    lineTo(0, 0);
    endFill();
  }
  target_mc.setMask(maskClip);
  target_mc._visible = true;
  var mask_tween:Object = new Tween(maskClip, "_yscale", Strong.easeOut,
  0, 100, 2, true);
};
this.createEmptyMovieClip("img_mc", 10);
var img_mcl:MovieClipLoader = new MovieClipLoader();
img_mcl.addListener(mclListener);
img_mcl.loadClip("http://www.helpexamples.com/flash/images/image1.jpg",
  img_mc);
```

This code example imports the Tween class and each of the classes in the easing package. Next, it creates an object that acts as the listener object for a MovieClipLoader instance that's created in a later section of the code. The listener object defines a single event listener, onLoadInit, which centers the dynamically loaded JPEG image on the Stage. After the code repositions the image, a new movie clip instance is created within the target_mc movie clip (which contains the dynamically loaded JPEG image). The Drawing API code draws a rectangle with the same dimensions as the JPEG image within this new movie clip. The new movie clip masks the JPEG image by calling the MovieClip.setMask() method. After the mask is drawn and set up, the mask uses the Tween class to animate, which causes the image to slowly reveal itself.

3. Save the Flash document and select Control > Test Movie to test the SWF file.

> **NOTE**
> To animate `_alpha` in the previous example instead of `_yscale`, tween the `target_mc` directly instead of the mask movie clip.

You can find a sample source file, drawingapi.fla, in the Samples folder on your hard disk, which shows you how to use the Drawing API in a Flash application.

- In Windows, browse to *boot drive*\Program Files\Macromedia\Flash 8\ Samples and Tutorials\Samples\ActionScript\DrawingAPI.

- On the Macintosh, browse to *Macintosh HD*/Applications/Macromedia Flash 8/ Samples and Tutorials/Samples/ActionScript/DrawingAPI.

Understanding scaling and slice guides

You can use 9-slice scaling (Scale-9) to specify component-style scaling for movie clips. 9-slice scaling lets you create movie clip symbols that scale appropriately for use as user interface components, as opposed to the type of scaling typically applied to graphics and design elements.

Understanding how 9-slice scaling works

The easiest way to explain how 9-slice scaling works is to look at an example of how 9-slice scaling works in Flash.

To understand scaling in Flash:

1. Create a new Flash document and save it as **dynmask.fla**.

2. Drag a copy of the Button component to the Stage from the Components panel (Window > Components).

3. Increase the Stage's zoom level to 400% by using the Zoom tool.

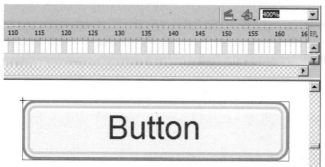

By default, the Button component instance is 100 pixels wide by 22 pixels high.

4. Resize the Button component instance to 200 pixels width by 44 pixels high by using the Property inspector.

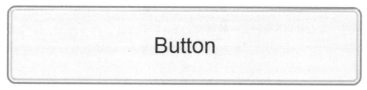

You can see that even though the component resized, the Button's border and text label do not distort. The button's label remained centered and maintained its font size. Although components of version 2 of the Macromedia Component Architecture do not use 9-slice scaling, components handle scaling in the version 2 component architecture so the outlines do not change size (as shown in the next figure).

Imagine that the button instance is sliced into 9 separate pieces, or a 3 by 3 grid, similar to a keypad on a telephone or keyboard. When you resize the button instance horizontally, only the three vertical segments in the center (numbers 2, 5, and 8 on a keypad) stretch so your content doesn't appear distorted. If you resized the button instance vertically, only the three horizontal segments in the center (numbers 4, 5, and 6 on a keypad) would resize. The four corners of the scaling grid are not scaled at all, which allows the component to grow without looking like it is being stretched (see the following images).

> **TIP** Strokes are created from the edges after the 9-slice scaling transformation, and therefore don't deform or lose detail.

You can enable slice guides for 9-slice scaling in the Flash environment within the Convert to Symbol dialog box or the Symbol Properties dialog box. The Enable guides for 9-slice scaling check box is available only if you are publishing for Flash Player 8 and the behavior is set to movie clip. The 9-slice scaling guides are not available for earlier versions of Flash or if you are creating a button or graphic symbol. 9-slice scaling can be enabled in ActionScript by setting the `scale9Grid` property on a movie clip instance.

Whether you created your slice guides by using the user interface or by using ActionScript, you can trace the *x* coordinate, y coordinate, width, and height by tracing the movie clip's `scale9Grid` property.

```
trace(my_mc.scale9Grid); // (x=20, y=20, w=120, h=120)
```

This snippet of code traces the value of the Rectangle object being used by the `scale9Grid` property. The rectangle has a *x* and *y* coordinates of 20 pixels, a width of 120 pixels and a height of 120 pixels.

Working with 9-slice scaling in ActionScript

In the following example, you use the drawing tools to draw a 300 pixel by 300 pixel square which is resized by using 9-slice scaling. The square is split up into nine smaller squares, each one approximately 100 pixels wide by 100 pixels high. When you resize the square, each segment that isn't a corner expands to match the specified width and height.

To use 9-slice scaling with ActionScript:

1. Create a new Flash document and save it as **ninescale.fla**.

2. Drag a Button component into the current document's library.

3. Select the Rectangle tool and draw a red square (300 pixels by 300 pixels) with a 15-pixel black stroke on the Stage.

4. Select the Oval tool and draw a purple circle (50 pixels by 50 pixels) with a 2-pixel black stroke on the Stage.

5. Select the purple circle and drag it into the upper-right corner of the red square created earlier.

6. Select the Oval tool and draw a new circle that is approximately 200 pixels by 200 pixels and position it off of the Stage.

7. Select the new circle on the Stage and drag it so that the circle's center-point is in the lower-left corner of the square.

8. Click outside of the circle instance to deselect the circle.

9. Double-click the circle again to select it and press backspace to delete the shape and remove a circular portion of the square.

10. Using the mouse, select the entire red square and inner purple circle.

11. Press F8 to convert the shape into a movie clip symbol.

12. Give the movie clip on the Stage an instance name of **my_mc**.

13. Add the following ActionScript to Frame 1 of the main Timeline:

```
import mx.controls.Button;
import flash.geom.Rectangle;

var grid:Rectangle = new Rectangle(100, 100, 100, 100);

var small_button:Button = this.createClassObject(Button, "small_button",
    10, {label:"Small"});
small_button.move(10, 10);
small_button.addEventListener("click", smallHandler);
function smallHandler(eventObj:Object):Void {
    my_mc._width = 100;
    my_mc._height = 100;
}

var large_button:Button = this.createClassObject(Button, "large_button",
    20, {label:"Large"});
large_button.move(120, 10);
large_button.addEventListener("click", largeHandler);
function largeHandler(eventObj:Object):Void {
    my_mc._width = 450;
    my_mc._height = 300;
}

var toggle_button:Button = this.createClassObject(Button,
    "toggle_button", 30, {label:"scale9Grid=OFF", toggle:true,
    selected:false});
toggle_button.move(420, 10);
toggle_button.setSize(120, 22);
toggle_button.addEventListener("click", toggleListener);
function toggleListener(eventObj:Object):Void {
    if (eventObj.target.selected) {
        eventObj.target.label = "scale9Grid=ON";
        my_mc.scale9Grid = grid;
    } else {
        eventObj.target.label = "scale9Grid=OFF";
        my_mc.scale9Grid = undefined;
    }
}
```

The preceding code is separated into five sections. The first section of code imports two classes: mx.controls.Button (the Button component class) and flash.geom.Rectangle. The second section of code creates a new Rectangle class instance and specifies x and y coordinates of 100 pixels as well as a width and height of 100 pixels. This rectangle instance is used to set up the 9-slice scaling grid for a movie clip shape created later on.

Next, you create a new Button component instance and give it an instance name of `small_button`. Whenever you click this button, the movie clip that you created earlier resizes to 100 pixels wide by 100 pixels high. The fourth section of code dynamically creates a new Button instance named `large_button` which, when clicked, resizes the target movie clip to 450 pixels wide by 300 pixels high. The final section of code creates a new Button instance that the user can toggle on and off. When the button is in the on state, the 9-slice grid is applied. If the button is in the off state, the 9-slice grid is disabled.

14. Save the Flash document and select Control > Test Movie to test the SWF file.

This code example adds and positions three Button component instances on the Stage and creates event listeners for each button. If you click the Large button with the 9-slice grid disabled, you can see that the image becomes distorted and looks stretched. Enable the 9-slice grid by clicking the toggle button and click the Large button again. With the 9-slice grid enabled, the circle in the upper-left corner should no longer appear distorted.

CHAPTER 14

Creating Interaction with ActionScript

In simple animations, Macromedia Flash Player plays the scenes and frames of a SWF file sequentially. In an interactive SWF file, your audience uses the keyboard and mouse to jump to different parts of a SWF file, move objects, enter information in forms, and perform many other interactive operations.

You use ActionScript to create scripts that tell Flash Player what action to perform when an event occurs. Some events that can trigger a script occur when the playhead reaches a frame, when a movie clip loads or unloads, or when the user clicks a button or presses a key.

A script can consist of a single command, such as instructing a SWF file to stop playing, or a series of commands and statements, such as first evaluating a condition and then performing an action. Many ActionScript commands are simple and let you create basic controls for a SWF file. Other actions require some familiarity with programming languages and are intended for advanced development.

For more information on creating interaction with ActionScript, see the following topics:

About events and interaction

Whenever a user clicks the mouse or presses a key, that action generates an event. These types of events are generally called *user events* because they are generated in response to some action by the user. You can write ActionScript to respond to, or *handle*, these events. For example, when a user clicks a button, you might want to send the playhead to another frame in the SWF file or load a new web page into the browser.

In a SWF file, buttons, movie clips, and text fields all generate events to which you can respond. ActionScript provides three ways to handle events: event handler methods, event listeners, and `on()` and `onClipEvent()` handlers. For more information about events and handling events, see Chapter 10, "Handling Events."

Controlling SWF file playback

The following ActionScript functions let you control the playhead in the timeline and load a new web page into a browser window:

- The `gotoAndPlay()` and `gotoAndStop()` functions send the playhead to a frame or scene. These are global functions that you can call from any script. You can also use the `MovieClip.gotoAndPlay()` and `MovieClip.gotoAndStop()` methods to navigate the timeline of a specific movie clip object. See "Jumping to a frame or scene" on page 576.
- The `play()` and `stop()` actions play and stop SWF files. See "Playing and stopping movie clips" on page 577.
- The `getURL()` action jumps to a different URL. See "Jumping to a different URL" on page 578.

For more information, see the following topics:

- "Jumping to a frame or scene" on page 576
- "Playing and stopping movie clips" on page 577
- "Jumping to a different URL" on page 578

Jumping to a frame or scene

To jump to a specific frame or scene in the SWF file, you can use the `gotoAndPlay()` and `gotoAndStop()` global functions or the equivalent `MovieClip.gotoAndPlay()` and `MovieClip.gotoAndStop()` methods of the MovieClip class. Each function or method lets you specify a frame to jump to in the current scene. If your document contains multiple scenes, you can specify a scene and frame where you want to jump.

The following example uses the global `gotoAndPlay()` function within a button object's `onRelease` event handler to send the playhead of the timeline that contains the button to Frame 10:

```
jump_btn.onRelease = function () {
  gotoAndPlay(10);
};
```

In the next example, the `MovieClip.gotoAndStop()` method sends the timeline of a movie clip instance named `categories_mc` to Frame 10 and stops. When you use the MovieClip methods `gotoAndPlay()` and `gotoAndStop()`, you must specify an instance to which the method applies.

```
jump_btn.onPress = function () {
  categories_mc.gotoAndStop(10);
};
```

In the final example, the global `gotoAndStop()` function is used to move the playhead to Frame 1 of Scene 2. If no scene is specified, the playhead goes to the specified frame in the current scene. You can use the scene parameter only on the root timeline, not within timelines for movie clips or other objects in the document.

```
nextScene_mc.onRelease = function() {
  gotoAndStop("Scene 2", 1);
}
```

Playing and stopping movie clips

Unless it is instructed otherwise, after a SWF file starts, it plays through every frame in the timeline. You can start or stop a SWF file by using the `play()` and `stop()` global functions or the equivalent MovieClip methods. For example, you can use `stop()` to stop a SWF file at the end of a scene before proceeding to the next scene. After a SWF file stops, it must be explicitly started again by calling `play()` or `gotoAndPlay()`.

You can use the `play()` and `stop()` functions or MovieClip methods to control the main timeline or the timeline of any movie clip or loaded SWF file. The movie clip you want to control must have an instance name and must be present in the timeline.

The following `on(press)` handler attached to a button starts the playhead moving in the SWF file or movie clip that contains the button object:

```
// Attached to a button instance
on (press) {
  // Plays the timeline that contains the button
  play();
}
```

This same `on()` event handler code produces a different result when attached to a movie clip object rather than a button. When attached to a button object, statements made within an `on()` handler are applied to the timeline that contains the button, by default. However, when attached to a movie clip object, statements made within an `on()` handler are applied to the movie clip to which the `on()` handler is attached.

For example, the following `onPress()` handler code stops the timeline of the movie clip to which the handler is attached, not the timeline that contains the movie clip:

```
// Attached to the myMovie_mc movie clip instance
myMovie_mc.onPress() {
  stop();
};
```

The same conditions apply to `onClipEvent()` handlers attached to movie clip objects. For example, the following code stops the timeline of the movie clip that bears the `onClipEvent()` handler when the clip first loads or appears on the Stage:

```
onClipEvent(load) {
  stop();
}
```

Jumping to a different URL

To open a web page in a browser window, or to pass data to another application at a defined URL, you can use the `getURL()` global function or the `MovieClip.getURL()` method. For example, you can have a button that links to a new website, or you can send timeline variables to a CGI script for processing in the same way as you would an HTML form. You can also specify a target window, the same as you would when targeting a window with an HTML anchor tag (`<a></a>`).

For example, the following code opens the macromedia.com home page in a blank browser window when the user clicks the button instance named `homepage_btn`:

```
// Attach to frame
homepage_btn.onRelease = function () {
  getURL("http://www.macromedia.com", "_blank");
};
```

You can also send variables along with the URL, using GET or POST methods. This is useful if the page you are loading from an application server, such as a ColdFusion server (CFM) page, expects to receive form variables. For example, suppose you want to load a CFM page named addUser.cfm that expects two form variables, firstName and age. To do this, you can create a movie clip named variables_mc that defines those two variables, as shown in the following example:

```
variables_mc.firstName = "Francois";
variables_mc.age = 32;
```

The following code then loads addUser.cfm into a blank browser window and passes variables_mc.name and variables_mc.age in the POST header to the CFM page:

```
variables_mc.getURL("addUser.cfm", "_blank", "POST");
```

The functionality of getURL() is dependent on what browser you use. The most reliable way to get all browsers to work the same is to call a JavaScript function in the HTML code that uses the JavaScript window.open() method to open a window. Add the following HTML and JavaScript within your HTML template:

```
<script language="JavaScript">
<--
  function openNewWindow(myURL) {
    window.open(myURL, "targetWindow");
  }
// -->
</script>
```

You can use the following ActionScript to call openNewWindow from your SWF file:

```
var myURL:String = "http://foo.com";
getURL("javascript:openNewWindow('" + String(myURL) + "');");
```

For more information, see %{getURL function}% in the *ActionScript 2.0 Language Reference* in Flash Help.

Creating interactivity and visual effects

To create interactivity and other visual effects, you need to understand the following techniques:

- "Creating a custom mouse pointer" on page 580
- "Getting the pointer position" on page 581
- "Capturing keypresses" on page 583
- "Setting color values" on page 586
- "Creating sound controls" on page 587
- "Detecting collisions" on page 590
- "Creating a simple line drawing tool" on page 592

Creating a custom mouse pointer

A standard mouse pointer is the operating system's on-screen representation of the position of the user's mouse. By replacing the standard pointer with one you design in Flash, you can integrate the user's mouse movement within the SWF file more closely. The sample in this section uses a custom pointer that looks like a large arrow. The power of this feature, however, is your ability to make the custom pointer look like anything—for example, a football to be carried to the goal line or a swatch of fabric pulled over a chair to change its color.

To create a custom pointer, you design the pointer movie clip on the Stage. Then, in ActionScript, you hide the standard pointer and track its movement. To hide the standard pointer, you use the `hide()` method of the built-in Mouse class (see %{hide (Mouse.hide method)}% in the *ActionScript 2.0 Language Reference* in Flash Help).

To create a custom pointer:

1. Create a movie clip to use as a custom pointer, and place an instance of the clip on the Stage.
2. Select the movie clip instance on the Stage.
3. In the Property inspector, type **cursor_mc** in the Instance Name text box.

4. Select Frame 1 of the Timeline, and type the following code in the Actions panel:

```
Mouse.hide();
cursor_mc.onMouseMove = function() {
  this._x = _xmouse;
  this._y = _ymouse;
  updateAfterEvent();
};
```

The `Mouse.hide()` method hides the pointer when the movie clip first appears on the Stage; the `onMouseMove` function positions the custom pointer at the same place as the pointer and calls `updateAfterEvent()` whenever the user moves the mouse.

The `updateAfterEvent()` function immediately refreshes the screen after the specified event occurs, rather than when the next frame is drawn, which is the default behavior. (See %{updateAfterEvent function}% in the *ActionScript 2.0 Language Reference* in Flash Help.)

5. Select Control > Test Movie to test your custom pointer.

Buttons still function when you use a custom mouse pointer. It's a good idea to put the custom pointer on the top layer of the timeline so that, as you move the mouse in the SWF file, the custom pointer appears in front of buttons and other objects in other layers. Also, the tip of a custom pointer is the registration point of the movie clip you're using as the custom pointer. Therefore, if you want a certain part of the movie clip to act as the tip of the pointer, set the registration point coordinates of the clip to be that point.

For more information about the methods of the Mouse class, see %{Mouse}% in the *ActionScript 2.0 Language Reference* in Flash Help.

Getting the pointer position

You can use the `_xmouse` and `_ymouse` properties to find the location of the pointer in a SWF file. These properties could be used, for example, in a map application that gets the values of the `_xmouse` and `_ymouse` properties and uses the values to calculate the longitude and latitude of a specific location.

Each timeline has an _xmouse and _ymouse property that returns the location of the pointer within its coordinate system. The position is always relative to the registration point. For the main timeline (_level0), the registration point is the upper left corner. For a movie clip, the registration point depends on the registration point set when the clip was created or its placement on the Stage.

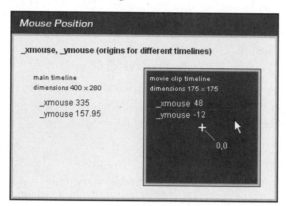

The _xmouse *and* _ymouse *properties within the main timeline and a movie clip timeline*

The following procedure shows several ways to get the pointer position within the main timeline or within a movie clip.

To get the current pointer position:

1. Create two dynamic text fields, and name them **box1_txt** and **box2_txt**.

2. Add labels for the text boxes: *x* position and *y* position, respectively.

3. Select Window > Actions to open the Actions panel if it is not already open.

4. Add the following code to the script pane:

```
var mouseListener:Object = new Object();
mouseListener.onMouseMove = function() {
  // returns the X and Y position of the mouse
  box1_txt.text = _xmouse;
  box2_txt.text = _ymouse;
};
Mouse.addListener(mouseListener);
```

5. Select Control > Test Movie to test the Flash movie. The box1_txt and box2_txt fields show the position of the pointer while you move it over the Stage.

For more information about the _xmouse and _ymouse properties, see %{_xmouse (MovieClip._xmouse property)}% and %{_ymouse (MovieClip._ymouse property)}% in the *ActionScript 2.0 Language Reference* in Flash Help.

Capturing keypresses

You can use the global on() handler to intercept the built-in behavior of keypresses in Flash Player, as shown in the following example:

```
/* When you press the Left or Right Arrow key, the movie clip to which the
   handler is attached changes transparency. */
on (keyPress "<Left>") {
  this._alpha -= 10;
}
on (keyPress "<Right>") {
  this._alpha += 10;
}
```

Make sure that you select Control > Disable Keyboard Shortcuts, or certain keys with built-in behavior won't be overridden when you use Control > Test Movie to test the application. See the keyPress parameter of %{on handler}% in the *ActionScript 2.0 Language Reference* in Flash Help.

You can use the methods of the built-in Key class to detect the last key that the user pressed. The Key class does not require a constructor function; to use its methods, you call the methods on the class, as shown in the following example:

```
Key.getCode();
```

You can obtain either virtual key codes or American Standard Code for Information Interchange (ASCII) values of keypresses:

- To obtain the virtual key code of the last key pressed, use the getCode() method.
- To obtain the ASCII value of the last key pressed, use the getAscii() method.

A virtual key code is assigned to every physical key on a keyboard. For example, the left arrow key has the virtual key code 37. By using a virtual key code, you ensure that your SWF file's controls are the same on every keyboard, regardless of language or platform.

ASCII values are assigned to the first 127 characters in every character set. ASCII values provide information about a character on the screen. For example, the letter "A" and the letter "a" have different ASCII values.

To decide which keys to use and determine their virtual key codes, use one of the following approaches:

- See the list of key codes in Appendix C, "Keyboard Keys and Key Code Values."

- Use a Key class constant. (In the Actions toolbox, click ActionScript 2.0 Classes > Movie > Key > Constants.)

- Assign the following `onClipEvent()` handler to a movie clip, and select Control > Test Movie and press the desired key:

```
onClipEvent(keyDown) {
  trace(Key.getCode());
}
```

The key code of the desired key appears in the Output panel.

A common place to use Key class methods is within an event handler. In the following example, the user moves the car using the arrow keys. The `Key.isDown()` method indicates whether the key being pressed is the right, left, up, or down arrow. The event listener, `Key.onKeyDown`, determines the `Key.isDown(keyCode)` value from the `if` statements. Depending on the value, the handler instructs Flash Player to update the position of the car and to show the direction.

The following example shows how to capture keypresses to move a movie clip up, down, left, or right on the Stage, depending on which corresponding arrow key (up, down, left, or right) is pressed. Also, a text field shows the name of the pressed key.

To create a keyboard-activated movie clip:

1. On the Stage, create a movie clip that can move in response to keyboard arrow activity.

    In this example, the movie clip instance name is `car_mc`.

2. Select Frame 1 in the Timeline; then select Window > Actions to open the Actions panel if it is not already visible.

3. To set how far the car moves across the screen with each keypress, define a `distance` variable and set its value to 10:

    ```
    var distance:Number = 10;
    ```

4. Add the following ActionScript code to the Actions panel below the existing code:

    ```
    this.createTextField("display_txt", 999, 0, 0, 100, 20);
    ```

5. To create the event handler for the car movie clip that checks which arrow key (left, right, up, or down) is currently pressed, add the following code to the Actions panel:

    ```
    var keyListener:Object = new Object();
    keyListener.onKeyDown = function() {
    };
    Key.addListener(keyListener);
    ```

6. To check if the Left Arrow key is pressed and to move the car movie clip accordingly, add code to the body of the `onEnterFrame` event handler.

Your code should look like the following example (new code is in boldface):

```
var distance:Number = 10;
this.createTextField("display_txt", 999, 0, 0, 100, 20);
var keyListener:Object = new Object();
keyListener.onKeyDown = function() {
   if (Key.isDown(Key.LEFT)) {
      car_mc._x = Math.max(car_mc._x - distance, 0);
      display_txt.text = "Left";
   }
};
Key.addListener(keyListener);
```

If the Left Arrow key is pressed, the car's _x property is set to the current _x value minus distance or the value 0, whichever is greater. Therefore, the value of the _x property can never be less than 0. Also, the word *Left* should appear in the SWF file.

7. Use similar code to check if the Right, Up, or Down Arrow key is being pressed.

Your complete code should look like the following example (new code is in boldface):

```
var distance:Number = 10;
this.createTextField("display_txt", 999, 0, 0, 100, 20);
var keyListener:Object = new Object();
keyListener.onKeyDown = function() {
   if (Key.isDown(Key.LEFT)) {
      car_mc._x = Math.max(car_mc._x - distance, 0);
      display_txt.text = "Left";
   } else if (Key.isDown(Key.RIGHT)) {
      car_mc._x = Math.min(car_mc._x + distance, Stage.width -
   car_mc._width);
      display_txt.text = "Right";
   } else if (Key.isDown(Key.UP)) {
      car_mc._y = Math.max(car_mc._y - distance, 0);
      display_txt.text = "Up";
   } else if (Key.isDown(Key.DOWN)) {
      car_mc._y = Math.min(car_mc._y + distance, Stage.height -
   car_mc._height);
      display_txt.text = "Down";
   }
};
Key.addListener(keyListener);
```

8. Select Control > Test Movie to test the file.

For more information about the methods of the Key class, see %{Key}% in the *ActionScript 2.0 Language Reference* in Flash Help.

Setting color values

You can use the methods of the built-in ColorTransform class (flash.geom.ColorTransform) to adjust the color of a movie clip. The `rgb` property of the ColorTransform class assigns hexadecimal red, green, blue (RGB) values to the movie clip. The following example uses `rgb` to change an object's color, based on which button the user clicks.

To set the color value of a movie clip:

1. Create a new Flash document and save it as **setrgb.fla**.

2. Select the Rectangle Tool and draw a large square on the Stage.

3. Convert the shape to a movie clip symbol and give the symbol an instance name of **car_mc** in the Property inspector.

4. Create a button symbol named colorChip, place four instances of the button on the Stage, and name them `red_btn`, `green_btn`, `blue_btn`, and `black_btn`.

5. Select Frame 1 in the main Timeline, and select Window > Actions.

6. Add the following code to Frame 1 of the main Timeline:

```
import flash.geom.ColorTransform;
import flash.geom.Transform;

var colorTrans:ColorTransform = new ColorTransform();
var trans:Transform = new Transform(car_mc);
trans.colorTransform = colorTrans;
```

7. To make the blue button change the color of the `car_mc` movie clip to blue, add the following code to the Actions panel:

```
blue_btn.onRelease = function() {
  colorTrans.rgb = 0x333399; // blue
  trans.colorTransform = colorTrans;
};
```

The preceding snippet of code changes the `rgb` property of the color transform object and reapplies the color tranform effect to the `car_mc` movie clip whenever the button is pressed.

8. Repeat step 7 for the other buttons (red_btn, green_btn, and black_btn) to change the color of the movie clip to the corresponding color.

Your code should now look like the following example (new code is in bold):

```
import flash.geom.ColorTransform;
import flash.geom.Transform;

var colorTrans:ColorTransform = new ColorTransform();
var trans:Transform = new Transform(car_mc);
trans.colorTransform = colorTrans;

blue_btn.onRelease = function() {
    colorTrans.rgb = 0x333399; // blue
    trans.colorTransform = colorTrans;
};
red_btn.onRelease = function() {
    colorTrans.rgb = 0xFF0000; // red
    trans.colorTransform = colorTrans;
};
green_btn.onRelease = function() {
    colorTrans.rgb = 0x006600; // green
    trans.colorTransform = colorTrans;
};
black_btn.onRelease = function() {
    colorTrans.rgb = 0x000000; // black
    trans.colorTransform = colorTrans;
};
```

9. Select Control > Test Movie to change the color of the movie clip.

For more information about the methods of the ColorTransform class, see %{ColorTransform (flash.geom.ColorTransform)}% in the *ActionScript 2.0 Language Reference* in Flash Help.

Creating sound controls

You use the built-in Sound class to control sounds in a SWF file. To use the methods of the Sound class, you must first create a Sound object. Then you can use the attachSound() method to insert a sound from the library into a SWF file while the SWF file is running.

The Sound class's setVolume() method controls the volume, and the setPan() method adjusts the left and right balance of a sound.

The following procedures show how to create sound controls.

To attach a sound to a timeline:

1. Select File > Import to import a sound.

2. Select the sound in the library, right-click (Windows) or Control-click (Macintosh), and select Linkage.

3. Select Export for ActionScript and Export in First Frame; then give the sound the identifier `a_thousand_ways`.

4. Add a button to the Stage and name it `play_btn`.

5. Add a button to the Stage and name it `stop_btn`.

6. Select Frame 1 in the main Timeline, and select Window > Actions.

   Add the following code to the Actions panel:

```
var song_sound:Sound = new Sound();
song_sound.attachSound("a_thousand_ways");
play_btn.onRelease = function() {
  song_sound.start();
};
stop_btn.onRelease = function() {
  song_sound.stop();
};
```

   This code first stops the speaker movie clip. It then creates a new Sound object (`song_sound`) and attaches the sound whose linkage identifier is `a_thousand_ways`. The `onRelease` event handlers associated with the `playButton` and `stopButton` objects start and stop the sound by using the `Sound.start()` and `Sound.stop()` methods, and also play and stop the attached sound.

7. Select Control > Test Movie to hear the sound.

To create a sliding volume control:

1. Using the Rectangle Tool, draw a small rectangle on the Stage, approximately 30 pixels high by 10 pixels wide.

2. Select the Selection Tool and double-click the shape on the Stage.

3. Press F8 to open the Convert to Symbol dialog box.

4. Select the Button type, enter a symbol name of **volume**, and click OK.

5. With the button symbol selected on the Stage, enter the instance name of **handle_btn** in the Property inspector.

6. Select the button, and select Modify > Convert to Symbol.

   Be careful to select the movie clip behavior. This creates a movie clip with the button on Frame 1.

7. Select the movie clip, and enter **volume_mc** as the instance name in the Property inspector.

8. Select Frame 1 of the main Timeline, and select Window > Actions.

9. Enter the following code into the Actions panel:

```
this.createTextField("volume_txt", 10, 30, 30, 200, 20);
volume_mc.top = volume_mc._y;
volume_mc.bottom = volume_mc._y;
volume_mc.left = volume_mc._x;
volume_mc.right = volume_mc._x + 100;
volume_mc._x += 100;

volume_mc.handle_btn.onPress = function() {
  startDrag(this._parent, false, this._parent.left, this._parent.top,
  this._parent.right, this._parent.bottom);
};
volume_mc.handle_btn.onRelease = function() {
  stopDrag();
  var level:Number = Math.ceil(this._parent._x - this._parent.left);
  this._parent._parent.song_sound.setVolume(level);
  this._parent._parent.volume_txt.text = level;
};
volume_mc.handle_btn.onReleaseOutside = slider_mc.handle_btn.onRelease;
```

The startDrag() parameters left, top, right, and bottom are variables set in a movie clip action.

10. Select Control > Test Movie to use the volume slider.

To create a sliding balance control:

1. Use the Rectangle Tool to draw a small rectangle on the Stage, approximately 30 pixels high by 10 pixels wide.

2. Select the Selection Tool and double-click the shape on the Stage.

3. Press F8 to launch the Convert to Symbol dialog box.

4. Select the Button type, enter a symbol name of **balance**, and click OK.

5. With the button symbol selected on the Stage, enter an instance name of **handle_btn** in the Property inspector.

6. Select the button, and select Modify > Convert to Symbol.

   Be careful to select the movie clip behavior. This creates a movie clip with the button on Frame 1.

7. Select the movie clip, and enter **balance_mc** as the instance name in the Property inspector.

8. Enter the following code into the Actions panel:

```
balance_mc.top = balance_mc._y;
balance_mc.bottom = balance_mc._y;
balance_mc.left = balance_mc._x;
balance_mc.right = balance_mc._x + 100;
balance_mc._x += 50;
balance_mc.handle_btn.onPress = function() {
   startDrag(this._parent, false, this._parent.left, this._parent.top,
   this._parent.right, this._parent.bottom);
};
balance_mc.handle_btn.onRelease = function() {
   stopDrag();
   var level:Number = Math.ceil((this._parent._x - this._parent.left -
   50) * 2);
   this._parent._parent.song_sound.setPan(level);
};
balance_mc.handle_btn.onReleaseOutside =
   balance_mc.handle_btn.onRelease;
```

The `startDrag()` parameters `left`, `top`, `right`, and `bottom` are variables set in a movie clip action.

9. Select Control > Test Movie to use the balance slider.

For more information about the methods of the Sound class, see %{Sound}% in the *ActionScript 2.0 Language Reference* in Flash Help.

Detecting collisions

The `hitTest()` method of the MovieClip class detects collisions in a SWF file. It checks to see if an object has collided with a movie clip and returns a Boolean value (`true` or `false`).

You would want to know whether a collision has occurred either to test if the user has arrived at a certain static area on the Stage, or to determine when one movie clip has reached another. With `hitTest()`, you can determine these results.

You can use the parameters of `hitTest()` to specify the *x* and *y* coordinates of a hit area on the Stage or use the target path of another movie clip as a hit area. When you specify *x* and *y*, `hitTest()` returns `true` if the point identified by (*x*, *y*) is a non-transparent point. When a target is passed to `hitTest()`, the bounding boxes of the two movie clips are compared. If they intersect, `hitTest()` returns `true`. If the two boxes do not intersect, `hitTest()` returns `false`.

You can also use `hitTest()` to test a collision between two movie clips.

The following example shows how to detect a collision between a mouse and movie clips on the Stage.

To detect a collision between a movie clip and the mouse pointer:

1. Select the first frame on Layer 1 in the Timeline.

2. Select Window > Actions to open the Actions panel, if it is not already open.

3. Add the following code in the Actions panel:

```
this.createEmptyMovieClip("box_mc", 10);
with (box_mc) {
    beginFill(0xFF0000, 100);
    moveTo(100, 100);
    lineTo(200, 100);
    lineTo(200, 200);
    lineTo(100, 200);
    lineTo(100, 100);
    endFill();
}

this.createTextField("status_txt", 999, 0, 0, 100, 22);

var mouseListener:Object = new Object();
mouseListener.onMouseMove = function():Void {
    status_txt.text = _level0.hitTest(_xmouse, _ymouse, true);
}
Mouse.addListener(mouseListener);
```

4. Select Control > Test Movie, and move the pointer over the movie clip to test the collision.

The value `true` appears whenever the pointer is over a non-transparent pixel.

To perform collision detection on two movie clips:

1. Drag two movie clips to the Stage, and give them the instance names car_mc and area_mc.

2. Select Frame 1 on the Timeline.

3. Select Window > Actions to open the Actions panel, if it is not already visible.

4. Enter the following code in the Actions panel:

```
this.createTextField("status_txt", 999, 10, 10, 100, 22);
area_mc.onEnterFrame = function() {
    status_txt.text = this.hitTest(car_mc);
};

car_mc.onPress = function() {
    this.startDrag(false);
    updateAfterEvent();
};
car_mc.onRelease = function() {
    this.stopDrag();
};
```

5. Select Control > Test Movie, and drag the movie clip to test the collision detection.

Whenever the bounding box of the car intersects the bounding box of the area, the status is `true`.

For more information, see %{hitTest (MovieClip.hitTest method)}% in the *ActionScript 2.0 Language Reference* in Flash Help.

Creating a simple line drawing tool

You can use methods of the MovieClip class to draw lines and fills on the Stage as the SWF file plays. This lets you create drawing tools for users and draw shapes in the SWF file in response to events. The drawing methods are `beginFill()`, `beginGradientFill()`, `clear()`, `curveTo()`, `endFill()`, `lineTo()`, `lineStyle()`, and `moveTo()`.

You can apply these methods to any movie clip instance (for example, `myClip.lineTo()`), or to a level (`_level0.curveTo()`).

The `lineTo()` and `curveTo()` methods let you draw lines and curves, respectively. You specify a line color, thickness, and alpha setting for a line or curve with the `lineStyle()` method. The `moveTo()` drawing method sets the current drawing position to the *x* and *y* Stage coordinates that you specify.

The `beginFill()` and `beginGradientFill()` methods fill a closed path with a solid or gradient fill, respectively, and `endFill()` applies the fill specified in the last call to `beginFill()` or `beginGradientFill()`. The `clear()` method erases what's been drawn in the specified movie clip object.

To create a simple line drawing tool:

1. In a new document, create a button on the Stage, and enter `clear_btn` as the instance name in the Property inspector.

2. Select Frame 1 in the Timeline.

3. Select Window > Actions to open the Actions panel, if it is not already visible.

4. In the Actions panel, enter the following code:

```
this.createEmptyMovieClip("canvas_mc", 999);
var isDrawing:Boolean = false;
//
clear_btn.onRelease = function() {
  canvas_mc.clear();
};
//
var mouseListener:Object = new Object();
mouseListener.onMouseDown = function() {
  canvas_mc.lineStyle(5, 0xFF0000, 100);
  canvas_mc.moveTo(_xmouse, _ymouse);
  isDrawing = true;
};
mouseListener.onMouseMove = function() {
  if (isDrawing) {
    canvas_mc.lineTo(_xmouse, _ymouse);
    updateAfterEvent();
  }
};
mouseListener.onMouseUp = function() {
  isDrawing = false;
};
Mouse.addListener(mouseListener);
```

5. Select Control > Test Movie to test the document.

6. Drag your pointer to draw a line on the Stage.

7. Click the button to erase what you've drawn.

Creating runtime data bindings using ActionScript

If you use components to create applications, it's often necessary to add bindings between those components so that you can interact with data or have components interact with each other. Interaction between components is necessary for creating usable forms or interfaces that your users can interact with. You can use the Bindings tab in the Component inspector to add bindings between components on the Stage. You can use the Bindings tab in the Component inspector to bind data between components on the Stage.

For more information on using the Bindings tab, see "Working with bindings in the Bindings tab (Flash Professional only)" in Flash Help. You can also find additional information in the following online articles: Building a Tip of the day Application (Part 2), Data Binding in Macromedia Flash MX Professional 2004, and Building a Google Search Application with Macromedia Flash MX Professional.

You can use ActionScript instead of the Bindings tab to create bindings between components. Adding code is often faster and more efficient than relying on the authoring environment. Using ActionScript to create bindings is necessary when you use code to add components to an application. You can choose to use the `createClassObject()` method to add components onto the Stage dynamically; however, you couldn't use the Bindings tab to create a binding because the components don't exist until runtime. Using ActionScript to add data binding is often called *runtime data binding*.

For more information, see the following topics:

- "Creating bindings between UI components using ActionScript" on page 594
- "Using components, bindings, and custom formatters" on page 598
- "Adding and binding components on the Stage" on page 601

Creating bindings between UI components using ActionScript

It isn't difficult to bind data between two components at runtime. You can do so in Flash Basic 8 or Flash Professional 8. You must remember to include the DataBindingClasses component in your document for it to work, because that component contains the classes that you need to work with.

To create a binding between two TextInput components using ActionScript:

1. Create a new Flash document called **panel_as.fla**.
2. Drag two copies of the TextInput component onto the Stage.
3. Give the components the following instance names: **in_ti** and **out_ti**.
4. Select Window > Common Libraries > Classes and open the new common library called Classes.fla.
5. Drag a copy of the DataBindingClasses component into the Library panel, or drag the component onto the Stage and then delete it.

   You can close the common library after you finish. After you delete the DataBindingClasses component from the Stage, Flash leaves a copy in the library.

TIP	If you forget to delete the DataBindingClasses component from the Stage, the component's icon is visible at runtime.

NOTE	When you created a binding using the Component inspector in the previous example, Flash added the DataBindingClasses component automatically to the FLA file. When you use ActionScript to create data bindings, you must copy that class into your library yourself, as shown in the following step.

6. Insert a new layer and name it **actions**.

7. Add the following ActionScript to Frame 1 of the actions layer:

```
var src:mx.data.binding.EndPoint = new mx.data.binding.EndPoint();
src.component = in_ti;
src.property = "text";
src.event = "focusOut";
var dest:mx.data.binding.EndPoint = new mx.data.binding.EndPoint();
dest.component = out_ti;
dest.property = "text";
new mx.data.binding.Binding(src, dest);
```

If you prefer the somewhat shortened version, you could import the binding classes and use the following code instead:

```
import mx.data.binding.*;
var src:EndPoint = new EndPoint();
src.component = in_ti;
src.property = "text";
src.event = "focusOut";
var dest:EndPoint = new EndPoint();
dest.component = out_ti;
dest.property = "text";
new Binding(src, dest);
```

This ActionScript creates two data binding end points, one for each component that you're binding. The first endpoint you create defines which component it is binding from (in_ti), which property to watch for (text), and which event will trigger the binding (focusOut). The second endpoint you create lists only the component and property (out_ti and text, respectively). Finally, you create the binding between the two endpoints when you call the constructor for the Binding class (new Binding(src, dest)).

You don't need to use fully qualified class names (such as mx.data.binding.EndPoint) in your ActionScript, as you saw in the first code snippet. If you use the import statement at the beginning of your code, you can avoid using fully qualified names. When you import all the classes in the mx.data.binding package using the wildcard (*) (the package includes both the EndPoint and Binding classes), you can shorten your code and directly reference the EndPoint and Binding classes. For more information on import statements, see the import entry in the *ActionScript 2.0 Language Reference* in Flash Help.

8. Select Control > Test Movie to test the code in the test environment. Enter some text into the in_ti text input field.

After the in_ti instance loses focus (click the Stage, press Tab, or click the second field), Flash copies any text that you input into in_ti to the out_ti text field.

9. Select File > Save to save your changes.

If you want to modify the text in the `out_ti` text input field from the previous exercise, your code can become a lot more complex. If you use the Component inspector to set up bindings, by default you create a two-way connection. This means that if you change either text field on the Stage, the other text field changes as well. When you use ActionScript to create bindings, your application works the opposite way. Runtime data bindings are one-way by default unless you specify otherwise, as demonstrated in the following example.

To use ActionScript to create a two-way binding, you need to make some small modifications to the code snippets from the previous procedure. This example uses the second, shortened ActionScript snippet from step 7.

To create a two-way binding:

1. Open **panel_as.fla** from the previous example.

2. Modify your ActionScript slightly (see **boldface** code) to match the following ActionScript:

```
import mx.data.binding.*;
var src:EndPoint = new EndPoint();
src.component = in_ti;
src.property = "text";
src.event = "focusOut";
var dest:EndPoint = new EndPoint();
dest.component = out_ti;
dest.property = "text";
dest.event = "focusOut";
new Binding(src, dest, null, true);
```

The two changes you make to the ActionScript do the following:

- Define an event property for the destination EndPoint instance.
- Define two additional parameters for the Binding constructor.

You use the first parameter for advanced formatting options; you can set that value to `null` or `undefined`. The second parameter defines whether the binding is two-way (`true`) or one-way (`false`).

You might wonder where the `focusOut` event comes from. That's where the ActionScript becomes complicated. You can investigate the TextInput class and use some of the listed methods (such as `change()` or `enter()`), but you won't find the `focusOut` event there. The TextInput class inherits from the UIObject and UIComponent classes. If you view the UIComponent class, which adds focus support to components, you see four additional events: `focusIn`, `focusOut`, `keyDown`, and `keyUp`. You can use these events with the TextInput component.

3. (Optional) If you want the previous example to update the value in the `out_ti` text input field, you can change the event from `focusOut` to `change`.

1. Select Control > Test Movie to test the document.

   Flash changes the second value in the in_ti text input field and updates the value for out_ti. You successfully created a two-way connection.

You can use the Binding classes with most user interface components of version 2 of the Macromedia Component Architecture, not just the TextInput component. The following example demonstrates how to use ActionScript to bind CheckBox instances and Label components during runtime.

To use binding classes with the CheckBox component:

1. Create a new Flash document.

2. Select File > Save As and name the new file **checkbox_as.fla**.

3. Select Window > Common Libraries > Classes.

4. Drag a copy of the DataBindingClasses class into the document's library.

5. Drag a copy of the CheckBox component onto the Stage and give it the instance name my_ch.

6. Drag a copy of the Label component onto the Stage and give it the instance name **my_lbl**.

7. Create a new layer and name it **actions**.

8. Add the following ActionScript to Frame 1 of the actions layer:

```
var srcEndPoint:Object = {component:my_ch, property:"selected",
    event:"click"};
var destEndPoint:Object = {component:my_lbl, property:"text"};
new mx.data.binding.Binding(srcEndPoint, destEndPoint);
```

You use objects to define the endpoints instead of creating new instances of the EndPoint class, as demonstrated in the previous exercises in this section. The code snippet in this step creates two objects, which act as endpoints for the binding. You create the binding when you call the constructor for the Binding class. To reduce the amount of code (and readability) even more, define the objects inline as shown in the following snippet:

```
new mx.data.binding.Binding({component:my_ch, property:"selected",
    event:"click"}, {component:my_lbl, property:"text"});
```

This ActionScript reduces the readability of your code, but it also reduces the amount of typing you have to do. If you share your FLA (or ActionScript) files, you might want to use the first snippet of ActionScript, because it is more reader friendly.

Using components, bindings, and custom formatters

Custom formatters help you format complex data in a specific way. You can also use custom formatting to help display images, HTML formatted text, or other components within a component such as the DataGrid. The following example illustrates how useful custom formatters can be.

To use custom formatters in a document:

1. Create a new FLA file and add the DataBindingClasses class to the library (Window > Common Libraries > Classes).

2. Drag a copy of the DateChooser component onto the Stage and give it the instance name **my_dc**.

3. Drag a copy of the Label component onto the Stage and give it the instance name **my_lbl**.

4. Insert a new layer and name it **actions**.

5. Add the following ActionScript code to Frame 1 of the actions layer:

   ```
   import mx.data.binding.*;
   var src:EndPoint = new EndPoint();
   src.component = my_dc;
   src.property = "selectedDate";
   src.event = "change";
   var dest:EndPoint = new EndPoint();
   dest.component = my_lbl;
   dest.property = "text";
   new Binding(src, dest);
   ```

   This code creates a binding between the DateChooser's `selectedDate` property and the `text` property of the Label component on the Stage. Each time you click a new date in the calendar, the selected date appears in the Label component.

6. Save the Flash document as **customformat.fla** in a convenient location on your hard disk. (You will recycle it in the next exercise.)

7. Select Control > Test Movie to test the document.

   Try to change the dates in the Calendar component and you'll see the currently selected date appear in the Label component. The Label component isn't wide enough to display the entire date, so Flash crops off the text.

8. Close the test SWF file and return to the authoring environment.

   Either resize the Label component on the Stage or select the Label component and set the `autoSize` property to `left` in the Parameters tab of the Property inspector.

9. Select Control > Test Movie to test the document again.

Now the text field displays the entire date, although it is awkward and lacks formatting. Depending on your own time zone and selected date, the date might appear similar to this: `Thu Nov 4 00:00:00 GMT-0800 2004`

Even though the binding works properly and displays the `selectedDate` property, these dates aren't very user friendly. Nobody wants to see time-zone offsets, and you might not want to display hours, minutes, and seconds. What you need is a way to format the date so that it's more readable and a little less mechanical. Custom formatters are particularly useful for formatting text.

Formatting data using the CustomFormatter class

The CustomFormatter class defines two methods, `format()` and `unformat()`, that provide the ability to transform data values from a specific data type to String, and the reverse. By default, these methods do nothing; you must implement them in a subclass of `mx.data.binding.CustomFormatter`. The CustomFormatter class lets you convert data types to strings and back. In this case, you want to convert the `selectedDate` property from the DateChooser component into a nicely formatted string when the value copies into the Label component.

The following example shows you how to create your own custom formatter, which displays the date as `NOV 4, 2004` instead of displaying a default date string.

> **NOTE**: You need to complete the exercise from "Using components, bindings, and custom formatters" on page 598 before you begin this one.

To format data using the CustomFormatter class:

1. Select File > New and then select ActionScript File to create a new AS file.

2. Select File > Save As and save the new file as **DateFormat.as**.

3. Enter the following code into the Script window:

```
class DateFormat extends mx.data.binding.CustomFormatter {
  function format(rawValue:Date):String {
    var returnValue:String;
    var monthName_array:Array =
["JAN","FEB","MAR","APR","MAY","JUN","JUL","AUG","SEP","OCT","NOV","D
EC"];
    returnValue = monthName_array[rawValue.getMonth()]+"
"+rawValue.getDate()+", "+rawValue.getFullYear();
    return returnValue;
  }
}
```

The first section of code defines the new class called DateFormat, which extends the CustomFormatter class in the `mx.data.binding` package. Remember that Flash compiles the binding classes in the DataBindingClasses component file, so you can't view them directly or find them within the Classes folder in the Flash install directory.

The only method you use is the `format()` method, which converts the date instance into a custom string format. The next step is to create an array of month names so that the end result looks closer to `NOV 4, 2004` rather than the default date format. Remember that arrays are zero-based in Flash, so if the value of `rawValue.getMonth()` returns 1, it represents February instead of January (because January is month 0). The remaining code builds the custom formatted string by concatenating values and returning the `returnValue` string.

A problem can arise when you work with classes within a compiled clip, which you can see in the previous snippet. Because you extend a class that's located in the DataBindingClasses class and it isn't readily available to Flash, you encounter the following error when you check the syntax in the previous class:

```
**Error** <path to DateFormat class>\DateFormat.as: Line 1: The class
   'mx.data.binding.CustomFormatter' could not be loaded.
      class DateFormat extends mx.data.binding.CustomFormatter {

Total ActionScript Errors: 1   Reported Errors: 1
```

Your code is probably fine. This problem occurs when Flash cannot locate the class, and because of this, syntax checking fails.

4. Save the DateFormat.as file.

5. Open customformat.fla from the exercise in "Using components, bindings, and custom formatters". Make sure you save or copy DateFormat.as in the same directory as this file.

6. In customformat.fla, modify the ActionScript code in Frame 1 of the actions layer to match the following code:

```
import mx.data.binding.*;
var src:EndPoint = new EndPoint();
src.component = my_dc;
src.property = "selectedDate";
src.event = "change";
var dest:EndPoint = new EndPoint();
dest.component = my_lbl;
dest.property = "text";
new Binding(src, dest, {cls:mx.data.formatters.Custom,
   settings:{classname:"DateFormat", classname_class:DateFormat}});
```

This time you define a `customFormatter` object, which tells Flash that you're using the newly created DateFormat class to format the endpoint on the binding.

7. Save the changes in your document and select Control > Test Movie to test your code.

Adding and binding components on the Stage

One of the biggest advantages to using the binding classes with ActionScript is that you can create bindings between components that Flash has added to the Stage at runtime. Imagine creating your own custom class that adds the appropriate text fields to the Stage at runtime, and then validates the necessary data and adds the necessary bindings. As long as you have the components in your library, you can add them dynamically and use a couple of extra lines of code to create bindings.

To add and then bind components on the Stage by using ActionScript:

1. Create a new Flash document.

2. Drag a ComboBox and a Label component into the document's library.

3. Insert a new layer and name it **actions**.

4. Add the following code to Frame 1 of the actions layer:
```
import mx.data.binding.*;
this.createClassObject(mx.controls.ComboBox, "my_cb", 1, {_x:10,
    _y:10});
this.createClassObject(mx.controls.Label, "my_lbl", 2, {_x:10, _y:40});
my_cb.addItem("JAN", 0);
my_cb.addItem("FEB", 1);
my_cb.addItem("MAR", 2);
my_cb.addItem("APR", 3);
my_cb.addItem("MAY", 4);
my_cb.addItem("JUN", 5);
var src:EndPoint = new EndPoint();
src.component = my_cb;
src.property = "value";
src.event = "change";
var dest:EndPoint = new EndPoint();
dest.component = my_lbl;
dest.property = "text";
new Binding(src, dest);
```

The first line of ActionScript imports the classes from the mx.data.binding package so that you don't need to use fully qualified paths in your code. The next two lines of ActionScript attach the components from the document's library to the Stage. Next you position the components on the Stage.

Finally you add data to the ComboBox instance and create the binding between the my_cb ComboBox and my_lbl Label component on the Stage.

Deconstructing a sample script

In the sample SWF file zapper.swf (which you can view in Using Flash Help), when a user drags the bug to the electrical outlet, the bug falls and the outlet shakes. The main timeline has only one frame and contains three objects: the ladybug, the outlet, and a reset button. Each object is a movie clip instance.

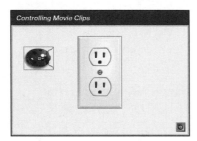

The following script is attached to Frame 1 of the main Timeline:

```
var initx:Number = bug_mc._x;
var inity:Number = bug_mc._y;
var zapped:Boolean = false;

reset_btn.onRelease = function() {
   zapped = false;
   bug_mc._x = initx;
   bug_mc._y = inity;
   bug_mc._alpha = 100;
   bug_mc._rotation = 0;
};

bug_mc.onPress = function() {
   this.startDrag();
};
bug_mc.onRelease = function() {
   this.stopDrag();
};
bug_mc.onEnterFrame = function() {
   if (this.hitTest(this._parent.zapper_mc)) {
      this.stopDrag();
      zapped = true;
      bug_mc._alpha = 75;
      bug_mc._rotation = 20;
      this._parent.zapper_mc.play();
   }
   if (zapped) {
      bug_mc._y += 25;
   }
};
```

The bug's instance name is bug_mc, and the outlet's instance name is zapper_mc. In the script, the bug is referred to as this because the script is attached to the bug and the reserved word this refers to the object that contains it.

There are event handlers with several different events: onRelease(), onPress(), and onEnterFrame(). The event handlers are defined on Frame 1 after the SWF file loads. The actions in the onEnterFrame() event handler executes every time the playhead enters a frame. Even in a one-frame SWF file, the playhead still enters that frame repeatedly and the script executes repeatedly.

Two variables, initx and inity, are defined to store the initial x and y positions of the bug_mc movie clip instance. A function is defined and assigned to the onRelease event handler of the reset_btn instance. This function is called each time the mouse button is pressed and released on the reset_btn button. The function places the ladybug back in its starting position on the Stage, resets its rotation and alpha values, and resets the zapped variable to false.

A conditional if statement uses the hitTest() method to check whether the bug instance is touching the outlet instance (this._parent.zapper_mc). The two possible outcomes of the evaluation are true or false:

- If the hitTest() method returns true, Flash calls the stopDrag() method, sets the zapper_mc variable to true, changes the alpha and rotation properties, and instructs the zapped instance to play.
- If the hitTest() method returns false, none of the code within the curly braces ({ }) immediately following the if statement runs.

The actions in the onPress() statement execute when the mouse button is pressed over the bug_mc instance. The actions in the onRelease() statement execute when the mouse button is released over the bug_mc instance.

The startDrag() action lets you drag the ladybug. Because the script is attached to the bug_mc instance, the keyword this indicates that the bug instance is the one you can drag:

```
bug_mc.onPress = function() {
  this.startDrag();
};
```

The stopDrag() action stops the drag action:

```
bug_mc.onRelease = function() {
  this.stopDrag();
};
```

CHAPTER 15

Working with Images, Sound, and Video

If you import an image or a sound while you author a document in Macromedia Flash Basic 8 or Macromedia Flash Professional 8, the image and sound are packaged and stored in a SWF file when you publish it. In addition to importing media while authoring, you can load external media, including other SWF files, at runtime. You might want to keep media outside of a Flash document for several reasons.

Reduce file size   By keeping large media files outside of your Flash document and loading them at runtime, you can reduce the initial downloading time for your applications and presentations, especially over slow Internet connections.

Modularize large presentations   You can divide a large presentation or application into separate SWF files and load those separate files as needed at runtime. This process reduces initial downloading time and also makes it easier to maintain and update the presentation.

Separate content from presentation   This theme is common in application development, especially data-driven applications. For example, a shopping cart application might display an image of each product. By loading each image at runtime, you can easily update a product's image without modifying the original FLA file.

Take advantage of runtime-only features   Some features, such as dynamically loaded Flash Video (FLV) and MP3 playback, are available only at runtime through ActionScript.

This section describes how to work with image files, sound files, and FLV video in your Flash applications. For more information, see the following topics:

About loading and working with external media

You can load several types of media files into a Flash application at runtime: SWF, MP3, JPEG, GIF, PNG, and FLV files. However, not all versions of Flash Player support each kind of media. For more information on the image file types that are supported in Macromedia Flash Player 8, see "Loading external SWF and image files" on page 607. For information on FLV video support in Flash Player, see "About using FLV video" on page 617

Macromedia Flash Player can load external media from any HTTP or FTP address, from a local disk using a relative path, or by using the `file://` protocol.

To load external SWF and image files, you can use the `loadMovie()` or `loadMovieNum()` function, the `MovieClip.loadMovie()` method, or the `MovieClipLoader.loadClip()` method. The class methods generally provide more function and flexibility than global functions and are appropriate for more complex applications. When you load a SWF or image file, you specify a movie clip or SWF file level as the target for that media. For more information on loading SWF and image files, see "Loading external SWF and image files" on page 607.

To play back an external MP3 file, use the `loadSound()` method of the Sound class. This method lets you specify whether the MP3 file should progressively download or complete downloading before it starts to play. You can also read the ID3 information embedded in MP3 files, if they're available. For more information, see "Reading ID3 tags in MP3 files" on page 615.

Flash Video is the native video format used by Flash Player. You can play FLV files over HTTP or from a local file system. Playing external FLV files provides several advantages over embedding video in a Flash document, such as better performance and memory management as well as independent video and Flash frame rates. For more information, see "Playing back external FLV files dynamically" on page 620.

You can also preload or track the downloading progress of external media. Flash Player 7 introduced the MovieClipLoader class, which you can use to track the downloading progress of SWF or image files. To preload MP3 and FLV files, you can use the `getBytesLoaded()` method of the Sound class and the `bytesLoaded` property of the NetStream class. For more information, see "Preloading FLV files" on page 623.

You can find samples of photo gallery applications on your hard disk. These files provide examples of how to use ActionScript to control movie clips dynamically while loading image files into a SWF file. You can find gallery_tree.fla and gallery_tween.fla, the sample source files, in the Samples folder on your hard disk.

- In Windows, browse to *boot drive*\Program Files\Macromedia\Flash 8\ Samples and Tutorials\Samples\ActionScript\Galleries.
- On the Macintosh, browse to *Macintosh HD*/Applications/Macromedia Flash 8/ Samples and Tutorials/Samples/ActionScript/Galleries.

Loading external SWF and image files

To load a SWF or image file, use the `loadMovie()` or `loadMovieNum()` global function, the `loadMovie()` method of the MovieClip class, or the `loadClip()` method of the MovieClipLoader class. For more information on the `loadClip()` method, see `MovieClipLoader.loadClip()` in the *ActionScript 2.0 Language Reference* in Flash Help.

For image files, Flash Player 8 supports the JPEG (progressive and non-progressive) image file type, GIF images (transparent and non-transparent, although only the first frame of an animated GIF will be loaded), and PNG files (transparent and non-transparent).

To load a SWF or image file into a level in Flash Player, use the `loadMovieNum()` function. To load a SWF or image file into a movie clip target, use the `loadMovie()` function or method. In either case, the loaded content replaces the content of the specified level or target movie clip.

When you load a SWF or image file into a movie clip target, the upper-left corner of the SWF file or image is placed on the registration point of the movie clip. Because this registration point is often the center of the movie clip, the loaded content might not appear centered. Also, when you load a SWF file or image to a root timeline, the upper-left corner of the image is placed on the upper-left corner of the Stage. The loaded content inherits rotation and scaling from the movie clip, but the original content of the movie clip is removed.

You can optionally send ActionScript variables with a `loadMovie()` or `loadMovieNum()` call. This is useful, for example, if the URL you're specifying in the method call is a server-side script that returns a SWF or image file according to data passed from the Flash application.

When you use the global `loadMovie()` or `loadMovieNum()` function, specify the target level or clip as a parameter. The following example loads the Flash application contents.swf into the movie clip instance named `image_mc`:

```
loadMovie("contents.swf", image_mc);
```

You can use `MovieClip.loadMovie()` to achieve the same result:

```
image_mc.loadMovie("contents.swf");
```

The following example loads the image1.jpg JPEG image into the `image_mc` movie clip instance:

```
image_mc.loadMovie("http://www.helpexamples.com/flash/images/image1.jpg");
```

For more information about loading external SWF and image files, see "About loading SWF files and the root timeline" on page 611.

To preload SWF and JPEG files into movie clip instances, you can use the MovieClipLoader class. This class provides an event listener mechanism to give notification about the status of file downloads into movie clips. To use a MovieClipLoader object to preload SWF and JPEG files, you must complete the following:

Create a new MovieClipLoader object   You can use a single MovieClipLoader object to track the downloading progress of multiple files or create a separate object for each file's progress. Create a new movie clip, load your contents into it, then create the MovieClipLoader object as shown in the following code:

```
this.createEmptyMovieClip("img_mc", 999);
var my_mcl:MovieClipLoader = new MovieClipLoader();
```

Create a listener object and create event handlers   The listener object can be any ActionScript object, such as a generic Object object, a movie clip, or a custom component.

The following example creates a generic listener object named loadListener and defines for itself onLoadError, onLoadStart, onLoadProgress, and onLoadComplete functions:

```
// Create listener object:
var mclListener:Object = new Object();
mclListener.onLoadError = function(target_mc:MovieClip, errorCode:String,
  status:Number) {
    trace("Error loading image: " + errorCode + " [" + status + "]");
};
mclListener.onLoadStart = function(target_mc:MovieClip):Void {
    trace("onLoadStart: " + target_mc);
};
mclListener.onLoadProgress = function(target_mc:MovieClip,
  numBytesLoaded:Number, numBytesTotal:Number):Void {
    var numPercentLoaded:Number = numBytesLoaded / numBytesTotal * 100;
    trace("onLoadProgress: " + target_mc + " is " + numPercentLoaded + "%
    loaded");
};
mclListener.onLoadComplete = function(target_mc:MovieClip,
  status:Number):Void {
    trace("onLoadComplete: " + target_mc);
};
```

> **NOTE**   Flash Player 8 allows you to check the HTTP status of a MovieClipLoader download within the onLoadComplete and onLoadError event listeners. This ability allows you to check why the file was unable to download—whether it was a server error, or the file was unable to be found, and so on.

Register the listener object with the MovieClipLoader object In order for the listener object to receive the loading events, you must register it with the MovieClipLoader object, as shown in the following code:

```
my_mcl.addListener(mclListener);
```

Begin loading the file (image or SWF) into a target clip To start downloading an image or SWF file, you use the `MovieClipLoader.loadClip()` method, as shown in the following code:

```
my_mcl.loadClip("http://www.helpexamples.com/flash/images/image1.jpg",
  img_mc);
```

> **NOTE** You can use MovieClipLoader methods only to track the downloading progress of files loaded with the `MovieClipLoader.loadClip()` method. You cannot use the `loadMovie()` function or `MovieClip.loadMovie()` method.

The following example uses the `setProgress()` method of the ProgressBar component to display the downloading progress of a SWF file. (See "ProgressBar.setProgress()" in *Components Language Reference* in Flash Help.)

To display downloading progress by using the ProgressBar component:

1. Create a new Flash document, and save it as **progress.fla**.

2. Open the Components panel (Window > Components).

3. Drag a ProgressBar component from the Components panel to the Stage.

4. In the Property inspector (Window > Properties > Properties), name the ProgressBar component my_pb.

5. Select Frame 1 in the Timeline, and open the Actions panel (Window > Actions).

6. Add the following code to the Actions panel:

```
var my_pb:mx.controls.ProgressBar;
my_pb.mode = "manual";

this.createEmptyMovieClip("img_mc", 999);

var my_mcl:MovieClipLoader = new MovieClipLoader();
var mclListener:Object = new Object();
mclListener.onLoadStart = function(target_mc:MovieClip):Void {
   my_pb.label = "loading: " + target_mc._name;
};
mclListener.onLoadProgress = function(target_mc:MovieClip,
   numBytesLoaded:Number, numBytesTotal:Number):Void {
   var pctLoaded:Number = Math.ceil(100 * (numBytesLoaded /
   numBytesTotal));
   my_pb.setProgress(numBytesLoaded, numBytesTotal);
};
my_mcl.addListener(mclListener);
my_mcl.loadClip("http://www.helpexamples.com/flash/images/image1.jpg",
   img_mc);
```

7. Test the document by selecting Control > Test Movie.

The image loads into the movie `img_mc` clip.

8. Select File > Publish > Formats, and make sure the SWF and HTML options are selected.

9. Click Publish and find the HTML and SWF files on your hard disk.

They're in the same folder as progress.fla that you saved in step 1.

10. Double-click the HTML document to open it in a browser and see the progress bar animate.

> **NOTE**
> When you load files in the test environment, make sure you load an uncached file from the Internet and not a local file if you want to see the progress bar work. A local file loads too quickly to see the progress. Alternatively, upload your SWF file and test your document on a server.

For related information, see "About loading SWF files and the root timeline" on page 611. For more information on the MovieClipLoader class, see %{MovieClipLoader}% in the *ActionScript 2.0 Language Reference* in Flash Help. For information on creating a progress bar animation, see "Creating a progress animation for loading SWF and image files" on page 638.

You can find samples of photo gallery applications on your hard disk. These files provide examples of how to use ActionScript to control movie clips dynamically while loading image files into a SWF file. You can find the sample source files, gallery_tree.fla and gallery_tween.fla, in the Samples folder on your hard disk.

- In Windows, browse to *boot drive*\Program Files\Macromedia\Flash 8\ Samples and Tutorials\Samples\ActionScript\Galleries.

- On the Macintosh, browse to *Macintosh HD*/Applications/Macromedia Flash 8/ Samples and Tutorials/Samples/ActionScript/Galleries.

About loading SWF files and the root timeline

The ActionScript property, `_root`, specifies or returns a reference to the root timeline of a SWF file. If you load a SWF file into a movie clip in another SWF file, any references to `_root` in the loaded SWF file resolve to the root timeline in the host SWF file, not to that of the loaded SWF file. This action can sometimes cause unexpected behavior at runtime (for example, if the host SWF file and the loaded SWF file both use `_root` to specify a variable).

In Flash Player 7 and later, you can use the `%{_lockroot (MovieClip._lockroot property)}%` property to force references to `_root` made by a movie clip to resolve to its own timeline rather than to the timeline of the SWF file that contains that movie clip. For more information, see "Specifying a root timeline for loaded SWF files" on page 362. For more information about using `_root` and `_lockroot`, see Chapter 19, "Best Practices and Coding Conventions for ActionScript 2.0," on page 745.

One SWF file can load another SWF file from any location on the Internet. However, for a SWF file to access data (variables, methods, and so forth) defined in another SWF file, the two files must originate from the same domain. In Flash Player 7 and later, cross-domain scripting is prohibited unless the loaded SWF file specifies otherwise by calling `System.security.allowDomain()`.

For more information on System.security.allowDomain, see `%{allowDomain (security.allowDomain method)}%` in the *ActionScript 2.0 Language Reference* in Flash Help and "About domains, cross-domain security, and SWF files" on page 708.

About loading and using external MP3 files

To load MP3 files at runtime, use the `loadSound()` method of the Sound class. First, you create a Sound object, as shown in the following example:

```
var song1_sound:Sound = new Sound();
```

Use the new object to call `loadSound()` to load an event or a streaming sound. Event sounds are loaded completely before being played; streaming sounds play as they download. You can set the `isStreaming` parameter of `loadSound()` to specify a sound as a streaming or event sound. After you load an event sound, you must call the `start()` method of the Sound class to make the sound play. Streaming sounds begin playing when sufficient data is loaded into the SWF file; you don't need to use `start()`.

For example, the following code creates a Sound object named `my_sound` and then loads an MP3 file named song1.mp3. Put the following ActionScript in Frame 1 on the Timeline:

```
var my_sound:Sound = new Sound();
my_sound.loadSound("http://www.helpexamples.com/flash/sound/song1.mp3",
   true);
```

In most cases, set the `isStreaming` parameter to `true`, especially if you're loading large sound files that should start playing as soon as possible—for example, when creating an MP3 "jukebox" application. However, if you download shorter sound clips and need to play them at a specified time (for example, when a user clicks a button), set `isStreaming` to `false`.

To determine when a sound IS completely downloaded, use the `Sound.onLoad` event handler. This event handler automatically receives a Boolean value (`true` or `false`) that indicates whether the file downloaded successfully.

For more information, see the following topics:

- "Loading an MP3 file" on page 613
- "Preloading MP3 files" on page 613
- "Reading ID3 tags in MP3 files" on page 615

You can find a sample source file that loads MP3 files, jukebox.fla, in the Samples folder on your hard disk. This sample demonstrates how to create a jukebox by using data types, general coding principles, and several components:

- In Windows, browse to *boot drive*\Program Files\Macromedia\Flash 8\ Samples and Tutorials\Samples\Components\Jukebox.
- On the Macintosh, browse to *Macintosh HD*/Applications/Macromedia Flash 8/ Samples and Tutorials/Samples/Components/Jukebox.

Loading an MP3 file

suppose you're creating an online game that uses different sounds that depend on what level the user has reached in the game. The following code loads an MP3 file (song2.mp3) into the game_sound Sound object and plays the sound when it IS completely downloaded.

To load an MP3 file:

1. Create a new FLA file called **loadMP3.fla**.

2. Select Frame 1 on the Timeline, and then type the following code in the Actions panel:

```
var game_sound:Sound = new Sound();
game_sound.onLoad = function(success:Boolean):Void {
   if (success) {
      trace("Sound Loaded");
      game_sound.start();
   }
};
game_sound.loadSound("http://www.helpexamples.com/flash/sound/song2.mp3"
   false);'
```

3. Select Control > Test Movie to test the sound.

Flash Player supports only the MP3 sound file type for loading sound files at runtime.

For more information, see Sound.loadSound(), Sound.start(), and Sound.onLoad in the *ActionScript 2.0 Language Reference* in Flash Help. For information on preloading MP3 files, see "Preloading MP3 files" on page 613. For information on creating a progress bar animation when you load a sound file, see "Creating a progress bar for loading MP3 files with ActionScript" on page 640.

You can find a sample source file that loads MP3 files, jukebox.fla, in the Samples folder on your hard disk. This sample demonstrates how to create a jukebox by using data types, general coding principles, and several components.

- In Windows, browse to *boot drive*\Program Files\Macromedia\Flash 8\ Samples and Tutorials\Samples\Components\Jukebox.

- On the Macintosh, browse to *Macintosh HD*/Applications/Macromedia Flash 8/ Samples and Tutorials/Samples/Components/Jukebox.

Preloading MP3 files

When you preload MP3 files, you can use the setInterval() function to create a *polling mechanism* that checks the bytes loaded for a Sound or NetStream object at predetermined intervals. To track the downloading progress of MP3 files, use the Sound.getBytesLoaded() and Sound.getBytesTotal() methods.

The following example uses `setInterval()` to check the bytes loaded for a Sound object at predetermined intervals.

To preload an MP3 file:

1. Create a new FLA file called **preloadMP3.fla.**

2. Select Frame 1 on the Timeline and type the following code in the Actions panel:

```
// Create a new Sound object to play the sound.
var songTrack:Sound = new Sound();
// Create the polling function that tracks download progress.
// This is the function that is "polled." It checks
// the downloading progress of the Sound object passed as a reference.
function checkProgress (soundObj:Object):Void {
  var numBytesLoaded:Number = soundObj.getBytesLoaded();
  var numBytesTotal:Number = soundObj.getBytesTotal();
  var numPercentLoaded:Number = Math.floor(numBytesLoaded /
  numBytesTotal * 100);
  if (!isNaN(numPercentLoaded)) {
    trace(numPercentLoaded + "% loaded.");
  }
};
// When the file has finished loading, clear the interval polling.
songTrack.onLoad = function ():Void {
  trace("load complete");
  clearInterval(poll);
};
// Load streaming MP3 file and start calling checkProgress(),
songTrack.loadSound("http://www.helpexamples.com/flash/sound/song1.mp3",
  true);
var poll:Number = setInterval(checkProgress, 100, songTrack);
```

3. Select Control > Test Movie to test the sound.

    The Output panel shows loading progress.

You can use the polling technique to preload external FLV files. To get the total bytes and current number of bytes loaded for an FLV file, use the `NetStream.bytesLoaded` and `NetStream.bytesTotal` properties (for more information, see %{bytesLoaded (NetStream.bytesLoaded property)}% and %{bytesTotal (NetStream.bytesTotal property)}%).

For more information, see `MovieClip.getBytesLoaded()`, `MovieClip.getBytesTotal()`, `setInterval()`, `Sound.getBytesLoaded()`, and `Sound.getBytesTotal()` in the *ActionScript 2.0 Language Reference* in Flash Help.

For information on creating a progress bar animation, see "Creating a progress bar for loading MP3 files with ActionScript" on page 640.

You can find a sample source file that loads MP3 files, jukebox.fla, in the Samples folder on your hard disk. This sample demonstrates how to create a jukebox by using data types, general coding principles, and several components.

- In Windows, browse to *boot drive*\Program Files\Macromedia\Flash 8\ Samples and Tutorials\Samples\Components\Jukebox.
- On the Macintosh, browse to *Macintosh HD*/Applications/Macromedia Flash 8/ Samples and Tutorials/Samples/Components/Jukebox.

Reading ID3 tags in MP3 files

ID3 tags are data fields that are added to an MP3 file. ID3 tags contain information about the file, such as the name of a song, album, and artist.

To read ID3 tags from an MP3 file, use the Sound.id3 property, whose properties correspond to the names of ID3 tags included in the MP3 file that you load. To determine when ID3 tags for a downloading MP3 file are available, use the Sound.onID3 event handler. Flash Player 7 supports version 1.0, 1.1, 2.3, and 2.4 tags; version 2.2 tags are not supported.

The following example loads an MP3 file named song1.mp3 into the song_sound Sound object. When the ID3 tags for the file are available, the display_txt text field shows the artist name and song name.

To read ID3 tags from an MP3 file:

1. Create a new FLA file called **id3.fla.**
2. Select Frame 1 on the Timeline and type the following code in the Actions panel:

```
this.createTextField("display_txt", this.getNextHighestDepth(), 0, 0,
    100, 100);
display_txt.autoSize = "left";
display_txt.multiline = true;
var song_sound:Sound = new Sound();
song_sound.onLoad = function() {
    song_sound.start();
};
song_sound.onID3 = function():Void {
    display_txt.text += "Artist:\t" + song_sound.id3.artist + "\n";
    display_txt.text += "Song:\t" + song_sound.id3.songname + "\n";
};
song_sound.loadSound("http://www.helpexamples.com/flash/sound/
    song1.mp3");
```

3. Select Control > Test Movie to test the sound.

    The ID3 tags appear on the Stage, and the sound plays.

Because ID3 2.0 tags are located at the beginning of an MP3 file (before the sound data), they are available as soon as the file starts downloading. ID3 1.0 tags, however, are located at the end of the file (after the sound data), so they aren't available until the entire MP3 file finishes downloading.

The `onID3` event handler is called each time new ID3 data is available. So, if an MP3 file contains ID3 2.0 tags and ID3 1.0 tags, the `onID3` handler is called twice because the tags are located in different parts of the file.

For a list of supported ID3 tags, see `%{id3 (Sound.id3 property)}%` in the *ActionScript 2.0 Language Reference* in Flash Help.

You can find a sample source file that loads MP3 files, jukebox.fla, in the Samples folder on your hard disk. This sample demonstrates how to create a jukebox by using data types, general coding principles, and several components:

- In Windows, browse to *boot drive*\Program Files\Macromedia\Flash 8\ Samples and Tutorials\Samples\Components\Jukebox.
- On the Macintosh, browse to *Macintosh HD*/Applications/Macromedia Flash 8/ Samples and Tutorials/Samples/Components/Jukebox.

Assigning linkage to assets in the library

You can assign linkage identifiers for assets in the library, such as movie clips and font symbols. In Flash Basic 8 and Flash Professional 8, you can set linkage identifiers to sound and image assets in the library. This supports using image and sound files with shared libraries and with the new BitmapData class.

The following example adds a bitmap image in the library with a linkage set to `myImage`. Then you add the image to the Stage and make it draggable.

To use linkage with bitmap files:

1. Create a new FLA file called **linkBitmap.fla**.
2. Import a bitmap image to the library.
3. Right-click (Windows) or Control-click (Macintosh) the image in the library, and select Linkage from the context menu.
4. Select Export for ActionScript and Export in first Frame and type **myImage** in the Identifier text box.
5. Click OK to set the linkage identifier.

6. Select Frame 1 on the Timeline, and type the following code in the Actions panel:

```
import flash.display.BitmapData;
// Create imageBmp and attach the bitmap from the library.
var imageBmp:BitmapData = BitmapData.loadBitmap("myImage");
// create movie clip and attach imageBmp
this.createEmptyMovieClip("imageClip", 10);
imageClip.attachBitmap(imageBmp, 2);
// make the clip draggable
imageClip.onPress = function() {
    this.startDrag();
};
imageClip.onRelease = function() {
    this.stopDrag();
}
```

7. Select Control > Test Movie to test the document.

The bitmap in the library appears on the Stage, and the image is draggable.

About using FLV video

The FLV file format contains encoded audio and video data for delivery by using Flash Player. For example, if you have a QuickTime or Windows Media video file, you use an encoder (such as Flash 8 Video Encoder, or Sorensen Squeeze) to convert that file to an FLV file.

Flash Player 7 supports FLV files that are encoded with the Sorenson Spark video codec. Flash Player 8 supports FLV files encoded with Sorenson Spark or On2 VP6 encoder in Flash Professional 8. The On2 VP6 video codec supports an alpha channel. Different Flash Player versions support FLV in different ways. For more information, see the following table:

Codec	SWF file version (publish version)	Flash Player version required for playback
Sorenson Spark	6	6, 7, or 8
	7	7, 8
On2 VP6	6	8*
	7	8
	8	8

* If your SWF file loads an FLV file, you can use the On2 VP6 video with having to republish your SWF file for Flash Player 8, as long as users use Flash Player 8 to view your SWF file. Only Flash Player 8 supports publish and playback of On2 VP6 video.

For information on video fundamentals, such as streaming, progressive download, dimensions, encoding, importing, and bandwidth concerns, see "Working with Video" in Flash Help.

This section discusses using FLV video without components. You can also use the FLVPlayback component to play FLV files or use the VideoPlayback class to create a custom video player that loads FLV files dynamically (see www.macromedia.com/devnet/flash or www.macromedia.com/support/documentation/). For information on using FLV video with the FLVPlayback and Media components, see the following sections:

- "FLVPlayback Component (Flash Professional Only)" in the *Components Language Reference* in Flash Help
- "Media components (Flash Professional only)" in the *Components Language Reference* in Flash Help

As an alternative to importing video directly into the Flash authoring environment, you can use ActionScript to dynamically play external FLV files in Flash Player. You can play FLV files from an HTTP address or from a local file system. To play FLV files, use the NetConnection and NetStream classes and the `attachVideo()` method of the Video class. For more information, see %{NetConnection}%, %{NetStream}%, and %{attachVideo (Video.attachVideo method)}% in the *ActionScript 2.0 Language Reference* in Flash Help.

You can create FLV files by importing video into the Flash authoring tool and exporting it as an FLV file. If you have Flash Professional 8, you can use the FLV Export plug-in to export FLV files from supported video-editing applications.

Using external FLV files provides certain capabilities that are not available when you use imported video:

- Longer video clips can be used in your Flash documents without slowing down playback. External FLV files play using *cached memory*, which means that large files are stored in small pieces and accessed dynamically, requiring less memory than embedded video files.
- An external FLV file can have a different frame rate than the Flash document in which it plays. For example, you can set the Flash document frame rate to 30 frames per second (fps) and the video frame rate to 21 fps. This setting gives you better control of the video than embedded video, to ensure smooth video playback. It also allows you to play FLV files at different frame rates without the need to alter existing Flash content.
- With external FLV files, Flash document playback does not have to be interrupted while the video file is loading. Imported video files can sometimes interrupt document playback to perform certain functions, such as accessing a CD-ROM drive. FLV files can perform functions independently of the Flash document, which does not interrupt playback.

- Captioning video content is easier with external FLV files because you can use event handlers to access metadata for the video.

 To load FLV files from a web server, you might need to register the file extension and MIME type with your web server; check your web server documentation. The MIME type for FLV files is video/x-flv. For more information, see "About configuring FLV files for hosting on a server" on page 636.

For more information on FLV video, see the following topics:

- "Creating a video object" on page 619
- "Playing back external FLV files dynamically" on page 620
- "Creating a video banner" on page 621
- "Preloading FLV files" on page 623
- "Working with cue points" on page 625
- "Working with metadata" on page 634
- "About configuring FLV files for hosting on a server" on page 636
- "About targeting local FLV files on Macintosh" on page 637

Creating a video object

Before you can load and manipulate video using ActionScript, you need to create a video object, drag it to the Stage, and give it an instance name. The following example describes how to add a video instance to an application.

To create a video object:

1. With a document open in the Flash authoring tool, select New Video from the pop-up menu in the Library panel (Window > Library).

2. In the Video Properties dialog box, name the video symbol and select Video (ActionScript controlled).

3. Click OK to create a video object.

4. Drag the video object from the Library panel to the Stage to create a video object instance.

5. With the video object selected on the Stage, type **my_video** in the Instance Name text box in the Property inspector (Window > Properties > Properties).

   Now you have a video instance on the Stage, for which you can add ActionScript to load video or manipulate the instance in a variety of ways.

For information on loading FLV files dynamically, see "Playing back external FLV files dynamically". For information on creating a video banner, see "Creating a video banner" on page 621.

Playing back external FLV files dynamically

You can load FLV files at runtime to play in a SWF file. You can load them into a video object or into a component such as the FLVPlayback component. The following example shows how to play back a file named clouds.flv in a video object.

To play back an external FLV file in a Flash document:

1. Create a new Flash document called **playFLV.fla**.

2. In the Library panel (Window > Library), select New Video from the Library pop-up menu.

3. In the Video Properties dialog box, name the video symbol and select Video (ActionScript controlled).

4. Click OK to create a video object.

5. Drag the video object from the Library panel to the Stage to create a video object instance.

6. With the video object selected on the Stage, type **my_video** in the Instance Name text box in the Property inspector (Window > Properties > Properties).

7. Select Frame 1 in the Timeline, and open the Actions panel (Window > Actions).

8. Type the following code in the Actions panel:

```
this.createTextField("status_txt", 999, 0, 0, 100, 100);
status_txt.autoSize = "left";
status_txt.multiline = true;
// Create a NetConnection object
var my_nc:NetConnection = new NetConnection();
// Create a local streaming connection
my_nc.connect(null);
// Create a NetStream object and define an onStatus() function
var my_ns:NetStream = new NetStream(my_nc);
my_ns.onStatus = function(infoObject:Object):Void {
    status_txt.text += "status (" + this.time + " seconds)\n";
    status_txt.text += "\t Level: " + infoObject.level + "\n";
    status_txt.text += "\t Code: " + infoObject.code + "\n\n";
};
// Attach the NetStream video feed to the Video object
my_video.attachVideo(my_ns);
// Set the buffer time
my_ns.setBufferTime(5);
// Begin playing the FLV file
my_ns.play("http://www.helpexamples.com/flash/video/clouds.flv");
```

9. Select Control > Test Movie to test the document.

For information on preloading FLV files, see "Preloading FLV files" on page 507. For information on dynamically loading FLV video into components, see "Creating an application with the FLVPlayback component" in the *Components Language Reference* in Flash Help. For information on FLV files and the server, and FLV files and playing FLV files locally on the Macintosh, see "About configuring FLV files for hosting on a server" on page 636.

Creating a video banner

Video content within banners and other Flash advertisements is often used for advertising, such as showing Flash movie previews or television advertisements. The following example shows how you might create a video instance and add ActionScript in a FLA file to create a banner advertisement that contains video.

To create a video banner:

1. Create a new Flash document called **vidBanner.fla**.
2. Select Modify > Document.
3. Change the dimensions of your FLA file, type **468** in the width text box and **60** in the height text box.
4. In the Library panel (Window > Library), select New Video from the Library options.
5. In the Video Properties dialog box, name the video symbol and select Video (ActionScript controlled).
6. Click OK to create a video object.
7. Drag the video object from the Library panel to the Stage to create a video instance.
8. With the video object selected on the Stage, type **my_video** in the Instance Name text box in the Property inspector (Window > Properties > Properties).
9. With the video instance still selected, type **105** in the width text box and **60** in the height text box in the Property inspector.
10. Drag the video instance to a position on the Stage, or use the Property inspector to set its *x* and *y* coordinates.
11. Select Frame 1 in the Timeline, and open the Actions panel (Window > Actions).
12. Add the following code to the Actions panel:
    ```
    var my_nc:NetConnection = new NetConnection();
    my_nc.connect(null);
    var my_ns:NetStream = new NetStream(my_nc);
    my_video.attachVideo(my_ns);
    my_ns.setBufferTime(5);
    my_ns.play("http://www.helpexamples.com/flash/video/vbanner.flv");
    ```

13. Select Insert > Timeline > Layer to create a new layer, and name it **button**.

14. Select the Rectangle tool in the Tools panel.

15. In the Colors section of the Tools panel, click the pencil icon to select the Stroke color control.

16. Select No Color, which disables the rectangle's outline.

17. Drag the pointer diagonally across the Stage to create a rectangle.

    The size of the rectangle does not matter because you'll resize it by using the Property inspector.

18. Click the Selection tool in the Tools panel then click the rectangle on the Stage to select it.

19. With the rectangle still selected, type **468** in the width text box and **60** in the height text box in the Property inspector. Then change the X and Y coordinates (X and Y text boxes) to **0**.

20. With the rectangle selected on the Stage, press F8 to change the rectangle into a symbol.

21. In the Convert to Symbol dialog box, type **invisible btn** in the Name text box, select Button, and then click OK.

22. Double-click the new button on the Stage to enter symbol-editing mode.

    The rectangle is currently on the first Up frame of the button you created. This is the Up state of the button—what users see when the button is on the Stage. However, you want the button to not be visible on the Stage, so you need to move the rectangle to the Hit frame, which is the hit area of the button (the active region that a user can click to activate the button's actions).

23. Click the keyframe at the Up frame, and hold down the mouse button while you drag the keyframe to the Hit frame.

    You can now click in the entire banner area, but there is no visual appearance of the button on your banner.

24. Click Scene 1 to return to the main Timeline.

    A teal rectangle appears over the banner area, representing the invisible button's hit area.

25. Select the button you created, open the Property inspector, and type **inv_btn** in the Instance Name text box.

26. Select Frame 1 on the Timeline, and then type the following code in the Actions panel:
    ```
    inv_btn.onRelease = function(){
      getURL("http://www.macromedia.com");
    };
    ```

27. Make other modifications to the banner, such as adding graphics or text.

28. Select Control > Test Movie to test the banner in Flash Player.

In this example, you created a banner and resized its dimensions to the established, standardized dimensions that the Interactive Advertising Bureau specifies. For information on standard advertising dimensions (and many other useful guidelines), see the Interactive Advertising Bureau's Standards and Guidelines page at www.iab.net/standards/adunits.asp.

Despite standardized guidelines, ensure that you confirm the advertising guidelines for the advertising service, client, or website that you're advertising with first. If you submit your banner to an advertising company, make sure the file meets a specified file size, dimension, target Flash Player version, and frame-rate guideline. Also, you might have to consider rules about the kinds of media you can use, button code you use in the FLA file, and so on.

Preloading FLV files

To track the downloading progress of FLV files, use the `NetStream.bytesLoaded` and `NetStream.bytesTotal` properties. To obtain the total bytes and current number of bytes loaded for an FLV file, use the `NetStream.bytesLoaded` and `NetStream.bytesTotal` properties.

The following example uses the `bytesLoaded` and `bytesTotal` properties that show the loading progress of video1.flv into the video object instance called my_video. A text field called loaded_txt is dynamically created to show information about the loading progress.

To preload an FLV file:

1. Create a new FLA file called **preloadFLV.fla**.
2. In the Library panel (Window > Library), select New Video from the Library pop-up menu.
3. In the Video Properties dialog box, name the video symbol and select Video (ActionScript controlled).
4. Click OK to create a video object.
5. Drag the video object from the Library panel to the Stage to create a video object instance.
6. With the video object selected on the Stage, type **my_video** in the Instance Name text box in the Property inspector (Window > Properties > Properties).
7. With the video instance still selected, type **320** in the width text box and **213** in the height text box in the Property inspector.
8. Select Frame 1 in the Timeline, and open the Actions panel (Window > Actions).

9. Type the following code in the Actions panel:

```
var connection_nc:NetConnection = new NetConnection();
connection_nc.connect(null);
var stream_ns:NetStream = new NetStream(connection_nc);
my_video.attachVideo(stream_ns);
stream_ns.play("http://www.helpexamples.com/flash/video/
  lights_short.flv");

this.createTextField("loaded_txt", this.getNextHighestDepth(), 10, 10,
  160, 22);
var loaded_interval:Number = setInterval(checkBytesLoaded, 500,
  stream_ns);
function checkBytesLoaded(my_ns:NetStream) {
  var pctLoaded:Number = Math.round(my_ns.bytesLoaded / my_ns.bytesTotal
  * 100);
  loaded_txt.text = Math.round(my_ns.bytesLoaded / 1000) + " of " +
  Math.round(my_ns.bytesTotal / 1000) + " KB loaded (" + pctLoaded +
  "%)";
  progressBar_mc.bar_mc._xscale = pctLoaded;
  if (pctLoaded >= 100) {
    clearInterval(loaded_interval);
  }
}
```

10. Select Control > Test Movie to test your code.

> **NOTE**
>
> If your progress bar loads instantly, the video has cached on your hard disk (either from testing this example or loading it in a different procedure). If this occurs, upload a FLV file to your server and load it instead.

Another way to preload FLV files is to use the `NetStream.setBufferTime()` method. This method takes a single parameter that indicates the number of seconds of the FLV stream to buffer before playback begins. For more information, see `%{setBufferTime (NetStream.setBufferTime method)}%`, `%{getBytesLoaded (MovieClip.getBytesLoaded method)}%`, `%{getBytesTotal (MovieClip.getBytesTotal method)}%`, `%{bytesLoaded (NetStream.bytesLoaded property)}%`, `%{bytesTotal (NetStream.bytesTotal property)}%`, and `%{setInterval function}%` in the *ActionScript 2.0 Language Reference* in Flash Help

Working with cue points

You can use several different kinds of cue points with Flash Video. You can use ActionScript to interact with cue points that you embed in an FLV file (when you create the FLV file), or that you create by using ActionScript.

Navigation cue points You embed navigation cue points in the FLV stream and FLV metadata packet when you encode the FLV file. You use navigation cue points to let users seek to a specified part of a file.

Event cue points You embed event cue points in the FLV stream and FLV metadata packet when you encode the FLV file. You can write code to handle the events that are triggered at specified points during FLV playback.

ActionScript cue points External cue points that you create by using ActionScript code. You can write code to trigger these cue points in relation to the video's playback. These cue points are less accurate than embedded cue points (up to a tenth of a second), because the video player tracks them separately.

Navigation cue points create a keyframe at the specified cue point location, so you can use code to move a video player's playhead to that location. You can set particular points in an FLV file where you might want users to seek. For example, your video might have multiple chapters or segments, and you can control the video by embedding navigation cue points in the video file.

If you plan to create an application in which you want users to navigate to a cue point, you should create and embed cue points when you encode the file instead of using ActionScript cue points. You should embed the cue points in the FLV file, because they are more accurate to work with. For more information on encoding FLV files with cue points, see "Embedding cue points (Flash Professional only)" in Flash Help.

You can access cue point parameters by writing ActionScript. Cue point parameters are a part of the event object received with the `cuePoint` event (`event.info.parameters`).

Tracing cue points from an FLV file

You can trace the cue points that are embedded in an FLV document using `NetStream.onMetaData`. You need to recurse the structure of the metadata that returns to see the cue point information.

The following code traces cue points in an FLV file:

```
var connection_nc:NetConnection = new NetConnection();
connection_nc.connect(null);
var stream_ns:NetStream = new NetStream(connection_nc);
stream_ns.onMetaData = function(metaProp:Object) {
    trace("The metadata:");
    traceMeta(metaProp);
    // traceObject(metaProp, 0);
};
my_video.attachVideo(stream_ns);
stream_ns.play("http://www.helpexamples.com/flash/video/cuepoints.flv");

function traceMeta(metaProp:Object):Void {
    var p:String;
    for (p in metaProp) {
        switch (p) {
        case "cuePoints" :
            trace("cuePoints: ");
            //cycles through the cue points
            var cuePointArr:Array = metaProp[p];
            for (var j:Number = 0; j < cuePointArr.length; j++) {
                //cycle through the current cue point parameters
                trace("\t cuePoints[" + j + "]:");
                var currentCuePoint:Object = metaProp[p][j];
                var metaPropPJParams:Object = currentCuePoint.parameters;
                trace("\t\t name: " + currentCuePoint.name);
                trace("\t\t time: " + currentCuePoint.time);
                trace("\t\t type: " + currentCuePoint.type);
                if (metaPropPJParams != undefined) {
                    trace("\t\t parameters:");
                    traceObject(metaPropPJParams, 4);
                }
            }
            break;
        default :
            trace(p + ": " + metaProp[p]);
            break;
        }
    }
}
function traceObject(obj:Object, indent:Number):Void {
    var indentString:String = "";
    for (var j:Number = 0; j < indent; j++) {
        indentString += "\t";
```

```
    }
    for (var i:String in obj) {
      if (typeof(obj[i]) == "object") {
        trace(indentString + " " + i + ": [Object]");
        traceObject(obj[i], indent + 1);
      } else {
        trace(indentString + "  " + i + ": " + obj[i]);
      }
    }
}
```

The following output appears:

```
The metadata:
canSeekToEnd: true
cuePoints:
  cuePoints[0]:
    name: point1
    time: 0.418
    type: navigation
    parameters:
      lights: beginning
  cuePoints[1]:
    name: point2
    time: 7.748
    type: navigation
    parameters:
      lights: middle
  cuePoints[2]:
    name: point3
    time: 16.02
    type: navigation
    parameters:
      lights: end
audiocodecid: 2
audiodelay: 0.038
audiodatarate: 96
videocodecid: 4
framerate: 15
videodatarate: 400
height: 213
width: 320
duration: 16.334
```

For information on using cue points with the FLVPlayback component, see "Using embedded cue points with the FLVPlayback component (Flash Professional only)".

Using embedded cue points with the FLVPlayback component (Flash Professional only)

You can view cue points for an FLV file in the Property inspector when you use the FLVPlayback component. After you set the `contentPath` property for the FLVPlayback instance, you can view any cue points that are embedded in the video file. Using the Parameters tab, find the `cuePoints` property, and click the magnifying glass icon to see a list of the cue points in the file.

> **NOTE**: To see the cue points on the Parameters tab, you must type the name of your FLV file in the contentPath text box instead of using code to assign the contentPath.

The following example shows how to use cue point information with the FLVPlayback component.

To use cue points with the FLVPlayback component:

1. Create a new Flash document called **cueFlv.fla**.

2. Open the Components panel (Window > Components), and drag an instance of the FLVPlayback and TextArea components to the Stage.

3. Select the TextArea component, and type **my_ta** in the Instance Name text box in the Property inspector (Window > Properties > Properties).

4. With the TextArea component still selected, type **200** in the width text box and **100** in the height text box.

5. Select the FLVPlayback instance on the Stage, and then type **my_flvPb** in the Instance Name text box.

6. Select Frame 1 on the Timeline, and type the following code in the Actions panel.

```
var my_flvPb:mx.video.FLVPlayback;
var my_ta:mx.controls.TextArea;
my_flvPb.contentPath = "http://www.helpexamples.com/flash/video/
    cuepoints.flv";
var listenerObject:Object = new Object();
listenerObject.cuePoint = function(eventObject:Object) {
    my_ta.text += "Elapsed time in seconds: " + my_flvPb.playheadTime +
    "\n";
};
my_flvPb.addEventListener("cuePoint",listenerObject);
```

7. Select Control > Test Movie to test the SWF file.

   The elapsed time appears in the TextArea instance when the playhead passes each cue point embedded in the document.

For more information on working with the FLVPlayback component, see "FLVPlayback Component (Flash Professional Only)" in the *Components Language Reference* in Flash Help.

Creating cue points with ActionScript to use with components (Flash Professional only)

You can create cue points with ActionScript, and then use them with a video object instance, or one of the video player components (FLVPlayback for Flash Player 8, or MediaPlayback for Flash Player 7). The following examples show you how easy it is to use ActionScript code to create cue points, and then use a script to access them.

> **NOTE**
>
> Embed navigation cue points in a document if you intend to add navigation functionality to an application. For more information, see "Working with cue points" on page 625. For an example of working with embedded cue points, see "Using embedded cue points with the FLVPlayback component (Flash Professional only)" on page 628.

To create and use cue points with the FLVPlayback component:

1. Create a new Flash document called **cueFlvPb.fla**.

2. Drag an instance of the FLVPlayback component from the Components panel (Window > Components) to the Stage.

   The component is in the FLVPlayback - Player 8 folder.

3. Select the component and open the Property inspector (Window > Properties > Properties).

4. Type **my_flvPb** in the Instance Name text box.

5. Drag an instance of the TextArea component from the Components panel to the Stage.

6. Select the TextArea component and type **my_ta** in the Instance Name text box.

7. With the TextArea component still selected, type **200** in the width text box and **100** in the height text box.

8. Select Frame 1 on the Timeline, and type the following code in the Actions panel:

```
var my_flvPb:mx.video.FLVPlayback;
my_flvPb.contentPath = "http://www.helpexamples.com/flash/video/
  clouds.flv";

// Create cuePoint object.
var cuePt:Object = new Object();
cuePt.time = 1;
cuePt.name = "elapsed_time";
cuePt.type = "actionscript";
// Add AS cue point.
my_flvPb.addASCuePoint(cuePt);

// Add another AS cue point.
my_flvPb.addASCuePoint(2, "elapsed_time2");

// Display cue point information in text field.
```

```
var listenerObject:Object = new Object();
listenerObject.cuePoint = function(eventObject) {
  my_ta.text += "Elapsed time in seconds: " + my_flvPb.playheadTime +
  "\n";
};
my_flvPb.addEventListener("cuePoint",listenerObject);
```

9. Select Control > Test Movie to test your code.

   The following cue points trace in the Output panel:

   ```
   Elapsed time in seconds: 1.034
   Elapsed time in seconds: 2.102
   ```

For information on `addASCuePoint()`, see "FLVPlayback.addASCuePoint()" in the *Components Language Reference* in Flash Help. For information on working with cue points and the FLVPlayback component, see "Using cue points" and "FLVPlayback Component (Flash Professional Only)" in the *Components Language Reference* in Flash Help.

The following example shows how to add cue points at runtime and then trace the cue points when a FLV file plays in the MediaPlayback component.

To create and use cue points with the MediaPlayback component:

1. Create a new Flash document called cuePointMP.fla

2. Drag an instance of the MediaPlayback component from the Components panel (Window > Components) to the Stage.

   The component is in the Media - Player 6 - 7 folder.

3. Select the component, and open the Property inspector (Window > Properties > Properties).

4. Type **my_mp** in the Instance Name text box.

5. Select the Parameters tab, and click Launch Component Inspector.

6. In the Component inspector, type **http://www.helpexamples.com/flash/video/clouds.flv** in the URL text box.

7. Open the Actions panel (Window > Actions), and type the following code in the Script pane:

```
import mx.controls.MediaPlayback;
var my_mp:MediaPlayback;
my_mp.autoPlay = false;
my_mp.addEventListener("cuePoint", doCuePoint);
my_mp.addCuePoint("one", 1);
my_mp.addCuePoint("two", 2);
my_mp.addCuePoint("three", 3);
my_mp.addCuePoint("four", 4);
function doCuePoint(eventObj:Object):Void {
    trace(eventObj.type + " = {cuePointName:" + eventObj.cuePointName +
  " cuePointTime:" + eventObj.cuePointTime + "}");
}
```

8. Select Control > Test Movie to test your code.

   The following cue points trace in the Output panel:

```
cuePoint = {cuePointName:one cuePointTime:1}
cuePoint = {cuePointName:two cuePointTime:2}
cuePoint = {cuePointName:three cuePointTime:3}
cuePoint = {cuePointName:four cuePointTime:4}
```

For more information on working with the MediaPlayback component, see "Media components (Flash Professional only)" in the *Components Language Reference* in Flash Help. For more information on working with the FLVPlayback component, see "FLVPlayback Component (Flash Professional Only)" in the *Components Language Reference* in Flash Help.

Adding seek functionality with cue points (Flash Professional only)

You can embed Navigation cue points in an FLV file to add seeking functionality to your applications. The seekToNavCuePoint() method of the FLVPlayback component locates the cue point in the FLV file with the specified name, at or after the specified time. You can specify a name as a string (such as "part1" or "theParty").

You can also use the seekToNextNavCuePoint() method, which seeks to the next navigation cue point, based on the current playheadTime. You can pass the method a parameter, time, which is the starting time from where to look for the next navigation cue point. The default value is the current playheadTime.

Alternatively, you can also seek to a specified duration of the FLV file, using the seek() method.

In the following examples, you add a button that you use to jump between cue points or a specified duration in a FLV file that plays in the FLVPlayback component, and a button to jump to a specified cue point.

To seek to a specified duration:

1. Create a new Flash document called **seekduration.fla**.

2. Drag an instance of the FLVPlayback component from the Components panel (Window > Components).

   The component is in the FLVPlayback - Player 8 folder.

3. Select the component and open the Property inspector (Window > Properties > Properties).

4. Type **my_flvPb** in the Instance Name text box.

5. Drag an instance of the Button component from the Components panel to the Stage.

6. Select the Button component and type **my_button** in the Instance Name text box.

7. Select Frame 1 on the Timeline and type the following code in the Actions panel:

```
import mx.controls.Button;
import mx.video.FLVPlayback;
var seek_button:Button;
var my_flvPb:FLVPlayback;
my_flvPb.autoPlay = false;
my_flvPb.contentPath = "http://www.helpexamples.com/flash/video/
  sheep.flv";
seek_button.label = "Seek";
seek_button.addEventListener("click", seekFlv);
function seekFlv(eventObj:Object):Void {
  // seek to 2 seconds
  my_flvPb.seek(2);
}
```

8. Select Control > Test Movie to test your code.

   When you click the button, the video playhead moves to the duration that you specify: 2 seconds into the video.

To add seeking functionality with the FLVPlayback component:

1. Create a new Flash document called **seek1.fla**.

2. Drag an instance of the FLVPlayback component from the Components panel (Window > Components).

   The component is in the FLVPlayback - Player 8 folder.

3. Select the component and open the Property inspector (Window > Properties > Properties).

4. Type **my_flvPb** in the Instance Name text box.

5. Drag an instance of the Button component from the Components panel to the Stage.

6. Select the Button component and type **my_button** in the Instance Name text box.

7. Select Frame 1 on the Timeline and type the following code in the Actions panel:

```
import mx.video.FLVPlayback;
var my_flvPb:FLVPlayback;
my_flvPb.autoPlay = false;
my_flvPb.contentPath = "http://www.helpexamples.com/flash/video/
    cuepoints.flv";
my_button.label = "Next cue point";

function clickMe(){
  my_flvPb.seekToNextNavCuePoint();
}
my_button.addEventListener("click", clickMe);
```

8. Select Control > Test Movie to test your code.

The cuepoints.flv file contains three navigation cue points: one each near the beginning, middle, and end of the video file. When you click the button, the FLVPlayback instance seeks to the next cue point until it reaches the last cue point in the video file.

You can also seek to a specified cue point in an FLV file by using the `seekToCuePoint()` method, as shown in the following example.

To seek to a specified cue point:

1. Create a new Flash document called **seek2.fla**.

2. Drag an instance of the FLVPlayback component from the Components panel (Window > Components).

The component is in the FLVPlayback - Player 8 folder.

3. Select the component, and open the Property inspector (Window > Properties > Properties).

4. Type **my_flvPb** in the Instance Name text box.

5. With the FLVPlayback instance still selected, click the Parameters tab.

6. Type **http://www.helpexamples.com/flash/video/cuepoints.flv** in the contentPath text box.

When you type the URL in the contentPath text box, the cue points appear in the Parameters tab (next to cuePoint parameter). Therefore, you can determine the name of the cue point that you want to find in your code. If you click the magnifying glass icon, you can view all of the video file's cue points and information about each cue point in a table.

7. Drag an instance of the Button component from the Components panel to the Stage.

8. Select the Button component and type **my_button** in the Instance Name text box.

9. Select Frame 1 on the Timeline and type the following code in the Actions panel:

```
import mx.video.FLVPlayback;
var my_flvPb:FLVPlayback;
my_flvPb.autoPlay = false;
my_button.label = "Seek to point2";

function clickMe(){
  my_flvPb.seekToNavCuePoint("point2");
}
my_button.addEventListener("click", clickMe);
```

10. Select Control > Test Movie to test your code.

The cuepoints.flv file contains three navigation cue points: one each near the beginning, middle, and end of the video file. When you click the button, the FLVPlayback instance seeks to the specified cue point (`point2`).

For more information on cue points, see "Using cue points" in the *Components Language Reference* in Flash Help. For more information on the FLVPlayback component, see "FLVPlayback Component (Flash Professional Only)" in the *Components Language Reference* in Flash Help.

Working with metadata

You can use the `onMetaData` method to view the metadata information in your FLV file. Metadata includes information about your FLV file, such as duration, width, height, and frame rate. The metadata information that is added to your FLV file depends on the software you use to encode your FLV file or the software you use to add metadata information.

> **NOTE**
> If your video file does not have metadata information, you can use tools to add metadata information to the file.

To work with `NetStream.onMetaData`, you must have Flash Video that contains metadata. If you encode FLV files using Flash 8 Video Encoder, your FLV file will have metadata information in it (see the following example for a list of metadata in a FLV file encoded with Flash 8 Video Encoder).

> **NOTE**
> Flash Video Exporter 1.2 and later (including Flash 8 Video Exporter), add the metadata to your FLV files. Sorenson Squeeze 4.1 and later also adds metadata to your video files.

The following example uses `NetStream.onMetaData` to trace the metadata information of an FLV file encoded with Flash 8 Video Encoder.

To use NetStream.onMetaData to view metadata information:

1. Create a new FLA file called **flvMetadata.fla**.

2. In the Library panel (Window > Library), select New Video from the Library pop-up menu.

3. In the Video Properties dialog box, name the video symbol and select Video (ActionScript controlled).

4. Click OK to create a video object.

5. Drag the video object from the Library panel to the Stage to create a video object instance.

6. With the video object selected on the Stage, type **my_video** in the Instance Name text box in the Property inspector (Window > Properties > Properties).

7. With the video instance still selected, type **320** in the width text box and **213** in the height text box.

8. Select Frame 1 in the Timeline, and open the Actions panel (Window > Actions).

9. Type the following code in the Actions panel:

```
// Create a NetConnection object.
var netConn:NetConnection = new NetConnection();
// Create a local streaming connection.
netConn.connect(null);
// Create a NetStream object and define an onStatus() function.
var nStream:NetStream = new NetStream(netConn);
// Attach the NetStream video feed to the Video object.
my_video.attachVideo(nStream);
// Set the buffer time.
nStream.setBufferTime(30);
// Being playing the FLV file.
nStream.play("http://www.helpexamples.com/flash/video/
  lights_short.flv");
// Trace the metadata.
nStream.onMetaData = function(myMeta) {
    for (var i in myMeta) {
        trace(i + ":\t" + myMeta[i])
    }
};
```

10. Select Control > Test Movie to test your code.

You see the following information in the Output panel:

```
canSeekToEnd:true
audiocodecid:2
audiodelay:0.038
audiodatarate:96
videocodecid:4
framerate:15
videodatarate:400
height:213
width:320
duration:8.04
```

> **NOTE** If your video does not have audio, the audio-related metadata information (such as `audiodatarate`) returns `undefined` because no audio information is added to the metadata during encoding.

You can also use the following format to display most metadata information. For example, the following code shows the duration of an FLV file:

```
nStream.onMetaData = function(myMeta) {
  trace("FLV duration: " + myMeta.duration + " sec.");
};
```

This format cannot trace `cuePoint` metadata information. For information on tracing cue points, see "Tracing cue points from an FLV file" on page 626.

About configuring FLV files for hosting on a server

When you work with FLV files, you might have to configure your server to work with the FLV file format. Multipurpose Internet Mail Extensions (MIME) is a standardized data specification that lets you send non-ASCII files over Internet connections. Web browsers and e-mail clients are configured to interpret numerous *MIME types* so that they can send and receive video, audio, graphics, and formatted text. To load FLV files from a web server, you might need to register the file extension and MIME type with your web server, so you should check your web server documentation. The MIME type for FLV files is `video/x-flv`. The full information for the FLV file type is as follows:

Mime Type: video/x-flv

File extension: .flv

Required parameters: none

Optional parameters: none

Encoding considerations: FLV files are binary files; some applications might require the application/octet-stream subtype to be set.

Security issues: none

Published specification: www.macromedia.com/go/flashfileformat.

Microsoft changed the way streaming media is handled in Microsoft Internet Information Services (IIS) 6.0 web server from earlier versions. Earlier versions of IIS do not require any modification to stream Flash Video. In IIS 6.0, the default web server that comes with Windows 2003, the server requires a MIME type to recognize that FLV files are streaming media.

When SWF files that stream external FLV files are placed on a Microsoft Windows 2003 server and are viewed in a browser, the SWF file plays correctly, but the FLV video does not stream. This issue affects all FLV files placed on Windows 2003 server, including files you make with earlier versions of the Flash authoring tool, the Macromedia Flash Video Kit for Dreamweaver MX 2004. These files work correctly if you test them on other operating systems.

For information about configuring Microsoft Windows 2003 and Microsoft IIS Server 6.0 to stream FLV video, see www.macromedia.com/go/tn_19439.

About targeting local FLV files on Macintosh

If you attempt to play a local FLV from a non-system drive on a Macintosh computer by using a path that uses a relative slash (/), the video will not play. *Non-system drives* include, but are not limited to, CD-ROMs, partitioned hard disks, removable storage media, and connected storage devices.

> **NOTE** The reason for this failure is a limitation of the operating system, not a limitation in Flash or Flash Player.

For an FLV file to play from a non-system drive on a Macintosh, refer to it with an absolute path using a colon-based notation (:) rather than slash-based notation (/). The following list shows the difference in the two kinds of notation:

Slash-based notation myDrive/myFolder/myFLV.flv

Colon-based notation (Macintosh) myDrive:myFolder:myFLV.flv

You can also create a projector file for a CD-ROM you intend to use for Macintosh playback. For the latest information on Macintosh CD-ROMs and FLV files, see www.macromedia.com/go/3121b301.

About creating progress animations for media files

ActionScript provides several ways to preload or track the downloading progress of external media. You can create progress bars or animations to visually show the loading progress or the amount of content that has loaded.

To preload SWF and JPEG files, use the MovieClipLoader class, which provides an event listener mechanism for checking downloading progress. For more information, see "Preloading SWF and JPEG files" on page 427.

To track the downloading progress of MP3 files, use the `Sound.getBytesLoaded()` and `Sound.getBytesTotal()` methods; to track the downloading progress of FLV files, use the `NetStream.bytesLoaded` and `NetStream.bytesTotal` properties. For more information, see "Preloading MP3 files" on page 420.

For information on creating progress bars to load media files, see the following topics:

- "Creating a progress animation for loading SWF and image files" on page 638
- "Creating a progress bar for loading MP3 files with ActionScript" on page 640
- "Creating a progress bar for loading FLV files with ActionScript" on page 643

You can find a sample source file that uses scripted animation to create a progress bar animation. Find tweenProgress.fla in the Samples folder on your hard disk:

- In Windows, browse to *boot drive*\Program Files\Macromedia\Flash 8\ Samples and Tutorials\Samples\ActionScript\Tween ProgressBar.
- On the Macintosh, browse to *Macintosh HD*/Applications/Macromedia Flash 8/ Samples and Tutorials/Samples/ActionScript/Tween ProgressBar.

Creating a progress animation for loading SWF and image files

When you load large SWF or image files into an application, you might want to create an animation that shows the loading progress. You might create a progress bar that shows increases as the animation loads. You might also create an animation that changes as the file loads. For information on loading SWF and image files, see "Loading external SWF and image files" on page 607.

The following example shows how to use the MovieClipLoader class and the Drawing API to show the loading progress of an image file.

To create a progress bar for loading image or SWF files:

1. Create a new Flash document called **loadImage.fla**.

2. Select Modify > Document, and type **700** into the width text box and **500** into the height text box to change the document's dimensions.

3. Select Frame 1 of the Timeline, and then type the following code in the Actions panel:

```
//create clips to hold your content
this.createEmptyMovieClip("progressBar_mc", 0);
progressBar_mc.createEmptyMovieClip("bar_mc", 1);
progressBar_mc.createEmptyMovieClip("stroke_mc", 2);
//use drawing methods to create a progress bar
with (progressBar_mc.stroke_mc) {
    lineStyle(0, 0x000000);
    moveTo(0, 0);
    lineTo(100, 0);
    lineTo(100, 10);
    lineTo(0, 10);
    lineTo(0, 0);
}
with (progressBar_mc.bar_mc) {
    beginFill(0xFF0000, 100);
    moveTo(0, 0);
    lineTo(100, 0);
    lineTo(100, 10);
    lineTo(0, 10);
    lineTo(0, 0);
    endFill();
    _xscale = 0;
}
progressBar_mc._x = 2;
progressBar_mc._y = 2;
// load progress
var mclListener:Object = new Object();
mclListener.onLoadStart = function(target_mc:MovieClip) {
    progressBar_mc.bar_mc._xscale = 0;
};
mclListener.onLoadProgress = function(target_mc:MovieClip,
    bytesLoaded:Number, bytesTotal:Number) {
    progressBar_mc.bar_mc._xscale = Math.round(bytesLoaded/
    bytesTotal*100);
};
mclListener.onLoadComplete = function(target_mc:MovieClip) {
    progressBar_mc.removeMovieClip();
};
mclListener.onLoadInit = function(target_mc:MovieClip) {
    target_mc._height = 500;
    target_mc._width = 700;
};
//Create a clip to hold the image.
```

```
this.createEmptyMovieClip("image_mc", 100);
var image_mcl:MovieClipLoader = new MovieClipLoader();
image_mcl.addListener(mclListener);
/* Load the image into the clip.
You can change the following URL to a SWF or another image file. */
image_mcl.loadClip("http://www.helpexamples.com/flash/images/gallery1/
   images/pic3.jpg", image_mc);
```

4. Select Control > Test Movie to see the image load and watch the progress bar.

> **NOTE** If you test this code a second time, the image will be cached and the progress bar will complete right away. To test multiple times, use different images and load them from an external source. A local source might cause problems with testing your application because the content loads too quickly.

You can find a sample source file that uses scripted animation to create a progress bar animation. Find tweenProgress.fla in the Samples folder on your hard disk.

- In Windows, browse to *boot drive*\Program Files\Macromedia\Flash 8\ Samples and Tutorials\Samples\ActionScript\Tween ProgressBar.

- On the Macintosh, browse to *Macintosh HD*/Applications/Macromedia Flash 8/ Samples and Tutorials/Samples/ActionScript/Tween ProgressBar.

You can also find samples of photo gallery applications. These files provide examples of how to use ActionScript to control movie clips dynamically while loading image files into a SWF file. You can find the sample source files, gallery_tree.fla and gallery_tween.fla, in the Samples folder on your hard disk.

- In Windows, browse to *boot drive*\Program Files\Macromedia\Flash 8\ Samples and Tutorials\Samples\ActionScript\Galleries.

- On the Macintosh, browse to *Macintosh HD*/Applications/Macromedia Flash 8/ Samples and Tutorials/Samples/ActionScript/Galleries.

Creating a progress bar for loading MP3 files with ActionScript

The following example loads several songs into a SWF file. A progress bar, created using the Drawing API, shows the loading progress. When the music starts and completes loading, information appears in the Output panel. For information on loading MP3 files, see "Loading an MP3 file" on page 613.

To create a progress bar for loading MP3 files:

1. Create a new Flash document called **loadSound.fla**.

2. Select Frame 1 on the Timeline and type the following code in the Actions panel.

```
var pb_height:Number = 10;
var pb_width:Number = 100;
var pb:MovieClip = this.createEmptyMovieClip("progressBar_mc",
   this.getNextHighestDepth());
pb.createEmptyMovieClip("bar_mc", pb.getNextHighestDepth());
pb.createEmptyMovieClip("vBar_mc", pb.getNextHighestDepth());
pb.createEmptyMovieClip("stroke_mc", pb.getNextHighestDepth());
pb.createTextField("pos_txt", pb.getNextHighestDepth(), 0, pb_height,
   pb_width, 22);

pb._x = 100;
pb._y = 100;

with (pb.bar_mc) {
   beginFill(0x00FF00);
   moveTo(0, 0);
   lineTo(pb_width, 0);
   lineTo(pb_width, pb_height);
   lineTo(0, pb_height);
   lineTo(0, 0);
   endFill();
   _xscale = 0;
}
with (pb.vBar_mc) {
   lineStyle(1, 0x000000);
   moveTo(0, 0);
   lineTo(0, pb_height);
}
with (pb.stroke_mc) {
   lineStyle(3, 0x000000);
   moveTo(0, 0);
   lineTo(pb_width, 0);
   lineTo(pb_width, pb_height);
   lineTo(0, pb_height);
   lineTo(0, 0);
}

var my_interval:Number;
var my_sound:Sound = new Sound();
my_sound.onLoad = function(success:Boolean) {
   if (success) {
      trace("sound loaded");
   }
};
my_sound.onSoundComplete = function() {
   clearInterval(my_interval);
```

```
    trace("Cleared interval");
}
my_sound.loadSound("http://www.helpexamples.com/flash/sound/song2.mp3",
    true);
my_interval = setInterval(updateProgressBar, 100, my_sound);

function updateProgressBar(the_sound:Sound):Void {
    var pos:Number = Math.round(the_sound.position / the_sound.duration *
    100);
    pb.bar_mc._xscale = pos;
    pb.vBar_mc._x = pb.bar_mc._width;
    pb.pos_txt.text = pos + "%";
}
```

3. Select Control > Test Movie to load the MP3 file and watch the progress bar.

> **NOTE**
>
> If you test this code a second time, the image will be cached and the progress bar will complete right away. To test multiple times, use different images and load them from an external source. A local source might cause problems with testing your application because the content loads too quickly.

For more information on using sound, see the Sound class entry, %{Sound}%, in the *ActionScript 2.0 Language Reference* in Flash Help.

You can find a sample source file that uses scripted animation to create a progress bar animation. Find tweenProgress.fla in the Samples folder on your hard disk.

- In Windows, browse to *boot drive*\Program Files\Macromedia\Flash 8\ Samples and Tutorials\Samples\ActionScript\Tween ProgressBar.

- On the Macintosh, browse to *Macintosh HD*/Applications/Macromedia Flash 8/ Samples and Tutorials/Samples/ActionScript/Tween ProgressBar.

You can also find a sample source file that loads MP3 files, jukebox.fla, in the Samples folder on your hard disk. This sample demonstrates how to create a jukebox by using data types, general coding principles, and several components.

- In Windows, browse to *boot drive*\Program Files\Macromedia\Flash 8\ Samples and Tutorials\Samples\Components\Jukebox.

- On the Macintosh, browse to *Macintosh HD*/Applications/Macromedia Flash 8/ Samples and Tutorials/Samples/Components/Jukebox.

Creating a progress bar for loading FLV files with ActionScript

You can create a progress bar to display the loading progress of an FLV file. For information on loading FLV files into a SWF file, see "Preloading FLV files" on page 623. For other information about FLV files and Flash, see "About using FLV video" on page 617.

The following example uses the Drawing API to create a progress bar. The example also uses the `bytesLoaded` and `bytesTotal` properties to show the loading progress of video1.flv into the video object instance called `my_video`. The `loaded_txt` text field is dynamically created to show information about the loading progress.

To create a progress bar that shows loading progress:

1. Create a new FLA file called **flvProgress.fla**.
2. In the Library panel (Window > Library), select New Video from the Library pop-up menu.
3. In the Video Properties dialog box, name the video symbol and select Video (ActionScript controlled).
4. Click OK to create a video object.
5. Drag the video object from the Library panel to the Stage to create a video object instance.
6. With the video object selected on the Stage, type **my_video** in the Instance Name text box in the Property inspector (Window > Properties > Properties).
7. With the video instance selected, type **320** into the width text box and **213** into the height text box.

8. Select Frame 1 in the Timeline and type the following code in the Actions panel:

```
var connection_nc:NetConnection = new NetConnection();
connection_nc.connect(null);
var stream_ns:NetStream = new NetStream(connection_nc);
my_video.attachVideo(stream_ns);
stream_ns.play("http://www.helpexamples.com/flash/video/
  typing_short.flv");

this.createTextField("loaded_txt", this.getNextHighestDepth(), 10, 10,
  160, 22);
this.createEmptyMovieClip("progressBar_mc", this.getNextHighestDepth());
progressBar_mc.createEmptyMovieClip("bar_mc",
  progressBar_mc.getNextHighestDepth());
with (progressBar_mc.bar_mc) {
  beginFill(0xFF0000);
  moveTo(0, 0);
  lineTo(100, 0);
  lineTo(100, 10);
  lineTo(0, 10);
  lineTo(0, 0);
  endFill();
  _xscale = 0;
}
progressBar_mc.createEmptyMovieClip("stroke_mc",
  progressBar_mc.getNextHighestDepth());
with (progressBar_mc.stroke_mc) {
  lineStyle(0, 0x000000);
  moveTo(0, 0);
  lineTo(100, 0);
  lineTo(100, 10);
  lineTo(0, 10);
  lineTo(0, 0);
}

var loaded_interval:Number = setInterval(checkBytesLoaded, 500,
  stream_ns);
function checkBytesLoaded(my_ns:NetStream) {
  var pctLoaded:Number = Math.round(my_ns.bytesLoaded /
  my_ns.bytesTotal * 100);
  loaded_txt.text = Math.round(my_ns.bytesLoaded / 1000) + " of " +
  Math.round(my_ns.bytesTotal / 1000) + " KB loaded (" + pctLoaded +
  "%)";
  progressBar_mc.bar_mc._xscale = pctLoaded;
  if (pctLoaded>=100) {
    clearInterval(loaded_interval);
  }
}
```

9. Select Control > Test Movie to test your code.

The video loads and an animating bar and changing text values communicate the loading progress. If these elements overlap your video, move the video object on the Stage. You can customize the color of the progress bar by modifying `beginFill` and `lineStyle` in previous code snippet.

> **NOTE**
>
> If your progress bar loads instantly, the video is cached on your hard disk (either from testing this example already, or loading it in a different procedure). If this occurs, upload a FLV file to your server and load it instead.

You can find a sample source file that uses scripted animation to create a progress bar animation. Find tweenProgress.fla in the Samples folder on your hard disk.

- In Windows, browse to *boot drive*\Program Files\Macromedia\Flash 8\ Samples and Tutorials\Samples\ActionScript\Tween ProgressBar.
- On the Macintosh, browse to *Macintosh HD*/Applications/Macromedia Flash 8/ Samples and Tutorials/Samples/ActionScript/Tween ProgressBar.

CHAPTER 16

Working with External Data

In Macromedia Flash Basic 8 and Macromedia Flash Professional 8, you can use ActionScript to load data from external sources to a SWF file. You can also send data, which could be provided by the user or the server, from a SWF file to an application server (such as Macromedia ColdFusion or Macromedia JRun) or another type of server-side script, such as PHP or Perl. Macromedia Flash Player can send and load data over HTTP or HTTPS or load from a local text file. You can also create persistent TCP/IP socket connections for applications that require low latency—for example, chat applications or stock quote services. New in Flash Player 8 is the ability to upload files from the user's computer to a server and download files from a server to the user's computer.

Data that you load into or send from a SWF file can be formatted as XML (Extensible Markup Language) or as name-value pairs.

Flash Player can also send data to and receive data from its host environment—a web browser, for example—or another instance of Flash Player on the same computer or web page.

By default, a SWF file can access only data that resides in exactly the same domain (for example, www.macromedia.com). (For more information, see "About domains, cross-domain security, and SWF files" on page 708.)

For more information on working with external data, see the following topics:

Sending and loading variables

A SWF file is a window for capturing and displaying information, much like an HTML page. However, SWF files can stay loaded in the browser and continuously update with new information without having to reload the entire page. Using ActionScript functions and methods, you can send information to and receive information from server-side scripts and receive information from text files and XML files.

In addition, server-side scripts can request specific information from a database and relay it to a SWF file. Server-side scripts can be written in different languages: some of the most common are CFML, Perl, ASP (Microsoft Active Server Pages), and PHP. By storing information in a database and retrieving it, you can create dynamic and personalized content for your SWF file. For example, you could create a message board, personal profiles for users, or a shopping cart that keeps track of a user's purchases.

Several ActionScript functions and methods let you pass information into and out of a SWF file. Each function or method uses a protocol to transfer information and requires information to be formatted in a certain way.

- The functions and MovieClip methods that use the HTTP or HTTPS protocol to send information in URL-encoded format are `getURL()`, `loadVariables()`, `loadVariablesNum()`, `loadMovie()`, and `loadMovieNum()`.

- The LoadVars methods that use the HTTP or HTTPS protocol to send and load information in URL-encoded format are `load()`, `send()`, and `sendAndLoad()`.

- The methods that use HTTP or HTTPS protocol to send and load information as XML are `XML.send()`, `XML.load()`, and `XML.sendAndLoad()`.

- The methods that create and use a TCP/IP socket connection to send and load information as XML are `XMLSocket.connect()` and `XMLSocket.send()`.

For more information, see the following topics:

- "Checking for loaded data" on page 648
- "Creating a progress bar to display data loading progress" on page 650

Checking for loaded data

Each function or method that loads data into a SWF file (except `XMLSocket.send()`) is *asynchronous*: the results of the action are returned at an indeterminate time.

Before you can use loaded data in a SWF file, you must check to see whether it has been loaded. For example, you can't load variables and manipulate their values in the same script because the data to manipulate doesn't exist in the file until it is loaded. In the following script, you cannot use the variable lastSiteVisited until you're sure that the variable has loaded from the file myData.txt. In the file myData.txt, you would have text similar to the following example:

```
lastSiteVisited=www.macromedia.com
```

If you used the following code, you could not trace the data that is loading:

```
loadVariables("myData.txt", 0);
trace(lastSiteVisited); // undefined
```

Each function or method has a specific technique you can use to check data it has loaded. If you use %{loadVariables function}% or %{loadMovie function}%, you can load information into a movie clip target and use the onData handler to execute a script. If you use %{loadVariables function}% to load the data, the onData handler executes when the last variable is loaded. If you use %{loadMovie function}% to load the data, the onData handler executes each time a fragment of the SWF file is streamed into Flash Player.

For example, the following ActionScript loads the variables from the file myData.txt into the movie clip loadTarget_mc. An onData() handler assigned to the loadTarget_mc instance uses the variable lastSiteVisited, which is loaded from the file myData.txt. The following trace actions appear only after all the variables, including lastSiteVisited, are loaded:

```
this.createEmptyMovieClip("loadTarget_mc", this.getNextHighestDepth());
this.loadTarget_mc.onData = function() {
    trace("Data loaded");
    trace(this.lastSiteVisited);
};
loadVariables("myData.txt", this.loadTarget_mc);
```

If you use the XML.load(), XML.sendAndLoad(), and XMLSocket.connect() methods, you should define a handler that processes the data when it arrives. This handler is a property of an XML or XMLSocket object to which you assign a function you defined. The handlers are called automatically when the information is received. For the XML object, use XML.onLoad() or XML.onData(). For the XMLSocket object, use XMLSocket.onConnect().

For more information, see "Using the XML class" on page 667 and "Using the XMLSocket class" on page 673. For more information on using LoadVars to send and load data that can be processed after the data is received, see "Using the LoadVars class" on page 653.

Creating a progress bar to display data loading progress

The following exercise dynamically creates a simple preloader using the Drawing application programming interface (API) and displays the loading progress for an XML document.

 TIP | If the remote XML file loads too quickly to see the preloading effect, try uploading a larger XML file to the internet and loading that file.

Creating a progress bar using the Drawing API:

1. Create a new Flash document and save it as **drawapi.fla**.

2. Add the following ActionScript to Frame 1 of the main Timeline:

```
var barWidth:Number = 200;
var barHeight:Number = 6;

this.createEmptyMovieClip("pBar_mc", 9999);
var bar:MovieClip = pBar_mc.createEmptyMovieClip("bar_mc", 10);
bar.beginFill(0xFF0000, 100);
bar.moveTo(0, 0);
bar.lineTo(barWidth, 0);
bar.lineTo(barWidth, barHeight);
bar.lineTo(0, barHeight);
bar.lineTo(0, 0);
bar.endFill();
bar._xscale = 0;

var stroke:MovieClip = pBar_mc.createEmptyMovieClip("stroke_mc", 20);
stroke.lineStyle(0, 0x000000);
stroke.moveTo(0, 0);
stroke.lineTo(barWidth, 0);
stroke.lineTo(barWidth, barHeight);
stroke.lineTo(0, barHeight);
stroke.lineTo(0, 0);

pBar_mc.createTextField("label_txt", 30, 0, barHeight, 100, 21);
pBar_mc.label_txt.autoSize = "left";
pBar_mc.label_txt.selectable = false;

pBar_mc._x = (Stage.width - pBar_mc._width) / 2;
pBar_mc._y = (Stage.height - pBar_mc._height) / 2;

var my_xml:XML = new XML();
my_xml.ignoreWhite = true;
my_xml.onLoad = function(success:Boolean) {
  pBar_mc.onEnterFrame = undefined;
  if (success) {
    trace("XML loaded successfully");
```

```
  } else {
    trace("Unable to load XML");
  }
};
my_xml.load("http://www.helpexamples.com/flash/xml/ds.xml");

pBar_mc.onEnterFrame = function() {
  var pctLoaded:Number = Math.floor(my_xml.getBytesLoaded() /
  my_xml.getBytesTotal() * 100);
  if (!isNaN(pctLoaded)) {
    pBar_mc.bar_mc._xscale = pctLoaded;
    pBar_mc.label_txt.text = pctLoaded + "% loaded";
    if (pctLoaded >= 100) {
      pBar_mc.onEnterFrame = undefined;
    }
  }
};
```

The previous code is broken down into seven sections. The first section defines the width
and height of the progress bar when it is drawn on the Stage. The progress bar will be
centered on the Stage in an upcoming section. The next section of code creates two movie
clips, pBar_mc and bar_mc. The bar_mc movie clip is nested inside pBar_mc, and draws a
red rectangle on the Stage. The bar_mc instance modifies its _xscale property as the
external XML file loads from the remote website.

Next, a second movie clip is nested inside of the pBar_mc movie clip, stroke_mc. The
stroke_mc movie clip draws an outline on the Stage that matches the dimensions
specified by the barHeight and barWidth variables defined in the first section. The
fourth section of code creates within the pBar_mc movie clip a text field that is used to
display what percentage of the XML file has already loaded, similar to the label on the
ProgressBar component. Next, the pBar_mc movie clip (which includes the nested
bar_mc, stroke_mc, and label_txt instances) is centered on the Stage.

The sixth section of code defines a new XML object instance, which is used to load an
external XML file. An onLoad event handler is defined and traces a message to the Output
panel. The onLoad event handler also deletes the onEnterFrame event handler (which is
defined in the next section) for the pBar_mc movie clip. The final section of code defines
an onEnterFrame event handler for the pBar_mc movie clip. This event handler monitors
how much of the external XML file has loaded and modifies the _xscale property for the
bar_mc movie clip. First the onEnterFrame event handler calculates what percentage of
the file has finished downloading. As long as the percentage of the file loaded is a valid
number, the _xscale property for bar_mc is set, and the text field within pBar_mc
displays what percentage of the file has loaded. If the file has completed loading (percent
loaded reaches 100%) the onEnterFrame event handler is deleted so download progress is
no longer monitored.

3. Select Control > Test Movie to test the Flash document.

As the external XML file loads, the nested `bar_mc` movie clip resizes to display the download progress of the XML. Once the XML file has completely loaded, the `onEnterFrame` event handler gets deleted so it doesn't continue to calculate the download progress. Depending on how fast the download completes, you should be able to see the bar slowly grow until the `bar_mc` is the same width as the `stroke_mc` movie clip. If the download occurs too fast, the progress bar may go from 0% to 100% too quickly, making the effect harder to see; in this case it may be necessary to try downloading a larger XML file.

Using HTTP to connect to server-side scripts

The %{loadVariables function}%, %{loadVariablesNum function}%, %{getURL function}%, %{loadMovie function}%, %{loadMovieNum function}% functions and the %{loadVariables (MovieClip.loadVariables method)}%, %{loadMovie (MovieClip.loadMovie method)}%, and %{getURL (MovieClip.getURL method)}% methods can communicate with server-side scripts using HTTP or HTTPS protocols. These functions and methods send all the variables from the timeline to which the function is attached. When used as methods of the MovieClip object, `loadVariables()`, `getURL()`, and `loadMovie()` send all the variables of the specified movie clip; each function (or method) handles its response as follows:

- The `getURL()` function returns any information to a browser window, not to Flash Player.
- The `loadVariables()` method loads variables into a specified timeline or level in Flash Player.
- The `loadMovie()` method loads a SWF file into a specified level or movie clip in Flash Player.

When you use `loadVariables()`, `getURL()`, or `loadMovie()`, you can specify several parameters:

- *URL* is the file in which the remote variables reside.
- *Location* is the level or target in the SWF file that receives the variables. (The `getURL()` function does not take this parameter.)

For more information about levels and targets, see "About Multiple Timelines and levels" in Flash Help.

- *Variables* sets the HTTP method, either GET (appends the variables to the end of the URL) or POST (sends the variables in a separate HTTP header), by which the variables are sent. When this parameter is omitted, Flash Player defaults to GET, but no variables are sent.

For example, if you want to track the high scores for a game, you could store the scores on a server and use loadVariables() to load them into the SWF file each time someone played the game. The function call might look like the following example:

```
this.createEmptyMovieClip("highscore_mc", 10);
loadVariables("http://www.helpexamples.com/flash/highscore.php",
  highscore_mc, "GET");
```

This example loads variables from the ColdFusion script called high_score.cfm into the movie clip instance scoreClip using the GET HTTP method.

Any variables loaded with the loadVariables() function must be in the standard MIME format *application/x-www-form-urlencoded* (a standard format used by CFM and CGI scripts). The file you specify in the *URL* parameter of loadVariables() must write out the variable and value pairs in this format so that Flash can read them. This file can specify any number of variables; variable and value pairs must be separated with an ampersand (&), and words within a value must be separated with a plus (+) sign. For example, the following phrase defines several variables:

```
highScore1=54000&playerName1=RGoulet&highScore2=53455&playerName2=
  WNewton&highScore3=42885&playerName3=TJones
```

> **NOTE** You might need to URL-encode certain characters, such as the plus (+) sign or ampersand (&) characters. For more information, see www.macromedia.com/go/tn_14143

For more information, see the following topic: "Using the LoadVars class" on page 653. Also, see %{loadVariables function}%, %{getURL function}%, %{loadMovie function}%, and the %{LoadVars}% entry in the *ActionScript 2.0 Language Reference* in Flash Help.

Using the LoadVars class

If you are publishing to Flash Player 6 or later and want more flexibility than loadVariables() offers, you can use the LoadVars class instead to transfer variables between a SWF file and a server.

The LoadVars class was introduced in Flash Player 6 to provide a cleaner, more object-oriented interface for the common task of exchanging CGI data with a web server. Advantages of the LoadVars class include the following:

- You don't need to create container movie clips for holding data or clutter existing movie clips with variables specific to client/server communication.
- The class interface is similar to that of the XML object, which provides some consistency in ActionScript. It uses the methods `load()`, `send()`, and `sendAndLoad()` to initiate communication with a server. The main difference between the LoadVars and XML classes is that the LoadVars data is a property of the LoadVars object rather than of an XML Document Object Model (DOM) tree stored in the XML object.
- The class interface is more straightforward—with methods named `load`, `send`, `sendAndLoad`—than the older loadVariables interface.
- You can get additional information about the communication, using the `getBytesLoaded` and `getBytesTotal` methods.
- You can get progress information about the download of your data (although you can't access the data until it is fully downloaded).
- The callback interface is through ActionScript methods (`onLoad`) instead of the obsolete, deprecated `onClipEvent` (data) approach required for loadVariables.
- There are error notifications.
- You can add custom HTTP request headers.

You must create a LoadVars object to call its methods. This object is a container to hold the loaded data.

The following procedure shows how to use ColdFusion and the LoadVars class to send an e-mail from a SWF file.

 NOTE You must have ColdFusion installed on your web server for this example.

To load data with the LoadVars object:

1. Create a CFM file in Macromedia Dreamweaver or in your favorite text editor. Add the following text to the file:

```
<cfif StructKeyExists(Form, "emailTo")>
<cfmail to="#Form.emailTo#" from="#Form.emailFrom#"
  subject="#Form.emailSubject#">#Form.emailBody#</cfmail>
&result=true
<cfelse>
&result=false
</cfif>
```

2. Save the file as **email.cfm**, and upload it to your website.

3. In Flash, create a new document.

4. Create four input text fields on the Stage, and give them the following instance names: **emailFrom_txt**, **emailTo_txt**, **emailSubject_txt**, and **emailBody_txt**.

5. Create a dynamic text field on the Stage with the instance name **debug_txt**.

6. Create a button symbol, drag an instance on to the Stage, and give it an instance name of **submit_btn**.

7. Select Frame 1 in the Timeline, and open the Actions panel (Window > Actions) if it isn't already open.

8. Enter the following code in the Actions panel:

```
this.submit_btn.onRelease = function() {
    var emailResponse:LoadVars = new LoadVars();
    emailResponse.onLoad = function(success:Boolean) {
    if (success) {
        debug_txt.text = this.result;
    } else {
        debug_txt.text = "error downloading content";
    }
    };
    var email:LoadVars = new LoadVars();
    email.emailFrom = emailFrom_txt.text;
    email.emailTo = emailTo_txt.text;
    email.emailSubject = emailSubject_txt.text;
    email.emailBody = emailBody_txt.text;
    email.sendAndLoad("http://www.yoursite.com/email.cfm", emailResponse,
    "POST");
};
```

This ActionScript creates a new LoadVars object instance, copies the values from the text fields into the instance, and then sends the data to the server. The CFM file sends the e mail and returns a variable (`true` or `false`) to the SWF file called `result`, which appears in the `debug_txt` text field.

 NOTE Remember to change the URL www.yoursite.com to your own domain.

9. Save the document as **sendEmail.fla**, and then publish it by selecting File > Publish.

10. Upload sendEmail.swf to the same directory that contains email.cfm (the ColdFusion file you saved and uploaded in step 2).

11. View and test the SWF file in a browser.

For more information, see the %{LoadVars}% entry in the *ActionScript 2.0 Language Reference* in Flash Help.

Flash Player 8 introduced the onHTTPStatus event handler for the LoadVars class, XML class, and MovieClipLoader class to allow users to access the status code from an HTTP request. This allows developers to determine *why* a particular load operation may have failed instead of only being able to determine that a load operation already has failed.

The following example shows how you can use the LoadVars class's onHTTPStatus event handler to check whether a text file successfully downloaded from the server and what the status code returned from the HTTP request was.

To check HTTP status with the LoadVars object:

1. Create a new Flash document and save it as **loadvars.fla**.

2. Add the following ActionScript to Frame 1 of the main Timeline:

```
this.createTextField("params_txt", 10, 10, 10, 100, 21);
params_txt.autoSize = "left";

var my_lv:LoadVars = new LoadVars();
my_lv.onHTTPStatus = function(httpStatus:Number) {
  trace("HTTP status is: " + httpStatus);
};
my_lv.onLoad = function(success:Boolean) {
  if (success) {
    trace("text file successfully loaded");
    params_txt.text = my_lv.dayNames;
  } else {
    params_txt.text = "unable to load text file";
  }
};
my_lv.load("http://www.helpexamples.com/flash/404.txt");
/* output:
  Error opening URL "http://www.helpexamples.com/flash/404.txt"
  HTTP status is: 404
*/
```

The previous code creates a new text field on the Stage and enables text field autosizing. Next, a LoadVars object is created and two event handlers: onHTTPStatus and onLoad. The onHTTPStatus event handler is new to Flash Player 8 and is invoked when a LoadVars.load() or LoadVars.sendAndLoad() operation has completed. The value passed to the onHTTPStatus event handler function (httpStatus in the previous code) contains the HTTP status code definition for the current load operation. If the SWF file was able to successfully load the text file, the value of httpStatus is set to 200 (HTTP status code for "OK"). If the file didn't exist on the server, the value of httpStatus is set to 404 (HTTP status code for "Not Found"). The second event handler, LoadVars.onLoad(), gets called after the file has finished loading. If the file successfully loaded, the value of the success parameter is set to true, otherwise the success parameter is set to false. Finally, the external file is loaded using the LoadVars.load() method.

3. Select Control > Test Movie to test the Flash document.

Flash displays an error message to the Output panel stating that it was unable to load the image because it doesn't exist on the server. The onHTTPStatus event handler traces the status code of 404 since the file could not be found on the server, and the onLoad event handler sets the params_txt text field's text property to "unable to load text file."

> **CAUTION** If a web server does not return a status code to the Flash Player, the number 0 is returned to the onHTTPStatus event handler.

About file uploading and downloading

The FileReference class lets you add the ability to upload and download files between a client and server. Your users can upload or download files between their computer and a server. Users are prompted to select a file to upload or a location for download in a dialog box (such as the Open dialog box on the Windows operating system).

Each FileReference object that you create with ActionScript refers to a single file on the user's hard disk. The object has properties that contain information about the file's size, type, name, creation date, and modification date. On the Macintosh, there is also a property for the file's creator type.

You can create an instance of the FileReference class in two ways. You can use the following new operator:

```
import flash.net.FileReference;
var myFileReference:FileReference = new FileReference();
```

Or, you can call the `FileReferenceList.browse()` method, which opens a dialog box on the user's system to prompt the user to select a file to upload and then creates an array of FileReference objects if the user selects one or more files successfully. Each FileReference object represents a file selected by the user from the dialog box. A FileReference object does not contain any data in the FileReference properties (such as `name`, `size`, or `modificationDate`) until the `FileReference.browse()` method or `FileReferenceList.browse()` method has been called and the user has selected a file from the file picker or until the `FileReference.download()` method has been used to select a file from the file picker.

> **NOTE** `FileReference.browse()` lets the user select a single file. `FileReferenceList.browse()` lets the user select multiple files.

After a successful call to the `browse()` method, you call `FileReference.upload()` to upload one file at a time.

You can also add download functionality to your Flash application. The `FileReference.download()` method prompts end users for a location on their hard disks to save a file from a server. This method also initiates downloading from a remote URL. When using the `download()` method, only the `FileReference.name` property is accessible when the `onSelect` event is dispatched. The rest of the properties are not accessible until the `onComplete` event is dispatched.

> **NOTE** When a dialog box appears on the end-user's computer, the default location that appears in the dialog box is the most recently browsed folder (if that location can be determined) or the desktop (if the recent folder cannot be determined). The FileReference and FileReferenceList APIs do not let you set the default file location

For information on the functionality and security of the FileReference API, see "About FileReference API functionality and security" on page 659. For an example of an application that uses the FileReference API, see "Adding file upload functionality to an application" on page 660. You can find the sample source file for this example, FileUpload.fla, in the Samples folder on your hard disk.

- In Windows, browse to *boot drive*\Program Files\Macromedia\Flash 8\Samples and Tutorials\Samples\ActionScript\FileUpload.
- On the Macintosh, browse to *Macintosh HD*/Applications/Macromedia Flash 8/Samples and Tutorials/Samples/ActionScript/FileUpload.

For information on each method, property, and event of the FileReference API, see `%{FileReference (flash.net.FileReference)}%` and `%{FileReferenceList (flash.net.FileReferenceList)}%` in the *ActionScript 2.0 Language Reference* in Flash Help.

About FileReference API functionality and security

Flash Player and the FileReference API (see "About file uploading and downloading" on page 657) support file uploading and downloading up to 100 MB. The FileReference API does *not* let the Flash application that initiates the file transfer do the following:

- Access the uploaded or downloaded file
- Access the path of the file on the user's computer

When a server requires authentication, the only potentially successful operation is to perform file downloading using the Flash Player browser plug-in. Uploading on all Flash players, or downloading through the stand-alone or external Flash Player, fails on a server that requires authentication. Use FileReference event listeners to determine whether operations completed successfully or to handle errors.

Both file uploading and downloading are restricted to the SWF file's domain, including any domains that you specify using a cross-domain policy file. You need to put a policy file on the server if the SWF file that initiates the uploading or downloading doesn't come from the same domain as the server. For more information on cross-domain policy files and security, see "About domains, cross-domain security, and SWF files" on page 708.

When calls to `FileReference.browse()`, `FileReferenceList.browse()`, or `FileReference.download()` are executing, playback of the SWF file pauses on the following platforms: Mac OS X Flash Player browser plug-ins, the Macintosh external Flash Player, and the Macintosh stand-alone player on Mac OS X 10.1 and earlier. The SWF file continues to run on all Windows players and in the Macintosh stand-alone Flash Player on Mac OS X 10.2 and later.

> **WARNING**
>
> When allowing users to upload files to a server, you should always be careful to check the file type before saving the file to the hard disk. For example, you wouldn't want to allow a user to upload a server-side script that could be used to delete folders or files on the server. If you only want to allow users to upload an image file, make sure the server-side script that uploads the files checks that the file being uploaded is a valid image.

For an example of an application that uses the FileReference API, see "Adding file upload functionality to an application" on page 660.

Adding file upload functionality to an application

The following procedure shows you how to build an application that lets you upload image files to a server. The application lets users select an image on their hard disks to upload and then send it to a server. The image that they upload then appears in the SWF file that they used to upload the image.

Following the example that builds the Flash application is an example that details the server-side code. Remember that image files are restricted in size: you can only upload images that are 200K or smaller.

To build a FLA application using the FileReference API:

1. Create a new Flash document and save it as **fileref.fla**.

2. Open the Components panel, and then drag a ScrollPane component onto the Stage and give it an instance name of **imagePane**. (The ScrollPane instance is sized and repositioned using ActionScript in a later step.)

3. Drag a Button component onto the Stage and give it an instance name of **uploadBtn**.

4. Drag two Label components onto the Stage and give them instance names of **imageLbl** and **statusLbl**.

5. Drag a ComboBox component onto the Stage and give it an instance name of **imagesCb**.

6. Drag a TextArea component onto the Stage and give it an instance name of **statusArea**.

7. Create a new movie clip symbol on the Stage, and open the symbol for editing (double-click the instance to open it in symbol-editing mode).

8. Create a new static text field inside the movie clip, and then add the following text:

   The file that you have tried to download is not on the server.

   In the final application, this warning might appear for one of the following reasons, among others:

   - The image was deleted from the queue on the server as other images were uploaded.
   - The server did not copy the image because the file size exceeded 200K.
   - The type of file was not a valid JPEG, GIF, or PNG file.

   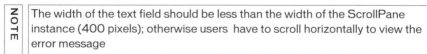

   NOTE: The width of the text field should be less than the width of the ScrollPane instance (400 pixels); otherwise users have to scroll horizontally to view the error message

9. Right-click the symbol in the Library and select Linkage from the context menu.

10. Select the Export for ActionScript and Export in First Frame check boxes, and type **Message** into the Identifier text box. Click OK.

11. Add the following ActionScript to Frame 1 of the Timeline:

```
import flash.net.FileReference;

imagePane.setSize(400, 350);
imagePane.move(75, 25);
uploadBtn.move(75, 390);
uploadBtn.label = "Upload Image";
imageLbl.move(75, 430);
imageLbl.text = "Select Image";
statusLbl.move(210, 390);
statusLbl.text = "Status";
imagesCb.move(75, 450);
statusArea.setSize(250, 100);
statusArea.move(210, 410);

/* The listener object listens for FileReference events. */
var listener:Object = new Object();

/* When the user selects a file, the onSelect() method is called, and
   passed a reference to the FileReference object. */
listener.onSelect = function(selectedFile:FileReference):Void {
   /* Update the TextArea to notify the user that Flash is attempting to
   upload the image. */
   statusArea.text += "Attempting to upload " + selectedFile.name + "\n";
   /* Upload the file to the PHP script on the server. */
   selectedFile.upload("http://www.helpexamples.com/flash/file_io/
   uploadFile.php");
};

/* When the file begins to upload, the onOpen() method is called, so
   notify the user that the file is starting to upload. */
listener.onOpen = function(selectedFile:FileReference):Void {
   statusArea.text += "Opening " + selectedFile.name + "\n";
};

/* When the file has uploaded, the onComplete() method is called. */
listener.onComplete = function(selectedFile:FileReference):Void {
   /* Notify the user that Flash is starting to download the image. */
   statusArea.text += "Downloading " + selectedFile.name + " to
   player\n";
   /* Add the image to the ComboBox component. */
   imagesCb.addItem(selectedFile.name);
   /* Set the selected index of the ComboBox to that of the most recently
   added image. */
   imagesCb.selectedIndex = imagesCb.length - 1;
   /* Call the custom downloadImage() function. */
```

```
    downloadImage();
};

var imageFile:FileReference = new FileReference();
imageFile.addListener(listener);

imagePane.addEventListener("complete", imageDownloaded);
imagesCb.addEventListener("change", downloadImage);
uploadBtn.addEventListener("click", uploadImage);

/* If the image does not download, the event object's total property will
   equal -1. In that case, display a message to the user. */
function imageDownloaded(event:Object):Void {
   if (event.total == -1) {
      imagePane.contentPath = "Message";
   }
}

/* When the user selects an image from the ComboBox, or when the
   downloadImage() function is called directly from the
   listener.onComplete() method, the downloadImage() function sets the
   contentPath of the ScrollPane in order to start downloading the image
   to the player. */
function downloadImage(event:Object):Void {
   imagePane.contentPath = "http://www.helpexamples.com/flash/file_io/
   images/" + imagesCb.value;
}

/* When the user clicks the button, Flash calls the uploadImage()
   function, and it opens a file browser dialog box. */
function uploadImage(event:Object):Void {
   imageFile.browse([{description: "Image Files", extension:
   "*.jpg;*.gif;*.png"}]);
}
```

This ActionScript code first imports the FileReference class and initializes, positions, and resizes each of the components on the Stage. Next, a listener object is defined, and three event handlers are defined: onSelect, onOpen, and onComplete. The listener object is then added to a new FileReference object named imageFile. Next, event listeners are added to the imagePane ScrollPane instance, imagesCb ComboBox instance, and uploadBtn Button instance. Each of the event listener functions is defined in the code that follows this section of code.

The first function, imageDownloaded(), checks to see if the amount of total bytes for the downloaded images is -1, and if so, it sets the contentPath for the ScrollPane instance to the movie clip with the linkage identifier of Message, which you created in a previous step. The second function, downloadImage(), attempts to download the recently uploaded image into the ScrollPane instance. When the image has downloaded, the imageDownloaded() function defined earlier is triggered and checks to see whether the image successfully downloaded. The final function, uploadImage(), opens a file browser dialog box, which filters all JPEG, GIF, and PNG images.

12. Save your changes to the document.

13. Select File > Publish settings and then select the Formats tab, and make sure that Flash and HTML are both selected.

14. (Optional) In the Publish Settings dialog box, select the Flash tab, and then select Access Network Only from the Local Playback Security pop-up menu.

If you complete this step, you won't run into security restrictions if you test your document in a local browser.

15. In the Publish Settings dialog box, click Publish to create the HTML and SWF files.

When you're finished, go on to the next procedure, in which you create the container for the SWF file.

You can find the sample source file for this example, FileUpload.fla, in the Samples folder on your hard disk.

- In Windows, browse to *boot drive*\Program Files\Macromedia\Flash 8\ Samples and Tutorials\Samples\ActionScript\FileUpload.

- On the Macintosh, browse to *Macintosh HD*/Applications/Macromedia Flash 8/ Samples and Tutorials/Samples/ActionScript/FileUpload.

The following procedure requires that PHP is installed on your web server and that you have write permissions to subfolders named images and temporary. You need to first complete the previous procedure, or use the finished SWF file available in the previously noted folders.

To create a server-side script for the image upload application:

1. Create a new PHP document using a text editor such as Dreamweaver or Notepad.

2. Add the following PHP code to the document. (A code overview follows this script.)

```php
<?php

$MAXIMUM_FILESIZE = 1024 * 200; // 200KB
$MAXIMUM_FILE_COUNT = 10; // keep maximum 10 files on server
echo exif_imagetype($_FILES['Filedata']);
if ($_FILES['Filedata']['size'] <= $MAXIMUM_FILESIZE) {
  move_uploaded_file($_FILES['Filedata']['tmp_name'], "./temporary/
  ".$_FILES['Filedata']['name']);
  $type = exif_imagetype("./temporary/".$_FILES['Filedata']['name']);
  if ($type == 1 || $type == 2 || $type == 3) {
    rename("./temporary/".$_FILES['Filedata']['name'], "./images/
  ".$_FILES['Filedata']['name']);
  } else {
    unlink("./temporary/".$_FILES['Filedata']['name']);
  }
}
$directory = opendir('./images/');
$files = array();
while ($file = readdir($directory)) {
  array_push($files, array('./images/'.$file, filectime('./images/
  '.$file)));
}
usort($files, sorter);
if (count($files) > $MAXIMUM_FILE_COUNT) {
  $files_to_delete = array_splice($files, 0, count($files) -
  $MAXIMUM_FILE_COUNT);
  for ($i = 0; $i < count($files_to_delete); $i++) {
    unlink($files_to_delete[$i][0]);
  }
}
print_r($files);
closedir($directory);

function sorter($a, $b) {
  if ($a[1] == $b[1]) {
    return 0;
  } else {
    return ($a[1] < $b[1]) ? -1 : 1;
  }
}
?>
```

This PHP code first defines two constant variables: $MAXIMUM FILESIZE and $MAXIMUM_FILE_COUNT. These variables dictate the maximum size (in kilobytes) of an image being uploaded to the server (200KB), as well as how many recently uploaded files can be kept in the images folder (10). If the file size of the image currently being uploaded is less than or equal to the value of $MAXIMUM_FILESIZE, the image is moved to the temporary folder.

Next, the file type of the uploaded file is checked to ensure that the image is a JPEG, GIF, or PNG. If the image is a compatible image type, the image is copied from the temporary folder to the images folder. If the uploaded file wasn't one of the allowed image types, it is deleted from the file system.

Next, a directory listing of the image folder is created and looped over using a while loop. Each file in the images folder is added to an array and then sorted. If the current number of files in the images folder is greater than the value of $MAXIMUM_FILE_COUNT, files are deleted until there are only $MAXIMUM_FILE_COUNT images remaining. This prevents the images folder from growing to an unmanageable size, as there can be only 10 images in the folder at one time, and each image can only be 200KB or smaller (or roughly 2 MB of images at any time).

3. Save your changes to the PHP document.

4. Upload the SWF, HTML, and PHP files to your web server.

5. View the remote HTML document in a web browser, and click the Upload Image button in the SWF file.

6. Locate an image file on your hard disk and select Open from the dialog box.

   The SWF file uploads the image file to the remote PHP document, and displays it in the ScrollPane (which adds scroll bars if necessary). If you want to view a previously uploaded image, you can select the filename from the ComboBox instance on the Stage. If the user tries to upload an image that isn't an allowed image type (only a JPEG, GIF, or PNG image is allowed) or the file size is too big (over 200 KB), Flash displays the error message from the Message movie clip in the Library.

You can find the sample source file for this example, FileUpload.fla, in the Samples folder on your hard disk.

- In Windows, browse to *boot drive*\Program Files\Macromedia\Flash 8\ Samples and Tutorials\Samples\ActionScript\FileUpload.

- On the Macintosh, browse to *Macintosh HD*/Applications/Macromedia Flash 8/ Samples and Tutorials/Samples/ActionScript/FileUpload.

For more information on local file security, see "About local file security and Flash Player" on page 693.

For more information on writing PHP, go to www.php.net/.

About XML

Extensible Markup Language (XML) is becoming the standard for exchanging structured data in Internet applications. You can integrate data in Flash with servers that use XML technology to build sophisticated applications, such as chat or brokerage systems.

In XML, as with HTML, you use tags to specify, or *mark up*, a body of text. In HTML, you use predefined tags to indicate how text should appear in a web browser (for example, the `<b>` tag indicates that text should be bold). In XML, you define tags that identify the type of a piece of data (for example, `<password>VerySecret</password>`). XML separates the structure of the information from the way it appears, so the same XML document can be used and reused in different environments.

Every XML tag is called a *node*, or an element. Each node has a type (1, which indicates an XML element, or 3, which indicates a text node), and elements might also have attributes. A node nested in a node is called a *child node*. This hierarchical tree structure of nodes is called the XML DOM—much like the JavaScript DOM, which is the structure of elements in a web browser.

In the following example, `<portfolio>` is the parent node; it has no attributes and contains the child node `<holding>`, which has the attributes `symbol`, `qty`, `price`, and `value`:

```
<portfolio>
   <holding symbol="rich"
     qty="75"
     price="245.50"
     value="18412.50" />
</portfolio>
```

For more information, see the following topics:

- "Using the XML class" on page 667
- "Using the XMLSocket class" on page 673

For more information on XML, see www.w3.org/XML.

There are several sample files on your hard disk that load XML into a SWF file at runtime. One sample demonstrates how to create a web log tracker by loading, parsing, and manipulating XML data. You can find the sample source file, xml_blogTracker.fla, in the Samples folder on your hard disk.

- In Windows, browse to *boot drive*\Program Files\Macromedia\Flash 8\ Samples and Tutorials\Samples\ActionScript\XML_BlogTracker.
- On the Macintosh, browse to *Macintosh HD*/Applications/Macromedia Flash 8/ Samples and Tutorials/Samples/ActionScript/XML_BlogTracker.

A second sample demonstrates how to use XML and nested arrays to select strings of different languages to populate text fields. You can find the sample source file, xml_languagePicker.fla, in the Samples folder on your hard disk.

- In Windows, browse to *boot drive*\Program Files\Macromedia\Flash 8\ Samples and Tutorials\Samples\ActionScript\XML_LanguagePicker.

- On the Macintosh, browse to *Macintosh HD*/Applications/Macromedia Flash 8/ Samples and Tutorials/Samples/ActionScript/XML_LanguagePicker.

A third sample demonstrates how to create a dynamic menu with XML data. The sample calls the ActionScript `XmlMenu()` constructor and passes it two parameters: the path to the XML menu file and a reference to the current timeline. The rest of the functionality resides in a custom class file, XmlMenu.as.

You can find the sample source file, xmlmenu.fla, in the Samples folder on your hard disk.

- On Windows, browse to *boot drive*\Program Files\Macromedia\Flash 8\ Samples and Tutorials\Samples\ActionScript\XML_Menu.

- On the Macintosh, browse to *Macintosh HD*/Applications/Macromedia Flash 8/ Samples and Tutorials/Samples/ActionScript/XML_Menu.

Using the XML class

The methods of the ActionScript XML class (for example, `appendChild()`, `removeNode()`, and `InsertBefore()`) let you structure XML data in Flash to send to a server and manipulate and interpret downloaded XML data.

The following XML class methods send and load XML data to a server by using the HTTP POST method:

- The `load()` method downloads XML from a URL and places it in an ActionScript XML object.

- The `send()` method encodes the XML object into an XML document and sends it to a specified URL using the POST method. If specified, a browser window displays returned data.

- The `sendAndLoad()` method sends an XML object to a URL. Any returned information is placed in an ActionScript XML object.

For example, you could create a brokerage system that stores all its information (user names, passwords, session IDs, portfolio holdings, and transaction information) in a database.

The server-side script that passes information between Flash and the database reads and writes the data in XML format. You can use ActionScript to convert information collected in the SWF file (for example, a user name and password) to an XML object and then send the data to the server-side script as an XML document. You can also use ActionScript to load the XML document that the server returns into an XML object to be used in the SWF file.

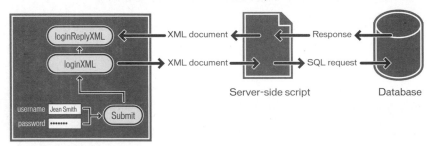

The flow and conversion of data between a SWF file, a server-side script, and a database

The password validation for the brokerage system requires two scripts: a function defined on Frame 1, and a script that creates and then sends the XML objects created in the document.

When a user enters information into text fields in the SWF file with the variables `username` and `password`, the variables must be converted to XML before being passed to the server. The first section of the script loads the variables into a newly created XML object called `loginXML`. When a user clicks a button to log in, the `loginXML` object is converted to a string of XML and sent to the server.

The following ActionScript is placed on the timeline and is used to send XML-formatted data to the server. To understand this script, read the commented lines (indicated by the characters //):

```
// ignore XML white space
XML.prototype.ignoreWhite = true;
// Construct an XML object to hold the server's reply
var loginReplyXML:XML = new XML();
// this function triggers when an XML packet is received from the server.
loginReplyXML.onLoad = function(success:Boolean) {
  if (success) {
    // (optional) Create two text fields for status/debugging
    // status_txt.text = this.firstChild.attributes.status;
    // debug_txt.text = this.firstChild;
    switch (this.firstChild.attributes.STATUS) {
    case 'OK' :
      _global.session = this.firstChild.attributes.SESSION;
      trace(_global.session);
      gotoAndStop("welcome");
      break;
    case 'FAILURE' :
      gotoAndStop("loginfailure");
      break;
    default :
      // this should never happen
      trace("Unexpected value received for STATUS.");
    }
  } else {
    trace("an error occurred.");
  }
};
// this function triggers when the login_btn is clicked
login_btn.onRelease = function() {
  var loginXML:XML = new XML();
  // create XML formatted data to send to the server
  var loginElement:XMLNode = loginXML.createElement("login");
  loginElement.attributes.username = username_txt.text;
  loginElement.attributes.password = password_txt.text;
  loginXML.appendChild(loginElement);
  // send the XML formatted data to the server
  loginXML.sendAndLoad("http://www.flash-mx.com/mm/main.cfm",
  loginReplyXML);
};
```

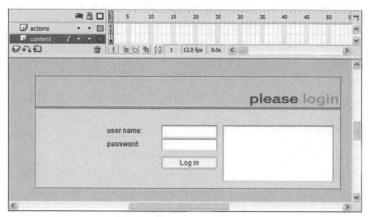

You can test this code by using a user name of JeanSmith and the password VerySecret. The first section of the script generates the following XML when the user clicks the login button:

```
<login username="JeanSmith" password="VerySecret" />
```

The server receives the XML, generates an XML response, and sends it back to the SWF file. If the password is accepted, the server responds with the following:

```
<LOGINREPLY STATUS="OK" SESSION="4D968511" />
```

This XML includes a session attribute that contains a unique, randomly generated session ID, which is used in all communications between the client and server for the rest of the session. If the password is rejected, the server responds with the following message:

```
<LOGINREPLY STATUS="FAILURE" />
```

The loginreply XML node must load into a blank XML object in the SWF file. The following statement creates the XML object loginreplyXML to receive the XML node:

```
// Construct an XML object to hold the server's reply
var loginReplyXML:XML = new XML();
loginReplyXML.onLoad = function(success:Boolean) {
```

The second statement in this ActionScript defines an anonymous (inline) function, which is called when the onLoad event triggers.

The login button (login_btn instance) is used to send the user name and password as XML to the server and to load an XML response back into the SWF file. You can use the sendAndLoad() method to do this, as shown in the following example:

```
loginXML.sendAndLoad("http://www.flash-mx.com.com/mm/main.cfm",
  loginReplyXML);
```

First, the XML-formatted data is created, using the values that the user inputs in the SWF file, and that XML object is sent using the `sendAndLoad` method. Similar to data from a `loadVariables()` function, the `loginreply` XML element arrives asynchronously (that is, it doesn't wait for results before being returned) and loads into the `loginReplyXML` object. When the data arrives, the `onLoad` handler of the `loginReplyXML` object is called. You must define the `loginReplyXML` function, which is called when the `onLoad` handler triggers, so it can process the `loginreply` element.

NOTE This function must always be on the frame that contains the ActionScript for the login button.

If the login is successful, the SWF file progresses to the `welcome` frame label. If the login is not successful, then the playhead moves to the `loginfailure` frame label. This is processed using a condition and case statement. For more information on case and break statements, see %{case statement}% and %{break statement}% in the *ActionScript 2.0 Language Reference* in Flash Help. For more information on conditions, see %{if statement}% and %{else statement}% in the *ActionScript 2.0 Language Reference* in Flash Help.

NOTE This design is only an example, and Macromedia can make no claims about the level of security it provides. If you are implementing a secure password-protected system, make sure you have a good understanding of network security.

For more information, see Integrating XML and Flash in a Web Application at www.macromedia.com/support/flash/interactivity/xml/ and the %{XML}% entry in the *ActionScript 2.0 Language Reference* in Flash Help. For more information on local file security, see "About local file security and Flash Player" on page 693.

You can find a sample source file, login.fla, in the Samples folder on your hard disk. This sample shows how to add simple login functionality to your websites using ActionScript 2.0. The sample uses ActionScript and components to create a small form in which you enter a user name and password and then click a button to enter a site.

- In Windows, browse to *boot drive*\Program Files\Macromedia\Flash 8\ Samples and Tutorials\Samples\ActionScript\Login.

- On the Macintosh, browse to *Macintosh HD*/Applications/Macromedia Flash 8/ Samples and Tutorials/Samples/ActionScript/Login.

Flash Player 8 introduced the `onHTTPStatus` event handler for the XML class, LoadVars class, and MovieClipLoader class to allow users to access the status code from an HTTP request. This allows developers to determine *why* a particular load operation may have failed instead of only being able to determine that a load operation already has failed.

The following example shows how you can use the XML class's `onHTTPStatus` event handler to check whether an XML file successfully downloaded from the server and what the status code returned from the HTTP request was.

Checking HTTP status codes using the XML class:

1. Create a new Flash document and save it as **xmlhttp.fla**.

2. Add the following ActionScript to Frame 1 of the main Timeline:

```
var my_xml:XML = new XML();
my_xml.ignoreWhite = true;
my_xml.onHTTPStatus = function(httpStatus:Number) {
  trace("HTTP status is: " + httpStatus);
};
my_xml.onLoad = function(success:Boolean) {
  if (success) {
    trace("XML successfully loaded");
    // 0 (No error; parse was completed successfully.)
    trace("XML status is: " + my_xml.status);
  } else {
    trace("unable to load XML");
  }
};
my_xml.load("http://www.helpexamples.com/crossdomain.xml");
```

The previous code defines a new XML object with the variable name `my_xml`, defines two event handlers (`onHTTPStatus` and `onLoad`), and loads an external XML file. The `onLoad` event handler checks to see whether the XML file was successfully loaded and if so sends a message to the Output panel as well as traces the XML object's status property. It is important to remember that the `onHTTPStatus` event listener returns the status code returned from the web server, whereas the `XML.status` property contains a numeric value that indicates whether the XML object was able to be parsed successfully.

3. Select Control > Test Movie to test the Flash document.

> **TIP**
>
> The `XML.onHTTPStatus` event handler is new to Flash Player 8.

> **WARNING**
>
> Don't confuse the HTTP httpStatus codes with the XML class's `status` property. The `onHTTPStatus` event handler returns the server's status code from an HTTP request and the `status` property automatically sets and returns a numeric value that indicates whether an XML document was successfully parsed into an XML object.

> **CAUTION**
>
> If a web server does not return a `status` code to the Flash Player, the number 0 is returned to the `onHTTPStatus` event handler.

There are several sample files on your hard disk that load XML into a SWF file at runtime. One sample demonstrates how to create a web log tracker by loading, parsing, and manipulating XML data. You can find the sample source file, xml_blogTracker.fla, in the Samples folder on your hard disk.

- In Windows, browse to *boot drive*\Program Files\Macromedia\Flash 8\ Samples and Tutorials\Samples\ActionScript\XML_BlogTracker.
- On the Macintosh, browse to *Macintosh HD*/Applications/Macromedia Flash 8/ Samples and Tutorials/Samples/ActionScript/XML_BlogTracker.

A second sample demonstrates how to use XML and nested arrays to select strings of different languages to populate text fields. You can find the sample source file, xml_languagePicker.fla, in the Samples folder on your hard disk.

- In Windows, browse to *boot drive*\Program Files\Macromedia\Flash 8\Samples and Tutorials\Samples\ActionScript\XML_LanguagePicker.
- On the Macintosh, browse to *Macintosh HD*/Applications/Macromedia Flash 8/Samples and Tutorials/Samples/ActionScript/XML_LanguagePicker.

A third sample demonstrates how to create a dynamic menu with XML data. The sample calls the ActionScript XmlMenu() constructor and passes it two parameters: the path to the XML menu file and a reference to the current timeline. The rest of the functionality resides in a custom class file, XmlMenu.as.

You can find the sample source file, xmlmenu.fla, in the Samples folder on your hard disk.

- On Windows, browse to *boot drive*\Program Files\Macromedia\Flash 8\Samples and Tutorials\Samples\ActionScript\XML_Menu.
- On the Macintosh, browse to *Macintosh HD*/Applications/Macromedia Flash 8/Samples and Tutorials/Samples/ActionScript/XML_Menu.

Using the XMLSocket class

ActionScript provides a built-in XMLSocket class, which lets you open a continuous connection with a server. A socket connection lets the server publish, or *push*, information to the client as soon as that information is available. Without a continuous connection, the server must wait for an HTTP request. This open connection removes latency issues and is commonly used for real-time applications such as chats. The data is sent over the socket connection as one string and should be formatted as XML. You can use the XML class to structure the data.

To create a socket connection, you must create a server-side application to wait for the socket connection request and send a response to the SWF file. This type of server-side application can be written in a programming language such as Java.

<table>
<tr><td>NOTE</td><td>The XMLSocket class cannot tunnel through firewalls automatically because, unlike the Real-Time Messaging Protocol (RTMP), XMLSocket has no HTTP tunneling capability. If you need to use HTTP tunneling, consider using Flash Remoting or Flash Communication Server (which supports RTMP) instead.</td></tr>
</table>

You can use the `connect()` and `send()` methods of the XMLSocket class to transfer XML to and from a server over a socket connection. The `connect()` method establishes a socket connection with a web server port. The `send()` method passes an XML object to the server specified in the socket connection.

When you invoke the `connect()` method, Flash Player opens a TCP/IP connection to the server and keeps that connection open until one of the following events happens:

- The `close()` method of the XMLSocket class is called.
- No more references to the XMLSocket object exist.
- Flash Player exits.
- The connection is broken (for example, the modem disconnects).

The following example creates an XML socket connection and sends data from the XML object myXML. To understand the script, read the commented lines (indicated by the characters //):

```
// Create XMLSocket object
var theSocket:XMLSocket = new XMLSocket();
// Connect to a site on unused port above 1024 using connect() method.
// Enter localhost or 127.0.0.1 for local testing.
// For live server, enter your domain www.yourdomain.com
theSocket.connect("localhost", 12345);
// displays text regarding connection
theSocket.onConnect = function(myStatus) {
  if (myStatus) {
    conn_txt.text = "connection successful";
  } else {
    conn_txt.text = "no connection made";
  }
};
// data to send
function sendData() {
  var myXML:XML = new XML();
  var mySend = myXML.createElement("thenode");
  mySend.attributes.myData = "someData";
  myXML.appendChild(mySend);
  theSocket.send(myXML);
}
// button sends data
sendButton.onRelease = function() {
  sendData();
};
// traces data returned from socket connection
theSocket.onData = function(msg:String):Void {
  trace(msg);
};
```

For more information, see the %{XMLSocket}% entry in the *ActionScript 2.0 Language Reference* in Flash Help.

For more information on local file security, see "About local file security and Flash Player" on page 693.

Sending messages to and from Flash Player

To send messages from a SWF file to its host environment (for example, a web browser, a Macromedia Director movie, or the stand-alone Flash Player), you can use the `fscommand()` function. This function lets you extend your SWF file by using the capabilities of the host. For example, you could pass an `fscommand()` function to a JavaScript function in an HTML page that opens a new browser window with specific properties.

To control a SWF file in Flash Player from web browser scripting languages such as JavaScript, VBScript, and Microsoft JScript, you can use Flash Player methods—functions that send messages from a host environment to the SWF file. For example, you could have a link in an HTML page that sends your SWF file to a specific frame.

For more information, see the following topics:

- "Using the fscommand() function" on page 676
- "About using JavaScript to control Flash applications" on page 679
- "About Flash Player methods" on page 679

Using the fscommand() function

> **NOTE**
>
> The External API is a replacement for `fscommand()` in Flash 8 for interoperating with a HTML page or a container application. The External API offers more robust functionality than `fscommand()` in this situation. For more information, see "About the External API" on page 680.

You use the `fscommand()` function to send a message to whichever program is hosting Flash Player, such as a web browser.

> **NOTE**
>
> Using the `fscommand()` to call JavaScript does not work on the Safari or Internet Explorer browsers for the Macintosh.

The `fscommand()` function has two parameters: *command* and *arguments*. To send a message to the stand-alone version of Flash Player, you must use predefined commands and arguments. For example, the following event handler sets the stand-alone player to scale the SWF file to the full monitor screen size when the button is released:

```
my_btn.onRelease = function() {
  fscommand("fullscreen", true);
};
```

The following table shows the values you can specify for the *command* and *arguments* parameters of fscommand() to control the playback and appearance of a SWF file playing in the stand-alone player, including projectors.

Command	Arguments	Purpose
quit	None	Closes the projector.
fullscreen	true or false	Specifying true sets Flash Player to full-screen mode. Specifying false returns the player to normal menu view.
allowscale	true or false	Specifying false sets the player so that the SWF file is always drawn at its original size and never scaled. Specifying true forces the SWF file to scale to 100% of the player.
showmenu	true or false	Specifying true enables the full set of context menu items. Specifying false dims all the context menu items except Settings and About Flash Player.
exec	Path to application	Executes an application from within the projector.

To use fscommand() to send a message to a scripting language such as JavaScript in a web browser, you can pass any two parameters in the *command* and *arguments* parameters. These parameters can be strings or expressions and are used in a JavaScript function that "catches," or handles, the fscommand() function.

An fscommand() function invokes the JavaScript function *moviename*_DoFSCommand in the HTML page that embeds the SWF file, where *moviename* is the name of Flash Player as assigned by the name attribute of the embed tag or the id attribute of the object tag. If the SWF file is assigned the name myMovie, the JavaScript function invoked is myMovie_DoFSCommand.

To use fscommand() to open a message box from a SWF file in the HTML page through JavaScript:

1. Create a new FLA file, and save it as **myMovie.fla**.

2. Drag two instances of the Button component to the Stage and give them the instance names **window_btn** and **alert_btn**, respectively, and the labels **Open Window** and **Alert**.

3. Insert a new layer on the Timeline, and rename it **Actions**.

4. Select Frame 1 of the Actions layer, and add the following ActionScript in the Actions panel:

```
window_btn.onRelease = function() {
  fscommand("popup", "http://www.macromedia.com/");
};
alert_btn.onRelease = function() {
  fscommand("alert", "You clicked the button.");
};
```

5. Select File > Publish Settings, and make sure that Flash with FSCommand is selected in the Template menu on the HTML tab.

6. Select File > Publish to generate the SWF and HTML files.

7. In an HTML or text editor, open the HTML file that was generated in step 6 and examine the code. When you published your SWF file using the Flash with FSCommand template on the HTML tab of the Publish Settings dialog box, some additional code was inserted in the HTML file. The SWF file's `NAME` and `ID` attributes are the filename. For example, for the file myMovie.fla, the attributes would be set to `myMovie`.

8. In the HTML file, add the following JavaScript code where the document says `// Place your code here.`:

```
if (command == "alert") {
  alert(args);
} else if (command == "popup") {
  window.open(args, "mmwin", "width=500,height=300");
}
```

(For more information about publishing, see "Publishing" in Flash Help)

Alternatively, for Microsoft Internet Explorer applications, you can attach an event handler directly in the `<SCRIPT>` tag, as shown in this example:

```
<script Language="JavaScript" event="FSCommand (command, args)"
  for="theMovie">
...
</script>
```

9. Save and close the HTML file.

When you're editing HTML files outside of Flash in this way, remember that you must deselect the HTML check box in File > Publish Settings, or your HTML code is overwritten by Flash when you republish.

10. In a web browser, open the HTML file to view it. Click the Open Window button; a window is opened to the Macromedia website. Click the Alert button; an alert window appears.

The fscommand() function can send messages to Macromedia Director that are interpreted by Lingo as strings, events, or executable Lingo code. If the message is a string or an event, you must write the Lingo code to receive it from the fscommand() function and carry out an action in Director. For more information, see the Director Support Center at www.macromedia.com/support/director.

In Visual Basic, Visual C++, and other programs that can host ActiveX controls, fscommand() sends a VB event with two strings that can be handled in the environment's programming language. For more information, use the keywords *Flash method* to search the Flash Support Center at www.macromedia.com/support/flash.

About using JavaScript to control Flash applications

Flash Player 6 (6.0.40.0) and later versions support certain JavaScript methods that are specific to Flash applications, as well as FSCommand, in Netscape 6.2 and later. Earlier versions do not support these JavaScript methods and FSCommand in Netscape 6.2 or later. For more information, see the Macromedia Support Center article, "Scripting With Flash," at www.macromedia.com/support/flash/publishexport/scriptingwithflash/.

For Netscape 6.2 and later, you do not need to set the swliveconnect attribute to true. However, setting swLiveConnect to true has no adverse effects on your SWF file. For more information, see the swLiveConnect attribute in "Parameters and attributes" in Flash Help.

About Flash Player methods

You can use Flash Player methods to control a SWF file in Flash Player from web-browser scripting languages such as JavaScript and VBScript. As with other methods, you can use Flash Player methods to send calls to SWF files from a scripting environment other than ActionScript. Each method has a name, and most methods take parameters. A parameter specifies a value upon which the method operates. The calculation performed by some methods returns a value that can be used by the scripting environment.

Two technologies enable communication between the browser and Flash Player: LiveConnect (Netscape Navigator 3.0 or later on Windows 95/98/2000/NT/XP or Power Macintosh) and ActiveX (Internet Explorer 3.0 and later on Windows 95/98/2000/NT/XP). Although the techniques for scripting are similar for all browsers and languages, there are additional properties and events available for use with ActiveX controls.

For more information, including a complete list of Flash Player scripting methods, use the keywords *Flash method* to search the Flash Support Center at www.macromedia.com/support/flash.

About the External API

The ExternalInterface class is also called the *External API*, which is a new subsystem that lets you easily communicate from ActionScript and the Flash Player container to an HTML page with JavaScript or to a desktop application that embeds Flash Player.

 NOTE This functionality replaces the older fscommand() function for interoperating with a HTML page or a container application. The External API offers more robust functionality than fscommand() in this situation. For more information, see "About the External API" on page 680.

The ExternalInterface class is available only under the following circumstances:

- In all supported versions of Internet Explorer for Windows (5.0 and later).
- In an embedded custom ActiveX container, such as a desktop application embedding the Flash Player ActiveX control.
- In any browser that supports the NPRuntime interface (which currently includes the following browsers:
  - Firefox 1.0 and later
  - Mozilla 1.7.5 and later
  - Netscape 8.0 and later
  - Safari 1.3 and later.

In all other situations, the ExternalInterface.available property returns false.

From ActionScript, you can call a JavaScript function on the HTML page. The External API offers the following improved functionality compared with fscommand():

- You can use any JavaScript function, not only the functions that you can use with %{fscommand function}%.
- You can pass any number of arguments, with any names; you aren't limited to passing a command and arguments.
- You can pass various data types (such as Boolean, Number, and String); you are no longer limited to String parameters.
- You can now receive the value of a call, and that value returns immediately to ActionScript (as the return value of the call you make).

You can call an ActionScript function from JavaScript on an HTML page. For more information, see %{ExternalInterface (flash.external.ExternalInterface)}%. For more information on local file security, see "About local file security and Flash Player" on page 693.

The following sections contain examples that use the External API:

- "Creating interaction with the External API" on page 681
- "Controlling Flash Video with the External API" on page 684

Creating interaction with the External API

You can create interaction between the browser and a SWF file that's embedded on a web page. The following procedure sends text to the HTML page that contains the SWF file, and the HTML sends a message back to the SWF file at runtime.

To create the Flash application:

1. Create a new Flash document and save it as **extint.fla**.

2. Drag two TextInput components onto the Stage and give them instance names of **in_ti** and **out_ti**.

3. Drag a Label component onto the Stage, assign it an instance name of **out_lbl**, position it above the out_ti TextInput instance, and set the text property in the Parameters tab of the Property inspector to **Sending to JS:**.

4. Drag a Button component onto the Stage, position it next to the out_lbl label, and give it an instance name of **send_button**.

5. Drag a Label component onto the Stage, assign it an instance name of **in_lbl**, position it above the in_ti TextInput instance, and set its text property in the Parameters tab to **Receiving from JS:**.

6. Add the following ActionScript to Frame 1 of the main Timeline:

```
import flash.external.ExternalInterface;

ExternalInterface.addCallback("asFunc", this, asFunc);
function asFunc(str:String):Void {
   in_ti.text = "JS > Hello " + str;
}

send_button.addEventListener("click", clickListener);
function clickListener(eventObj:Object):Void {
   trace("click > " + out_ti.text);
   ExternalInterface.call("jsFunc", out_ti.text);
}
```

The previous code is split into three sections. The first section imports the ExternalInterface class so you don't have to use its fully qualified class name. The second section of code defines a callback function, asFunc(), which is called from JavaScript in an HTML document created in an upcoming example. This function sets the text within a TextInput component on the Stage. The third section of code defines a function and assigns it as an event listener for when the user clicks the Button component instance on the Stage. Whenever the button is clicked, the SWF file calls the jsFunc() JavaScript function in the HTML page and passes the text property of the out_ti text input instance.

7. Select File > Publish Settings and then select the Formats tab and make sure that Flash and HTML are both selected.

8. Click Publish to create the HTML and SWF files.

   When you're finished, go on to the next procedure to create the container for the SWF file.

Before you can test the previous Flash document, you need to modify the generated HTML code and add some additional HTML and JavaScript. The following procedure modifies the HTML container for the SWF file so the two files can interact when they run in a browser.

To create the HTML container for the SWF file:

1. Complete the previous procedure.

2. Open the extint.html file that Flash creates when you publish the application.

   It's in the same folder as the Flash document.

3. Add the following JavaScript code between the opening and closing head tags:

```
<script language="JavaScript">
<!--
   function thisMovie(movieName) {
     var isIE = navigator.appName.indexOf("Microsoft") != -1;
     return (isIE) ? window[movieName] : document[movieName];
   }

   function makeCall(str) {
     thisMovie("extint").asFunc(str);
   }

   function jsFunc(str) {
     document.inForm.inField.value = "AS > Hello " + str;
   }
// -->
</script>
```

This JavaScript code defines three methods. The first method returns a reference to the embedded SWF file based on whether the user's browser is Microsoft Internet Explorer (IE) or a Mozilla browser. The second function, makeCall(), calls the asFunc() method that you defined within the Flash document in the previous example. The "extint" parameter in the thisMovie() function call refers to the object ID and embed name of the embedded SWF file. If you saved your Flash document with a different name, you need to change this string to match the values in the object and embed tags. The third function, jsFunc(), sets the value of the inField text field in the HTML document. This function is called from the Flash document when a user clicks the send_button Button component.

4. Add the following HTML code before the closing </body> tag:

```
<form name="outForm" method="POST"
   action="javascript:makeCall(document.outForm.outField.value);">
   Sending to AS:<br />
   <input type="text" name="outField" value="" /><br />
   <input type="submit" value="Send" />
</form>

<form name="inForm" method="POST" action="">
   Receiving from AS:<br />
   <input type="text" name="inField">
</form>
```

This HTML code creates two HTML forms similar to the forms created in the Flash environment in the previous exercise. The first form submits the value of the outField text field to the makeCall() JavaScript function defined in an earlier step. The second form is used to display a value that gets sent from the SWF file when the user clicks the send button instance.

5. Save the HTML document and upload both the HTML and SWF files to a web server.

6. View the HTML file in a web browser, enter a string in the out_ti TextInput instance, and click the Send button.

   Flash calls the jsFunc() JavaScript function and passes the contents of the out_ti text field, which displays the contents in the HTML form inForm inField input text field.

7. Type a value into the outField HTML text field and click the Send button.

   Flash calls the SWF file's asFunc() function, which displays the string in the in_ti TextInput instance.

You can find the sample source file, ExtInt.fla, in the Samples folder on your hard disk.

- In Windows, browse to *boot drive*\Program Files\Macromedia\Flash 8\
  Samples and Tutorials\Samples\ActionScript\ExternalAPI\simple example.

- On the Macintosh, browse to *Macintosh HD*/Applications/Macromedia Flash 8/
  Samples and Tutorials/Samples/ActionScript/ExternalAPI/simple example.

For a more complex example that uses the External API, see "Controlling Flash Video with the External API" on page 684. For more information on local file security, see "About local file security and Flash Player" on page 693.

> **NOTE**
>
> Avoid using other methods of accessing the plug-in object, such as `document.getElementById("pluginName")` or `document.all.pluginName`, because these other methods do not work consistently across all browsers.

Controlling Flash Video with the External API

The following procedure shows you how to control Flash Video (FLV) files using controls in an HTML page and displays information about the video in an HTML text field. This procedure uses the External API to achieve this functionality.

To build a Flash application using the External API:

1. Create a new Flash document and save it as **video.fla**.

2. Add a new video symbol to the library by selecting New Video from the pop-up menu in the Library panel.

3. Drag the video symbol to the Stage and give it an instance name of **selected_video**.

4. Select the `selected_video` instance and then the Property inspector to resize the instance to **320** pixels wide by **240** pixels high.

5. Set both the *x* and *y* coordinates for the video's position to **0**.

6. Select the Stage and use the Property inspector to resize its dimensions to **320** pixels by **240** pixels.

   Now the Stage matches the dimensions of the video instance.

7. Add the following ActionScript to Frame 1 of the main Timeline:

```
import flash.external.ExternalInterface;

/* Register playVideo() and pauseResume() so that it is possible
to call them from JavaScript in the container HTML page. */
ExternalInterface.addCallback("playVideo", null, playVideo);
ExternalInterface.addCallback("pauseResume", null, pauseResume);

/* The video requires a NetConnection and NetStream object. */
var server_nc:NetConnection = new NetConnection();
server_nc.connect(null);
var video_ns:NetStream = new NetStream(server_nc);

/* Attach the NetStream object to the Video object on Stage so
that the NetStream data is displayed in the Video object. */
selected_video.attachVideo(video_ns);

/* The onStatus() method is called automatically when the status of
the NetStream object is updated (the video starts playing, for example).
When that occurs, send the value of the code property to the HTML page by
calling the JavaScript updateStatus() function via ExternalInterface. */
video_ns.onStatus = function(obj:Object):Void {
   ExternalInterface.call("updateStatus", "   " + obj.code);
};

function playVideo(url:String):Void {
   video_ns.play(url);
}

function pauseResume():Void {
   video_ns.pause();
}
```

The first part of this ActionScript code defines two ExternalInterface callback functions, playVideo() and pauseResume(). These functions are called from the JavaScript in the next procedure. The second part of the code creates a new NetConnection and NetStream object, which you use with the video instance to dynamically play back FLV files.

The code in the next procedure defines an onStatus event handler for the video_ns NetStream object. Whenever the NetStream object changes its status, Flash uses the ExternalInterface.call() method to trigger the custom JavaScript function, updateStatus(). The final two functions, playVideo() and pauseResume(), control the playback of the video instance on the Stage. Both of these functions are called from JavaScript written in the following procedure.

8. Save the Flash document.

9. Select File > Publish Settings and then select the Formats tab, and make sure that HTML and Flash are both selected.

10. Click Publish to publish the SWF and HTML files to your hard disk.

When you're finished, go on to the next procedure to create the container for the SWF file.

You can find the sample source file, external.fla, in the Samples folder on your hard disk.

- In Windows, browse to *boot drive*\Program Files\Macromedia\Flash 8\ Samples and Tutorials\Samples\ActionScript\ExternalAPI.

- On the Macintosh, browse to *Macintosh HD*/Applications/Macromedia Flash 8/ Samples and Tutorials/Samples/ActionScript/ExternalAPI.

In the following procedure, you modify the HTML code generated by Flash in the previous procedure. This procedure creates the JavaScript and HTML required to make the FLV files play back within the SWF file.

To create the container for the SWF file:

1. Complete the previous procedure.

2. Open the video.html document that you published in the last step of the previous procedure.

3. Modify the existing code so that it matches the following code:

> **NOTE** Review the code comments in the following example. A code overview follows this code example.

```
<!DOCTYPE html PUBLIC "-//W3C//DTD XHTML 1.0 Transitional//EN" "http://
  www.w3.org/TR/xhtml1/DTD/xhtml1-transitional.dtd">
<html xmlns="http://www.w3.org/1999/xhtml" xml:lang="en" lang="en">
<head>
<meta http-equiv="Content-Type" content="text/html; charset=iso-8859-1"
  />
<title>ExternalInterface</title>

<script language="JavaScript">
  // Use a variable to reference the embedded SWF file.
  var flashVideoPlayer;

  /* When the HTML page loads (through the onLoad event of the <body>
  tag), it calls the initialize() function. */
  function initialize() {
    /* Check whether the browser is IE. If so, flashVideoPlayer is
  window.videoPlayer. Otherwise, it's document.videoPlayer. The
  videoPlayer is the ID assigned to the <object> and <embed> tags. */
    var isIE = navigator.appName.indexOf("Microsoft") != -1;
    flashVideoPlayer = (isIE) ? window['videoPlayer'] :
  document['videoPlayer'];
  }
```

```
    /* When the user clicks the play button in the form, update the
    videoStatus text area, and call the playVideo() function within the
    SWF file, passing it the URL of the FLV file. */
    function callFlashPlayVideo() {
       var comboBox = document.forms['videoForm'].videos;
       var video = comboBox.options[comboBox.selectedIndex].value;
       updateStatus("____" + video + "____");
       flashVideoPlayer.playVideo("http://www.helpexamples.com/flash/
    video/" + video);
    }

    // Call the pauseResume() function within the SWF file.
    function callFlashPlayPauseVideo() {
       flashVideoPlayer.pauseResume();
    }

    /* The updateStatus() function is called from the SWF file from the
    onStatus() method of the NetStream object. */
    function updateStatus(message) {
       document.forms['videoForm'].videoStatus.value += message + "\n";
    }
</script>
</head>
<body bgcolor="#ffffff" onLoad="initialize();">

<object classid="clsid:d27cdb6e-ae6d-11cf-96b8-444553540000"
   codebase="http://fpdownload.macromedia.com/pub/shockwave/cabs/flash/
   swflash.cab#version=8,0,0,0" width="320" height="240" id="videoPlayer"
   align="middle">
<param name="allowScriptAccess" value="sameDomain" />
<param name="movie" value="video.swf" />
<param name="quality" value="high" />
<param name="bgcolor" value="#ffffff" />
<embed src="video.swf" quality="high" bgcolor="#ffffff" width="320"
   height="240" name="videoPlayer" align="middle"
   allowScriptAccess="sameDomain" type="application/x-shockwave-flash"
   pluginspage="http://www.macromedia.com/go/getflashplayer" />
</object>

<form name="videoForm">
   Select a video:<br />
   <select name="videos">
      <option value="lights_long.flv">lights_long.flv</option>
      <option value="clouds.flv">clouds.flv</option>
      <option value="typing_long.flv">typing_long.flv</option>
      <option value="water.flv">water.flv</option>
   </select>
   <input type="button" name="selectVideo" value="play"
   onClick="callFlashPlayVideo();" />
```

```
·<br /><br />

Playback <input type="button" name="playPause" value="play/pause"
onClick="callFlashPlayPauseVideo();" />

<br /><br />
Video status messages <br />
<textarea name="videoStatus" cols="50" rows="10"></textarea>
</form>

</body>
</html>
```

This HTML code defines four JavaScript functions: `initialize()`,
`callFlashPlayVideo()`, `callFlashPlayPauseVideo()`, and `updateStatus()`. The
`initialize()` function is called within the `body` tag in the `onLoad` event. Both the
`callFlashPlayVideo()` and `callFlashPlayPauseVideo()` functions are called when
the user clicks on either the play button or play/pause button within the HTML
document, and trigger the `playVideo()` and `pauseResume()` functions in the SWF file.

The final function, `updateStatus()`, gets called by the SWF file whenever the `video_ns`
NetStream object's `onStatus` event handler is triggered. This HTML code also defines a
form that has a combo box of videos that the user can choose from. Whenever the user
selects a video and clicks the play button, the `callFlashPlayVideo()` JavaScript function
is called, which then calls the `playVideo()` function within the SWF file. This function
passes the URL of the SWF file to load into the video instance. As the video plays back
and the NetStream object's status changes, the contents of the HTML text area on the
Stage are updated.

4. Save your changes to the HTML document, and then upload both the HTML and SWF
   files to a website.

5. Open the remote video.html document from the website, select a video from the combo
   box, and click the play button.

   Flash plays the selected FLV file and updates the contents of the videoStatus text area
   within the HTML document.

You can find the sample source file, external.fla, in the Samples folder on your hard disk.

■ In Windows, browse to *boot drive*\Program Files\Macromedia\Flash 8\
  Samples and Tutorials\Samples\ActionScript\ExternalAPI.

■ On the Macintosh, browse to *Macintosh HD*/Applications/Macromedia Flash 8/
  Samples and Tutorials/Samples/ActionScript/ExternalAPI.

For more information on the External API, see %{ExternalInterface (flash.external.ExternalInterface)}% in the *ActionScript 2.0 Language Reference* in Flash Help.

For more information on local file security, see "About local file security and Flash Player" on page 693.

NOTE

Avoid using other methods of accessing the plug-in object, such as document.getElementById("pluginName") or document.all.pluginName, because these other methods do not work consistently across all browsers.

CHAPTER 17

Understanding Security

17

In Macromedia Flash Basic 8 and Macromedia Flash Professional 8, you can use ActionScript to load data from external sources into a SWF file or send data to a server. When you load data into a SWF file, you need to understand and accommodate the Flash 8 security model. When you open a SWF file on your hard disk, you might need to make special configurations so you can test your file locally.

For information on local file security, see "About local file security and Flash Player" on page 693. For information on the changes between the Flash Player 7 and Flash Player 8 security model, see "About compatibility with previous Flash Player security models" on page 691. For information on how to load and parse data from a server, read Chapter 16, "Working with External Data," on page 647. For more information on security, see www.macromedia.com/devnet/security and www.macromedia.com/software/flashplayer/security/.

For more information on security in Flash 8, see the following topics:

About compatibility with previous Flash Player security models

As a result of the security feature changes in Flash Player 7, content that runs as expected in Flash Player 6 or earlier might not run as expected in later versions of Flash Player. For example, in Flash Player 6, a SWF file that resides in www.macromedia.com could read data on a server located at data.macromedia.com; that is, Flash Player 6 allowed a SWF file from one domain to load data from a similar domain.

In Flash Player 7 and later, if a version 6 (or earlier) SWF file attempts to load data from a server that resides in another domain, and that server doesn't provide a policy file that allows reading from that SWF file's domain, the Macromedia Flash Player Settings dialog box appears. The dialog box asks the user to allow or deny the cross-domain data access.

If the user clicks Allow, the SWF file can access the requested data; if the user clicks Deny, the SWF file cannot access the requested data.

To prevent this dialog box from appearing, you should create a security policy file on the server providing the data. For more information, see "Allowing cross-domain data loading" on page 716.

Flash Player 7 and later do not allow cross-domain access without a security policy file.

Flash Player 8 changed the way it handles `System.security.allowDomain`. A Flash 8 SWF file that calls `System.security.allowDomain` with any argument, or any other SWF file that uses the wildcard (*) value, permits access only to itself. There is now support for a wildcard (*) value, for example: `System.security.allowDomain("*")` and `System.security.allowInsecureDomain("*")`. If a SWF file of version 7 or earlier calls `System.security.allowDomain` or `System.security.allowInsecureDomain` with an argument other than wildcard (*), this will affect all SWF files of version 7 or lower in the calling SWF file's domain, as it did in Flash Player 7. However, this kind of call does not affect any Flash Player 8 (or later) SWF files in the calling SWF file's domain. This helps minimize legacy content breaking in Flash Player.

For more information, see "About domains, cross-domain security, and SWF files" on page 708, %{allowDomain (security.allowDomain method)}%, and %{allowInsecureDomain (security.allowInsecureDomain method)}%.

Flash Player 8 does not allow local SWF files to communicate with the Internet without a specific configuration on your computer. Suppose you have legacy content that was published before these restrictions were in effect. If that content tries to communicate with the network or local file system, or both, Flash Player 8 stops the operation, and you must explicitly provide permission for the application to work properly. For more information, see "About local file security and Flash Player" on page 693

About local file security and Flash Player

Flash Player 8 has made enhancements to the security model, in which Flash applications and SWF files on a local computer are not allowed to communicate with *both* the Internet and the local file system by default. A *local SWF file* is a SWF file that is locally installed on a user's computer, not served from a website, and does not include projector (EXE) files.

When you create a FLA file, you can indicate whether a SWF file is allowed to communicate with a network or with a local file system. In previous versions of Flash Player, local SWF files could interact with other SWF files and load data from any remote or local location. In Flash Player 8, a SWF file cannot make connections to the local file system *and* the Internet. This is a safety change, so a SWF file cannot read files on your hard disk and then send the contents of those files across the Internet.

This security restriction affects all locally deployed content, whether it is legacy content (a FLA file created in an earlier version of Flash) or created in Flash 8. Suppose you deploy a Flash application, using Flash MX 2004 or earlier, that runs locally and also accesses the Internet. In Flash Player 8, this application now prompts the user for permission to communicate with the Internet.

When you test a file on your hard disk, there are a series of steps to determine whether the file is a local trusted document or a potentially untrusted document. If you create the file in the Flash authoring environment (for example, when you select Control > Test Movie), your file is trusted because it is in a test environment.

In Flash Player 7 and earlier, local SWF files had permissions to read from both a local file system and the network (such as the Internet). In Flash Player 8, local SWF files can have the following levels of permission:

Access the local file system only (default)   A local SWF file can read from the local file system and universal naming convention (UNC) network paths but cannot communicate with the Internet. For more information on local file access SWF files, see "Access local files only (default)" on page 700.

Access the network only   A local SWF file can access the network (such as the Internet) but not the local file system where it is installed. For more information on network-only SWF files, see "Access network only" on page 701.

Access to the local file system and the network A local SWF file can read from the local file system where it is installed, read and write to and from servers, and can cross-script other SWF files on either the network or the local file system. These files are trusted, and behave like they did in Flash Player 7. For more information on local and network access SWF files, see "Access file system and network" on page 701.

For more information on local file security in Flash 8 as it pertains to the authoring tool, see the following sections:

- "Understanding local security sandboxes" on page 694
- "About Flash Player security settings" on page 695
- "About local file security and projector files" on page 697
- "About troubleshooting legacy SWF files" on page 698
- "Fixing legacy content deployed on local computers" on page 698
- "Publishing files for local deployment" on page 699

For information about local file security for users, see "About Flash Player security settings" on page 695. For more information on security, see www.macromedia.com/devnet/security/ and www.macromedia.com/software/flashplayer/security/.

Understanding local security sandboxes

There are several different security sandboxes in the Flash Player. Each one determines how a SWF file can interact with the local file system, the network, or both the local file system and network at the same time. Restricting how a file can interact with the local file system, or the network helps keep your computer and files safe. Understanding security sandboxes helps you develop and test Flash applications on your computer without encountering unexpected errors.

Local-with-file-system

For security purposes, Flash Player 8 places all local SWF files, including all legacy local SWF files, in the local-with-file-system sandbox, by default (unless some other setting is made). For some legacy (earlier than Flash Player 8) SWF files, operations could be affected by enforcing restrictions on their access (no outside network access), but this provides the most secure default for the users' protection.

From this sandbox, SWF files may read from files on local file systems or UNC network paths (by using the XML.load() method, for example), but they may not communicate with the network in any way. This assures the user that local data cannot be leaked out to the network or otherwise inappropriately shared.

Local-with-networking

When local SWF files are assigned to the local-with-networking sandbox, they forfeit their local file system access. In return, the SWF files are allowed to access the network. However, a local-with-networking SWF file still is not allowed to read any network-derived data unless permissions are present for that action. Therefore, a local-with-networking SWF file has no local access, yet it has the ability to transmit data over the network and can read network data from those sites that designate site-specific access permissions.

Local-trusted

SWF files assigned to the local-trusted sandbox can interact with any other SWF files, and load data from anywhere (remote or local).

About Flash Player security settings

Macromedia has designed Flash Player to provide security settings that do not require you to explicitly allow or deny access in most situations. You might occasionally encounter legacy Flash content that was created using older security rules for Flash Player 7 or earlier. In these cases, Flash Player lets you allow the content to work as the developer intended, using the older security rules; or, you can choose to enforce the newer, stricter rules. The latter choice ensures that you only view or play content that meets the most recent standards of security, but it may sometimes prevent older Flash content from working properly.

All users who view SWF files (including non-Flash developers) can set permissions globally through the Global Security Settings panel in Flash Player's Settings Manager (shown in the following figure).

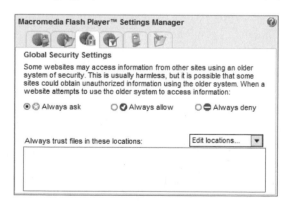

When older content runs in a newer version of the player, and Flash Player needs you to make a decision about enforcing newer rules or not, you may see one of the following pop-up dialog boxes. These dialog boxes ask your permission before allowing the older Flash content to communicate with other locations on the Internet:

- A dialog box might appear alerting you that the Flash content you are using is trying to use older security rules to access information from a site outside its own domain, and that information might be shared between two sites. Flash Player asks if you want to allow or deny such access.

  In addition to responding to the dialog box, you can use the Global Security Settings panel to specify whether Flash Player should always ask for your permission, through the dialog box, before allowing access; always deny access, without asking first; or always allow access to other sites or domains without asking your permission.

- (Flash Player 8 only) A dialog box might appear alerting you that a SWF file is trying to communicate with the Internet. Flash Player 8 doesn't let local Flash content communicate with the Internet, by default.

Click Settings to access the Global Security Settings panel, where you can specify that certain Flash applications on your computer may communicate with the Internet.

To change your security settings or learn more about your options, you use the Global Security Settings panel. Use this panel to reset the privacy settings in Macromedia Flash Player:

- If you select *Always Deny* and then confirm your selection, any website that tries to use your camera or microphone is denied access. You are not asked again whether a website can use your camera or microphone. This action applies both to websites you have already visited and to those you haven't yet visited.

- If you select *Always Ask* and then confirm your selection, any website that tries to use your camera or microphone must ask your permission. This action applies both to websites you have already visited and to those you haven't yet visited.

If you previously selected Remember in the Privacy Settings panel (see the following figure) to permanently allow or deny access for one or more websites, selecting Always Ask or Always Deny has the effect of deselecting Remember for all those websites. In other words, the selection you make here overrides any previous selections you may have made in the Privacy Settings panel, shown in the following figure.

After you select either Always Ask or Always Deny (or instead of doing so), you can specify privacy settings for individual websites that you have already visited. For example, you might select Always Deny here, then use the Website Privacy Settings panel and select Always Allow for individual websites that you know and trust.

For locally deployed content and local data, users have another option: They can specify which SWF files may access the Internet using the Global Security Settings panel. For more information on specifying settings in the Global Security Settings panel, see "Specifying trusted files using the Settings Manager" on page 702. For more information on the Global Security Settings panel, see www.macromedia.com/support/documentation/en/flashplayer/help/settings_manager04a.html.

 NOTE | The selections users make in the Global Security Settings panel override any decisions made in the security pop-up dialog box.

About local file security and projector files

Projector files and the SWF files contained within them or loaded into the projector at runtime are not affected by local file security restrictions, because the end user must run the executable to use the SWF file. There are no changes to security and projector files in Flash Player 8; it has the same level of access and security as earlier versions of Flash Player.

Remember that users are often cautious about executing projector files. A projector file is an executable EXE or Macintosh application, and users should be careful about running such files on their computers. If you distribute an application using projector files, some users might not install it.

In addition, a projector file embeds a specific version of Flash Player inside the projector, which might be older than the latest version of Flash Player available for download from the Macromedia website. The Flash Player that's embedded within the projector file might be a legacy version if the projector was created with an older version of Flash, or an edition of Flash Player was released after the current version of the Flash authoring tool. For these reasons, you should distribute applications using SWF files when possible.

About troubleshooting legacy SWF files

Some legacy FLA and SWF files (created with Flash MX 2004 and earlier) might not work when you test or deploy them locally (on a hard disk) because of security changes in Flash 8. This might happen when a SWF file tries to access websites outside its domain, and, in this case, you need to implement a cross-domain policy file.

You might have FLA or SWF files created in Flash MX 2004 or earlier that have been distributed to users who do not use the Flash 8 authoring tool but have upgraded to Flash Player 8. If your locally tested or deployed legacy content (an old SWF file on a user's hard disk) breaks because it tries to communicate with the Internet when playing in Flash Player 8, you must rely on users to explicitly trust your content in order for it to play properly (by clicking a button in a dialog box).

To learn how to fix legacy content for playback on a local computer, see "Fixing legacy content deployed on local computers" on page 698.

Fixing legacy content deployed on local computers

If you published SWF files for Flash Player 7 or earlier that are deployed on local computers and communicate with the Internet, users must explicitly allow Internet communication. Users can stop content from breaking by adding the location of the SWF file on their local computer to the trusted sandbox in the Settings Manager.

To fix SWF files for local playback, use any of the following options:

Redeploy   Run the Local Content Updater. The Local Content Updater reconfigures your SWF file to make it compatible with the Flash Player 8 security model. You reconfigure the local SWF file so it can either access only the network or only the local file system. For more information, and to download the Local Content Updater, see www.macromedia.com/support/flashplayer/downloads.html.

Republish and redeploy   Republish the file with Flash Basic 8 or Flash Professional 8. The authoring tool requires you to specify in the Publish Settings dialog box whether a local SWF file can access the network or the local file system—but not both. If you specify that a local SWF file can access the network, you also must enable permissions for that SWF file (and all local SWF files) in the SWF, HTML, data, and/or server files that it accesses. For more information, see "Publishing files for local deployment" on page 699.

Deploy new content   Use a configuration (.cfg) file in the #Security/FlashPlayerTrust folder. You can use this file to set network and local access permissions. For more information, see "Creating configuration files for Flash development" on page 704.

> **NOTE**
> Any of these options require that you either republish or redeploy your SWF file.

Publishing files for local deployment

You might send your Flash 8 FLA or SWF files to a user to test or approve and need the application to access the Internet. If your document plays back on a local system but accesses files on the Internet (for example, loading XML or sending variables), your user might need a configuration file for the content to function properly, or you might need to set up the FLA file so the SWF file that you publish can access the network. Alternatively, you can set up a configuration file inside the FlashPlayerTrust directory. For more information on setting up configuration files, see "Creating configuration files for Flash development" on page 704.

Use Flash Basic 8 or Flash Professional 8 to create content for local deployment that works with Flash Player 8 local file security. In Flash 8 publish settings, you must specify whether local content can access the network or access the local file system, but not both.

You can set permission levels for a FLA file in the Publish Settings dialog box. These permission levels affect the local playback of the FLA file, when it plays locally on a hard disk.

> **NOTE**
> If you specify network access for a local file, you must also enable permissions in the SWF, HTML, data, and server files that are accessed by the local SWF file.

Network SWF files   SWF files that download from a network (such as an online server) are placed in a separate *sandbox* that corresponds to their unique website origin domains. Local SWF files that specify they have network access are placed in the *local-with-networking* sandbox. By default, these files can read data from only the same site from which they originated. Exact-domain matching applies to these files. Network SWF files can access data from other domains if they have the proper permissions. For more information on network SWF files, see "Access network only" on page 701.

Local SWF files   SWF files that operate with local file systems or UNC network paths are placed into one of three sandboxes in Flash Player 8. By default, local SWF files are placed in the *local-with-file-system* sandbox. Local SWF files that are registered as trusted (using a configuration file) are placed in the *local-trusted* sandbox. For information on the three sandboxes, see "Access local files only (default)" on page 700.

For more information on the security sandbox, see "Understanding local security sandboxes" on page 694.

The first two permission levels are set in the Flash authoring environment, and the third is set using the Global Security Settings panel or the FlashAuthor.cfg file. The following example shows what options are available when you publish a file for testing on your local hard disk.

To publish a document with a specified permission level:

1. Open the FLA file for which you want to specify a permission level.

2. Select File > Publish Settings > Flash.

3. Find the Local Playback Security dialog box, and select one of the following options from the pop-up menu:

   - Access local files only (See "Access local files only (default)")
   - Access network only (See "Access network only")

4. Click OK to continue authoring the FLA file, or click Publish to create the SWF file.

For more information on levels of permission that you can set for your applications, see "Access local files only (default)" on page 700, "Access network only" on page 701, and "Access file system and network" on page 701.

Access local files only (default)

To set this permission level, select Publish Settings > Flash, and then select Access Local Files Only from the Local Playback Security pop-up menu. This permission level lets a local SWF file access only the local file system where the SWF file is running. The SWF file can read from known files on the local disk without any restrictions. However, the following restrictions apply to the application accessing the network:

- The SWF file cannot access the network in any way. The SWF file cannot cross-script network SWF files, or be cross-scripted by network SWF files.
- The SWF file cannot communicate with local SWF files that have permission to access the network only, and the SWF file cannot communicate with HTML pages. However, in some cases communication is allowed, such as if the HTML is trusted and `allowScriptAccess` is set to `always` or if `allowScriptAccess` is not set and the SWF file is Flash Player 7 or earlier.

Access network only

To set this permission level, select Publish Settings > Flash, and then select Access Network Only from the Local Playback Security pop-up menu. Local SWF files with network access can read from a server if the server contains a cross-domain policy file with `<allow-access-from-domain="*">`. Local SWF files with network access may cross script other SWF files if the other SWF files, which are being accessed, contain `System.security.allowDomain("*")`. A local SWF file with network access can be cross-scripted by network SWF files if the local SWF file contains `allowDomain("*")`. The SWF file can never read from local files. In some cases, the type of SWF file affects the access. For information, see %{allowDomain (`security.allowDomain method`)}% in the *ActionScript 2.0 Language Reference* in Flash Help.

The wildcard (*) value indicates that *all* domains, including local hosts, are allowed access. Be certain you want to provide this broad level of access before using the wildcard argument.

Without any of these permissions, local SWF files with network access can communicate only with other local SWF files that have network access, and they can send data to servers (using `XML.send()`, for example). In some cases, access is allowed if the HTML file is trusted.

Access file system and network

This level is the highest level of permission. A local SWF file that has these permissions is a *trusted local SWF file*. Trusted local SWF files can read from other local SWF files, interact with any server, and write ActionScript for other SWF files or HTML files that have not explicitly forbidden the file permission (for example, with `allowScriptAccess="none"`). This level of permission can be granted by the user or Flash developer in the following ways:

- Using the Global Security Settings panel in the Settings Manager.
- Using a global configuration file.

A configuration file can be installed with the SWF file, created by a Flash developer, or added by an administrator (for all users or the current user) or any Flash developer (for the current user).

For more information on configuration files and the Global Security Settings panel, see "About Flash Player security settings" on page 695 and "Specifying trusted files using the Settings Manager" on page 702 and "Creating configuration files for Flash development" on page 704.

Testing content locally with Flash 8 local file security restrictions

As a Flash developer, you frequently test Flash applications locally, so you might see a dialog box prompt when a local Flash application tries to communicate with the Internet. You might see this dialog box when you test a SWF file in Flash Player if the SWF file does not have network access. For more information on publishing SWF files with specified permission levels, see "Publishing files for local deployment" on page 699. Publishing a SWF file with one of these options means you can communicate with the network *or* the local file system.

At times, you might need to communicate with the local file system and the network when you are testing a document. Because the new security model might interrupt your workflow when you are authoring Flash applications, you can use the Global Security Settings panel in Flash Player's Settings Manager to specify which Flash applications on your computer can always communicate with both the Internet and the local file system. Or, you can modify the configuration file to specify trusted directories on your hard disk.

For more information, see the following sections:

- "Specifying trusted files using the Settings Manager" on page 702
- "Creating configuration files for Flash development" on page 704

Specifying trusted files using the Settings Manager

You can specify what Flash content on your computer may always use the older security rules by adding the location of the content to the Global Security Settings panel in the Flash Player Settings Manager. After you add a location on your computer to the Security panel, content in that location is *trusted*. Flash Player won't ask you for permission and is always allowed to use the older security rules, even if Always Deny is selected in the Security panel. The Always Trust Files in These Locations list overrides the options in the Settings panel. That is, if you select to always deny local and web content the right to use the older security rules, the local files in your trusted list are always allowed to use the older rules.

The Always trust files list at the bottom of the panel applies specifically to Flash content that you have downloaded to your computer, not content that you use while visiting a website.

The following example shows how to specify that a local SWF file can communicate with the Internet. When you test a file in a browser locally (File > Publish Preview > HTML), a security dialog box might appear. If you click Settings, the Settings Manager Global Security Settings panel appears

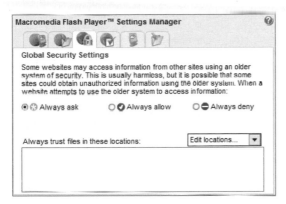

To specify that a local SWF file can communicate with the Internet and local file system:

1. In the Global Security Settings panel, click the pop-up menu and select Add Location.

   The Add Location box opens.

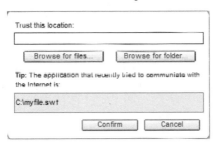

If you arrived at the Settings Manager by clicking the Settings button in a dialog box, the Add Location box contains a path that is similar to C:*directoryname**filename.swf* or /*Users/directoryname/filename.swf*; this path tells you which file tried to communicate with the Internet and was stopped by Flash Player security. If the path contains the content that you want to let communicate with the Internet, copy and paste the path into the Trust This Location box. Or, click one of the Browse buttons and find the content yourself.

You can add an individual file or an entire directory. If you add an entire directory, all the files and subdirectories in that directory are trusted. Some Flash content consists of multiple related files, and you might need to trust the entire directory where all the related files are located. In general, avoid trusting top-level directories.

2. Click Confirm.

The location is added to the Security Settings panel. Locations listed are always allowed to use the older security rules, even if the Always Deny or Always Ask options at the top of the Security panel are selected.

After you add trusted locations, you must restart the local Flash content by either refreshing the browser or restarting the player.

If you click Always Allow, it only applies that setting to always allow legacy content (Flash Player 7 and earlier). The setting does not "always allow" Flash Player 8 content. It is recommended that you specify the Flash applications and directories on your computer that can communicate with both the Internet and the local file system.

Creating configuration files for Flash development

The Flash 8 authoring tool sets a flag on your hard disk to identify you as a developer to direct you to a specific developer-oriented version of the Global Security Settings panel instead of a user-oriented Global Security Settings panel. The flag is in the FlashAuthor.cfg file on your hard disk, which installs automatically when the Flash Basic 8 and Flash Professional 8 authoring tool installs.

The FlashAuthor.cfg file is located in the following approximate directories:

Windows *boot disk*\Documents and Settings\<*UserName*>\Application Data\Macromedia\Flash Player\#Security

Macintosh /Users/<*UserName*>/Library/Preferences/Macromedia/Flash Player/#Security/

By default, this file is set to `LocalSecurityPrompt=Author`, which means the warnings you see on your computer treat you as a Flash developer as opposed to a user without the authoring tool installed.

You can test your local applications as an end user and see the warning dialog boxes that an end user would encounter. To do so, open FlashAuthor.cfg in a text editor, and change the LocalSecurityPrompt in the FlashAuthor.cfg file to match the following:

```
LocalSecurityPrompt=User
```

You might want to provide a FlashAuthor.cfg file, with `LocalSecurityPrompt` set to `Author`, to other developers in your design or development process or to users who test Flash applications on their local hard disk and do not have the Flash 8 authoring tool installed. This helps you mimic the end user's experience with your locally deployed content.

> **NOTE** If the FlashAuthor.cfg file is deleted, the file is recreated when you launch the Flash 8 authoring tool.

In the #Security directory on your hard disk, you can create a FlashPlayerTrust directory where you can store unique configuration files. Inside these files, you can specify directories or applications to trust on your hard disk. This directory does not require administrative access, so users without administrative permissions can set permissions for SWF files and test applications.

If you do not specify a directory, your content might not function as intended. Configuration files inside a FlashPlayerTrust directory contain directory paths. The file can contain a list of several directories, and you can append new paths to the file. Flash Player expects one path per line in configuration files. Any line that begins with a # punctuator (with no leading space before it) is treated as a comment.

To create a configuration file to trust a directory:

1. Locate the #Security folder on your hard disk.

2. Create a folder called **FlashPlayerTrust** inside the #Security folder.

3. Create a new file in the FlashPlayerTrust directory using a text editor, and save it as **myTrustFiles.cfg**.

    You can use any unique name for your configuration file.

4. Locate the directory where you test Flash applications.

5. Type or paste each directory path (any directory path on your hard disk) on a new line in the file. You can paste multiple directory paths on separate lines. When you finish, your file looks similar to the following example:

    ```
    C:\Documents and Settings\<yourname>\My Documents\files\
    C:\Documents and Settings\<yourname>\My Documents\testapps\
    ```

6. Save your changes to myTrustFiles.cfg.

7. Test a document that accesses local and network files from the directory you added to the file.

    Flash applications saved in this directory can now access local files and the network.

There can be numerous directory paths saved in each configuration file, and numerous *.cfg files saved in the FlashPlayerTrust directory.

If you create applications that install on an end user's hard disk, you might need to create a configuration file in FlashPlayerTrust to specify a trusted directory for your application. You can create configuration files inside the FlashPlayerTrust directory that specify the location of the trusted application. See the pervious procedure for information on this directory and creating configuration files.

NOTE | An installer is run by a user with administrative permission on a computer.

You should develop a unique naming scheme to avoid conflicts with other applications that might install files in this directory. For example, you might want to use your unique company and software name in the filename to avoid conflicts.

 TIP If you do not want to use configuration files, you could publish your Flash applications to a separate, testing server instead of providing clients or other developers SWF files to run on their local hard disks.

For more information on configuration files, see www.macromedia.com/go/flashauthorcfg. You can also create a unique configuration file to trust one or more directories. For detailed information on security, see www.macromedia.com/devnet/security/and www.macromedia.com/software/flashplayer/security/.

About the sandboxType property

Flash Player 8's `System.security.sandboxType` property returns the type of security sandbox in which the calling SWF file is operating.

The `sandboxType` property has one of the four following values:

remote   The SWF file is hosted on the Internet and operates under domain-based sandbox rules.

localTrusted   The SWF file is a local file that has been trusted by the user, using either the Global Security Settings Manager or a FlashPlayerTrust configuration file. The SWF file can both read from local data sources and communicate with the network (such as the Internet).

localWithFile   The SWF file is a local file that has not been trusted by the user, and was not published with a networking designation. The SWF file can read from local data sources but cannot communicate with the network (such as the Internet).

localWithNetwork   The SWF file is a local file that has not been trusted by the user, and was published with Access Network Only selected in the Publish Settings dialog box (Flash tab). The SWF file can communicate with the network but cannot read from local data sources.

You can check the `sandboxType` property from any SWF file, although a value is returned only in files published for Flash Player 8. This means that when you publish for Flash Player 7 or earlier, you do not know whether the `sandboxType` property is supported at runtime. If the property isn't supported at runtime, the value is `undefined`, which occurs when the Flash Player version (indicated by the `System.capabilities.version` property) is less than 8. If the value is `undefined`, you can determine the sandbox type according to whether your SWF file's URL is a local file or not. If the SWF file is a local file, Flash Player classifies your SWF as `localTrusted` (which is how all local content was treated prior to Flash Player 8); otherwise Flash Player classifies the SWF file as `remote`.

About local-with-file-system restrictions

A local-with-file-system file has not been registered using the configuration file inside the FlashPlayerTrust directory, the Global Security Settings panel in the Settings Manager, or has not been granted network permission in the Publish Settings dialog box in the Flash authoring environment.

> **NOTE** For information on security sandboxes, see "Understanding local security sandboxes" on page 694.

These files include legacy content that plays in Flash Player 8. If you are developing content in Flash 8, or you have content that falls into one of the following categories, you (or your users) should register the file as trusted. For information on registering a file as trusted, see "Specifying trusted files using the Settings Manager" on page 702. For information on granting permission for local file playback using configuration files, see "Creating configuration files for Flash development" on page 704.

Local-with-file-system SWF files have the following restrictions:

- Cannot access the network, which includes the following:
  - Loading other SWF files from the network (*except* using non-Internet UNC paths)
  - Sending HTTP requests
  - Making connections using XMLSocket, Flash Remoting, or NetConnection
  - Calling `getURL()` *except* if you use `getURL("file:...")` or `getURL("mailto:...")`

- Can interact with other local-with-file-system files, but includes restrictions to the following:
  - Cross-scripting (such as ActionScript access to objects in other SWF files).
  - Calling `System.security.allowDomain`
  - Using `LocalConnection` as sender or listener and regardless of `LocalConnection.allowDomain` handlers.

> **NOTE** Local-with-file-system SWF files can interact with other local-with-file-system, non-network SWF files. However, they cannot interact with local-with-network SWF files.

Local-with-file-system SWF files have read access to known files on the local file system. For example, you can use `XML.load()` in a local-with-file-system SWF file as long as you load from the local file system and not the Internet.

- Local-with-file-system SWF files cannot communicate with HTML pages, which includes the following:
  - Inbound scripting (such as ExternalInterface API, ActiveX, LiveConnect, and XPConnect)
  - Outbound scripting (such as custom `fscommand` calls, and `getURL("javascript:...")`)

> **NOTE** An exception to this is if the HTML page is trusted.

About domains, cross-domain security, and SWF files

By default, Flash Player 7 and later versions prevent a SWF file served from one domain from reading data, objects, or variables from SWF files that are served from different domains. In addition, content that is loaded through nonsecure (non-HTTPS) protocols cannot read content loaded through a secure (HTTPS) protocol, even when both are in exactly the same domain. For example, a SWF file located at http://www.macromedia.com/main.swf cannot load data from https://www.macromedia.com/data.txt without explicit permission; neither can a SWF file served from one domain load data (using `loadVars()`, for example) from another domain.

Identical numeric IP addresses are compatible. However, a domain name is not compatible with an IP address, even if the domain name resolves to the same IP address.

The following table shows examples of compatible domains:

www.macromedia.com	www.macromedia.com
data.macromedia.com	data.macromedia.com
65.57.83.12	65.57.83.12

The following table shows examples of incompatible domains:

www.macromedia.com	data.macromedia.com
macromedia.com	www.macromedia.com
www.macromedia.com	macromedia.com
65.57.83.12	www.macromedia.com (even if this domain resolves to 65.57.83.12)
www.macromedia.com	65.57.83.12 (even if www.macromedia.com resolves to this IP address)

Flash Player 8 does not allow local SWF files to communicate with the Internet without a proper configuration. For information on setting up a configuration file to test content locally, see "Creating configuration files for Flash development" on page 704.

For more information on security, see www.macromedia.com/devnet/security/ and www.macromedia.com/software/flashplayer/security/.

For more information, see the following topics:

- "Domain name rules for settings and local data" on page 709
- "Cross-domain and subdomain access between SWF files" on page 710
- "Allowing cross-domain data loading" on page 716

Domain name rules for settings and local data

In Flash Player 6, superdomain matching rules are used by default when accessing local settings (such as camera or microphone access permissions) or locally persistent data (shared objects). That is, the settings and data for SWF files hosted at here.xyz.com, there.xyz.com, and xyz.com are shared and are all stored at xyz.com.

In Flash Player 7, exact-domain matching rules are used by default. That is, the settings and data for a file hosted at here.xyz.com are stored at here.xyz.com, the settings and data for a file hosted at there.xyz.com are stored at there.xyz.com, and so on. `System.exactSettings` lets you specify which rules to use. This property is supported for files published for Flash Player 6 or later. For files published for Flash Player 6, the default value is `false`, which means superdomain matching rules are used. For files published for Flash Player 7 or 8, the default value is `true`, which means exact-domain matching rules are used. If you use settings or persistent local data and want to publish a Flash Player 6 SWF file for Flash Player 7 or 8, you might need to set this value to `false` in the ported file. For more information, see `%{exactSettings (System.exactSettings property)}%` in the *ActionScript 2.0 Language Reference* in Flash Help.

Cross-domain and subdomain access between SWF files

When you develop a series of SWF files that communicate with each other online—for example, when using `loadMovie()`, `MovieClip.loadMovie()`, `MovieClipLoader.LoadClip()`, or Local Connection objects—you might host the SWF files in different domains or in different subdomains of a single superdomain.

In files published for Flash Player 5 or earlier, there were no restrictions on cross-domain or subdomain access.

In files published for Flash Player 6, you could use the `LocalConnection.allowDomain` handler or `System.security.allowDomain()` method to specify permitted cross-domain access (for example, to let a file at someSite.com be accessed by a file at someOtherSite.com), and no command was needed to permit subdomain access (for example, a file at www.someSite.com could be accessed by a file at store.someSite.com).

Files published for Flash Player 7 implement access between SWF files differently from earlier versions in two ways. First, Flash Player 7 implements exact-domain matching rules instead of superdomain matching rules. Therefore, the file being accessed (even if it is published for a Flash Player version earlier than Flash Player 7) must explicitly permit cross-domain or subdomain access; this topic is discussed in this section. Second, a file hosted at a site using a secure protocol (HTTPS) must explicitly permit access from a file hosted at a site using an insecure protocol (HTTP or FTP); this topic is discussed in the next section (see "HTTP to HTTPS protocol access between SWF files" on page 721).

You usually call `System.security.allowDomain` in your applications. However, when the LocalConnection receiver is an HTTPS SWF file and the sender is not, `allowInsecureDomain` is called instead.

The following issue affects only SWF files published for Flash Player 7. When the receiver is HTTPS, and the sender is a local SWF file, allowDomain() is called, even though allowInsecureDomain() should be called. However, in Flash Player 8, when an HTTPS LocalConnection receiver is Flash Player 8, and the sender is a local file, allowInsecureDomain() is called.

Files that run in Flash Player 8 are subject to changes from how they run in Flash Player 7. Calling System.security.allowDomain permits cross-scripting operations only where the SWF file being accessed is the one that called System.security.allowDomain. In other words, a SWF file that calls System.security.allowDomain now permits access only to itself. In previous versions, calling System.security.allowDomain permitted cross-scripting operations where the SWF file being accessed could be any SWF file in the same domain as the one that called System.security.allowDomain. Doing so opened up the entire domain of the calling SWF file.

Support has been added for the wildcard (*) value to System.security.allowDomain("*") and System.security.allowInsecureDomain("*"). The wildcard (*) value permits cross-scripting operations where the accessing file is any file and can be loaded from any location (such as global permission). Wildcard permissions can be useful, but they must adhere to the new local file security rules in Flash Player 8. Specifically, local files do not come from a domain, so the wildcard value must be used. However, use caution when using the wildcard value because any domain has access to your file. For more information, see %{allowInsecureDomain (security.allowInsecureDomain method)}%.

You might encounter a situation when you load a child SWF file from a different domain than the one calling it. You might want to allow that file to script the parent SWF file, but you don't know the final domain from which the child SWF file will come. This situation can happen, for example, when you use load-balancing redirects or third-party servers. In this situation, you can use the MovieClip._url property as an argument to this method. For example, if you load a SWF file into my_mc, you can call System.security.allowDomain(my_mc._url). If you do this, you must wait until the SWF file in my_mc begins loading because the _url property does not have its final, correct value yet. To determine when a child SWF file has started to load, use MovieClipLoader.onLoadStart.

The opposite situation can also occur; that is, you might create a child SWF file that wants to allow its parent to script it, but doesn't know what the domain of its parent SWF file will be (meaning, it's a SWF file that might be loaded by a variety of domains). In this situation, call `System.security.allowDomain(_parent._url)` from the child SWF file. You don't have to wait for the parent SWF file to load because it is loaded before the child file loads.

> **NOTE** If the Internet SWF file being accessed is loaded from an HTTPS URL, the Internet SWF file must call `System.security.allowInsecureDomain("*")`.

The following table summarizes domain-matching rules in different versions of Flash Player:

Files published for Flash Player	Cross-domain access between SWF files (allowDomain() is needed)	Subdomain access between SWF files
5 or earlier	No restrictions	No restrictions
6	Superdomain matching: `allowDomain()` is needed if superdomains do not match.	No restrictions
7 and later	Exact domain matching Explicit permission for HTTPS-hosted files to access HTTP- or FTP-hosted files	Exact domain matching Explicit permission for HTTPS-hosted files to access HTTP- or FTP-hosted files

> **NOTE** You need `System.security.allowInsecureDomain` in Flash Player 7 and later if you are performing HTTP-to-HTTPS access, even if you have exact-domain matching.

The versions that control the behavior of Flash Player are SWF file versions (the specified Flash Player version of a SWF file), not the version of Flash Player itself. For example, when Flash Player 8 is playing a SWF file published for version 7, Flash Player applies behavior that is consistent with version 7. This practice ensures that player upgrades do not change the behavior of `System.security.allowDomain()` in deployed SWF files.

Because Flash Player 7 and later versions implement exact-domain matching rules instead of superdomain matching rules, you might have to modify existing scripts if you want to read them from files that are published for Flash Player 7 or 8. (You can still publish the modified files for Flash Player 6.) If you used any `LocalConnection.allowDomain()` or `System.security.allowDomain()` statements in your files and specified superdomain sites to permit, you must change your parameters to specify exact domains instead. The following example shows changes you might have to make if you have Flash Player 6 code:

```
// Flash Player 6 commands in a SWF file at www.anyOldSite.com
// to allow access by SWF files that are hosted at www.someSite.com
// or at store.someSite.com
System.security.allowDomain("someSite.com");
my_lc.allowDomain = function(sendingDomain) {
  return(sendingDomain=="someSite.com");
}
// Corresponding commands to allow access by SWF files
// that are published for Flash Player 7 or later
System.security.allowDomain("www.someSite.com", "store.someSite.com");
my_lc.allowDomain = function(sendingDomain) {
  return(sendingDomain=="www.someSite.com" ||
    sendingDomain=="store.someSite.com");
}
```

You might also have to add statements such as these to your files if you aren't currently using them. For example, if your SWF file is hosted at www.someSite.com and you want to allow access by a SWF file published for Flash Player 7 or later at store.someSite.com, you must add statements such as the following example to the file at www.someSite.com (you can still publish the file at www.someSite.com for Flash Player 6):

```
System.security.allowDomain("store.someSite.com");
my_lc.allowDomain = function(sendingDomain) {
  return(sendingDomain=="store.someSite.com");
}
```

In addition, consider that if a Flash Player 6 application running in Flash Player 7 tries to access data outside its exact domain, Flash Player 7 and later domain-matching rules are enforced and the user is prompted to allow or deny access.

To summarize, you might have to modify your files to add or change `allowDomain` statements if you publish files for Flash Player 7 or later that meet the following conditions:

- You implemented cross-SWF file scripting (see "Allowing data access between cross-domain SWF files" on page 714).
- The called SWF file (of any version) is not hosted at a site using a secure protocol (HTTPS), or the calling and called SWF files are both hosted at HTTPS sites. (If only the called SWF file is HTTPS, see "HTTP to HTTPS protocol access between SWF files" on page 721.)

- The SWF files are not in the same domain (for example, one file is at www.domain.com and one is at store.domain.com).

You must make the following changes:

- If the called SWF file is published for Flash Player 7 or later, include `System.security.allowDomain` or `LocalConnection.allowDomain` in the called SWF file, using exact domain-name matching.

- If the called SWF file is published for Flash Player 6, modify the called file to add or change a `System.security.allowDomain` or `LocalConnection.allowDomain` statement, using exact domain-name matching, as shown in the code examples earlier in this section. You can publish the modified file for either Flash Player 6 or 7.

- If the called SWF file is published for Flash Player 5 or earlier, port the called file to Flash Player 6 or 7 and add a `System.security.allowDomain` statement, using exact domain-name matching, as shown in the code examples earlier in this section. (LocalConnection objects aren't supported in Flash Player 5 or earlier.)

For information on local security sandboxes, see "About local file security and Flash Player" on page 693.

Allowing data access between cross-domain SWF files

For two SWF files to access each other's data (variables and objects), the two files must originate from the same domain. By default, in Flash Player 7 and later, the two domains must match exactly for the two files to share data. However, a SWF file can grant access to SWF files served from specific domains by calling `LocalConnection.allowDomain` or `System.security.allowDomain()`.

`System.security.allowDomain()` lets SWF files and HTML files in specified domains access objects and variables in the SWF file that contains the `allowDomain()` call.

If two SWF files are served from the same domain—for example, http://mysite.com/movieA.swf and http://mysite.com/movieB.swf—then movieA.swf can examine and modify variables, objects, properties, methods, and so on in movieB.swf, and movieB can do the same for movieA. This is called cross-movie scripting, or *cross-scripting*.

If two SWF files are served from different domains—for example, http://mysite.com/movieA.swf and http://othersite.com/movieB.swf—then, by default, Flash Player does not allow movieA.swf to script movieB.swf, nor movieB to script movieA. If you call `System.security.allowDomain("mysite.com")`, movieB.swf gives movieA.swf permission to script movieB.swf. A SWF file gives SWF files from other domains permission to script it by calling `System.security.allowDomain()`. This is called *cross-domain scripting*.

For further information on `System.security.allowDomain()`, cross-scripting, and cross-domain scripting, see %{allowDomain (security.allowDomain method)}% in the *ActionScript 2.0 Language Reference* in Flash Help.

For example, suppose main.swf is served from www.macromedia.com. That SWF file then loads another SWF file (data.swf) from data.macromedia.com into a movie clip instance that's created dynamically using `createEmptyMovieClip()`.

```
// In macromedia.swf
this.createEmptyMovieClip("target_mc", this.getNextHighestDepth());
target_mc.loadMovie("http://data.macromedia.com/data.swf");
```

Suppose that data.swf defines a method named `getData()` on its main Timeline. By default, main.swf cannot call the `getData()` method defined in data.swf after that file has loaded because the two SWF files do not reside in the same domain. For example, the following method call in main.swf, after data.swf has loaded, fails:

```
// In macromedia.swf, after data.swf has loaded:
target_mc.getData(); // This method call will fail
```

However, data.swf can grant access to SWF files served from www.macromedia.com by using the `LocalConnection.allowDomain` handler and the `System.security.allowDomain()` method, depending on the type of access required. The following code, added to data.swf, allows a SWF file served from www.macromedia.com to access its variables and methods:

```
// Within data.swf
this._lockroot = true;
System.security.allowDomain("www.macromedia.com");
var my_lc:LocalConnection = new LocalConnection();
my_lc.allowDomain = function(sendingDomain:String):Boolean {
  return (sendingDomain == "www.macromedia.com");
};
function getData():Void {
  var timestamp:Date = new Date();
  output_txt.text += "data.swf:" + timestamp.toString() + "\n\n";
}
output_txt.text = "**INIT**:\n\n";
```

Now the `getData` function in the loaded SWF file can be called by the macromedia.swf file. Notice that `allowDomain` permits any SWF file in the allowed domain to script any other SWF file in the domain permitting the access, unless the SWF file being accessed is hosted on a site using a secure protocol (HTTPS).

For more information on domain-name matching, see "Cross-domain and subdomain access between SWF files" on page 710.

Server-side policy files for permitting access to data

A Flash document can load data from an external source by using one of the following data loading calls: `XML.load()`, `XML.sendAndLoad()`, `LoadVars.load()`, `LoadVars.sendAndLoad()`, `loadVariables()`, `loadVariablesNum()`, `MovieClip.loadVariables()`, `XMLSocket.connect()`, and Macromedia Flash Remoting (`NetServices.createGatewayConnection`). Also, a SWF file can import runtime shared libraries (RSLs), or assets defined in another SWF file, at runtime. By default, the data or RSL must reside in the same domain as the SWF file that is loading that external data or media.

To make data and assets in runtime shared libraries available to SWF files in different domains, you should use a *cross-domain policy file*. A cross-domain policy file is an XML file that provides a way for the server to indicate that its data and documents are available to SWF files served from certain domains, or from all domains. Any SWF file that is served from a domain specified by the server's policy file is permitted to access data, assets, or RSLs from that server.

If you are loading external data, you should create policy files even if you don't plan to port any files to Flash Player 7. If you are using RSLs, you should create policy files if either the calling or called file is published for Flash Player 7.

For more information, see the following topics:

- "Allowing cross-domain data loading" on page 716
- "About custom policy file locations" on page 718
- "About XMLSocket policy files" on page 719

Allowing cross-domain data loading

When a Flash document attempts to access data from another domain, Flash Player automatically attempts to load a policy file from that domain. If the domain of the Flash document that is attempting to access the data is included in the policy file, the data is automatically accessible.

Policy files must be named crossdomain.xml, and can reside either at the root directory or in another directory on the server that is serving the data with some additional ActionScript (see "About custom policy file locations" on page 718). Policy files function only on servers that communicate over HTTP, HTTPS, or FTP. The policy file is specific to the port and protocol of the server where it resides.

For example, a policy file located at https://www.macromedia.com:8080/crossdomain.xml applies only to data loading calls made to www.macromedia.com over HTTPS at port 8080.

An exception to this rule is the use of an XMLSocket object to connect to a socket server in another domain. In that case, an HTTP server running on port 80 in the same domain as the socket server must provide the policy file for the method call.

An XML policy file contains a single `<cross-domain-policy>` tag, which, in turn, contains zero or more `<allow-access-from>` tags. Each `<allow-access-from>` tag contains an attribute, `domain`, which specifies either an exact IP address, an exact domain, or a wildcard domain (any domain). Wildcard domains are indicated by either a single asterisk (*), which matches all domains and all IP addresses, or an asterisk followed by a suffix, which matches only those domains that end with the specified suffix. Suffixes must begin with a dot. However, wildcard domains with suffixes can match domains that consist of only the suffix without the leading dot. For example, foo.com is considered to be part of *.foo.com. Wildcards are not allowed in IP domain specifications.

If you specify an IP address, access is granted only to SWF files loaded from that IP address using IP syntax (for example, http://65.57.83.12/flashmovie.swf), not those loaded using domain-name syntax. Flash Player does not perform DNS resolution.

The following example shows a policy file that permits access to Flash documents that originate from foo.com, www.friendOfFoo.com, *.foo.com, and 105.216.0.40, from a Flash document on foo.com:

```
<?xml version="1.0"?>
<!-- http://www.foo.com/crossdomain.xml -->
<cross-domain-policy>
  <allow-access-from domain="www.friendOfFoo.com" />
  <allow-access-from domain="*.foo.com" />
  <allow-access-from domain="105.216.0.40" />
</cross-domain-policy>
```

You can also permit access to documents originating from any domain, as shown in the following example:

```
<?xml version="1.0"?>
<!-- http://www.foo.com/crossdomain.xml -->
<cross-domain-policy>
  <allow-access-from domain="*" />
</cross-domain-policy>
```

Each `<allow-access-from>` tag also has the optional `secure` attribute. The `secure` attribute defaults to `true`. You can set the attribute to `false` if your policy file is on an HTTPS server, and you want to allow SWF files on an HTTP server to load data from the HTTPS server.

Setting the `secure` attribute to `false` could compromise the security offered by HTTPS.

If the SWF file you are downloading comes from an HTTPS server, but the SWF file loading it is on an HTTP server, you need to add the `secure="false"` attribute to the `<allow-access-from>` tag, as shown in the following code:

`<allow-access-from domain="www.foo.com" secure="false" />`

A policy file that contains no `<allow-access-from>` tags has the same effect as not having a policy on a server.

About custom policy file locations

Flash Player 7 (7.0.19.0) supports a method called `System.security.loadPolicyFile`. This method lets you specify a custom location on a server where a cross-domain policy file can be found, so it does not need to be in the root directory. Flash Player 7 (7.0.14.0) only searched for policy files in the root location of a server, but it can be inconvenient for a site administrator to place this file in the root directory. For more information on the `loadPolicyFile` method and XMLSocket connections, see "About XMLSocket policy files" on page 719 and `%{loadPolicyFile (security.loadPolicyFile method)}%` in the *ActionScript 2.0 Language Reference* in Flash Help.

If you use the `loadPolicyFile` method, a site administrator can place the policy file in any directory, as long as the SWF files that need to use the policy file call `loadPolicyFile` to tell Flash Player where the policy file is located. However, policy files not placed in the root directory have a limited scope. The policy file allows access only to locations at or below its own level in the server's hierarchy.

The `loadPolicyFile` method is available only in Flash Player 7 (7.0.19.0) or later. Authors of SWF files using the `loadPolicyFile` method must do one of the following:

- Require Flash Player 7 (7.0.19.0) or later.
- Arrange for the site where the data is coming from to have a policy file in the default location (the root directory) as well as in the nondefault location. Earlier versions of Flash Player use the default location.

Otherwise, authors must create SWF files so a failure of a cross-domain loading operation is implemented.

> **CAUTION**
> If your SWF file relies on `loadPolicyFile`, visitors with Flash Player 6 or earlier or Flash Player 7 (7.0.19.0) or later do not have problems. However, visitors with Flash Player 7 (7.0.14.0) do not have support for `loadPolicyFile`.

If you want to use a policy file in a custom location on the server, you must call
`System.security.loadPolicyFile` *before* you make any requests that depend on the policy
file, such as the following:

```
System.security.loadPolicyFile("http://www.foo.com/folder1/folder2/
   crossdomain.xml");
var my_xml:XML = new XML();
my_xml.load("http://www.foo.com/folder1/folder2/myData.xml");
```

You can load several policy files with overlapping scopes using `loadPolicyFile`. For all
requests, Flash Player tries to consult all the files whose scope includes the location of the
request. If one policy file fails to grant cross-domain access, another file is not prevented from
granting access to data. If all access attempts fail, Flash Player looks in the default location of
the crossdomain.xml file (in the root directory). The request fails if no policy file is found in
the default location.

About XMLSocket policy files

For an XMLSocket connection attempt, Flash Player 7 (7.0.14.0) looked for crossdomain.xml
on an HTTP server on port 80 in the subdomain to which the connection attempt was being
made. Flash Player 7 (7.0.14.0) and all earlier versions restricted XMLSocket connections to
ports 1024 and above. However, in Flash Player 7 (7.0.19.0) and later, ActionScript can
inform Flash Player of a nondefault location for a policy file using
`System.security.loadPolicyFile`. Any custom locations for XMLSocket policy files must
still be on an XML socket server.

In the following example, Flash Player retrieves a policy file from a specified URL:

```
System.security.loadPolicyFile("http://www.foo.com/folder/policy.xml");
```

Any permissions granted by the policy file at that location apply to all content at the same
level or below in the server's hierarchy. Therefore, if you try to load the following data, you
discover you can only load data from certain locations:

```
myLoadVars.load("http://foo.com/sub/dir/vars.txt"); // allowed
myLoadVars.load("http://foo.com/sub/dir/deep/vars2.txt"); // allowed
myLoadVars.load("http://foo.com/elsewhere/vars3.txt"); // not allowed
```

To work around this, you can load more than one policy file into a single SWF file using
`loadPolicyFile`. Flash Player always waits for the completion of any policy file downloads
before denying a request that requires a policy file. Flash Player consults the default location of
crossdomain.xml if no other policies were authorized in the SWF file.

Special syntax allows policy files to be retrieved directly from an XMLSocket server:

```
System.security.loadPolicyFile("xmlsocket://foo.com:414");
```

In this example, Flash Player tries to retrieve a policy file from the specified host and a port. Any port can be used if the policy file is not in the default (root) directory; otherwise the port is limited to 1024 and higher (as with earlier players). When a connection is established to the specified port, Flash Player sends `<policy-file-request />`, terminated by a null byte.

The XML socket server might be configured to serve policy files in the following ways:

- To serve policy files and normal socket connections over the same port. The server should wait for `<policy-file-request />` before transmitting a policy file.

- To serve policy files over a separate port from normal connections, in which case it might send a policy file as soon as a connection is established on the dedicated policy file port.

The server must send a null byte to terminate a policy file before it closes the connection. If the server does not close the connection, Flash Player does so upon receiving the terminating null byte.

A policy file served by an XML socket server has the same syntax as any other policy file, except that it must also specify the ports to which access is granted. The allowed ports are specified in a `to-ports` attribute in the `<allow-access-from>` tag. If a policy file is less than port 1024, it can grant access to any port; when a policy file comes from port 1024 or higher, it can grant access only to other ports above 1024. Single port numbers, port ranges, and wildcards are allowed. The following code is an example of an XMLSocket policy file:

```
<cross-domain-policy>
<allow-access-from domain="*" to-ports="507" />
<allow-access-from domain="*.foo.com" to-ports="507,516" />
<allow-access-from domain="*.bar.com" to-ports="516-523" />
<allow-access-from domain="www.foo.com" to-ports="507,516-523" />
<allow-access-from domain="www.bar.com" to-ports="*" />
</cross-domain-policy>
```

Because the ability to connect to ports lower than 1024 is available in Flash Player 7 (7.0.19.0) and later, a policy file loaded with `loadPolicyFile` is always required to authorize this, even when a SWF file is connecting to its own subdomain.

HTTP to HTTPS protocol access between SWF files

You must use an `allowDomain` handler or method to permit a SWF file in one domain to be accessed by a SWF file in another domain. However, if the SWF file being accessed is hosted at a site that uses a secure protocol (HTTPS), the `allowDomain` handler or method doesn't permit access from a SWF file hosted at a site that uses an insecure protocol. To permit such access, you must use the `LocalConnection.allowInsecure Domain()` or `System.security.allowInsecureDomain()` statements. See "Allowing HTTP to HTTPS protocol access between SWF files" on page 721 for more information.

Allowing HTTP to HTTPS protocol access between SWF files

In addition to the exact-domain matching rules, you must explicitly permit files hosted at sites using a secure protocol (HTTPS) to be accessed by files hosted at sites using an insecure protocol. Depending on whether the called file is published for Flash Player 6, 7, or 8, you must implement either one of the `allowDomain` statements (see "Cross-domain and subdomain access between SWF files" on page 710), or use the `LocalConnection.allowInsecure Domain` or `System.security.allowInsecureDomain()` statements.

For example, if the SWF file at https://www.someSite.com/data.swf must allow access by a SWF file at http://www.someSite.com, the following code added to data.swf allows this access:

```
// Within data.swf
System.security.allowInsecureDomain("www.someSite.com");
my_lc.allowInsecureDomain = function(sendingDomain:String):Boolean {
  return (sendingDomain == "www.someSite.com");
};
```

> **WARNING** Implementing an `allowInsecureDomain()` statement compromises the security offered by the HTTPS protocol. You should make these changes only if you can't reorganize your site so that all SWF files are served from the HTTPS protocol.

The following code shows an example of the changes you might have to make:

```
// Commands in a Flash Player 6 SWF file at https://www.someSite.com
// to allow access by Flash Player 7 SWF files that are hosted
// at http://www.someSite.com or at http://www.someOtherSite.com
System.security.allowDomain("someOtherSite.com");
my_lc.allowDomain = function(sendingDomain) {
  return(sendingDomain=="someOtherSite.com");
}
// Corresponding commands in a Flash Player 7 SWF file
// to allow access by Flash Player 7 SWF files that are hosted
// at http://www.someSite.com or at http://www.someOtherSite.com
System.security.allowInsecureDomain("www.someSite.com",
  "www.someOtherSite.com");
my_lc.allowInsecureDomain = function(sendingDomain) {
  return(sendingDomain=="www.someSite.com" ||
    sendingDomain=="www.someOtherSite.com");
}
```

You might also have to add statements such as these to your files if you aren't currently using them. A modification might be necessary even if both files are in the same domain (for example, a file in http://www.domain.com is calling a file in https://www.domain.com).

To summarize, you might have to modify your files to add or change statements if you publish files for Flash Player 7 or later that meet the following conditions:

- You implemented cross-SWF file-scripting (using `loadMovie()`, `MovieClip.loadMovie()`, `MovieClipLoader.LoadClip()`, or Local Connection objects).

- The calling file is not hosted using an HTTPS protocol, and the called file is HTTPS.

You must make the following changes:

- If the called file is published for Flash Player 7, include `System.security.allowInsecureDomain` or `LocalConnection.allowInsecureDomain` in the called file, using exact domain-name matching, as shown in the code examples earlier in this section.

- If the called file is published for Flash Player 6 or earlier, and both the calling and called files are in same domain (for example, a file in http://www.domain.com is calling a file in https://www.domain.com), no modification is needed.

- If the called file is published for Flash Player 6, the files are not in same domain, and you don't want to port the called file to Flash Player 7, modify the called file to add or change a `System.security.allowDomain` or `LocalConnection.allowDomain` statement, using exact domain-name matching, as shown in the code examples earlier in this section.

- If the called file is published for Flash Player 6 and you want to port the called file to Flash Player 7, include `System.security.allowInsecureDomain` or `LocalConnection.allowInsecureDomain` in the called file, using exact domain-name matching, as shown in the code examples earlier in this section.

- If the called file is published for Flash Player 5 or earlier, and both files are not in the same domain, you can do one of two things. You can either port the called file to Flash Player 6 and add or change a `System.security.allowDomain` statement, using exact domain-name matching, as shown in the code examples earlier in this section, or you can port the called file to Flash Player 7, and include a `System.security.allowInsecureDomain` statement in the called file, using exact domain-name matching, as shown in the code examples earlier in this section.

CHAPTER 18

Debugging Applications

18

Macromedia Flash Basic 8 and Macromedia Flash Professional 8 provide several tools for testing ActionScript in your SWF files. The Debugger lets you find errors in a SWF file while it's running in the Flash Debug Player (see "Debugging your scripts" on page 725). Flash also provides the following additional debugging tools:

- The Output panel, which shows error messages, including some runtime errors, and lists of variables and objects (see "Using the Output panel" on page 738)
- The `trace` statement, which sends programming notes and values of expressions to the Output panel (see "Using the trace statement" on page 742)
- The `throw` and `try..catch..finally` statements, which let you test and respond to runtime errors from within your script.

This section describes how to debug your scripts and Flash applications by using the Debugger, and how to use the Output panel. For more information, see the following topics:

Debugging your scripts

The Debugger in Flash 8 helps you find errors in your SWF file while it runs in Flash Player. You must view your SWF file in a special version of Flash Player, which is called *Flash Debug Player*. When you install the authoring tool, Flash Debug Player is installed automatically. So if you install Flash and browse a website that has Flash content, or use the Test Movie option, you're using Flash Debug Player. You can also run the installer in the following directory in Windows or Macintosh: *Flash install directory*\Players\Debug\ directory or start the stand-alone Flash Debug Player from the same directory.

When you use the Control > Test Movie command to test SWF files that implement keyboard controls (tabbing, keyboard shortcuts created using `Key.addListener()`, and so on), select Control > Disable Keyboard Shortcuts. Selecting this option prevents the authoring environment from "grabbing" keystrokes, and lets them pass through to the player. For example, in the authoring environment, Control+U opens the Preferences dialog box. If your script assigns Control+U to an action that underlines text onscreen, when you use Test Movie, pressing Control+U opens the Preferences dialog box instead of running the action that underlines text. To let the Control+U command pass through to the player, you must select Control > Disable Keyboard Shortcuts.

> **CAUTION** When you use a non-English application on an English system, the Test Movie command fails if any part of the SWF file path has characters that cannot be represented with the MBCS encoding scheme. For example, Japanese paths on an English system do not work. All areas of the application that use the external player are subject to this limitation.

The Debugger shows a hierarchical display list of movie clips currently loaded in Flash Player. Using the Debugger, you can display and modify variable and property values as the SWF file plays, and you can use breakpoints to stop the SWF file and step through ActionScript code line by line.

You can use the Debugger in test mode with local files, or you can use it to test files on a web server in a remote location. The Debugger lets you set breakpoints in your ActionScript that stop Flash Player and step through the code as it runs. You can then go back to your scripts and edit them so that they produce the correct results.

After it's activated, the Debugger status bar displays the URL or local path of the file, tells whether the file is running in test mode or from a remote location, and shows a live view of the movie clip display list. When movie clips are added to or removed from the file, the display list reflects the changes immediately. You can resize the display list by moving the horizontal splitter.

To activate the Debugger in test mode:

- Select Control > Debug Movie.

  This command exports the SWF file with debugging information (the SWD file) and enables debugging of the SWF file. It opens the Debugger and opens the SWF file in test mode.

> **NOTE**
> If necessary, you can resize the various regions of the Debugger panel. When your pointer changes between each region, you can drag to resize the Display list, Watch list, and code view.

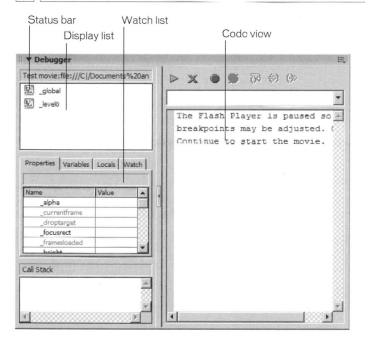

For more information, see the following topics:

- "Debugging a SWF file from a remote location"
- "Displaying and modifying variables" on page 730
- "Using the Watch list" on page 732
- "Displaying movie clip properties and changing editable properties" on page 733
- "Setting and removing breakpoints" on page 734
- "About working through lines of code" on page 736

Debugging a SWF file from a remote location

You can debug a remote SWF file by using the stand-alone, ActiveX, or plug-in version of Flash Player. To find these versions of Flash Player, look in the following directory in Windows or Macintosh: *Flash install directory*\Players\Debug\.

When you export a SWF file, you can enable debugging in the file and create a debugging password. If you don't enable debugging, the Debugger is not activated.

To ensure that only trusted users can run your SWF files in the Flash Debug Player, you can publish your file with a debugging password. As in JavaScript or HTML, users can view client-side variables in ActionScript. To store variables securely, you must send them to a server-side application instead of storing them in your file. However, as a Flash developer, you may have other trade secrets, such as movie clip structures, that you do not want to reveal. You can use a debugging password to protect your work.

To enable remote debugging of a SWF file:

1. Select File > Publish Settings.

2. On the Flash tab of the Publish Settings dialog box, select Debugging permitted.

3. To set a password, enter a password in the Password box.

   After you set this password, no one can download information to the Debugger without the password. However, if you leave the Password box blank, no password is required.

4. Close the Publish Settings dialog box, and select one of the following commands:

   - Control > Debug Movie
   - File > Export > Export Movie
   - File > Publish

   Flash creates a debugging file, with the extension .swd, and saves it in the same directory as the SWF file. The SWD file is used to debug ActionScript, and contains information that lets you use breakpoints and step through code.

5. Place the SWD file in the same directory as the SWF file on the server.

   If the SWD file is not in the same directory as the SWF file, you can still debug remotely; however, the Debugger has no breakpoint information, so you can't step through code.

6. In Flash, select Window > Debugger.

7. In the Debugger, select Enable Remote Debugging from the pop-up menu (at the upper right of the panel).

To activate the Debugger from a remote location:

1. Open the Flash authoring application.

2. In a browser or in the debug version of the stand-alone player, open the published SWF file from the remote location.

   The Remote Debug dialog box appears.

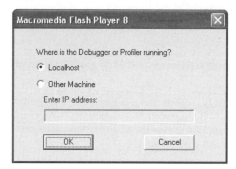

> **NOTE**
>
> If the Remote Debug dialog box doesn't appear, Flash can't find the SWD file. In this case, right-click (Windows) or Control-click (Macintosh) in the SWF file to display the context menu, and select Debugger.

3. In the Remote Debug dialog box, select Localhost or Other Machine:

   ■ Select Localhost if the Debug player and the Flash authoring application are on the same computer.

   ■ Select Other Machine if the Debug player and the Flash authoring application are not on the same computer. Enter the IP address of the computer running the Flash authoring application.

4. When a connection is established, a password prompt appears.

   Enter your debugging password if you set one.

   The display list of the SWF file appears in the Debugger. If the SWF file doesn't play, the Debugger might be paused, so click Continue to start it.

Displaying and modifying variables

The Variables tab in the Debugger shows the names and values of any global and timeline variables in the SWF file that are selected in the display list. If you change the value of a variable on the Variables tab, you can see the change reflected in the SWF file while it runs. For example, to test collision detection in a game, you can enter the variable value to position a ball in the correct location next to a wall.

The Locals tab in the Debugger shows the names and values of any local variables that are available in the line of ActionScript where the SWF file is currently stopped, at a breakpoint or anywhere else within a user-defined function.

To display a variable:

1. Select the movie clip containing the variable from the display list.

   To display global variables, select the _global clip in the display list.

    If necessary, you can resize the various regions of the Debugger panel. When your changes between each region, you can drag to resize the Display list, Watch list, and code view.

2. Click the Variables tab.

The display list updates automatically as the SWF file plays. If a movie clip is removed from the SWF file at a specific frame, that movie clip, along with its variable and variable name, is also removed from the display list in the Debugger. However, if you mark a variable for the Watch list (see "Using the Watch list" on page 732), the variable is removed from the Variables tab, but can still be viewed in the Watch tab.

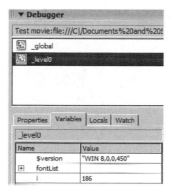

To modify a variable value:

■ Double-click the value, and enter a new value.

The value cannot be an expression. For example, you can use "Hello", 3523, or "http://www.macromedia.com", and you cannot use x + 2 or eval("name:" +i). The value can be a string (any value surrounded by quotation marks [""]), a number, or a Boolean value (true or false).

> **NOTE**
>
> To write the value of an expression to the Output panel in test mode, use the trace statement. See "Using the trace statement" on page 742.

Using the Watch list

To monitor a set of critical variables in a manageable way, you can mark variables to appear in the Watch list. The Watch list shows the absolute path to the variable and the value. You can also enter a new variable value in the Watch list the same way as in the Variables tab. The Watch list can show only variables and properties that you can access by using an absolute target path, such as _global or _root.

If you add a local variable to the Watch list, its value appears only when Flash Player is stopped at a line of ActionScript where that variable is in scope. All other variables appear while the SWF file is playing. If the Debugger can't find the value of the variable, the value is listed as undefined.

> **NOTE**
>
> If necessary, you can resize the various regions of the Debugger panel. When your changes between each region, you can drag to resize the Display list, Watch list, and code view.

The Watch list can show only variables, not properties or functions.

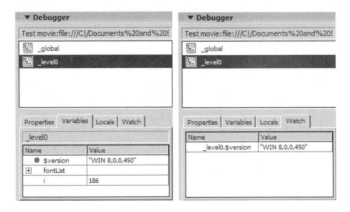

Variables marked for the Watch list and variables in the Watch list

To add variables to the Watch list, do one of the following:

- On the Variables or Locals tab, right-click (Windows) or Control-click (Macintosh) a selected variable and then select Watch from the context menu. A blue dot appears next to the variable.

- On the Watch tab, right-click (Windows) or Control-click (Macintosh) and select Add from the context menu. Double-click in the name column, and enter the target path to the variable name in the field.

To remove variables from the Watch list:

- On the Watch tab or the Variables tab, right-click (Windows) or Control-click (Macintosh) and select Remove from the context menu.

Displaying movie clip properties and changing editable properties

The Debugger's Properties tab shows all the property values of any movie clip on the Stage. You can change a value and see its effect in the SWF file while it runs. Some movie clip properties are read-only and cannot be changed.

> **NOTE** If necessary, you can resize the various regions of the Debugger panel. When your pointer changes between each region, you can drag to resize the Display list, Watch list, and code view.

To display a movie clip's properties in the Debugger:

1. Select a movie clip from the display list.

2. Click the Properties tab in the Debugger.

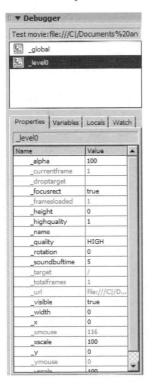

To modify a property value:

- Double-click the value, and enter a new value.

  The value cannot be an expression. For example, you can enter **50** or **"clearwater"**, but you cannot enter **x + 50**. The value can be a string (any value surrounded by quotation marks [""]), a number, or a Boolean value (`true` or `false`). You can't enter object or array values (for example, {id: "rogue"} or [1, 2, 3]) in the Debugger.

> **NOTE**
> To write the value of an expression to the Output panel in test mode, use the `trace` statement. See "Using the trace statement" on page 742.

Setting and removing breakpoints

A breakpoint lets you stop a Flash application running in Flash Debug Player at a specific line of ActionScript. You can use breakpoints to test possible trouble spots in your code. For example, if you've written a set of `if..else if` statements and can't determine which one is executing, you can add a breakpoint before the statements and examine them one by one in the Debugger.

You can set breakpoints in the Actions panel, Script window, or in the Debugger. Breakpoints set in the Actions panel are saved with the FLA file. Breakpoints set in the Debugger and Script window are not saved in the FLA file and are valid only for the current debugging session.

> **CAUTION**
> If you set breakpoints in the Actions panel or Script window and press the Auto Format button, you might notice that some breakpoints are no longer in the correct location. ActionScript might be moved to a different line when your code is formatted because sometimes empty lines are removed. You might need to check and modify your breakpoints after you click Auto Format, or to auto format your scripts before you set breakpoints.

To set or remove a breakpoint in the Actions panel or Script window during a debugging session, do one of the following:

- Click in the left margin. A red dot indicates a breakpoint.
- Click the Debug options button above the Script pane.
- Right-click (Windows) or Control-click (Macintosh) to display the context menu, and select Set Breakpoint, Remove Breakpoint, or Remove Breakpoints in this File.

> **NOTE**
> In the Script window, you can also select Remove Breakpoints in all AS Files.

- Press Control+Shift+B (Windows) or Command+Shift+B (Macintosh).

> **NOTE** In some previous versions of Flash, clicking in the left margin of the Script pane selected the line of code; now it adds or removes a breakpoint. To select a line of code, use Control-click (Windows) or Command-click (Macintosh).

To set and remove breakpoints in the Debugger, do one of the following:

- Click in the left margin. A red dot indicates a breakpoint.
- Click the Toggle Breakpoint or Remove All Breakpoints button above the code view.
- Right-click (Windows) or Control-click (Macintosh) to display the context menu, and select Set Breakpoint, Remove Breakpoint, or Remove All Breakpoints in the File.
- Press Control+Shift+B (Windows) or Command+Shift+B (Macintosh).

After Flash Player stops at a breakpoint, you can step into, over, or out of that line of code. (See "About working through lines of code" on page 736.)

You can set breakpoints in the Script window, and have them show up in the debugger if the debugger has the same path to the ActionScript file as the one that was opened in the Script window. Likewise, you can set breakpoints in the debugger during a debug session, and have the breakpoints appear in the ActionScript file if you open it in the Script window.

> **NOTE** Do not set breakpoints on comments or empty lines; if breakpoints are set on comments or empty lines, the breakpoints are ignored.

About the breakpoints XML file

When you work with breakpoints in an external script file in the Script window, the AsBreakpoints.xml file lets you store breakpoint information. The AsBreakpoints.xml file is written to the Local Settings directory, in the following locations:

Windows:

Hard Disk\Documents and Settings*User*\Local Settings\Application Data\Macromedia\ Flash 8*language*\Configuration\Debugger\

Macintosh:

Macintosh HD/Users/*User*/Library/Application Support/Macromedia Flash 8/Configuration/ Debugger/

An example of the AsBreakpoints.xml is as follows:

```xml
<?xml version="1.0"?>
<flash_breakpoints version="1.0">
  <file name="c:\tmp\myscript.as">
    <breakpoint line="10"></breakpoint>
    <breakpoint line="8"></breakpoint>
    <breakpoint line="6"></breakpoint>
  </file>
  <file name="c:\tmp\myotherscript.as">
    <breakpoint line="11"></breakpoint>
    <breakpoint line="7"></breakpoint>
    <breakpoint line="4"></breakpoint>
  </file>
</flash_breakpoints>
```

The XML file consists of the following tags:

flash_breakpoints   This node has an attribute, called `version`, that indicates the version of the XML file. Flash 8 is version 1.0.

file   A child node of `flash_breakpoints`. This node has one attribute, called `name`, that indicates the name of the file that contains breakpoints.

breakpoint   A child node of `file`. This node has an attribute, called `line`, that indicates the line number where the breakpoint exists.

The AsBreakpoints.xml file is read when you launch Flash, and generated again when you shut down Flash. AsBreakpoints.xml is used to keep track of the breakpoints between Flash development sessions. An internal data structure maintains the breakpoints as you set and remove them while developing in Flash.

About working through lines of code

When you start a debugging session, Flash Player is paused so that you can toggle breakpoints. If you set breakpoints in the Actions panel, you can click Continue to play the SWF file until it reaches a breakpoint. If you didn't set breakpoints in the Actions panel, you can use the jump menu in the Debugger to select any script in the SWF file. When you have selected a script, you can add breakpoints to it.

After adding breakpoints, you must click Continue to start the SWF file. The Debugger stops when it reaches the breakpoint. For example, in the following code, suppose a breakpoint is set inside a button on the `myFunction()` line:

```
on(press){
  myFunction();
}
```

When you click the button, the breakpoint is reached and Flash Player pauses. You can now bring the Debugger to the first line of myFunction() wherever it is defined in the document. You can also continue through or exit out of the function.

As you step through lines of code, the values of variables and properties change in the Watch list and in the Variables, Locals, and Properties tabs. A yellow arrow on the left side of the Debugger's code view indicates the line at which the Debugger stopped. Use the following buttons along the top of the code view:

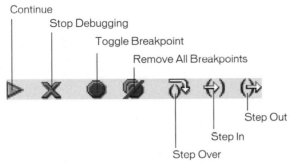

Step In advances the Debugger (indicated by the yellow arrow) into a function. Step In works only for user-defined functions.

In the following example, if you place a breakpoint at line 7 and click Step In, the Debugger advances to line 2, and another click of Step In advances you to line 3. Clicking Step In for lines that do not have user-defined functions in them advances the Debugger over a line of code. For example, if you stop at line 2 and select Step In, the Debugger advances to line 3, as shown in the following example:

```
1 function myFunction() {
2 x = 0;
3 y = 0;
4 }
5
6 mover = 1;
7 myFunction();
8 mover = 0;
```

> **NOTE** The numbers in this code snippet denote line numbers. They are not part of the code.

Step Out advances the Debugger out of a function. This button works only if you are currently stopped in a user-defined function; it moves the yellow arrow to the line after the line where that function was called. In the previous example, if you place a breakpoint at line 3 and click Step Out, the Debugger moves to line 8. Clicking Step Out at a line that is not within a user-defined function is the same as clicking Continue. For example, if you stop at line 6 and click Step Out, the player continues to execute the script until it encounters a breakpoint.

Step Over advances the Debugger over a line of code. This button moves the yellow arrow to the next line in the script. In the previous example, if you are stopped at line 7 and click Step Over, you advance directly to line 8 without stepping through `myFunction()`, although the `myFunction()` code still executes.

Continue leaves the line at which the player is stopped and continues playing until a breakpoint is reached.

Stop Debugging makes the Debugger inactive but continues to play the SWF file in Flash Player.

Using the Output panel

In test mode, the Output panel shows information to help you troubleshoot your SWF file. Some information (such as syntax errors) appear automatically. You can show other information by using the List Objects and List Variables commands. (See "Listing a SWF file's objects" on page 740 and "Listing a SWF file's variables" on page 741.)

If you use the `trace` statement in your scripts, you can send specific information to the Output panel as the SWF file runs. This could include notes about the SWF file's status or the value of an expression. (See "Using the trace statement" on page 742.)

To display or hide the Output panel, do one of the following:

- Select Window > Output
- Press F2.

To work with the contents of the Output panel, click the pop-up menu in the upper right corner to see your options.

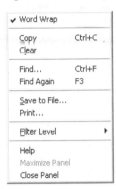

The following table lists the options available on the Output panel's pop-up menu:

Menu item	What it does
Word wrap	Toggles whether long lines wrap automatically, so the user does not have to use the horizontal scroll bar to view the entire line of characters. If selected, lines wrap; otherwise, lines do not wrap.
Copy	Copies the entire contents of the Output panel to the computer's Clipboard. To copy a selected portion of the output, select the area you want to copy and then select Copy.
Clear	Clears all output currently in the Output panel.
Find	Opens a dialog box that you can use to find a keyword or phrase within the Output panel contents.
Find Again	Attempts to locate the next instance of a keyword or phrase in the Output panel contents.
Save to File	Saves the current contents of the Output panel to an external text file.
Print	Shows the Print dialog box, which lets you print the current contents of the Output panel to an Installed printer or installed programs such as Flash Paper or Acrobat.
Filter level	Lets you select two possible levels of output: None or Verbose. Selecting None suppresses all output sent to the browser.
Maximize Panel	Maximizes the Output panel when it is docked.
Close Panel	Closes the Output panel and clears the contents of the panel.

For more information on the Output panel, see the following topics:

- "Listing a SWF file's objects" on page 740
- "Listing a SWF file's variables" on page 741
- "About displaying text field properties for debugging" on page 742
- "Using the trace statement" on page 742
- "Updating Flash Player for testing" on page 743

Listing a SWF file's objects

In test mode, the List Objects command shows the level, frame, object type (shape, movie clip, or button), target paths, and instance names of movie clips, buttons, and text fields in a hierarchical list. This option is especially useful for finding the correct target path and instance name. Unlike the Debugger, the list does not update automatically as the SWF file plays; you must select the List Objects command each time you want to send the information to the Output panel.

> **CAUTION**
> Selecting the List Objects command clears any information that currently appears in the Output panel. If you do not want to lose information in the Output panel, select Save to File from the Output panel Options pop-up menu or copy and paste the information to another location before selecting the List Objects command.

The List Objects command does not list all ActionScript data objects. In this context, an object is considered to be a shape or symbol on the Stage.

To display a list of objects in a SWF file:

1. If your SWF file is not running in test mode, select Control > Test Movie.

2. Select Debug > List Objects.

   A list of all the objects currently on the Stage appears in the Output panel, as shown in the following example:

```
Level #0: Frame=1 Label="Scene_1"
  Button: Target="_level0.myButton"
    Shape:
  Movie Clip: Frame=1 Target="_level0.myMovieClip"
    Shape:
  Edit Text: Target="_level0.myTextField" Text="This is sample text."
```

Listing a SWF file's variables

In test mode, the List Variables command shows a list of all the variables currently in the SWF file. This list is especially useful for finding the correct variable target path and variable name. Unlike the Debugger, the list does not update automatically as the SWF file plays; you must select the List Variables command each time you want to send the information to the Output panel.

The List Variables command also shows global variables declared with the _global identifier. The global variables appear at the top of the List Variables output in a Global Variables section, and each variable has a _global prefix.

In addition, the List Variables command shows getter/setter properties—properties that are created with the Object.addProperty() method and start get or set methods. A getter/setter property appears with any other properties in the object to which it belongs. To make these properties easily distinguishable from other variables, the value of a getter/setter property is prefixed with the string [getter/setter]. The value that appears for a getter/setter property is determined by evaluating the get function of the property.

> **CAUTION** Selecting the List Variables command clears any information that appears in the Output panel. If you do not want to lose information in the Output panel, select Save to File from the Output panel Options pop-up menu or copy and paste the information to another location before selecting the List Variables command.

To display a list of variables in a SWF file:

1. If your SWF file is not running in test mode, select Control > Test Movie.

2. Select Debug > List Variables.

   A list of all the variables currently in the SWF file appears in the Output panel, as shown in the following example:

   ```
   Global Variables:
     Variable _global.mycolor = "lime_green"
   Level #0:
   Variable _level0.$version = "WIN 7,0,19,0"
   Variable _level0.myArray = [object #1, class 'Array'] [
       0:"socks",
       1:"gophers",
       2:"mr.claw"
     ]
   Movie Clip: Target="_level0.my_mc"
   ```

About displaying text field properties for debugging

To obtain debugging information about TextField objects, you can use the Debug > List Variables command in test mode. The Output panel uses the following conventions to show TextField objects:

- If a property is not found on the object, it does not appear.
- No more than four properties appear on a line.
- A property with a string value appears on a separate line.
- If any other properties are defined for the object after the built-in properties are processed, they are added to the display by using the rules in the second and third points of this list.
- Color properties appear as hexadecimal numbers (0x00FF00).
- The properties appear in the following order: `variable`, `text`, `htmlText`, `html`, `textWidth`, `textHeight`, `maxChars`, `borderColor`, `backgroundColor`, `textColor`, `border`, `background`, `wordWrap`, `password`, `multiline`, `selectable`, `scroll`, `hscroll`, `maxscroll`, `maxhscroll`, `bottomScroll`, `type`, `embedFonts`, `restrict`, `length`, `tabIndex`, `autoSize`.

The List Objects command in the Debug menu (during test mode) lists TextField objects. If an instance name is specified for a text field, the Output panel shows the full target path including the instance name in the following form:

```
Target = "target path"
```

For more information on the List Variables or List Objects command, see "Using the Output panel" on page 738.

Using the trace statement

When you use the `trace` statement in a script, you can send information to the Output panel. For example, while testing a SWF file or scene, you can send specific programming notes to the panel or have specific results appear when a button is pressed or a frame plays. The `trace` statement is similar to the JavaScript `alert` statement.

When you use the `trace` statement in a script, you can use expressions as parameters. The value of an expression appears in the Output panel in test mode, as shown by the following code snippet and image of the Output panel.

To use the trace statement in a script:

1. Select Frame 1 of the Timeline, and add the following code in the Actions panel:

```
this.createEmptyMovieClip("img_mc", 10);
var mclListener:Object = new Object();
mclListener.onLoadInit = function(target_mc:MovieClip) {
    trace(target_mc+" loaded in "+getTimer()+" ms");
};
mclListener.onLoadError = function(target_mc:MovieClip,
    errorCode:String, httpStatus:Number) {
    trace(">> error downloading image into "+target_mc);
    trace(">>\t errorCode="+errorCode+", httpStatus="+httpStatus);
};
var img_mcl:MovieClipLoader = new MovieClipLoader();
img_mcl.addListener(mclListener);
img_mcl.loadClip("http://www.helpexamples.com/flash/images/404.jpg",
    img_mc);
```

2. Select Control > Test Movie to test the SWF file.

   The Output panel displays the following message:

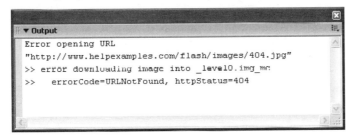

Updating Flash Player for testing

You can download the latest version of Flash Player from the Macromedia Support Center at www.macromedia.com/support/flash and use it to test your SWF files.

Best Practices and Coding Conventions for ActionScript 2.0

Macromedia Flash designers and developers must write code and structure applications in a way that is intuitive and beneficial to themselves as well as to the other people who are working on the same project. This is particularly important in FLA files with lots of assets, or long code files. When you follow best practices and coding conventions, everyone on the design and development team can understand the file structure and ActionScript code and can work more efficiently. This document helps formalize the Flash development and coding process.

Because it is common for more than one designer or developer to work on a single Flash project, teams benefit when everyone follows a standard set of guidelines for using Flash, organizing FLA files, and writing ActionScript 2.0 code. The sections in this chapter outline the best practices for writing ActionScript, and some sections of *Using Flash* in Flash Help cover best practices when using the Flash authoring tool.

The following guidelines encourage consistency for people learning how to use Flash and write ActionScript code. Adopt best practices at all times, whether you are a designer or developer, or working alone or as part of a team.

- When you work on Flash or ActionScript documents

  Adopting consistent and efficient practices helps you speed up your workflow. It is faster to develop using established coding conventions, and easier to understand and remember how you structured your document when you want to edit it further. Additionally, your code is often more portable within the framework of a larger project, and easier to reuse.

- When you share FLA or AS files

  Other people editing the document can quickly find and understand ActionScript, consistently modify code, and find and edit assets.

- When you work on applications

  Multiple authors can work on an application with fewer conflicts and greater efficiency. Project or site administrators can manage and structure complex projects or applications with fewer conflicts or redundancies if you follow best practices and coding conventions.

- When you are learning or teaching Flash and ActionScript

  Learning how to build applications by using best practices and following coding conventions reduces the need to relearn particular methodologies. If students learning Flash practice consistent and better ways to structure code, they might learn the language more quickly and with less frustration.

Consistent techniques and the following guidelines help people learning Flash, or people working effectively in team environments. Consistent methods help you remember how you structured your document when you work by yourself, particularly if you have not worked on the FLA file recently.

These are only a few of the reasons to learn and follow best practices. You are bound to discover many more when you read these best practices and develop your own good habits. Consider the following topics as a guideline when you are working with Flash; you might choose to follow some or all of the recommendations. You can also modify the recommendations to suit the way you work. Many of the guidelines in this chapter help you develop a consistent way of working with Flash and writing ActionScript code.

This chapter covers the following subjects on coding conventions and best practices:

Naming conventions

Typically, you spend 80% of your development time debugging, troubleshooting, and practicing general maintenance, especially on larger projects. Even when you work on small projects, you'll spend a significant amount of time analyzing and fixing code. The readability of your code is important for your benefit and the benefit of your team members. When you follow naming conventions, you increase readability, which increases workflow and enables you to find and fix any errors in your code. All programmers follow a standardized way of writing code; this improves the project in many ways.

Using naming conventions for your variable names can serve the following important functions:

- They make your code readable so that you can immediately identify a variable's data type. This can help students, those learning code, or developers unfamiliar with your code.
- They are easy to search for and replace when necessary.
- They help reduce conflicts with reserved words and language constructs.
- They can help you distinguish between variables from different scopes (local variables, class properties, parameters, and so on).

The following sections contain naming guidelines for writing ActionScript code, such as naming files, variables, constants, components, and so on. "Formatting ActionScript syntax" on page 777 discusses formatting conventions that are specific to ActionScript, and common in other programming languages. "ActionScript coding conventions" on page 759 discusses coding conventions that are specific to writing ActionScript and developing with Flash 8.

 NOTE

Flash Player 7 and 8 loosely follow the ECMAScript (ECMA-262) edition 3 language specification. It is useful to see this specification for information on how the language works. (See www.ecma-international.org/publications/standards/Ecma-262.htm.)

This section includes the following topics:

General naming guidelines

This section reviews naming guidelines for writing ActionScript code. Naming conventions are important for writing logical code. The primary purpose is to improve the readability of your ActionScript 2.0 code. Remember that all variables must have unique names. Names are case-sensitive in Flash Player 7 and later. Do not use the same name with a different case, because this can be confusing to programmers reading your code and can cause problems in earlier versions of Flash that do not force case sensitivity. Keep the following guidelines in mind when you name items such as variables, files, and classes in Flash:

- Limit your use of abbreviations.

  Use abbreviations consistently. An abbreviation must clearly stand for only one thing. For example, the abbreviation "sec" might represent "section" and "second."

- Concatenate words to create names.

  Use mixed-cases (upper and lower case) when you concatenate words to distinguish between each word for readability. For example, select `myPelican` rather than `mypelican`.

- Name a file by describing the process or item, such as `addUser`.

- Don't use nondescriptive names for methods or variables.

  For example, if you retrieve a piece of data that is the visitor's user name, you might use the `getUserName()` method instead of the less descriptive `getData()` method. This example expresses what is happening rather than how you accomplish it.

- Keep all names as short as possible.

  Remember to keep names descriptive.

The following sections offer more detail on naming items such as variables, classes, packages, and constants in your code.

Avoiding reserved words or language constructs

When naming instances and variables, avoid using reserved words, which can cause errors in your code. Reserved words include *keywords* in the ActionScript language.

Also, do not use any word in the ActionScript 2.0 languages (called a *language construct*) as an instance or variable name. ActionScript constructs include class names, component class names, method and property names, and interface names.

> **WARNING**
>
> Never use different cases to avoid conflicting with reserved words. For example, naming an instance of the `textfield` TextField class (which doesn't conflict with TextField because Flash is case-sensitive) is a poor coding practice.

The following table lists reserved keywords in ActionScript 2.0 that cause errors in your scripts when used as variable names:

add	and	break	case
catch	class	continue	default
delete	do	dynamic	else
eq	extends	false	finally
for	function	ge	get
gt	if	ifFrameLoaded	implements
import	In	instanceof	interface
intrinsic	le	it	ne
new	not	null	on
onClipEvent	or	private	public
return	set	static	super
switch	tellTarget	this	throw
try	typeof	var	void
while	with		

The following words are reserved for future use in Flash, from the ECMAScript (ECMA-262) edition 4 draft language specification. Avoid using these words because they might be used in future releases of Flash.

as	abstract	Boolean	bytes
char	const	debugger	double
enum	export	final	float
goto	is	long	namespace
native	package	protected	short
synchronized	throws	transient	use
volatile			

Naming variables

Variable names can only contain letters, numbers, and dollar signs ($). Do not begin variable names with numbers. Variables must be unique and they are case-sensitive in Flash Player 7 and later. For example, avoid the following variable names:

```
my/warthog = true;    // includes a slash
my warthogs = true;   // includes a space
my.warthogs = true;  // includes a dot
5warthogs = 55;       // begins with a number
```

Use strict data typing with your variables whenever possible because it helps you in the following ways:

- Adds code completion functionality, which speeds up coding.

- Generates errors in the Output panel so you don't have a silent failure when you compile your SWF file. These errors help you find and fix problems in your applications.

To add a data type to your variables, you must define the variable using the `var` keyword. In the following example, when creating a LoadVars object, you would use strict data typing:

```
var paramsLv:LoadVars = new LoadVars();
```

Strict data typing provides you with code completion, and ensures that the value of `paramsLv` contains a LoadVars object. It also ensures that the LoadVars object will not be used to store numeric or string data. Because strict typing relies on the `var` keyword, you cannot add strict data typing to global variables or properties within an object or array. For more information on strict typing variables, see "About assigning data types and strict data typing" on page 83.

 Strict data typing does not slow down a SWF file. Type checking occurs at compile time (when the SWF file is created), not at runtime.

Use the following guidelines when you name variables in your code:

- All variables must have unique names.

- Don't use the same variable name with different cases.

  Don't use, for example, `firstname` and `firstName` as different variables in your application. Although names are case-sensitive in Flash Player 7 and later, using the same variable name with a different case can be confusing to programmers reading your code and can cause problems in earlier versions of Flash that do not force case sensitivity.

- Don't use words that are part of the ActionScript 1.0 or 2.0 language as variable names.

  In particular, never use keywords as instance names, because they cause errors in your code. Don't rely on case sensitivity to avoid conflicts and get your code to work.

- Don't use variables that are parts of common programming constructs.

  Don't use language constructs if you are aware of them in other programming languages, even if Flash does not include or support these language constructs. For example, do not use the following keywords as variables:

```
textfield = "myTextfield",
switch = true;
new = "funk";
```

- Always add data type annotations to your code.

  Also referred to as "using strict data types with your variables," or "strong typing your variables," adding type annotations to your variables is important in order to:

  - Generate errors at compile time so your application doesn't silently fail.
  - Trigger code completion.
  - Helps users understand your code.

  For information on adding type annotations, see "About assigning data types and strict data typing" on page 83.

- Don't overuse the Object type.

  Data type annotations should be precise to improve performance. Use an Object type only when there is no reasonable alternative.

- Keep variables as short as possible while retaining clarity.

  Make sure your variable names are descriptive, but don't go overboard and use overly complex and long names.

- Only use single-character variable names for optimization in loops.

  Optionally, you can use single-character variables for temporary variables in loops (such as i, j, k, m, and n). Use these single-character variable names only for short loop indexes, or when performance optimization and speed are critical. The following example shows this usage:

```
var fontArr:Array = TextField.getFontList();
fontArr.sort();
var i:Number;
for (i = 0; i<fontArr.length; i++) {
  trace(fontArr[i]);
}
```

- Start variables with a lowercase letter.

  Names with capital first letters are reserved for classes, interfaces, and so on.

- Use mixed case for concatenated words.

  For example, use myFont instead of myfont.

- Don't use acronyms and abbreviations.

  The exception to this rule is if acronyms or abbreviations represent the standard way to use a term (such as HTML or CFM). For commonly used acronyms, use mixed cases for improved readability, such as `newHtmlParser` instead of `newHTMLParser`.

- Use complementary pairs when you create a related set of variable names.

  For example, you might use complementary pairs to indicate a minimum and maximum game score, as follows:

```
var minScoreNum:Number = 10; // minimum score
var maxScoreNum:Number = 500; // maximum score
```

Naming constants

You can use constants for situations in which you need to refer to a property whose value never changes. This helps you find typographical mistakes in your code that you might not find if you used literals. It also lets you change the value in a single place.

Variables should be lowercase or mixed-case letters; however, use the following guidelines for naming static constants (variables that do not change):

- Constants should be uppercase.
- Separate words should contain underscores.

You can see these guidelines at work in the following ActionScript code snippet:

```
var BASE_URL:String = "http://www.macromedia.com";  // constant
var MAX_WIDTH:Number = 10;  // constant
```

Do not directly code numerical constants unless the constant is 1, 0, or -1, which you might use in a `for` loop as a counter value.

Naming Boolean variables

Start Boolean variables with the word "is" (because a Boolean value either "is" or "is not" because of its nature). Therefore, you might use the following for whether a baby is a girl or not (which is a Boolean value):

```
isGirl
```

Or for a variable indicating whether a user is logged in (or not), you might use the following:

```
isLoggedIn
```

Naming functions and methods

Use the following guidelines when you name functions and methods in your code. For information on writing functions and methods, see Chapter 6, "Functions and Methods."

- Use descriptive names.
- Use mixed case for concatenated words.

  A good example would be singLoud().
- Start function and method names with a lowercase letter.
- Describe what value is being returned in the function's name.

  For example, if you are returning the name of a song title, you might name the function getCurrentSong().
- Establish a naming standard for relating similar functions.

  ActionScript 2.0 does not permit overloading. In the context of object-oriented programming, *overloading* refers to the ability to make your functions behave differently depending on which data types are passed into them.
- Name methods as verbs.

  You might concatenate the name, but it should contain a verb. You use verbs for most methods because they perform an operation on an object.

Examples of method names include the following:

```
sing();
boogie();
singLoud();
danceFast();
```

Naming classes and objects

When you create a new class file, use the following guidelines when you name the class and ActionScript file. For proper formatting, see the following examples of class names:

```
class Widget;
class PlasticWidget;
class StreamingVideo;
```

You might have public and private member variables in a class. The class can contain variables that you do not want users to set or access directly. Make these variables private and allow users to access the values only by using getter/setter methods.

The following guidelines apply to naming classes:

- Begin a class name with an uppercase letter.
- Write class names in mixed case when it's a compound or concatenated word.

  Begin with an uppercase letter for a compound or concatenated word. A good example is `NewMember`.
- Class names are usually nouns or qualified nouns.

  A qualifier describes the noun or phrase. For example, instead of "member," you might qualify the noun by using `NewMember` or `OldMember`.
- Clear names are more important than short names.
- Don't use acronyms and abbreviations.

  The exception to this rule is if acronyms or abbreviations represent the standard way to use a term (such as HTML or CFM). For commonly used acronyms, use mixed cases such as `NewHtmlParser` instead of `NewHTMLParser` for improved readability.
- Use meaningful and simple names that are descriptive of the class contents.

  To avoid being vague or misleading, use generic names.
- Sometimes a class name is a compound word.

  A qualifier might describe the noun or phrase. For example, instead of "member," you might qualify the noun using `NewMember` or `OldMember`.
- Do not pluralize the words you use in the class name (such as `Witches` or `BaldPirates`).

  In most cases, it is better to leave the words as qualified nouns instead. A qualifier describes the noun or phrase. For example, instead of "cat" or "buccaneer," you might qualify the noun by using `BlackCat` or `OldBuckaneer`.
- Don't use a class name in the properties of that class because it causes redundancy.

  For example, it does not make sense to have `Cat.catWhiskers`. Instead, `Cat.whiskers` is much better.
- Don't use nouns that also might be interpreted as verbs.

  For example, `Running`, or `Gardening`. Using these nouns might lead to confusion with methods, states, or other application activities.
- Use unique class names for each class in a single application.
- Do not name classes so that they conflict with the names of built-in classes in Flash.
- Try to communicate the relationship that a class has within a hierarchy.

  This helps display a class's relationship within an application. For example, you might have the Widget interface, and the implementation of Widget might be PlasticWidget, SteelWidget, and SmallWidget.

For information on interfaces, see Chapter 9, "Interfaces."

Naming packages

It's common for package names to use "reverse domain" naming convention. Examples of reverse domain names include `com.macromedia` for macromedia.com, and `org.yourdomain` for yourdomain.org.

Use the following guidelines when you name packages:

- Put the prefix for a package name in all lowercase letters.

  For example, `com`, `mx`, or `org`.

- Put related classes (classes with related functionality) in the same package.

- Begin package names with a consistent prefix.

  For example, you might use `com.macromedia.projectName` to maintain consistency. Another example would be `com.macromedia.docs.learnAS2.Users` for the *Learning ActionScript 2.0 Reference*.

- Use a clear and self-explanatory package name.

  It's important to explain the package's responsibilities. For example, you might have a package named `Pentagons`, which is responsible for using the Flash drawing API to draw various kinds of pentagons in documentation examples; its name would be `com.macromedia.docs.as2.Pentagons`.

- Use mixed capitalization for compound or concatenated package names.

  `packageName` is an example of a compound, concatenated package name. Remember to use all lowercase letters for the prefix (com, org, and so on).

- Do not use underscores or dollar sign characters.

Naming interfaces

Starting interface names with an uppercase "I" helps you distinguish an interface from a class. The following interface name, `IEmployeeRecords`, uses an initial uppercase letter and concatenated words with mixed case, as follows:

```
interface IEmployeeRecords{}
```

The following conventions also apply:

- Interface names have an uppercase first letter.
  This is the same as class names.

- Interface names are usually adjectives.
  `Printable` is a good example.

For more information on interfaces, see Chapter 9, "Interfaces."

Naming custom components

Component names have an uppercase first letter, and any concatenated words are written in mixed case. For example, the following default user-interface component set uses concatenated words and mixed case:

- CheckBox
- ComboBox
- DataGrid
- DateChooser
- DateField
- MenuBar
- NumericStepper
- ProgressBar
- RadioButton
- ScrollPane
- TextArea
- TextInput

Components that do not use concatenated words begin with an uppercase letter.

If you develop custom components, use a naming convention to prevent naming incompatibilities with Macromedia components. The names of your components must be different from those of the default set that is included with Flash. If you adopt your own consistent naming convention, it helps you prevent naming conflicts.

Remember that the naming conventions in this section are guidelines. It is most important to use a naming scheme that works well for you and to use it consistently.

Using comments in your code

This section describes how to use comments in your code. Comments document the decisions you make in the code, answering both *how* and *why*. For example, you might describe a work-around in comments. Another developer would be able to find the related code easily for updating or fixing. And finally, the issue might be addressed in a future version of Flash or Flash Player, hence the work-around would no longer be necessary.

For more information on writing comments in your ActionScript code, see the following sections:

- "Writing good comments" on page 757
- "Adding comments to classes" on page 758

Writing good comments

Using comments consistently in your ActionScript 2.0 code allows you to describe complex areas of code or important interactions that are not otherwise clear. Comments must clearly explain the intent of the code and not just translate the code. If something is not readily obvious in the code, add comments to it.

If you use the Auto Format tool with your code, you will notice that trailing comments (see "Trailing comments" on page 138) move to the next line. You can add these comments after you format your code, or you must modify the comment's new placement after you use the Auto Format tool.

For information on using comments in classes, see "Adding comments to classes" on page 758.

Use the following guidelines when you add comments to your code:

- Use block comments (/* and */) for multiline comments and single-line comments (//) for short comments.

  You can also use a *trailing comment* on the same line as the ActionScript code if necessary.

- Make sure you don't use comments to translate your ActionScript code.

  You don't need to comment on elements that are obvious in the ActionScript code.

- Comment on elements that are not readily obvious in the code.

  In particular, add comments when the subject is not described in the surrounding paragraphs.

- Do not use cluttered comments.

  A line of cluttered comments often contains equal signs (=) or asterisks (*). Instead, use white space to separate your comments from ActionScript code.

  > **NOTE**
  >
  > If you use the Auto Format tool to format ActionScript, you remove the white space. Remember to add it back or use single- line comments (//) to maintain spacing; these lines are easy to remove after you format your code.

- Remove any superfluous comments from the code before you deploy your project.

  If you find that you have many comments in your ActionScript code, consider whether you need to rewrite some of it. If you feel you must include many comments about how the ActionScript code works, it is usually a sign of poorly written code.

  > **NOTE**
  >
  > Using comments is most important in ActionScript code that is intended to teach an audience. For example, add comments to your code if you are creating sample applications for the purpose of teaching Flash, or if you are writing tutorials about ActionScript code.

Adding comments to classes

The two kinds of comments in a typical class or interface file are *documentation comments* and *implementation comments*.

> **NOTE**
> Documentation and implementation comments are not formally represented in the ActionScript language. However, they are commonly used by developers when writing class and interface files.

You use documentation comments to describe the code's specifications, but not the implementation. You use implementation comments to comment out code or to comment on the implementation of particular sections of code. Documentation comments are delimited with /** and */, and implementation comments are delimited with /* and */.

Use documentation comments to describe interfaces, classes, methods, and constructors. Include one documentation comment per class, interface, or member, and place it directly before the declaration. If you have additional information to document that does not fit into the documentation comments, use implementation comments (in the format of block comments or single-line comments).

Start classes with a standard comment, which uses the following format:

```
/**
  User class
  version 1.2
  3/21/2004
  copyright Macromedia, Inc.
*/
```

After the documentation comments, declare the class. Implementation comments should directly follow the declaration.

> **NOTE**
> Don't include comments that do not directly relate to the class that's being read. For example, don't include comments that describe the corresponding package.

Use block, single-line, and trailing comments within the body of your class to comment on your ActionScript code. For more information on using comments in class files, see "Adding comments to classes" on page 758.

ActionScript coding conventions

One of the most important aspects about programming is consistency, whether it relates to variable naming schemes (covered in "Naming conventions" on page 746), formatting code (covered in "Formatting ActionScript syntax" on page 777), or coding standards and the placement of your ActionScript 2.0 code, which is covered in this section. You dramatically simplify code debugging and maintenance if your code is organized and adheres to standards.

For more information on coding conventions, see the following topics:

- "Keeping your ActionScript code in one place" on page 759
- "Attaching code to objects" on page 760
- "Handling scope" on page 761
- "Structuring a class file" on page 764
- "About using functions" on page 773

Keeping your ActionScript code in one place

Whenever possible, put your ActionScript 2.0 code in a single location, such as in one or more external ActionScript files or on Frame 1 of the Timeline (when placed on the timeline, the code is called a *frame script*).

If you put your ActionScript code in a frame script, put the ActionScript code on the first or second frame on the Timeline, in a layer called *Actions*, which is the first or second layer on the Timeline. Sometimes you might create two layers—an acceptable practice—for ActionScript to separate functions. Some Flash applications do not always put all your code in a single place (in particular, when you use screens or behaviors).

Despite these rare exceptions, you can usually put all your code in the same location. The following are the advantages of placing your ActionScript in a single location:

- Code is easy to find in a potentially complex source file.
- Code is easy to debug.

One of the most difficult parts of debugging a FLA file is finding all the code. After you find all the code, you must figure out how it interacts with other pieces of code along with the FLA file. If you put all your code in a single frame, it is much easier to debug because it is centralized, and these problems occur less frequently. For information on attaching code to objects (and decentralizing your code), see "Attaching code to objects" on page 760. For information on behaviors and decentralized code, see "Best practices for using behaviors" in Flash Help.

Attaching code to objects

You must avoid attaching ActionScript code to objects (such as button or movie clip instances) in a FLA file, even in simple or prototype applications. Attaching code to an object means that you select a movie clip, component, or button instance, open the ActionScript editor (the Actions panel or Script window), and add ActionScript code by using the `on()` or `onClipEvent()` handler functions.

This practice is strongly discouraged for the following reasons:

- ActionScript code that is attached to objects is difficult to locate, and the FLA files are difficult to edit.
- ActionScript code that is attached to objects is difficult to debug.
- ActionScript code that is written on a timeline or in classes is more elegant and easier to build upon.
- ActionScript code that is attached to objects encourages poor coding style.
- ActionScript code that is attached to objects forces students and readers to learn additional syntax as well as different coding styles that are often poor and limited.
- Users typically have to relearn how to write functions and so on, on a timeline at a later date.

Some Flash users might say it is easier to learn ActionScript by attaching code to an object. Some also say it might be easier to add simple code, or write about or teach ActionScript this way. However, the contrast between two styles of coding (code placed on objects, and frame scripts) can be confusing to developers who are learning ActionScript and should be avoided. Also, users who learn how to write code attached to objects often have to relearn how to place the equivalent code as a frame script at a later date. This is why consistency throughout the learning process, by learning how to write frame scripts, has advantages.

Attaching ActionScript code to a button called `myBtn` appears as follows. Avoid this method:

```
on (release) {
  // Do something.
}
```

However, placing the equivalent ActionScript code on a timeline appears as follows:

```
// good code
myBtn.onRelease = function() {
  // Do something.
};
```

For more information on ActionScript syntax, see "Formatting ActionScript syntax" on page 777.

Handling scope

Scope is the area where the variable is known and can be used in a SWF file, such as on a timeline, globally across an application, or locally within a function. Typically, you can reference scope in more than one way when you write code. Using scope correctly means that you can create portable and reusable ActionScript code, and you don't risk breaking your applications as you build new modules.

It is important to understand the difference between the global and root scopes. The root scope is unique for each loaded SWF file. The global scope applies to all timelines and scopes within SWF files. You use relative addressing rather than references to root timelines, because relative addressing makes your code reusable and portable. For more information on handling scope in your applications, see the following sections:

"About variables and scope" on page 99

"About scope and targeting" on page 127

"Understanding classes and scope" on page 289.

Avoiding absolute targets (_root)

You can use several methods to target instances that let you avoid using _root; these methods are discussed later in this section. Avoid using _root in ActionScript 2.0 because SWF files that load into other SWF files might not work correctly. The _root identifier targets the base SWF file that is loading, not the SWF file using relative addressing instead of _root. This issue limits code portability in SWF files that are loaded into another file, and, particularly, in components and movie clips. You can help resolve problems by using _lockroot, but only use _lockroot when necessary (such as when you are loading a SWF file but do not have access to the FLA file). For more information on using _lockroot, see "Using _lockroot" on page 762.

Use this, this._parent, or _parent keywords rather than _root, depending on where your ActionScript 2.0 code is located. The following example shows relative addressing:

```
myClip.onRelease = function() {
  trace(this._parent.myButton._x);
};
```

All variables must be scoped, except for variables that are function parameters, and local variables. Scope variables relative to their current path whenever possible, using relative addressing, such as the this property. For more information on using the this property, see %{this property}% in the *ActionScript 2.0 Language Reference* in Flash Help.

Using _lockroot

You can use _lockroot to target content as a way to solve the scoping issues sometimes associated with the inappropriate use of _root. Although this solves many problems with applications, consider _lockroot as a work-around for problems caused by using _root. If you experience problems loading content into a SWF file or a component instance, try applying _lockroot to a movie clip that loads the content. For example, if you have a movie clip called myClip loading content, and it stops working after it is loaded, try using the following code, which is placed on a timeline:

```
this._lockroot = true;
```

Using the this keyword

Whenever possible, use the this keyword as a prefix instead of omitting the keyword, even if your code works without it. Use the this keyword to learn when a method or property belongs to a particular class. For example, for a function on a timeline, you write ActionScript 2.0 code by using the following format:

```
circleClip.onPress = function() {
   this.startDrag();
};
circleClip.onRelease = function() {
   this.stopDrag();
};
```

For a class, use the following format to write code:

```
class User {
   private var username:String;
   private var password:String;
   function User(username:String, password:String) {
     this.username = username;
     this.password = password;
   }
   public function get username():String {
     return this.username;
   }
   public function set username(username:String):Void {
     this.username = username;
   }
}
```

If you consistently add the this keyword in these situations, your ActionScript 2.0 code will be much easier to read and understand.

About scope in classes

When you port code to ActionScript 2.0 classes, you might have to change how you use the this keyword. For example, if you have a class method that uses a callback function (such as the LoadVars class's onLoad method), it can be difficult to know if the this keyword refers to the class or to the LoadVars object. In this situation, you might need to create a pointer to the current class, as the following example shows:

```
class Product {
  private var m_products_xml:XML;
  // Constructor
  // targetXmlStr contains the path to an XML file
  function Product(targetXmlStr:String) {
    /* Create a local reference to the current class.
       Even if you are within the XML's onLoad event handler, you
       can reference the current class instead of only the XML packet. */
    var thisObj:Product = this;
    // Create a local variable, which is used to load the XML file.
    var prodXml:XML = new XML();
    prodXml.ignoreWhite = true;
    prodXml.onload = function(success:Boolean) {
      if (success) {
        /* If the XML successfully loads and parses,
           set the class's m_products_xml variable to the parsed
           XML document and call the init function. */
        thisObj.m_products_xml = this;
        thisObj.init();
      } else {
        /* There was an error loading the XML file. */
        trace("error loading XML");
      }
    };
    // Begin loading the XML document
    prodXml.load(targetXmlStr);
  }
  public function init():Void {
    // Display the XML packet
    trace(this.m_products_xml);
  }
}
```

Because you are trying to reference the private member variable within an onLoad handler, the this keyword actually refers to the prodXml instance and not to the Product class, which you might expect. For this reason, you must create a pointer to the local class file so that you can directly reference the class from the onLoad handler.

For more information on classes, see "Understanding classes and scope" on page 289. For more information on scope, see "Handling scope" on page 761.

Structuring a class file

You create classes in separate ActionScript 2.0 files that are imported into a SWF file when it is compiled.

You create classes in separate ActionScript 2.0 files that are imported into a SWF file when you compile an application. To create a class file, you write code that can have a certain methodology and ordering. This methodology is discussed in the following sections.

The following conventions for structuring a class file show how you can order parts of a class to increase the efficiency and improve the readability of your code.

To structure a class file, use the following elements:

1. Add documentation comments that include a general description of the code, in addition to author information and version information.

2. Add your import statements (if applicable).

3. Write a class declaration, or interface declaration, such as the following:

   ```
   UserClass{...}
   ```

4. Include any necessary class or interface implementation comments.

   In this comment, add information that is pertinent for the entire class or interface.

5. Add all your static variables.

   Write the public class variables first and follow them with private class variables.

6. Add instance variables.

   Write the public member variables first, and follow them with private member variables.

7. Add the constructor statement, such as the one in the following example:

   ```
   public function UserClass(username:String, password:String) {...}
   ```

8. Write your methods.

   Group methods by their functionality, not by their accessibility or scope. Organizing methods this way helps to improve the readability and clarity of your code.

9. Write the getter/setter methods into the class file.

Guidelines for creating a class

Remember the following guidelines when you create a class file:

- Place only one declaration per line.
- Don't place multiple declarations on a single line.

  For example, format your declarations as shown in the following example:

  ```
  var prodSkuNum:Number;      // Product SKU (identifying) number
  var prodQuantityNum:Number; // Quantity of product
  ```

  This example shows better form than putting both declarations on a single line. Place these declarations at the beginning of a block of code.

- Initialize local variables when they are declared.

  A class's properties should only be initialized in the declaration if the initializer is a compile-time constant.

- Declare variables before you first use them.

  This includes loops.

- Avoid using local declarations that hide higher-level declarations.

  For example, don't declare a variable twice, as the following example shows:

  ```
  var counterNum:Number = 0;
  function myMethod() {
    for (var counterNum:Number = 0; counterNum<=4; counterNum++) {
      // statements;
    }
  }
  ```

  This code declares the same variable inside an inner block, which is a practice to avoid.

- Don't assign many variables to a single value in a statement.

  Follow this convention because otherwise your code is difficult to read, as the following ActionScript code shows:

  ```
  playBtn.onRelease = playBtn.onRollOut = playsound;
  ```

  or

  ```
  class User {
    private var m_username:String, m_password:String;
  }
  ```

- Make a method or property public only if it needs to be public for a reason. Otherwise, make your methods and properties private.

- Don't *overuse* getter/setter functions in your class file.

  Getter/setter functions are excellent for a variety of purposes (see "About getter and setter methods" on page 261), however overuse might indicate that you could improve upon your application's architecture or organization.

- Set most member variables to private unless you have a good reason for making them public.

  From a design standpoint, it is much better to make member variables private and allow access to those variables through a group of getter/setter functions only.

Using the this prefix in class files

Use the `this` keyword as a prefix within your classes for methods and member variables. Although it is not necessary, it makes it easy to tell that a property or method belongs to a class when it has a prefix; without it, you cannot tell if the property or method belongs to the superclass.

You can also use a class name prefix for static variables and methods, even within a class. This helps qualify the references you make. Qualifying references makes for readable code. Depending on what coding environment you are using, your prefixes might also trigger code completion and hinting. The following code demonstrates prefixing a static property with a class name:

```
class Widget {
  public static var widgetCount:Number = 0;
  public function Widget() {
    Widget.widgetCount++;
  }
}
```

> **NOTE** You don't have to add these prefixes, and some developers feel it is unnecessary. Macromedia recommends that you add the `this` keyword as a prefix, because it can improve readability and it helps you write clean code by providing context.

About initialization

For the initial values for variables, assign a default value or allow the value of undefined, as the following class example shows. When you initialize properties inline, the expression on the right side of an assignment must be a compile-time constant. That is, the expression cannot refer to anything that is set or defined at runtime. Compile time constants include string literals, numbers, Boolean values, null, and undefined, as well as constructor functions for the following top-level classes: Array, Boolean, Number, Object, and String. This class sets the initial values of m_username and m_password to empty strings:

```
class User {
  private var m_username:String = "";
  private var m_password:String = "";
  function User(username:String, password:String) {
    this.m_username = username;
    this.m_password = password;
  }
}
```

Delete variables or make variables null when you no longer need them. Setting variables to null can still enhance performance. This process is commonly called *garbage collection*. Deleting variables helps optimize memory use during runtime, because unneeded assets are removed from the SWF file. It is better to delete variables than to set them to null. For more information on performance, see "Optimizing your code" on page 776.

> **NOTE**
> Flash Player 8 has made improvements in garbage collection within Flash Player.

For information on naming variables, see "Naming variables" on page 750. For more information on deleting objects, see %{delete statement}% in *ActionScript 2.0 Language Reference* in Flash Help.

One of the easiest ways to initialize code by using ActionScript 2.0 is to use classes. You can encapsulate all your initialization for an instance within the class's constructor function, or abstract it into a separate method, which you would explicitly call after the variable is created, as the following code shows:

```
class Product {
  function Product() {
    var prodXml:XML = new XML();
    prodXml.ignoreWhite = true;
    prodXml.onLoad = function(success:Boolean) {
      if (success) {
        trace("loaded");
      } else {
        trace("error loading XML");
      }
    };
    prodXml.load("products.xml");
  }
}
```

The following code could be the first function call in the application, and the only one you make for initialization. Frame 1 of a FLA file that is loading XML might use code that is similar to the following ActionScript:

```
if (init == undefined) {
  var prodXml:XML = new XML();
  prodXml.ignoreWhite = true;
  prodXml.onLoad = function(success:Boolean) {
    if (success) {
      trace("loaded");
    } else {
      trace("error loading XML");
    }
  };
  prodXml.load("products.xml");
  init = true;
}
```

Use trace statements

Use `trace` statements in your documents to help you debug your code while authoring the FLA file. For example, by using a `trace` statement and `for` loop, you can see the values of variables in the Output panel, such as strings, arrays, and objects, as the following example shows:

```
var dayArr:Array = ["sun", "mon", "tue", "wed", "thu", "fri", "sat"];
var numOfDays:Number = dayArr.length;
for (var i = 0; i<numOfDays; i++) {
  trace(i+": "+dayArr[i]);
}
```

This displays the following information in the Output panel:

```
0: sun
1: mon
2: tue
3: wed
4: thu
5: fri
6: sat
```

Using a `trace` statement is an efficient way to debug your ActionScript 2.0.

You can remove your `trace` statements when you publish a SWF file, which makes minor improvements to playback performance. Before you publish a SWF file, open Publish Settings and select Omit Trace Actions on the Flash tab. For more information on using a trace, see %{trace function}% in the *ActionScript 2.0 Language Reference* in Flash Help.

The Debugger tool is also useful for debugging ActionScript code. For more information, see Chapter 18, "Debugging Applications."

About the super prefix

If you refer to a method in the parent class, prefix the method with `super` so that other developers know from where the method is invoked. The following ActionScript 2.0 snippet demonstrates the use of proper scoping by using the `super` prefix:

In the following example, you create two classes. You use the super keyword in the Socks class to call functions in the parent class (Clothes). Although both the Socks and Clothes classes have a method called getColor(), using super lets you specifically reference the base class's methods and properties. Create a new AS file called Clothes.as, and enter the following code:

```
class Clothes {
   private var color:String;
   function Clothes(paramColor) {
      this.color = paramColor;
      trace("[Clothes] I am the constructor");
   }
   function getColor():String {
      trace("[Clothes] I am getColor");
      return this.color;
   }
   function setColor(paramColor:String):Void {
      this.color = paramColor;
      trace("[Clothes] I am setColor");
   }
}
```

Create a new class called Socks that extends the Clothes class, as shown in the following example:

```
class Socks extends Clothes {
   private var color:String;
   function Socks(paramColor:String) {
      this.color = paramColor;
      trace("[Socks] I am the constructor");
   }
   function getColor():String {
      trace("[Socks] I am getColor");
      return super.getColor();
   }
   function setColor(paramColor:String):Void {
      this.color = paramColor;
      trace("[Socks] I am setColor");
   }
}
```

Then create a new AS or FLA file and enter the following ActionScript in the document:

```
import Socks;
var mySock:Socks = new Socks("maroon");
trace(" -> "+mySock.getColor());
mySock.setColor("Orange");
trace(" -> "+mySock.getColor());
```

The following result is displayed in the Output panel:

```
[Clothes] I am the constructor
[Socks] I am the constructor
[Socks] I am getColor
[Clothes] I am getColor
-> Maroon
[Socks] I am setColor
[Socks] I am getColor
[Clothes] I am getColor
-> Orange
```

If you forgot to put the super keyword in the Socks class's getColor() method, the
getColor() method could call itself repeatedly, which would cause the script to fail because
of infinite recursion problems. The Output panel would display the following error if you
didn't use the super keyword:

```
[Socks] I am getColor
[Socks] I am getColor
...
[Socks] I am getColor
256 levels of recursion were exceeded in one action list.
This is probably an infinite loop.
Further execution of actions has been disabled in this SWF file.
```

Avoid the with statement

One of the more confusing concepts to understand for people learning ActionScript 2.0 is
using the with statement. Consider the following code that uses the with statement:

```
this.attachMovie("circleClip", "circle1Clip", 1);
with (circle1Clip) {
    _x = 20;
    _y = Math.round(Math.random()*20);
    _alpha = 15;
    createTextField("labelTxt", 100, 0, 20, 100, 22);
    labelTxt.text = "Circle 1";
    someVariable = true;
}
```

In this code, you attach a movie clip instance from the library and use the with statement to
modify its properties. When you do not specify a variable's scope, you do not always know
where you are setting properties, so your code can be confusing. In the previous code, you
might expect someVariable to be set within the circle1Clip movie clip, but it is actually
set in a timeline of the SWF file.

It is easier to follow what is happening in your code if you explicitly specify the variables scope, instead of relying on the with statement. The following example shows a slightly longer, but better, ActionScript example that specifies the variables scope:

```
this.attachMovie("circleClip", "circle1Clip", 1);
circle1Clip._x = 20;
circle1Clip._y = Math.round(Math.random()*20);
circle1Clip._alpha = 15;
circle1Clip.createTextField("labelTxt", 100, 0, 20, 100, 22);
circle1Clip.labelTxt.text = "Circle 1";
circle1Clip.someVariable = true;
```

An exception to this rule is, when you are working with the drawing API to draw shapes, you might have several similar calls to the same methods (such as lineTo or curveTo) because of the drawing API's functionality. For example, when you draw a simple rectangle, you need four separate calls to the lineTo method, as the following code shows:

```
this.createEmptyMovieClip("rectangleClip", 1);
with (rectangleClip) {
    lineStyle(2, 0x000000, 100);
    beginFill(0xFF0000, 100);
    moveTo(0, 0);
    lineTo(300, 0);
    lineTo(300, 200);
    lineTo(0, 200);
    lineTo(0, 0);
    endFill();
}
```

If you wrote each lineTo or curveTo method with a fully qualified instance name, the code would quickly become cluttered and difficult to read and debug.

About using functions

Reuse blocks of code whenever possible. One way you can reuse code is by calling a function multiple times, instead of creating different code each time. Functions can be generic pieces of code; therefore, you can use the same blocks of code for slightly different purposes in a SWF file. Reusing code lets you create efficient applications and minimize the ActionScript 2.0 code that you must write, which reduces development time. You can create functions on a timeline, in a class file, or write ActionScript that resides in a code-based component, and reuse them in a variety of ways.

If you are using ActionScript 2.0, avoid writing functions on a timeline. When you use ActionScript 2.0, place functions into class files whenever possible, as the following example shows:

```
class Circle {
public function area(radius:Number):Number {
   return (Math.PI*Math.pow(radius, 2));
}
public function perimeter(radius;Number):Number {
   return (2 * Math.PI * radius);
}
public function diameter(radius:Number):Number {
   return (radius * 2);
}
}
```

Use the following syntax when you create functions:

```
function myCircle(radius:Number):Number {
  //...
}
```

Avoid using the following syntax, which is difficult to read:

```
myCircle = function(radius:Number):Number {
  //...
}
```

The following example puts functions into a class file. This is a best practice when you choose to use ActionScript 2.0, because it maximizes code reusability. To reuse the functions in other applications, import the existing class rather than rewrite the code from scratch, or duplicate the functions in the new application.

```
class mx.site.Utils {
  static function randomRange(min:Number, max:Number):Number {
    if (min>max) {
      var temp:Number = min;
      min = max;
      max = temp;
    }
    return (Math.floor(Math.random()*(max-min+1))+min);
  }
  static function arrayMin(numArr:Array):Number {
    if (numArr.length == 0) {
      return Number.NaN;
    }
    numArr.sort(Array.NUMERIC | Array.DESCENDING);
    var min:Number = Number(numArr.pop());
    return min;
  }
  static function arrayMax(numArr:Array):Number {
    if (numArr.length == 0) {
      return undefined;
    }
    numArr.sort(Array.NUMERIC);
    var max:Number = Number(numArr.pop());
    return max;
  }
}
```

You might use these functions by adding the following ActionScript to your FLA file:

```
import mx.site.Utils;
var randomMonth:Number = Utils.randomRange(0, 11);
var min:Number = Utils.arrayMin([3, 3, 5, 34, 2, 1, 1, -3]);
var max:Number = Utils.arrayMax([3, 3, 5, 34, 2, 1, 1, -3]);
trace("month: "+randomMonth);
trace("min: "+min);
trace("max: "+max);
```

About stopping code repetition

The `onEnterFrame` event handler is useful because Flash can use it to repeat code at the frame rate of a SWF file. However, limit the amount of repetition that you use in a Flash file as much as possible so that you do not affect performance. For example, if you have a piece of code that repeats whenever the playhead enters a frame, it is processor intensive. This behavior can cause performance problems on computers that play the SWF file. If you use the `onEnterFrame` event handler for any kind of animation or repetition in your SWF files, delete the `onEnterFrame` handler when you finish using it. In the following ActionScript 2.0 code, you stop repetition by deleting the `onEnterFrame` event handler:

```
circleClip.onEnterFrame = function() {
  circleClip._alpha -= 5;
  if (circleClip._alpha<=0) {
    circleClip.unloadMovie();
    delete this.onEnterFrame;
    trace("deleted onEnterFrame");
  }
};
```

Similarly, limit the use of `setInterval`, and remember to clear the interval when you finish using it to reduce processor requirements for the SWF file.

ActionScript and Flash Player optimization

If you compile a SWF file that contains ActionScript 2.0 with publish settings set to Flash Player 6 and ActionScript 1.0, your code functions as long as it does not use ActionScript 2.0 classes. No case sensitivity is involved with the code, only Flash Player. Therefore, if you compile your SWF file with Publish Settings set to Flash Player 7 or 8 and ActionScript 1.0, Flash enforces case sensitivity.

Data type annotations (strict data types) are enforced at compile time for Flash Player 7 and 8 when you have publish settings set to ActionScript 2.0.

ActionScript 2.0 compiles to ActionScript 1.0 bytecode when you publish your applications, so you can target Flash Player 6, 7, or 8 while working with ActionScript 2.0.

For more information on optimizing your applications, see "Optimizing your code".

Optimizing your code

Remember the following guidelines when you optimize your code:

- Avoid calling a function multiple times from within a loop.

  It is better to include the contents of a small function inside the loop.

- Use native functions when possible.

  Native functions are faster than user-defined functions.

- Don't overuse the Object type.

  Data-type annotations should be precise, because it improves performance. Use the Object type only when there is no reasonable alternative.

- Avoid using the eval() function or array access operator.

  Often, setting the local reference once is preferable and more efficient.

- Assign the Array.length to a variable before a loop.

  Assign Array.length to a variable before a loop to use as its condition, rather than using myArr.length itself. For example,

  ```
  var fontArr:Array = TextField.getFontList();
  var arrayLen:Number = fontArr.length;
  for (var i:Number = 0; i < arrayLen; i++) {
    trace(fontArr[i]);
  }
  ```

  instead of:

  ```
  var fontArr:Array = TextField.getFontList();
  for (var i:Number = 0; i < fontArr.length; i++) {
    trace(fontArr[i]);
  }
  ```

- Focus on optimizing loops, and any repeating actions.

  Flash Player spends a lot of time processing loops (such as those that use the setInterval() function).

- Add the var keyword when declaring a variable.

- Don't use class variables or global variables when local variables will suffice.

Formatting ActionScript syntax

Formatting ActionScript 2.0 code in a standardized way is essential to writing maintainable code, and it's easier for other developers to understand and modify. For example, it would be extremely difficult to follow the logic of a FLA file that has no indenting or comments, as well as inconsistent naming conventions and formatting. By indenting blocks of code (such as loops and if statements), you make the code easy to read and debug.

For more information on formatting code, see the following topics:

- "General formatting guidelines" on page 777
- "Writing conditional statements" on page 780
- "Writing compound statements" on page 781
- "Writing a for statement" on page 782
- "Writing while and do..while statements" on page 783
- "Writing return statements" on page 783
- "Writing switch statements" on page 783
- "Writing try..catch and try..catch..finally statements" on page 784
- "About using listener syntax" on page 785

General formatting guidelines

When you use spaces, line breaks, and tab indents to add white space to your code, you increase your code's readability. White space enhances readability because it helps show the code hierarchy. Making your ActionScript 2.0 easier to understand by making it more readable is important for students as well as for experienced users working on complex projects. Legibility is also important when you are debugging ActionScript code, because it is much easier to spot errors when code is formatted correctly and is properly spaced.

You can format or write a piece of ActionScript 2.0 code several ways. You'll find differences in the way developers choose to format the syntax across multiple lines in the ActionScript editor (the Actions panel or Script window), such as where you put brackets ({ }) or parentheses [( )]).

Macromedia recommends the following formatting points to help promote readability in your ActionScript code.

- Put one blank line between paragraphs (modules) of ActionScript.

  Paragraphs of ActionScript code are groups of logically related code. Adding a blank line between them helps users read the ActionScript code and understand its logic.

- Use consistent indentation in your code to help show the hierarchy of the code's structure.

  Use the same indentation style throughout your ActionScript code, and make sure that you align the braces ({ }) properly. Aligned braces improve the readability of your code. If your ActionScript syntax is correct, Flash automatically indents the code correctly when you press Enter (Windows) or Return (Macintosh). You can also click the Auto Format button in the ActionScript editor (the Actions panel or Script window) to indent your ActionScript code if the syntax is correct.

- Use line breaks to make complex statements easier to read.

  You can format some statements, such as conditional statements, in several ways. Sometimes formatting statements across several lines rather than across a single line makes your code easier to read.

- Include a space after a keyword that is followed by parentheses [( )].

  The following ActionScript code shows an example of this:

  ```
  do {
    // something
  } while (condition);
  ```

- Don't put a space between a method name and parentheses.

  The following ActionScript code shows an example of this:

  ```
  function checkLogin():Boolean {
    // statements;
  }
  checkLogin();
  ```

  or

  ```
  printSize("size is " + foo + "\n");
  ```

- Include a space after commas in a list of arguments.

  Using spaces after commas makes it easier to distinguish between method calls and keywords, as the following example shows:

  ```
  function addItems(item1:Number, item2:Number):Number {
    return (item1 + item2);
  }
  var sum:Number = addItems(1, 3);
  ```

- Use spaces to separate all operators and their operands.

  Using spaces makes it is easier to distinguish between method calls and keywords, as the following example shows:

  ```
  //good
  var sum:Number = 7 + 3;
  //bad
  var sum:Number=7+3;
  ```

  An exception to this guideline is the dot (.) operator.

- Don't include a space between unary operators and their operands.

  For example, increment (++) and decrement(--), as shown in the following example:

  ```
  while (d++ = s++)
  -2, -1, 0
  ```

- Don't include spaces after an opening parenthesis and before a closing parenthesis.

  The following ActionScript code shows an example of this:

  ```
  //bad
  ( "size is " + foo + "\n" );
  //good
  ("size is " + foo + "\n");
  ```

- Put each statement on a separate line to increase the readability of your ActionScript code.

  The following ActionScript code shows an example of this:

  ```
  theNum++;         // Correct
  theOtherNum++;    // Correct
  aNum++; anOtherNum++;   // Incorrect
  ```

- Don't embed assignments.

  Embedded statements are sometimes used to improve performance in a SWF file at runtime, but the code is much harder to read and debug. The following ActionScript code shows an example of this (but remember to avoid single-character naming in the actual code):

  ```
  var myNum:Number = (a = b + c) + d;
  ```

- Assign variables as separate statements.

  The following ActionScript code shows an example of this (but remember to avoid single-character naming in the actual code):

  ```
  var a:Number = b + c;
  var myNum:Number = a + d;
  ```

- Break a line before an operator.

- Break a line after a comma.

- Align the second line with the start of the expression on the previous line of code.

> **NOTE**
> You can control auto-indentation and indentation settings by selecting Edit ›
> Preferences (Windows) or Flash › Preferences (Macintosh), and then selecting the
> ActionScript tab.

Writing conditional statements

Use the following guidelines when you write conditional statements:

- Place conditions on separate lines in if, else..if, and if..else statements.
- Use braces ({ }) for if statements.
- Format braces as shown in the following examples:

```
// if statement
if (condition) {
  // statements
}

// if..else statement
if (condition) {
  // statements
} else {
  // statements
}

// else..if statement
if (condition) {
  // statements
} else if (condition) {
  // statements
} else {
  // statements
}
```

When you write complex conditions, it is good form to use parentheses [()] to group conditions. If you don't use parentheses, you (or others working with your ActionScript 2.0 code) might run into operator precedence errors.

For example, the following code does not use parentheses around the conditions:

```
if (fruit == apple && veggie == leek) {}
```

The following code uses good form by adding parentheses around conditions:

```
if ((fruit == apple) && (veggie == leek)) {}
```

You can write a conditional statement that returns a Boolean value in two ways. The second example is preferable:

```
if (cartArr.length>0) {
  return true;
} else {
  return false;
}
```

Compare this example with the previous one:

```
// better
return (cartArr.length > 0);
```

The second snippet is shorter and has fewer expressions to evaluate. It's easier to read and to understand.

The following example checks if the variable *y* is greater than zero (0), and returns the result of x/y or a value of zero (0).

```
return ((y > 0) ? x/y : 0);
```

The following example shows another way to write this code. This example is preferable:

```
if (y>0) {
  return x/y;
} else {
  return 0;
}
```

The shortened if statement syntax from the first example is known as the conditional operator (?:). It lets you convert simple if..else statements into a single line of code. In this case, the shortened syntax reduces readability.

If you must use conditional operators, place the leading condition (before the question mark [?]) inside parentheses to improve the readability of your code. You can see an example of this in the previous code snippet.

Writing compound statements

Compound statements contain a list of statements within braces ({ }). The statements within these braces are indented from the compound statement. The following ActionScript code shows an example of this:

```
if (a == b) {
  // This code is indented.
  trace("a == b");
}
```

Place braces around each statement when it is part of a control structure (`if..else` or `for`), even if it contains only a single statement. The following example shows code that is written poorly:

```
// bad
if (numUsers == 0)
  trace("no users found.");
```

Although this code validates, it is poorly written because it lacks braces around the statements. In this case, if you add another statement after the `trace` statement, the code executes regardless of whether the `numUsers` variable equals 0:

```
// bad
var numUsers:Number = 5;
if (numUsers == 0)
  trace("no users found.");
  trace("I will execute");
```

Executing the code despite the `numUsers` variable can lead to unexpected results. For this reason, add braces, as shown in the following example:

```
var numUsers:Number = 0;
if (numUsers == 0) {
  trace("no users found");
}
```

When you write a condition, don't add the redundant `==true` in your code, as follows:

```
if (something == true) {
  //statements
}
```

If you are compare against `false`, you could use `if (something==false)` or `if(!something)`.

Writing a for statement

You can write the `for` statement using the following format:

```
for (init; condition; update) {
  // statements
}
```

The following structure demonstrates the `for` statement:

```
var i:Number;
for (var i = 0; i<4; i++) {
  myClip.duplicateMovieClip("newClip" + i + "Clip", i + 10, {_x:i*100,
  _y:0});
}
```

Remember to include a space following each expression in a `for` statement.

Writing while and do..while statements

You can write `while` statements using the following format:

```
while (condition) {
  // statements
}
```

You can write `do-while` statements using the following format:

```
do {
  // statements
} while (condition);
```

Writing return statements

Don't use parentheses [()] with any return statements that have values. The only time to use parentheses with `return` statements is when they make the value more obvious, as shown in the third line of the following ActionScript code snippet:

```
return;
return myCar.paintColor;
// parentheses used to make the return value obvious
return ((paintColor)? paintColor: defaultColor);
```

Writing switch statements

- All `switch` statements include a default case.

  The default case is the last case in a `switch` statement. The `default` case includes a `break` statement that prevents a fall-through error if another case is added.

- If a case does not have a break statement, the case will *fall through* (see `case A` in the following code example).

  Your statement should include a comment in the `break` statement's place, as you can see in the following example after `case A`. In this example, if the condition matches case A, both cases A and B execute.

You can write `switch` statements using the following format:

```
switch (condition) {
case A :
  // statements
  // falls through
case B :
  // statements
  break;
case Z :
  // statements
  break;
default :
  // statements
  break;
}
```

Writing try..catch and try..catch..finally statements

Write `try..catch` and `try..catch..finally` statements using the following formats:

```
var myErr:Error;
// try..catch
try {
  // statements
} catch (myErr) {
  // statements
}

// try..catch..finally
try {
  // statements
} catch (myErr) {
  // statements
} finally {
  // statements
}
```

About using listener syntax

You can write listeners for events in several ways in Flash 8. Some popular techniques are shown in the following code examples. The first example shows a properly formatted listener syntax, which uses a Loader component to load content into a SWF file. The `progress` event starts when content loads, and the `complete` event indicates when loading finishes.

```
var boxLdr:mx.controls.Loader;
var ldrListener:Object = new Object();
ldrListener.progress = function(evt:Object) {
  trace("loader loading:" + Math.round(evt.target.percentLoaded) + "%");
};
ldrListener.complete = function(evt:Object) {
  trace("loader complete:" + evt.target._name);
};
boxLdr.addEventListener("progress", ldrListener);
boxLdr.addEventListener("complete", ldrListener);
boxLdr.load("http://www.helpexamples.com/flash/images/image1.jpg");
```

A slight variation on the first example in this section is to use the `handleEvent` method, but this technique is slightly more cumbersome. Macromedia does not recommend this technique because you must use a series of `if..else` statements or a `switch` statement to detect which event is caught.

```
var boxLdr:mx.controls.loader;
var ldrListener:Object = new Object();

ldrListener.handleEvent = function(evt:Object) {
  switch (evt.type) {
  case "progress" :
    trace("loader loading:" + Math.round(evt.target.percentLoaded) + "%");
    break;
  case "complete" :
    trace("loader complete:" + evt.target._name);
    break;
  }
};
boxLdr.addEventListener("progress", ldrListener);
boxLdr.addEventListener("complete", ldrListener);
boxLdr.load("http://www.helpexamples.com/flash/images/image1.jpg");
```

Error Messages

A

Macromedia Flash Basic 8 and Macromedia Flash Professional 8 provide compile-time error reporting when you publish to ActionScript 2.0 (the default). The following table contains a list of error messages that the Flash compiler can generate:

Error number	Message text
1093	A class name was expected.
1094	A base class name is expected after the 'extends' keyword.
1095	A member attribute was used incorrectly.
1096	The same member name may not be repeated more than once.
1097	All member functions need to have names.
1099	This statement is not permitted in a class definition.
1100	A class or interface has already been defined with this name.
1101	Type mismatch.
1102	There is no class with the name '<ClassName>'.
1103	There is no property with the name '<propertyName>'.
1104	A function call on a non-function was attempted.
1105	Type mismatch in assignment statement: found [lhs-type] where [rhs-type] is required.
1106	The member is private and cannot be accessed.
1107	Variable declarations are not permitted in interfaces.
1108	Event declarations are not permitted in interfaces.
1109	Getter/setter declarations are not permitted in interfaces.
1110	Private members are not permitted in interfaces.
1111	Function bodies are not permitted in interfaces.

Error number	Message text
1112	A class may not extend itself.
1113	An interface may not extend itself.
1114	There is no interface defined with this name.
1115	A class may not extend an interface.
1116	An interface may not extend a class.
1117	An interface name is expected after the 'implements' keyword.
1118	A class may not implement a class, only interfaces.
1119	The class must implement method 'methodName' from interface 'interfaceName'.
1120	The implementation of an interface method must be a method, not a property.
1121	A class may not extend the same interface more than once.
1122	The implementation of the interface method doesn't match its definition.
1123	This construct is only available in ActionScript 1.0.
1124	This construct is only available in ActionScript 2.0.
1125	Static members are not permitted in interfaces.
1126	The expression returned must match the function's return type.
1127	A return statement is required in this function.
1128	Attribute used outside class.
1129	A function with return type Void may not return a value.
1130	The 'extends' clause must appear before the 'implements' clause.
1131	A type identifier is expected after the ':'.
1132	Interfaces must use the 'extends' keyword, not 'implements'.
1133	A class may not extend more than one class.
1134	An interface may not extend more than one interface.
1135	There is no method with the name '<methodName>'.
1136	This statement is not permitted in an interface definition.
1137	A set function requires exactly one parameter.
1138	A get function requires no parameters.
1139	Classes may only be defined in external ActionScript 2.0 class scripts.
1140	ActionScript 2.0 class scripts may only define class or interface constructs.

Error number	Message text
1141	The name of this class, '<A.B.C>', conflicts with the name of another class that was loaded, '<A.B>'. (This error occurs when the ActionScript 2.0 compiler cannot compile a class because of the full name of an existing class is part of the conflicting class' name. For example, compiling class `mx.com.util` generates error 1141 if class `mx.com` is a compiled class.)
1142	The class or interface '<Class or Interface Name>' could not be loaded.
1143	Interfaces may only be defined in external ActionScript 2.0 class scripts.
1144	Instance variables cannot be accessed in static functions.
1145	Class and interface definitions cannot be nested.
1146	The property being referenced does not have the static attribute.
1147	This call to super does not match the superconstructor.
1148	Only the public attribute is allowed for interface methods.
1149	The import keyword cannot be used as a directive.
1150	You must export your Flash movie as Flash 7 to use this action.
1151	You must export your Flash movie as Flash 7 to use this expression.
1152	This exception clause is placed improperly.
1153	A class must have only one constructor.
1154	A constructor may not return a value.
1155	A constructor may not specify a return type.
1156	A variable may not be of type Void.
1157	A function parameter may not be of type Void.
1158	Static members can only be accessed directly through classes.
1159	Multiple implemented interfaces contain same method with different types.
1160	There is already a class or interface defined with this name.
1161	Classes, interfaces, and built-in types may not be deleted.
1162	There is no class with this name.
1163	The keyword '<keyword>' is reserved for ActionScript 2.0 and cannot be used here.
1164	Custom attribute definition was not terminated.
1165	Only one class or interface can be defined per ActionScript 2.0 .as file.

Error number	Message text
1166	The class being compiled, '‹A.b›', does not match the class that was imported, '‹A.B›'. (This error occurs when a class name is spelled with a different case from an imported class. For example, compiling class `mx.com.util` generates error 1166 if the statement `import mx.Com` appears in the util.as file.)
1167	You must enter a class name.
1168	The class name you have entered contains a syntax error.
1169	The interface name you have entered contains a syntax error.
1170	The base class name you have entered contains a syntax error.
1171	The base interface name you have entered contains a syntax error.
1172	You must enter an interface name.
1173	You must enter a class or interface name.
1174	The class or interface name you have entered contains a syntax error.
1175	'variable' is not accessible from this scope.
1176	Multiple occurrences of the 'get/set/private/public/static' attribute were found.
1177	A class attribute was used incorrectly.
1178	Instance variables and functions may not be used to initialize static variables.
1179	Runtime circularities were discovered between the following classes: ‹list of user-defined classes›. This runtime error indicates that your custom classes are incorrectly referencing each other.
1180	The currently targeted Flash Player does not support debugging.
1181	The currently targeted Flash Player does not support the releaseOutside event.
1182	The currently targeted Flash Player does not support the dragOver event.
1183	The currently targeted Flash Player does not support the dragOut event.
1184	The currently targeted Flash Player does not support dragging actions.
1185	The currently targeted Flash Player does not support the loadMovie action.
1186	The currently targeted Flash Player does not support the getURL action.
1187	The currently targeted Flash Player does not support the FSCommand action.

Error number	Message text
1188	Import statements are not allowed inside class or interface definitions.
1189	The class '‹A.B›' cannot be imported because its leaf name is already resolved to the class that is being defined, '‹C.B›'. (For example, compiling class util generates error 1189 if the statement import mx.util appears in the util.as file.)
1190	The class '‹A.B›' cannot be imported because its leaf name is already resolved to a previously imported class '‹C.B›'. (For example, compiling import jv.util generates error 1190 if the statement import mx.util also appears in the AS file.)
1191	A class' instance variables may only be initialized to compile-time constant expressions.
1192	Class member functions cannot have the same name as a superclass' constructor function.
1193	The name of this class, '‹ClassName›', conflicts with the name of another class that was loaded.
1194	The superconstructor must be called first in the constructor body.
1195	The identifier '‹className›' will not resolve to built-in object '‹ClassName›' at runtime.
1196	The class '‹A.B.ClassName›' needs to be defined in a file whose relative path is '‹A.B›'.
1197	The wildcard character '*' is misused in the ClassName '‹ClassName›'.
1198	The member function '‹classname›' has a different case from the name of the class being defined, '‹ClassName›', and will not be treated as the class constructor at runtime.
1199	The only type allowed for a for-in loop iterator is String.
1200	A setter function may not return a value.
1201	The only attributes allowed for constructor functions are public and private.
1202	The file 'toplevel.as', which is required for typechecking ActionScript 2.0, could not be found. Please make sure the directory '$(LocalData)/Classes' is listed in the global classpath of the ActionScript Preferences.
1203	Branch between ‹spanStart› and ‹spanEnd› exceeds 32K span.
1204	There is no class or package with the name '‹packageName›' found in package '‹PackageName›'.
1205	The currently targeted Flash Player does not support the FSCommand2 action.

Error number	Message text
1206	Member function '‹functionName›' is larger than 32K.
1207	Anonymous function around line ‹lineNumber› exceeds 32K span.
1208	Code around line ‹lineNumber› exceeds 32K span.
1210	The package name '‹PackageName›' cannot also be used as a method name.
1211	The package name '‹PackageName›' cannot also be used as a property name.
1212	The ASO file for the class '‹ClassName›' could not be created. Please make sure the fully-qualified class name is short enough so that the ASO filename, '‹ClassName.aso›', is less than 255 characters.
1213	This type of quotation mark is not allowed in ActionScript. Please change it to a standard (straight) double quote.

Deprecated Flash 4 operators

B

The following table lists Flash 4 only operators, which are deprecated in ActionScript 2.0. Do not use these operators unless you are publishing to Flash Player 4 and earlier.

Operator	Description	Associativity
not	Logical NOT	Right to left
and	Logical AND	Left to right
or	Logical OR (Flash 4)	Left to right
add	String concatenation (formerly &)	Left to right
instanceof	Instance of	Left to right
lt	Less than (string version)	Left to right
le	Less than or equal to (string version)	Left to right
gt	Greater than (string version)	Left to right
ge	Greater than or equal to (string version)	Left to right
eq	Equal (string version)	Left to right
ne	Not equal (string version)	Left to right

Keyboard Keys and Key Code Values

The following tables list all the keys on a standard keyboard and the corresponding key code values and ASCII key code values that are used to identify the keys in ActionScript:

- "Letters A to Z and standard numbers 0 to 9" on page 796
- "Keys on the numeric keypad" on page 798
- "Function keys" on page 799
- "Other keys" on page 800

You can use key constants to intercept the built-in behavior of keypresses. For more information on the on() handler, see %{on handler}% in the *ActionScript 2.0 Language Reference* in Flash Help. To capture key code values and ASCII key code values using a SWF file and key presses, you can use the following ActionScript code:

```
var keyListener:Object = new Object();
keyListener.onKeyDown = function() {
  trace("DOWN -> Code: " + Key.getCode() + "\tACSII: " + Key.getAscii() +
  "\tKey: " + chr(Key.getAscii())));
};
Key.addListener(keyListener);
```

For more information on the Key class, see %{Key}% in *ActionScript 2.0 Language Reference* in Flash Help. To trap keys when you test a SWF file in the authoring environment (Control > Test Movie), make sure that you select Control > Disable Keyboard Shortcuts.

Letters A to Z and standard numbers 0 to 9

The following table lists the keys on a standard keyboard for the letters A to Z and the numbers 0 to 9, with the corresponding key code values that are used to identify the keys in ActionScript:

Letter or number key	Key code	ASCII key code
A	65	65
B	66	66
C	67	67
D	68	68
E	69	69
F	70	70
G	71	71
H	72	72
I	73	73
J	74	74
K	75	75
L	76	76
M	77	77
N	78	78
O	79	79
P	80	80
Q	81	81
R	82	82
S	83	83
T	84	84
U	85	85
V	86	86
W	87	87
X	88	88
Y	89	89
Z	90	90

Letter or number key	Key code	ASCII key code
0	48	48
1	49	49
2	50	50
3	51	51
4	52	52
5	53	53
6	54	54
7	55	55
8	56	56
9	57	57
a	65	97
b	66	98
c	67	99
d	68	100
e	69	101
f	70	102
g	71	103
h	72	104
i	73	105
j	74	106
k	75	107
l	76	108
m	77	109
n	78	110
o	79	111
p	80	112
q	81	113
r	82	114
s	83	115
t	84	116

Letter or number key	Key code	ASCII key code
u	85	117
v	86	118
w	87	119
x	88	120
y	89	121
z	90	122

Keys on the numeric keypad

The following table lists the keys on a numeric keypad, with the corresponding key code values that are used to identify the keys in ActionScript:

Numeric keypad key	Key code	ASCII key code
Numpad 0	96	48
Numpad 1	97	49
Numpad 2	98	50
Numpad 3	99	51
Numpad 4	100	52
Numpad 5	101	53
Numpad 6	102	54
Numpad 7	103	55
Numpad 8	104	56
Numpad 9	105	57
Multiply	106	42
Add	107	43
Enter	13	13
Subtract	109	45
Decimal	110	46
Divide	111	47

Function keys

The following table lists the function keys on a standard keyboard, with the corresponding key code values that are used to identify the keys in ActionScript:

Function key	Key code	ASCII key code
F1	112	0
F2	113	0
F3	114	0
F4	115	0
F5	116	0
F6	117	0
F7	118	0
F8	119	0
F9	120	0
F10	This key is reserved by the system and cannot be used in ActionScript.	This key is reserved by the system and cannot be used in ActionScript.
F11	122	0
F12	123	0
F13	124	0
F14	125	0
F15	126	0

Other keys

The following table lists keys on a standard keyboard other than letters, numbers, numeric keypad keys, or function keys, with the corresponding key code values that are used to identify the keys in ActionScript:

Key	Key code	ASCII key code
Backspace	8	8
Tab	9	9
Enter	13	13
Shift	16	0
Control	17	0
Caps Lock	20	0
Esc	27	27
Spacebar	32	32
Page Up	33	0
Page Down	34	0
End	35	0
Home	36	0
Left Arrow	37	0
Up Arrow	38	0
Right Arrow	39	0
Down Arrow	40	0
Insert	45	0
Delete	46	127
Num Lock	144	0
ScrLk	145	0
Pause/Break	19	0
; :	186	59
= +	187	61
- _	189	45
/ ?	191	47
` ~	192	96

Key	Key code	ASCII key code
[{	219	91
\ |	220	92
] }	221	93
" '	222	39
,	188	44
.	190	46
/	191	47

For additional key code and ASCII values, use the ActionScript at the beginning of this appendix and press the desired key to trace its key code.

Writing Scripts for Earlier Versions of Flash Player

ActionScript has changed considerably with each release of the Macromedia Flash authoring tools and Flash Player. When you create content for Macromedia Flash Player 8, you can use the full power of ActionScript. You can still use Flash 8 to create content for earlier versions of Flash Player, but you can't use every ActionScript element.

This chapter provides guidelines to help you write scripts that are syntactically correct for the player version you are targeting.

> **NOTE**
> You can review surveys for Flash Player version penetration on the Macromedia website; see www.macromedia.com/software/player_census/flashplayer/.

About targeting earlier versions of Flash Player

When you write scripts, use the Availability information for each element in the *ActionScript 2.0 Language Reference* in Flash Help to determine if an element you want to use is supported by the Flash Player version you are targeting. You can also determine which elements you can use by showing the Actions toolbox; elements that are not supported for your target version appear in yellow.

If you create content for Flash Player 6, 7 or 8, you should use ActionScript 2.0, which provides several important features that aren't available in ActionScript 1.0, such as improved compiler errors and more robust object-oriented programming capabilities.

To specify the player and ActionScript version you want to use when publishing a document, select File > Publish Settings and make your selections on the Flash tab. If you need to target Flash Player 4, see the next section.

Using Flash 8 to create content for Flash Player 4

To use Flash 8 to create content for Flash Player 4, specify Flash Player 4 on the Flash tab of the Publish Settings dialog box (File > Publish Settings).

Flash Player 4 ActionScript has only one basic primitive data type, which is used for numeric and string manipulation. When you write an application for Flash Player 4, you must use the deprecated string operators located in the Deprecated > Operators category in the ActionScript toolbox.

You can use the following Flash 8 features when you publish for Flash Player 4:

- The array and object access operator ([])
- The dot operator (.)
- Logical operators, assignment operators, and pre- and post-increment/decrement operators
- The modulo operator (%), and all methods and properties of the Math class

The following language elements are not supported natively by Flash Player 4. Flash 8 exports them as series approximations, which creates results that are less numerically accurate. In addition, because of the inclusion of series approximations in the SWF file, these language elements need more space in Flash Player 4 SWF files than they do in Flash Player 5 or later SWF files.

- The for, while, do..while, break, and continue actions
- The print() and printAsBitmap() actions
- The switch action

For additional information, see "About targeting earlier versions of Flash Player" on page 803.

Using Flash 8 to open Flash 4 files

Flash 4 ActionScript had only one true data type: string. It used different types of operators in expressions to indicate whether the value should be treated as a string or as a number. In subsequent releases of Flash, you can use one set of operators on all data types.

When you use Flash 5 or later to open a file that was created in Flash 4, Flash automatically converts ActionScript expressions to make them compatible with the new syntax. Flash makes the following data type and operator conversions:

- The = operator in Flash 4 was used for numeric equality. In Flash 5 and later, == is the equality operator and = is the assignment operator. Any = operators in Flash 4 files are automatically converted to ==.

- Flash automatically performs type conversions to ensure that operators behave as expected. Because of the introduction of multiple data types, the following operators have new meanings:

  +, ==, !=, <>, <, >, >=, <=

  In Flash 4 ActionScript, these operators were always numeric operators. In Flash 5 and later, they behave differently, depending on the data types of the operands. To prevent semantic differences in imported files, the Number() function is inserted around all operands to these operators. (Constant numbers are already obvious numbers, so they are not enclosed in Number().) For more information on these operators, see the operator table in "About operator precedence and associativity" on page 183 and "Deprecated Flash 4 operators" on page 793.

- In Flash 4, the escape sequence \n generated a carriage return character (ASCII 13). In Flash 5 and later, to comply with the ECMA-262 standard, \n generates a line-feed character (ASCII 10). An \n sequence in Flash 4 FLA files is automatically converted to \r.

- The & operator in Flash 4 was used for string addition. In Flash 5 and later, & is the bitwise AND operator. The string addition operator is now called add. Any & operators in Flash 4 files are automatically converted to add operators.

- Many functions in Flash 4 did not require closing parentheses; for example, Get Timer, Set Variable, Stop, and Play. To create consistent syntax, the getTimer function and all actions now require parentheses [()]. These parentheses are automatically added during the conversion.

- In Flash 5 and later, when the getProperty function is executed on a movie clip that doesn't exist, it returns the value undefined, not 0. The statement undefined == 0 is false in ActionScript after Flash 4 (in Flash 4, undefined == 1). In Flash 5 and later, solve this problem when converting Flash 4 files by introducing Number() functions in equality comparisons. In the following example, Number() forces undefined to be converted to 0 so the comparison will succeed:

```
getProperty("clip", _width) == 0
Number(getProperty("clip", _width)) == Number(0)
```

> **NOTE** If you used any Flash 5 or later keywords as variable names in your Flash 4 ActionScript, the syntax returns an error when you compile it in Flash 8. To solve this problem, rename your variables in all locations. For information, see "About reserved words" on page 143 and "About naming variables" on page 94.

Using slash syntax

Slash syntax (/) was used in Flash 3 and 4 to indicate the target path of a movie clip or variable. In slash syntax, slashes are used instead of dots and variables are preceded with a colon, as shown in the following example:

```
myMovieClip/childMovieClip:myVariable
```

To write the same target path in dot syntax, which is supported by Flash Player 5 and later versions, use the following syntax:

```
myMovieClip.childMovieClip.myVariable
```

Slash syntax was most commonly used with the `tellTarget` action, but its use is also no longer recommended. The `with` action is now preferred because it is more compatible with dot syntax. For more information, see %{tellTarget function}% and %{with statement}% in the *ActionScript 2.0 Language Reference* in Flash Help.

Object-Oriented Programming with ActionScript 1.0

E

The information in this appendix comes from the Macromedia Flash MX documentation and provides information on using the ActionScript 1.0 object model to write scripts. It is included here for the following reasons:

- If you want to write object-oriented scripts that support Flash Player 5, you must use ActionScript 1.0.

- If you already use ActionScript 1.0 to write object-oriented scripts and aren't ready to switch to ActionScript 2.0, you can use this appendix to find or review information you need while writing your scripts.

If you have never used ActionScript to write object-oriented scripts and don't need to target Flash Player 5, you should not use the information in this appendix because writing object-oriented scripts using ActionScript 1.0 is deprecated. Instead, for information on using ActionScript 2.0, see Chapter 7, "Classes," on page 231.

This chapter contains the following sections:

> **NOTE**
> Some examples in this appendix use the Object.registerClass() method. This method is supported only in Flash Player 6 and later versions; don't use this method if you are targeting Flash Player 5.

About ActionScript 1.0

> **NOTE**
> Many Flash users can greatly benefit from using ActionScript 2.0, especially with complex applications. For information on using ActionScript 2.0, see Chapter 7, "Classes," on page 231.

ActionScript is an object-oriented programming language. Object-oriented programming uses *objects*, or data structures, to group together properties and methods that control the object's behavior or appearance. Objects let you organize and reuse code. After you define an object, you can refer to it by name without having to redefine it each time you use it.

A *class* is a generic category of objects. A class defines a series of objects that have common properties and can be controlled in the same ways. Properties are attributes that define an object, such as its size, position, color, transparency, and so on. Properties are defined for a class, and values for the properties are set for individual objects in the class. Methods are functions that can set or retrieve properties of an object. For example, you can define a method to calculate the size of an object. As with properties, methods are defined for an object class and then invoked for individual objects in the class.

ActionScript includes several built-in classes, including the MovieClip class, Sound class, and others. You can also create custom classes to define categories of objects for your applications.

Objects in ActionScript can be pure containers for data, or they can be graphically represented on the Stage as movie clips, buttons, or text fields. All movie clips are instances of the built-in MovieClip class, and all buttons are instances of the built-in Button class. Each movie clip instance contains all the properties (for example, `_height`, `_rotation`, `_totalframes`) and all the methods (for example, `gotoAndPlay()`, `loadMovie()`, `startDrag()`) of the MovieClip class.

To define a class, you create a special function called a *constructor function*. (Built-in classes have built-in constructor functions.) For example, if you want information about a bicycle rider in your application, you could create a constructor function, `Biker()`, with the properties `time` and `distance` and the method `getSpeed()`, which tells you how fast the biker is traveling:

```
function Biker(t, d) {
   this.time = t;
   this.distance = d;
   this.getSpeed = function() {return this.time / this.distance;};
}
```

In this example, you create a function that needs two pieces of information, or *parameters*, to do its job: t and d. When you call the function to create new instances of the object, you pass it the parameters. The following code creates instances of the object Biker called emma and hamish, and it traces the speed of the emma instance, using the getSpeed() method from the previous ActionScript:

```
emma = new Biker(30, 5);
hamish = new Biker(40, 5);
trace(emma.getSpeed()); // traces 6
```

In object oriented scripting, classes can receive properties and methods from each other according to a specific order, which is called *inheritance*. You can use inheritance to extend or redefine the properties and methods of a class. A class that inherits from another class is called a *subclass*. A class that passes properties and methods to another class is called a *superclass*. A class can be both a subclass and a superclass.

An object is a complex data type containing zero or more properties and methods. Each property, like a variable, has a name and a value. Properties are attached to the object and contain values that can be changed and retrieved. These values can be of any data type: String, Number, Boolean, Object, MovieClip, or undefined. The following properties are of various data types:

```
customer.name = "Jane Doe";
customer.age = 30;
customer.member = true;
customer.account.currentRecord = 609;
customer.mcInstanceName._visible = true;
```

The property of an object can also be an object. In line 4 of the previous example, account is a property of the object customer, and currentRecord is a property of the object account. The data type of the currentRecord property is Number.

Creating a custom object in ActionScript 1.0

NOTE Many Flash users can greatly benefit from using ActionScript 2.0, especially with complex applications. For information on using ActionScript 2.0, see Chapter 7, "Classes," on page 231.

To create a custom object, you define a constructor function. A constructor function is always given the same name as the type of object it creates. You can use the keyword `this` inside the body of the constructor function to refer to the object that the constructor creates; when you call a constructor function, Flash passes `this` to the function as a hidden parameter. For example, the following code is a constructor function that creates a circle with the property `radius`:

```
function Circle(radius) {
  this.radius = radius;
}
```

After you define the constructor function, you must create an instance of the object. Use the `new` operator before the name of the constructor function, and assign a variable name to the new instance. For example, the following code uses the `new` operator to create a Circle object with a radius of 5 and assigns it to the variable `myCircle`:

```
myCircle = new Circle(5);
```

NOTE An object has the same scope as the variable to which it is assigned.

Assigning methods to a custom object in ActionScript 1.0

> **NOTE**
> Many Flash users can greatly benefit from using ActionScript 2.0, especially with complex applications. For information on using ActionScript 2.0, see Chapter 7, "Classes," on page 231.

You can define the methods of an object inside the object's constructor function. However, this technique is not recommended because it defines the method every time you use the constructor function. The following example creates the methods `getArea()` and `getDiameter():` and traces the area and diameter of the constructed instance `myCircle` with a radius set to 55:

```
function Circle(radius) {
  this.radius = radius;
  this.getArea = function(){
    return Math.PI * this.radius * this.radius;
  };
  this.getDiameter = function() {
    return 2 * this.radius;
  };
}
var myCircle = new Circle(55);
trace(myCircle.getArea());
trace(myCircle.getDiameter());
```

Each constructor function has a `prototype` property that is created automatically when you define the function. The `prototype` property indicates the default property values for objects created with that function. Each new instance of an object has a `__proto__` property that refers to the `prototype` property of the constructor function that created it. Therefore, if you assign methods to an object's `prototype` property, they are available to any newly created instance of that object. It's best to assign a method to the `prototype` property of the constructor function because it exists in one place and is referenced by new instances of the object (or class). You can use the `prototype` and `__proto__` properties to extend objects so that you can reuse code in an object-oriented manner. (For more information, see "Creating inheritance in ActionScript 1.0" on page 815.)

The following procedure shows how to assign an `getArea()` method to a custom Circle object.

To assign a method to a custom object:

1. Define the constructor function `Circle()`:

```
function Circle(radius) {
  this.radius = radius;
}
```

2. Define the `getArea()` method of the Circle object. The `getArea()` method calculates the area of the circle. In the following example, you can use a function literal to define the `getArea()` method and assign the `getArea` property to the circle's prototype object:

```
Circle.prototype.getArea = function () {
    return Math.PI * this.radius * this.radius;
};
```

3. The following example creates an instance of the Circle object:

```
var myCircle = new Circle(4);
```

4. Call the `getArea()` method of the new `myCircle` object using the following code:

```
var myCircleArea = myCircle.getArea();
trace(myCircleArea); // traces 50.265...
```

ActionScript searches the `myCircle` object for the `getArea()` method. Because the object doesn't have a `getArea()` method, its prototype object `Circle.prototype` is searched for `getArea()`. ActionScript finds it, calls it, and traces `myCircleArea`.

Defining event handler methods in ActionScript 1.0

 NOTE Many Flash users can greatly benefit from using ActionScript 2.0, especially with complex applications. For information on using ActionScript 2.0, see Chapter 7, "Classes," on page 231.

You can create an ActionScript class for movie clips and define the event handler methods in the prototype object of that new class. Defining the methods in the prototype object makes all the instances of this symbol respond the same way to these events.

You can also add an onClipEvent() or on() event handler methods to an individual instance to provide unique instructions that run only when that instance's event occurs. The onClipEvent() and on() methods don't override the event handler method; both events cause their scripts to run. However, if you define the event handler methods in the prototype object and also define an event handler method for a specific instance, the instance definition overrides the prototype definition.

To define an event handler method in an object's prototype object:

1. Create a movie clip symbol and set the linkage identifier to theID by selecting the symbol in the Library panel and selecting Linkage from the Library pop-up menu.

2. In the Actions panel (Window > Actions), use the function statement to define a new class, as shown in the following example:

```
// define a class
function myClipClass() {}
```

This new class is assigned to all instances of the movie clip that are added to the application by the timeline or that are added to the application with the attachMovie() or duplicateMovieClip() method. If you want these movie clips to have access to the methods and properties of the built-in MovieClip object, you need to make the new class inherit from the MovieClip class.

3. Enter code, such as the following example:

```
// inherit from MovieClip class
myClipClass.prototype = new MovieClip();
```

Now, the class myClipClass inherits all the properties and methods of the MovieClip class.

4. Enter code, such as the following example, to define the event handler methods for the new class:

```
// define event handler methods for myClipClass class
myClipClass.prototype.onLoad = function() {trace("movie clip loaded");}
myClipClass.prototype.onEnterFrame = function() {trace("movie clip
  entered frame");}
```

5. Select Window > Library to open the Library panel if it isn't already open.

6. Select the symbols that you want to associate with your new class, and select Linkage from the Library panel pop-up menu.

7. In the Linkage Properties dialog box, select Export for ActionScript.

8. Enter a linkage identifier in the Identifier text box.

The linkage identifier must be the same for all symbols that you want to associate with the new class. In the myClipClass example, the identifier is theID.

9. Enter code, such as the following example, in the Actions panel:

```
// register class
Object.registerClass("theID", myClipClass);
this.attachMovie("theID","myName",1);
```

This step registers the symbol whose linkage identifier is theID with the class myClipClass. All instances of myClipClass have event handler methods that behave as defined in step 4. They also behave the same as all instances of the MovieClip class because you told the new class to inherit from the class MovieClip in step 3.

The complete code is shown in the following example:

```
function myClipClass(){}

myClipClass.prototype = new MovieClip();
myClipClass.prototype.onLoad = function(){
   trace("movie clip loaded");
}
myClipClass.prototype.onPress = function(){
   trace("pressed");
}

myClipClass.prototype.onEnterFrame = function(){
   trace("movie clip entered frame");
}

myClipClass.prototype.myfunction = function(){
   trace("myfunction called");
}

Object.registerClass("myclipID",myClipClass);
this.attachMovie("myclipID","clipName",3);
```

Creating inheritance in ActionScript 1.0

NOTE | Many Flash users can greatly benefit from using ActionScript 2.0, especially with complex applications. For information on using ActionScript 2.0, see Chapter 7, "Classes," on page 231.

Inheritance is a means of organizing, extending, and reusing functionality. Subclasses inherit properties and methods from superclasses, and add their own specialized properties and methods. For example, reflecting the real world, Bike would be a superclass and MountainBike and Tricycle would be subclasses of the superclass. Both subclasses contain, or *inherit*, the methods and properties of the superclass (for example, wheels). Each subclass also has its own properties and methods that extend the superclass (for example, the MountainBike subclass would have a gears property). You can use the elements prototype and __proto__ to create inheritance in ActionScript.

All constructor functions have a prototype property that is created automatically when the function is defined. The prototype property indicates the default property values for objects created with that function. You can use the prototype property to assign properties and methods to a class. (For more information, see "Assigning methods to a custom object in ActionScript 1.0" on page 811.)

All instances of a class have a __proto__ property that tells you the object from which they inherit. When you use a constructor function to create an object, the __proto__ property is set to refer to the prototype property of its constructor function.

Inheritance proceeds according to a definite hierarchy. When you call an object's property or method, ActionScript looks at the object to see if such an element exists. If it doesn't exist, ActionScript looks at the object's __proto__ property for the information (myObject.__proto__). If the property is not a property of the object's __proto__ object, ActionScript looks at myObject.__proto__.__proto__, and so on.

The following example defines the constructor function Bike():

```
function Bike(length, color) {
   this.length = length;
   this.color = color;
   this.pos = 0;
}
```

The following code adds the roll() method to the Bike class:

```
Bike.prototype.roll = function() {return this.pos += 20;};
```

Then, you can trace the position of the bike with the following code:

```
var myBike = new Bike(55, "blue");
trace(myBike.roll());   // traces 20.
trace(myBike.roll());   // traces 40.
```

Instead of adding `roll()` to the MountainBike class and the Tricycle class, you can create the MountainBike class with Bike as its superclass, as shown in the following example:

```
MountainBike.prototype = new Bike();
```

Now you can call the `roll()` method of MountainBike, as shown in the following example:

```
var myKona = new MountainBike(20, "teal");
trace(myKona.roll());   // traces 20
```

Movie clips do not inherit from each other. To create inheritance with movie clips, you can use `Object.registerClass()` to assign a class other than the MovieClip class to movie clips.

Adding getter/setter properties to objects in ActionScript 1.0

> **NOTE**
>
> Many Flash users can greatly benefit from using ActionScript 2.0, especially with complex applications. For information on using ActionScript 2.0, see Chapter 7, "Classes," on page 231.

You can create getter/setter properties for an object using the `Object.addProperty()` method.

A *getter function* is a function with no parameters. Its return value can be of any type. Its type can change between invocations. The return value is treated as the current value of the property.

A *setter function* is a function that takes one parameter, which is the new value of the property. For instance, if property x is assigned by the statement x = 1, the setter function is passed the parameter 1 of type Number. The return value of the setter function is ignored.

When Flash reads a getter/setter property, it invokes the getter function, and the function's return value becomes a value of `prop`. When Flash writes a getter/setter property, it invokes the setter function and passes it the new value as a parameter. If a property with the given name already exists, the new property overwrites it.

You can add getter/setter properties to prototype objects. If you add a getter/setter property to a prototype object, all object instances that inherit the prototype object inherit the getter/setter property. You can add a getter/setter property in one location, the prototype object, and have it propagate to all instances of a class (similar to adding methods to prototype objects). If a getter/setter function is invoked for a getter/setter property in an inherited prototype object, the reference passed to the getter/setter function is the originally referenced object, not the prototype object.

The Debug > List Variables command in test mode supports getter/setter properties that you add to objects using `Object.addProperty()`. Properties that you add to an object in this way appear with other properties of the object in the Output panel. Getter/setter properties are identified in the Output panel with the prefix `[getter/setter]`. For more information on the List Variables command, see "Using the Output panel" on page 738.

Using Function object properties in ActionScript 1.0

> **NOTE**
>
> Many Flash users can greatly benefit from using ActionScript 2.0, especially with complex applications. For information on using ActionScript 2.0, see Chapter 7, "Classes," on page 231.

You can specify the object to which a function is applied and the parameter values that are passed to the function, using the `call()` and `apply()` methods of the Function object. Every function in ActionScript is represented by a Function object, so all functions support `call()` and `apply()`. When you create a custom class using a constructor function, or when you define methods for a custom class using a function, you can invoke `call()` and `apply()` for the function.

Invoking a function using the Function.call() method in ActionScript 1.0

> **NOTE**
>
> Many Flash users can greatly benefit from using ActionScript 2.0, especially with complex applications. For information on using ActionScript 2.0, see Chapter 7, "Classes," on page 231.

The `Function.call()` method invokes the function represented by a Function object.

In almost all cases, the function call operator (`()`) can be used instead of the `call()` method. The function call operator creates code that is concise and readable. The `call()` method is primarily useful when the `this` parameter of the function invocation needs to be explicitly controlled. Normally, if a function is invoked as a method of an object, within the body of the function, `this` is set to `myObject`, as shown in the following example:

```
myObject.myMethod(1, 2, 3);
```

In some situations, you might want `this` to point somewhere else; for instance, if a function must be invoked as a method of an object but is not actually stored as a method of that object, as shown in the following example:

```
myObject.myMethod.call(myOtherObject, 1, 2, 3);
```

You can pass the value `null` for the *thisObject* parameter to invoke a function as a regular function and not as a method of an object. For example, the following function invocations are equivalent:

```
Math.sin(Math.PI / 4)
Math.sin.call(null, Math.PI / 4)
```

To invoke a function using the Function.call() method:

■ Use the following syntax:

myFunction`.call(`*thisObject, parameter1, ..., parameterN*`)`

The method takes the following parameters:

■ The parameter *thisObject* specifies the value of `this` within the function body.

■ The parameters *parameter1...*, *parameterN* specify parameters to be passed to *myFunction*. You can specify zero or more parameters.

Specifying the object to which a function is applied using Function.apply() in ActionScript 1.0

 Many Flash users can greatly benefit from using ActionScript 2.0, especially with complex applications. For information on using ActionScript 2.0, see Chapter 7, "Classes," on page 231.

The `Function.apply()` method specifies the value of `this` to be used within any function that ActionScript calls. This method also specifies the parameters to be passed to any called function.

The parameters are specified as an Array object. This is often useful when the number of parameters to be passed is not known until the script actually executes.

For more information, see `%{apply (Function.apply method)}%` in the *ActionScript 2.0 Language Reference* in Flash Help.

To specify the object to which a function is applied using Function.apply():

- Use the following syntax:

```
myFunction.apply(thisObject, argumentsObject)
```

The method takes the following parameters:

- The parameter *thisObject* specifies the object to which *myFunction* is applied.
- The parameter *argumentsObject* defines an array whose elements are passed to *myFunction* as parameters.

Terminology

As with all scripting languages, ActionScript uses its own terminology. Macromedia Flash also uses unique terminology. The following list provides an introduction to important ActionScript terms, and Flash terms that relate to programming with ActionScript and that are unique to working in the Flash authoring environment.

ActionScript editor is the code editor in the Actions panel and Script window. The ActionScript editor consists of a number of features, such as Auto formatting, showing hidden characters, and color coding parts of your scripts. (Also see: Script window, Actions panel).

Actions panel is a panel in the Flash authoring environment where you write ActionScript code.

Anonymous function is an unnamed function that references itself; you reference the anonymous function when you create it. For information and an example, see "Writing anonymous and callback functions" on page 212.

Alias refers to aliased text that does not use color variations to make its jagged edges appear smoother, unlike anti-aliased text (see following definition).

Anti-alias refers to anti-aliasing characters in order to smooth text so the edges of characters that appear onscreen look less jagged. The Anti-Alias option in Flash makes text more legible by aligning text outlines along pixel boundaries, and is effective for clearly rendering smaller font sizes.

Arrays are objects whose properties are identified by numbers representing their positions in the structure. Essentially, an array is a list of items.

Authoring environment is the Flash workspace including all elements of the user interface. You create FLA files or script files (in the Script window) using the authoring environment.

Bitmap graphics (or *raster* graphics) are typically photo-realistic images, or graphics with a high amount of detail. Each pixel (or *bit*) in the image contains a piece of data, and together these bits form the image itself. Bitmaps might be saved in the JPEG, BMP or GIF file formats. Another graphic type, different than bitmap, is *vector*.

Boolean is a true or false value.

Caching refers to information that is reused in your application, or information that is stored on your computer so it can be reused. For example, if you download an image from the internet, it's often cached so you can view it again without downloading the image data.

Callback functions are anonymous functions that you associate with a certain event. A function calls a callback function after a specific event occurs, such as after something finishes loading (`onLoad()`) or finishes animating (`onMotionFinished()`). For more information and an examples, see "Writing anonymous and callback functions" on page 212.

Characters are letters, numerals, and punctuation that you combine to make up strings. They are sometimes called *glyphs*.

Classes are data types that you can create to define a new type of object. To define a class, you use the `class` keyword in an external script file (not in a script you are writing in the Actions panel).

Classpath refers to the list of folders in which Flash searches for class or interface definitions. When you create a class file, you need to save the file to one of the directories specified in the classpath, or a subdirectory within that. Classpaths exist at the global (application) level, and at the document level.

Constants are elements that don't change. For example, the constant `Key.TAB` always has the same meaning: it indicates the Tab key on a keyboard. Constants are useful for comparing values.

Constructor functions (or *constructors*) are functions that you use to define (initialize) the properties and methods of a class. By definition, constructors are functions within a class definition that have the same name as the class. For example, the following code defines a Circle class and implements a constructor function:

```
// file Circle.as
class Circle {
   private var circumference:Number;
// constructor
   function Circle(radius:Number){
     this.circumference = 2 * Math.PI * radius;
   }
}
```

The term *constructor* is also used when you create (instantiate) an object based on a particular class. The following statements are calls to the constructor functions for the built-in Array class and the custom Circle class:

```
var my_array:Array = new Array();
var my_circle:Circle = new Circle(9);
```

Data types describe the kind of information a variable or ActionScript element can contain. The built-in ActionScript data types are String, Number, Boolean, Object, MovieClip, Function, null, and undefined. For more information, see "About data types" on page 74.

Device fonts are special fonts in Flash that are not embedded in a Flash SWF file. Instead, Flash Player uses whatever font on the local computer most closely resembles the device font. Because font outlines are not embedded, SWF file size is smaller than when embedded font outlines are used. However, because device fonts are not embedded, the text that you create with them looks different than expected on computer systems that do not have a font installed that corresponds to the device font. Flash includes three device fonts: _sans (similar to Helvetica and Arial), _serif (similar to Times Roman), and _typewriter (similar to Courier).

Dot syntax refers to when you use a dot (.) operator (dot syntax) to access properties or methods that belong to an object or instance on the Stage using ActionScript. You also use the dot operator to identify the target path to an instance (such as a movie clip), variable, function, or object. A dot syntax expression begins with the name of the object or movie clip, followed by a dot, and it ends with the element you want to specify.

Events occur while a SWF file is playing. For example, different events are generated when a movie clip loads, the playhead enters a frame, the user clicks a button or movie clip, or the user types on the keyboard.

Event handlers are special events that manage when the mouse is clicked, or when data finishes loading. There are two kinds of ActionScript event handlers: event handler methods and event listeners. (There are also two event handlers, %{on handler}% and %{onClipEvent handler}%, that you can assign directly to buttons and movie clips.) In the Actions toolbox, each ActionScript object that has event handler methods or event listeners has a subcategory called Events or Listeners. Some commands can be used both as event handlers and as event listeners and are included in both subcategories. For more information on event management, see "Handling Events" on page 335.

Expressions are any legal combination of ActionScript symbols that represent a value. An expression consists of operators and operands. For example, in the expression x + 2, x and 2 are operands and + is an operator.

Flash Player container refers to the system that holds the Flash application, such as a browser or the desktop application. You can add ActionScript and JavaScript to facilitate communication between the Flash Player container and a SWF file.

FlashType refers to the advanced font rendering technology in Flash 8. For example, Alias Text for Readability uses the FlashType rendering technology, and Alias Text for Animation does not. For information, see "About font rendering and anti-alias text" on page 415.

Frame scripts are blocks of code that you add to a frame on a timeline.

Functions are blocks of reusable code that can be passed parameters and can return a value. For more information, see "About functions and methods" on page 206.

Function literals are unnamed functions that you declare in an expression instead of in a statement. Function literals are useful when you need to use a function temporarily, or to use a function in your code where you might use an expression instead.

IDE refers to an "integrated development environment," which is an application in which a developer can code, test, and debug applications in an interactive environment. The Flash authoring tool is sometimes called an IDE.

Identifiers are names used to indicate a variable, property, object, function, or method. The first character must be a letter, underscore (_), or dollar sign ($). Each subsequent character must be a letter, number, underscore, or dollar sign. For example, firstName is the name of a variable.

Instances are objects that contain all the properties and methods of a particular class. For example, all arrays are instances of the Array class, so you can use any of the methods or properties of the Array class with any array instance.

Instance names are unique names that let you target instances you create, or movie clip and button instances on the Stage. For example, in the following code, "names" and "studentName" are instance names for two objects, an array and a string:

```
var names:Array = new Array();
var studentName:String = new String();
```

You use the Property inspector to assign instance names to instances on the Stage. For example, a master symbol in the library could be called counter and the two instances of that symbol in the SWF file could have the instance names scorePlayer1_mc and scorePlayer2_mc. The following code sets a variable called score inside each movie clip instance by using instance names:

```
this.scorePlayer1_mc.score = 0;
this.scorePlayer2_mc.score = 0;
```

You can use strict data typing when creating instances so that code hints appear as you type your code.

Keywords are reserved words that have special meaning. For example, var is a keyword used to declare local variables. You cannot use a keyword as an identifier. For example, var is not a legal variable name. For a list of keywords, see "About keywords" on page 142 and "About reserved words" on page 143.

Literals represent values that have a particular type, such as numeric literals or string literals. Literals are not stored in a variable. A literal is a value that appears directly in your code, and is a constant (unchanging) value within your Flash documents. Also see *function literal*, and *string literal*.

Methods are functions associated with a class. For example, sortOn() is a built-in method associated with the Array class. You can also create functions that act as methods, either for objects based on built-in classes or for objects based on classes that you create. For example, in the following code, clear() becomes a method of a controller object that you have previously defined:

```
function reset(){
   this.x_pos = 0;
   this.y_pos = 0;
}
controller.clear = reset;
controller.clear();
```

The following examples show how you create methods of a class:

```
//ActionScript 1.0 example
A = new Object();
A.prototype.myMethod = function() {
   trace("myMethod");
}

//ActionScript 2.0 example
class B {
   function myMethod() {
      trace("myMethod");
   }
}
```

Named function is a kind of function that you commonly create in your ActionScript code to carry out all kinds of actions. For information and an example, see "Writing named functions" on page 211.

Object code is ActionScript that you attach to instances. To add object code, you select an instance on the Stage and then type code into the Actions panel. Attaching code to objects on the Stage is not recommended. For information on best practices, see "Best Practices and Coding Conventions for ActionScript 2.0" on page 745.

Objects are collections of properties and methods; each object has its own name and is an instance of a particular class. Built-in objects are predefined in the ActionScript language. For example, the built-in Date class provides information from the system clock.

Operators are terms that calculate a new value from one or more values. For example, the addition (+) operator adds two or more values together to produce a new value. The values that operators manipulate are called *operands*.

Parameters (also called *arguments*) are placeholders that let you pass values to functions. For example, the following `welcome()` function uses two values it receives in the parameters `firstName` and `hobby`:

```
function welcome(firstName:String, hobby:String):String {
var welcomeText:String = "Hello, " + firstName + ". I see you enjoy " +
    hobby +".";
    return welcomeText;
}
```

Packages are directories that contain one or more class files and reside in a designated classpath directory (see "About packages" on page 234).

Pinning scripts lets you pin multiple scripts from various objects and work with them simultaneously in the Actions panel. This feature works best with the Script navigator.

Progressive JPEG images are gradually constructed and displayed as they download from a server. A normal JPEG image is displayed line-by-line while it downloads from a server.

Properties are attributes that define an object. For example, `length` is a property of all arrays that specifies the number of elements in the array.

Punctuators are special characters that help you form ActionScript code. There are several language punctuators in Flash. The most common type of punctuators are semicolons (;), colons (:), parentheses [()] and braces ({}). Each of these punctuators has a special meaning in the Flash language and helps define data types, terminate statements or structure ActionScript.

Script Assist is a new assisted mode in the Actions panel. Script Assist lets you more easily create scripts without having detailed knowledge of ActionScript. It helps you build scripts by selecting items from the Actions toolbox in the Actions panel, and provides an interface of text fields, radio buttons, and check boxes that prompt you for the correct variables and other scripting language constructs. This feature is similar to *normal mode* in earlier editions of the Flash authoring tool.

Script pane is a pane in the Actions panel or Script window, and is the area where you type your ActionScript code.

Script window is a code editing environment where you can create and modify external scripts, such as Flash JavaScript files or ActionScript files. For example, select File > New and then select ActionScript File to use the Script window to write a class file.

Statements are language elements that perform or specify an action. For example, the `return` statement returns a result as a value of the function in which it executes. The `if` statement evaluates a condition to determine the next action that should be taken. The `switch` statement creates a branching structure for ActionScript statements.

String is a sequence of characters, and a data type. See "About strings and the String class" on page 459 for more information.

String literal is a sequence of characters enclosed by straight quote characters. The characters are themselves a data value, not a reference to data. A string literal is not a String object. For more information, see "About strings and the String class" on page 459.

Surface is a movie clip that has its bitmap caching flag turned on. For information on bitmap caching, see "Caching a movie clip" on page 379.

Syntax refers to the grammar and spelling of a language that you program with. The compiler cannot understand incorrect syntax, so you see errors or warnings displayed in the Output panel when you try to test the document in the test environment. Therefore, syntax is a collection of rules and guidelines that help you form correct ActionScript.

Target paths are hierarchical addresses of movie clip instance names, variables, and objects in a SWF file. You name a movie clip instance in the movie clip Property inspector. (The main timeline always has the name _root.) You can use a target path to direct an action at a movie clip, or to get or set the value of a variable or property. For example, the following statement is the target path to the volume property of the object named stereoControl:

    stereoControl.volume

Text is a series of one or more strings that can be displayed in a text field, or within a user interface component.

Text fields are visual elements on the Stage that let you display text to a user, which you can create using the Text tool or using ActionScript code. Flash lets you set text fields as editable (read-only), allow HTML formatting, enable multiline support, password masking, or apply a CSS style sheet to your HTML formatted text.

Text formatting can be applied to a text field, or certain characters within a text field. Some examples of text formatting options that can be applied to text are: alignment, indenting, bold, color, font size, margin widths, italics, and letter spacing.

Top-level functions are functions that don't belong to a class (sometimes called *predefined* or *built-in functions*), meaning that you can call them without a constructor. Examples of functions that are built in to the top level of the ActionScript language are trace() and setInterval();.

User-defined functions are functions that you create to use in applications, as opposed to functions in built-in classes that perform predefined functions. You name the functions yourself and add statements in the function block.

Variables are identifiers that hold values of any data type. Variables can be created, changed, and updated. The values they store can be retrieved for use in scripts. In the following example, the identifiers on the left side of the equal signs are variables:

```
var x:Number = 5;
var name:String = "Lolo";
var c_color:Color = new Color(mcinstanceName);
```

For more information on variables, see "About variables" on page 89.

Vector graphics describe images using lines and curves, called vectors, that also include color and position properties. Each vector uses mathematical calculations, instead of bits, to describe the shape, which allows them be scaled without degrading in quality. Another graphic type is *bitmap*, which is represented by dots or pixels.

Index

Symbols

\" 469
\' 469
\b 469
\f 469
\n 469
\r 469
\t 469
\unnnn 469
\xnn 469
_lockroot, using 762
_root scope 127

Numerics

9-slice scaling
  about 568
  enabling 570
  scale9Grid property 570
  understanding 568
  using 571

A

Actions panel
  about 36, 37
  Actions toolbox 37
  coding in 39
  defined 821
  pop-up menu 42
  Script navigator 37
  Script pane 38
Actions toolbox, yellow items in 53
actions, coding standards 759
ActionScript
  about 69, 70
  comparing versions 71
  creating cue points with 629
  editing preferences 44
  Flash Player 775
  formatting 52
  publish settings 64
ActionScript 2.0
  assigning ActionScript 2.0 class to movie clips 384
  compiler error messages 787
ActionScript editing
  check syntax 57
  code hints 50
  escape shortcut keys 54
  find tool 56
  importing and exporting scripts 57
  line numbers 54
  pin scripts 60
  showing hidden characters 55
  syntax highlighting 53
  word wrap 54
ActionScript editor 821
ActiveX controls 679
adaptively sampled distance field (ADF) 417
adaptively sampled distance fields 420
ADFs 417, 420
alias, defined 821
alpha channel masking 383
animation
  brightness 537
  creating a progress bar 638
  filters 543
  frame rate 481, 502
  with glow filter 508
animation, symbols and 79
animations
  continuing 503
  that run continuously 504

E

easing
  about 498
  defining 492
  with code 500
ECMA-262 specification 119
effects
  blending modes 549
  brightness 536
  brightness and color 484
  brightness tween 486
  fading 481
  grayscale 485
  noise 546
  panning an image 488
effects. *See* filters
elements, of an array 167
embedded characters
  adding and removing 406
  using with text fields 407
embedded fonts
  embedding a font symbol 408
  using with TextField class 413
enable remote debugging 729
encapsulation
  about 240
  using 267
encoding text 59
endpoints 597
equality operators 193
error handling and filters 514
error messages 787
escape character 469
escape sequences 82
Escape shortcut keys 54
event handler methods
  and on() and onClipEvent() 343
  assigning functions to 338
  attaching to buttons or movie clips 343
  attaching to objects 347
  defined 335, 823
  defined by ActionScript classes 336
  in ActionScript 2.0 352
  scope 349
event handler mthods
  checking for XML data 649
event listeners 338
  classes that can broadcast 339
  scope 349

event model
  for event handler methods 336
  for event listeners 339
  for on() and onClipEvent() handlers 343
events
  and movie clips 384
  broadcasting 348
  defined 335, 823
exporting scripts and language encoding 59
expressions
  defined 823
  manipulating values in 180
extends keyword 308
  about 308
  syntax 309
Extensible Markup Language. *See* XML
External API
  about 680
  using 681
external class files
  using classpaths to locate 246
external media 605
  about loading 606
  and the root timeline 611
  creating progress bar animations 638
  loading images and SWF files 607
  loading MP3 files 640
  loading SWF and image files 638
  loading SWF files and JPEG files 607
  MP3 files 612
  playing FLV files 618
  preloading 623, 638
  ProgressBar component 609
  reasons for using 605
external sources, connecting Flash with 647, 691
ExternalInterface class
  about 680
  using 681

F

fading objects 481
FileReference class
  about 657
  and download() method 658
  and security 659
  building an application 660
files, uploading 657

gradient glow filter
    about 525
    using 526
grayscale image 485
grid fit types, using 426

H

handlers. *See* event handlers
hitTest() method 590
HTML
    example of using with styles 439
    styling built-in tags 439
    supported tags 446
    tags enclosed in quotation marks 446
    text field 394
    using <img> tag to flow text 445, 448, 454
    using cascading style sheets to define tags 442
    using in text fields 445
HTTP protocol
    communicating with server-side scripts 652
    with ActionScript methods 648
HTTPS protocol 648

I

icons
    above Script pane 40
    in Debugger 737
ID3 tags 615
IDE (integrated development environment), defined 824
identifiers, defined 824
if..else if statements, writing 150
if..else statements, writing 149
IIS 6.0 web server 637
images
    applying blending modes 549
    embedding in text fields 454
    loading into movie clips 363
    See also external media
IME (input method editor)
    about 464
    using 465
import
    about the statement 510
    multiple classes within package 510
    using wildcard 510

importing
    class files 245
    scripts, and language encoding 59
indentation in code, enabling 53
indexed array 168, 173
information, passing between SWF files 648
inheritance
    about 307
    and OOP 238
    and subclasses 308
    example 310
initialization, writing ActionScript 767
initializing movie clip properties 386
input method editor
    about 464
    using 465
input text 391
instance names
    and target paths 123
    compared with variable names 395
    defined 357, 824
instances 481
    and OOP 238
    applying filters to 513
    defined 302, 824
    targeting 123
    targeting dynamic 125
    targeting nested 124
instantiation
    defined 232
    of objects 302
interactivity, in SWF files
    creating 575
    techniques for 580
interface keyword 321
interfaces
    about 319
    and OOP 239
    complex interface example 330
    creating 322
    creating as data type 324
    defining and implementing 322
    example 328
    naming 321
    understanding inheritance and 326
IP addresses
    policy files 717
    security 708

M

vector graphics 828

video

about 617

about external FLV files 618

adding seek functionality 631

and Macintosh 637

configuring the server for FLV 636

creating a banner 621

creating a progress bar to load FLV 643

creating a video object 619

creating FLV files 618

cue points 625

metadata 634

navigating a FLV file 631

playing FLV files at runtime 620

preloading 623

seek to a specified duration 632

seek to cue point 632, 633

tracing cue points 626

using the onMetaData handler 635

working with cue points 628

video, alternative to importing 618

View Options pop-up menu 54, 55

void data type 83

volume, creating sliding control 588

W

Watch tab, Debugger 732

web applications, continuous connection 673

while loops 164

with statement 771

word wrapping in code, enabling 54

writing ActionScript

super prefix 769

trace 769

with statement 771

writing syntax and statements

listener 785

return 783

switch 783

X

XLIFF files 462

XML 666

DOM 666

example of using with styles 443

hierarchy 666

in server-side scripts 668

loading and displaying text 405

sample variable conversion 667

sending information via TCP/IP socket 648

sending information with XML methods 648

XML class, methods 667

XML files, updating for Flash 8 installation 10

XML Localization Interchange File Format 462

XML Socket object

checking for data 649

loadPolicyFile 719

methods 674

using 673

Z

Zoom transition behavior 493

Training from the Source

Macromedia's *Training from the Source* series is one of the best-selling series on the market. This series offers you a unique self-paced approach that introduces you to the major features of the software and guides you step by step through the development of real-world projects.

Each book is divided into a series of lessons. Each lesson begins with an overview of the lesson's content and learning objectives and is divided into short tasks that break the skills into bite-size units. All the files you need for the lessons are included on the CD that comes with the book.

Macromedia Flash 8: Training from the Source
ISBN 0-321-33629-1

Macromedia Flash Professional 8: Training from the Source
ISBN 0-321-38403-2

Macromedia Flash 8 ActionScript: Training from the Source
ISBN 0-321-33619-4

Macromedia Studio 8: Training from the Source
ISBN 0-321-33620-8

Macromedia Dreamweaver 8: Training from the Source
ISBN 0-321-33626-7

Macromedia Dreamweaver 8 with ASP, PHP and ColdFusion: Training from the Source
ISBN 0-321-33625-9

Macromedia Fireworks 8: Training from the Source
ISBN 0-321-33591-0

macromedia®
PRESS

www.macromediapress.com